UTAH AND PIONEER MARRIAGES

Volume I

A compilation of marriages from *Pioneer Women of Faith and Fortitude*
1787 – 1935

by:
Colleen Liechty
2014

ISBN-13: 978-0692236017
ISBN-10: 0692236015

Table of Contents

MARRIAGES BY MALE SURNAME

A

Aagard	Anders Jensen	Jensen	Anne	1865 03 14	UT, Moroni
Aagard	Andrew James	Christensen	Christina Caroline	1921 03 23	UT, Moroni
Aagard	Jens Pedersen	Andersen	Maren	1826 10 25	Denmark
Aasen	Svend Jakobsen	Jonson	Johanna	1822 07 21	
Abbott	Joshua	Markham	Ruth	1834	
Abbott	Lewis	Marsh	Ann	1829 06 22	MA, Wayland
Abbott	Myron	Allen	Laura Josephine	1861 04 25	UT, Ogden
Abbott	Stephen J.	Smith	Abigail	1825 12 11	NY, Steuben
Abbott	Thomas Marsh	Smith	Alma Janette	1859 04 25	UT, Salt Lake City
Abel	Elijah	Adams	Mary Ann	1847 02 16	OH, Hamilton
Abplanalp	Peter	Eggler	Margaretha	1856 11 30	Switzerland
Abraham	James	Phelps	Martha	1852 11 08	ENG
Adair	Samuel	Hunter	Rachel	1853 05 09	UT, Payson
Adair	Thomas Jefferson	Rogers	Francis		
Adair	Thomas Jefferson	Vancil	Mary		
Adair	Wesley	Williams	Harriet Cordelia	1849 02 08	
Adams	Azra Matson	Clark	Sabina	1831 03 23	Canada
Adams	Barnabas L.	Chase	Hannah Gove	1856 11 16	UT, Salt Lake City
Adams	Charles	Davenport	Sarah Ann	1863 03 31	UT, Parowan
Adams	David Barclay	Mann	Lydia Catherine	1849 05 30	IA
Adams	Elias	Harris	Elizabeth Rose	1863 11 29	UT, Kaysville
Adams	Elias	Railey	Malinda Jane	1837 06 01	IL, Quincy
Adams	George Pilling	Sheen	Ann Eliza	1876 12 30	
Adams	Jerome J.	Frost	Mary Angeline	1854 01 29	IA, Freemont
Adams	John	Howells	Mary Price	1857 09 14	UT, Tooele
Adams	John	Nash	Mary	1816	ENG, Kent
Adams	John N.	Marshall	Lovinia	1866 05 29	UT, Franklin
Adams	John Vorley	Bailey	Mary Ann	1857 04 09	UT, Salt Lake City
Adams	Joshua	Boggard	Mary	1862 07 26	UT, Salt Lake City
Adams	Joshua	Logan	Mary Bathgate	1859 12 22	
Adams	Nathan W.	Plunkett	Mary Melinda	1855 02 15	UT, American Fork
Adams	Orson Bennett	Gingell	Charlotte E.	1859 07 21	UT, Parowan
Adams	Samuel Ferry	Eskelson	Johanna Maria	1878 11 28	UT, Richmond
Adams	Samuel Lorenzo	Jackson	Almira Lucinda	1885 10 25	
Adams	Samuel Lorenzo	Jackson	Emma	1852 02 05	ENG, Liverpool
Adams	Samuel Lorenzo	Morgan	Mary Ann	1863 10 10	UT, Salt Lake City
Adams	Thomas	Durrant	Jane	1868 12 18	UT, Porterville
Adams	William	Bolanz	Maria Barbara	1864 01 16	UT, Salt Lake City
Adams	William	Leech	Mary Ann	1842 10 10	IRE, Down
Adams	William Henry	Jennings	Martha	1839 11 03	ENG, Dover
Adams	William Henry	Otten	Frances Ann	1858	
Adamson	Dougal	McAuslin	Ann	1855 11	UT, Murray
Adamson	John	Cameron	Helen (Ellen)	1836 12 31	Scotland
Adamson	Peter	Kelly	Emily	1894 07 17	

Male	Female	Date	Place
Adamson ....Thomas C.	Sneddon..............Agnes	1869 11 15	UT, Salt Lake City
Adamson ....William	Baird...................Agnes	1799 12 11	Scotland
Adamson ....William	Gallafent.............Elizabeth	1868 07 25	UT, Salt Lake City
Adcock............Charles	Johnson ....Hannah Edith	1869	
Adkinson.........Charles	McMeans ....Margaret T.	1826 12 28	
Adshed ....William	Gibbs.................Ruth		
Ager................John	Coolbear ....Caroline	1861 01 05	
Agramonte.......Clarence H. M.	Stenhouse..........Clara Fedarata	1879 06	UT, Richfield
Ahrens ....Claus Johann	Christensen........Dorthea Elizabeth	1859 11 15	Denmark
Aiken ....Samuel Ruggles	Daggett ....Hannah	1851 09 13	
Aiken ....Samuel Ruggles	Livingston............Isabella	1857 04 22	UT, Salt Lake City
Ainscough.......William	Clarke.................Mary	1843	IL, Nauvoo
Aird ....William	McLean ....Elizabeth	1853 02	Scotland
Akes ....Harmon J.	Frost...................Martha M.	1839 03 14	IA, Jefferson Co.
Aland ....John Sparrow	Harding ....Ellen Sarah	1832 11 12	ENG
Alden ....Briggs	Harrington ....Lydia	1841 05 09	NY, Henderson
Alder ....Alfred	Field ....Susan	1848 03 26	MO, St. Louis
Alder ....George	Hamilton.............Mary Ann		ENG
Alder ....George Alfred	Dunford ....Lydia	1864 04 01	MO, St. Louis
Alder ....Johannes	Alder..................Anna Barbara	1849 07 02	Switzerland
Alder ....William	Beven.................Elizabeth	1814 01 14	ENG
Aldous ....Charles	Drake ....Lucy	1860 11 26	UT, Ogden
Aldous ....George Parkin	Thurston.............Christiane M.	1865 12 24	
Aldous ....Robert F.	Parkin................Mary Anne	1835 12 24	ENG, London
Aldredge ....Joseph	Williams.............Ann		
Alexander ....Alvah	Houston..............Phoebe	1822 05 09	NH, Acworth
Alexander ....Horace Martin	Burwell ....Martha	1849	
Alexander ....Horace Martin	Houston..............Catherine	1849	
Alexander ....Horace Martin	Walker................Nancy Reeder	1834 09 14	
Alexander ....John	Davidson ....Eleanor	1863 03 27	
Alexander ....Thomas Murphy	Lublin ....Kate	1864 07 26	UT
Alexanderson ..Knud	Larsen ....Ingeborg Kristine	1836 02 29	
Alger ....John	Pulsipher ....Sarah	1842 01 11	IL, Nauvoo
Alger ....Samuel	Hancock ....Clarissa		
Allan ....Charles Edward	Watkins ....Elizabeth	1869 07 24	UT, Salt Lake City
Alleman ....John	Stentz.................Christiana	1832 12 11	PA, Middletown
Allen ....Alanson David	Hadlock ....Chastina	1850 11 10	UT
Allen ....Albern	Allen ....Marcia	1826	NY, Otsego Co.
Allen ....Albern	Hoopes...............Mary Ann		
Allen ....Ammon	Hislop ....Isabelle	1881 11 03	UT, Huntsville
Allen ....Andrew	Miner..................Eunice	1806 01 03	VT, Montpelier
Allen ....Andrew Jackson	Andrews ....Delilah E. B.	1841 04 29	KY
Allen ....Andrew Lee	Knapp.................Clarinda	1824 12 11	NY, Allegany
Allen ....Elihu M.	Clawson ....Lola Ann	1827	NY
Allen ....Elihu Moroni	Graham ....Mary Elizabeth	1853	UT
Allen ....Elijah	Bickmore ....Eliza Ann	1852 05 03	IA, Mills
Allen ....Ezra Hale	Fiske ....Sarah Beriah	1837 12 25	
Allen ....Gideon	Hand ....Rachel	1799 10 03	CT, Litchfield
Allen ....Ira	Bass ....Calista	1834 11 28	CT
Allen ....Ira	Benson................Cynthia Elizabeth	1858 08 25	
Allen ....James Carson	Lowe ....Betsy	1883 03 01	UT, Salt Lake City
Allen ....James Carson	Lowe ....Ellen	1884	UT
Allen ....James D.	Hardy ....Sarah Ann	1825 03 02	NJ, Salem
Allen ....Joseph	Player.................Zillah	1844 09 16	IL, Nauvoo

Male	Female	Date	Place
Allen ....Joseph Stewart	Hansen.............Karen Maria	1854 01 28	UT
Allen ....Joseph Stewart	Jesperson ....Ingeborg Kristine	1857 09 11	
Allen ....Joseph Stewart	Morley ....Lucy Diantha	1835 09 02	MO, Clay Co.
Allen ....Jude	Anglesey ....Martha	1859 02 23	UT, Bountiful
Allen ....Jude	Anglesey ....Sarah	1866 02 03	UT, Salt Lake City
Allen ....Jude	Nicholas ....Mary Ann	1837	
Allen ....Marshall F.	Holmes..............Emma	1859 02 27	UT, Ogden
Allen ....Orin Daniel	Bindrup..............Annie Christine	1878 02 01	
Allen ....Orville Morgan	Ward ....Susannah	1848 06 20	IA
Allen ....Peter	Sneddon.............Agnes	1857	MO, St. Louis
Allen ....Rufus	Phelps...............Mary	1861 06 03	
Allen ....Samuel	Moore................Harriet	1854 04 10	UT, Salt Lake City
Allen ....Simeon F.	Johnson ....Boletta Marie	1863 12 05	UT, Salt Lake City
Allen ....William L. N.	Jackson..............Hannah	1848 08 14	
Alley................George	Symonds ....Mary	1822 09 15	MA
Alley...............Stephen Webb	Turner ....Emma	1868 10 03	UT, Salt Lake City
Allman ....Thomas	Phillips...............Almira	1863 02 21	UT, Salt Lake City
Allphin.............Israel	Damron ....Susan Emaline	1858 03 17	UT, Salt Lake City
Allred ....Isaac	Calvert...............Mary	1811 02 14	
Allred ....Isaac	Henderson ....Mary	1846 01 15	
Allred ....Isaac	Stewart...............Matilda	1852 11 05	
Allred ....Isaac	Taylor ....Julia Ann	1832 10 11	TN, Bedford
Allred ....James	Patrick ....Elizabeth	1846 02 03	IL, Nauvoo
Allred ....James	Warren ....Elizabeth	1803 11 17	NC, Randolph
Allred ....James A.	Pollard ....Mary Ann	1866 01 06	UT, Spring City
Allred ....James Franklin	McKenzie ....Jane T.	1860 07 01	
Allred ....James Martin	Vance................Mary Francis	1860 03 21	UT, Mt. Pleasant
Allred ....John Allen	Knight................Mary Jane	1856 04	UT, Slaterville
Allred ....John Jones	Bridgeman..........Mary Young	1852 09 23	MO, Smithville
Allred ....Medwin Newton	Stock ....Maria Josephine	1875 05 31	UT, Salt Lake City
Allred ....Paulinus H.	Norton ....Melissa Isabel	1848 02 03	IA, Council Bluffs
Allred ....Reddin Alexander	Cannon ....Leonora	1857 02 08	
Allred ....Reuben Warren	Butler.................Lucy Ann	1836 12 04	TN
Allred ....Thomas Butler	Stoddart ....Hannah	1885	
Allred ....William Lansing	Wilkes ....Sarah Ann	1867 01 25	UT, Salt Lake City
Allred ....William Moore	Bates.................Orissa Angelia	1842 01 09	IL, Nauvoo
Allsop...............John	Eskelson ....Johanna Maria	1867 03 16	UT, Salt Lake City
Allsop...............John	Wood.................Mary Ellen	1854 09 12	
Allsop...............Thomas	Johnson ....Sarah	1863 02	
Alsop ....Thomas Hill	Steele................Betsy		IA
Alston ....James	Molyneaux...........Ann	1852 11 08	ENG
Alton ....Abel	Sanger ....Irene	1794 11 27	CT
Alvord ....Gideon W.	Shupe................Sarah Ann	1860 09 16	UT, North Ogden
Amatt...............James	Bryan.................Elizabeth	1837	ENG
Ames ....Ira	Slawson ....Catherine	1857 09 11	UT, Salt Lake City
Ames ....Samuel	Leishman ....Isabella	1864 01 13	UT, Salt Lake City
Amundsen ....Dyre	Olsen.................Gjertrude Marie	1833 11 10	Norway
Amundsen ....Ole	Halvorson...........Marie	1845 04 29	Norway
Amundson ....Dyre	Nilson ....Maria Sophie	1865 10 29	UT, Salt Lake City
Andelin ....Olof A.	Lofdahl ....Oliva Maria	1866 02 10	
Andersen ....Andrew	Henderson ....Janet	1875 10 11	UT, Salt Lake City
Andersen ....Christen	Hansen...............Karen Marie	1817 03 14	Denmark
Andersen ....Christen	Jensen ....Karen	1829 05 08	Denmark
Andersen ....Christen	Nielsen ....Mette Kirsten	1806 07 13	Denmark

Male	Female	Date	Place
Andersen.........Christian	Nielsen...............Kersten	1852 05 04	Denmark
Andersen.........Hans Frederik	Pedersen............Else Marie	1836 10 21	Denmark
Andersen.........Jans	Thomasen..........Maren	1839 11	Denmark
Andersen.........Jens	Pedersen............Ane	1846 12 01	Denmark
Andersen.........Lars	Pedersen............Maren	1842	Denmark
Andersen.........Lars C.	Jensen...............Clara Christine	1864 11 06	
Andersen.........Peder	Larsen...............Maren	1836 04 08	Denmark
Andersen.........Peder Christian	Jensen...............Carolina	1866 11 04	UT, Salt Lake City
Andersen.........Thomas C.	Andersen............Sidse	1863 01 28	
Anderson.........Alexander	McKenzie...........Catherine	1836 08 14	Scotland
Anderson.........Anders	Jensen...............Jensine S. P.	1827 10 02	Denmark
Anderson.........Anders	Olafson...............Sarah Britta		
Anderson.........Anders Christian	Christensen.........Anna	1857 12 27	
Anderson.........Anders Christian	Jensson..............Annie	1874 02 17	
Anderson.........Anders J.	Jespersen...........Mariane	1833 10 08	Denmark
Anderson.........Anders P.	Lovell..................Martha Ann	1873 04 14	UT, Salt Lake City
Anderson.........Andreas	Brodin.................Augusta Matilda	1865 01 18	UT, Salt Lake City
Anderson.........Andrew	Brooks.................Alice	1857 03 26	UT, Salt Lake City
Anderson.........Andrew R.	Christensen.........Nelsina Maria	1871	
Anderson.........Archibald	Adamson..............Agnes	1826	
Anderson.........Archibald A.	Rees....................Sarah Jane	1859 08 23	UT, Spanish Fork
Anderson.........Charles A.	Fredricksen.........Martine	1865 11 02	UT, Salt Lake City
Anderson.........Christian	Christensen.........Annie	1871 04 17	UT, Salt Lake City
Anderson.........Christoffer	Amundson...........Anne Gurine	1838 07 29	Norway
Anderson.........Enos	Ballam.................Elizabeth		UT, Snowville
Anderson.........George	Thorn..................Mary Ann	1860 02 15	UT, Salt Lake City
Anderson.........Gustave	Esbjornsson.........Anna	1858 03 22	UT, Salt Lake City
Anderson.........Gustave	Haroldsen............Maren	1861 09 28	UT
Anderson.........Gustave	Larsen.................Mary	1874 11 23	UT, Clover
Anderson.........Gustave	Svensson.............Caroline W.	1868 09 19	UT, Salt Lake City
Anderson.........Gustave	Torstensen...........Maren	1842 12 27	Norway
Anderson.........Hans	Jensen...............Ane Katrina	1885 02 25	
Anderson.........Hans	Jensen...............Maren	1845 10 17	Denmark
Anderson.........James	Peterson.............Annie Christine	1876 11 19	UT, Spring City
Anderson.........James Pace	Morton.................Eliza	1857 03 10	UT, Parowan
Anderson.........Jens	Nielsen...............Caroline J. K. S.	1863 04 06	Denmark
Anderson.........Johannes	Olson..................Johanna	1852 12 18	Sweden
Anderson.........Johannes	Persson..............Martha	1844 05 10	Sweden
Anderson.........John Larsen	Christiansen........Johanna	1860 12 10	UT, Salt Lake City
Anderson.........Joseph S.	Nielson...............Anne Margreth	1875 12 06	UT, Salt Lake City
Anderson.........Joseph Smith	Christensen.........Annie	1878	
Anderson.........Lars	Berg...................Helena Catrine	1838 09 30	Sweden
Anderson.........Lars Jacob	Bengtson.............Anna Britta	1853 11 05	Sweden
Anderson.........Miles	Pace...................Nancy	1821 08 09	TN, Rutherford
Anderson.........Mons	Benson.................Christina	1854 07 03	UT, Salt Lake City
Anderson.........Mons	Jorgensen...........Anne Catherine	1850	Denmark
Anderson.........Neils	Pedersen............Maria Petrea	1876 05 08	UT, Salt Lake City
Anderson.........Niel	Pierson...............Hannah	1862 10 25	UT, West Jordan
Anderson.........Niels	Paulsen..............Ingaborg	1857 11 15	UT, Ephraim
Anderson.........Nils	Larsson...............Arna	1844 01 28	Sweden
Anderson.........Ola	Borkerson............Anna	1839 02 20	Sweden
Anderson.........Ola	Shenstrom...........Bengta	1856 12 06	
Anderson.........Ove C.	Morgansen..........Maren	1838 10 19	Denmark
Anderson.........Paul	Hakansson..........Kjerstena	1846	Sweden

Male		Female		Date	Place
Anderson	Peter L.	Poulsen	Else Margretha	1865 04 25	UT, Ephraim
Anderson	Peter N.	Larsson	Kjarsta P.	1854 11 03	Sweden
Anderson	Rasmus Peter	Jensen	Jensine S. P.	1857 10	Denmark
Anderson	William	Gourlay	Elizabeth	1823 11 28	Scotland
Anderson	William O.	Erickson	Elsie	1866 03 30	UT, Salt Lake City
Andreasen	Andrew Carl	Jorgensen	Sophia Petronella	1880 12 02	UT, Salt Lake City
Andreasen	Casper	Anderson	Caroline	1887	UT, Logan
Andrew	Frederick C,	Fisher	Mary Ann	1854 11 19	
Andrews	Charles A. B.	Button	Keturah Eliza	1824	NY, Onondago
Andrews	John	Wright	Elizabeth	1857	
Andrus	Milo	Alexander	Adeline	1852 03 27	
Andrus	Milo	Boyce	Margaret Ann	1857 02 15	
Andrus	Milo	Brooks	Ann	1855 11 22	
Andrus	Milo	Brooks	Elizabeth	1855 11 22	
Andrus	Milo	Covert	Mary Emma	1858 02 28	
Andrus	Milo	Daley	Abigail Jane	1833 02 21	OH, Huron
Andrus	Milo	Daley	Abigail Jane	1886 03 17	ID, Oxford
Andrus	Milo	Loomis	Lucy	1851 06 01	UT
Andrus	Milo	Miles	Sarah Ann	1848 01 01	NE
Andrus	Milo	Munday	Jane	1855 11 22	
Andrus	Milo	Webster	Mary Ann	1852 12 23	
Angell	James William	Morton	Phoebe Ann	1804	
Angell	Solomon	Johanson	Anna Cajia	1863 10 31	UT, Salt Lake City
Angell	Solomon	Very	Lucy Ann N.		
Angell	Solomon	Young	Eunice Clark	1828 04 13	RI, North Prov.
Angell	Truman O.	Johnson	Polly Ann	1832 10 07	NY, Genesee
Anthony	John	Evans	Alice	1835 02 23	Wales
Arave	Nelson	Wadsworth	Susan Aroline	1855 02 18	UT, Salt Lake City
Archibald	James R.	Mark	Janel	1866 12 01	UT
Archibald	James R.	Mark	Mary	1857 01 07	NY, New York
Archibald	Thomas	Russell	Elizabeth	1835 04 18	Scotland
Archibald	William R.	Halliday	Elizabeth	1857 09 08	Scotland
Argyle	Joseph	Finch	Rebecca Jane	1840 12 24	ENG, Birmingham
Argyle	Joseph Jr.	Holroyd	Ellen Taylor	1867 09 28	UT, Salt Lake City
Armstrong	David	Weaver	Julia Cecelia	1862	UT
Armstrong	Francis	Siddoway	Isabella	1864 12 10	
Armstrong	Thomas K.	Hutchison	Margaret S.	1869 01 19	UT, Salt Lake City
Armstrong	William	Craddock	Catherine	1838 10 22	
Arneson	Augustinus	Johannesen	Caroline M.	1855 04 26	Norway
Arnold	Henry	Green	Elizabeth	1857 02 20	UT, Salt Lake City
Arnold	John	Snarr	Mary Ann	1869 01 11	UT, Salt Lake City
Arnold	Josiah	Bliss	Elizabeth	1831	NY
Arnold	Orson Pratt	Read	Alicia Quilley	1860 11 04	UT, Salt Lake City
Arrowsmith	Josiah Thomas	Smith	Hannah	1854 11 15	UT, Salt Lake City
Arrowsmith	William	Taylor	Elizabeth	1840	
Arthur	Christopher J.	Haight	Caroline Eliza	1854 12 30	
Ash	James	Ackerly	Phoebe	1844	ENG
Ash	Joseph	Lundblad	Mary Christina	1876	
Ashby	Benjamin	Chester	Ann	1857	
Ashby	Nathaniel	Garr	Mary Virginia	1858 02 13	UT, Salt Lake City
Ashby	Nathaniel	Hammond	Susan	1826 11 30	MA, Salem
Ashby	Samuel	Ward	Hannah	1847 04 15	ENG, Thornby
Ashby	William Hardin	Badger	Nancy Maria	1865 01 14	UT, Salt Lake City
Ashcraft	James Eli	Fullmer	Lavinia Elizabeth	1859 01 23	UT, Springville

Male	Female	Date	Place
Ashcraft ....Joseph	Land ....Narcissa B.	1840	
Ashcroft ....Henry	Barton ....Elizabeth Ann	1861 10 26	UT, Salt Lake City
Ashdown.........Richard	Bengtsson ....Sophia		
Ashdown.........Richard	Burgess ....Ann	1841 11 10	
Ashton ....Edward	Treharne ....Jane	1854 02 05	UT, Salt Lake City
Ashton ....Richard	Higgenbotham.....Alice	1837 12 17	ENG
Ashton ....Samuel	Bunting ....Mary		
Ashworth ....Benjamin	Dorsey...............Eliza	1839 06 02	ENG, Yorkshire
Asper ....Elias	Morrow ....Jane McCune	1849 03 07	
Astle ....Francis	Raynor ....Felicia	1836 03 21	ENG, Nottingham.
Astle ....John	Bradshaw ....Isabelle Jane	1866 12 09	UT, Hyrum
Aston ....John	Harris ....Mary Ann	1886 11 02	
Aston ....William Henry	Johnson ....Hannah Edith		
Atkin ....Thomas	Morley ....Mary	1826 02 13	ENG
Atkin ....Thomas Jr.	Maughan ....Mary Ann	1856 05 20	UT, Salt Lake City
Atkin ....William	Stucki ....Rosetta	1879 10 02	UT, St. George
Atkin ....William	Thompson ....Rachel	1854 12 18	ENG
Atkinson..........Alfred Henry	Peterson.............Johanna Mathilda	1871 07 10	UT, Salt Lake City
Atkinson..........Alfred John	Botting...............Ann	1848 04 27	ENG
Atkinson..........Charles John	Smith.................Ann	1814 11 20	ENG, Surrey
Atkinson..........William	Campbell............Phoebe	1833 12 26	Canada
Atwood ....Simeon E.	Bolton................Fanny	1865 09 25	UT, Salt Lake City
Atwood ....Simeon E.	Turrell................Melissa	1834 09 30	NY, Chautaugua
Atwood ....Walter Henry	Dibble................Julia Frances	1865 07 08	UT, Salt Lake City
Atwood ....William Turrell	Wade.................Laura	1867 11 30	
Atwood ....William Turrell	Wade.................Sarah Jane	1868 10 31	UT, Salt Lake City
Auerbach ....Samuel H.	Brooks...............Eveline	1879 12 16	UT, Salt Lake City
Auger.............Jabez	Cosgrove............Sarah Ann	1855 01 01	PA, Philadelphia
Austin ....John	Wilkinson............Elizabeth		
Austin ....William	McIntyre ....Agnes	1853 07 15	UT
Aver ....Ulrich	Cutcliffe ....Mary Jane	1873 02 18	UT, Salt Lake City
Averett ....Elijah	Carlsen..............Johanne Kristine	1855 07 03	UT, Salt Lake City
Averett ....Elijah	Grimes ....Cherrizade	1830 02 09	IL, Hamilton
Averett ....George W. G.	Turnbeaugh........Nancy Ann	1853 02 24	IL, Pike
Averett ....Jeduthan	Tingle ....Holly Jane	1835 08 11	AL, Marion Co.
Avery ....Charles Edward	Harrington ....Mary Miranda	1843 12 30	IA, Lee
Avery ....Vernile Thomas	Jones ....Sarah Rebecca	1872 02 05	UT, Salt Lake City
Avery ....William H.	Garlick...............Talitha Cumi	1845 03 12	IL, Nauvoo
Ayers ....Caleb	Haggerty ....Lucinda Catherine	1832 01 11	NJ, Stanhope
Ayling............Christian	Christensen........Mary Elizabeth	1881 12 01	UT, Salt Lake City
Ayrton ....John	Lambert..............Isabella	1824 11 27	ENG, Yorkshire
Ayrton ....William	Davis ....Elizabeth	1878 08 22	UT, Salt Lake City

B

Male	Female	Date	Place
Babbitt ....Almon W.	Johnson ....Delcena D.	1846 01 24	IL, Nauvoo
Babbitt ....Almon W.	Johnson ....Julia Ann	1833 11 23	OH
Babbitt ....Don Carlos	Johnson ....Melissa Almera	1864 01 24	
Babcock...........Adolphus	Chapman ....Hannah	1858 05 25	UT, Spanish Fork
Babcock...........George	Jorgensen ....Anne Catherine	1862 10 20	UT, Spanish Fork
Babcock...........John	McKee ....Harriet Persis	1867 02 26	UT, Salt Lake City
Babcock...........Nathaniel	Fisher ....Lydia Rebecca	1880	UT, Spanish Fork
Babcock...........William Lorenzo	Faulkner ....Louisa	1889 06 18	

Male	Female	Date	Place
Backhouse........James	Williams..............Jane	1847	ENG
Backman ....Olaus A.	Johannas..........Engelina	1847	Sweden
Bacon ....Chauncy	Sission ....Celestia Falinda	1841 03 17	IL, Nauvoo
Badcock..........Moses	Webb..................Mary	1842 07 14	ENG, Littlington
Badcock (Webb)William	Dellow ....Sara	1866 05 21	ENG, Litlington
Badcock (Webb)William	Jarvis..................Amelia	1869 09 15	UT, Sat Lake City
Baddley ....George	DeGrey..............Charlotte	1861 10 04	UT, Salt Lake City
Baddley ....George	Parker ....Eliza	1845 11 02	ENG
Badger.............John C.	Haines................Kindness Ann	1855	UT, Grantsville
Badger............Rodney	Garr....................Nancy	1845 03 09	IL, LaHarpe
Bagg ....Thomas Vognsen	Kristensen...........Mette		
Bagley ....Daniel	Wood..................Mary	1849 05 10	IA, Appanoose
Bagley ....John Grant	Allen ....Margaret Mary J.	1861 03 27	UT, Draper
Bailey.............Calvin	Goldthwaite ....Lydia	1828	
Bailey.............Charles R.	Adamson.............Johannah	1863 11 07	UT, Salt Lake City
Bailey.............Charles R.	Hawkins ....Susannah	1863 11 07	UT, Salt Lake City
Bailey.............George Brown	Andrews ....Elsie		
Bailey.............George Brown	Young.................Elizabeth	1853 02 10	ENG, Gloucester.
Bailey.............James	Tucker ....Mary Ann	1846	IL, Nauvoo
Bailey.............Job T.	Stevenson...........Elizabeth	1845 06 24	IA, Charleston
Bailey.............John	Tompkins ....Eliza	1850 02 26	ENG
Bailey.............John Cook	Robbins..............Ellen Jane	1827	ENG
Bailey.............Joseph	Smith..................Ann	1818 07 13	
Bailey.............Nephi	Mackelprang ....Annie Eva A.	1873 12 11	UT, Cedar City
Bailey.............William	Montgomery ....Mary Elizabeth	1864 03 01	UT, Ogden
Bailey.............William Henry	Read ....Amelia	1837	
Bain ....Robert Angus	Mitchell..............Euphemia	1857 01	
Bair ....John	Bigelow ....Mary Jane	1856 04 08	
Bair ....John	Owens................Lucinda	1843 10 19	
Bair ....John	Richardson..........Jerusha Ann	1846 01 27	IL, Nauvoo
Baird ....Richard A.	Camp ....Margaret H.	1870 10 03	UT, Salt Lake City
Baird ....Robert	Bell.....................Agnes	1831 01 21	Scotland
Baird ....Robert Erwin	Hadley................Jane		
Baird ....Robert Erwin	Hadley................Mary	1858 08 12	UT, Salt Lake City
Baird ....Robert II	Cumming.............Jane	1853 06 08	Scotland
Baird ....Samuel	Rutledge..............Matilda		
Baker ....Amenzo White	Steele.................Agnes	1864 11 19	
Baker ....George	Thompson ....Rhoda Ann	1840 10 05	
Baker ....Henry	Griffiths...............Jean Rio	1832 09 24	ENG
Baker ....Henry Walker	Elliott ....Eliza Anne	1851 01 05	ENG, London
Baker ....Job	Bowthorpe ....Maria Ann	1859 10 06	UT, Salt Lake City
Baker ....John	Simmons ....Mary Ann	1832 10 25	ENG
Baker ....Joseph	Pack...................Lucy Amelia	1859 07 10	UT, Salt Lake City
Baker ....Phillip Jr.	Thompson ....Harriet Ann	1860 03 02	
Baker ....Simon	Young.................Mercy	1829 12 31	NY, Herker
Baker ....Thomas	Evans ....Mary	1817 10 13	ENG, Warwick
Baker ....William Evans	Cole...................Esther Celestia	1865 03 08	UT, Riverdale
Baldwin...........David	Cole...................Elizabeth Ann	1825 02 01	ENG, Birmingham
Baldwin...........Nathan Bennett	Oler ....Margaretta		
Ball ....James Henry	Williams..............Mary Jane	1876 10 21	UT, Salt Lake City
Ballam ....Henry R.	Drake ....Elizabeth Jefford	1852 07 13	ENG, London
Ballantyne........David	Bannerman ....Ann	1808 10 28	Scotland
Ballantyne........Richard	Clark..................Huldah Meriah	1847 02 17	
Ballantyne........Richard	Pearce................Mary	1855 11 25	

Male	Female	Date	Place
Ballantyne........Richard	Sanderson...........Caroline A.	1857 03 16	
Ballard ....Henry	McNeil ....Emily Reid	1867 10 04	
Ballard ....Henry	McNeil ....Margaret Reid	1861 05 05	UT, Logan
Ballard ....William	Russell ....Hannah	1820 10 16	ENG, Hampshire
Ballif................Serge Louis	Lecoultre ....Elsie Marie	1849 04 27	
Ballou ....Richard	Simmons ....Sarah		
Balls................John	Baxter.................Sarah	1848 11 03	ENG, Suffolk
Bancroft...........William C.	Newham..............Mary	1849 03 02	
Bancroft...........William N.	Moore.................Olivia Sophia	1871 05 15	
Banford............Samuel	Tarrant ....Charlotte	1845 06 12	ENG, Warwick
Bankhead ....Alexander	Redd ....Marinda	1862	UT, Spanish Fork
Banks ....William Ellis	Hobbs.................Alice Lavina	1877 04 11	UT, St. George
Barber..............George	Hatch..................Adeline	1852 02 05	
Barbour............Peter	Caldwell ....Margaret	1814 01 14	Scotland
Bardsley ....William	Duffin.................Martha Ann	1868 06 08	UT, Gunnison
Barkdull ....Isaiah Jones	Fausett ....Narcissus R.		
Barkdull ....Michael	Tremayne............Prudence	1824 05 06	OH, Akron
Barkdull ....Solomon M.	Clark...................Lucy Jane	1848 08 20	IA, Council Bluffs
Barker.............Byron	Hubbard ....Julia Cynthia	1867 12 07	UT, Salt Lake City
Barker.............Frederick	Bligh ....Ann	1822 02 18	ENG, Norfolk
Barker.............Fredrick	Barbour ....Jane	1857	
Barker.............George	Bligh ....Ann	1855 11 03	UT, Salt Lake City
Barker.............James	Blodgett..............Polly Emiline	1851 03 02	UT, Ogden
Barker.............James	Malan ....Mary Catherine	1856 06 06	UT, Ogden
Barker.............John Henry	Dermott ....Susan Ann	1862 06 28	NE, Florence
Barker.............John Newman	Smart ....Mary Ann Maria	1849 02 19	ENG
Barker.............John T.	Pickett ....Jane	1870 06 20	UT, Salt Lake City
Barker.............Joseph	Doidge................Mary Ann	1860 06 11	ENG, Stonehouse
Barker.............Josiah	Woodhead..........Alice	1853 10	
Barker.............William	Holt....................Mary Ann	1855 10 05	UT, Salt Lake City
Barker.............William	Spencer..............Henrietta	1871 07	
Barlow ....Israel	Haven.................Elizabeth	1840 02 23	IL, Quincy
Barlow ....Israel Jr.	Yates..................Annie Hannah	1863 04 26	UT, Bountiful
Barlow ....Joseph Smith	Morgan...............Amanda	1867 11 30	UT, Cedar Fort
Barlow ....Thomas	Hulme.................Ann	1847 11 05	
Barnard............Ezra J.	Leach ....Harriet Josephine	1856 04 15	
Barnard............John Porter	Wycoff................Eliza Ann	1826 08 31	NY, Tomkins
Barnes ....Daniel Hays	Standley ....Sarah Jane	1842 05 17	MO, Randolph Co.
Barnes ....George	Howard...............Jane	1836 05 01	ENG
Barnes ....John M.	Wilson ....Eleanor	1852	
Barnes ....John Richard	Shelton...............Emily	1853 03 23	ENG, Lancashire
Barnes ....Richard	Allen...................Mary	1840 02 17	ENG, Bury
Barnes ....William	Howard...............Jane	1857 03 12	
Barnes ....William	Jeffries ....Elizabeth	1816 11 04	ENG, Bedfordshire
Barnes ....William Henry	Clegg.................Margaret Ellen	1873 12 28	UT, Salt Lake City
Barnes ....William Jeffries	Chapman ....Frances F.	1841 02 07	ENG, Bedfordshire
Barnett............George	Mathews.............Mary Ann	1850 09 17	ENG, Ashton
Barnett............Henry W.	Mitchell..............Elizabeth	1862 03 25	ENG, Tyne
Barnett............James	Berrett ....Ann	1822 08 22	ENG, Ashton
Barnett............James	Riden..................Hannah		
Barney ....Alma	Gardner..............Alice Ann	1871 09 22	UT, Kanarraville
Barney ....Benjamin F.	Beard ....Caroline	1849 04 27	IA, Council Bluffs
Barney ....Edson	Ballou.................Lillis	1831 01 01	OH, Lorain Co.
Barney ....Edson	Walker................Louisa	1847 05 10	

Male	Female	Date	Place
Barney ....Henry	Lucas ....Marcy Jane	1846	
Barney ....Royal	Wright................Esther B.	1857 07 18	UT, Salt Lake City
Barney ....Royal Alonzo	Taylor ....Elizabeth Agnes	1881 05 19	UT, Salt Lake City
Barney ....William Street	Stoddart ....Hannah	1864	
Barnhurst........Samuel	Jensen ....Anna Marie	1857 11 29	UT, Salt Lake City
Barnson ....Bernard	Braithwaite ....Elizabeth Hannah	1881 12 28	UT, Manti
Barnson ....Christian	Anderson............Maria	1853 01 08	ENG, Liverpool
Barrett.............John	Filby ....Mary	1869 04 05	
Barron............Alexander F.	Miller ....Mary	1848 01 04	TX, Harris Co.
Barrus.............Benjamin F.	Steele................Lovina Ann	1861	
Barrus.............Emery	Nickerson ....Huldah Abigail	1833 12 19	
Bartholomew ...Edwin	Lyman ....Lelia Deseret	1871 12 25	UT, Fillmore
Bartholomew ...John	Metcalf ....Eliza Roxie	1868 10 11	UT, Manti
Bartholomew ...Joseph	Benson...............Polly	1843 12 10	IL, Hancock
Bartholomew ...Noah Willis	Catlin ....Mary Altaina	1848 06 17	UT
Bartholomew ...Noah Willis	Catlin ....Marinda		
Bartlett ....Charles C.	Jensen ....Annie Katrina	1868 09 12	UT, Salt Lake City
Barton.............Hyrum	Crabb ....Georgina Calder	1880 01 01	UT, Salt Lake City
Barton.............John	Bell ....Elizabeth		ENG, Lancashire
Barton.............John	Wilkinson............Susannah	1835 12 29	PA, Shamokin
Barton.............Joseph Alma	Lundblad ....Mary Christina	1870	
Barton.............Peter	Beazer................Ellen Ann	1870 12 26	UT, Salt Lake City
Barton.............William	Kay.....................Nancy	1840 04 08	ENG, Lancashire
Barton.............William Bell	Foster.................Sarah	1867 06 08	UT, Salt Lake City
Bascom ....Joel Almon	Bell ....Alice Jane	1857 12 06	UT
Bassett ....Charles Henry	Knight................Mary Elizabeth	1853 03 05	UT, Salt Lake City
Bassett ....Loren Elias	Durfee ....Emma	1865 12 24	
Bassett ....Loren Elias	Vaughn...............Hulda Dimeras	1844	IL
Bassett ....Oliver H.	Stanton...............Lucy Celesta		
Bastholm ....Niels P.	Christensen.........Johanna Kristine	1855 01 30	Denmark
Bastian ....Jacob	Hansen...............Kirsten	1861 02 07	UT, Moroni
Bastian ....Jacob	Sanders..............Matta Marie	1867 10 28	UT, Salt Lake City
Baston ....Andrew	Rowley ....Ann Jewel	1857	UT, Parowan
Batchelor ....Edward	Pullen ....Caroline	1841 01 26	
Bate ....Peter	Cross.................Margaret	1837	ENG
Bateman ....Jeremiah	Baker.................Mary Ann		ENG
Bateman ....Samuel	Allen ....Marinda	1854 11 27	
Bateman ....Thomas	Street ....Mary	1829 08 18	ENG, Manchester
Bateman ....Thomas Jr.	Lavender............Mary	1861 09 18	UT, West Jordan
Bates ....Cyrus	Harrington ....Lydia	1813 02 18	
Bates ....Cyrus W.	Mathews.............Harriet Eliza	1846 12 13	
Bates ....John	Draycott.............Hannah	1837 05 16	ENG, Stapenhill
Bates ....Joseph	Redding..............Maria	1847 01 04	ENG, Warwick
Bates ....Joseph William	Billington ....Harriet	1850 12 10	
Batty ....George Jr.	Woodcock ....Encora	1844	ENG, Pilley
Batty ....Miles	Mecham ....Mary Henrietta	1864 07 24	UT, Salt Lake City
Baum ....Jacob	Harris ....Agnes Nancy	1826 10 12	PA, Manor
Bawden ....Henry	Howard...............Sarah Freelove	1857 03 18	UT
Bawden ....Henry	Ireland ....Ann	1844 03 17	ENG, Barnstable
Baxter.............Isaac	Harvey................Elizabeth	1825 07 25	ENG, Chester
Baxter ....Robert Wright	Love ....Jane	1848 03 27	Scotland
Baxter.............Robert Wright	McKinnon............Jane	1856 12 28	UT, Salt Lake City
Baxter.............Robert Wright	Stuart ....Marion	1868 10 11	UT, Wellsville
Baxter.............Zimri Harford	Seavey ....Eunice	1832 05 02	ME, Milton

Male	Female	Date	Place
Bayles.............Herman D.	Jensen ....Dorthea	1858 12 28	UT, Parowan
Beach ....Rufus	Williams............Harriet Cordelia	1846	IA, Council Bluffs
Beagley ....John	Howarth.............Dorothy	1868 12 24	
Beal ....Henry Allen	Bjerregaard ....Anna Christena	1863 03 28	UT, Salt Lake City
Beal ....Henry Allen	Nielsen ....Marianne	1868 04 28	UT, Salt Lake City
Beal ....Henry Allen	Thorpe.............Mary	1854 07 04	UT, Ephraim
Beal ....John	Deacon.............Mary Ann	1822 03 04	
Beal ....John	Pectol ....Jemima Bell		
Bean ....George W.	Baum.................Elizabeth	1853 01 06	UT, Salt Lake City
Bean ....James	Lewis.................Elizabeth	1824 07 27	MO, Lincoln
Bean ....James Addison	Fausett ....Harriet Catherine	1853 02 10	UT, Provo
Bean ....Joseph William	Beanland............Sarah	1842 07 25	
Beard ....Stephen	Roberts ....Mary Ann	1863 06 22	UT, Henefer
Beard ....William	Holt.................Mary	1854 08 27	ENG, Wochester
Beardall ....Francis	Gabbitas............Emma	1853 06 25	ENG, Yorkshire
Beardshall ......William	Clegg................Catherine		
Beardshall ....William	Clegg.................Mary		
Beatie ....Hampden S.	Clawson ....Helen Cordelia	1855 12 02	UT, Salt Lake City
Beazer ....Mark	Hodges..............Hannah	1849 01 14	ENG
Beck ....Alfred R. M.	Thomas ....Margaret	1867 12 14	UT, Salt Lake City
Beck ....George	Simmons ....Margaret	1910 11 23	
Beck ....John Forsyth	Hopkin..............Mary	1868 02 15	UT, Salt Lake City
Beck ....Joseph Ellison	Forsyth ....Hannah Harrison	1835 12 17	PA, Philadelphia
Beck ....Joseph Ellison	Robbins.............Margaret Burtis	1862 12 13	UT, Salt Lake City
Beck ....Stephen	Jacobsen............Inger Kerstine	1847	Denmark
Beckman ....Andreas	Anderson............Christina Amalia	1855 10 21	Sweden
Beckstead.......Alexander	Gilson.................Clarissa Ann	1856 02 03	
Beckstead.......Alexander	Lense ....Catherine	1823 01 25	Canada
Beckstead.......George W.	Davies ....Elinor	1859 04 28	UT, Provo
Beckstead.......Henry	Marsden............Emma	1862 04 01	UT, Salt Lake City
Beckstead.......Sidney M.	Rollins ....Ann Sophia	1850 06 11	NE, Bellevue
Beckstead.......Thomas W.	Ashton...............Sarah Ellen	1864	UT, Salt Lake City
Beckstrand ......Elias A.	Hegglund...........Anna Sophia	1862 01 24	
Beckstrand ......Elias A.	Nielsen ....Henrietta C.	1869 06 07	UT, Salt Lake City
Beckstrand ......Karl J.	Peterson............Carren	1862 02 28	UT, Salt Lake City
Beckstrom ......Andrew J.	Rosengren ....Kjersti Lovisa	1863 10 28	UT, Mt. Pleasant
Beckstrom ....Hogan	Bauer ....Fredrica Eleonora	1851 05 11	Sweden
Beddo ....George	Simons ....Jane Meredith	1845 10 21	Wales
Bedford............James	Smith.................Elizabeth	1844 10 20	ENG
Bee ....George	Aitcheson ....Jennette	1826	Scotland
Beebe ....William Albert	Newton..............Louisa	1835	NY
Beech ....John	Lewis.................Eliza	1842 12 25	ENG, Longport
Beech ....Thomas Lewis	Allgood ....Jane	1868 01 09	UT, Salt Lake City
Beecher ....Ransom Asa	Wheeler..............Sylvia Desire	1838 11 22	KS
Beemus ....George M.	Jones ....Margaret	1865 08	UT, Salt Lake City
Beers ....Phillip Zend	Hansen..............Martha Kirstine		
Beers ....William	Dennis...............Delia C. C.	1868 08 08	UT, Salt Lake City
Beesley...........William	Flint ....Hannah	1857 04 11	UT, Salt Lake City
Beirdneau ....Nehemiah	Steele................America Ann	1846 04 30	IA, Pottawattamie
Belcher ....Edward Everett	Perkins ....Elizabeth Jane	1863 12 02	NV, Washoe
Bell ....Alfred	Montgomery........Martha Louisa	1832 09 08	IL, Shelby Co.
Bell ....Eli	McClellan ....Louisa Jane	1858 08 16	UT, Payson
Bell ....James	McGregor...........Annie Louisa	1858 02 15	UT, Salt Lake City
Bell ....John Watson	Fish ....Ann	1834 10	ENG

Male		Female		Date	Place
Bell	Philander	Bigelow	Mary Jane	1868 04 09	
Bell	Thomas	Elwood	Mahala	1854	UT, Salt Lake City
Bell	Thomas	Lundquist	Henrietta E.	1865 11 07	UT, Salt Lake City
Bell	William Milton	Benson	Martha Kerstine	1859 04 09	UT, Lehi
Belnap	Gilbert	Knight	Adaline	1845 12 21	IL, Nauvoo
Belnap	Gilbert	McBride	Henrietta	1852 06 26	UT, Salt Lake City
Bemis	Alvin	Gurnsey	Jerusha	1824	NY, Jefferson Co.
Bemus	Linus	Jewell	Martha Amelia	1827 02 25	IL, Fulton
Benbow	John	Holmes	Jane	1826 10 16	ENG, Worcester
Benbow	John	Wright	Rosetta	1851 09 03	
Benbow	Thomas	Holmes	Sarah	1845 02 10	IL, Nauvoo
Bench	William	Bradshaw	Ellen		
Bench	William	Longman	Ann	1836 10 14	ENG
Bench	William	Tatton	Frances Ann	1862 12 25	UT, Salt Lake City
Benedict	Joshua Northrop	Moses	Fidelia	1843 11 30	
Bengtsson	Jons	Peterson	Elsa	1820 12 19	Sweden
Bengtsson	Nils	Johanson	Johannah	1830 07 04	Sweden
Bennett	Benjamin	Jones	Catherine	1818 12 31	Wales
Bennett	David Van Horn	Summers	Emma	1864	UT, Manti
Bennett	Edward	Wood	Elizabeth Jane	1877 03 02	UT, St. George
Bennett	Eli	Simmons	Margaret	1868 07 11	UT, Salt Lake City
Bennett	Eli	Zufelt	Louisa	1851 03 28	IA, Harris Grove
Bennett	George A.	Saxey	Lucy Ann S.		UT
Bennett	Hyrum Bell	Greenhalgh	Sarah Ellen	1866 10 04	UT, Salt Lake City
Bennett	Hyrum Bell	Smith	Martha	1845 08 17	IA, Lee Co.
Bennett	James	Pincock	Ellen	1833 06 30	ENG, Lancashire
Bennett	John	Roberts	Jane	1843 10 22	
Bennett	John Bell	Senior	Mary Elizabeth	1863 02 02	
Bennett	Randle	Bolton	Fanny		
Bennett	Richard	Bell	Mary	1811 02 28	TN, Sumner Co.
Bennett	Richard	Foster	Maria	1863	ENG, Birmingham
Bennett	Thomas	Driggs	Maria	1862 01 14	UT, Kaysville
Bennett	Thomas	Lacey	Ann	1839 12 25	ENG, Bromsgrove
Bennett	Thomas	Wattis	Mary Twinberrow	1836 06 30	ENG
Bennett	Thomas M.	Wilson	Margaret Lovina	1837 11 09	IL
Bennett	William B.	Chapple	Sarah	1866 10 27	UT, Salt Lake City
Bennett	William J.	Bell	Elizabeth	1814 02 24	TN, Sumner Co.
Bennion	Alfred	Slade	Amelia Eliza	1882 08 28	UT, Salt Lake City
Bennion	John	Birch	Esther Ann	1856 07 20	UT, Salt Lake City
Bennion	John	Turpin	Mary	1857 04 19	UT, Salt Lake City
Bennion	John	Wainwright	Esther	1842 02 15	ENG, Liverpool
Bennion	Samuel	Bushell	Mary	1839 04 28	ENG, Liverpool
Bennion	Samuel	Jones	Rhoda	1868 10 25	UT, Salt Lake City
Bennion	Samuel	Williams	Sarah	1853 02 13	UT, Salt Lake City
Benson	Alford B.	Yager	Hetty Elizabeth	1841 06 17	IL, Nauvoo
Benson	Alva	Vail	Cynthia	1820 08 11	
Benson	Benjamin	Messenger	Keziah	1795 12 15	NY, Ramslea Co.
Benson	Ezra Taft	Andrus	Adeline Brooks	1844 04 27	IL, Nauvoo
Benson	Ezra Taft	Andrus	Pamelia	1832 01 01	MA, Uxbridge
Benson	Ezra Taft	Fullmer	Desdemona W.	1846 01 21	IL, Nauvoo
Benson	Ezra Taft	Gallaher	Elizabeth	1853 06 04	UT, Salt Lake City
Benson	Ezra Taft	Knight	Olive Mary	1858 03 19	UT, Salt Lake City
Benson	Ezra Taft	Larsen	Maren	1866 09 15	UT, Salt Lake City
Benson	George Taft	Ballif	Louisa A.	1867 12 20	UT, Salt Lake City

Male	Female	Date	Place
Benson ....Jens Peter	Ericksen ....Kirsten M.	1857 10 16	UT, Lehi
Benson ....Jens Peter	Ericksen ....Mette Christina	1855 04 15	UT, Salt Lake City
Benson ....Jerome M.	Rhodes................Mary	1830 10	
Benson ....Richard	Forrester ....Phoebe	1844 06 30	
Benson ....Yeppa	Koefoed................Maren K.	1819 06 03	Denmark
Bent ....Samuel	Burgess................Elizabeth	1846 01 28	IL, Nauvoo
Bent ....Samuel	Harris ....Naomi		
Bent ....Samuel	Slafter................Asenath	1845 12	IL, Nauvoo
Bent ....Samuel	Thompson ....Marial	1846 01 14	IL, Nauvoo
Bentley ....John	Middlefell............Elizabeth	1831	
Bentley ....Joseph	Tull ....Ann	1877	UT
Bentley ....Richard	Price..................Elizabeth	1843 09 09	IL, Nauvoo
Bernhisel ....John Milton	Haight.................Julia Ann	1846 01 20	IL, Nauvoo
Berntson ....Rasmus	....	1867 05 25	UT
Berntson ....Rasmus	Lundberg............Laura	1861 12 22	Sweden
Berrett............Charles Henry	Jones ....Charlotte E.	1872 04 10	UT
Berrett............Charles Henry	Titus ....Melissa	1861 12 25	UT, Ogden
Berrett............John Watts	Hookway ....Eliza	1865 12 16	UT, Mill Creek
Berrett............Richard T.	Nuns...................Mary Ann	1860 01 01	UT, Ogden
Berrett............Robert Griffin	Woodhead..........Sarah Ann	1855 03 04	
Berry................Jesse Woods	Shanks ....Armelia	1820 02 08	TN, Wilson Co.
Berry................John Francis	Cherrington ....Elizabeth	1862 03 26	UT, Salt Lake City
Berry................John Williams	Thomas ....Jane Elizabeth	1851 05 08	UT, Salt Lake City
Berry..............William Shanks	Beck...................Rebecca Rosina	1860 11 22	UT, Spanish Fork
Bertelsen ....Andreas	Olsen..................Olena	1886	
Bertelsen ....Jens	Jessen................Anne	1827 11 11	Denmark
Bertelsen ....Niels	Larsen ....Maren	1831 12 01	Denmark
Bess ....James L.	Dykman..............Maria Alida	1870 03 14	UT, Salt Lake City
Bess ....James L.	Fullmer...............Joanna Price	1854	
Bess ....Joel	Richardson..........Laura	1830	NY, Steuben Co.
Bethers ....William S.	McMillian ....Phebe Hannah	1866 09 14	UT, Heber
Betts ....James	Powell ....Margaret	1867 04 03	UT, Payson
Betts ....Peter	Franklin ....Elizabeth	1822 04 28	ENG, Middlesex
Beus ....Michael	Combe ....Marianne	1836 11 14	Italy
Bevan ....James	McPherson..........Isabella	1859 11 03	UT, Salt Lake City
Bevan ....James	Shields ....Mary	1850 05 09	IA, Council Bluffs
Bickley ....Thomas	Lishman ....Maria	1850 01 11	
Bickley ....William Green	Walton................Jane	1867 03 21	UT, Pine Valley
Bickmore ....David	Dickey ....Margaret	1793 08 31	ME, Knox Co.
Bickmore ....Gilbert M.	Huntsman............Catharine J.	1849 03 13	IA, Council Bluffs
Bickmore ....Isaac M.	Harville ....Martha	1829 03 01	ME, Friendship
Bickmore ....Thomas	Cullumber............Martha	1866 05 10	
Bickmore ....William M.	Bagley ....Christina	1825	IL, Madison Co.
Biddlecome......George R.	Davis ....Mary	1873 06 14	UT, Tooele
Bigelow............Daniel	Mecham ....Permelia	1865 07 23	UT, Silver Creek
Bigelow............Nahum	Gibbs.................Mary	1826 12 12	IL, Laurenceville
Bigler ....Adam C.	Miller ....Isabella Clarinda	1867 04 04	UT, Farmington
Bigler ....David George	Betts...................Eliza	1867 10 16	UT, Salt Lake City
Bigler ....Jacob G.	Keller..................Nancy Ann	1855 11 25	UT, Nephi
Bilby................John	Ludvigsen............Ann Kirstine	1861 05 10	UT, Salt Lake City
Billings ....Alfred Nelson	Patten................Deborah	1851 12 09	UT, Salt Lake City
Billings ....George Pierce	Shomaker............Jerusha Lois	1856 04 27	UT, Provo
Billings ....Titus	Morley ....Diantha	1817 02 16	
Billings ....Titus	Tuttle ....Mary Ann	1854 01 20	

Male	Female	Date	Place
Billings ....William W.	Greenhalgh ....Margaret Alice	1882 01 19	UT, Manti
Bills ....John	Hall....................Elizabeth	1848 01 06	IL, Nauvoo
Bills ....John	Scott..................Elizabeth	1834 01 07	PA, Allegheny Co.
Bills ....William Andrew	Amundsen..........Matilda	1869 03 01	UT, Salt Lake City
Bills ....William Andrew	Beckstead ....Emeline	1852 07 04	
Binderup ....Christen C.	Petersen.............Martena Arup	1854 06 22	Denmark
Bingham ....Alonzo	Thorn..................Sarah	1854 03 04	UT
Bingham ....Edwin	Burke..................Phoebe Jane	1854 12 28	
Bingham ....Erastus	Barber ....Sally Maria	1853 04 07	
Bingham ....Erastus	Gates ....Lucinda	1820 03 21	VT, Essex Co.
Bingham ....Erastus	Perkins ....Patience	1852 04 04	
Bingham ....Erastus Jr.	Freeman.............Olive Hovey	1843 10 29	IL, Nauvoo
Bingham ....Sanford	Fife ....Agnes (Ann)	1863 10 10	UT, Salt Lake City
Bingham ....Sanford	Lewis..................Martha Ann	1847 07 18	NE, Platte River
Bingham ....Thomas	Holladay ....Caron Happoch	1849 09 06	UT, Salt Lake City
Bingham ....Willard	Gates ....Genet	1853 04 24	UT, Salt Lake City
Binnall.............Charles	Leach ....Rosannah	1856 02 06	UT, Salt Lake City
Birch ....James	Hale...................Mary Ann	1847 04 12	ENG
Birch ....Joseph	Chambers ....Dorothy	1851 05 27	ENG, Lancashire
Birch ....Joseph	Sylvester ....Mary Elizabeth	1861 11 17	UT, Salt Lake City
Birch ....Richard	Hale...................Mary Ann	1858	
Birch ....Thomas	Plitcroft ....Mary	1814 05 02	ENG, Manchester
Birch ....Thomas Francis	Boot....................Sarah	1866 10 18	
Birch ....William	Coleman.............Elizabeth	1856	
Bird	Goble ....Harriet		
Bird ....Andrew	Shill ....Ann		
Bird ....Charles	Dunsdon.............Sarah Ann	1853 02 03	
Bird ....Charles	Kennedy.............Mary Ann	1826 03 22	PA, Tioga Co.
Bird ....James	Carpenter ....Jane Mott	1831	
Bird ....Jasper Thomas	Starr ....Eunice Ann		UT, Salt Lake City
Bird ....John	Russon................Ann	1830	
Bird ....Richard	Crandall..............Emeline	1845 03 07	NY
Bird ....Richard	Crandall..............Laura	1855 03 06	UT, Salt Lake City
Bird ....Richard Leroy	Mendenhall ....Elizabeth Wells	1871 09 18	UT, Salt Lake City
Bird ....William F. II	Jones ....Sarah Rebecca		
Birkinshaw ....William	Greensmith ....Zillah	1863 03 28	UT, Salt Lake City
Bishop ....Mahonri M.	Gibbs..................Mary Amanda	1868 07 18	UT, Salt Lake City
Bishop ....William Evans	Morris ....Harriet	1863 09 28	UT, Salt Lake City
Bishop ....William Henry	Pratt ....Eliza	1841 03 21	IN, La Port
Bissell ....Henry	Plummer.............Dorothy E.	1816	MA, Boston
Bissell ....Joseph	Alleman ....Anna Catherine	1852 03 21	IA, Council Bluffs
Bitner ....Abraham	Barr ....Anna	1835 05 12	PA, Washington
Bitter ....Traugott	Aust...................Rosina W.	1859	Germany
Bitton ....John Evington	Wintle ....Sarah S.	1856 05 13	ENG, Norfolk
Bjarnson ....Manus	Eramusson..........Gudney	1862 12 13	
Bjork ....Gustave	Bjork..................Anna		Sweden
Black................George	Jacaway ....Susannah	1850 04 06	MO, St. Louis
Black................George	McRee................Mary	1838	MS, Copiah
Black................James	Bertelsen............Johanne B.	1854 11	
Black................John	Paxton................Jane	1864 08 15	UT, Parowan
Black................William	Johnston ....Jane	1822 07 31	IRE, Antrim
Black................William Morley	Hansen...............Anna Marie	1859 10 26	UT, Manti
Black................William Morley	Thompson ....Sarah Marinda	1874 05 10	UT, Glendale
Black................William Morley	Washburn............Emma Jane	1851 02 02	UT, Manti

Male	Female	Date	Place
Black...............William V.	Ayers..................Almira Murray	1855 02 28	UT, Salt Lake City
Black...............William V.	Ayers..................Victoria	1857 04 04	UT, Salt Lake City
Blackburn ....Elias Hicks	Crompton ....Virtue Leah	1862 01 31	UT, Salt Lake City
Blackburn ....Elias Hicks	Lane...................Nancy Phipps	1852 04 12	UT, Salt Lake City
Blackburn ....Jehu	Pilch...................Lydia		
Blackburn ....Thomas M.	Bowen.................Elizabeth	1801 12 02	PA
Blackham........James	Tucker ....Harriet	1853 11 20	UT, Salt Lake City
Blackham.........Samuel	Robinson.............Martha	1826	ENG
Blackner ....James Henry	Allen...................Jane	1852 10 25	ENG, Yorkshire
Blackner ....Richard	Hall.....................Elizabeth	1820 05 29	ENG, Heckington
Blain ....John	Graham................Isabell	1838 12 25	ENG, Gretne Green
Blair ....Edward	Chase.................Hannah Gove	1873 05 13	UT, Salt Lake City
Blair ....Harrison	McNutt................Mary Ann	1852	IL, Adams Co.
Blair ....Isaac	Desaules ....Adele	1899 12 13	
Blair ....Isaac	Suddery...............Ruth	1850 04 20	ENG, Middlesex
Blake	Allen..................Laura Josephine		
Blake ....Benjamin F.	Hollis ....Harriet	1841 05 31	ENG
Blake ....Fredrick	Green.................Eliza		
Blake ....Fredrick	Green.................Emily	1868 09 12	UT, Salt Lake City
Blake ....Walter	Banford ....Martha C.	1923	
Blake ....William	Barrow.................Sarah	1838 03 05	ENG, Devon
Blanch ....Wealthy	Larsen ....Dorothea		
Blanch ....Wealthy	Mikkelsen ....Inger Marie	1865 03 19	
Blanchard ....John Reid	Bailey ....Eliza	1853 11 19	UT, Salt Lake City
Blanchard ....John Reid	Potts...................Sarah	1854 03 08	
Blanchard ....William C.	Walker.................Jerusha Celesta	1867 10 12	UT, Salt Lake City
Bland ....John II	Bland...................Chloe	1834 11 30	MS, Carroll
Blazzard ....John H.	Miller ....Mary Jane	1846 03 30	NE
Bleak ....James G.	Gosnold..............Caroline B.	1860 11 24	UT, Salt Lake City
Bleak ....James Godson	Moore.................Elizabeth	1849 10 14	ENG, London
Bleak ....James Godson	Thompson...........Jane	1861 10 26	UT, Salt Lake City
Bleasdale.........William	Moss ....Margaret	1820 09 27	ENG
Blickenstorfer...Gottleib	Stucki ....Rosena	1873 08 04	UT, Salt Lake City
Bliss................Norman Ingles	Bird....................Elizabeth Ann	1845	IL, Hancock
Bliss................Norman Ingles	Stout...................Lydia M. F.	1871 04 30	
Blodgett ....Greenleaf	Garrard...............Sarah S.	1871 12 25	
Blood ....William	Hooper ....Jane Wilkie	1861 09	
Blood ....William	Stretton ....Mary	1836 02 16	ENG
Bloomfield........John	Barton ....Elizabeth Ann	1869 01 11	UT, Salt Lake City
Bloomfield........John	Riches ....Martha	1822 10 28	ENG, Bungay
Bloomfield........John	Wilkinson.............Harriet	1857 11 11	NJ, Chancerville
Bluemel ....Oswald Karl	Olpin...................Julia	1871 05 22	UT, Morgan
Blunt ....Joseph	Meears ....Salina	1863 05 24	ENG, Whiton
Boam ....Thomas	McGhie...............Elizabeth	1854 05	MO, St. Louis
Boardman.......Robert	Green.................Mary	1844 06 18	ENG, Lincolnshire
Boardman.......Robert Jr.	Strong ....Elizabeth Ann	1868 06 12	UT, Salt Lake City
Boden ....James	Coleman.............Annora	1847 03 10	Wales
Bodily.............Robert	Pittam.................Jane	1840 12 27	ENG
Bodily.............Robert Jr.	Roberts ....Harriet Ann	1869 02 02	UT, Salt Lake City
Boggs ....Francis	Martin.................Eveline	1832	
Bohman..........John W.	Soderstrom ....Maria Christiana	1857 02 25	
Bohn..............Adolph Joseph	Bonelli ....Suzetta	1858 03 23	UT, Cedar City
Bohn..............Adolph Joseph	Nielsen ....Karen Marie	1846	Denmark
Bohn..............Jacob J. M.	Thorning.............Marie	1849 04 10	Denmark

Male	Female	Date	Place
Bohn ....Magnus Carl F.	Hjetting ....Helsine	1843 01 29	Denmark
Boice ....Benjamin	Philpot ....Martha Eliza	1859 06 09	UT, Salt Lake City
Boice ....John	Barzee.................Mary Ann	1840 05 07	
Boice ....John	Daggett ....Hannah	1862 11 15	
Boice ....John	Herns ....Martha Jane	1835	Canada
Bolton ....Charles G.	Osguthorpe ....Lydia		
Bolton ....Charles G.	Osguthorpe ....Priscilla M.	1873 02 05	UT, Salt Lake City
Bolton ....Curtis Edwin	Bunker.................Rebecca Baks	1839 09 12	NY
Bolton ....Curtis Edwin	Merritt..................Ellen Coil	1846 02 06	IL, Nauvoo
Bolton ....John	Judd ....Hannah	1878 03	
Bond ....Stephen A.	Clark.................Sarah Ann	1860 12 06	UT, Lehi
Bond ....William	Alger..................Sarah Lydia		UT, Millard Co.
Bond ....William	Barker ....Mary Ann	1838 08 02	ENG, Manchester
Bone ....John	Slater.................Hannah	1860 08 28	UT, Salt Lake City
Bone ....William	Wagstaff.............Fanny	1867 07 26	UT, Lehi
Bone ....William	Wagstaff.............Mary	1833 12 05	ENG, Bedfordshire
Bonelli............Hans George	Ammann..............Anna Maria	1835 08 04	Switzerland
Bonner.............George Jr.	Edmundston........Margaret	1849 10 22	Scotland
Booth	Blake ....Caroline Lucy		
Booth ....George	Bedford ....Sarah		
Booth ....John	Lythgoe ....Ann	1856 04	ENG, Eccles
Booth ....Richard T.	Edge..................Elsie	1846 08 13	ENG, Bedford Leigh
Booth ....William	Hunt ....Sarah	1833	
Boothe ....Willis Henry	Neff ....Susanna	1860 03 08	
Boram ....Alfred	Homer ....Mary Ann	1890 07 04	ID, Rigby
Boren..............Coleman	Keller.................Melinda	1830 03 07	IL, Union Co.
Boren..............William Jasper	Mecham ....Lucina	1859 07 03	UT, Provo
Boren..............Willis	Dutton ....Sophia	1857 12 10	
Borg................Pehr	Jonsson..............Ingar	1830 12 17	Sweden
Borgquist ....Rasmus	Jonson ....Anna Cecelia	1866 11 05	UT, Salt Lake City
Borresen..........Niels H.	Evensen..............Anniken Johanne	1864 02	
Borresen..........Niels H.	Nielsen ....Johanne Marie	1851 11 01	Denmark
Boserup ....Christian R.	Mogensen ....Kristine	1835 05 24	Denmark
Bosnell.............	Benson...............Jane		
Boss ....Phillip	Brown.................Obedience	1818	NC, Rowan Co.
Bosshard ....Johannes	Egli ....Anna Katherina	1840 10 12	Switzerland
Boswell ....Abraham	Betts ....Matilda	1865 07 01	UT, Salt Lake City
Boswell ....Abraham	Hambleton...........Gerusha Lucretia	1853 06 13	
Bosworth ....James B.	Chapman ....Frances C.	1874	UT, Croyden
Bosworth ....John	Bunting................Sarah Ann	1841 09 27	ENG
Boulter ....John	Munro.................Ester Ann	1855 01 29	UT, Draper
Boulter ....Thomas	Davis ....Comfort	1822 05 07	ENG
Boulton ....Martin Cook	Clark..................Mary Alice	1870 11 14	UT, Salt Lake City
Boulton ....Thomas	Cook..................Sarah Harris	1849 03 26	ENG, Worchester
Boulton ....Thomas	Thompson ....Martha		
Bourne ....Charles	Alder..................Jane	1842 06	ENG
Bowden ....Joseph	Norris ....Emily	1872 01 08	UT, Salt Lake City
Bowden ....William	Churchill.............Elizabeth	1830 09 20	ENG, Bristol
Bowen ....Benjamin L.	Gowens.............Barbara	1876 07 24	UT, Salt Lake City
Bowen ....Israel	Durham ....Charlotte L.	1825	NY
Bowen ....John Morris	Densley ....Ann	1872 02 26	UT, Salt Lake City
Bowen ....John Morris	Densley ....Mary	1883 09 13	UT, Salt Lake City
Bowen ....Lewis	Harris ....Mary Ann	1836 09 28	Wales
Bowen ....Thomas	Evans ....Hannah	1834	Wales

Male	Female	Date	Place
Bowering ....George Kirkham	Cosgrove..............Sarah Ann	1869 09 20	UT, Salt Lake City
Bowering ....Isaac	Riden....................Hannah	1812 01 22	Wales
Bowers ....James	Lay ....Maria	1831 04 01	ENG, Stafford
Bowers ....John	Leach ....Rosannah	1835 11 08	ENG, Oldbury
Bowles..............Enoch	Webb.....................Amelia Emily	1865 12 08	UT, Nephi
Bowman ....Hyrum W.	Eskildsen..............Maren Katrina	1867 05 25	UT, Salt Lake City
Bowman ....William	Sneddon..............Margaret	1820 10 28	Scotland
Box ....John Henry	Haynes................Elizabeth	1837 11 30	IN, Lawrence Co.
Boyack..............James	Mealmaker ....Elizabeth	1827 11 14	Scotland
Boyce ....Benjamin	Judd ....Susannah C.	1836 02 08	Canada
Boyes ....George	Geldard ....Ann		ENG
Boyes ....George	Taylor ....Elizabeth	1847 07 16	Trail
Boyce ....John	Despain..............Ella Eugenia	1879 01 30	
Boyce ....Martin Calvin	Marshall ....Louisa	1865 05 07	
Boyd ....George Albert	Roe......................Isabella Jane	1866 11 10	UT, Salt Lake City
Boyer ....Augustus Sell	Houtz...................Catharine	1839	PA
Boyer ....John Sell	Crandall...............Julia Ann	1866 02 08	
Bracken ....Levi	Clark....................Elizabeth	1810	OH
Bradfield ....George	Vockins ....Sarah	1840 10 25	
Bradford..........Jehial Lee	Sprague ....Abigail	1830 08 21	
Bradford..........Pleasant S.	Jones ....Jane	1864 10 15	UT, Salt Lake City
Bradley ....George Henry	Love ....Elizabeth A.	1857 03 10	UT, Nephi
Bradley ....George W.	Kroll.....................Elizabeth	1835 03 02	NY
Bradley ....George W.	Wagle..................Cynthia	1854 03 14	
Bradley ....Thomas	Miller ....Ann		
Bradley ....Thomas J.	Kroll.....................Elizabeth	1828	NY, Clarence
Bradshaw ....Edward	Bagshaw ....Sarah	1848 09 06	ENG, Derbyshire
Bradshaw ....John	White...................Ann	1817 08 27	ENG, Derbyshire
Bradshaw ....Richard	Simpson ....Elizabeth	1844 03 11	
Bradshaw ....Richard T.	Bone....................Mary Ann	1867 07 26	UT, Lehi
Bradshaw ....Samuel	Elsey ....Mary Ann	1852	UT, Salt Lake City
Brady ....Charles	Turple..................Susan Ann E.	1841	
Brady ....Jordan	Howell ....Mary Lavina	1861 12 10	UT, Fairview
Brady ....Lindsay A.	Hendrickson........Elizabeth Ann	1831 10 18	KY, Washington
Brady ....Lindsay A.	Ward ....Susannah	1852 06 11	UT, Salt Lake City
Brady ....Marion H.	Richards..............Frances	1855 02 06	UT
Brady ....Marion H.	Richards..............Lucy Ann	1858 03 22	UT, Salt Lake City
Braffitt ....George W.	Webber ....Sarah	1852 12 02	
Braithwaite.......Rowland	Askew ....Hannah	1822 03 04	ENG
Bramall ....Samuel	Coffman ....Susan Elmina	1875 11 01	UT, Salt Lake City
Bramall ....William	Drayson...............Ann	1849 11 26	ENG
Brandon...........George W.	Fowler ....Keziah	1831 10 06	
Brandon...........Thomas J.	Cherry ....Mary Margaret	1856 05 09	UT, Salt Lake City
Brandon...........Thomas J.	Palmer................Lovina	1847	IA
Brandow ....Alfred H.	Cordon ....Rachel Ann	1888 11 04	UT, Willard
Brantley ....Thomas Berges	Camp ....Margaret H.	1866 07 01	
Breinholt ....Jens Christian	Hansen................Christiane	1874 03 30	
Breinholt ....Lars J.	Nielsen ....Ane Sophia		
Brett.................James	Colston................Catherine E.	1879 03 27	UT, Salt Lake City
Brewer ....Myron	Proctor ....Ellen	1854 03	UT, Salt Lake City
Brewer ....William	Grinnel ....Jane	1806 04 07	
Brewerton ....George	Pilley ....Ann	1822 08 06	ENG, Lincolnshire
Brewerton ....Thomas W.	Crooks................Sarah Ann	1850 12 25	ENG, Nottingham
Brian ....Daniel Gross	Ashworth ....Martha E.	1860 12 31	UT, Salt Lake City

Male	Female	Date	Place
Bridge ....Joseph	Walsh ....Mary Ann	1865 07 08	UT, Salt Lake City
Bridges ....Charles Henry	Pearson..............Frances E.	1859 06 20	UT, Salt Lake City
Bridges ....Henry M.	Lowe ....Sarah Louisa	1824	ENG
Bridges ....Robert Albert	Powell ....Eliza Mary	1880	
Bridges ....William Erskine	Morse ....Teresa	1831	
Briggs ....Hugh L.	Vine...................Susanna		
Briggs ....John	Butterworth.........Ruth	1835	
Briggs ....Thomas	Burgess..............Ann	1877 05 25	UT, St. George
Bright ....Gilbert	Hill ....Alice	1869 12 06	
Bright ....John	Ginther ....Susannah	1796	
Bright ....John Jr.	Pugh...................Susan	1835 08 13	TN
Brimhall ....George W.	Mayer ....Rachel Ann	1852 02 02	UT, Salt Lake City
Brimhall ....John	Harris ....Anaretta	1850 06	UT, Woods Cross
Brindle ....Benjamin W.	Pouney...............Sarah	1839 12 25	ENG
Brinkerhoff ......James	Henderson ....Eliza Jane	1854 06 11	UT, Salt Lake City
Brinkerhoff ......James	Snider................Sally Ann	1836 01 01	NY, Cayuga
Brinkerhoff ......Levi	Cameron ....Eliza Jane	1870 04 25	
Brinton ....David	Dilworth ....Harriet W.	1848 01 14	NE
Brinton ....David	Halstensen ....Hilda Mathilda	1867 10 19	UT, Salt Lake City
Briscoe ....George	Ward ....Mary	1862	ENG
Bristol ....William	Jensen ....Ane Marie S.		
Broadbent........Enoch	Lunn ....Keturah Ann	1842 07 05	ENG
Broadbent........Francis G.	Steers................Sarah Frances	1860 12 24	UT, Salt Lake City
Broadbent........James W.	Greenwood ....Mary	1835	ENG
Broadbent........Joseph	Schofield ....Elizabeth		
Broadbent........Levi	Code ....Eliza	1848 06 15	ENG, Lincolnshire
Broadbent........Thomas	Nuttall................Mary Jane	1863 04 11	UT, Salt Lake City
Broadhead.......David	Betts..................Elizabeth	1868 05 04	UT, Salt Lake City
Broadhead.......David	Betts..................Harriet	1850 01 29	ENG, Coventry
Broadhead.......David	Morris ....Mary	1856 02 17	UT, Salt Lake City
Broadhead.......Robert	Clegg.................Alice	1861 01 15	UT, Heber
Broadhead.......William	Golding..............Sarah	1830	
Brockbank ....Isaac	Brown................Sarah	1852 10 02	
Brockbank ....Isaac	Mainwaring.........Elizabeth	1835	ENG, Liverpool
Brockbank ....Isaac Jr.	Howard...............Katherine Alice	1860 06 25	
Brockbank ....Isaac Jr.	Park...................Mary Ann	1865 01	
Brockbank ....Joshua	Jex ....Sarah Ann T.	1868 03 07	UT, Salt Lake City
Bronson ....Clinton D.	Andrews.............Lovisa	1850 09 25	UT, Salt Lake City
Bronson ....Lemon	Brass.................Lucy	1817 01 02	OH, Geauga
Brooks ....Francis William	Williams.............Harriet Cordelia	1851	IL, Warren
Brotherson.......Hans	Jensen ....Frederickka A.	1869 10 18	UT, Salt Lake City
Brough............Samuel Richard	Bott...................Elizabeth	1858 02 01	ENG
Brough............Thomas	Paterson.............Jane	1851 11 09	ENG
Brower ....Ariah Coats	Humphrey ....Mary Jane	1854 03 05	UT, Salt Lake City
Brower ....Ariah Coats	Hussey...............Margaret E.	1838 09 06	IL
Brower ....Ariah Coats	Thompson ....Margaret	1853 02 06	UT, Salt Lake City
Browett ....Daniel	Harris ....Elizabeth	1834 06 02	ENG
Brown ....Abia William	Cadwallader........Abigail	1830 04 30	
Brown ....Abraham	Sheldon..............Harriet	1834 03 26	VT, Simonsville
Brown ....Alfred	Doty...................Eliza	1848 04 30	
Brown ....Ben	Cadwallader........Abigail		
Brown ....Benjamin F.	Leavitt ....Lucinda	1848 02 12	MI, Hillsdale
Brown ....Charles	Sanders..............Zillah		
Brown ....Cornelius	Hamer ....Sarah	1852	IA

Male	Female	Date	Place
Brown ....Ebenezer	Draper ....Phebe	1842 08 26	IL, Pike
Brown ....Ezekiel	Slawson ....Catherine	1825 03 20	PA, Erie
Brown ....George	Bitely ....Sarah Adams		
Brown ....George W.	Barrows.............Emma Lorena	1858 08 16	UT, Salt Lake City
Brown ....Hans Jorgen	Larsen ....Anna Christina	1867 04 20	UT, Salt Lake City
Brown ....Hans Jorgen	Nielsen ....Anna Amelia	1862 04 13	Ocean
Brown ....Henry	Beck ....Elizabeth Ann	1876 10 01	UT, Salt Lake City
Brown ....James	McRee...............Mary	1846 07 16	IL, Nauvoo
Brown ....James	Smith..................Abigail	1846 02 08	IL, Nauvoo
Brown ....James	Steadwell ....Sarah (Sally)	1845 01 10	IL, Nauvoo
Brown ....James Andrew	Brown.................Mary Eliza	1851 04 12	IA, Kanesville
Brown ....James Henry	Bullock ....Ann Elizabeth	1852 02 10	ENG, Offchurch
Brown ....James Polly	Hansen...............Petrea	1855	
Brown ....James Polly	Reasor ....Eunice	1836 04 13	IN, Floyd Co.
Brown ....John	Crosby................Elizabeth	1844 05 21	
Brown ....John	Snyder.................Amy	1854 02 22	
Brown ....John	Wilkins................Jane	1851 03 15	ENG
Brown ....John	Young.................Mary	1836 12 17	
Brown ....John	Zimmerman........Margaret		
Brown ....John Weaver	Eckersley ....Fannie	1859 11	
Brown ....Jonathan	Cousins ....Sarah	1838 10 31	ENG, Berkshire
Brown ....Jonathan	Langfield ....Ann	1856 11	UT
Brown ....Joseph G.	Brown.................Esther	1857 01 18	UT, Draper
Brown ....Joseph G.	Manhard.............Lovina	1857	
Brown ....Joseph G.	Young.................Harriet Maria	1851 12 31	UT, Salt Lake City
Brown ....Joshua Woods	Bailey ....Sarah R.	1856 04 03	UT, Salt Lake City
Brown ....Neuman	Pectol ....Jemima Bell	1857 05	
Brown ....Neuman	Petty...................Sarah Geraldine	1851 05 08	
Brown ....Neuman	Taylor ....Lora Ann	1852 06 18	UT, Manti
Brown ....Norman	Smith..................Annie	1858 12 01	
Brown ....Robert	Beveridge...........Elizabeth	1837 11 04	Scotland
Brown ....Robert	Davies ....Mary	1872 09 21	UT, Beaver
Brown ....Robert	Evans ....Ann	1852 11 18	ENG, Bristol
Brown ....Robert H.	Tuttle ....Elizabeth Ann	1861 04 16	UT, Manti
Brown ....Samuel	Munday ....Jane	1853 04 19	
Brown ....Thomas B.	Brown.................Eliza	1870 05 09	
Brown ....Thomas D.	Willis..................Mary Lucretia	1855 10 19	UT, Cedar City
Brown ....William	Saxton................Frances	1814 04 18	ENG, Warwick
Brown ....William Albert	Todd...................Emily	1890 01 15	UT, Taylorsville
Brown ....William Jr.	Burnett...............Ellen	1867 07 13	
Brown ....William P.	Blanchard...........Mary Ann	1854 12 24	MO, St. Louis
Brownell..........Gideon	Wheeler..............Elizabeth	1814	MA, Dartmouth
Browning ....David H.	Garner................Elizabeth Jane	1854 05 28	
Browning ....James Green	Chase.................Harriet Louise	1855 07 20	
Browning ....James Green	Hills ....Olive	1852 03 22	UT, Salt Lake City
Browning ....James Green	Neal....................Mary Ann	1827 11 20	TN, Sumner
Bryant ....Edwin	Grassing.............Ann	1826	ENG, Gloucester
Bryce ....Ebenezer	Park....................Mary Ann	1854 04 16	UT, Salt Lake City
Bryne (Byrne) ..Moses	Beus...................Ann	1857 11 30	
Bryne (Byrne) ..Moses	Cardon ....Catherine	1854 11 05	UT, Salt Lake City
Bryner ....Hans Ulrich	Wintsch ....Verena	1826 03 29	Switzerland
Bryner ....Hans Ulrich Jr.	Mathis ....Anna Maria D.	1849	Switzerland
Bryson ....John	Cowan.................Margaret	1815 06 15	IRE
Bryson ....Samuel	Connery ....Sarah Ann	1839	IRE, Downs

Male	Female	Date	Place
Bryson ....Samuel	Fairchild ....Polly Tryphena	1867 05 25	UT, Salt Lake City
Buchanan ....Archibald W. O.	Brown.................Mary Ann	1860 01 01	UT, Manti
Buchanan ....Archibald W. O.	Whiting ....Helen Amelia	1855 08 22	
Buchanan ....James	Land ....Narcissa B.	1879 01 27	CO, Huerfano Co.
Buchanan ....John	Bache..................Nancy Ann	1812 04 12	KY, Lexington
Buchanan ....John	Coons.................Adaline	1851 02 23	IA, Coonsville
Buchanan ....John	Wilkinson............Sarah	1866 04 28	UT, Salt Lake City
Buck ....Charles	Chantry ....Hannah	1859 12 22	ENG, Nottingham
Buckland.........Alondus	Aldrich ....Nancy Laura	1846 10 10	CA, Mission D.
Buckland.........James D. Jr.	Aldrich ....Nancy Laura	1855 07 09	UT, Bountiful
Buckland.........Joseph	Daggett ....Hannah	1823 02 16	VT, Orange
Buckley ....Samuel	Dawtry ....Mary Ann	1837	ENG
Buckwalter.......John	Shuler.................Sarah	1828 02 21	PA
Buckwalter.......John E.	Morris ....Susan	1863 07 23	UT, American Fork
Budge ....Thomas Scott	Ponton.................Huldah	1862 05	
Budge ....William	Stratford ....Julia	1856 11 24	ENG, Baxex
Buell ....Norman	Huntington...........Presendia L.	1827 01 08	NY, Jefferson Co.
Bulkley............Newman	Draper.................Jane	1844 01 07	IL, Nauvoo
Bulkley............Newman	Palmer.................Lovina	1857	
Bulkley............Noah	Newman..............Nancy Ann	1807	NY, Tioga
Bulkley............Samuel	Giles...................Louisa	1872 03 04	UT, Salt Lake City
Bull ....Charles	Round ....Flora Jane	1861 12 08	
Bull ....Daniel Berry	Tantam................Elizabeth	1840 10 25	ENG, Warwick
Bull ....Joseph	Bullock ....Sarah	1812	ENG
Bullock............Benjamin III	Kimball...............Dorothy	1818 01 24	NH, Grafton
Bullock............Henry	Griffin ....Sarah	1859 04 21	ENG, Stafford
Bullock............Isaac	..............................Ann		
Bullock............Isaac	Stott....................Emma	1856 12 14	
Bullock............Isaac	Wood..................Electa	1856 12 14	UT, Salt Lake City
Bullock............James	Bromwich ....Elizabeth	1827 11 10	
Bullock............James	Hill......................Mary	1836 03 28	Canada
Bullock............James Jr.	Bailey ....Margaret	1860 12 08	Scotland
Bullock............Thomas	Rushton...............Henrietta	1838 06 25	
Bullock............Thomas Henry	McBride...............Jane		
Bullock............Thomas Henry	Wagstaff..............Mary Ann	1864 06 25	UT
Bunker ....Edward	Abbott.................Emily	1846 02 19	IL, Nauvoo
Bunker ....Edward	Browning ....Sarah Ann	1852 06 26	UT, Salt Lake City
Bunker ....Edward	McQuarrie ....Mary M.	1861 04 20	UT, Salt Lake City
Bunnell ....Daniel Kimball	Muir....................Mary	1874 02 01	UT, Salt Lake City
Bunnell ....David Edwin	Conrad ....Sarah Helen	1830 04 15	NY, Fayette
Bunnell ....Stephen	Grover.................Percia C.	1856 09 19	UT, Provo
Bunnell ....Zuriel	Van Benthuysen..Keziah K.		
Bunting ....James	Slater..................Ann	1819 03 15	ENG, Derbyshire
Bunting ....James Lovett	Dye.....................Harriet	1859 05 15	
Bunting ....John Slater	Doxey..................Mary	1865 10 20	UT, Salt Lake City
Burbank ....Daniel M.	Southworth..........Sarah Zurviah	1864 07 18	UT, Salt Lake City
Burbidge ....James R.	Brown.................Mary	1836 03 21	ENG
Burbidge ....James W.	Humphreys..........Sarah Jane	1858 07 05	UT, Salt Lake City
Burchell ....Joseph	Llewellyn ....Mary	1839 07 18	ENG, Birmingham
Burgess ....Harrison	Foster.................Sophia Minerva	1835 07 01	OH, Kirtland
Burgess ....Harrison	Hammond ....Amanda M.	1846 02 06	IL, Nauvoo
Burgess ....Hyrum	Dykes ....Eliza Jane	1852	
Burgess ....Hyrum	Smith..................Agnes	1872 03 06	
Burgess ....Melanchton	McIntire ....Margaret	1855 04 10	

Male	Female	Date	Place
Burgess ....William	Chamberlain........Catherine	1859	
Burgess ....William	Keeling ....Dorcas	1854 12 17	UT, Salt Lake City
Burgess ....William	Leggett ....Charlotte E.	1853	
Burgess ....William	Pulsipher ....Mariah	1840 09 14	
Burgess ....William	Stockwell............Vilate	1813 05 01	NH, Chesterfield
Burke ....John Matthias	Van Benthuysen..Keziah K.	1832	MO
Burlingame ......Orson	Kelsey ....Cecelia	1854	UT, Union Fort
Burnett............David R.	Ruxton...............Isabella	1831 10 19	Scotland
Burnett............David R.	Wilde ....Sarah Jane		UT, Tooele
Burnham ....George Franklin	Smith.................Sarah Marinda	1862 11 07	UT, Richmond
Burnham.........James L.	Huntley..............Mary Ann	1834 12 01	VT, Waitsfield
Burnham.........Luther C.	Barnett ....Matilda	1863 11 19	UT, Salt Lake City
Burnham.........Luther C.	Stewart..............Mary Lucinda	1875	
Burnham.........Wallace C.	Hansen...............Anna Christine	1878 10 12	UT, Salt Lake City
Burnham.........Wallace K.	Standley ....Lydia	1865 04 11	UT, Salt Lake City
Burningham .....Alfred	Barrett ....Mary Ann	1865 09 09	UT, Salt Lake City
Burningham .....Thomas	Hook...................Ellen	1861 08	UT, Salt Lake City
Burningham .....Thomas	White..................Sarah Elizabeth	1826 05 29	ENG, Surrey
Burns ....Joseph	Hancock ....Ellen	1831 03 20	ENG, Brampton
Burrell ....John Battish	Pulsipher ....Mary	1850	IA, Council Bluffs
Burridge..........George W.	Shaw ....Hannah Jane	1847 11 18	Scotland
Burriston ....John	Stewart..............Mary Priscilla	1858 11 09	
Burrows ....William Creeland	Louder................Catherine	1857 01 01	
Burrup.............Edward	Dutson...............Susanna	1798 03 28	ENG, St. Clement
Burrup.............James	Cocker...............Mary	1867 02 09	UT, Salt Lake City
Burrup.............James Phillips	Bennett..............Mary Ann	1855 01 26	
Burt.................John Davidson	Howell ....Ann	1875 08 09	
Burton.............James	Walton...............Isabella	1825 03 05	ENG, Yorkshire
Burton.............Joseph	Cusworth............Eliza	1846 06 08	ENG
Burton.............Joseph	Hudson..............Ann	1843 04 30	ENG
Burton.............Joseph F.	Driver ....Mary Ann E.	1886 03 30	UT, Logan
Burton.............Robert Lamb	Holmes..............Ann	1849	ENG
Burton.............Robert Walton	Marriott..............Elizabeth	1845 02 06	IL, Nauvoo
Burton.............Samuel Jr.	Shipley ....Hannah	1804 01 11	ENG, Yorkshire
Burton.............William G.	Tregale..............Hannah	1852 05 09	ENG, Devonshire
Burton.............William Hudson	Marshall ....Mary Jane	1876 10 23	
Burton.............William W.	Fielding ....Ellen	1861 09 02	UT, Salt Lake City
Burton.............William W.	Fielding ....Rachel	1856 03 28	UT, Salt Lake City
Busby ....William	Meadows............Maria	1846 10 23	ENG, Lancaster
Busenbark ....Elias M.	Smith.................Sarah Ann	1876 10 15	
Busenbark ....Henry D.	Epperson............Martha Jane	1852 06	IA, Honey Creek
Busenbark ....Isaac	Manning ....Abigail	1824	NY, Seneca Co.
Busenbark ....Isaac	Patterson............Lovina	1853	
Bush ....William James	Luddington ....Angeline A.	1864 09 12	UT, Pleasant Grove
Bushman ....Martin	Degen ....Elizabeth	1827 05 20	PA, Lancaster
Bushnell...........John	Brockbank ....Elizabeth	1854 08 15	UT, Fillmore
Butler ....Alva	Labrum...............Jane Elizabeth	1867 03 16	UT, Salt Lake City
Butler ....James	Harris ....Elizabeth	1858	
Butler ....John	Hall....................Elizabeth	1834 06 18	ENG
Butler ....John Lowe	Blythe ....Henrietta Eaton	1857 09 05	UT, Salt Lake City
Butler ....John Lowe	Skeen.................Caroline F.	1831 02 03	KY, Simpson Co.
Butler ....John Ockford	Thompson...........Mary Ann L.	1868 06 06	UT, Salt Lake City
Butler ....Pehr Larson	Hanson...............Ellen Elna	1811	Sweden
Butler ....Peter	Nelson................Anne	1845	Sweden

Male	Female	Date	Place
Butler ....Richard	Morris ....Elizabeth Ann	1841 09 20	Wales
Butler ....William	Harvey................Emma	1856 01 23	ENG, Herefordshire
Butt ....Uriah R.	Pucell ....Margaret Augusta	1857 02 18	
Buttars ....David	Keep...................Sarah	1866 12 16	UT, Lehi
Buttars ....David	Spaulding ....Margaret	1848 12 14	Scotland
Butterfield ....Almon	Farmer ....Elizabeth Ann	1866 01 27	UT, Salt Lake City
Butterfield ....George	Cook...................Emma	1870 02 14	
Butterfield ....Jacob K.	Hayes.................Sarah	1855 02 28	UT, Salt Lake City
Butterfield ....Jacob Kemp	Jennings.............Sarah	1850 10 20	UT, Salt Lake City
Butterfield ....Thomas J.	Parker ....Mary Jane	1835 02 15	ME, Farmington
Buttle ....William	Acomb...............Elizabeth	1856 11 16	UT, Salt Lake City
Buys ....Edward	Bromley..............Celesta C.	1867 03 23	UT, Salt Lake City
Buys ....Edward	Hamilton.............Margaret	1876	
Bybee ....Byram	Knudsen.............Else Marie	1856 08 15	UT, Salt Lake City
Bybee ....Byram	Lane ....Elizabeth Ann	1820 01 05	KY, Barren Co.
Bybee ....David Bowman	Penrod ....Mary Elizabeth	1857 02 28	UT, Salt Lake City
Byington ....Hiram N.	Hawkins ....Sarah	1828 01 27	NY, Oneida Co.
Byington ....Joseph H.	Molland ....Hannah	1864 02 27	UT, Salt Lake City
Byrne ....John Phillip	Clare ....Edith Ann	1884 02 17	WY, Uinta

C

Male	Female	Date	Place
Cable ....John	Cornelius............Mary Ann		
Cahoon............Andrew	Carruth ....Janet	1848 07 16	
Cahoon............Andrew	Carruth ....Margaret	1848 07 17	
Cahoon............Daniel Stiles	Spencer..............Martha	1846 01 16	
Cahoon............Mahonri M.	Romney..............Sarah	1853 11 02	
Cahoon............Rais Bell C. R.	Johnson ....Mary Charlotte	1867 11 16	UT, Salt Lake City
Cahoon............Reynolds	Roberts ....Lucina	1842	
Cahoon............Reynolds	Stiles ....Thirza	1810 12 11	NY, Herkimer
Cain ....John T.	Nightingale ....Margaret	1850 10 22	
Cain ....Joseph	Whittaker............Elizabeth	1847 02 01	ENG
Calder..............George	Bennion..............Mary	1861 04 06	UT, Taylorsville
Calderwood .....Alexander	Salmon...............Margaret	1862 12 28	
Caldwell...........David	Vaughan.............Mary Ann	1813 05 14	Scotland
Caldwell...........David Henry	Johnson ....Fanny C.	1856 01 24	UT, Taylorsville
Caldwell...........Matthew	Guymon ....Barzilla	1843 10 17	IL, Carthage
Caldwell...........Robert	Vallier ....Mary Jane	1860	Trail
Caldwell...........Robert	Vallier ....Mary Jane	1909 11 23	IA, Logan
Caldwell...........Robert C.	Hill ....Margaret Ann	1854	
Calkins............William	Bennett...............Martha	1852 05 31	
Calkins............William	Parneby..............Elizabeth	1875 02 20	
Call ....Anson	Bowen ....Ann Mariah	1851 04 16	UT, Salt Lake City
Call ....Anson	Clark..................Margaretta U.	1857 02 07	
Call ....Anson	Flint ....Mary	1833 10 03	OH, Lake Co.
Call ....Anson	Summers.............Emma	1857 02 27	UT, Salt Lake City
Call ....Anson Vasco	Holbrook.............Charlotte	1853 01 28	
Call ....Chester	Barlow ....Pamela E.	1888	
Call ....Cyril	Tiffany ....Sarah (Sally)	1806 04 06	VT, Franklin Co.
Call ....Israel	Judd ....Jane Lucinda	1880 06 11	UT, St. George
Callan ....Stephen J. P.	Marshall ....Sarah	1888 07 18	
Callaway.........Levi H.	Van Buren ....Mary Francis	1850 11 17	IA, Garden Grove
Callister ....Thomas	Smith..................Caroline Clara	1845 08 31	

Male	Female	Date	Place
Calvert ....Charles	Borsen................Annie Bolliti		
Cambron..........Joseph	Jensen ....Ane Marie S.	1875	UT, Nephi
Cameron..........William	Lint ....Jane Francis	1837 11 23	
Camp ....Reuben	Warn ....Elizabeth Pollow		
Camp ....Richard	Evans ....Amelia	1857	UT, Salt Lake City
Camp ....Williams W.	Greer..................Diannah	1822 01 18	
Camp ....Williams W.	Lindsay...............Marion	1865	UT, Salt Lake City
Campbell ....Alexander	Mattatahl ....Barbara E.	1817	
Campbell ....Daniel	Cady...................Maria	1845	
Campbell ....David	Izatt ....Jane	1832	
Campbell ....David William	Butler.................Elizabeth	1866 10 11	
Campbell ....Eli	Ash....................Hannah	1881 12 10	UT, Mendon
Campbell ....Isaiah	Garrard...............Sarah S.	1854 01 21	UT, Salt Lake City
Campbell ....Jared LeRoy	Tice ....Polly	1842 03 13	NY, Steuben Co.
Campbell ....Joseph H.	Mathews.............Elizabeth	1861 01 01	UT, Providence
Campbell ....Orson Grant	Dewsnup............Ann	1871 05 21	
Campbell ....Solomon L.	Campbell.............Lovina	1848 12 23	MO
Campkin ....George	Bell ....Elizabeth	1837 01 05	ENG
Campkin ....Isaac	Webb..................Martha	1847 02 13	ENG
Candland ....David	Barton ....Mary Ann	1844 03 27	IL, Nauvoo
Candland ....David	Woodhouse.........Annie	1855 11 05	UT, Salt Lake City
Cannon ....Angus Munn	Hughes...............Martha Maria	1884 10 06	UT, Salt Lake City
Cannon ....Angus Munn	Mousley..............Ann Amanda	1858 07 18	UT, Salt Lake City
Cannon ....Angus Munn	Mousley..............Sarah Maria	1858 07 18	UT, Salt Lake City
Cannon ....David Henry	Crossgrove..........Josephine L.	1867 10 19	UT, Salt Lake City
Cannon ....George Q.	Telle ....Martha	1868	UT, Salt Lake City
Cannon ....George Q.	Tenney ....Eliza L.	1865 07 29	UT, Salt Lake City
Cantwell...........James Sherlock	Hamer ....Elizabeth C.	1838 04 27	ENG, Lancashire
Capener...........William	Rigby..................Ellen	1861 03 23	
Capson ....Charles	Ranck..................Sarah Jane	1852 08 12	
Capsson ....Nils	Lundstrom ....Gustava Amelea	1854 02 05	Ocean
Carbine ....Edmund Zebulon	Rider ....Adelia	1823 02 15	
Carbine ....William V.	Miller ....Sarah Jane	1879 05 30	UT, Salt Lake City
Card.................Amasa	Richardson..........Jerusha Ann	1842 01 08	
Card.................Cyrus William	Booth..................Emma	1859 11 07	
Card.................William Fuller	Sabin..................Sarah Ann	1811 12 28	NY, Dutchess Co.
Cardon.............Jean Paul	Goudin ....Susanna	1857 03 16	UT, Ogden
Cardon.............John	Furrer ....Anna Regula	1856 10	
Cardon.............Philippe	Gaudin-Moise......Jeanne Marie	1863 03 21	UT, Hyrum
Cardon.............Philippe	Tourn..................Martha Marie	1821 02 01	Italy
Carlile ....George	Giles...................Laura Ann	1856 11 25	
Carlile ....James	Lee.....................Fanny	1863 04 18	
Carlile ....John	Williamson...........Elizabeth	1844	ENG, Lincolnshire
Carlile ....Robert	Spouncer.............Christiana		ENG
Carling ....Isaac V.	Browning.............Asenath E.	1854	UT, Salt Lake City
Carling ....John	Green..................Ann	1844 06 10	IL, Nauvoo
Carlisle ....John	Hocquard ....Elizabeth	1857 02 08	UT, Salt Lake City
Carlisle ....Thomas Fields	Hocquard ....Fanny Sophia	1854 01 22	UT, Pleasant Grove
Carlsen ....Ole	Hansen................Ane Margaret	1845 08 09	Denmark
Carlsen ....Peter	Anderson.............Annie E.	1856 12 27	
Carlson ....James	Jensen ....Caroline	1870 02 14	UT, Salt Lake City
Carlson ....Swen	Hammer ....Johanna C.	1865 12 01	UT, Salt Lake City
Carlson ....Swen	Larsson ....Bengta	1852 12 17	Sweden
Carothers........John Thomas	Clark...................Kate Arabel	1866 01 11	CA, Sacramento

Male	Female	Date	Place
Carpenter ....Daily	Baldwin ....Phebe	1842 03 13	
Carroll.............Patrick	Robinson............Margaret E.	1854	Canada
Carroll.............Willard	Moulton ....Charlotte	1869 03 16	UT, Salt Lake City
Carruth ....William	Wilde ....Emma	1870 05 09	
Carson............George	Hough ....Ann	1817	PA, Mifflin Co.
Carson............Valentine	Waggle...............Hannah	1862	UT, Nephi
Carstensen ......Peter Cornelius	Hansen...............Elsie Sophie		
Carstensen ......Peter Cornelius	Petersen.............Karen	1864 04 27	Ocean
Carter ....Dominicus	Mecham ....Sylvia Amaret	1839 03 28	MO, Far West
Carter ....Edwin J.	Stockdale ....Mary Ann	1830	ENG, Devonshire
Carter ....Erastus Francis	Green ....Alice Elisabeth	1870 11 21	
Carter ....George	Brown................Frances	1868 12 14	UT, Salt Lake City
Carter ....Gideon H.	Woods...............Charlotte	1833 12 31	
Carter ....James	Adams................Alice	1874 03 16	UT, Salt Lake City
Carter ....John	Libby ....Hannah Knight	1805 03 02	ME, Cumberland
Carter ....John Benbow	Blake ....Emma	1873 06 04	UT, Salt Lake City
Carter ....John Russell	Powell ....Eliza Mary	1856	UT, Parowan
Carter ....Samuel	Davis.................Sarah E.	1861	UT, Salt Lake City
Carter ....Samuel	James ....Sarah	1879	
Carter ....Samuel	Masser ....Ellen	1860 03 08	ENG, Stafford.
Carter ....William	Benbow ....Ellen	1843 12 05	IL, Nauvoo
Carter ....William	Turnbow..............Sophronia E. L. H.	1857 02 08	
Carter ....William	Utley..................Harriet T.	1853 11 23	UT, Salt Lake City
Carter ....William F.	Howard...............Mary Elizabeth	1854 09 10	UT, Salt Lake City
Carter ....William F.	Mecham ....Roxena	1847 03 13	NE
Carter ....William F.	Mecham ....Sally Ann	1857 12 02	
Carter ....William F.	York...................Sarah	1831	
Cartwright ....John	Hardwick ....Ann	1859 01 30	ENG, Derbyshire
Carver.............John	Eames................Mary Ann	1850 03 10	Ocean
Carver.............John	Eames................Sarah Ann	1871 01 09	UT, Salt Lake City
Carver.............John	Tellefsen ....Rachel Fredrica	1864 12 10	UT, Salt Lake City
Case ....George W.	Stephenson.........Eliza Ann		
Case ....George W.	Thorn.................Sarah	1866 02 04	UT, Salt Lake City
Case ....James	Wiard.................Hannah	1815 12 12	OH, Austinburg
Case ....Solomon Cowles	Pectol ....Elizabeth	1851 09 06	UT, Springville
Case ....Solomon Cowles	Richey ....Emily		
Case ....Solomon Cowles	Sampson............Sarah	1855 12 04	
Casey ....John Albert	Carter ....Elizabeth	1881 03 10	
Cash ....James	Jones ....Ann		
Casper............Duncan Spears	Allison ....Matilda	1845 05 24	IL, Nauvoo
Casper............James Moroni	McFarland...........Sarah Jean	1876 02 14	UT, Salt Lake City
Casper............William	Durbin ....Avarilla	1809 05 06	OH, Knox Co.
Casper............William Wallace	Bean..................Sarah Ann	1844 08 24	IL, Adams Co.
Cassity............Edward Penale	Churchill ....Elizabeth		
Cast ....Eric Magnus	Harrison ....Alice	1864 12 25	
Casteel ....James Nolan	Weaver...............Miranda Bridget	1855	CA, San Bern.
Castleton ....James Joseph	Brown................Frances Sarah	1853 01 02	ENG
Casto ....Abel	Galland...............Mary	1812 06 03	
Casto ....Mathew Gailand	Daniels...............Elizabeth	1846 02 07	IL, Nauvoo
Casto ....William W.	Nielsen...............Petrasanne C.	1867 11 16	UT, Salt Lake City
Catlin ....Richard	Harrison ....Alice		
Cazier.............Adelbert	Parkes................Mary Ann	1880 10 12	
Cazier.............David C.	Mangum.............Sarah Frances	1857 06 07	UT, Nephi
Cazier.............David C.	Naylor................Eliza		

Male	Female	Date	Place
Cederlof...........John Monson	Bjork...............Mary	1865	Ocean
Chadwick.........Abraham	Foxall ....Mary	1850 12	
Chadwick.........Abraham	Garner.............Mary Marinda	1866 12 13	UT, North Ogden
Chadwick.........Abraham	Siebenaller.........Anna	1899	
Chadwick.........Abraham	Wheeler.............Mary	1853 05 22	
Chadwick.........James	Candland.............Mary Catherine	1866 01 20	UT, Salt Lake City
Chadwick.........Joseph	Goode ....Sarah	1857	
Chadwick.........Joseph	Whitehead..........Mary	1832 11 19	ENG, Lancashire
Chalmers ....Horace S.	Miles...................Malinda Ann		UT, Salt Lake City
Chamberlain ....John Allen	Watmough..........Amanda S.	1864 12 29	UT, Salt Lake City
Chamberlain ....Solomon	Morse ....Teresa	1848	UT, Salt Lake City
Chamberlain ....William	Allen ....Mary Ellen	1836 11 12	ENG, Oxford
Chandler..........Calvin H.	Treseder.............Elizabeth	1874 05 25	UT, Salt Lake City
Chandler..........Frank	Stark...................Gustavia Sophia	1866 06 29	UT, Coalville
Chandler..........Frank	Trower................Sarah	1857 11 07	ENG, Sussex
Chandler..........Henry	Wall ....Fanny Maria	1903 09 01	UT, Millville
Chaney	Tucker ....Mary Ann		
Chapman.........Hyrum	Fullmer ....Rhoda Ann	1871 04 10	UT, Salt Lake City
Chapman.........Isaac Moroni	Ashworth ....Sarah Ann	1856 11 23	
Chapman.........Robert	Skellington ....Elizabeth		
Chapman.........Welcome	Mackey...............Ann	1855 10 05	UT, Manti
Chapman.........Welcome	Marsden ....Harriet Zelnora	1876	
Chapman.........Welcome	Risley ....Susan Amelia	1831	NY, Madison
Chapman.........William	Ward ....Emma Ellen	1875 08	UT, Salt Lake City
Chapman.........William	Watson...............Rachel S.	1848 09 12	ENG
Chappell ....William E.	Lake ....Hannah	1859 01 08	ENG, Devonshire
Charman..........George	Smith..................Caroline	1844	ENG, Nottingham
Chase ....Abner	Scott...................Amy	1808 11 02	VT, Addison Co.
Chase ....Eli	Hills ....Olive	1840 07 25	NY
Chase ....Elisha Wells	Barker ....Harriet	1857 02 20	UT, Salt Lake City
Chase ....Ezra	Wells ....Tirzah	1818 08 22	MA, Franklin Co.
Chase ....Isaac	Ogden ....Phoebe	1818 08	NY
Chase ....John Darwin	Higgins ....Almira	1847 02 17	CO, Pueblo
Chase ....Sisson A. D.	Gove ....Miriam	1832 05 16	
Chase ....Solomon Drake	Thorn...................Lydia Ann	1840 04 19	NY, Sparta
Chase ....Stephen	Rowe...................Orryanna	1799 05 12	NY
Chatterley ....Joseph	Clark...................Catherine	1852 02 21	UT, Salt Lake City
Chatterly ....Morton	Mackelprang ....Christina J.	1866 02 01	UT, Cedar City
Chatwin ....Henry	Lee ....Fanny	1869 06 07	UT, Heber
Chatwin ....William	Luce ....Caroline	1865 08	
Cheney ....Aaron	Wells ....Mehetable	1813	
Cheney ....Elam	Garlick................Talitha Cumi	1854 02 13	
Cheney ....Elijah	Harmon ....Sarah	1846 06	
Cheney ....Joseph T.	Austin ....Louise Maria	1860 04 12	UT, Farmington
Cheney ....Nathan C.	Beebe.................Eliza Ann	1834 04 22	NY, Freedom
Cherrington......John	Belcher...............Sarah	1845 05 11	ENG, Stafford
Cherrington......Joseph	Straw..................Prudence	1877 02 01	UT, Springville
Cherry.............Aaron B.	Yelton.................Mary Margaret	1829 05 21	KY, Pendleton
Cheshire ....George	Keys ....Elizabeth P.	1841 06 11	ENG
Chesnut ....Henry	Cherrington ....Elizabeth	1876 07 05	UT, Salt Lake City
Chesson ....John	Tokelove ....Mary	1822 07	ENG, London
Chester...........Thomas	Chapman ....Hannah	1833 01 28	ENG
Chidester ....John Madison	Parker ....Mary Josephine	1836 12 28	
Chidester ....John P.	Gifford ....Mary Ann	1806	

Male	Female	Date	Place
Chidester ....John Peck	Foy ....Susannah	1851 10 23	UT, Salt Lake City
Chidester ....Myron Alphonzo	Jackson ....Sarah Ann	1881 03 31	
Child ....Alfred B.	Barber ....Polly	1817 03 19	NY, Saratoga
Child ....Thomas	Milnes..................Tabitha	1847 03 28	ENG, Bradford
Child ....Warren Gould	Wilder...................Hannah Austin	1853 01 06	UT, Ogden
Chilton ....Isaac	Jones ....Mary	1878	
Chipman ....James	Green	1858 12 25	UT, American Fork
Chipman ....James	Huntsman............Salena	1863 08 01	
Chipman ....Stephen	Washburn............Amanda	1826	Canada
Chipman ....Washburn	Mayhew...............Caroline Abigail	1868 05 30	UT, Salt Lake City
Chipman ....William H.	Binns ....Sarah	1861 04 07	UT, Salt Lake City
Chipman ....William H.	Filcher ....Eliza	1859	
Chittock ....John	Bloomfield ....Mary Ann	1835 11 14	ENG
Chlarson ....Hans Nadrian	Scherlin ....Johanna C.	1861 09 20	
Christensen .....Anders	..........................Kirsten		
Christensen .....Anders	Pedersen...........Nilla		UT, Salt Lake City
Christensen .....Anders	Sorensen............Karen	1831	Denmark
Christensen .....Anders C.	Jensen ....Kirsten Marie	1857 03 03	Denmark
Christensen .....Anders C.	Pedersen............Elsie Christine	1889	UT, Ephraim
Christensen .....Andrew	Nielsen ....Kirsten	1864 01 18	UT, Mt. Pleasant
Christensen .....Berthel	Pedersen............Maren		
Christensen .....Bothel	Jacobson.............Cajsa C. C.	1820 10 18	Sweden
Christensen .....Carl C. A.	Peterson..............Maren F.	1868 11 30	UT, Salt Lake City
Christensen .....Carl C. A.	Scheel ....Elise R. S.	1857 04 24	
Christensen .....Christen	Mortensen ....Boldid (Boletta)	1837	Denmark
Christensen .....Christen	Thomsen ....Johanne Marie	1867 02 17	
Christensen .....Hans	Christensen.........Johanna	1832 06 06	Denmark
Christensen .....Jacob	Andersen.............Ingaborg	1865 01 14	
Christensen .....Jacob	Meyer ....Marie Theresa	1855 07 29	Denmark
Christensen .....James	Christensen.........Karen Caroline	1862 05 17	Denmark
Christensen .....James	Madsen ....Christina	1859 12	
Christensen .....Jens	Christensen.........Ane	1818 10 04	Denmark
Christensen .....Jens	Jensen ....Mariane	1846 01 01	
Christensen .....Jens	Munk ....Amelia Thomsen	1858	
Christensen .....Jens	Nielsen ....Kirsten	1855 11 01	UT, Salt Lake City
Christensen .....Jens Christian	Pedersen............Johanne K.	1859 10	
Christensen .....Jens Peter	Christiansen ....Severene	1869 06 08	UT, Salt Lake City
Christensen .....Jeppe	Sorensen............Ellen	1858	UT, Salt Lake City
Christensen .....Jeppe	Sorensen............Elsie	1858 08 15	UT, Salt Lake City
Christensen .....Johan	Knudsen..............Johanne	1824	
Christensen .....John Nicolai	Nielsen ....Kirstine Marie	1869 06 28	UT, Salt Lake City
Christensen .....Lars M. C.	Andersen.............Else Kathrine	1866 04 22	Denmark
Christensen .....Lays	Sorensen............Jensine Helene	1847 12 07	
Christensen .....Mads	Jensen ....Maren Johanne	1854 11 24	Denmark
Christensen .....Mads	Tranum...............Dorthea C.	1831 03 31	Denmark
Christensen .....Mads F. T.	Rasmussen ....Sophia C.	1861 06 03	
Christensen .....Martin	Rasmussen ....Maren Johanna	1866 10 28	UT, Salt Lake City
Christensen .....Niels	Pederson.............Anne Marie	1840 09 20	Denmark
Christensen .....Niels Christian	Thomsen ....Christine		
Christensen .....Niels Christian	Thomsen ....Johanne Marie	1868 02 05	
Christensen .....Niels Thomas	Pedersen............Mette Marie		
Christensen .....Otto E. W. T.	Anderson.............Maren Annette	1865 09 23	UT, Fairview
Christensen .....Peter Christian	Mikkelsen ....Fredrikka	1869 05 17	
Christensen .....Rasmus	Mitchell...............Priscilla V.	1857 01 28	UT, Tooele

Male		Female		Date	Place
Christensen	Soren C.	Jacobsen	Christine Marie	1862 05 31	UT, Mt. Pleasant
Christiansen	Carl F. W.	Anderson	Mary	1871 07 03	UT, Salt Lake City
Christiansen	Christian	Christensen	Anne Marie	1814 12 29	Denmark
Christiansen	Christian	Iversen	Ane Marie		UT
Christiansen	Christian	Rasmussen	Anne Magdalene		
Christiansen	Christian Peter	Naser	Caroline	1865 07 08	UT, Salt Lake City
Christiansen	Frederick J.	Anderson	Kristine Marie	1856 01 13	Ocean
Christiansen	Lars Nielsen	Hansen	Karen M.	1869 04 26	UT, Salt Lake City
Christiansen	Lars Nielsen	Jorgensen	Maren Kirstine	1850 12 29	
Christiansen	Neils Christian	Mortensen	Catherine	1845 10 28	
Christiansen	Peter	Hansen	Ane Marie	1867 05 24	UT, Salt Lake City
Christiansen	Peter	Rasmussen	Marie	1841 11 12	
Christiansen	Soren	Larsen	Elsie Marie		
Christopherson	Martin	Ledingham	Janet F.	1874 12 27	UT, Salt Lake City
Church	Hayden Wells	Arterbury	Sarah Ann	1844 12 19	AL, Perry Co.
Church	Hayden Wells	Rutledge	Matilda	1870 10 15	
Clapp	Benjamin L.	Mortensen	Ann Christine	1856 10 12	UT, Salt Lake City
Clare	Richard	Gutteridge	Mary Ann	1861 08 26	ENG, Lancaster
Clark	Benjamin T.	Butterworth	Ruth	1857 06 28	
Clark	Daniel	Gower	Elizabeth	1839 10 27	ENG
Clark	Daniel Porter	Hakes	Sarah Melissa	1845 08 31	
Clark	David	Williams	Myra	1849 11 26	MO, St. Louis
Clark	Edward Watkins	Ashby	Lucy	1843 07 25	ENG, Stafford
Clark	Edward Watkins	Mellor		1857 02 03	
Clark	Ezra Thompson	Leggett	Susan	1861 11 08	UT, Salt Lake City
Clark	Ezra Thompson	Stevenson	Mary	1845 05 18	IA, Lee Co.
Clark	George	Gascoigne	Catherine	1850 10 21	
Clark	George Sheffer	Dalley	Susannah	1850 03 23	IA, Council Bluffs
Clark	Hiram William	Wood	Nancy Ann	1843	
Clark	Isaac	Herrick	Dianna	1851 06 10	UT, Ogden
Clark	Isaac	Lemmons	Mary		
Clark	Israel Justes	Pearson	Emily Jane	1853	
Clark	James	Osborne	Annie	1869 03 01	UT, Salt Lake City
Clark	James	Pearson	Elizabeth		ENG
Clark	John	Barbour	Lillias	1837 12 18	Scotland
Clark	John	Brindle	Amelia Charlotte	1860 11 26	ENG
Clark	John	Hopkins	Caroline	1852 05 31	
Clark	John	Noddings	Mary	1832	
Clark	John Haslem	Cox	Therissa E.	1867 05 01	UT, Manti
Clark	John Norman	Santifer	Eliza Branch	1816 04 24	VA, Patrick Co.
Clark	John Wesley	Brown	Evaline	1841 11 18	
Clark	Joseph	Topham	Sarah	1849 10 17	UT, Provo
Clark	Joshua R.	Woolley	Mary Louisa	1870 07 11	UT, Salt Lake City
Clark	Lorenzo	Hunt	Mary		UT, Salt Lake City
Clark	Michael	Smuin	Eliza	1861 10 28	UT, Salt Lake City
Clark	Michael	Smuin	Harriet	1859 09 24	UT, Salt Lake City
Clark	Raymond	Gill	Louisa	1827 09 16	
Clark	Raymond	Miller	Hannah	1847 05 02	MO, Platte Co.
Clark	Riley Garner	Williams	Amanda	1850 03 20	
Clark	Samuel	Garner	Rebecca	1827 07 18	OH, Clark
Clark	Thomas B.	Neal	Sarah Charlotte	1853 11 15	UT, Salt Lake City
Clark	Thomas Henry	Gailey	Charlotte	1825 11 28	
Clark	Wheeler	Clark	Julia Ann		
Clark	William	Boardman	Margaret	1867 04 20	UT, Salt Lake City

Male		Female		Date	Place
Clark	William	Underhill	Charlotte	1853	ENG
Clark	William Henry	Godfrey	Sarah	1877 10 10	UT, Salt Lake City
Clarke	Amos	Johnstone	Ann	1853 11 13	Wales
Clarke	Francis	Teeples	Harriet Elvira	1867 01 28	UT, Eden
Clarke	John Henry	Heaver	Elizabeth	1854 01 08	ENG, London
Clarkson	John	Turner	Mary	1857 07 04	UT, Fillmore
Clarkson	Thomas	McCoy	Catherine	1821 10 21	ENG
Clawson	Hiram B.	Judd	Margaret Gay	1852 08 21	UT, Salt Lake City
Clawson	James	Larsen	Sarah	1873 01 29	UT, Spring City
Clawson	Moses	Brown	Cornelia	1820	NY
Clawson	Moses	Inkley	Sarah Ann	1853 09 25	UT, Salt Lake City
Clawson	Zephaniah	Reese	Catherine	1824 01 08	NY
Clayfield	Richard	Gill	Maria	1825	
Clayson	Nathan	Butler	Annie Harriet	1868 02 24	UT, Payson
Clayson	Thomas	Essom	Frances	1835 11 02	
Clayson	Thomas Jr.	Sims	Priscilla	1868 02 24	UT, Payson
Clayton	Albert	Higgenbotham	Frances	1851 07 10	ENG
Clayton	Edward	Morrison	Ellen	1867 01 08	ID, Franklin
Clayton	John	Tonks	Elizabeth	1874 08 13	UT, Morgan
Clayton	Nephi Willard	Johnson	Sybella White	1884 06 26	
Clayton	William	Higgs	Annie Elizabeth	1870 12 30	UT, Salt Lake City
Clayton	William	Moon	Margaret	1843 04 27	IL, Nauvoo
Clayton	William	Moon	Ruth	1836 10 09	ENG, Lancashire
Clayton	William	Walters	Sarah	1856 11 30	UT, Salt Lake City
Clegg	Benjamin	Dodd	Elizabeth	1850	UT, Salt Lake City
Clegg	Henry	Griffiths	Margaret Ann		
Clegg	Henry Jr.	Lewis	Ann	1855 12 03	UT, Salt Lake City
Clegg	Jonathan	Walmsley	Ellen	1836	
Clegg	William	Cocker	Mary	1853 12 19	ENG
Clemensen	Niels	Nielsen	Kirstine Marie	1863 10 24	UT, Salt Lake City
Clements	Albert	Winchell	Ada	1821 01 28	NY, Washington
Clements	Albert N.	Boice	Elizabeth Ann	1865	
Clements	James	Wilds	Ann		
Clemons	William	Wilds	Ann	1840	ENG
Cliff	Edward	Cresswell	Eliza	1863 04 27	ENG
Clifford	Benjamin Rush	Griffin	Susannah	1875 09 14	
Clifford	Leander H.	Mathias	Ada	1854	UT, Fort Brigham
Clifton	Charles	Frith	Elizabeth	1864 03 26	UT, Salt Lake City
Clinger	James	Chapin	Harriet	1845 12 07	IL
Clinger	James Henry	Williamson	Pauline Mary	1868 02 09	UT, Provo
Cloggie	William	Harvey	Elizabeth		
Cloward	Daniel	Logan	Ruth Bailey	1840 10 15	PA, Unionville
Cloward	Jacob	Pluck	Catherine Ann	1815 02 17	PA, Bucks Co.
Cloward	Jacob Jr.	Mendenhall	Susannah	1848 12 05	IA, Council Bluffs
Cloward	Thomas P.	Gardner	Mary Amelia	1853 09 01	UT, Provo
Cloward	William	Searle	Rebecca Ann	1848	
Cluff	Benjamin	Foster	Eliza Arnette	1856 02 20	UT, Salt Lake City
Cluff	David Jr.	Fleming	Sarah Ann	1851 03 19	UT, Salt Lake City
Cluff	Moses	Bond	Ann	1857 02 14	UT, Salt Lake City
Cluff	Moses	Johnson	Margaret Jane	1857 04 22	
Cluff	Moses	Langman	Rebecca C.	1856 12 25	UT, Salt Lake City
Clutton	George	King	Mary	1826	
Clyde	George W.	Davis	Cynthia	1824 10 30	NY, Ogdensburg
Clyde	George W. Jr.	McDonald	Jane	1851 09 30	

Male	Female	Date	Place
Clyde ....William M.	McDonald............Eliza	1851 01 24	UT, Alpine
Coates ....William B.	Fullmer ....Lavinia Elizabeth	1855	
Cobb................James T.	Meith ....Camilla Clara	1864 11 14	
Cochrane.........John	Gill.....................Caroline		
Cocker............Joseph	Dawtry ....Mary Ann	1832 12 10	ENG
Cockerill...........John	Barrow...............Sarah		
Coffin ....William B.	Starbuck............Abigail	1833 09 21	IN
Coffman...........William M.	Wood.................Margaret S.	1854 05 11	MO, Putnam Co.
Coldiron ....William H.	Damron ....Susan Emaline	1850 12 02	
Coldwell..........John	Land ....Narcissa B.	1837 05 22	MO, Jackson Co.
Cole ....Barnet	Van Alstyne.........Phoebe	1820 12 15	OH, Sheffield
Cole ....Charles Martin	Banford ....Martha C.	1864 12 20	UT, Cherry Creek
Cole ....James Barnet	Ward ....Lucy	1856 11 02	WY, Fort Bridger
Cole ....John	Jenkins...............Charlotte	1843 08 25	IL, Nauvoo
Cole ....John	Voss ....Mary Ann	1873	UT, Willard
Cole ....Martin Richard	Pillings...............Elizabeth	1840	ENG
Cole ....Walter Charles	Beirdneau............Louisa A.	1872 01 08	UT, Salt Lake City
Cole ....William George	Larnder...............Sarah	1837 02 12	ENG, London
Cole ....William Riley	Parrish................Nancy Sarepta	1840 03 19	IL, Quincy
Colebrook ....Charles	Bowthorpe..........Virtue Ann	1854 01 07	UT, Salt Lake City
Colebrook ....Charles	Purser................Maria	1846 03 10	ENG, Worchester
Coleman ....George	Reeves...............Mary	1840	NY, Niagra
Coleman ....George	Smith.................Jane	1857 01 28	UT, Lehi
Coleman ....Henry	Johnson ....Sarah	1892	
Coleman ....Louis	O'Neil ....Rachel Ellis	1876 03 20	UT, Salt Lake City
Coleman ....Prime	Thornton.............Sarah	1826 08 28	ENG, Bedfordshire
Colemere........George	Burgess..............Rachel	1844 11 03	IL, Nauvoo
Collard ....James E.	Hunt ....Hannah	1865 10 01	
Collett ....Daniel	Jones ....Esther	1833 04 14	ENG
Collett ....Reuben	Merrill ....Elthura R.	1861 01 17	UT, Smithfield
Collings...........Fredrick John	Beard ....Fannie Jane	1872 12 13	
Collings...........James	Bewick...............Elizabeth	1834	ENG
Collings...........Richard	Lawrence ....Emma Hannah	1844 05 26	ENG, London
Collings...........William R.	Bohman..............Augusta E.	1887 12 28	UT, St. George
Collins............Albert W.	Thomas ....Ann Bingham	1851 03 03	
Collins............Albert W.	Thomas ....Susan Newman	1841 03 03	GA
Collins............Aquilla	Hillier.................Lemira	1860 07 04	ENG, Wiltshire
Collins............John	Goddard ....Mary	1863	
Collins............John	Shefford ....Priscilla	1824 11 06	ENG
Collins............Joseph Smith	Bennett...............Emma	1874 12	ID, Blackfoot
Collins............Nathan N.	Daggett ....Hannah	1847	
Collyer ....Samuel	Vine...................Susanna	1881 05 02	
Colton ....Philander	Merrill ....Polly Matilda	1833 07 13	MI, Macomb
Coltrin ....Graham	Hickman ....Harriet		
Coltrin ....Henry Clay	Duncan...............Matilda Ann	1906 05 02	
Coltrin ....Zebedee	Fullmer ....Lavinia Elizabeth	1857 02 25	
Coltrin ....Zebedee	Mott...................Mary	1843 02 05	IL, Nauvoo
Colvin ....Alvin	Waite.................Martha	1856	UT, North Ogden
Comish ....John	Stanford ....Esther E.	1862 11 22	UT, Salt Lake City
Comish ....William	Kegg..................Elizabeth	1831 02 12	Isle of Man
Compton.........John Allen	Miller ....Mary Elmira	1865 12 09	UT, Salt Lake City
Comstock ....Fitch	Ballou................Lillis	1823 05 01	
Conder...........Edward	Pierce................Helen (Ellen)	1846	MO, St. Louis
Conder...........Edward	Shelley ....Sarah Elizabeth	1854 11 19	

Male	Female	Date	Place
Condie ....Gibson	Robinson............Elizabeth	1857 02 24	UT, Salt Lake City
Conklin ....Clarence	Wilds ....Ann	1851	UT
Connell ....James	Pendleton............Sarah E.	1869 10 04	UT, Salt Lake City
Connell ....Samuel	Tegan.................Methine	1883 10 03	UT, St. George
Connell ....William Michael	Hollis ....Sophia	1859	ENG
Connelly ....John	Jessop................Elizabeth		
Conover..........Abram Golden	Owen..................Ann	1857 02 26	UT, Provo
Conrad............Charles F.	Bitely ....Sarah Adams	1830 02 08	NY, Ontario
Cook...............Alonzo H.	Laker..................Amy Ellen	1878 11 14	UT, Salt Lake City
Cook...............Daniel	Fuller.................Mary Maria	1820	Canada
Cook...............David	Holden................Mary Ann	1852 12 15	UT, Provo
Cook...............David Patterson	Hunter ....Elizabeth	1859 02 04	UT, Salt Lake City
Cook...............David S.	Hunter ....Janet	1852 09 24	UT, Salt Lake City
Cook...............Fredrick	Picton................Mary Ann	1863 01 13	UT, Salt Lake City
Cook...............George	Burrows..............Hannah	1854 01 31	ENG, Kent
Cook...............Henry F.	Strobridge ....Sophronia	1837 04 09	
Cook...............Henry Lyman	Turple................Susan Ann E.	1852 09 28	UT, Goshen
Cook...............James Benjamin	Tucker...............Mary Ann	1860	
Cook...............John	Denley................Ann	1836	ENG, Compton
Cook...............John	Frith..................Elizabeth	1839 03 01	ENG, Derbyshire
Cook...............John	Rostron ....Sarah	1858 03 17	UT, Salt Lake City
Cook...............Joseph Wood	Lawson...............Mary	1864 03 12	UT, Salt Lake City
Cook...............Melvin Darwin	Duncombe...........Sarah	1870 12 19	UT, Salt Lake City
Cook...............Milton	Smith..................Olive Amanda		
Cook...............Phineas W.	Howland..............Ann Eliza	1840 01 01	MI
Cook...............Thomas	Meredith ....Mary		
Cook...............Washington N.	Morrow ....Mary Parmelia	1845	
Cook...............William	Chapman ....Lucy	1805 12 19	
Cook...............William	Horrocks..............Mary	1876	UT, Heber City
Cook...............William	Rodeback............Rebecca H.	1875 10 25	UT, Salt Lake City
Cook...............William S.	Bowman..............Christine	1854 07 23	UT, Salt Lake City
Cooke.............Charles M.	Fawson ....Ann Marie	1865 12 24	
Cooke.............Henry	Morris.................Martha	1832 06 03	ENG, Sussex
Coolbear.........John	Barnard ....Mary Ann	1832 09 24	
Cooley ....Andrew Wood	Coon ....Rachel Caroline	1868 02 22	UT, Salt Lake City
Cooley ....Andrew Wood	Hazen.................Ann	1870 02 14	UT, Salt Lake City
Cooley ....Andrew Wood	Huntington...........Mary Asenath	1866 02 17	UT, Grantsville
Cooley ....Andrew Wood	Jenkins...............Mary Jane	1868 02 22	UT, Salt Lake City
Coon...............Abraham	Yarbrough ....Elizabeth	1829	IL, St. Claire Co.
Coon...............John	York...................Mary Tabitha	1854 03 12	UT, Salt Lake City
Coon...............John Abraham	Hirst...................Charlotte	1881 01 06	UT, Salt Lake City
Coons.............Libbeus T.	King...................Sarah	1846 01 24	IL, Nauvoo
Coons.............Libbeus T.	Minchell..............Esther	1867	
Coons.............Libbeus T.	Williamson...........Mary Ann	1831	NY
Coons.............Sidney	Sorensen.............Christiana	1877 05 20	
Cooper............David	Crossley ....Hannah Mariah	1870	UT, Richmond
Cooper............Frederick A.	McGregor............Agnes	1870 06 13	
Cooper............Isaac	Lance ....Nancy	1852 05 01	
Cooper............Isaac	Stuart ....Mary Elizabeth	1857 03 18	
Cooper............James	Guest ....Elizabeth C.		
Cooper............William	Maslen ....Elizabeth	1858 05 08	NE, Monroe
Cooper............William	Olpin..................Sarah Ann W.	1865 11 09	UT, Salt Lake City
Cooper............William	Robinson............Millizzer	1843 07 21	ENG, Eastwood
Cooper............William Darby	Rochester...........Lydia Ellen	1846 10 13	

Male	Female	Date	Place
Cooper............William H.	Jackson...............Anne	1861 12 07	ENG, Yorkshire
Coray..............Howard	Knowlton.............Martha Jane	1841 02 06	IL, Hancock
Coray..............William	Burton.................Melissa	1846 06 22	IA, Mt. Pisgah
Corbett............Daniel D.	Wright.................Elmira	1834	
Corbett............John W.	Woodard.............Emily Jane	1863 10 31	UT, Salt Lake City
Corbett............Samuel	Jacobsen.............Cammilla D.	1860 10 02	
Corbett............Thomas	Brett...................Sarah Ann	1857 02 23	UT, Payson
Corbridge.........Edward	Parker................Alice	1843 07 17	ENG
Corbridge.........William	Howard...............Emma	1870 04 14	UT, Salt Lake City
Cordon............Alfred	Parker................Emma	1836 12 19	ENG
Cordon............Alfred	Pridmore............Emily Maria	1856 10 09	UT, Salt Lake City
Cordon............Alfred	Voss...................Mary Ann	1865 04 22	UT, Salt Lake City
Cordon............Edwin P.	Voss...................Sarah	1867 12 14	UT, Salt Lake City
Corless............Edward	Stephenson.........Catherine	1829 08 21	ENG
Corless............John	Knox..................Dorothy	1862 02 11	UT, Salt Lake City
Corless............John	Knox..................Mary Ann	1872 07 22	UT, Salt Lake City
Corlett.............James	Clark..................Catherine	1837 05 23	
Cornaby..........Samuel	Last...................Hannah	1851 01 30	ENG, Norfolk
Cornia.............Peter/Pierre	Carter................Ruth Clarissa	1856 05 02	UT, Salt Lake City
Cornum...........Jens C.	Pedersen.............Ane T. M.	1862 06 17	NE, Florence
Cornwall.........William	George................Elizabeth		
Cottam............John	Livesay...............Catherine	1816	
Cottam............Thomas	Smith..................Caroline	1847 10 09	
Cotterell..........William	Hughes...............Elizabeth A.	1871 07 03	UT, Salt Lake City
Cottrell............George	Messam.............Catherine	1841 12 14	ENG
Couche...........Sam	Gill....................Eliza		
Coulam...........George	Harrocks.............Elizabeth	1869 12 27	
Court..............William Lee	Judd..................Hannah	1853 06 27	ENG, Coventry
Covey.............Benjamin	Mack..................Almira	1836 10 23	
Covey.............Hyrum	Parkinson............Ellen	1867 07 19	UT, Salt Lake City
Covington........Berrill	Hodges...............Elizabeth	1812 11 08	ENG, Bedford
Cowan............Alexander	Mitchell...............Jane	1860 01 22	UT, Salt Lake City
Cowan............Robert	Read..................Naomi	1875 05 01	UT, Slaterville
Cowell............John	Singleton............Mary	1841 01 21	ENG, Lancashire
Cowley............Charles	Killip..................Ann	1833 12 26	Isle of Man
Cowley............James	Caine.................Isabelle Ann	1827 04 28	United Kingdom
Cowley............Joseph Enos	Worley...............Catherine	1875 07 05	UT, Salt Lake City
Cowley............Matthias	Foss..................Sarah Elizabeth	1857 10 17	
Cowley............Matthias	Hyde..................Abbie		
Cowley............William E.	Alger.................Sarah Ann	1863 01 11	UT, Beaver
Cowley............William M.	Wall...................Sarah Emily	1860 02 22	UT, Salt Lake City
Cox................Daniel William	Smith..................Lucy Maria	1847 06 17	IL, Green Co.
Cox................Frederick Walter	Darrow...............Mary Ann	1858 01 09	UT, Manti
Cox................Fredrick W.	Losee.................Jemimah	1844 01 27	IL, Nauvoo
Cox................Fredrick W.	Morley...............Cordella C.	1846 01 27	IL, Nauvoo
Cox................Jacob	Snow..................Julia Marie	1871 01 23	
Cox................Jehu	Pyle...................Sarah Riddle	1824 01 13	IN, Monroe
Cox................Jehu Jr.	Merrill................Laura Cordelia	1854 12 24	UT, Salt Lake City
Cox................John Jr.	Stiff...................Hannah	1858 08 22	ENG, Hampshire
Cox................Joseph Daniel	Snow..................Julia Marie	1865 12 31	
Cox................Levi Ashton	Sharp................Mary	1853 10 02	
Cox................Orville S.	Mills..................Elvira Pamela	1839 10 03	IL, Adams Co.
Cragun...........Simeon	Mower................Susan	1849	IA, Kanesville
Cragun...........Wilford Elisha	Ellis..................Mary Ann	1871 01 02	UT, Salt Lake City

Male	Female	Date	Place
Cram...............Charles S.	Prescott..............Eliza Jane	1846 11 10	NY, New York
Cram...............Charles S. Jr.	Greenhalgh ....Ruth Elizabeth	1888 01 17	
Cram...............Victor Doe P.	Johnson ....Esther A.	1879 12 17	UT, St. George
Cramer ....Christopher	Otterstrom...........Josephine	1879 01 23	UT, Salt Lake City
Cramer ....John Charles	Larsson ....Anna Christina	1883 12 06	UT, Salt Lake City
Crandall ....Hyrum O.	Guymon ....Harriet		
Crandall ....Hyrum O.	Guymon ....Margaret E.	1864 03 06	UT, Springville
Crandall ....Martin Pardon	Hurst ....Mary Jane	1862 10 04	UT, Springville
Crandall ....Myron Nathan	Bisbee ....Tryphena	1841 01 26	IL, Nauvoo
Crandall ....Myron Nathan	Hurst ....Mary Jane	1857 03 13	UT, Salt Lake City
Crane...............Elias	Smith..................Elizabeth	1857 06 13	NE, Florence
Crane...............George	Howe..................Ann	1868 02 01	ENG, London
Crane...............James	Briggs.................Rachel	1869 03 28	
Crane...............James	Davis ....Alice	1858 04 05	IA, Iowa City
Crane...............James	Stewart................Elizabeth	1864 09 20	UT, Salt Lake City
Crane...............James S.	Dansie.................Sarah Ann	1878 10 11	UT, Salt Lake City
Crane...............John L.	Stannard ....Sarah	1849 11 16	
Cranshaw ....Richard	Lofthouse ....Ann	1852 07 18	ENG
Crapo...............Joseph G.	Collins ....Mary Hicks	1826 06 18	
Crapo...............Leonides L.	Holbrook..............Alice Matilda	1867 02 24	UT, Paradise
Cravath............Austin	Doty....................Eliza	1828 12 25	NY, Gainsville
Crawford..........John	Sharp ....Cecelia	1853 04 06	UT, Salt Lake City
Crawford..........John	Snow ....Elizabeth C.	1856 02 02	UT, Manti
Crawford..........John	Terry...................Marilla	1841 01 20	IL
Crawford..........Samuel Sinclair	Smith..................Jane Louisa	1862 10 03	UT, Salt Lake City
Crawley ....Thomas	Ritchie ....Betsy	1863 03 21	Ocean
Creer ....Edward	Morris..................Ann	1835 06 20	ENG, Lancashire
Creer ....William	Bradley................Sarah Jane M.	1858 01 22	UT, Spanish Fork
Criddle ....Henry	Bull.....................Mary	1837 06 22	ENG, Somerset
Criddle ....John	Taylor..................Elizabeth Ann	1854 06	UT, Salt Lake City
Cripps ....Charles	Baker..................Elizabeth	1825 11 13	ENG, Surrey
Crisman ....Peter	Williams...............Mary	1824 05 21	KY, Hopkinville
Crismon ....Charles	Hessell ....Christina Amelia	1867 10 12	UT, Salt Lake City
Crismon ....Charles	Hill.....................Mary	1830 05 06	
Critchlow..........Benjamin	Garner.................Martha Ann	1861 01 01	UT, Ogden
Critchlow..........William	Brown..................Nancy	1852 11 06	UT, Salt Lake City
Critchlow..........William	Hawkins ....Harriet	1832 02 14	PA, Butler
Crittenden........Chauncey S.	Wareing...............Elizabeth	1865 02 01	
Crockett ....Alvin	Reed ....Mary Sophia	1852 06 29	UT, Payson
Crockett ....David	Young..................Lydia	1830 12 20	ME, Knox Co.
Crockett ....Edward Hall	Rogers ....Sarah	1832	ENG, Lincolnshire
Crockett ....Wilford W.	Reed ....Mary Mahala	1860 07 29	UT, Payson
Crockwell.........George	Davey..................Eliza Louisa	1871 10 23	UT, Salt Lake City
Croft................Jacob	Land ....Sebrina	1854 01	OK
Crofts ....John	Rothwell ....Ellen	1854 01 01	ENG, Manchester
Cromar ....William T.	Turner ....Selina	1861 04 15	ENG, Sheffield
Crompton........John	Hardy ....Hannah	1850 03 01	IA, Council Bluffs
Crook..............James	Mason ....Sophia	1811	
Crook..............Samuel Lane	Haines................Sarah Ann	1856 05 29	Ocean
Crook..............William Joshua	Howell ....Harriet Jane	1880 10 14	UT, Salt Lake City
Crookston ....Robert	Welch ....Ann	1847 06 20	NE
Cropper ....George Waters	Land ....Sebrina	1841	TX, Harris Co.
Cropper ....Leigh Richmond	Powell ....Fanny Louisa	1864 09 17	UT, Deseret
Crosby ....David B.	Thompson...........Marial	1834 09 21	

Male	Female	Date	Place
Crosby ....John P.	Coleman..............Elizabeth Glenn	1804 12 18	
Crosland ....Benjamin	Smith..................Catherine	1852 06 14	UT, Salt Lake City
Crossgrove ......Charles	Raymond.............Theresa	1830 09 01	PA, Peansbury
Crossland ....Junius	Otten ....Frances Ann	1841 05 29	ENG, London
Crossley ....William	Eckersall ....Lettice Brown	1835	ENG, Pilkington
Crouch............Ebenezer	Russell ....Sarah	1846 10 20	ENG, Sussex
Crow ....Robert	Brown.................Elizabeth	1817 09 05	MO
Crowther.........Edwin Dugard	Seamons.............Lydia	1861 06 09	UT, Salt Lake City
Crowther.........George	Dugard ....Sarah Ann	1833	ENG
Crump.............William Charles	James ....Margaret	1853	
Crystal ....Andrew	Cousin................Elizabeth	1850 05 30	Scotland
Cufley ....William	Irvin ....Jennet	1857	UT, Salt Lake City
Cullen ....Martin	Mole ....Mary	1875 06 26	UT, Morgan
Cullimore ....James	Fowlke................Clara	1864 02 10	UT, Lindon
Cummings ....Benjamin F.	Yearsley ....Mary Jane	1856 05 27	UT, Salt Lake City
Cummings ......John	Canada ....Rachel	1834 03 16	TN, Gibson Co.
Cunningham ....Andrew	Rawlins ....Lucinda	1841 04 22	IL, Adams Co.
Cunningham ....James	Nicholson ....Elizabeth	1834 02 15	
Currie..............John	Washburn............Amanda	1855	UT
Curtis ....Benjamin G.	Dunn ....Maria	1825 03 24	OH, Brown Co.,
Curtis ....Enos	Durfee ....Tamma	1850 10 20	UT, Salt Lake City
Curtis ....Enos	Franklin ....Ruth	1805 12 15	NY, New York
Curtis ....Erastus	Fullmer ....Joanna Price	1860 02 14	UT, Spanish Fork
Curtis ....Hyrum	Haws ....Lydia Catherine	1884 08 06	
Curtis ....Hyrum	Haws ....Mary Eliza	1859 10 04	UT, Provo
Curtis ....John White	Durfee ....Tamma	1857 04 07	UT, Salt Lake City
Curtis ....John White	Miner ....Matilda	1855 10 21	UT, Salt Lake City
Curtis ....Joseph H.	Morrell ....Sarah	1835 06 21	ENG, Middlesex
Curtis ....Lyman	Alvord................Charlotte	1834 07 26	MO, Caldwell
Curtis ....Lyman	Hartley...............Sarah Wells	1862 07 26	UT, Salt Lake City
Curtis ....Nahum	Byam..................Delia Deliverance	1839 10 29	IL, Warsaw
Curtis ....Theodore	Fluskey...............Charlotte		
Curtis ....Theodore	Morgan...............Margaret	1846 01 17	IL, Nauvoo
Cushing ....Arthur John	Cushing..............Ellen Maria	1869 12 24	UT, Salt Lake City
Cushing ....Hosea	Murray................Helen Janet	1847 02 04	IA, Winter Quarters
Cushing ....James	Long ....Maria	1850 10 13	ENG, Norfolk
Cushing ....Phillip Hosea	Nisonger.............Pheobe	1871 09 07	UT, Santaquin
Cushing ....William Ellis	Fillmore ....Miranda Ann	1872 08 18	
Cutler..............	Perry ....Phebe Roxy	1889 03 20	UT
Cutler.............Harmon	McGregor ....Agnes	1859 12 19	UT, Salt Lake City
Cutler.............Harmon	Pettegrew............Lucy Ann	1842 08 29	IA, Zarahemla
Cutler.............Isaac	Cole...................Elizabeth Ann	1849 11 15	
Cutler.............Mason Jr.	Bengtsson ....Anna	1867	
Cutler.............Perley	Freeman..............Caroline Sophia	1828 02 28	
Cutler.............Ransom	Cope ....Emily	1885 12 03	
Cutler.............Royal James	Ross...................Margaret	1857 12 08	UT, Salt Lake City
Cutler.............Sheldon Bela	Jensen ....Maren	1861 03 02	UT, Salt Lake City
Cutler.............Sheldon Bela	Wight..................Sarah (Sally)	1850 02 09	IA, Kanesville
Cutler.............Thomas R.	Coons.................Laura Elizabeth	1870 12 26	UT, Salt Lake City

D

Male	Female	Date	Place
Dack ....Philip	Maxham ....Cynthia Sildona	1859 05 15	

Male	Female	Date	Place
Dade.............John	Halliday ....Mary		
Dahl.................Endre (Andrew)	Jonson ....Johanna	1832	
Dahle...............Hans Hansen	Johansen ....Anna	1822 07 06	Norway
Dahle...............Johannes	Helgesen............Marta Karena	1862	
Dahle...............Johannes	Malmberg...........Johanna C.	1872 03 04	
Daines ....Robert	Seamons............Jemima	1859 05 01	
Dale ....James Robert	Hutchison...........Euphemia	1867 11 16	UT, Salt Lake City
Daley ....John	Ennis ....Elizabeth	1809	
Daley ....Matthew H.	Wightman...........Mary Elizabeth	1863 03 01	UT, Payson
Daley ....Moses	Barber ....Almira	1819 01 22	
Daley ....Phineas	Grover ....Adeline	1853 01 27	CA, San Bern.
Daley ....William	Graham ....Mary Ann	1834 03 12	
Dall ....Henry David	Carrier ....Rebecca	1839 04 29	
Dalley ....James	Bertelsen............Johanne B.	1856 10 09	UT, Salt Lake City
Dalley ....James	Bertelsen............Petrina	1861 10 09	UT, Salt Lake City
Dalley ....James	Wright................Emma	1850 08 15	IA, Keg Creek
Dalley ....William	Davies ....Ann	1818	ENG, Leominster
Dalley ....William	Hillman ....Mandana	1846 09 04	IA, Trading Point
Dallin ....William	Sutherland..........Eliza	1862 10 18	
Dalrymple ....Andrew	Holland...............Caroline	1861 01 05	UT, Salt Lake City
Dalton ....Charles W.	Bowen ....Juliette E.	1847 01 13	
Dalton ....Edward	Benson...............Jane	1855 10 09	
Dalton ....John	Goldthwaite ....Lydia	1851 09 18	
Dalton ....Matthew W.	Miller ....Alice Ophelia	1868 04 05	
Dalton ....Matthew W.	Whitaker.............Rozilla	1850 12 15	
Dalton ....Simon C.	Durham ....Charlotte L.	1872	
Dand................Thomas	Hind...................Mary Ann	1807 01 26	ENG, Harrington
Daniels ....Aaron	Rogers ....Hannah Caroline	1845 12 14	
Daniels ....James E.	Salthouse...........Elizabeth	1816 10 13	ENG, Manchester
Daniels ....Sheffield	Warren ....Abigail		
Daniels ....Thomas E.	Olsen.................Anna	1864 06 04	UT, Salt Lake City
Daniels ....Thomas E.	Sheffield.............Jane Ann	1855 11 25	UT, Payson
Dansie ....Robert	Rudland..............Charlotte	1849 04 08	
Darley ....William F.	Thirkell ....Jemima Brown	1857 03 22	
Darrow............George	Gifford ....Mary Ann		
Dart.................John	Roberts ....Lucy Ann	1831 11 24	
Davenport........Edward W.	Crapo ....Clarissa D.	1848 08 10	
Davenport........James	Phelps ....Almira	1822 09 04	NY, Olean
Davenport........James B.	Pass ....Rachel	1872 10 07	UT, Salt Lake City
Davenport........Joseph C.	Sperry ....Charlotte Ellen	1871 02 05	
Davenport........Thomas	Burrows..............Sarah	1836 08 28	ENG, Yorkshire
Davey ....Charles B.	Maddox ....Louisa	1860 01 20	UT, Salt Lake City
Davey ....Charles B.	Maddox ....Susanna M. A.	1851 08 24	ENG, London
Davidson ....Hans Christian	Jensen ....Anna Maria	1852 11 02	Denmark
Davidson ....Robert	Hemingway ....Ada Cemantha	1861 11 08	UT, Salt Lake City
Davidson ....Robert	McNeil ....Janet Jane	1880 06 10	
Davies ....David	Evans.................Alice	1826 04 10	Wales
Davies ....Edward	Jasper ....Elizabeth	1827 11 17	ENG, Kinnerly
Davies ....Henry	Bolton................Sarah	1848 08 28	ENG, Lancashire
Davies ....James G.	Williams..............Polly	1856	UT, Ft. Harmony
Davies ....John	Cadwallader ....Elizabeth	1831 04 17	Wales
Davies ....Morgan	Keep...................Ann	1865 03 01	UT, Lehi
Davies ....Thomas	Allen ....Eliza	1858 07 26	NE, Nance Co.
Davies ....Thomas T.	Jones ....Mary	1843 01 06	Wales

Male	Female	Date	Place
Davies ....William R.	Morris ....Rachel	1824	Wales
Davis	Cocks ....Emily Ann		
Davis ....Albert Westly	Lambson ....Melissa Jane	1865 11 25	UT, Salt Lake City
Davis ....Charles A.	Kennan...............Ruth	1839 04 11	MA, Worcester
Davis ....Daniel C.	Davis ....Charlotte Ann	1859 02 10	
Davis ....Daniel George	Drake ....Elizabeth Jefford	1860 04 29	
Davis ....Daniel Kelley	Garrett................Ann Priscilla	1888 01 12	UT, Bountiful
Davis ....David	Angell ....Caroline Francis	1843 03 26	IL, Nauvoo
Davis ....David	Davis ....Ann H.	1853 12 25	Wales
Davis ....David Evan	Jenkins...............Jane	1867 06 22	
Davis ....David Lazarus	Jeremy ....Esther	1866 11 29	UT, Salt Lake City
Davis ....David Thomas	Williams..............Mary	1860 11 28	UT, Spanish Fork
Davis ....David W.	Davis ....Ann H.	1859 06 10	UT, Logan
Davis ....Edward G.	Mudd ....Sarah Esther	1847 07 25	ENG, Middlesex
Davis ....Edward W.	Drabble ....Sarah	1822 01 13	ENG, London
Davis ....Edward W. Jr.	Nightingale ....Jemima	1857 02 26	UT, Salt Lake City
Davis ....Elisha H.	Mitchell...............Mary Ann	1846 12 25	ENG, London
Davis ....Elisha H.	Stewart...............Sarah Ellen	1871 01 30	UT, Salt Lake City
Davis ....Henry	Hunter ....Rachel	1825 11 14	
Davis ....Henry Tames	Fretwell ....Mary Elizabeth	1864 04 23	UT, Salt Lake City
Davis ....Isaac	Salisbury ....Sarah Ann	1815	
Davis ....James Duane	Davis ....Roxanna	1831 01 16	
Davis ....John	Weston...............Mary Ann	1840 12 23	
Davis ....Jonathan G.	Hancock.............Alta	1858 01 28	UT, Springville
Davis ....Joseph C.	Williams..............Louisa		
Davis ....Joseph C.	Williams..............Maria	1859 04 01	Wales
Davis ....Joshua	Cole...................Susan Ann	1840 11 12	IL, Madison Co.
Davis ....Mormon	Walters...............Louisa	1876 10 16	UT, Salt Lake City
Davis ....Nathan	....	1862	
Davis ....Nathan	Woolley ....Sarah	1836 03 31	OH, Columbus
Davis ....Nathan Cutler	Wells ....Isabella	1840 11 11	NY, Warren Co.
Davis ....Richard J.	Morgan...............Rebecca	1849 07 22	Wales
Davis ....Thomas William	Vickery ....Sophia Caroline	1861	OH
Davis ....William	Bishop ....Elizabeth	1831 05 31	
Davis ....William	Evans ....Amelia	1864 12	UT, Salt Lake City
Davis ....William	Goddard ....Mary	1865 04 10	UT, Salt Lake City
Davis ....William	Haidon...............Sarah	1842 12 19	ENG
Davis ....William B.	Llewellyn ....Elizabeth	1876 04 16	UT, Goshen
Davis ....William C.	Hull....................Isabelle Forbes	1867 11 08	UT, Salt Lake City
Davis ....William C.	Vilhelmsen ....Annie J.	1869 11 22	UT, Salt Lake City
Dawson ....Alexander	Fowle ....Elizabeth Jane	1860 02 22	South Africa
Dawson ....Meredith	Bird....................Ann	1873 12 19	
Dawson ....William	Smith..................Lucy Maria	1863 01 20	UT, Lehi
Day ....Abraham	Broomhead ....Charlotte C.	1851 11 30	UT, Salt Lake City
Day ....Abraham	Buckley ....Elmira	1838 06 16	VT, Windhall
Day ....David	Davis ....Elizabeth	1857 04 03	UT, Salt Lake City
Day ....Henry Eastman	Cottrell...............Elizabeth	1862 11 01	UT, Salt Lake City
Day ....Hugh	Judd ....Susannah C.	1847 09 07	NE, Florence
Day ....James	Roberts ....Mary Ann M.	1867 03 23	UT, Salt Lake City
Day ....James Henry	Stringfellow ....Lucy	1874 11	UT, Draper
Day ....Joseph	Harvey...............Ann	1839 01 28	ENG, Essex
Day ....Richard	Smith..................Elizabeth	1846 02 23	ENG, Elkstone
Daybell ....Finity	Draper................Mary	1841 03 09	ENG, Falkingham
Daybell ....William	Price...................Annie	1877 11 12	UT, Heber

Male	Female	Date	Place
Dayley ....Jacob	Eliasson ....Anna Christina	1879 01 09	UT, Salt Lake City
Dayley ....James	McBride..............Isabelle	1834 03 18	OH
Dayton ....Hiram	Lance ....Nancy	1846 02 24	IA, Winter Quarters
De La Mare......Philippe	Chevalier............Marie	1852 03 10	MO, St. Louis
Deaken ....John	Griffin ....Lydia	1868 10 24	UT
Deal ....John Wesley	Crandall..............Eliza	1842 10 28	IL, Adams Co.
Dean...............Heber C.	Swindlehurst ....Sophia	1879 04 02	UT, St. George
Dean...............John	Holdsworth..........Martha	1832 01 06	ENG, Pendle
Dean...............John	Singleton ....Mary		
Dean...............Joseph	Lacey ....Amelia	1865 01 05	UT, Salt Lake City
Dearden..........Thomas	Davies ....Charlotte	1867 03 10	ENG
Debenham.......Henry W.	Cracroft ....Sarah	1870 10 03	UT, Salt Lake City
Decker ....Charles F.	Young.................Vilate	1847 02 04	IA
Decker ....Isaac Perry	Wheeler..............Harriet Page	1821	NY, Phelps
Decker ....Zachariah B.	Bean...................Nancy	1849 03 06	UT, Salt Lake City
Decloux ....Maurice	Romeril...............Fanny Mary Ann	1859 08 19	UT, Salt Lake City
Dee.................Thomas D.	Taylor ....Annie	1871 04 10	UT, Salt Lake City
DeGraw ....Jacob	Dutton ....Sophia	1833 08 24	
Degrey............Alfred	Raybold..............Anna Maria	1853 09 20	ENG, Dudley
Degrey............John	Brooks ....Mariah	1827	ENG, Kingswinford
Degrey............Samuel	Jarman ....Marie	1888 03 20	UT, Salt Lake City
Delitch ....Radovan N.	Bransford ....Susanna	1930	
Demill ....Elias	Winget................Melvina	1863 06 12	
Demill ....Freeborn	Knight.................Anna	1819 03 11	
Denison ....Hans	Christofferson......Johanna	1846 11 22	Denmark
Dennett............Daniel Quinby	Very....................Lucy Ann N.		
Denney ....Charles	Gold ....Sarah Ann	1872 12 02	UT, Salt Lake City
Denning ....James	Merrifield ....Sarah	1849 07 08	Wales
Dennis ....William T.	Bankhead............Talitha C. A.	1836 12 08	
Dennis ....William T.	Fullmer...............Ann Adelaide	1857 09 06	UT, Salt Lake City
Densley ....Daniel	Beech.................Sarah	1851	ENG
Denton............John	Broadhead ....Elizabeth	1852 03	
Deournso........Lewis	Kempton..............Hannah	1875	
Derrick ....Zachariah W.	Shepherd ....Mary	1836 04 16	ENG
DeSaules........Daniel H.	Dessoulavy ....Marie Elizabeth	1818 02 17	Switzerland
Despain ....Henry Waters	Erickson ....Joanna Matilda	1879 05 24	
Despain ....James H.	Reynolds ....Celia Ann	1846 11 10	
Despain ....Solomon J.	Newell ....Ruth Amelia	1842 06 30	
Deuel..............Osmyn M.	Thorn.................Mary Ann	1855 11 26	UT, Salt Lake City
Deuel..............Osmyn M.	Tonks ....Sarah R. R.	1868 08 22	UT, Salt Lake City
Deuel..............William H.	Whiting...............Eliza Avery	1837 01 01	NY, Freedom
Devey ....John	Timms ....Hannah A. A.	1868 06 20	ENG, Liverpool
Dewey ....John Cook	Allen...................Mary	1854 04 21	UT, Bountiful
Dewey ....John Cook	May ....Harriet	1857 02 11	
Dewitt ....Abel A.	Watson...............Margaret Miller	1860 03 15	
Dewsnup ....John D.	Topham ....Jemima	1836 03 13	ENG, Lancashire
Dibble ....John W.	Bouton...............Amanda	1837	
Dibble ....Philo	Dubois................Hannah Ann		
Dick ....David	Duff ....Helen	1867 06	Scotland
Dickerson ....Joseph	Bales ....Mary Ann	1858 04 14	NE, Florence
Dickerson ....William	Dunkley ....Frances	1820 01 05	ENG, Bedford
Dickson...........Billa	Stoddard ....Mary Ann	1837 04 10	
Dickson...........Stuart	Champlin............Mary Jane	1849 08 27	IA
Dickson...........William H.	Slade.................Martha	1872 03 22	UT, Richville

Male	Female	Date	Place
Dilworth ....Caleb	Woolerton...........Eliza	1812	
Dimick..............Albert Stanley	Wimmer..............Eliza Jane	1861 11 09	
Dimick..............Thomas J.	Gates ....Mary Anne	1827 02	NY, Monroe
Dinwoodey.......Henry	Gore ....Ellen	1846 02 08	
Dinwoodey.......Henry	Kinnersley ....Sarah Emily	1864 09 24	UT, Salt Lake City
Dinwoodey......James	Wool..................Elizabeth	1821	ENG, Liverpool
Dittmore...........Henry	Smuin.................Rachel	1864 03 01	UT, Salt Lake City
Dixon ....Charles	Humphrey ....Elizabeth	1799 10 13	Canada
Dixon ....Christopher F.	Wightman............Jane Elizabeth	1844 09 01	Canada
Dixon ....Harvey	Harmon ....Susan	1876	
Dixon ....Harvey	Pritchett..............Kittie Evelyn	1870 03 07	UT, Salt Lake City
Dixon ....Henry A.	Degrey ....Sarah	1865 01 21	
Dixon ....Henry A.	Smith..................Mary Ann	1869 04 13	UT, Salt Lake City
Dixon ....William W.	Lake ....Sabra	1842 08 16	IL, Scott Co.
Dobson ....Joseph	Aitcheson ....Jennette	1851	MO, St. Louis
Dobson ....William Frain	Hill......................Ann	1868 12 28	UT, Salt Lake City
Doddis ....Harry	Crowther ....Hannah		
Dodds ....George	Davies ....Mary Emiah	1873 04 16	UT, New Harmony
Dodds ....Thomas	Farrow.................Mary	1868 02 29	UT, Salt Lake City
Dodge.............Augustas E.	Clark...................Marion Wallace	1850 09 05	UT, Salt Lake City
Dodge.............Nathaniel Morgan	Hadden ....Duritha	1862	
Dofflemeyer .....George	Mabey ....Esther	1902	
Domgaard........Niels P.	Nielsen ....Else Kirstine	1845 10 12	Denmark
Don.................William	Squire.................Janet		
Donald ....Malcolm	Shaw ....Mary	1822 09 27	Scotland
Done................Abraham	Hancock ....Ann	1825	
Done................George	Smith..................Alice	1858 09 09	UT, Cottonwood
Done................John	Barker ....Sarah	1852 02 15	ENG, Lancashire
Donelson ....Charles M.	Jolley..................Caroline Carson	1850 05 01	IA, Harris Grove
Doney..............John	George ....Ann Temperance	1853 01 22	ENG, Cornwall
Dopp................Peter	Standley ....Sarah Jane	1850 07 02	IA, Kanesville
Dorius ....John F. F.	Frantzen.............Karen	1857 04 25	
Dorius ....Lewis Olsen	Firth...................Mary Ann	1862 10 04	UT, Salt Lake City
Dorius ....Lewis Olsen	Jensen ....Caroline Maria	1867 05 11	UT, Salt Lake City
Dorney............William	Davis ....Mary	1816	ENG
Dorrity.............Dennis	Berry ....Martha Elizabeth	1860	
Dorrity.............Dennis	Jolley..................Diana Louisa	1835	TN, Dresden
Dorton.............Joseph A.	Clayton...............Martha	1858 04	
Dotson ....William	Landrum..............Henrietta	1853 07 03	AL
Doty ....Benjamin	Butterfield...........Mary Jane	1874 05 12	
Doty ....Benjamin	Hofhine...............Mary Jane	1856 12 01	UT, Salt Lake City
Douglas ....George	Briggs.................Ellen	1823	ENG, Downham
Douglass ....Samuel	Dixon..................Emma Jane	1874 10 26	UT, Salt Lake City
Douglass ....William	Cross..................Agnes	1842 10 14	IRE
Dowdle ....Robert	Robinson.............Sarah Ann	1818 05 27	SC
Downs ....James	Greathouse ....Mary Ann	1847 03 03	IA, Council Bluffs
Downs ....Reuben John	Wagle.................Cynthia	1861 05 19	UT, Nephi
Doxey ....Thomas	Hunt ....Ann Elizabeth	1853 07 10	IA, Council Bluffs
Drake..............Daniel	Perkins ....Patience	1813 12 02	
Drake..............Daniel N.	Johnson ....Cynthia Parker	1844 01 04	IL, Hancock Co.
Drake..............Daniel N.	Kempton............Hannah	1849	UT
Drake..............Jacob	Hayden...............Flora	1834 07 01	NY, Pompey
Drake..............Richard	Beecher..............Phoebe Lavina	1864 07 24	UT, Willard
Draper ....Almon	Hansen..............Amy	1866 12 11	UT, Rockville

Male		Female		Date	Place
Draper	Nephi	Johnson	Charlotte E.	1870 11 15	UT, Rush Valley
Draper	Thomas Jr.	Mosier	Mary	1805	
Draper	William	Allard	Marie Louise	1849 06 03	IA, Pottawattamie
Draper	William	Mosier	Mary		
Draper	William	Staker	Elizabeth	1827 06 11	Canada
Draper	William	Thompson	Marial	1848 05 06	NE
Draper	William Jr.	Newton	Ruth Hannah	1854 04 17	UT, Draper
Draper	William Jr.	Raymer	Martha	1846 01 28	IL, Nauvoo
Draper	William Lathrop	Eckersley	Fannie	1864	
Draper	Zemira	Terry	Amy	1842 01 31	IL, Pleasant Vale
Dredge	Jesse R.	Rhees	Ellen	1854 04 29	Wales
Driggs	Benjamin W.	Pratt	Olivia Thankful	1857 02 16	UT, Pleasant Grove
Driggs	Samuel	Taylor	Elizabeth Ann	1840 10 04	IL, Nauvoo
Driggs	Shadrach F.	Harvey	Cecelia		
Driggs	Shadrach F.	White	Eliza Elizabeth	1836 06	Ohio
Driver	William	Boulter	Charlotte Emblen	1858 08 16	ENG, Middlesex
Drollinger	Samuel	Cook	Rachel	1819 12 21	OH, Bulter Co.
Druce	Henry	Jinks	Harriet	1845 05 04	ENG, Stratford
Druce	John	Jinks	Julia Ann	1842 06 19	ENG, Manchester
Dudley	William Davis	Durfee	Delana	1838 10 28	MO, Far West
Duel	Benjamin	Harris	Naomi	1823	NY, Palmyra
Duerden	Richard	Starkey	Sarah Ann	1866 02 17	ENG
Duffin	Isaac	Fielding	Mary	1849 06 03	PA, Philadelphia
Dugdale	Edmund	Waddell	Ann	1869	
Duke	James	Moore	Almira	1851 10 10	UT, Wallsburg
Duke	Jonathan O.	Stone	Mary	1828 12 30	ENG, Derby
Duke	Jonathan O.	Thompson	Martha	1855 12 03	
Duke	Jonathan O.	Thompson	Sarah Ann	1855 10 19	UT, Provo
Duke	Robert Stone	Horrocks	Rachel	1872 11 11	UT, Salt Lake City
Duncan	Adam	Robb	Isabella	1869 06 21	UT, Salt Lake City
Duncan	Homer	Banker	Asenath M. R.	1841 11 07	NY
Duncan	Homer	Trippess	Sarah	1863 07 11	
Duncan	James	Snedden	Jennet	1851	PA
Duncan	John C.	Farrell	Teresa Ann	1872 05 27	UT, Cedar City
Duncan	William	Brown	Mary	1835 02 27	Scotland
Dunford	Isaac	Bailey	Leah	1845 11 02	ENG, Wiltshire
Dunkley	Joseph	Wright	Margaret	1868 11 14	UT, Salt Lake City
Dunlap	Joseph	Cowan	Margaret	1860 10 09	UT, Salt Lake City
Dunn	James	Fielding	Hannah	1861 01 10	UT, Salt Lake City
Dunn	John	Bates	Harriet Elizabeth	1868 08 15	UT, Salt Lake City
Dunn	John Barker	Maguire	Juley Ann	1853 02 11	UT, North Ogden
Dunn	Joseph Moroni	White	Susanna E.	1866 12 27	UT, Tooele
Dunn	Simeon Adams	Caldwell	Jane	1846 05	
Dunn	William G.	Fleming	Elizabeth	1837 10 02	ENG, Lancashire
Dunton	James Harvey	Doidge	Mary Ann	1878 06 14	UT, St. George
Dunyon	John	Brown	Ann Kempton	1853 10 14	UT, Salt Lake City
Durfee	Abraham	Curtis	Ursula	1846	
Durfee	Abraham A.	Nielsen	Olevia Dorthea	1884 02 08	
Durfee	Edmund	Pickle	Magdelena	1809 10 18	RI, Tiverton
Durfee	Henry D.	Barker	Jane Isabelle	1857	UT, Ogden
Durfee	Jabez	Curtis	Celestia	1850 12 25	UT, Salt Lake City
Durfee	Jabez	Pickle	Magdelena	1846 01 21	IL, Nauvoo
Durfee	Nephi	Thomas	Amanda	1857	UT, Springville
Durham	Thomas	Mortensen	Caroline	1867 10 14	UT, Salt Lake City

Male	Female	Date	Place
Durrant ....James	Coolbear ....Caroline		
Dusenberry......Mahlon	Coray ....Aurilla	1831 05 21	PA, Easton
Dustin ....Seth	Everington...........Ann Reed	1870	
Dutson ....John	Green ....Ann	1826 02 07	ENG, Herefordshire
Dutson ....John W.	Jenkins..............Caroline Geneva	1858 09 07	UT, Fillmore
Dutson ....John William	Cowley ....Elizabeth Jane	1850 08 10	MO, St. Louis
Dye ....Robert	Coman ....Harriet	1841 08 12	ENG
Dye ....William	McKenzie ....Catherine	1869 04 12	UT, Salt Lake City
Dyer................Gideon	Brown................Eliza	1831 08 15	ENG
Dykes ....George Parker	Keeling ....Dorcas	1837	MO
Dymock ....E. George	Caldwell ....Caroline E.	1868	UT

E

Male	Female	Date	Place
Eagle ....Elias	Crook ....Mary	1844 02 23	
Eardley ....James	Fuller ....Zurviah Gleason	1852 03 15	MO, St. Louis
Eardley ....John	Cross.................Ann	1846 08 03	ENG, Derbyshire
Earl ....Jonathan	Wright.................Jane	1847 03 22	ENG
Earnshaw ....Mark	Green ....Harriet Ann	1864 10 01	UT, Salt Lake City
Earnshaw ....Thomas	Nowell ....Alice	1804 06 16	ENG, Yorkshire
Easton ....John	Fife ....Margaret	1850	MO, Grovie
Eatough ....George	Ollerton ....Sarah	1874	
Eccles.............Thomas	Hardman ....Alice	1843 08 06	ENG
Eckersell..........James B.	McPhail ....Henrietta	1861 04 21	
Eckersley.........Joseph	Hulme................Alice	1845 05 23	
Eckersley........William	Hardy ....Hannah	1833 10 21	ENG, Middleton
Edman ....Hans Odahl	Sandell ....Anna Caroline	1856 12 19	Sweden
Edminson ....Stokley	Gingell...............Charlotte E.	1866	
Edmiston ....John Jr.	Snow ....Martha Jane	1842	IL, Hancock
Edmunds ....Nathaniel	Jones ....Jane	1851 12 06	Wales
Edwards ....Caleb G.	Shephard ....Cynthia	1846 02 05	
Edwards ....David	Morgan...............Sarah Ann	1839 06 22	Wales
Edwards ....Esaias	Miles..................Belinda	1847 10 24	IA, Council Bluffs
Edwards ....Philip	Simmons.............Mary	1860 02 19	ENG, Sussex
Edwards ....Samuel James	Tingle ....Holly Jane	1857 03 15	UT, Salt Lake City
Egan ....Howard	Parshley ....Tamson	1838 12 01	MA, Essex
Egan ....Howard	Tuttle ....Mary Ann	1849	
Egan ....Howard Ransom	Andrus................Amanda Ann	1863 10 10	UT, Salt Lake City
Egan ....William Hyrum	Preator ....Mary Salome	1872 01 30	UT, Deep Creek
Egbert............Hyrum Smith	McGhie...............Annie Rebecca	1890 09 25	UT, Salt Lake City
Egbert............John	Hahn ....Susannah	1809 11 11	KY, Nelson Co.
Egbert............John Calvert	Bennett...............Ellen	1861	
Egbert............Joseph	Allred.................Mary Carolyn	1840 12 04	IL, Nauvoo
Egbert............Joseph	Taylor.................Louisa	1852 06 17	
Egbert............Robert Cowden	Cunningham........Seviah	1846 04 01	IL, Nauvoo
Egbert............Samuel	Beckstead ....Margaret Mariah	1839 04 18	MO, Clay Co.
Ekins..............George	Sykes ....Eleanor	1851 02 04	ENG, Brampton
Elder ....Claybourne	Pedersen.............Mica M. C. M.	1858 01 31	
Elder ....David	Montgomery ....Martha Louisa	1825 11 07	
Eldredge ....Alanson	Neff ....Martha Elizabeth	1870 05 09	UT, East Mill Creek
Eldredge ....Elnathan	Baker.................Ruth	1839 09 04	
Eldredge ....Horace S.	Gibbs.................Sarah Waterous	1851 04 21	UT, Salt Lake City
Eldredge ....Hyrum	Phippen..............Julia Ann	1866 07 28	UT, Coalville

Male		Female		Date	Place
Eldredge	Ira	Black	Nancy	1833 07 04	
Eldredge	Ira	Jensen	Helvig Maria	1861 11 22	
Eldredge	Ira	Savage	Hannah Maria	1852 02 28	
Eldridge	John S.	Chipman	Sinah Ceneth	1849 03 24	
Eldridge	Joseph	Radburn	Eliza	1847 04 20	ENG
Eliason	Andreas P.	Ericksson	Anna Marie	1863 09 12	UT, Salt Lake City
Eliason	Andrew	Swenson	Johanna	1867 11 16	UT, Salt Lake City
Eliason	Johan	Pedersen	Ane Margrethe	1847 04 24	Denmark
Eliason	Johannes L.	Larsen	Helena	1867 03 04	UT, Salt Lake City
Eliason	Lars A.	Olsson	Hanna	1836 12 02	Sweden
Ellett	John James	Davidson	Eleanor	1840 04 22	
Ellett	John James	Turner	Mary	1861 11 11	
Elliott	Peter Mack	Alvord	Charlotte	1857 02 01	UT, Salt Lake City
Ellis	Alexander G.	Elsmore	Maria	1863 05 14	ENG
Ellis	David Moroni	Jackson	Sophronia Ann	1879 06 19	
Ellis	Edmund	Barnaby	Sarah Grace	1854 01 16	ENG, Wiltshire
Ellis	Frederick W.	Davis	Susan Keziah	1869 09 06	UT, Salt Lake City
Ellis	James	Phillips	Ann	1845 05 11	Wales
Ellis	John	Hales	Harriet	1839 10 31	IL, Adams Co.
Ellis	John E.	Barber	Hannah	1841 10 30	ENG, Sussex
Ellis	John E.	Fuller	Martha Jane	1879	
Ellison	James	Halliwell	Alice	1842 06 01	ENG, Lancashire
Ells		Dubois	Hannah Ann		
Ellsworth	Edmund L.	Young	Elizabeth	1842 07 10	
Ellwood	Robert	Underwood	Elizabeth	1849 12 24	ENG
Elmer	Elijah	Williams	Mary	1840 04 29	
Elmer	Henry	Beckstead	Sarah Ann	1866 03 31	UT, Salt Lake City
Elmer	Hyrum K.	Huffman	Mary	1845 06 09	IA, Lee Co.
Elsey	Joseph	Lane	Sarah	1827 01 08	ENG
Elsmore	Thomas	Sandall	Martha	1845 06 01	ENG, Glou.
Elvers	Carl	Rivers	Mary	1864	UT, Salt Lake City
Emery	Albion B.	Bransford	Susanna	1884 11 11	
Emery	Henry	Brewerton	Elizabeth	1851 05 18	IA, Council Bluffs
Emmons	Charles Henry	Thompson	Sarah Ann	1870 11 14	UT, Salt Lake City
Engalitchell	Nicolas V.	Bransford	Susanna	1935	
Engberson	Henry	Borsen	Annie Bolliti	1872 12 16	UT, Salt Lake City
England	Daniel	Medler	Mary Ann	1828 02 11	ENG
England	John	Hope	Emma Eliza	1920 10 20	UT, Logan
England	Thomas	Hayball	Ellen Jane	1885 04 26	
England	William	Seamons	Eliza	1860 06 05	IA, Council Bluffs
Englested	Rasmus Madsen	Ohlsen	Margrethe	1858 03 25	UT, Emery
Engstrom	Carl Gustaf	Jensen	Kirsten Marie	1871 12 04	UT
Engstrom	Magnus	Jansson	Caisa Lisa	1863 10	UT
Enniss	John	Boulter	Elizabeth	1845 12 14	ENG
Ensign	Horace	Bronson	Mary	1825 09 28	
Ensign	Horace D.	Stewart	Eliza Jane	1850 01	UT, Ogden
Ensign	Isaac	Bryant	Mary	1803 11 03	MA, Westfield
Ensign	Martin Luther	Dunn	Mary	1852 01 08	UT, Salt Lake City
Ensign	Samuel	Gordon	Mary Everett	1832 11 29	MA
Enslow	Elza	Harding	Mary	1848 03	
Epperson	Sidney Hiram	Robey	Mary Jane	1853 11 07	UT, Provo
Ercanbrack	William T.	Seabury	Ruth Ann	1864 11 11	
Erekson	Jonas	Benbow	Isabella Markham	1869 08 30	
Erekson	Jonas	Powell	Mary J.	1852 12 31	UT, Salt Lake City

Male		Female		Date	Place
Ericksen	Henrik S.	Jonassen	Magla	1822 06 12	Norway
Ericksen	Jorgen	Pedersen	Sidse	1846 07 31	Denmark
Ericksen	Marcus	Christensen	Kersten	1833	Denmark
Erickson	Engebret	Olsen	Olena	1849	
Erickson	John A.	Anderson	Hilda	1882 01 23	UT, Salt Lake City
Erickson	Swen	Bengtson	Maria Kristina	1853	Sweden
Ericson	John M.	Graham	Christina Burns	1887 08 17	UT, Salt Lake City
Erskine	Archibald	McFarlane	Ann	1851 06 03	Scotland
Eskildsen	Niels C.	Larsen	Mette Maria	1846 05 23	Denmark
Esklund	Lars P. H.	Christensen	Brita K. B.	1847 11 05	Sweden
Esplin	John	Webster	Margaret	1853 11 10	UT, Salt Lake City
Etherington	John	Hemsley	Elizabeth	1818 03 29	
Etherington	Thomas	Tarrant	Charlotte	1869	
Etherington	Thomas	Wheeler	Sarah	1858 03 09	UT, Salt Lake City
Evans	Abel	Jones	Mary	1850 05 05	LA, New Orleans
Evans	Abram	Davis	Mary	1832 12 17	Wales
Evans	Benjamin Bowen	Phippen	Julia Ann	1886 10 22	UT, Logan
Evans	David	Coleman	Rebecca		
Evans	David	Ewell	Barbara Ann	1841 11 23	IL
Evans	David	Hinchcliff	Edna	1854 11 03	
Evans	David	Holm	Margrethe K.	1861 05 04	UT, Salt Lake City
Evans	David	Morris	Jane	1811 08 01	ENG, Prestwich
Evans	David	Rees	Phoebe	1825 07 16	Wales
Evans	David	Shaw	Clemina		
Evans	David Rees	Lloyd	Gwen W.	1853 07 08	UT, Brigham City
Evans	David W.	Alldredge	Elizabeth	1862 06 15	UT, Salt Lake City
Evans	Edward	Morgan	Hannah	1804 12 09	Wales
Evans	George	Hone	Emma	1867 03 31	UT, Salt Lake City
Evans	James R.	Foster	Elizabeth	1851 04 15	ENG, Birmingham
Evans	John	Hardcastle	Elizabeth	1858 07 24	NY, Oneida
Evans	John	Stead	Mary	1817 12 11	ENG
Evans	John	Wool	Elizabeth	1839	
Evans	John Jr.	Ellison	Mary	1854 12 25	MO, St. Louis
Evans	John Robert	Woolley	Mary Edna	1830 08 24	ENG, Louth
Evans	John Thomas	Lloyd	Elizabeth Ann	1855 11 25	
Evans	Moses	Pollard	Louisa	1866 03 09	
Evans	Richard	Yarnell	Sarah	1844 09 23	ENG
Evans	Samuel L.	Manning	Anna Eliza	1846 09 07	ENG, Bristol
Evans	Thomas	Commander	Matilda	1859 05 03	ENG, Birmingham
Evans	Thomas	Norris	Mary	1854 03 09	Wales
Evans	Thomas David	Merriman	Priscilla	1856 04 03	Wales
Evans	William	Jordan	Mary	1864 05 22	Ocean
Evans	William M.	Hyder	Charlotte J.	1852 07 15	UT, Salt Lake City
Evensen	Henrik	Gahrson	Tarjer Serine	1843 09 22	Norway
Everts	Joshua	Arms	Charity	1830	VT
Ewell	William Fletcher	Bland	Mary Lee	1834	KY
Ewing	Anderson	Parker	Exile Liberty	1865	UT, Provo
Ewing	Samuel	Smith	Susanna	1853 07 16	
Ewings	Alexander	Lehman	Sarah Ann	1820	
Eyre	George	Hopkin	Rebekah	1861 04 17	ENG, Sheffield

F

Male	Female	Date	Place
Fackrell..........David B.	Sumner ....Susannah	1855 11 10	UT, Bountiful
Fackrell..........James	Crumb ....Amy	1819	VT
Fackrell..........James Jr.	Chapman ....Martha Ann	1850 01 13	UT, Salt Lake City
Fackrell..........Joseph C.	Dempsey............Clarissa	1845 08 28	MI, Bertrand
Fairbanks........David	Mandeville..........Susan	1838 11 26	NJ
Fairbanks........John B.	Van Wagoner......Sarah	1844 08 31	
Fairbanks........Joseph	Brooks................Mary	1803 10 03	
Fairchild..........Joshua Jr.	Fenner................Prudence	1827	OH, Marion
Fairchild..........Moroni F.	McMurray...........Harriet Lucinda	1855 01 18	UT, Grantsville
Farley ....Edward	Moore................Mary	1821 08 09	VA, Greenbriar
Farley ....Isaac Robeson	Malan ....Madeleine	1855 03 11	UT, Salt Lake City
Farley ....Isaac Robeson	Malan ....Pauline Amelia	1855 03 11	UT, Salt Lake City
Farley ....James	Lakeman ....Rebecca		
Farley ....Winthrop	Hastings ....Mary Elizabeth	1863 01 24	UT, Salt Lake City
Farley ....Winthrop	Pons...................Lydia	1857 03 08	CO, Manasa
Farmer............Edward John	Wright................Elizabeth E.	1858 09 26	PA, Philadelphia
Farmer............James	Biddle ....Mary Ann	1854 10 27	ENG
Farmer............James B.	Blain ....Jane	1865 03 10	UT, Salt Lake City
Farmer............Richard	Morris ....Elizabeth	1810	ENG
Farnes ....Thomas S.	Harrison ....Sarah Ann	1861 03 02	ENG, London
Farnham.........Augustus A.	Pill ....Caroline	1858 02 07	UT, Salt Lake City
Farnsworth ......Albert S.	Johnson ....Mary Ann	1874 01 12	UT, Salt Lake City
Farnsworth ......Alonzo L.	Bertelsen............Christianna D.	1877 03 09	UT, Salt Lake City
Farnsworth ......Alonzo L.	Heinrich..............Eda Henrietta	1875 04 08	UT, Salt Lake City
Farnsworth ......Alonzo L.	Staker.................Mary Ann	1866 09 08	UT, Salt Lake City
Farnsworth ......Philo T.	Adams................Margaret	1857 08 24	UT, Beaver
Farnsworth ......Philo T.	Griffiths...............Mary Priscilla	1860 06 15	UT, Salt Lake City
Farnsworth ......Philo T.	Patterson............Agnes Ann	1858 12 10	
Farnsworth ......Philo T.	Yates..................Margaret	1848 10 29	UT, Salt Lake City
Farnsworth ......Stephen M.	Lewis..................Eliza	1854 05 30	UT, Salt Lake City
Farnsworth ......Stephen M.	Showell ....Ellen Louisa	1856 02 26	UT, Salt Lake City
Farr..................Elbridge	Russ...................Sarah	1828 07 03	MA, Hunsdale
Farr..................Franklin R.	Jones ....Anne	1866 12 22	UT, Salt Lake City
Farr..................Lorin	Chase.................Nancy Bailey	1845 01 01	IL, Nauvoo
Farr..................Lorin	Giles...................Sarah	1851 07 26	
Farr..................Winslow	Freeman.............Olive Hovey	1816 12 05	VT, Waterford
Farr..................Winslow Jr.	Covington............Emily Jane	1858 10 17	UT
Farrell ....John	McMillan.............Sarah Ann		
Farrow ....Nicholas	Cairnes...............Ruth	1830	Scotland
Faulkner ....Edward	Taylor.................Jane	1838 11 11	
Faulkner ....John	Bratt ....Mary	1828 04 29	ENG
Fausett ....John McKee	Shelton...............Mary Ann	1852 07 28	UT, Salt Lake City
Fausett ....Nephi R.	Orchard..............Ruth	1868 09 26	UT, Salt Lake City
Fausett ....William M.	Butcher...............Matilda Caroline	1826 03 02	TN, Maury Co.
Fausett ....William M.	Logan ....Ruth Bailey		
Faux ....Jabez	Danielson...........Hanna	1862 12 24	UT, Moroni
Fawcett............William	Smith..................Jane Corner	1837 08 03	
Fawson............Abraham	Hodierne ....Ann	1838 05 06	ENG, Foleshill
Fawson............Abraham	Kilpack ....Louisa	1862 12 15	ENG
Fechser ....Johann F.	Hafen ....Anna Katharina	1867 09 14	UT, Salt Lake City
Fellows ....Albert G.	Anderson............Ann	1867 06 29	UT, Salt Lake City
Felshaw ....William	Gilbert ....Mary Harriet	1827 02 01	NY

Male	Female	Date	Place
Felt ....John Johnson	Peterson............Stina Kajsa	1862 06 21	UT, Salt Lake City
Felt ....John Johnson	Stromberg ....Kajsa Lisa	1863 09 12	UT, Salt Lake City
Felt ....John Johnson	Stromberg ....Maria Kristina		
Felt ....Joseph Henry	Bouton................Sarah Louise	1866 12 24	UT, Salt Lake City
Felt ....Joseph Henry	Mineer................Elizabeth		
Felt ....Marcus	Allen................Laura Josephine		
Felt ....Nathaniel Henry	Pile ....Mary Louise	1857 12 07	UT, Salt Lake City
Felt ....Nathaniel Henry	Preston................Eliza Ann	1839 10 03	MA, Salem
Fenn ....William	Yarnell................Sarah	1859	UT, Provo
Fenton ....Thomas	Wilson ....Annie Mariah	1866 05 12	
Ferguson ....Jacob S.	Humble................Francis E.	1851 08 31	ENG
Ferrin ....Jacob S.	McBride...............Janetta Ann	1857 03 29	UT, Ogden
Ferrin ....Samuel	Howard................Margaret Ann	1857 05 03	UT, Ogden
Ferrin ....Samuel	Powell ....Sallie Clotilda	1833 01 21	PA
Field................John	Lavender ....Alice	1862 04 05	UT, Salt Lake City
Field................William	Harding ....Mary	1825 02 14	ENG, Rosebury
Fielding............Amos H.	Benson................Jane		
Fielding............Amos H.	Hobbs.................Ellen Agnes	1871	UT, Parowan
Fielding............James H.	Dawtry................Mary Ann	1861 04 27	UT, Salt Lake City
Fielding............Joseph	Greenwood ....Hannah	1838 06 11	ENG, Preston
Fife ....Adam	Sharp ....Helen (Ellen)	1825	Scotland
Fife ....James	Mathieson ....Margaret	1824 09 19	Scotland
Fifield..............Matthew P.	Gibson................Almira Jane	1852 04 05	UT, Bountiful
Fifield..............Matthew P.	Hoopes...............Rebecca Ann	1862 03 03	UT, Richmond
Fillerup............Anders P.	Rasmussen ....Caroline Rasmine	1867 06 30	Ocean
Fillmore............Daniel B.	Grant..................Thankful Ann	1839 09 22	WI, Muskego
Finch................William	Holt....................Mary	1863 12 31	UT, Salt Lake City
Findlay............Hugh	Partington............Catherine Ann	1856 03 25	UT, Salt Lake City
Findlay............Williams	Muir....................Agnes	1868 12 14	
Finlayson ....David	Johnston ....Margaret	1850 02 26	
Finley..............David	Ford....................Margaret Jane		
Finlinson ....George	Trimble ....Susan	1866	UT, Fillmore
Firth ....Arthur	Firth....................Emily Mary	1869 11 25	UT, South Weber
Firth ....John	Kendell................Jane	1845 05 12	ENG, Yorkshire
Firth ....William	Stead..................Ann	1818 08 08	ENG
Fischer............Hans Jacob	Sigrist.................Elizabeth	1862 12 06	UT, Salt Lake City
Fish................Horace	Leavitt ....Hannah	1824 05 18	Canada
Fish................Joseph	Lewis..................Eliza Jane	1869	UT, Salt Lake City
Fish................Joseph	Steele.................Mary Campbell	1859 03 22	
Fisher ....James	Burrows..............Emma	1840 11 17	ENG, London
Fisher ....James	Ross...................Jane Duncan	1869 10 11	UT, Salt Lake City
Fisher ....James	Stott...................Hannah Lees	1844 11 17	ENG
Fisher ....John	Pearson...............Jane	1841 05 31	ENG
Fisher ....Moroni	Peterson.............Mary	1875 09 27	UT, Salt Lake City
Fisher ....Thomas F.	Christton..............Jane	1834 01 25	ENG, Camberwell
Fisher ....Thomas F.	Smith..................Sarah Ann	1857 04 10	UT, Salt Lake City
Fisher ....Vardis J.	Chapman ....Jane	1832 07 02	
Fitt ....George	Wakefield ....Caroline Rachel	1877 11 14	UT, Salt Lake City
Fitt ....William	Hansen................Annie Marie	1868 07 31	UT, Salt Lake City
Fitzgerald........John	Williams..............Sarah Ann	1858 02 17	UT, Salt Lake City
Fitzgerald........Perry	Casot..................Mary Ann	1839 01 10	IL, Vermillion
Flack..............John Logan	Burchell ....Emma	1860 06 07	UT, Bates Creek
Flaherty ....Michael	Carter.................Elizabeth	1850	
Flake..............Green	Crosby................Martha Vilate	1854	NC

Male		Female		Date	Place
Flamm	Jacob Henry	Bock	Helene	1859 11 27	CT, Norwalk
Flanigan	Thomas	Very	Lucy Ann N.	1842 10 08	MA, Salem
Fleet	Henry	Hayter	Annetta	1841 10 24	ENG
Fleming	Josiah W.	Bigler	Nancy	1828 06 05	WV
Fletcher	Benjamin	Leavitt	Roxanna	1838 04 12	IL
Fletcher	Francis	Wright	Esther B.	1839 07 03	MA, Middlesex
Flint	John	Spencer	Mary	1838 12 05	ENG
Flint	William	Goodridge	Mary Jane	1850 12 24	UT, Salt Lake City
Florence	Henry	Taylor	Sarah Jane	1861 11 13	UT, Big Cottonwood
Floyd	Leonard	Foster	Emma E.	1873 08 27	ID, St. Charles
Fluiett	William	Day	Mary Ann	1855 07 15	
Fogelburg	Wilhelm	Lyon	Sophia Margaret	1885 08 20	UT, Logan
Folkman	Christopher O.	Lindvall	Maximiliana M. O.	1869 04 26	UT, Salt Lake City
Folkman	Jens Peter	Funk	Matilda K.	1857 03 31	Denmark
Folkman	Jens Peter	Thomasen	Maren Catherine	1865 09 02	UT, Salt Lake City
Folland	Henry	Wright	Harriet	1849 05 05	ENG, Upton Pyne
Follett	William T.	Bayliss	Esther	1853 10	UT, Salt Lake City
Folsom	Hyrum P.	Broadbent	Nancy	1866 12 29	UT, Salt Lake City
Folsom	William H.	Clark	Zerviah Eliza	1837 08 21	NY, Pembroke
Foote	Thomas	Barrett	Eliza Ann	1857	NY
Forbes	Henry Clay	Seddon	Ester	1860	UT
Forbes	James	Norris	Mary	1860 09 21	
Forbush	Rufus	Clark	Polly	1811 11 05	MA, Royalston
Forbush	Sanford	Gaylord	Mary S.	1844 05 27	IL, Hancock Co.
Forbush	Sanford	Jensen	Christina	1871 03 27	
Ford	Alford	Tegan	Methine	1870 01 17	
Ford	Alfred Charles	Rasmussen	Matilda	1863 12 26	UT, Salt Lake City
Ford	John	Chandler	Rebecca	1833 06 23	ENG, Cambridge
Ford	Jonathan	Roberson	Rachel	1826 04 16	IN, Bartholomew
Ford	Joseph	Voss	Phebe	1875	UT
Ford	Luke	Rowley	Ann Jewel	1857 10 14	
Ford	Thomas	Voss	Phebe	1867 12 07	UT, Salt Lake City
Ford	William	Durfee	Delana	1845 08 03	IL, Nauvoo
Ford	William	Marsh	Mary Jane	1857 03 05	
Ford	William	Mecham	Elizabeth Lucena	1853	
Ford	William M.	Stoker	Zebiah Mariba	1852 11	IA, Trader's Point
Fordham	Elijah	Brown	Amelia	1856 04 06	
Foreman	James	Campbell	Mary Ann	1818 01 12	ENG
Foreman	Thomas J.	Biggs	Eliza Frances	1842 08 17	NC, Careret Co.
Foremaster	Fredrick W.	Lindau	Christina S. M.	1859 08 24	Prussia
Forrester	Robert	Christensen	Sara Kristine		
Forsyth	Thomas R.	Donald	Isabella	1839 04 01	Scotland
Forsyth	Thomas R.	Goheen	Fredonia Melissa	1863 04 05	
Foss	Calvin	Carter	Sarah Bracket	1823 11 01	ME, Scarboro
Foster	Charles Allan	Hinkle	Mary Rhodes	1851	UT, Ogden
Foster	William Jr.	Morris	Ann	1830	ENG
Fotheringham	John	Gentle	Charlotte	1819 04 18	Scotland
Fotheringham	John	Smith	Susanna	1862 06 24	
Fotheringham	William	Wardrobe	Mary	1857 01 25	UT, Salt Lake City
Foulger	Herbert John	Hall	Charlotte Maria	1881 10 11	UT, Salt Lake City
Foutz	Jacob	Mann	Margaret	1822 07 22	
Foutz	Jacob Jr.	Thorne	Sarah Ann	1866 01 07	
Fowers	Jesse	Johnson	Sarah	1841 11	ENG
Fowler	William	Bradshaw	Ellen	1855 01 24	ENG

Male		Female		Date	Place
Fowles	Timothy	Saunders	Eliza	1839 08 13	ENG
Fox	Charles Wilson	Brook	Elizabeth	1862 02 02	UT, Lehi
Fox	George Sellman	Jones	Mary Elizabeth	1842 02 21	ENG, Aston
Fox	Isaac W.	Simmons	Catherine Sophia	1869 05 31	UT, Salt Lake City
Fox	Jesse W. Jr.	May	Ruth	1873 05 08	UT, Salt Lake City
Fox	Jesse Williams	Foss	Sarah Elizabeth	1871 03 13	UT, Salt Lake City
Fox	Jesse Williams	Gibbs	Eliza Jerusha	1849 06 02	IA, Council Bluffs
Fox	Thomas James	Green	Margaret Florenza	1875 11 27	UT, Union
Foy	John Moroni	Chestnut	Sarah Mary	1862 12 13	UT, Salt Lake City
Foy	Martin W.	Hoy	Susannah	1872 05 27	UT, Salt Lake City
Foy	Thomas Birk		Louisa	1861	
Foy	Thomas Birk	Fink	Catherine R.		
Frame	Archibald	Dick	Janet	1864 09 23	Scotland
Frame	Archibald	Duff	Helen	1882 03 13	UT, Salt Lake City
Frampton	David	Hough	Elizabeth	1829 03 26	IL, Nauvoo
Frampton	Nathaniel	Farnsworth	Laura	1824 05 27	OH, Burlington
Frampton	William M.	Terry	Mary Abby	1855 05 27	UT, Draper
France	Joseph	Harrod	Ellen	1856 10 12	UT, Salt Lake City
France	Joseph	Kuder	Mary Eleanor	1850 01 01	UT, Salt Lake City
Francis	Frederic Nelson	Shepard	Rozina	1862 11 01	
Francis	Samuel	Weisbrodt	Esther C. E.	1857 07 01	Switzerland
Francis	Thomas R.	Keep	Sarah	1865	
Francom	William	Harding	Amy	1837 09 03	ENG, Somerset
Franganillo	A. E.	Yeates	Elizabeth Lavinia		
Frankland	William Richard	Anderson	Elizabeth Ann	1870 10 11	UT, Salt Lake City
Fransen	Christian A.	Jensen	Anne C. C.	1878 11 14	UT, Salt Lake City
Frantzen	Anders	Hald	Trine Marie	1864 10 29	UT, Salt Lake City
Freckleton	John O.	Gardner	Jessie	1860 07 05	Scotland
Fredricksen	Anders	Nielsen	Karen	1848 02 12	Denmark
Fredricksen	Carl Antone	Christensen	Sara Kristine	1873 05 26	UT, Ephraim
Free	Absalom P.	Hicks	Annie	1857 03 05	UT, Salt Lake City
Free	Absalom P.	Strait	Elizabeth	1823 08 02	
Free	Preston Strait	Titcomb	Mary Jane A.	1855 08 22	UT, Salt Lake City
Freeman	John	Smoot	Nancy Beal	1826 02 09	KY, Calloway Co.
Freeman	John W.	Collins	Sarah Adaline		
Freestone	George	Lind	Jenny	1872 08 12	UT, Salt Lake City
Freestone	James F.	Lind	Maria Magdelene	1869 04 12	UT, Salt Lake City
Freestone	James F.	Poulsen	Pauline Kerstine	1868 02 15	UT, Salt Lake City
Freestone	Thomas	Fall	Ann	1837 08 01	Canada
Freshwater	William	Phillips	Hannah Elizabeth	1877 08 14	UT, St. George
Frew	John	Clotworthy	Jane	1846 05 01	Scotland
Friel	Edward	Harbell	Margaret Ann E.	1855 11 16	UT, Salt Lake City
Froerer	Frederick G.	Sabin	Elizabeth	1851 07 19	UT, Salt Lake City
Frost	Allen	Harrison	Annie Hester	1861 11 20	UT, Bountiful
Frost	Anders S.	Christensen	Else Marie	1827 03 17	Denmark
Frost	Jens C. S.	Andersen	Johanna Marie	1862 04 14	Ocean
Frost	Jens C. S.	Mortensen	Mette Marie	1866 12 15	UT, Ephraim
Frost	Jens C. S.	Petersen	Sena	1872 04 10	
Frost	McCaslin	Smith	Peninah	1809 11 28	NC
Fry	John J.	Toomer	Ann	1837 07 03	
Fry	Richard	Rawle	Ann Blackmore	1860 03 25	ENG, Liverpool
Fry	William	Collier	Mary	1844	
Fryer	Thomas C.	Rogers	Mary	1857	
Fryer	William	Colton	Ann	1833 06 18	

Male	Female	Date	Place
Fuller ....Amos B.	Smith...............Esther	1832 03 08	
Fuller ....Cornelius	Lewis.................Annie Elizabeth	1865 01 01	UT, Harrisburg
Fuller ....Edmund B.	Jelly...................Adelaide	1851 06 26	MO, St. Louis
Fuller ....Elijah K.	Walker...............Harriet (Alice)	1866 11 17	UT, Salt Lake City
Fuller ....Elijah K.	Woodward..........Ellen Celeste	1851 03 11	
Fuller ....Sanford	Bromley..............Mary Ann	1869	
Fuller ....Sanford	Spafford ....Martha Jane	1853 03 10	
Fullmer ....Almon L.	Follett ....Sarah Ann	1843 12 17	
Fullmer ....Almon L.	Neyman...............Rachel	1852 01 10	UT, Salt Lake City
Fullmer ....Almon L. II	Griffiths...............Jane Ellenor	1864 07 31	UT, Salt Lake City
Fullmer ....David	Marvin ....Rhoda Ann	1831 09 18	PA, Union
Fullmer ....David	Oysterbanks........Sarah Sophronia	1845 12 07	IL, Nauvoo
Fullmer ....Eugene B.	Mitchell...............Sarah Jane	1854 03 20	UT, Salt Lake City
Fullmer ....John S.	Price...................Mary Ann	1837 05 24	TN, Nashville
Fullmer ....John S.	Smith..................Olive Amanda	1846 01 21	IL, Nauvoo
Fullmer ....John S.	Stevenson ....Sarah Ann	1856	UT, Salt Lake City
Fullmer ....Junius Sextus	Ellyer ....Lucy	1866 09 16	UT, Salt Lake City
Fullmer ....Peter	Zerfass ....Susannah	1802	PA, Schuykill Co.
Fullmer ....William P.	Sainsbury ....Elizabeth Alice	1884 06 19	UT, Salt Lake City
Funk ....Daniel B.	Demill ....Mariah	1841 04 22	IL, Adams Co.
Funk ....Diderick	Hansen...............Christine	1825 11 12	
Furner............William Jr.	Ostler ....Sarah Ann	1862 12 22	UT, Nephi

G

Male	Female	Date	Place
Gadd...............Alfred	Hobbs................Mary Ann	1864 01 10	UT, Nephi
Gailey ....John	Greaves ....Ann	1843 06 27	IL, Nauvoo
Gailey ....John	Henwood............Elizabeth T.	1858 08 25	UT, Salt Lake City
Gaisford...........Isaac	Raikes ....Ellen	1851 06 13	ENG, Wiltshire
Galagher..........John	Brittingham..........Amelia	1848 01 11	MO, St. Louis
Galbraith..........George	Wilkie ....Ann	1832 07 13	Scotland
Gale ....Henry	Halliday ....Mary	1865 03 18	
Gale ....James	Derrick................Mary Ann S.	1854 01 01	UT, Salt Lake City
Gali ....Peter	Schneider............Anna Marie	1864 10 22	
Gallagher.........John	Neal....................Sarah Charlotte		
Gallian ....Jesse	Taylor ....Eliza	1854 04 02	MO, St. Louis
Galloway..........Charles Wesley	Cutler ....Anna	1849	
Gallup ....Luke William	Cook...................Lydia	1850 04 30	MO, Linden
Gammon..........Thomas	Day.....................Elizabeth	1840 10 27	ENG, Devon
Gange.............Thomas E. Jr.	Taylor ....Agnes	1873 09 20	UT, Salt Lake City
Gardner ....Alexander	Knox....................Ann	1832 10 06	Scotland
Gardner ....Archibald	Armitage..............Harriet	1857 06 21	UT, Salt Lake City
Gardner ....Archibald	Bradford ....Mary Ann	1849 04 19	UT, Salt Lake City
Gardner ....Archibald	Dowding..............Elizabeth	1867 03 02	UT, Salt Lake City
Gardner ....Archibald	Gahrson ....Tarjer Serine	1856 11 10	
Gardner ....Archibald	Hamilton..............Sarah Jane	1857 06 21	UT, Salt Lake City
Gardner ....Archibald	Hansen................Sidse Marie	1869 12 20	
Gardner ....Archibald	Lewis..................Elizabeth E.	1851 04 20	UT, Salt Lake City
Gardner ....Archibald	Livingston............Margaret	1839 02 19	Canada
Gardner ....Archibald	Park....................Jane	1852 08 24	UT, Salt Lake City
Gardner ....Archibald	Sprague ....Abigail	1849 04 19	
Gardner ....Archibald	Thompson ....Laura Althea	1852	
Gardner ....Benjamin	Lamport..............Electa	1822 05 29	

Male	Female	Date	Place
Gardner ....Charles	Kellogg ....Rhoda Elizabeth	1855 08 12	
Gardner ....Charles	Rigby ....Susannah	1867 01 11	UT, Salt Lake City
Gardner ....Charles A.	Timothy ....Martha	1878 12 05	UT, Salt Lake City
Gardner ....Elias	Abbott.................Ellen Elizabeth	1852 02 09	
Gardner ....Elias	Markham ....Ruth		
Gardner ....Fredrick	Smith..................Sarah Isabel	1853	
Gardner ....George B.	Beebe.................Harriet Mariah	1852 10 16	UT, Salt Lake City
Gardner ....George B.	Bird.....................Elizabeth Ann	1848 05 12	IA
Gardner ....Henry Bone	Ingram................Harriet	1845 11 22	ENG, Sussex
Gardner ....James	Rogers ....Eliza	1860 12	
Gardner ....James	Threlfall ....Jane	1855 03 03	
Gardner ....John	Hill ....Elizabeth Bryce	1856 01	
Gardner ....Matthew A.	Leggett ....Elizabeth	1838 06 24	
Gardner ....Milo Van Dusen	Montgomery ....Margaret	1859 09 29	UT, North Ogden
Gardner ....Moses Isaac	Pierson...............Polly Ann	1815 02 02	NY, Seneca Co.
Gardner ....Neil	Evensen ....Ingeborg Regine	1863 01 10	UT, Salt Lake City
Gardner ....Robert	Berry ....Cynthia Lovina	1851 08 05	
Gardner ....Robert	Calender ....Margaret	1800 05 25	Scotland
Gardner ....Robert	Cannon ....Leonora	1863 06 23	UT, Salt Lake City
Gardner ....Robert	Carr....................Mary Ann	1856 07 20	
Gardner ....Robert	McKeown ....Jane	1841 03 17	Canada
Gardner ....Walter Elias	Tuttle ....Mary Ann	1866 11 28	
Gardner ....William	Bennett...............Susan Ann	1857 10	UT
Gardner ....William	Gardner...............Agnes		
Garlick ....David Gaston	Buck....................Elizabeth	1816 10 01	
Garlick ....Joseph	Gillespie ....Mary Jane	1872 02 13	UT, Fairview
Garlick ....Joseph G.	Jones ....Amy Amillia	1851 10 31	UT, Salt Lake City
Garn ....Thomas	Eldredge.............Esther Ann	1868 03 14	UT, Salt Lake City
Garner ....David	Durfee ....Dolly	1842 10 18	IL, Lima
Garner ....David E.	Davis..................Sarah Rebecca	1870	UT, Salt Lake City
Garner ....Philip	Hedrick...............Mary	1830 04 04	IL, Carthage
Garner ....William Jr.	Field ....Mary	1856 11 01	UT, Slaterville
Garrard ....Timothy	Quantrille...........Susannah Evered	1827	
Garrett ....Levi Clutcher	Currie ....Christina	1863 01 10	UT, Salt Lake City
Garrett ....William	Maycock..............Maria	1841 04 04	ENG, Coventry
Garrett ....William A.	Wilkins................Ann Priscilla	1860 04 23	Ocean
Garrity.............Pat	Reynolds ....Celia Ann	1886 01 13	
Gates ....Charles Henry	Butler..................Elizabeth	1858 10 24	UT, Ogden
Gates ....Jacob	Ware ....Mary	1862 10 25	UT, Provo
Gates ....Reuben	Bryant.................Sarah Jane	1855 11 13	UT, Logan
Gates ....Samuel	Waite..................Martha	1858 01 08	UT, Salt Lake City
Gates ....Samuel Jr.	Downer................Lydia	1830 02 04	
Gay ....Alexander	Covington............Martha Ann	1841 08 24	NC
Gay ....Moses B.	Davis..................Lucretia	1830 12 02	
Gaydou ....Anthony	Malan.................Mary Catherine	1850 09 10	
Geddes ....Robert	Gibson................Marion	1793	
Geddes ....William	Hope ....Emma Eliza	1870 02 21	UT, Salt Lake City
Geddes ....William	Stewart...............Elizabeth	1855 06 03	UT, Salt Lake City
Geddes ....William	Stewart...............Martha	1856 07 10	UT, Plain City
Gee.................William	Walsom...............Mary Ann	1866 07 17	UT, Fayette
George ....John	Weight.................Amelia	1875	
George ....William	Ormond ....Mary	1852 10 31	UT, Salt Lake City
Gerber ....Johannes	Akeret.................Anna Maria	1843 11 23	
Gerber ....John T.	Rupp ....Anna Marie	1864 08 28	WY

Male	Female	Date	Place
Gerber ....John T.	Schuebel ....Eva	1865 11 22	UT, Salt Lake City
Germer ....Johann M. J. T.	Faasch ....Maria C. E.	1834 04 01	
Germer ....John M.	Lattmann ....Barbara	1858 03 12	UT, Plain City
Gheen.............Stephen H.	Hardy ....Mary Adelia	1856 11 06	
Gheen.............William	Harmon ....Aseneth	1841	
Gibb................John Lye	Simmons ....Hannah	1878 01 31	UT, Salt Lake City
Gibbons ....William B.	Wilkes ....Mary	1852 02 16	UT, Salt Lake City
Gibbs ....Carl F. W. C.	Pedersen............Mica M. C. M.	1852 05 31	Denmark
Gibbs ....Horace Dewitt	Underhill.............Charlotte	1855 01 10	UT, Salt Lake City
Gibbs ....John	Langton ....Mary Catherine	1852 12 24	
Gibbs ....John Duggan	Tompkins ....Julia Ann	1840	ENG
Gibbs ....William	Dana ....Elizabeth	1844 04 16	NY, Lockport
Gibbs ....William	Wilgus ....Mary Jane	1870	
Gibby ....John	Olpin..................Dorcas	1867 11 23	UT, Salt Lake City
Gibby ....John	Olpin..................Ellen	1860 06 17	
Gibby ....William D.	Stevenson...........Catherine	1857 05 26	UT, Salt Lake City
Gibson ....Benjamin	Covington............Martha Ann		
Gibson ....William	Barbour ....Lillias	1856 02 17	
Gifford.............Alpheus	Nash...................Anna	1817 04 27	NY, Butternuts
Gifford.............Henry Dill	Braffett ....Almira Ann	1848 11 05	IA, Pottawattamie
Gifford.............Levi	Wing..................Deborah	1816	
Gifford.............Levi Jr.	Jaques ....Caroline	1859	UT
Gifford.............Oliver D.	Allred.................Alice Virginia	1873 09 11	UT, Shonesburg
Gifford.............Samuel K.	Curtis.................Ursula	1870	
Gifford.............Samuel K.	Demille ....Lora Ann	1848 10 01	IA, Pottawattamie
Gilbert ....Algernon S.	Van Benthuysen..Elizabeth	1823 09 21	OH
Gilchrist ....Neil II	Scorey...............Elizabeth	1866 06 02	UT, Salt Lake City
Giles ....George	Thorn.................Elizabeth	1868 03 16	
Giles ....George Thomas	Daybell ....Sarah	1867 01 28	UT, Heber
Giles ....Thomas	Davis ....Maria	1807 12 18	Wales
Giles ....Thomas	Kirkham..............Mariah	1832 05 30	ENG, Nottingham.
Giles ....Thomas Davis	Evans ....Hannah		
Giles ....Thomas H.	Capener ....Jane Maria	1890 11 12	UT, Logan
Giles ....Thomas H.	Moore.................Elizabeth S.	1845 02 13	ENG
Giles ....William	Huskinson ....Sarah		ENG
Gillespie...........Alexander	McKinley ....Marion	1849 02 11	Scotland
Gillespie...........John Scott	Ross...................Catherine	1852 11 16	UT, Salt Lake City
Gillespie...........Peter	Knox...................Ann	1856 11 07	UT
Gillett ....Samuel	Chappell.............Naomi	1865 12 12	
Gillies.............Ebenezer	Graitus ....Ann	1853 02	ENG
Gillins.............Henry	Green ....Susannah	1866 11 10	IA, Council Bluffs
Gillins.............John T.	Collin ....Elizabeth	1826 06 26	ENG
Gillions...........John	Coleman.............Elizabeth	1860	
Gingell ....William	Woodhams..........Mary Ann	1840 11 01	ENG
Givens ....James	Thacker ....Anna Maria	1885 11 12	UT, Wallsburg
Glade.............James	Dyer ....Mary	1855 12 25	
Glade.............James	Litson ....Eliza Mary	1863 10	UT
Glade.............James	Love ....Isabell	1869 06 28	
Glazier ....Charles Dean	Dusenberry ....Martha Jane	1864 10 04	UT, Provo
Glazier ....Shepherd	Dean ....Rosetta	1841 10 13	IL, LaHarpe
Gleason ....John S.	Chase.................Desdemona	1839 11 08	NY, Livingston Co.
Gleason ....John S.	Sutherland..........Mary Ann	1864 07 16	UT, Salt Lake City
Gledhill ....Edward	Hague ....Betty		ENG
Gledhill ....John E.	Handley ....Elizabeth	1860 12 31	ENG, Oldham

Male	Female	Date	Place
Goaslind ....John C.	Allen....................Susan	1858 07 04	
Goaslind ....John Henry Jr.	Alder...................Mary Jane	1867 05 29	
Goates............William	Larkin ....Susan	1844 06 07	ENG
Goates............William	Pilgrim ....Rececca	1857 04 07	UT, Salt Lake City
Goble..............Edwin	Langshaw...........Mary	1868 10 24	UT, Salt Lake City
Goble..............William	Penfold...............Mary	1841 01 12	ENG, Brighton
Godbe.............Antoine Peter	Stenhouse...........Emelia Eliza	1873 06 07	UT, Salt Lake City
Goddard ....Robert	Woolfenden........Margaret	1843	ENG
Godfrey...........John	Pittaway ....Mary	1845 09 15	ENG, Dodderhill
Godfrey...........Joseph	Reeves...............Ann Eliza	1840	NJ
Godfrey...........Joseph	Reeves...............Mary	1857 03 07	UT, Salt Lake City
Godfrey...........Thomas	Jensen ....Caroline	1880 06 17	UT, Salt Lake City
Godfrey...........Thomas	Jensen ....Karen Marie	1867 04 01	UT, Clarkston
Godfrey...........Thomas	Whimlett.............Elizabeth	1821 04 26	ENG, Hanbury
Goff.................Heber	Ellwood ....Ellen	1874 05 03	UT, Salt Lake City
Goff.................Isaac	Naylor.................Mary Ann	1833 08 26	ENG
Goff.................James	Sampson.............Sarah	1852 04 12	UT, Salt Lake City
Goff.................Thomas	Smith..................Harriet	1856 05 11	ENG
Goheen...........Michael Roup	Moody ....Dorinda Melisa	1837 04 25	TX, Bastrop
Golding ....Johnathon E.	Cherrington ....Elizabeth	1869	UT, Salt Lake City
Golightly ....Richard	Jessop................Elizabeth	1855 01 20	UT, Salt Lake City
Golightly ....Richard	Richardson..........Isabella	1828	ENG
Goodale..........Isaac N.	Bingham.............Maria Louisa	1849 01 17	UT, Salt Lake City
Goodliffe ....Arnold	Ballam ....Elizabeth		
Goodman.........William	Crisp..................Matilda	1839 11 11	ENG, Bedfordshire
Goodrich.........Benjamin F.	Gardner..............Penelope R.	1823 04 01	
Goodrich.........George A.	Slade..................Rhoda	1879 10 09	UT, Salt Lake City
Goodrich.........George A.	Taggart...............Eliza Ann	1862 11 10	
Goodrich.........George A.	Taggart...............Harriet Maria	1866 05 05	UT, Salt Lake City
Goodridge.......William	Platt....................Ann Jane Griffin	1839 06 02	MA
Goodwin ....Edwin Abijah	Harwood.............Anna	1860 10	
Goodwin ....William	Benson...............Isabella	1866 10 09	UT, Logan
Goodworth.......Joseph	Chapman ....Hannah	1845 10 29	ENG, Yorkshire
Goodworth.......Richard	Evans.................Joanne	1866	
Gordge ....Samuel	Hancock ....Merab	1847 11 14	
Gordon ....James P.	Ballantyne ....Mary	1843 04 04	IL, Nauvoo
Gordon ....James P.	Park....................Marion Ellen	1854 02 07	UT, Salt Lake City
Gottfredson......Jens	Pedersen.............Karen Marie	1856 08 12	
Gottfredson......Peter	Gledhill...............Amelia Jane	1872 04 22	UT, Salt Lake City
Gough.............Joseph Hollings	Walker................Sarah	1853 04 06	Ocean
Gould..............Robert	Simpson..............Joan	1855 01 08	PA, Philadelphia
Gould..............Samuel	Aubrey................Elizabeth Jane	1885 02 03	UT, Salt Lake City
Gould..............Samuel	Ward ....Fanny	1850	IA, Council Bluffs
Gourley...........Alexander	Brady..................Amelia	1863 07 19	UT, Eureka
Gourley...........Paul	Japp ....Ellison	1853 06 03	Scotland
Gover..............Morris	Tucker................Sarah	1848 06 11	ENG
Gowans ....Andrew	McLiesh..............Ann	1823 06 20	Scotland
Gowans ....Hugh S.	Gowans..............Betsy	1854 08 11	Scotland
Gower.............Thomas	.......................Martha		
Graehl............George L.	Leuba.................Charlotte L.	1841	
Graham ....Alexander	Nutman ....Elizabeth Jane	1859 06 26	MO, St. Louis
Graham ....George	Fox.....................Elizabeth Mary	1877 05 12	
Graham ....James	Gregory..............Christianna		
Graham ....James	Read ....Hannah		

Male	Female	Date	Place
Graham ....John	McKenzie ....Christina P.	1820 05 12	Scotland
Graham ....John Duren	Forbush...............Louisa Maria	1860 02 28	UT, Salt Lake City
Graham ....Richard	Woodcock ....Mary	1841 03 08	
Graham ....Robert D.	Hutchison............Annie	1876 10 28	UT, Salt Lake City
Graham ....Robert Dundas	Burns.................Margaret M.	1845 09 14	Scotland
Graham ....Thomas B.	McCrary ....Sarah Ann	1825 06 27	AL, Green Co.
Graham ....William	Ross...................Jane Duncan	1848 01	Scotland
Grange ....Samuel	Stevenson...........Esther	1864 02 11	UT, Salt Lake City
Grant ....George D.	Dubois...............Elizabeth	1851 02 02	UT, Salt Lake City
Grant ....George D.	Noble.................Susan F.	1858 01 01	UT, Bountiful
Grant ....George Roberts	Carbine ....Mary Adelia	1857 12 17	
Grant ....Jedediah M.	Noble.................Susan F.	1849 02 11	
Grant ....Jedediah M.	Ivins.................Rachel	1855 11 29	UT, Salt Lake City
Grant ....Jedediah M.	Van Dyke ....Caroline	1844 07 02	
Grant ....Robert Collier	Hamilton............Susannah	1823 03 23	Scotland
Grant ....Thomas T.	Adamson............Jannett	1913 02 01	UT, Wellsville
Grant ....Thomas T.	Adamson............Margaret	1861 10 19	
Graves............Daniel	Newman..............Mary	1840 06 07	ENG, London
Gray................John	Brittingham.........Amelia		
Greaves...........Joseph	Cluley ....Sarah Priscilla	1853 02 22	ENG, Liverpool
Green ....Alphonso	Murdock.............Betsey Bonney	1838 12 29	NY, Madison Co.
Green ....Alva A.	Buckwalter ....Elizabeth	1858 12 25	UT, American Fork
Green ....Alva A.	Shelley ....Ellen Gibson		
Green ....Alvin Greely	Gibson................Francis Abigail	1850 12 27	UT, Salt Lake City
Green ....Austin G.	Hawker...............Sarah Ann	1870 05 16	UT, Salt Lake City
Green ....Austin G.	Marchant............Mary Ann	1856 09 06	UT, Salt Lake City
Green ....Benjamin	Cook..................Harriet Agnes	1862 02 22	
Green ....Charles	Francis ....Mary Ann	1862 11 24	
Green ....Cornelius	Hansen...............Karen C.	1859 10 16	UT, Salt Lake City
Green ....Henry T.	Mander...............Sarah Ann	1879 10 22	UT, Salt Lake City
Green ....Hervey	Rich...................Jane Ann	1837 11 14	OH, Huron Co.
Green ....John	Bradshaw ....Mary		ENG
Green ....John	Kirkman..............Margaret Mitelda	1835 12 23	South Africa
Green ....John	Stafford ....Mary	1857 12 25	UT, Provo
Green ....Silas Sprague	Gibbons..............Laura Caroline	1872 10 21	UT, Salt Lake City
Green ....Thomas	Shaw ....Rebecca	1862 05 03	
Green ....William	Mikesell ....Cynthia Ann	1856	IA, Pott. Co.
Green ....William	Saunders............Eliza	1867 10 26	UT, Salt Lake City
Green ....William	Staff...................Willoughby	1822 07 15	ENG, Norwich
Greene ....Evan M.	Kent...................Susan	1835 08 29	
Greene ....Evan M.	Platte.................Susie	1869 04 12	UT, Salt Lake City
Greenhalgh......Ezekiel	Arneson..............Emma Caroline		
Greenwell ....Ambrose	Hill....................Elizabeth B.	1854 09 25	ENG
Greenwell ....Ambrose	Mills..................Hannah	1861	
Greenwood......William	Hartley...............Ann	1839 11 24	ENG, Burnley
Greenwood......William Houghton	Wood.................Charlotte	1870 10 31	UT, Salt Lake City
Greer ....Dixon Hamlin	Camp ....Harriet Diannah	1864 02 25	UT, Salt Lake City
Greer ,............John Black	Leishman ....Ann McGregor	1853 05 19	UT, Salt Lake City
Greer ....Nathaniel Hunt	Roberts ....Nancy Ann T.	1821	GA
Greer ....William F.	Rutledge............Matilda	1854 06 27	
Greflo.............Julius	Land ....Narcissa B.	1869 08 26	MO, Jackson Co.
Gregory ....John	Singleton ....Mary	1869 10 04	
Gregory ....Robert	Marshall ....Selina	1863 01 02	ID, Franklin
Gribble............John	Hanks................Elizabeth	1852	ENG

Male	Female	Date	Place
Grier ....John	Stenhouse..........Margaret	1859 01 13	Scotland
Griffin ....Albert B.	Varney................Abigail		
Griffin ....Charles E.	Smith.................Sarah	1854 01 16	UT, Salt Lake City
Griffin ....Charles E.	Stout.................Lydia M. F.	1866 09 22	
Griffin ....Henry	Allen...................Maria		
Griffin ....Herbert Loyal	Nelson................Mary Eunice	1880 07 24	UT, Salt Lake City
Griffin ....John	Keep...................Ruth	1870 02 21	
Griffin ....William	Pitts ....Mary	1839 08 19	ENG, Worcester
Griffin ....William Hyrum	Clarke................Elizabeth Jane		
Griffith ....David	Allen...................Mary	1865 11 10	UT, Salt Lake City
Griffith ....David	Stead.................Mary	1802 03 28	
Griffith ....G. Andrew	Thurman.............Mary Elizabeth	1869 12 13	
Griffith ....Patison D.	Carson ....Elizabeth	1846 04 26	IL, Nauvoo
Griffith ....Patison D.	Roberts ....Sarah Elizabeth	1863 02 07	UT, Salt Lake City
Griffiths ....John Bishop	Griffin ....Theophenia	1863 11 22	
Griffiths ....Joseph	Pidd...................Sarah	1854 03 27	UT, Salt Lake City
Griffiths ....Joseph	Roberts ....Ann	1843 01 03	ENG, Liverpool
Grimshaw ....Duckworth	Moyes ....Mary Jane	1867 04 04	UT, Beaver
Grimshaw ....John	Whittaker............Alice	1836 01 01	ENG, Lancashire
Groesbeck ......Harmon	Bovee.................Maria (Polly)	1807	NY
Groesbeck ......Nicholas	Thompson ....Elizabeth	1841 03 25	IL, Springfield
Gronemann .....George	Rose...................Andrea Petrea	1851 11 07	Denmark
Grouard ....Benjamin F.	Mode..................Caroline	1839 05 30	PA
Grover ....Thomas	Heiner ....Elizabeth	1865 02 10	UT, Salt Lake City
Grover ....Thomas	Nickerson............Carolina Eliza	1841 02 20	IL, Nauvoo
Grover ....Thomas	Tupper................Hannah	1844 12 17	IL, Nauvoo
Grover ....Thomas	Tupper................Luduska Solome	1846	IL, Nauvoo
Grover ....Thomas	Walker................Elizabeth	1857 03 27	UT, Salt Lake City
Grover ....Thomas	Walker................Emma	1856 10 29	UT, Salt Lake City
Groves............Elisha Hurd	Simmons ....Lucy (Sally)	1836 01 16	OH, Kirtland
Groves............Elisha Samuel	Willis..................Mary Lucretia	1863 10 10	
Grow...............Henry	Moyer.................Mary	1834 01 24	PA
Grow...............John Wood	McKay ....Catherine	1869 11 08	UT, Salt Lake City
Gubler.............Casper	Akerman.............Magdalena	1868 05 30	UT, Salt Lake City
Gubler.............Casper	Gubler ....Anna Katherina	1861 11 09	UT, Salt Lake City
Gubler.............Heinrich	Dietschweiler.......Anna Maria	1861 10 18	
Guilliford	Morris.................Susan		
Gulbransen......Hans	Jensen ....Ane Marie S.	1867 07 06	
Gull ....John	Criddle................Charlotte	1867 01 12	UT, Salt Lake City
Gullies ....Martin	Ollerton ....Sarah		
Gunderson.......Erick	Johnson ....Caroline Cecelia		
Gunn...............John	Brazier................Ann	1820 11 10	ENG
Gunn...............Thomas	Houghton ....Ann	1855 02 28	ENG, London
Gunn...............William B.	Mills...................Sarah Ellen	1872 01 27	UT, Enterprise
Gunnell ....Francis W.	Baxter................Jane McPhall	1869 04 15	
Gunnell ....Francis W.	Bickmore ....Sarah Elizabeth	1859 04 04	UT, Wellsville
Gunnell ....Francis W.	Jeffs ....Emma	1869 04 05	UT, Salt Lake City
Gunnell ....Francis W.	Lewis.................Esther	1864 07 02	UT, Salt Lake City
Guppy.............John	Welch.................Ann		
Gurr ....Enoch Eldredge	Buckman............Ruth	1838	Australia
Gurr ....William	Barker ....Sarah Elizabeth	1854 04 27	Australia
Gutteridge........Robert	Grover ....Hannah	1841 01 09	ENG
Guymon..........James	Boden.................Mary	1857 10 08	UT, Salt Lake City
Guymon..........James	Christensen........Christene	1870 08 01	UT, Salt Lake City

Male		Female		Date	Place
Guymon	James	Nease	Rhoda Leech	1847 03 13	
Guymon	James	Park	Martha Jane	1866 11 24	UT, Salt Lake City
Guymon	James Neils	Couch	Mary Ann	1839 10 02	
Guymon	Lafayette	Mortensen	Anna Margaret	1861 02 20	UT, Parowan
Guymon	Noah T.	Johnson	Margaret	1845 11 25	IL, Nauvoo
Guymon	Noah T.	Jones	Elizabeth Ann	1847 02 12	NE
Guymon	Noah T.	Rowley	Louisa	1857 03 02	UT, Salt Lake City
Guymon	Thomas	Gordon	Sarah	1809 02 23	NC, Stokes
Gyllenskog	Neils N.	Anderson	Celia		
Gyllenskog	Neils N.	Truedsson	Hannah Pernilla	1846	

H

Male		Female		Date	Place
Haag		Peterson	Johanna		NE
Haarby	Niels Schaug	Arnesen	Andrea	1839 11 15	Norway
Hacking	James	Pearson	Jane	1827 01 27	ENG
Hacking	John S.	Clark	Jane	1856 05 16	MO, St. Louis
Hadden	William	Barrow	Sarah	1870	
Hadley	Richard D.	Shooter	Mary	1826 04 04	ENG
Hadlock	Stephen	Alton	Salley	1816 12 05	VT
Hafen	John George	Bosshard	Susette	1861 10 18	UT, Salt Lake City
Hafen	John George	Stucki	Rosena	1885 02 28	
Hafledasson	Arna	Erasmuson	Gudney	1828 10 04	Iceland
Haggie	James	Bailey	Eliza	1814 05 28	
Haigh	William	Simpson	Elizabeth	1834 10 10	
Haight	Hector Caleb	Van Orden	Julia	1829 12 18	NY, Greene Co.
Haight	Isaac C.	Price	Eliza Ann	1853 10 10	
Haight	Isaac C.	Snyder	Eliza Ann	1836 12 31	NY, Cayuga Co.
Haight	William V. O.	Turner	Louise	1861 07 04	UT, Farmington
Hakansson	Johannes	Pehrson	Elena	1817 08 02	Sweden
Hakes	Collins Rowe	Rollins	Mary Amelia	1909 11 19	UT, Salt Lake City
Halbom	John	Sawyer	Mary Ann		
Hale	Alma Helaman	Clark	Ellen Victoria	1865 08 19	UT, Salt Lake City
Hale	Alma Helaman	Clark	Sarah Ann	1861 12 24	UT, Grantsville
Hale	Aroet	Cooke	Charlotte	1865 03 18	
Hale	Aroet	Whittle	Olive Amelia	1849 09 05	UT, Salt Lake City
Hale	Aroet L.	Lee	Eliza Ann	1869 09 11	UT, Grantsville
Hale	Job	Walton	Jane	1861 09 20	UT, Salt Lake City
Hales	Charles Henry	Lockwood	Julie Ann	1852 10 31	IL, Quincy
Hales	George	Eddins	Louisa Ann	1852 10 17	UT, Salt Lake City
Hales	George Gillett	Bradford	Tryphena	1864 10 15	UT, Salt Lake City
Hales	George Gillett	Gay	Mariah Henrietta	1873 05 05	
Hales	Henry William	McKinney	Sarah Jane	1857 01 11	UT, Salt Lake City
Hales	Stephen	Hales	Mary Ann	1816 08 31	ENG
Hales	Stephen	Keyes	Henrietta	1851 12 23	UT, Salt Lake City
Hales	Stephen F.	Johnson	Hilma Caroline	1878 11 14	UT, Salt Lake City
Hall	Alfred Lorenzo	Hansen	Julia Elzina	1882 01 18	UT, St. George
Hall	Allen	Dowding	Elizabeth	1875 01 29	UT, Salt Lake City
Hall	Edward	Ballinger	Nancy Eleanor	1842 02 01	IL, Brown Co.
Hall	Job Pitcher	Jones	Mary Elizabeth	1848 02 25	IA, Winter Quarters
Hall	John	Bates	Mary	1830 01 27	ENG
Hall	John	Selston	Susanna	1830 01 24	
Hall	John Charles	Degrey	Keziah	1857 09 25	UT, Salt Lake City

Male		Female		Date	Place
Hall	John Charles	Degrey	Selina	1853 04 26	ENG, Dudley
Hall	Joseph	Hartley	Hannah	1837 10 29	ENG, Wakefield
Hall	Joseph Smith	Hill	Margaret	1865 01 20	
Hall	Joshua Challis	Bybee	Sally Ann	1834	
Hall	Miles	Johnson	Sarah Ellen	1850	IA, Leon
Hall	Newton D.	Busenbark	Sarah Jane	1843 10	
Hall	Newton D.	Mather	Sarah Ann	1856 02 07	UT, Ogden
Hall	Samuel Parley	Williamson	Margaret Rae	1864 02 02	UT, Wellsville
Hall	Thomas	Hughes	Ann	1839 12 30	Wales
Hall	Timothy	Thorn	Elizabeth	1865 03	UT, Salt Lake City
Hall	William	Larsen	Ansine Marie	1881 08 09	UT, Salt Lake City
Halladay	Abraham	Beesley	Mary Ann	1845 01 27	ENG, Chilvers
Halling	Jorgen (John)	Ludvigsen	Maren	1861 11 02	UT, Brigham City
Halling	Lars	Christophersen	Johanne M. K.	1862 12 24	UT, Brigham City
Halling	Peder J.	Rogo	Anne M.	1823 02 08	Denmark
Halls	William	Enderby	Louisa Carritt	1861 04 15	ENG
Halls	William	Frandson	Johanne Marie	1871	
Halls	William	Howard	Eleanor	1880 01 08	
Halsett	Antone Ludwig	Halstensen	Hilda Mathilda	1879	UT, Salt Lake City
Halversen	Jonas	Johansen	Kirstina	1865	UT, Hyrum
Halverson	Oliver H.	Erickson	Josephine	1881 02 17	UT, Gunnison
Hamblin	Francis M.	Lay	Rhoda Elizabeth	1861 10 21	UT, Santa Clara
Hamblin	Frederick	Prudum	Frances Jane	1859 05	
Hamblin	Isaiah	Haynes	Daphne	1812 11 30	
Hamblin	Jacob	Bonelli	Louisa	1865 11 16	
Hamblin	Oscar	Corbridge	Mary Ann	1854 02 18	UT, Salt Lake City
Hamblin	William H.	Leavitt	Betsy	1854 05 01	UT, Tooele
Hamblin	William H.	Leavitt	Mary		
Hamer	John	Wilding	Elizabeth Ann	1850 09 24	IA, Ferryville
Hamilton	Eli	Green	Elizabeth		
Hamilton	Henry	Johnston	Janet	1857 11 07	
Hamilton	Henry	Simpson	Euphemia		
Hamilton	James C.	Hill	Isabella Hood	1870 11 28	UT, Salt Lake City
Hamilton	James Lang	Campbell	Mary Ann	1840 07 13	Canada
Hamilton	John	Lang	Sarah	1806 03 05	IRE
Hamilton	John C.	Nott	Maria Seaburn	1866 08 18	UT, Salt Lake City
Hamilton	John Jr.	Cochrane	Janet	1901 05 15	UT, Salt Lake City
Hammer	Austin	Elston	Nancy Jane	1826 12 26	IN, Wayne Co.
Hammon	Levi	Bybee	Polly Chapman	1840 09 10	IN, Clay
Hammond	Francis A.	Dilworth	Mary Jane	1848 11 17	UT, Salt Lake City
Hammond	John	Osborne	Charlotte	1853 01 19	UT, Salt Lake City
Hammond	John	Parker	Mary Lovisa	1819 12 15	NY, Malone
Hammond	Joseph	Rommrell	Jane Nancy	1858	
Hammond	Milton Datus	Miller	Freelove	1864 01 29	
Hammond	Milton Datus	Miller	Lovisa	1853 12 11	UT, Farmington
Hampton	James T.	Bracken	Martha Ruth	1843	
Hancock	Alvah B.	Eames	Juletta	1823	
Hancock	Benjamin	Sampson	Sarah		
Hancock	Cyrus M.	Bracken	Martha Ann	1860 12 09	UT, Payson
Hancock	George W.	Hancock	Amy	1852 04 04	UT, Salt Lake City
Hancock	James	Hughes	Ann Melsome	1846	ENG
Hancock	Levi W.	Morgansen	Maren	1868 08 09	
Hancock	Levi W.	Reed	Clarissa	1831 03 29	
Hancock	Solomon	Adams	Phoebe	1836 06 28	NY

Male	Female	Date	Place
Hancy ....James	Seamons ....Rachel	1855 10 11	ENG, Rumburg
Hand ....George Edward	Mitchell ....Marian Elizabeth	1877 12 25	UT, Payson
Handy ....Samuel	Watts ....Hannah	1842 10 25	ENG
Handy ....William	Day.....................Mary Ann	1866 11 11	
Hanks ....Ehpraim K.	Capener ....Jane Maria	1856 05 26	UT, Pleasant Creek
Hanks ....Ephraim K.	Decker................Harriet Amelia	1848 09 22	
Hanks ....Ephraim K.	Read ....Thisbe Quilley	1862 04 05	UT, Salt Lake City
Hanks ....George William	Edwards ....Elizabeth	1865 07 23	UT, Paragonah
Hanks ....William	Hanks.................Elizabeth	1829	
Hannibal ....Peter C.	Siversen ....Sophia Maria	1845 02 08	
Hansen ....Anders	Knudsen ....Abelone	1839 07 25	Denmark
Hansen ....Andrew Janus	Pedersen.............Caroline	1878 07 25	UT, Salt Lake City
Hansen ....Carl C.	Clausen...............Margrethe K.	1847 06 14	
Hansen ....Christian	Eriksen ....Elizabeth	1850 11 01	Denmark
Hansen ....Embreth	Ohlsen................Margrethe		
Hansen ....Frederick Emil	Knoppel..............Amelia F. J.	1869 05 14	
Hansen ....Hans	Johansen ....Annie	1851 12 12	
Hansen ....Hans Godfred	Neilson ....Mette Marie	1845 11 07	Denmark
Hansen ....Hans Peter	Ipsen ....Andrea Hansine		
Hansen ....Hans Petrus A.	Eskland ....Emma Johannah	1884 01 14	UT, Scipio
Hansen ....Hendrick	Nielsen ....Ane	1857 04	Denmark
Hansen ....James	Jensen ....Anna Katherine	1851 04 06	
Hansen ....James	Petersen.............Karen	1856 02 03	UT, Salt Lake City
Hansen ....James Peter	Hansen................Bendicta C.	1855	Denmark
Hansen ....Jens	Andersen.............Karen	1857 12 20	
Hansen ....Jens	Anderson............Maren	1863 09 17	UT, Salt Lake City
Hansen ....Jens	Hansen................Mettie Marie	1868 01 23	UT, Salt Lake City
Hansen ....Jens	Johansen ....Kirstina	1855 05 06	Denmark
Hansen ....John Johannes	Ipsen ....Andrea Hansine	1861 05 16	Ocean
Hansen ....Jorgen L.	Madsen ....Ane	1848 10 14	Denmark
Hansen ....Lars (Lewis)	Madsen ....Christine Marie	1871 03 06	UT, Salt Lake City
Hansen ....Mads L.	Mortensen ....Ane K.	1874 12	
Hansen ....Michael A.	Christensen.........Ansine K.	1857	Denmark
Hansen ....Mourtis	Jesperson ....Ingeborg Kristine	1834 11 08	Denmark
Hansen ....Niels	Jensen ....Elizabeth	1843 05 28	Denmark
Hansen ....Niels Miller	Hansen................Karen Marie	1868 06 20	Ocean
Hansen ....Niels Peter	Heaton ....Hannah	1870 03 27	NV, Overton
Hansen ....Nils	Terry....................Marilla	1846 01 28	
Hansen ....Paul	Larsen ....Andrea Marie	1868 06 06	UT, Salt Lake City
Hansen ....Paul	Larsen ....Anna Christine	1885 08 17	UT, Providence
Hansen ....Peder	Grimethsson........Hanne Laurine	1862 10 18	
Hansen ....Peder	Hansen................Johanne M.	1835 05 29	Denmark
Hansen ....Peder	Post....................Annie	1853 03 23	Denmark
Hansen ....Peder Niels	Jensen ....Marie	1862 10 06	UT, Fairview
Hansen ....Peter	Borjesson ....Beata Gustafva	1863 11 16	UT, Manti
Hansen ....Peter	Butterfield...........Mary Jane		
Hansen ....Peter	Larsen ....Anne Kristine	1862 09 24	Denmark
Hansen ....Peter	Petersen.............Karen	1851 04 24	Denmark
Hansen ....Peter Henrick	Carlsen...............Anemena C.	1876 06 12	UT, Salt Lake City
Hansen ....Rasmus	Pedersen.............Ane Kirstine	1849 11 11	Denmark
Hansen ....Rasmus	Wilhelmsen ....Maren	1832 10 09	Denmark
Hanson ....George	Booth..................Frances Hiley	1853 09 22	ENG, Aston
Hanson ....Nels	Bengtsson ....Sophia	1863 09 06	UT, Salt Lake City
Hanson ....Niels C.	Jensen ....Mariane	1863 05 05	Denmark

Male	Female	Date	Place
Hanson ....Ole	Johansen ....Julia Teoa	1866 05 16	UT, Salt Lake City
Hanson ....William L.	Judson ....Mary Jane	1857 08 21	UT, Salt Lake City
Harbertson.......James	Garner.................Roemma		
Hardcastle ....William	Goff ....Naomi	1890 03 20	UT, Sandy
Hardcastle ....William	Hall......................Ann	1830 04 22	ENG
Harding............Alma	Jones ....Margaret Ann	1867 11 02	UT, Salt Lake City
Harding............Dwight	Holbrook.............Phebe	1833 02 12	NY, Weathersfield
Harding............George	Jones ....Mary	1864 07 02	UT, Salt Lake City
Harding............Thomas	Bull.....................Sophronia Ann	1875 01 17	UT, Morgan
Hardman..........Abraham W.	Walters...............Martha	1860 09 09	UT, Pleasant Grove
Hardman..........Lehi Nephi	Coon ....Frances Ann	1860 06 15	UT, Salt Lake City
Hardman..........Richard	Holden................Margaret	1828 01 07	ENG, Brindle
Hardy ....Joseph	Blanden..............Lucy Thorndyke	1832 04 26	ME, Lincolnville
Hardy ....Joseph	Davis ....Lydia Rebecca	1868 10 03	UT, Salt Lake City
Hardy ....Kimball	Bird.....................Elizabeth Ann	1854	
Hardy ....Leonard W.	Goodridge ....Sophia Lois	1850 11 28	UT, Salt Lake City
Hardy ....Samuel B.	Finley ....Sarah	1854 07 02	UT, Salt Lake City
Hardy ....Samuel B.	Rogers ....Caroline Bacon	1826 01 17	MA, Georgetown
Hardy ....Samuel P.	Lamb...................Almyra	1856 12 04	UT, Salt Lake City
Hardy ....Warren	Blake...................Caroline Lucy	1864 03 05	
Hardy ....Zachariah	Philbrook ....Elizabeth Ann	1822 07 17	ME, Belfast
Harman............Charles M.	Davis ....Margaret Ann	1882 03 30	UT, Salt Lake City
Harmer ....Elias	Cloward...............Charlotte R.	1845	PA, Chester
Harmon............Alpheus	Vaughn................Hulda Dimeras	1823 02 01	PA, Erie Co.
Harmon............Ansel P.	Chandler ....Roseline	1862 11 29	UT, Salt Lake City
Harmon............Appleton M.	Stringham............Elemeda	1846 01 01	IL, Nauvoo
Harmon............Henry Martin	Marler..................Susan	1856	UT, Ogden
Harmon............James	Smithson ....Mary Ann Blanks	1828	SC, Pendleton
Harmon............Levi N.	Chidester.............Eunice	1854 11 08	UT, Salt Lake City
Harmon............Norton	Tanner.................Thankful Loretta	1843 01 04	
Harmon............Oliver	Harmon ....Sarah	1810	
Harper ....Charles Alfred	Dilworth ....Lavina W.	1839 12 19	PA
Harper ....Charles Alfred	Taylor..................Harriet	1855 12 02	UT, Salt Lake City
Harper ....James	Thacker...............Anna Maria	1893 03 12	UT, Wallsburg
Harper ....Richard	Faulkner..............Susann	1849 08 16	ENG, Anwick
Harper ....Thomas	Jones ....Hannah Jane	1854 10 29	UT, Salt Lake City
Harper ....Thomas	Lewis..................Rachel Stapleton		
Harriman..........Henry H.	Hobbs.................Sarah Elizabeth	1871 09 23	UT, St. George
Harrington........Jonathan	Clark...................Julia Ann	1824 10 16	PA, Bucks Co.
Harris ....Alexander	Craner.................Harriet Ann	1855 06 21	UT, Salt Lake City
Harris ....Charles	Hall.....................Louisa Maria	1855 04 20	UT, Ogden
Harris ....Daniel	Harris ....Lydia	1853 10 05	CA, San Bern.
Harris ....David	David...................Ann	1851 08 23	
Harris ....Emer	Chappel..............Parna	1826 05 29	PA
Harris ....George H. A.	Loader.................Sarah	1862 05 30	UT, Pleasant Grove
Harris ....George W.	Funk....................Diddrikke Helena	1862 02 07	UT, Richmond
Harris ....Isaac	Bowering ....Esther Ellen	1833 12 25	Wales
Harris ....James Harvey	Woodward...........Emmeline B. B.	1843 07 29	
Harris ....John	Evans ....Rachel Jones	1855 08 12	
Harris ....John	Gilmore ....Mary Elizabeth	1812	Wales
Harris ....John	Stanley ....Ann	1846 01 29	
Harris ....John Smith	Aldridge..............Nancy Lydia	1850 04 04	UT, Bountiful
Harris ....Martin H.	Sargent ....Louisa	1859 04 03	UT, Ogden
Harris ....Martin Jr.	Corbett ....Mary		

Male	Female	Date	Place
Harris............Martin Jr.	Homer................Nancy Ann	1859 11 01	UT, Salt Lake City
Harris.............Martin Lot	Larsen................Winka	1879 12 18	UT, St. George
Harris.............McGee	Givens................Mary (Polly)	1826 12 29	TN, Wilson Co.
Harris.............McGee	Simmons............Mary Ann		UT, Salt Lake City
Harris.............Micah Francis	Bond...................Mary Jane	1868 01 15	UT, Coalville
Harris.............Moses	Smith..................Francis	1824 01 01	IN, Cork Co.
Harris.............Robert	Eagles................Hannah Maria	1825 09 28	ENG
Harris.............Silas	Aldridge..............Sariah	1849 09 02	WY, Ind. Rock
Harris.............Thomas	Williams..............Ann	1844 03 01	ENG
Harris.............William	Whittle................Emeline	1861 08 20	UT, Richmond
Harris.............William Jasper	Smith..................Martha Ann	1857 04 24	UT, Provo
Harris.............William M.	Carter.................Jane	1858 07 04	NY, Williamsburg
Harris.............Zachariah	Hill......................Emily	1834	IL, Macoupin Co.
Harrison..........George R.	Edmonds............Mary Jane	1846 08 30	ENG, London
Harrison..........James	Brownell.............Mary Ann	1870 05 04	UT, Salt Lake City
Harrison..........John	Vest....................Margaret Ann	1881 06 19	UT, Mona
Harrison..........John Heber	Eldridge..............Ellen Eliza	1870 10 24	UT, Salt Lake City
Harrison..........John William	Platt...................Nancy Ellen	1854 09 27	ENG, Lancashire
Harrison..........Richard	Fryer..................Jane	1855 02 25	UT, Salt Lake City
Harrison..........Richard	Whitaker.............Mary Ann	1836 09 10	
Harrison..........William	Adams................Hannah	1856 03 24	Ocean
Harrison..........William	Ellis ....Hannah Louise	1836 07 24	ENG
Harrocks ....Daniel	Rutter ....Ann	1840 09 07	ENG
Harrod ....Charles	Matty ....Elizabeth	1855 10 20	ENG
Harrop ....James	Kilner..................Rachel	1836 10 29	ENG, Eccles
Hart..................James	Loader................Mary	1873 01 20	UT, Salt Lake City
Hart..................James Henry	Scheib ....Sabina	1861 05 04	UT, Salt Lake City
Hart..................John Isaac	Barton ....Martha	1863 04 11	UT, West Weber
Hart..................Samuel Cornelius	Leah ....Sarah Ann	1849 03 31	ENG, Manchester
Hart..................Samuel Walter	Raymond.............Martha	1880 02 20	UT, Woodruff
Hart..................Stephen James	Orgill..................Sarah	1876 09 25	UT, Salt Lake City
Hartley ....Charles	Horne ....Eliza	1840 11 01	ENG
Hartley ....Charles R.	Cooper ....Sariah	1874 01 04	UT, Salt Lake City
Hartley ....Jesse Thompson	Bullock ....Mary Ann		
Hartley ....S. John	Gill.....................Eliza	1836 01 31	ENG
Hartvigsen ....Peter A.	Nielsen ....Teralina F.	1864 07 18	NE, Florence
Harvey ....Alfred	Brown.................Betsey Agnes	1869 06 27	UT, Pleasant Grove
Harvey ....J. Frederick	Player.................Sarah Ann	1886 01 01	
Harvey ....James	Burns..................Agnes	1851 12 21	Scotland
Harvey ....James	Ellis ....Martha		
Harvey ....John	Coope ....Ann	1854	UT, Salt Lake City
Harvey ....Jonathan L.	Harbert...............Sarah B.	1819 01 31	WV, Harrison
Harward...........Thomas	Curtis..................Sabrina	1851 04 06	
Harwood ....James T.	Taylor.................Sarah Jane	1858 06 30	UT, Lehi
Haskell............Ashbel Green	Billings................Ursula	1822 03 03	
Haskell............Chester K.	Haws ....Lydia Catherine	1853 03 12	UT, Provo
Haskell............George Niles	Runnels..............Sarah Elizabeth	1816	VT, Dixon
Haskell............Thales	Edwards..............Margaret J.	1857	UT, Salt Lake City
Haskell............Thales	Woodbury...........Hannah Marie	1855 10 04	
Haslam ....Henry H.	Jones ....Ann	1865 01 20	UT, Salt Lake City
Haslam ....James Holt	Redford...............Ann Eckersall	1869 04 05	UT, Salt Lake City
Haslam ....John	Hulme.................Alice	1834	
Haslam ....Robert	Nuttall.................Mary	1828 10 19	ENG, Prestwich
Hastings ....John	Burdett ....Jane	1843 10 11	ENG

Male	Female	Date	Place
Hastings ....John Jr.	Ringrose..............Mary Ann	1870 06 20	UT, Salt Lake City
Hastings ....William	Smith...................Sarah Jane	1859 04 16	MA, Boston
Hatch ....Alvah A.	Nelson.................Mary Elizabeth	1868 12 07	UT, Salt Lake City
Hatch ....Ira Stearns	Bee.......................Jane	1852 11 27	UT, Salt Lake City
Hatch ....Ira Stearns	Stewart...............Jane Ann	1857 03 20	UT, Salt Lake City
Hatch ....Isaac Burres	Garlick.................Mary Jane	1845 09 10	IA, Charleston
Hatch ....Isaac Burres Jr.	Michael...............Mary Ann	1880 01 29	UT, Salt Lake City
Hatch ....Jeremiah	Alexander...........Louisa Pool	1842 12 26	IL, Nauvoo
Hatch ....Jeremiah	Haight.................Elizabeth	1789 11 23	VT, Addison Co.
Hatch ....Josephus	Durfee ....Melinda	1822 12 06	
Hatch ....Lorenzo Hill	Eastman..............Sylvia Savonia	1851 02 28	UT, Salt Lake City
Hatch ....Lorenzo Hill	Hanson................Alice	1860 01 02	
Hatch ....Lorenzo Hill	Karren ....Catherine	1854 11 11	UT, Lehi
Hatch ....Lorenzo L.	Scarborough ....Annie	1873 12 01	UT, Salt Lake City
Hatch ....Meltiar	Ellis ....Mary Ann	1856 05 06	UT, Salt Lake City
Hatch ....Meltiar	Snyder.................Permelia	1845 01 01	
Hatch ....Orin	Perry ....Elizabeth Melissa	1855 11 10	UT, Salt Lake City
Hatch ....Orin	Thompson ....Maria	1856 05 02	UT, Salt Lake City
Hatch ....Orson Samuel	Dibble.................Ida Elizabeth	1870 12 12	UT, Salt Lake City
Hatch ....Ransom	Atkinson ....Frances E.	1854 12 18	UT, Salt Lake City
Hatch ....Ransom Osborn	Ford.....................Emma	1863 05 15	
Hatch ....Wilder	Wheeler...............Phoebe Marietta	1872 10 03	
Hatch ....William	Garlick.................Mary Jane	1858	UT, Payson
Hatch ....William Edson	Malan ....Jane Dinah	1865 03 03	UT, Salt Lake City
Havens ....John	Van Waggoner ....Harriet Ann	1839 02 13	NJ
Hawkes............Joseph Bryant	Baldwin ....Phoebe Ann	1837 12	
Hawkes............Joseph Bryant	Durham ....Charlotte L.	1850	
Hawkey............Foster	Middleton ....Hannah	1847 12 06	ENG
Hawkins	Livermore ....Almeda Melissa		
Hawkins ....Benjamin	Freeman..............Caroline Sophia	1857 04 07	
Hawkins ....James R. A.	Sewell ....Ann	1843 05 01	ENG
Hawkins ....John Bennett	Moulton ....Sarah	1856 12 05	UT, Salt Lake City
Hawkins ....Jonah W.	Hansen................Martha Kirstine	1864 12 10	UT, Salt Lake City
Hawkins ....Thomas S.	Davis ....Sarah		
Hawkins ....William C.	Germer................Henrietta C. C.	1860 02 09	
Hawks..............Amos	White...................Agnes M. M. J.	1859 01 23	UT, Spanish Fork
Hawley............Asa Smith	Stewart................Mary Priscilla	1866 04 11	
Hawley............William John	Smith...................Elsa Ellis	1821	Canada
Haws ....Amos W.	Bean....................Mary Elizabeth	1855 12 27	UT, Provo
Haws ....Elijah	Pease...................Catherine Floyd	1829 06	
Haws ....George W.	Scoville...............Eliza Rebecca	1892 01	
Haws ....Gilberth	Whitcomb ....Hannah	1822 06 02	
Haws ....Jason	Hillman................Sarah	1851 09 07	IA, Coonville
Haws ....Peter	Durham ....Charlotte L.	1852	
Haws ....William W.	Mills....................Barbara Belinda	1853 12 01	UT, Provo
Hayball ....George S.	Hancock..............Louisa	1850 09 20	ENG
Hayball ....Hyrum	Nelson.................Ellen	1872 05 06	UT, Salt Lake City
Hayes ....John J.	Wagstaff..............Rachel Eleanor	1853 02 23	Ocean
Hayes ....William W.	Jennings..............Sarah	1838 04 16	ENG
Haynes ....John	Francis ....Ann	1863	
Hayward ....Gammon	Cripps.................Sarah Ann	1850 06 01	ENG
Hazen ....Robert	Bainbridge..........Mary Ann	1853 08 29	ENG, Newcastle
Heaps.............Thomas	Goldthrope ....Susannah	1854 07 30	ENG
Heath..............Frederick	Butcher...............Harriet	1855 12 02	UT, Salt Lake City

Male	Female	Date	Place
Heath............John	Hulme...............Barbara	1825	ENG
Heath..............Nicholas	Freeman.............Hannah	1828 05 13	
Heaton............Jonathan	O'Dwyer ....Frances	1822	ENG
Heaton............William	Bielby ....Esther	1851 02 10	ENG, Yorkshire
Heder..............Johannes O.	Erickson ....Christina	1845	Sweden
Heelis ....Thomas B.	Benson...............Mary	1863 07 27	NE, Florence
Heggie ....Andrew W.	Stewart..............Annie Thompson	1865 02 03	UT, Salt Lake City
Hegsted ....Hans C. S.	Iverson ....Ane Christena	1866 01 20	UT, Salt Lake City
Heiner.............George	Henderson ....Mary	1866 12 22	UT, Salt Lake City
Heiner.............Johann Martin	Dietzel...............Adelgunda	1838 01 06	
Heiselt ....Hans C.	Pederson............Laurssine	1860	
Heiselt ....Niels Christian	Hansen...............Karen Kirstine	1859 04 17	Ocean
Hellebrant........Oliver Lastie	Gibbs..................Mary Amanda	1894 04 09	
Hellewell ....George E.	Burrup ....Mary Ann	1878 07 24	UT, Salt Lake City
Hellewell ....Joseph H.	Horspool.............Martha Jane	1879 11 27	UT, Salt Lake City
Hellewell ....Robert	Frost...................Rachael	1844 07 04	ENG
Hellewell ....Robert	Pillings...............Elizabeth	1854 05 24	
Helm ....Thomas	Cady...................Maria	1904 12	
Hemenway ......Jonathan	Brown.................Joanna Ward	1855 03 11	
Hemmert.........Mathias	Langgaard...........Marie Kirstine	1863	
Hemrot............	Wilhelmsen ....Maren		
Hemsley ....Edward P.	Brown.................Margaret Daniels	1866 03 17	UT, Salt Lake City
Henderson.......Robert	Ross...................Mary	1846 09 26	Scotland
Henderson.......Samuel Goforth	Cutler ....Helen Mar	1855 05 06	UT, Salt Lake City
Hendricks ....James	Dorris ....Drusilla	1827 05 31	
Hendricks ....Josiah	Potts...................Sarah	1869 10 05	
Hendricks ....William D.	Smith..................Alvira Lavona	1851	
Hendricksen ....Carl F.	Anderson.............Anna Marie	1864 05	Ocean
Hendrickson ....Henry	Madsen ....Mary Christina	1873 11 01	UT, Glenwood
Hendrickson ....Niels	Olsen..................Olena	1868	
Hendry............John Mark	Archibald ....Margaret	1854 10 16	Scotland
Hendry............John Mark	Kerr ....Mary	1875	
Henefer...........James	Hulks ....Sarah Ann	1846 08 30	
Henefer...........William	Hays...................Rebecca Ann	1850 01 01	NJ, Trenton
Henrichson ......Soren P.	Gylenskog...........Christina	1866 11 16	
Henrie.............Daniel	Bradley...............Amanda	1849 10 29	UT, Salt Lake City
Henrie.............James	Hatch..................Wealtha Rhoana	1850 12 28	UT, Bountiful
Henrie.............James	Schow ....Christena R.	1861 12 06	UT, Salt Lake City
Henrie.............Joseph	Duncan...............Susan	1852 01 29	UT, Salt Lake City
Henrie.............Joseph Ozro	Andersen.............Mary Christine	1877 07 25	UT, Logan
Henrie.............Joseph Ozro	Weaver...............Christiana Martha		
Henrie.............William	Mayall.................Myra	1824 11 17	OH, Cincinnati
Henriod...........Eugene A.	Mallett ....Mary Thorne	1854 11 05	UT, Salt Lake City
Henry..............Robert	Bacon.................Elizabeth	1865 12 17	UT, Fillmore
Henthorn..........	Clegg..................Mary		ENG
Hepworth.........Edmund	Cowling ....Hannah S.	1862 09 17	ENG
Hepworth.........Joseph	Hirst...................Mary	1837 04 09	ENG, Yorkshire
Hepworth.........Thomas	Fletcher..............Mary	1848 08 27	ENG, Liverpool
Herman...........Henry	Oldfield...............Martha		ENG
Herold.............Robert William	Cordon ....Rachel Ann	1879	
Herrick ....Lester James	McQuarrie ....Agnes	1867 06 12	UT, Salt Lake City
Hess ....Alma	Miller ....Mary Elmira	1862 05 10	UT, Salt Lake City
Hess ....Jacob	Foutz..................Elizabeth	1816	PA, Franklin Co.
Hess ....Johannes	Dietschweiler.......Anna Maria	1850 01 17	

Male	Female	Date	Place
Hess ....John W.	Bigler..................Emeline	1845 11 02	IL, Nauvoo
Hess ....John W.	Card ....Emily	1852 03 30	UT, Salt Lake City
Hess ....John W.	Pearson..............Julia Helena	1856 11 16	
Hess ....John W.	Steed..................Mary Ann	1857 03 27	UT, Salt Lake City
Hess ....John W.	Workman.............Caroline	1861 04 12	
Hessel ....Peter	Svenson ....Anna Margareta	1840 12 26	
Heward ....John	Terry..................Elizabeth	1844 05 20	IL, Nauvoo
Hewitson.........George	Hobson...............Mary	1843 08 26	ENG, York
Hewitt ....Wilkerson	Calhoun..............Margaret G.		
Hewlett ....Thomas	Longhurst ....Amelia Ann	1865 04 22	UT, Salt Lake City
Heyborne.........John	McMillan..............Sarah Ann	1842 09 14	ENG
Heybourne.......Charles M.	Rollins ....Melissa Kezia	1921 10 31	
Heywood ....Joseph L.	Bell.....................Mary	1855 10 31	UT, Salt Lake City
Hibbard...........George	Williams..............Hannah	1855	
Hibbert............Benjamin	Mills...................Mary	1862 01 01	
Hibbert............James	Brown.................Hannah	1828 11 10	ENG, Manchester
Hicken ....Addison	Moulton ....Sophia Elizabeth	1873 12 22	UT, Salt Lake City
Hicken ....Thomas	Fewkes...............Catherine	1845 06 30	
Hicken ....Thomas	Powell ....Margaret	1865 08 15	UT, Salt Lake City
Hickenlooper ...John T.	Fullmer ....Elvira Martha	1856 11 16	UT, Salt Lake City
Hickenlooper ...William	Ham ....Ann		
Hickenlooper ...William	Hawkins ....Sarah	1829 08 29	
Hickerson ....James M. F.	Winters...............Helen Melissa	1867 09	
Hickman ....William	Case...................Martha Diana	1855	
Hickman ....William A.	...........................Margaret	1855 09 15	UT, Salt Lake City
Hickman ....William A.	Johnson..............Sarah Eliza V.	1855 09 15	UT, Salt Lake City
Hickman ....William A.	Wade..................Minerva	1849 05 01	IA, Council Bluffs
Hicks...............William B.	Roberts ....Cyrene Elsie	1837	IL, Carlton
Higbee............Isaac	Woods................Charlotte	1841 04 30	
Higbee............John S.	Granger..............Ann	1852 03	
Higginbotham ..William Elliott	Ward ....Louisa	1831 09 08	
Higgins ....Nelson	Blackman ....Sarah	1826 12 14	OH, Fitchville
Higginson ....George B.	Gardner..............Elizabeth		
Higginson ....James G.	Buchanan...........Eliza Jane	1857 01 10	UT, Spanish Fork
Higginson ....William T.	Taylor.................Hattie Jane	1873 02 10	
Higginson ....William T.	Young.................Christina	1863 09 27	
Higgs ....Thomas	Stowe ....Elizabeth	1844 05 21	NY, Utica
Higley ....Clark	Cheney...............Malinda	1837 09 17	
Higley ....Myron Spencer	Eberson..............Priscilla	1826 06	
Higley ....Oliver	Higley ....Lucretia	1801 06 20	VT, Marlboro
Hill ....Alexander	Broom ....Jenette	1834 10 10	
Hill ....Alexander	Currie ....Elizabeth	1806 05 30	Scotland
Hill ....Alexander	Meiklejohn..........Mary	1857 01 28	
Hill ....Alexander B.	Wimmer..............Eliza Jane	1857 03 23	
Hill ....Alexander Hood	Park...................Jane	1857 01 19	
Hill ....Daniel Brice	Leishman ....Jane	1865 01 20	UT, Salt Lake City
Hill ....Daniel Currie	Bryce.................Elizabeth		
Hill ....George W.	Stewart...............Cynthia Utley	1845 09 18	
Hill ....Heamon Alison	Chase.................Lurancy	1860 11 25	UT, Salt Lake City
Hill ....Isaac	Miller..................Martha	1852 10 27	UT, Salt Lake City
Hill ....Isaac	Miller..................Mary Jane	1852 10 27	UT, Salt Lake City
Hill ....James	Yarwood.............Mary	1836 04 05	ENG, Manchester
Hill ....James Allen	Mellor ....Clara Althera	1873 11 03	UT, Salt Lake City
Hill ....James Bennett	....	1865 06 10	UT

Male	Female	Date	Place
Hill .... James Bennett	Smith .... Elizabeth	1839 09 01	ENG, Cheshire
Hill .... John	Bryce .... Margaret	1837	Canada
Hill .... John	Steele .... Agnes	1859 11 26	
Hill .... Return Richard	Wheeler .... Rhoda	1841	
Hill .... Richard	Strait .... Sarah	1816 03 31	OH
Hill .... Samuel	Hollis .... Sophia	1847 05 10	ENG, Birmingham
Hill .... William	Syer .... Mary Ann		
Hill .... William Brown	Price .... Mary Jane	1859 08 31	UT, Salt Lake City
Hill .... William Henry	Briggett .... Isabella Wells	1864 10 31	UT, Coalville
Hill .... William James	Hadlock .... Henrietta	1867 09 21	UT
Hill .... William James	Hadlock .... Sally Cilicia	1855 02 25	
Hill .... William John	Humphris .... Elizabeth	1863 05 03	UT, North Ogden
Hillier .... George C.	Lashbrook .... Annie	1861 11 25	ENG, Croyden
Hillman .... Ira King	Baker .... Emma	1857 02 22	UT, Salt Lake City
Hillman .... Ira King	Petty .... Mary Prianna	1851 06 08	UT, Salt Lake City
Hillman .... Mayhew	King .... Sarah	1807	NY, Cambridge
Hillman .... Silas	Cocks .... Emily Ann	1850 02 16	IA, Pottawattamie
Hillman .... Silas	Hulet .... Electa Fidelia	1842 09 10	IL, Nauvoo
Hillyard .... Thomas	Heaps .... Mary Ann	1852 01 28	ENG
Hillyard .... Thomas	Wool .... Elizabeth	1830	ENG, Doddington
Hillyard .... William	Harper .... Emma Louisa	1884 10 15	UT; Logan
Hilton .... Hugh	Frost .... Isabella P.	1852 04 09	
Hinchcliff .... Elijah	Field .... Hannah	1812 11 02	ENG, High Holyland
Hinckley .... Ira Nathaniel	Noble .... Angeline Wilcox	1855 07 22	UT, Salt Lake City
Hinckley .... Ira Nathaniel	Rock .... Elizabeth	1878 05 23	UT, Salt Lake City
Hinman .... Lyman	Lewis .... Aurelia	1819 08 16	NY, New Lebanon
Hinton .... John Nocks	Spendlove .... Emma	1861 05 19	Ocean
Hipwell .... William	Barton .... Elizabeth	1863 03 01	UT, West Weber
Hirschi .... Gottlieb	Rupp .... Mary Ann	1861 09 14	UT, Salt Lake City
Hirst .... John	Brooks .... Charlotte	1837 11 05	ENG, Yorkshire
Hiss .... Johann Friedrich	Bates .... Emma	1876 04 19	UT, Stockton
Hjorring .... Nicolai	Sorensen .... Anna Marie	1836 06 14	Denmark
Hjort .... William Lauritz	Nielsen .... Marthine N. M.	1868 11 07	UT, Salt Lake City
Hjorth .... Niels Peder	Hansen .... Dorthea	1844 07 08	Denmark
Hjorth .... Niels Peter	Jonson .... Sissa	1879	UT, Fairview
Hjorth .... Peter Herman	Jensson .... Annie	1868 12 07	UT, Salt Lake City
Hoagland .... Lucas	Hale .... Rachel J. S.	1848 12 24	UT, Salt Lake City
Hobbs .... Charles W.	Emms .... Mary Ann	1854 08 28	ENG, Cheltenham
Hobbs .... Willon Down	Pope .... Mary Ann	1835 11 09	ENG, Brighton
Hochstrasser ... Rudolf	Muller .... Margaritha	1839 01 25	Switzerland
Hochstrasser ... Rudolf	Sutter .... Maria	1859 09 10	Ocean
Hocking .... William H.	Crompton .... Harriet Maria	1862 11 08	UT, Salt Lake City
Hocklippe .... James	Lavender .... Alice	1853	
Hocquard .... Francis	Jeune .... Elizabeth H.	1819	Channel Isle
Hodges .... Nathaniel M.	Weston .... Anna	1873	UT
Hodges .... Nathaniel M.	Weston .... Louisa	1869 10 11	UT, Salt Lake City
Hodges .... Richard	Brazier .... Martha	1830 03 26	ENG, Worcester
Hodgson .... Henry W. S.	Shaw .... Mary	1845 04 10	ENG, Yorkshire
Hodnett .... Andrew	Fall .... Ann	1861 08 05	UT, Alpine
Hofheins .... Jacob	Braffett .... Amanda Lucretia	1851 11 05	UT, Parowan
Hofheins .... Jacob	Hadden .... Duritha	1859 01 04	
Hofheins .... Peter	Fisher .... Verena	1855	UT
Hofheins .... Peter	Mode .... Sarah Ann	1835 11 25	PA, Philadelphia
Hogan .... Eric G. M.	....	1858	

Male	Female	Date	Place
Hogan.............Eric G. M.	Knudsen.............Helge	1829 03 26	Norway
Hogan.............Eric G. M.	Nilson.................Hannah	1862 12 20	UT, Bountiful
Hogan.............Goudy	Nelson.................Ann		
Hogan.............Goudy	Nelson.................Bergetta	1853 12 24	UT, Salt Lake City
Hogan.............Goudy	Nelson.................Christiana	1853 12 24	UT, Salt Lake City
Hogg.................Robert	McNiven.............Janet	1862 11 26	UT, Salt Lake City
Hoggan.............George D.	Harrison.............Edith Frances	1877 11 29	UT, Salt Lake City
Hoggan.............George W.	Drummond.........Margaret	1843 10 30	Scotland
Hoggan.............Thomas A.	Hoggan..............Margaret	1872 12 16	UT, Salt Lake City
Hoggan.............Walter	Jamison.............Agnes	1851 07 18	
Hoggard.............James	Blacknell.............Emily	1842 02 26	ENG, Calverton
Hogge.............Charles	Stanger..............Ann	1852 06 26	ENG, Yorkshire
Holbrook.........Chandler	Dunning.............Eunice	1831 06 22	NY, Wethersfield
Holbrook.........Joseph	Angell.................Caroline Francis	1850 12 31	UT, Salt Lake City
Holbrook.........Joseph	Flint.....................Hannah	1843 01 01	IL, Nauvoo
Holbrook.........Joseph H. A.	Cooper...............Catherine	1878 01 13	UT, Salt Lake City
Holdaway.........David Oscar	Prater.................Elizabeth A.	1855	UT, Provo
Holdaway.........Shadrack	Haws...................Eliza	1853 01 06	UT, Provo
Holdaway.........Shadrack	Haws...................Lucinda	1848 12 24	UT, Salt Lake City
Holden.............John Wyley	Covert.................Mary Emma		
Holden.............Joshua	Tally....................Mary	1819 09 23	TN
Holden.............Willey H.	Emmett...............Mary Jane	1843 05 11	IL, Nauvoo
Holding.............Daniel	Middleton............Sarah	1844 03 02	ENG, Chester
Holladay.........David Hollis	Taylor..................Henrietta	1852 02 01	CA, San Bern.
Holladay.........John D.	Higgins...............Catherine B.	1822 04 16	SC, Kershaw
Holladay.........John D. III	Dall.....................Rebecca Fannie	1870 01 01	UT, Santaquin
Holladay.........John D. Jr.	Blake..................Johanna	1867 10 20	
Holladay.........John D. Jr.	Matthews............Mahala Ann R.	1848 11 02	UT, Holladay
Holland.............Thomas	Nerdin.................Harriet	1866 02 17	
Holley..............James	Ingram................Lucy Jane	1852 05 10	ENG
Hollingshead....Nelson	Evans..................Elizabeth	1861 06 29	UT, Salt Lake City
Hollingshead....Thomas	Matthews............Aurelia	1823 02 06	Canada
Hollist..............Henry	Chandler.............Elizabeth	1837 12 25	ENG
Holm................Jens Neilson	Ipsen..................Margaret C.	1842 04 30	Denmark
Holman.............James Alonzo	Mathis................Sarah Ann	1855 11 30	UT, Payson
Holman.............James Sawyer	Lebaron..............Naomi Roxanna	1833 03 24	
Holman.............John G.	....	1856	
Holman.............John G.	....	1875	
Holman.............John G.	Clark...................Nancy	1849 08 23	IA, Kanesville
Holman.............John G.	Loader................Sarah	1875 12 22	
Holmes............Edward Francis	Bransford............Susanna	1900	
Holmes............Henry	Anderson............Helen (Ellen)	1857 03 29	UT, Salt Lake City
Holmes............John	White..................Mary Ann	1829 06 22	ENG
Holmes............Jonathan H.	Cowles...............Elvira Annie	1844 12 01	IL, Nauvoo
Holroyd............Seth	Halliday..............Mary	1828 12 24	ENG
Holt.................Edward David	Billings................Emma	1865 03 10	
Holt.................James	Overton..............Parthenia	1845 02 11	
Holt.................James Cooper	Rostron..............Sarah	1847 03 24	ENG
Holt.................Jesse Payton	Carr....................Sarah Naomi	1856 11 30	UT, Spanish Fork
Holt.................John	Redd..................Mary	1814 11	NC, Onslow Co.
Holt.................Matthew	Harrison.............Ann	1851 05 09	ENG
Holt.................William	Bjornson.............Vigdis	1861 04 14	UT, Salt Lake City
Holt.................William	Childs.................Patience Dolly	1853 07 28	UT, Salt Lake City
Holt.................William	Mabey.................Jane	1862 05 04	ENG

Male	Female	Date	Place
Holyoak .... George	Brazier .... Ann		
Holyoak .... George Jr.	Ferguson .... Elizbaeth Ann	1866 10 09	UT, Salt Lake City
Holyoak .... George	Green .... Sarah	1825 01 17	ENG
Holyoak .... Henry	Robinson .... Sarah Ann	1865 01 02	UT, Paragonah
Homer .... Henry	Johnson .... Inger K.	1874 10 01	UT, Salt Lake City
Homer .... Russell King	Petty .... Mary Prianna	1867 11 23	UT, Clarkston
Homer .... Russell King	Thornton .... Eliza	1861 03 29	UT, Salt Lake City
Homer .... Russell King	Williamson .... Eliza	1836 12 20	NY
Hone .... David	Adams .... Sarah	1860 09 23	ENG, Coventry
Hone .... George	Boss .... Mary	1833 12 25	ENG, Banbury
Hone .... George Jr.	Mills .... Jane	1864 04 26	ENG
Hoogensen ...... Christen	Nielsen .... Karen Petra	1859 05 06	Ocean
Hook .... Richard	Ashdown .... Alice B.	1834	ENG, Heathfield
Hookway .... Thomas	Chatters .... Ann Marie	1815 11 09	ENG
Hooley .... Thomas	Nerdin .... Harriet	1858	UT, Pleasant Grove
Hooper .... John	Hillyer .... Ann	1812 05 17	ENG
Hooper .... John	Wilkie .... Ann	1844 07	
Hoops .... Jonathan	Watts .... Rebecca	1812	
Hoops .... Warner	Gifford .... Priscilla	1839 10 18	
Hopkin .... Morgan	Williams .... Hannah	1841 04 25	Wales
Hopkins .... Charles	Edds .... Mary	1852 10 11	UT, Salt Lake City
Hopkins .... Ezekiel	Ditchfield .... Mary	1861 11 16	
Hopkins .... Ezekiel	Zimmerman .... Christina	1854 08 06	UT, Salt Lake City
Hopkins .... Ezekiel Jr.	Hendrickson .... Frances Anna	1865 01 21	UT, Salt Lake City
Horne .... Joseph	Hales .... Mary Isabella	1836 05 09	Canada
Horne .... Joseph	Shepherd .... Mary Park	1856 11 30	UT, Salt Lake City
Horne .... Moses	Hodgkins .... Angeline	1835 11 08	ME, Friendship
Horrocks .... Edward	Clark .... Eliza Ann		MA, Boston
Horrocks .... Edward G.	Mitchell .... Elizabeth	1864 06 04	UT, Salt Lake City
Horsely .... Robert	Ward .... Mary Ann	1868 07	ENG
Hortin .... Edmund	Mead .... Maria	1834 12 07	ENG
Hortin .... John	Wilkinson .... Maria	1864 12 03	UT, Salt Lake City
Hoskin .... Benjamin H.	Hoskin .... Elizabeth	1848 08 25	
Hough .... William	Drabwell .... Jemima	1833 05	ENG
Houghton .... Ornon	Curtis .... Mary	1845 07	IA, Montrose
Housley .... George F.	Jacobsen .... Maria Christina	1859 07 24	UT, Draper
Houston .... Isaac	Brown .... Eliza	1853 04 19	
Houston .... John H.	Bennett .... Susan Ann	1860 02 28	UT
Houtz .... John Christian	Pauling .... Susanna	1830	PA
Houtz .... Phillip	Hall .... Sarah Jane	1864 05 01	UT, Springville
Hovey .... Joseph Grafton	Goodridge .... Lusannah E.	1852 01 14	
Howard .... George Jr.	Christensen .... Ansine K.	1866 02 16	UT, Salt Lake City
Howard .... James	Fackrell .... Juliette	1869 04 19	UT, Salt Lake City
Howard .... John Richards	Brooks .... Harriet Spinks	1866 09	UT, Salt Lake City
Howard .... Joseph	Shelton .... Ann	1842 11 24	ENG
Howard .... Joseph	Woodall .... Caroline		
Howard .... Lockwood A.	Crystal .... Mary	1876 03 20	UT, Salt Lake City
Howard .... Samuel Lorenzo	Hamilton .... Sarah Jane	1865 04 01	UT, Salt Lake City
Howard .... Thomas	Lowe .... Mary Dudley	1864 12 25	UT, West Bountiful
Howard .... William	Anderson .... Elizabeth	1841	IRE
Howard .... William	Pead .... Mary	1868 12 21	UT, Salt Lake City
Howarth .... John	Kay .... Elizabeth	1853 02 27	ENG
Howd .... Simeon Fuller	Morgan .... Lucinda	1847 03 16	IA, Council Bluffs
Howe .... Amos	Cruse .... Julia	1851 06 09	MO, St. Louis

Male	Female	Date	Place
Howe ....Amos	Miller ....Amy	1876	UT
Howe ....Richard	Turner ....Ann	1862	
Howe ....William	Jenkins................Jane	1833 05 07	Wales
Howell............Edmond W.	Vail....................Sarah	1836 10 05	
Howell............Henry	Goble ....Frances	1855 03 10	ENG
Howell............Henry Nelson	Bird....................Elizabeth W.	1861 12 16	UT, Salt Lake City
Howell............Louis W.	Williams..............Mary	1878 06 27	UT, Salt Lake City
Howell............Thomas C. D.	Stuart ....Sarah	1835 07 05	TN, Gibson Co.
Howell............William	Williams..............Martha	1829 09 26	Wales
Howell............William J.	Beebe................Lydia Ann	1860 01 09	UT, Payson
Howell............William John	Taylor................Eliza	1859 10 03	UT, Salt Lake City
Howland ....Henry	Case..................Martha Diana	1842 12 27	IL, Ogle
Howlett ....William Titus	Waller................Margaret	1855 10 29	
Howls..............Thomas	Jones ....Eliza	1842 04 11	ENG, Worcester
Howsley..........Charles D.	Cook..................Harriet Agnes	1831 10 21	
Hoyt ....Israel	Cook..................Hannah Elizabeth	1855 11 25	UT, Nephi
Hoyt ....Israel	Miller ....Clarissa Amanda	1848 11 25	UT, Salt Lake City
Hoyt ....James	Sabin..................Beulah	1807	NY, Boonville
Hoyt ....Samuel Pierce	Burbidge.............Catherine Emma	1856 01 17	UT, Fillmore
Hoyt ....Samuel Pierce	Smith..................Emily	1832 04 17	
Hoyt ....Silas	Ingram................Harriet	1854 11 21	UT, Parowan
Hubbard..........Charles W.	Bosworth ....Mary Ann	1832 10 30	
Hubbard..........Charles W.	Edwards ....Mary	1856 02	UT, Salt Lake City
Hubbard..........Charles W.	Pollard................Sophia	1856 06 04	UT, Salt Lake City
Hubbard..........Elisha F.	Wilson................Almira	1885 04 02	
Hubbard..........Marshall M.	Nickerson............Caroline Eliza	1827 09 18	NY, Perrysburg
Huber..............Johannes	Munz ....Maria M.	1863 10 18	UT, Payson
Hudson............William	White..................Mary Elizabeth	1839	ENG, Derbyshire
Huey ....Robert French	Hayes.................Clara W. T.	1844 05 20	South Africa
Huff..................James	Nybolle...............Hansine Jacobine	1858	UT, Manti
Huff..................Joseph	Adamson.............Eliza Jane		
Huff..................Joseph	Losee ....Mary Jane	1836 11 10	Canada
Huff..................Thaddeus W.	Russell ....Frances M.	1864 12 17	UT, Salt Lake City
Huff..................Thomas	Adams................Betsey Elizabeth	1815 03 07	GA, Hancock Co.
Huffaker...........Simpson D.	Richardson..........Elizabeth Melvina	1846 01 18	IL, Nauvoo
Hughes ....Francis David	Davies................Ellen	1869 05 03	UT, Salt Lake City
Hughes ....Francis David	Davies................Harriet	1864 04 24	Wales
Hughes ....Peter	Evans.................Elizabeth	1854 03 04	Wales
Hughes ....Robert	Collier.................Mary	1862	
Hughes ....Robert	Holt....................Mary		
Hughes ....Ross Burton	Muir....................Mary	1871 01 23	UT, Salt Lake City
Huish ....James William	Niblet..................Helen	1842 02 14	ENG, Avening
Huish ....Lorenzo Snow	Fillmore ....Antha Elmira	1875 06 22	
Huish ....Walter Henry	Smith..................Ann	1848 06 12	
Hulet ....Charles	Lawson................Mary	1857 03 23	UT, Salt Lake City
Hulet ....Charles	Noah ....Margaret	1816 10 10	OH, Ravenna
Hulet ....Orin Sylvester	Holt....................Mary		
Hulet ....Sylvanus Cyrus	Stoker.................Catherine	1850 05 19	IA, Mt. Pisgah
Hull ....Robert McClellan	Chadwick ....Mary Ann	1863 06 01	ID, Franklin
Hulme ....William	Daniels................Phebe	1860 11 04	UT, Payson
Hulse ....Charles Wesley	Smith..................Ann	1845 06 26	ENG, Manchester
Hulse ....Hyrum Smith	Hjorth ....Johanne D. A.	1873 04 01	UT, Salt Lake City
Humble ....George	Gates ....Mary Ann A.	1828 07 27	
Humble ....Henry	Larsen................Anna Kirstine	1866 05 17	

Male	Female	Date	Place
Humphreys ......Hyrum T.	Rich...................Caroline Whiting	1873 10 07	
Humphreys ......Thomas	Sudbury..............Mary	1831 12 26	ENG, Mansfield
Humphries ....John S.	Baugh..................Hannah	1855 02 14	UT, Salt Lake City
Hundley ....Jordan Y.	Wooldridge..........Permelia Emily	1817 10 27	AL, Madison
Hunsaker ....Abraham	Beckstead ....Harriet Vernitia	1850 11 22	
Hunsaker ....Abraham	Collins ....Eliza	1833 01 03	IL, Quincy
Hunsaker ....Isaac	Hansen...............Eliza Marie	1868 11 01	UT, Salt Lake City
Hunt...............Amos	Welborne............Nancy Garrett	1840 12 21	KY, Greenville
Hunt...............Andrew Jackson	Wilson ....Nancy Jane	1864 12 11	
Hunt...............Bethuel Howard	Marshall ....Tryphena	1864 11 09	ID, Franklin
Hunt...............Daniel Durham	Bigelow...............Mary Jane	1859 02 14	
Hunt...............Emanuel	Fellows...............Phoebe Louisa	1857 03	UT, Salt Lake City
Hunt...............Gilbert	Gibson.................Lydia Ardilca	1847 03	CO, Pueblo
Hunt...............Isaac	Newling ....Ann	1854 03 27	UT, Salt Lake City
Hunt...............James Wilson	Vaughan.............Elizabeth	1865 03 23	UT
Hunt...............Jefferson	Mounts ....Celia	1823 12 01	IL
Hunt...............Jefferson	Neese.................Matilda Jane		
Hunt...............Jefferson	Stucki ....Rosetta	1900 12 21	UT, St. George
Hunt...............John	Bardell................Sarah		
Hunt...............John	Pratt ....Lois	1857 07 04	
Hunt...............John Cook	Olson..................Anna	1866 11 19	UT, Salt Lake City
Hunt...............John Jackson	Woodfield ....Mary	1854 07 26	MO, Lawrence
Hunt...............John Jr.	Coates................Jane	1810 02 01	
Hunt...............Levi	Fellows...............Phoebe Louisa	1863 04 01	UT, Gunnison
Hunt...............Marshall	Runyon...............Sarah Ann	1851 03 15	UT, Holladay
Hunt...............Thomas	Moon..................Hannah	1847 12 27	ENG
Hunt...............William	Holmes...............Mary Ann	1816 02 13	ENG
Hunt...............Wilson	Sumner ....Perselia	1840 12 27	KY, Belton
Hunter............Adam P.	Patterson............Elizabeth	1842 04 25	Scotland
Hunter............David P.	Hughes...............Mary	1867 08 09	UT, Farmington
Hunter............Edward	Hyde...................Martha Ann	1856 03 30	
Hunter............Edward	Spencer..............Henrietta	1856 05 20	UT, Salt Lake City
Hunter............Edward	Wann..................Susanna	1846 01 29	
Hunter............Edward	Whitesides ....Mary Ann	1843 11 05	IL, Nauvoo
Hunter............George	Muir...................Mary	1858 12 23	UT, Cedar City
Hunter............George F.	McGill ....Helen Adams	1870 01 17	UT, Salt Lake City
Hunter............James Forbes	Coutts................Christina	1846 07 27	
Hunter............James William	Snadon...............Mary	1813 05 13	Scotland
Hunter............John Davidson	Bennett...............Elizabeth	1863 10 27	UT, Fillmore
Hunter............Robert	Hunter ....Agnes Ann	1835 04 21	Scotland
Hunter............William	Erskine...............Jessie	1880 11 04	UT, Salt Lake City
Hunting ....Nathan	Radmall..............Elizabeth Ann	1861 04 17	UT, Gunnison
Hunting ....William	Clisbee...............Lydia	1841	IL, Nauvoo
Huntington ....Oliver B.	Neal...................Mary Melissa	1845 08 17	NY, Cambria
Huntington ....Oliver B.	Sanders..............Hannah M.	1852 11 25	UT, Salt Lake City
Huntsman ....Isaiah	Cunningham........Seviah	1868	
Huntsman ....James W.	Davis ....Hannah	1831 12 28	MI, White Pidgeon
Huntsman ....John	Leavitt ....Roxanna	1841 06 23	
Huntsman ....John	Prater ....Elizabeth A.	1846 06 07	OH, Perry
Huntsman ....William	Bickmore ....Mary Jane	1853	UT, Fillmore
Hurren ....James David	Reeder ....Eliza	1850 09 22	
Hurst...............Phillip	Guymon ....Lucinda Harris	1857 01 01	UT
Hurst...............William	Webley...............Susannah	1830 07 11	ENG
Hussey ....Elijah	Hartford ....Caroline Iown	1834 08 28	

Male	Female	Date	Place
Hutchens ....William B.	Stone.................Mary Eliza	1854 11 02	UT, Salt Lake City
Hutcheson ....Thomas	Bathgate.............Mary	1827 04 18	
Hutchings ....Elias	Cox....................Sarah S.	1816 12 29	OH, Avery
Hutchings ....Shepherd P.	Pectol ....Eliza Ann	1850 01 01	UT, Salt Lake City
Hutchings ....William Burch	Allred.................Amanda Jane	1857 03 27	
Hutchings ....William Burch	Stone.................Eliza	1857 03 27	
Hutchinson .....Jacob F.	Langdon ....Clementina C. E.	1837	
Hutchinson .....Jacob F.	Wasden ....Alice P.	1861 06 09	UT, Gunnison
Hutchinson .....Thomas C.	Adamson............Jannett	1861 06 06	Ocean
Hutchison ....David	Nish...................Agnes	1840 12 30	Scotland
Hutchison ....William	Penmen..............Jane (Jean)	1845 10	Scotland
Hyde ....Herman	Griffeth ....Phoebe Ann	1884	ID, Fairview
Hyde ....Herman	Tilton ....Polly Wyman	1810 12 05	
Hyde ....Orson	Lyon ....Sophia Margaret	1865 10 10	
Hyde ....Orson	Price..................Mary Ann		IL, Nauvoo
Hyde ....Rosel	Simmons ....Hannah Maria	1862 02 22	UT, Salt Lake City
Hyde ....Rosel James	Driggs................Jane	1865 03 10	UT, Salt Lake City
Hyde ....William	Allred.................Sally	1850 09 01	
Hyde ....William	Bullard...............Elizabeth Howe	1842 02 23	IL, Nauvoo
Hyde ....William	Gloyd.................Abigail	1860 01 01	UT, Salt Lake City
Hyde ....William	Griffeth ....Phoebe Ann	1867 08 31	UT, Salt Lake City
Hyder.............Richard Hugh	Jarrold ....Sarah	1828 04	ENG, London
Hyer...............Christian Larsen	Hogan ....Caroline	1850 11 23	UT, Bountiful
Hyer...............Christian Larsen	Hogan ....Lovina		
Hyer...............Christian Larsen	Shepard ....Rozina	1869 02 15	UT, Salt Lake City

I

Male	Female	Date	Place
Igguldin............John	Ware ....Mary Bigg	1834	ENG
Ingersoll..........Jonas	Gutteridge ....Mary Ann	1867 03 12	UT, Salt Lake City
Ingram ....Edward Jr.	Smith.................Ann	1838 08 12	ENG, Warwickshire
Ingram ....John	Hall....................Harriet	1862 03 30	ENG, Warwick
Ipson...............Niels Peter	Madsen ....Inger Kerstine	1864 10 10	UT, Salt Lake City
Isaacson ....Neils	Aagesen..............Bertha Catherine	1850 09 18	Norway
Isaacson ....Peter	Clemmensen.......Martha Kristina	1857 04 21	UT, Salt Lake City
Isom................Owen	Howard...............Elizabeth	1835 03 11	ENG, Warwickshire
Isom................William	Wolfe.................Catherine	1861 03 24	ENG, Birmingham
Itten ....John	Schneider...........Magdalena	1861 10 18	UT, Salt Lake City
Ivers...............William D.	Proctor ....Ellen	1868	
Iversen............Hans	Nielsen ....Brigitte	1870 12 05	UT, Salt Lake City
Ivie................Benjamin M.	Memmott............Martha Ann	1864 07 21	UT, Mt. Pleasant
Ivie................Hyrum Lewis	Thacker ....Anna Maria	1894 12 29	UT, Provo
Ivie................James R.	Faucett ....Eliza McKee	1824 06	TN, Maury Co.
Ivie................James Thomas	Smith.................Eliza Jane	1871 01 08	UT, Scipio
Ivie................John Lehi	Barton ....Mary Catherine	1852 05 16	UT, Bountiful
Ivins...............Israel	Hill....................Julia	1857 02 13	UT, Salt Lake City
Ivins...............Israel	Ivins..................Anna Laurie	1844 03 19	NJ, Horrerstown
Ivory..............George W.	Collard...............Mercie Hunt	1879 10 02	
Ivory..............Mathew Hayes	Bemus...............Mary Judith E.	1854 12 14	IL, Fulton Co.
Izatt................Alexander S.	Angus................Jane	1870 01 29	UT, Salt Lake City
Izatt................Alexander S.	Williamson..........Janetta	1864 02 27	UT, Salt Lake City

Male	Female	Date	Place
	J		
Jackman.........Levi	Byam.................Delia Deliverance	1850	
Jackman.........Levi	Harmon..............Lucinda	1849 11 18	UT, Salt Lake City
Jackman.........Parmeno	Heiner................Susannah C.	1892 02 14	UT, Salt Lake City
Jackson..........Aaron	Horrocks............Elizabeth	1848 05 28	ENG, Cheshire
Jackson..........James Jr.	Bedford..............Annis	1859 11 24	UT, Lehi
Jackson..........James Jr.	McFate...............Martha	1863	
Jackson..........James Jr.	Stapley..............Sarah Ann	1863	
Jackson..........John	Robinson............Alice	1861 06 16	ENG
Jackson..........Jonathan	Robinson............Alice	1869 01 11	
Jackson..........Thomas	Crompton............Alice	1842 08 14	ENG, Manchester
Jackson..........Thomas	Staples..............Joyce	1836 08 21	ENG, Westerham
Jackson..........William	Fuller.................Martha Jane	1846 11 19	
Jackson..........William	Wooley...............Ann Esther	1853 03	Ocean
Jackson..........William W.	Wright................Ellen	1854 07 08	UT, Salt Lake City
Jacob.............Udney Hay	Green.................Phylotte	1856 03 11	UT, Salt Lake City
Jacobs............John	Coleman.............Elizabeth	1853 10 27	UT, Salt Lake City
Jacobs............John	Payne.................Priscilla	1862	UT, Grantsville
Jacobs............John	Sabey.................Sarah Jane	1874 08 10	UT, Salt Lake City
Jacobsen........Christian L.	Nielsen...............Thora	1882 01 12	UT, Salt Lake City
Jacobsen........David	Sorensen............Karen	1828 11 14	Denmark
Jacobsen........Jorgen	Peterson.............Bertha Kirstine	1843 04 02	Denmark
Jacobsen........Lars	Nielsen...............Anna Marie	1854 04 08	Denmark
Jacobsen........Lars	Ohlsen................Margrethe		
Jacobson........Franz Leonard	Berg..................Helena Catrine	1869 07 12	UT, Salt Lake City
Jacobson........Hans	Hansen...............Maren	1840 07 04	Denmark
Jacobson........James	Rasmussen.........Anne	1865 05 10	Ocean
Jacobson........Ole Hans	Dutson...............Rebecca Deseret	1878 03 14	UT, Salt Lake City
Jacques..........Thomas	Phillips...............Hannah Elizabeth	1855 03 08	UT, Provo
Jakeman.........Henry	Jackson..............Maria	1859 06 02	UT, Moroni
Jakeman.........James	Field..................Ann	1833 11 13	ENG
Jakobsen........Peder S.	Olsen.................Gjertrude Marie	1828 09 20	Norway
James.............Daniel	Peasnall.............Love	1877 10 22	UT, Tooele
James.............David	Griffin................Lydia	1871 11 07	UT, Salt Lake City
James.............David Jenkins	Webb.................Fannie	1875 11 15	UT, Salt Lake City
James.............Howell	Jones.................Mary Ann	1837 03 27	Wales
James.............Isaac	Manning.............Jane Elizabeth	1845	IL, Nauvoo
James.............James	Richards.............Mary	1854 02 14	UT, Salt Lake City
James.............John Sanders	Williams.............Elizabeth Henry	1866 10 06	Wales
James.............Joseph	Holyoak..............Sarah	1854 10 02	UT, Salt Lake City
James.............Reuben	Allen..................Sarah Briggs	1878 02 20	UT, St. George
James.............Thomas	George...............Elizabeth	1855	
James.............Thomas	Williams.............Eleanor	1821 06 06	ENG, Lugwardine
James.............Thomas John	Newton...............Elizabeth	1864 11 18	UT, Salt Lake City
James.............William	Haynes...............Jane	1835 06 15	ENG, Pinvin
James.............William Bowen	Jenkins...............Sarah	1854 10 22	Wales
James.............William Francis	Whitehead..........Julia Ellen	1877 08 09	UT, Ogden
Jameson.........Alexander	Ewell.................Pirene Brown	1853 08 07	UT, Provo
Janes.............Jacob	Harrison.............Mary Ann	1869 01 11	UT, Salt Lake City
Janes.............Josiah	Slafter...............Asenath	1832 12 06	CT, Mansfield
Jansson..........Jan Peter	Jansson..............Maria Katerina	1832 02 03	Sweden
Jardine...........James	White.................Isabelle Elizabeth	1840 07 17	Scotland
Jardine...........John	Beveridge...........Agnes	1850 08 15	Scotland

Male	Female	Date	Place
Jarvis ....George	Webb..................Mary	1878 04 04	UT, St. George
Jarvis ....George Franklin	Prior ....Ann	1846 09 17	ENG, Southwark
Jarvis ....Henry	Turner ....Elizabeth	1837 08 04	ENG, Essex
Jarvis ....Joshua	Johnson ....Mary Ann	1861 04 20	ENG, Bethnel
Jeffery.............Thomas Alfred	Cowper..............Elizabeth	1862 02 22	UT, Salt Lake City
Jeffery.............Thomas Alfred	Hibbitt................Mary Ann	1853 12 29	ENG, Birmingham
Jeffs................Mark Walker	Carlile................Mary	1865	UT, Heber
Jeffs................William W.	Summers............Emma	1851 08 25	ENG, Warwickshire
Jeffs................William Yem	Hatchard ....Mary Ann	1847	ENG, Gloucester
Jenkins ....David	Evans ....Anna	1842 11 19	Wales
Jenkins ....David	Ferguson...........Jane	1807	
Jenkins ....Henry	John ....Martha	1843 07 09	
Jenkins ....Henry Laird	Stanfield ....Emily Hill	1819 05 01	UT, Goshen
Jenkins ....James	Davis ....Elizabeth	1842 05 09	Wales
Jenkins ....James Hardie	Laird..................Janet	1842 10 22	Scotland
Jenkins ....James Hardie	Sanders............Marian	1880	UT
Jenkins ....John	Morris ....Rosella N.	1870 11 25	UT, Salt Lake City
Jenkins ....John	Pritchard............Elizabeth	1852 01 17	UT, Salt Lake City
Jenkins ....Lewis	Harrison ....Eliza Ann	1870 05 22	UT, Salt Lake City
Jenkins ....Morgan	Hall....................Elizabeth	1867 10 26	UT, Salt Lake City
Jenkins ....Richard	Ostler ....Sarah Ann	1870 03 14	UT, Salt Lake City
Jenkins ....Thomas	Irvin ....Jennet	1884 05	
Jenkins ....Thomas	Marshall ....Joanna	1838 04 19	
Jenkins ....William	Rosser................Elizabeth	1845 12 13	Wales
Jenkins ....William	Rowberry...........Mary Parry	1840 07 01	ENG
Jennings ....Alexander	Anderson............Ane Margrethe	1876 04 09	UT, Levan
Jennings ....Cyrus M.	Hansen...............Hannah Jane	1874 02 05	UT, Rockville
Jennings ....Cyrus M.	Stout...................Lydia M. F.	1884	
Jennings ....Henry	Morgan................Ann	1848 05 14	MO, St. Louis
Jennings ....Mansfield C.	Perris..................Fanny Jane	1857 12 29	NV, Las Vegas
Jennings ....Schuyler P.	Barnett ....Polly M. V.	1835	TN, Perry
Jennings ....Schuyler P.	Barnett ....Polly M. V.		Remarried
Jensen.............Anders	Christensen.........Anne	1844 08 31	Denmark
Jensen.............Anders	Pedersen.............Maren	1856 05 25	Denmark
Jensen.............Andreas	Lauritzen ....Maria	1868 01 30	UT, Salt Lake City
Jensen.............Andrew	Pedersen.............Ellen Bendixen	1866	UT, Moroni
Jensen.............Andrew C.	Carlson................Anne Marie	1866 02 13	UT, Brigham City
Jensen.............Andrew L.	Christensen.........Christina Caroline	1872 05 18	UT, Salt Lake City
Jensen.............Anton C.	Mouritsen ....Maren	1865 11 20	UT, Smithfield
Jensen.............Christen	Andersen............Kirsten	1848	Denmark
Jensen.............Christen	Hansen...............Laurentze	1870 07 11	UT, Salt Lake City
Jensen.............Christen	Mikkelsen ....Anna Johanna	1848 05 03	Denmark
Jensen.............Christen	Mogensen ....Jacobine Kirstine	1854 06 02	
Jensen.............Christian	Anderson............Mary	1868 05 03	UT, Salt Lake City
Jensen.............Christian	Christensen.........Barbara	1850 10 29	Denmark
Jensen.............Christian G.	Christiansen........Else Marie	1853 04 03	MO, St. Louis
Jensen.............Christian G.	Nielsen ....Ane Johanna	1857 09 27	
Jensen.............David	Petersen.............Julia Konstance	1868 11 18	
Jensen.............David	Simonsen ....Bertha Serina	1859 08 20	Norway
Jensen.............David	Simonsen ....Julia		
Jensen.............Fredrick C.	Pedersen.............Johanne Marie	1842 11 26	Denmark
Jensen.............Gregers	Christensen.........Kirstine	1832 11 02	Denmark
Jensen.............Hans	Hansen...............Ane Kjerstine	1837	Denmark
Jensen.............Hans	Jacobsen.............Sidse Marie	1840 11 09	Denmark

Male	Female	Date	Place
Jensen............Hans Christian	Olsen..................Hedvig Marie	1846 06 05	Denmark
Jensen............Hans Peter	Eriksen...............Nicoline	1859 11 06	UT, Salt Lake City
Jensen............Hans R.	Andersen............Josephine	1871 11 06	UT, Salt Lake City
Jensen............Hans Severin	Neilson...............Mette Marie	1837 03 17	Denmark
Jensen............James	Larson...............Hannah	1875 01 01	UT, Hyrum
Jensen............James	Madsen..............Marie	1873	UT
Jensen............James	Sorensen............Mette J. P.	1865 09 21	UT, Salt Lake City
Jensen............Jens	Andersen............Maren	1839 07 12	Denmark
Jensen............Jens	Hansen...............Johanna	1852 10 22	Denmark
Jensen............Jens	Knudsen.............Anna Maria	1861 05 04	UT, Salt Lake City
Jensen............Jens	Kristensen...........Mette	1835 10 23	Denmark
Jensen............Jens	Larsen................Bodil Marie	1856 02 22	Denmark
Jensen............Jens	Pedersen............Sophia	1866	UT, Salt Lake City
Jensen............Jens	Sorensen............Karen Sophie		
Jensen............Jens Christian	Christensen.........Karen Marie	1840 12 01	Denmark
Jensen............Jens Christian	Larsen................Anna Christine	1870	UT, Logan
Jensen............Jens Iver	Nielsen...............Inger	1867 05 24	
Jensen............Jens Martinus	Thomson.............Caroline	1863 03 12	UT, Pleasant Grove
Jensen............Jens P.	Gregersen...........Dorthea	1866 10 23	UT, Salt Lake City
Jensen............Jens Peter	Nielsen...............Inger	1861 10 22	
Jensen............Jens Peter	Nielsen...............Karen C.	1878 06 05	UT, St. George
Jensen............Jes	Henriksen............Anna Maria	1851 01 29	Denmark
Jensen............Jes	Nelson................Katherine		
Jensen............Johannes C.	Nielsen...............Ansine Elizabeth	1855 11 16	Denmark
Jensen............Jorgen C.	Pedersen............Caroline	1851 05 21	Denmark
Jensen............Knud	Olsen..................Bodil	1834 04 28	Denmark
Jensen............Lars	Anderson............Inger	1852 03	Sweden
Jensen............Lars (Louis)	Rath...................Maria Christina	1858	Denmark
Jensen............Lars Christian	Kristensen...........Mette		
Jensen............Lars Christian	Munk..................Amelia Thomsen	1874 07 08	UT, Salt Lake City
Jensen............Lars Christian	Nielsen...............Margrethe	1857 03 31	UT, Salt Lake City
Jensen............Lars Rove	Freestone............Elizabeth Ann	1864 08 27	UT, Salt Lake City
Jensen............Mads Christian	Hansen...............Maren	1845 06 10	Denmark
Jensen............Mads Christian	Pedersen............Gertrude Marie	1855 01 27	UT, Salt Lake City
Jensen............Michael	Higgs..................Annie Elizabeth	1881 05 11	UT, Manti
Jensen............Michael	Pedersen............Anna Lena	1868 01 01	UT, Manti
Jensen............Morten	Christensen.........Anna	1826 03 27	Denmark
Jensen............Niels	Holm..................Ane Marie	1857 08 07	UT, Salt Lake City
Jensen............Niels	Langgaard...........Marie Kirstine	1849 01 30	
Jensen............Niels	Sorensen............Jensine Christine	1861 11 16	UT, Salt Lake City
Jensen............Ole	Hansen...............Karen Marie	1843 11 18	Denmark
Jensen............Ole	Jolly...................Margaret Ann	1868 02 29	UT, Clarkston
Jensen............Olof	Rasmussen.........Anne Maria	1841 06 23	Denmark
Jensen............Paul Martines	Olsen..................Mette Christina	1851 04 15	Denmark
Jensen............Peder	Sorensen............Karen	1850 04 18	Denmark
Jensen............Peter	Larsen................Christena	1886 12 29	UT, Logan
Jensen............Peter (Peder)	Mortensen..........Mary	1867 12 06	
Jensen............Peter Christen	Andersen............Maren	1853 12 09	Denmark
Jensen............Peter Christen	Jensen................Kjirste		
Jensen............Peter Christian	Pedersen............Ane Kirstine	1854 12 05	Denmark
Jensen............Peter George	Jensen................Anna Johanna	1882 11 30	UT, Salt Lake City
Jensen............Peter Jens	Oman..................Christina C.	1863 09 13	UT, Mt. Pleasant
Jensen............Peter Madsen	Hansen...............Anne Marie	1859 03 09	Denmark
Jensen............Peter Y.	Jensen................Jensine Christine	1868 05 30	UT, Salt Lake City

Male	Female	Date	Place
Jensen............Soren	Rasmussen.........Kjerstine	1867 03 09	UT, Salt Lake City
Jensen............Soren Peter	Christensen.........Maren	1866 11 08	UT, Salt Lake City
Jensen............Thomas C.	Iverson ....Karen Marie	1841 10 28	Denmark
Jenson............Jens	Roseberg............Emma Caroline	1874 01 02	
Jeppersen........Niels Jacob	Matisen ....Suzannah S. A.	1847 11	
Jeppesen.........Rasmus	Pedersen............Inger	1867 01 05	UT, Salt Lake City
Jeppeson.........Jacob	Klemmetson........Hannah	1837 03 20	Sweden
Jeppson...........Jeppa H.	Hansen...............Gunnell Marie	1854 10 11	
Jeppson...........Jeppa H.	Peterson.............Christina	1865 01 27	UT, Salt Lake City
Jepson............Martin	Anderson............Anna	1862 10 11	UT
Jeremy............Thomas Evans	Evans ....Sarah	1838 03 16	Wales
Jerman ....Daniel Smith	Egbert ....Susanna	1877 12 17	UT, Salt Lake City
Jerman ....James A.	Lundy ....Rachel Bunn	1843	
Jesperson........James Peter	Johnson ....Emma Ida	1880 09 19	UT, Richfield
Jessen ....Ebbe	Bertelsen............Anne Marie	1863 02 21	UT, Salt Lake City
Jessen ....Mads Peter	Bertelsen............Anne Marie	1858 09 07	
Jessop ....Thomas	Jensson..............Annie	1879 04 10	UT, Salt Lake City
Jewkes ....Samuel R.	Barentsen...........Susannah	1871 06 12	UT, Salt Lake City
Jex.................Richard	Goodson ....Eliza	1847 10 12	ENG, Crostwick
Jex.................William	Cox...................Jemima	1865 01	UT, Salt Lake City
Jex.................William	Goodson ....Eliza	1854 02 22	
Jinks ....John Jr.	Woodfield ....Mary	1823 05 12	ENG, Stone
Job.................Thomas	Daniels ....Hannah	1848 05 02	Wales
Job.................Thomas	Davies ....Elizabeth	1855 08 18	
Johansen.........Lars	Sorensen............Anna Margrethe	1816 08 25	Denmark
Johansen.........Ole	Iversen ....Ane Marie	1805 06 28	
Johansen.........Peter	Christensen.........Ane Kerstine	1858 11 21	UT
John...............David	Cree ....Jane	1865 10 08	UT, Salt Lake City
John...............David	Wride.................Mary	1860 02 08	
Johnsen..........Olaus	Amundsen..........Anna H.	1863 09 09	UT, Echo Canyon
Johnson..........Aaron	Ford..................Margaret Jane	1855 05 08	UT, Springville
Johnson..........Aaron	James ....Sarah	1857 03 01	UT, Salt Lake City
Johnson..........Aaron	Kelsey ....Polly Zehviah	1827 09 13	CT, New Haven
Johnson..........Aaron	Sanford ....Cecilla Elmina	1857 03 01	
Johnson..........Alfred F. T.	Bengtsson ....Anna	1870 01 11	UT, Salt Lake City
Johnson..........Andrew G.	Bjork.................Anna Sophia	1863 10 08	UT, Salt Lake City
Johnson..........Andrew John	Pehrson.............Elna Petronella	1855 12 22	Sweden
Johnson..........Augustus	Magnusson ....Carolina W.	1859 03 13	Sweden
Johnson..........Benjamin	Budd..................Charlotte	1836 04 01	
Johnson..........Benjamin F.	Gleason..............Flora Clarinda	1846 01 23	IL, Nauvoo
Johnson..........Benjamin F.	LeBaron ....Melissa B.	1841 12 25	OH, Kirtland
Johnson..........Benjamin F.	Spooner ....Sarah Jane	1857 04 05	UT, Salt Lake City
Johnson..........Benjamin Henry	Tidwell...............Mary Jane	1852 08 06	
Johnson..........Charles M.	Mathews.............Joan	1871 11 27	UT, Providence
Johnson..........Christian	Butler.................Caroline	1878 05 09	UT, Salt Lake City
Johnson..........Ezekiel	Hills ....Julia	1801 01 12	MA, Grafton
Johnson..........George W.	Burdick ....Eveline Jewell	1851 09 30	UT, Salt Lake City
Johnson..........George W.	Johnston ....Maria Jane	1844 04 14	IL, Macedonia
Johnson..........Gustav	Anderson............Mary	1862	UT, Deseret
Johnson..........Hans Jorge J.	Nielsen ....Inger Christine	1844 05	Norway
Johnson..........James	Larsen ....Mary (Marie)	1850 11 29	
Johnson..........Jarvis	Ainsworth ....Mary Jane	1870	
Johnson..........Jarvis	Angell.................Sarah Jane	1860 09 16	UT, Salt Lake City
Johnson..........Jarvis	Jackson..............Hester Ann	1849 08 05	NE

Male	Female	Date	Place
Johnson...........Jens	Nilsson ....Johanna	1845 07 04	Sweden
Johnson...........Joel Hills	Fife......................Janet	1845 10 25	OH, Kirtland
Johnson...........John	Anderson.............Karen Kirstine	1835 08 08	Denmark
Johnson...........John	Jonason ....Anna	1850 10 26	Sweden
Johnson...........John	Larsen ....Bergitte	1843 04 26	Norway
Johnson...........John	Madsen ....Mette Marie	1868 04 18	UT, Salt Lake City
Johnson...........John	Nielsen ....Anna Marie	1865 12 01	UT, Salt Lake City
Johnson...........John	Peterson.............Hannah Sophia	1879 01 02	UT, Salt Lake City
Johnson...........John	Sward..................Inger	1870 06 13	UT, Salt Lake City
Johnson...........John	Swenson ....Louisa	1858 07 27	Sweden
Johnson...........John Ellis	Goddard ....Hannah Maria	1849 12	IA, Kanesville
Johnson...........John James	Mortensen ....Inger Katherine	1870 07 11	
Johnson...........John P. R.	Taft......................Karen Marie	1845	Denmark
Johnson...........John Peter	Feltman ....Anna Barbara	1863 11 21	UT, Salt Lake City
Johnson...........Joseph E.	Fillmore ....Thankful R.	1869	UT, Spring Lake
Johnson...........Joseph Ellis	Snyder.................Harriet	1840 10 01	IL, Nauvoo
Johnson...........Joseph W.	Knight..................Elizabeth	1842 02 03	IL, Nauvoo
Johnson...........Julius	Liljenquist............Clara J. J.	1871 10 22	UT, Salt Lake City
Johnson...........Lorenzo	Hall.....................Mary Ann	1857 03 01	UT, Salt Lake City
Johnson...........Lorenzo	James ....Emma	1857 03 01	UT, St. George
Johnson...........Marion Maroni	Hall.....................Sarah Jane	1897 12 08	UT, Springville
Johnson...........Niels Peter	Johnson ....Josephine C. M.	1869 05 03	UT, Salt Lake City
Johnson...........Nils Toman	Peterson.............Johanna	1848 10 22	Sweden
Johnson...........Olaus	Syverson ....Paulina	1867 01 13	UT, Salt Lake City
Johnson...........Peter (Pehr)	Olsson.................Matta	1845 07 05	Sweden
Johnson...........Peter Henry	Roberts ....Lucina	1824 11 24	VT, Addison Co.
Johnson...........Rasmus	Jensen ....Mette	1857 02 13	UT, Salt Lake City
Johnson...........Richard	Bevan..................Husseler	1844 08 25	ENG, Stafford
Johnson...........Robert	Jenson ....Sophia Elizabeth	1862 12 09	
Johnson...........Robert	Johnston ....Elizabeth	1845 01 12	ENG, Lancaster
Johnson...........Robert L.	Guymon ....Melissa Jane	1862 08 16	UT, Salt Lake City
Johnson...........Robert L.	Guymon ....Polly Ann	1846 04 30	IL, Nauvoo
Johnson...........Theodore	Smith...................Susanna	1849 04 30	
Johnson...........Thomas Smith	Haines.................Kindness Ann	1849 02 04	
Johnson...........Warren M.	Nelson.................Samantha	1872 10 28	UT, Salt Lake City
Johnson...........William	Johnson ....Elizabeth Ann	1818 03 03	ENG
Johnson...........William D.	Brown..................Jane Cadwalladar	1848 11 29	IL, Nauvoo
Johnson...........William Derby Jr.	Cram ....Charlesetta P.	1879 05 29	UT, St. George
Johnson...........William Henry	Snyder.................Eliza	1858 04 16	UT, Springville
Johnson...........Willis Kelsey	Crandall...............Laura	1849 12 27	IA, Pottawattamie
Johnston..........Andrew	Bennet.................Margaret	1848 11 19	Scotland
Johnston..........Hugh	Yorston................Cecelia	1826 12 12	
Johnston..........James	Barbour ....Jane	1843	IL, LaHarpe
Johnston..........James	Gibson.................Bianca Jane	1862 09 01	UT, Salt Lake City
Johnston..........William J.	Perks...................Ellen	1863 01 26	
Johnston..........William James	Harris ....Elizabeth	1867 07 20	
Jolley ....Henry B. M.	Mayo ....Brittanna	1833 10 31	TN, Dresden
Jolley ....Reuben M.	Pippen.................Sarah	1829 01 13	TN, Weekly Co.
Jolley ....William J.	Curtis..................Serepta Lorinda	1850 04 25	IA, Council Bluffs
Jones...............Benjamin	Higgins ....Catherine B.		
Jones..............Calvin T.	Jolley..................Diana Louisa	1832	TN, Dresden
Jones..............Charles	Weeks ....Mary Ann	1846 09 20	ENG
Jones..............David	Morris..................Jane	1837	Wales
Jones..............David	Welch..................Ann	1869 12 27	UT, South Cotton.

Male	Female	Date	Place
Jones .... Edward	Markland .... Elizabeth	1826 11 06	ENG, Manchester
Jones .... Elias	Williams .... Hannah	1856 01 02	
Jones .... Elisha	Talbott .... Margaret	1831 09 03	OH, Smithfield
Jones .... Elisha Warren	Pierce .... Jane Ann	1871 03 06	UT, Heber
Jones .... Frederick W.	Marshall .... Ellen	1864 08 17	
Jones .... Frederick W.	Snow .... Julia Marie	1887 09 02	
Jones .... Hyrum	Ryan .... Alice	1888 07 02	UT, Heber
Jones .... Jacob	Cox .... Emma	1861 05 14	UT, Fairview
Jones .... James Naylor	Mallarnee .... Sarah Ann	1829 10 17	OH, Steubenville
Jones .... John Lee	Simkins .... Rachel	1862 01 07	UT, Cedar City
Jones .... John Markland	Mulliner .... Elizabeth Smith	1853 07 23	UT, Salt Lake City
Jones .... John Pidding	Chapman .... Fanny Ridsdale	1882	
Jones .... John Pidding	Lee .... Margaret	1839 09 23	ENG
Jones .... John Rodderick	Evans .... Ann	1857 01 05	ENG, Tredegar
Jones .... John Smith	Birch .... Ellen	1872 12 09	UT, Salt Lake City
Jones .... Joseph	Parry .... Jane	1847	Wales
Jones .... Levinas Jr.	Chorlton .... Harriet	1856 03 02	ENG
Jones .... Llewellyn	Creer .... Alice Ann	1868 03 28	UT, Salt Lake City
Jones .... Llewellyn G.	John .... Marie Jeanette	1840 07 11	Wales
Jones .... Merlin	Ives .... Roxana	1820 08 17	CT, Wellingford
Jones .... Nathaniel Vary	Brown .... Mary Eliza	1857 05 31	UT, Salt Lake City
Jones .... Peter	Bland .... Chloe	1854	
Jones .... Peter	Bland .... Mary Lee	1854	UT, Ogden
Jones .... Richard	Parsons .... Naomi	1849 11 19	ENG, Middlesex
Jones .... Richard George	Jeffcott .... Sarah	1860 07 11	UT, Salt Lake City
Jones .... Ricy Davis	Howell .... Ann	1854 07 01	
Jones .... Ricy Davis	Morse .... Margaret	1868 10 18	UT, Salt Lake City
Jones .... Robert	Thomas .... Sarah		Wales
Jones .... Samuel	Bradshaw .... Sarah Ann	1836 08 03	ENG
Jones .... Thomas	Morgan .... Mary	1840 07 13	ENG, Aberystruth
Jones .... Thomas	Thomas .... Ruth	1827 03 07	Wales
Jones .... Thomas English	Mailes .... Mary Ann	1842 01 16	IL, Nauvoo
Jones .... Thomas English	Nelson .... Jane	1857 07 05	UT, Salt Lake City
Jones .... William	Hughes .... Elizabeth	1825	NY, New York
Jones .... William Edward	Davis .... Sarah	1871 10 03	UT, Salt Lake City
Jones .... William Edward	Newman .... Eliza	1857 08 12	UT, Paragonah
Jones .... William Ellis	Davies .... Dinah	1856 02 03	MO, St. Joseph
Jones .... William Ellis	Vaughan .... Martha	1859 06	
Jones .... William Parsons	Shaw .... Elizabeth	1858 02 25	UT, Kaysville
Jones .... William Richard	Penrose .... Jessie Lucetta	1883 12 16	UT, Salt Lake City
Jones .... William Roberts	Wright .... Sarah Ann	1853 10 12	UT, Salt Lake City
Jonson .... Anders Paul	Anderson .... Elna	1831 12 28	Sweden
Jonson .... Jons	Nilsson .... Elsa	1842 07 15	Sweden
Jonson .... Truls	Larson .... Ingeborg	1852	Sweden
Jordan .... James F.	Cannon .... Sarah	1846 04 30	ENG
Jordan .... Justus Perry	Brady .... Tranquilla Ann	1921 06 29	
Jordan .... Nathaniel	Coon .... Lois	1847 11 27	IA, Pott. Co.
Jorden .... Frank	Fryer .... Jane	1842	ENG
Jorganson .... Lars	Larson .... Kjersti	1858	
Jorgensen	Poulsen .... Antonette		
Jorgensen .... Christian	Petersen .... Petrine Antomena	1878 09 26	UT, Salt Lake City
Jorgensen .... Hans	Andersen .... Dorthea	1853 07 04	IA, Council Bluffs
Jorgensen .... Hans	Henricksen .... Karen Marie	1864	Denmark
Jorgensen .... Jasper	Jensen .... Maren	1845 07 16	Denmark

Male	Female	Date	Place
Jorgensen........Jens	Bertelsen.............Kjersten	1863 02 21	UT, Salt Lake City
Jorgensen........Jorgen	Mickelson ....Maren	1838 05 04	Denmark
Jorgensen.......Jorgen C.	Knoppel...............Amelia F. J.	1859 10 23	NY, New York City
Jorgensen........Lars	Jorgensen ....Maren Kirstine	1841 04 02	
Jorgensen........Rasmus	Mogensen ....Jacobine Kirstine	1861 05 20	Ocean
Jost................Samuel Edward	Baker..................Elizabeth Ann	1872 04 02	UT, Ogden
Joyce ....Thomas	Ford...................Mary Ann	1838 02 13	ENG
Juchau.............James Joseph	Littlewood...........Elizabeth Tyrene	1860 08	UT, Salt Lake City
Judd................George	Paskett...............Jane Belbin	1869 12 06	UT, Salt Lake City
Judd................Hyrum	Fuller ....Lisania	1844 06 27	IL, Warsaw
Judd................James	Harrop ....Mary Jane	1866 11 04	UT, Coalville
Judd................Thomas	Redding..............Ann	1841 05 31	ENG
Judd................Thomas Alfred	Hastings ....Teresa	1830 12 27	Canada
Judd................William Riley	Norton ....Isabelle	1854 03 23	UT, Salt Lake City
Judd................William Riley	Reid...................Anna Jane	1856 11 26	UT, Salt Lake City
Judd................Zadok Knapp	Dart ....Mary Minerva	1852 11 14	UT, Parowan
Justesen ....Lars A.	Jensen ....Matilda	1862 10 25	
Justesen ....Lars Alexander	Rasmussen.........Karen (Caroline)	1841 11 10	Denmark

K

Male	Female	Date	Place
Karren.............Charles Hopkins	Davis ....Sarah Agnes	1871 12 25	UT, Lehi
Karren..............Thomas	Ratcliff................Ann	1832 05 04	ENG, Liverpool
Kartchner.........William Decatur	Casteel...............Margaret Jane	1844 03 17	IL, Hancock Co.
Kay ....John Rushton	Chatterly.............Sarah	1840 05 31	ENG, Prestwich
Kay ....John Thomas	Vest...................Margaret Ann	1864 04 15	UT, Mona
Kay ....Joseph	Howarth...............Mary	1855	ENG
Kay ....Joseph Chatterly	Walker................Margaret Ann	1869 02 15	UT, Salt Lake City
Kay ....William	Nelson................Mary Eunice	1853 04 07	
Kay ....William	Wattis ....Mary Twinberrow	1844 02 07	IL, Nauvoo
Kearl................James	Burton ....Ann	1853 09 18	ENG, Brockenhurst
Keele ....Richard John	McCullough.........Nancy Eleanor	1808 09 18	TN, Bedford
Keeler ....Daniel A.	Merrick ....Fanny	1846 02 06	
Keeler ....Daniel Hutchinson	Brown..................Ann	1853 01 10	UT, Salt Lake City
Keeler ....Daniel Hutchinson	Eldredge.............Philinda	1843 02 06	IL, Nauvoo
Keep ....James Joseph	Miller ....Ann	1836 07 24	ENG, Reading
Keetch ....Charles G.	Barker ....Mercy Truth	1860 12 14	NE, Florence
Keller ....Alva	Elliott ....Roxcy Lucina	1833 07 23	
Keller ....Alva	Saunders............Eliza	1854 07	UT, Salt Lake City
Keller ....James Morgan	Larsen ....Anna Christena	1860 01 05	UT, Salt Lake City
Kelley..............James H.	Bates..................Mary Maria	1876	UT
Kelley..............Joseph	Pine...................Thankful Lucy	1856 04 22	UT
Kelley..............Russel Samuel	Bingham.............Abigail		
Kelley..............Russel Thomas	Bingham.............Abigail		
Kelley..............Russel Thomas	Hudson...............Deseret McBride		
Kelley..............Russel Thomas	Moore.................Harriet	1858 01 31	UT, Salt Lake City
Kelley..............Russel Thomas	Skriggins ....Mary Ellen		
Kellman ....Johannes	Jonson ....Anna Cecelia	1860	
Kellogg ....Ezekiel	Harris ....Naomi	1826 10	NY, Palmyra
Kelly................	Steadwell ....Sarah (Sally)		
Kelly................George	Slater..................Mary Ann		
Kelly................John Phillip	Long ....Eliza	1838 12 25	ENG, Bromyard
Kelly................William Edward	Cunningham........Elizabeth	1858 07 19	UT, American Fork

Male	Female	Date	Place
Kelsey............Eli B.	Caldwell.............Jane		IL, Nauvoo
Kelsey............Eli B.	Caldwell.............Jane		Remarried
Kempe............Christopher J.	Johnson.............Anna Dorthea	1866 03 10	UT, Salt Lake City
Kempe............Christopher J.	Olsen.................Olena	1866 03 10	UT, Salt Lake City
Kempton..........Nathan	Cooper..............Rachel Russell	1837	TX
Kempton..........Nathan	Hall...................Mary Maria		
Kempton..........Nathan	Hardy.................Pamelia Anne	1856	UT
Kendall...........Levi Newell	Clements............Elizabeth	1852 11 29	UT, Salt Lake City
Kendall...........William	Peek...................Joanna	1853 12 07	ENG, Sohom
Kennedy..........Frank	Gordge...............Ann		
Kennedy..........John	Smith.................Annie Lorimer	1907 04 04	UT, Salt Lake City
Kenney...........John	Alden.................Phebe	1861 10 26	UT, Salt Lake City
Kenney...........John	Bennett..............Elizabeth	1861 10 26	UT, Salt Lake City
Kennington......William Henry	Lee....................Elizabeth Ann	1874	UT
Kennington......William Henry	Seward...............Annie Rebecca	1865 04 01	UT, Salt Lake City
Kent................Daniel	Young.................Nancy	1803 01 03	
Kent................Samuel	Standley.............Sarah Jane	1828 02 05	CT, Hartford
Kerr................George Mercer	Affleck...............Jane	1863 04 16	ENG, Byker
Kerr................Joseph	Rowe.................Margaret		
Kerr................Joseph	Rowe.................Ruth	1852	
Kerr................Robert Marion	Rawlins.............Elzira		
Kerr................Robert Marion	Rawlins.............Nancy Jane	1860 01 01	UT, Draper
Kershaw..........George F. W.	Byard.................Eliza	1849 12 17	South Africa
Kesler.............Frederick	Parker...............Emeline	1836 05 19	IA, Augusta
Kesler.............Frederick	Pratt.................Jane Elizabeth	1854 03 20	UT, Salt Lake City
Kesler.............Frederick	Snow.................Abigail Dow	1857 04 21	UT, Salt Lake City
Kesler.............Joseph	Pitts.................Annie Elizabeth	1864 02 04	UT, Salt Lake City
Keyes.............Alma	Tracy.................Marie Evaline	1861 04 27	OR
Keyes.............Elisha B.	Worden...............Johanna Case	1838 03 26	OH, Grafton
Keyes.............William Henry H.	Herrick...............Eliza Ann	1834 04 12	MO, Clay Co.
Kidd................Alexander	Bickmore............Fidelia	1852 05 03	
Kidgell............Charles Jr.	Cashmore...........Sarah Ann	1853 12 25	ENG, Bedford
Kilbourn..........Ozias Jr.	Granteer.............Electa	1832 11 28	CT, Canton
Kilpack............John	Sheriff...............Frances		
Kimball...........David Patten	Williams.............Caroline Marion	1857 04 13	UT, Salt Lake City
Kimball...........Heber Chase	Doty..................Eliza	1856 04 11	UT
Kimball...........Heber Chase	Fielding.............Mary	1844 09 14	
Kimball...........Heber Chase	Gheen.................Amanda Trimble	1845 12 01	IL, Nauvoo
Kimball...........Heber Chase	Gheen.................Ann Alice	1844 09 10	IL, Nauvoo
Kimball...........Heber Chase	Golden...............Christeen	1846 02 03	IL, Nauvoo
Kimball...........Heber Chase	Huntington..........Presendia L.	1846 11 07	
Kimball...........Heber Chase	McBride..............Martha	1846 01 26	IL, Nauvoo
Kimball...........Heber Chase	Murray...............Vilate	1822 11 07	NY, Mendon
Kimball...........Heber Chase	Sanders.............Ellen	1846 01 07	IL, Nauvoo
Kimball...........Heber Chase	Sanders.............Harriet	1846 01 07	IL, Nauvoo
Kimball...........Heber Chase	Shuler.................Sarah	1846 02 07	IL, Nauvoo
Kimball...........Heber Chase	Smithies.............Mary	1857 01 25	UT, Salt Lake City
Kimball...........Heber Chase	Swain.................Rebecca		
Kimball...........Heber Chase	Walker...............Lucy	1845 02 08	
Kimball...........Heber Chase	Whitney.............Sarah Ann	1846 01 12	IL, Nauvoo
Kimball...........Jeremiah H.	Davey.................Josephine		UT, Salt Lake City
Kimball...........William	Burton...............Melissa		
Kimball...........William Henry	Pack...................Lucy Amelia	1857 02 12	
Kimber...........Charles	Selwood.............Caroline	1841 08 02	ENG, Thatcham

Male		Female		Date	Place
Kinder	John Henry	Rusk	Hannah Mariah	1857 04 12	ENG, Dunkinfield
King	Daniel	Green	Mary	1855 10 29	UT, Salt Lake City
King	David A.	Hicks	Anna Hannah	1866	
King	Eleazer Jr.	Fowler	Mary Caroline	1853 04 27	UT, Salt Lake City
King	Enoch Marvin	Ware	Mary Bigg	1841 03 30	IL, Nauvoo
King	Franklin Ernest	Hall	Lulu May	1896 07 03	
King	George	Curtis	Sabrina	1846	
King	Hyrum Smith	Bennett	Alice	1864 01 01	UT, Kaysville
King	John	Griffin	Elizabeth	1868 11 01	UT, Salt Lake City
King	John	Serman	Eliza Hannah	1861 11 15	UT, Salt Lake City
King	Solomon	Leonard	Catherine Isabell	1876 01 17	
King	Thaddeus	Wright	Rosetta	1838 01	
King	Thomas Franklin	Ogden	Lucy Ann	1863 01 01	UT, Salt Lake City
King	Thomas J.	Olin	Rebecca E.	1827 07 08	VT, Shaftsbury
King	Thomas Rice	Robison	Matilda	1831 12 25	NY, Cicero
Kinghorn	Alexander Patrick	Campbell	Jane	1859 08	
Kingsbury	Joseph C.	Moore	Dorcas Adelia	1845 03 04	
Kingsbury	Joseph C.	Pond	Loenza	1846 01 27	IL, Nauvoo
Kingsford	Edward	Olsen	Helge	1861 12 25	
Kingsford	William	Horrocks	Elizabeth	1857 07 06	
Kinnersley	Henry	Statham	Martha	1836 05 17	
Kinney	Loren	Tucker	Mary Ann	1851 10 05	UT, Salt Lake City
Kinney	Loren	Tucker	Mary Ann		Remarried
Kinsman	Marshall C.	Snow	Sarah Jane	1853 12 05	UT, Provo
Kinyon	Aldric	Fenner	Prudence		
Kirby	Francis	Terry	Elizabeth	1833 07 18	
Kirk	William	Gheen	Louisa	1886	
Kirkham	George William	Astington	Mary Ann	1844 12 14	ENG, London
Kirkman	John	Jackson	Elizabeth	1856 12 13	UT, Salt Lake City
Kirkman	Robert L.	Lawson	Mary	1845 01 01	
Kite		Richards	Alice Howell		
Kjaer	Christian N.	Pedersen	Gertrude Marie	1847 08 31	Denmark
Kjar	Lars Christian	Christensen	Mette Marie	1843 12 01	Denmark
Kjar	Louis Christian	Jensen	Annie Edith	1884 11 14	UT, Logan
Kjar	Sixtus	Nybolle	Hansine Jacobine	1863 09 03	
Kleinman	Conrad	Benz	Anna	1857 02 08	UT, Salt Lake City
Kleinman	Conrad	Germer	Mary Ann	1857 04 08	UT, Salt Lake City
Kleinman	Conrad	Malholm	Elizabeth	1839 04	
Klemmensen	Peter Ankjar	Mathiason	Anna Emilie	1869	UT, Salt Lake City
Klingensmith	Phillip	Cattle	Betsy	1855 10 09	UT, Salt Lake City
Klingensmith	Phillip	Creemar	Hannah		
Klingensmith	Phillip	Elliker	Margaretha		
Knapp	Albert	Shepard	Rozina	1849 01 07	UT, Salt Lake City
Knapp	John Claus	Roberts	Cyrene Elsie	1860	
Knell	Robert	Crook	Mary	1855 02 23	UT, Kaysville
Knight	Charles	Lampitt	Elizabeth	1840	ENG, Worcester.
Knight	James Philander	Jones	Elizabeth	1860 08 08	
Knight	John	Watson	Mary Amelia	1835	ENG
Knight	Joseph	Judd	Jane Lucinda	1863 02 17	
Knight	Joseph Jr.	Covert	Betsy	1832 03 22	OH, Kirtland
Knight	Newel	Goldthwaite	Lydia	1835 11 23	OH, Kirtland
Knight	Vinson	McBride	Martha	1826 07 26	NY
Knight	William Thomas R.	Holden	Jane Eliza	1868 03 21	UT, Salt Lake City
Knighton	George	Wrigley	Catherine	1824 08 23	ENG, Eastwood

Male	Female	Date	Place
Knowles..........William H.	Croft...................Elizabeth	1851 08 10	ENG, Preston
Knowlton..........Benjamin Franklin	Richards.............Rhoda Ann J.	1863 10 13	UT, Salt Lake City
Knowlton..........Sidney A.	Burnham ....Harriet	1816 06 30	
Knowlton..........Sidney A.	Mortensen..........Maren	1863 01 17	
Knowlton..........Sidney A.	Yorston..............Cecelia	1855 03 25	
Knox ....William	Tweddle ....Elizabeth	1842 08 01	ENG, Durham
Knudsen ....Hans	Larsen ....Bergitte	1850 04 16	Norway
Knudsen ....John	Andersen............Karen	1857 08 21	
Knudsen ....Jorgen	Nielsen ....Anna Sophia	1855 01 13	UT, Salt Lake City
Knudsen ....Neils	Johansen ....Laurine W.	1869 05 30	UT, Deweyville
Koepernick ......Charles Robert	Kelly ....Emily	1862 11 06	UT, Salt Lake City
Kofford............Paul Ernest	Merrick ....Fanny	1849 07 29	MO, St. Louis
Kofoed ....Hans A.	Christensen........Karen Marie		
Kofoed ....Hans A.	Munch ....Cecillia	1838 11 17	Denmark
Kotter ....Herman H. L.	Boserup..............Petrina Henrietta	1866 07 29	NE, Wyoming
Koyle ....Hyrum	McCurdy..............Nancy	1838	
Koyle ....John Hyrum	Hillman ....Adalinda	1861 11 25	UT, Spanish Fork
Krogue ....Jens Peter	Nelson................Charlotte Amelia	1857	UT, Salt Lake City

L

Male	Female	Date	Place
Labrum ....Thomas	George ....Elizabeth	1837 11 12	ENG
Laird ....James	Renny.................Mary	1847 08 20	Scotland
Lake................Bailey	Marler.................Sarah Jane		
Lake................James Jr.	Smith..................Philomela	1823 09 03	
Lake................Joseph	Tristram..............Lucy	1872 11	UT, Henefer
Lake................William	Court ....Emmeline	1832 02 12	ENG, North Molton
Lake................William B.	Marler.................Sarah Jane	1850 12 26	
Laker ....Lashbrook	Bryceson ....Annie	1855 08 19	ENG
Lamb	Davey.................Rosina		
Lamb ....Abel	Merrill ....Almira	1826	
Lamb ....Benjamin Rush	Dubois................Elizabeth	1842 09 26	PA, Philadelphia
Lamb ....Brigham Young	Inkley.................Sarah Ann	1883	UT
Lamb ....Erastus	Jackson..............Abigail Mindwell	1829	NY
Lamb ....James Jackson	Ross...................Sarah Elizabeth	1863 03 21	UT, Salt Lake City
Lamb ....James Orrin	Fillmore..............Mary Jane	1854 02 22	NY, Rochester
Lamb ....Lisbon	Smith..................Sobrina	1866 02 03	UT, Salt Lake City
Lambert ....Abial	Philbrook............Sophia Wing	1823	
Lambert ....Charles	Cannon ....Mary Alice	1844 11 28	IL, Nauvoo
Lambert ....Charles John	Druce ....Lilly Harriet A.	1867 10 26	UT, Salt Lake City
Lambert ....John	Groesbeck..........Adelia	1846 02 06	IL, Nauvoo
Lambert ....John	Larsen ....Elena Hancena	1855 06 10	UT, Salt Lake City
Lambert ....Richard	Vay.....................Patience	1811 10 06	ENG
Lambert ....William	Greenfield ....Ann	1839	ENG
Lambourne ......William Jr.	Wernham ....Martha	1868 02 29	UT, Salt Lake City
Lambson..........Alfred B.	Keller..................Nancy Ann	1852 04 18	
Lamoreaux ......David Burlock	Gribble ....Mary Ann	1838 05 31	OH, Chardon
Lance..............Lewis	Tomlinson ....Temperance	1861 05 21	TX
Lance..............Samuel	Allard..................Marie Louise	1815	Canada
Lang ....Benjamin	Tull ....Ann	1856 02 18	ENG
Lang ....John	Stanfield ....Elizabeth	1867 10 10	UT, Salt Lake City
Lang ....William	Baker..................Mary Ann	1861 03 29	UT, Salt Lake City
Lang ....William	Bowden ....Mary	1822 02 11	ENG, Moulton

Male	Female	Date	Place
Lang ....William	Puglsey ....Mary	1851 07 04	IL, Troy
Lang ....William T.	Browning ....Sarah Ann	1847 05 29	
Langford ....James H.	Turnbaugh..........Mary Caroline	1856 09 14	
Langley............George W.	Frost....................Martha M.	1846 01 20	IL, Nauvoo
Langton ....James	Haydock..............Ellen	1826 04 09	ENG
Langston..........John	Freestone............Elizabeth Ann	1857 03 07	
Lapish..............Joseph	Settle..................Hannah	1853 07 03	ENG
Larsen ....Anders	Jensen ....Maren	1841 05 21	Denmark
Larsen ....Anders	Nielsen..............Margrethe	1827 10 23	Denmark
Larsen ....Bent Rolfson	Sorensen............Julianna Marie	1873 06 30	UT, Salt Lake City
Larsen ....Christian	Larsen ....Marianne	1868 12 21	UT, Salt Lake City
Larsen ....Christian	Peterson............Johanna	1866 02	UT, Spanish Fork
Larsen ....Christian Greis	Christiansen........Anna Marie	1860 01 15	UT, Salt Lake City
Larsen ....Christian Greis	Johnson ....Annetta	1864 04 09	UT, Salt Lake City
Larsen ....Christian Greis	Sorensen............Karen Marie	1857 04 01	Denmark
Larsen ....Christian Jens	Olsen..................Barbara J. D.	1853 10 30	Denmark
Larsen ....Gunder	Poulsen ....Antonette	1840 04 04	Denmark
Larsen ....Hans	Bentzen..............Elina D. S.	1836 08 05	Denmark
Larsen ....Hans	Hansen................Karen Kirstine	1849 11 14	Denmark
Larsen ....Hans	Mikkelsen ....Jensine Dorthea	1862	UT, Salt Lake City
Larsen ....Jens	Jacobsen..............Christine Marie	1836 09 02	Denmark
Larsen ....Jens	Sorensen............Ingeborg	1829 11 11	Denmark
Larsen ....Johane	Lausten ....Johanna Kirstine	1836 10 07	Denmark
Larsen ....Johannes	Jensen ....Anna	1866 11 25	UT, Salt Lake City
Larsen ....Johannes	Jorgensen ....Anna	1850	Denmark
Larsen ....John Christian	Mortensen..........Sarah	1872 09 30	UT, Salt Lake City
Larsen ....John Christian	Tittensor ....Mary Ellen	1877 02 07	UT, Logan
Larsen ....John Christian	Tittensor ....Susannah	1877 02 07	UT, Logan
Larsen ....John Niels	Larson ....Kjersti	1869 09 15	
Larsen ....Lars	Mathiesen ....Karen Sophia	1864	UT, Cottonwood
Larsen ....Lars	Pedersen............Inger	1857 11 13	Denmark
Larsen ....Lars	Pedersen............Kirsten	1856 11 16	UT, Brigham City
Larsen ....Lars Christian	Bertelsen............Maren		Denmark
Larsen ....Lars Kervin	Petersen..............Josephine M.	1870 05 10	UT, Logan
Larsen ....Lars Peter	Andersen............Bertha Christine	1874 10 14	UT, Salt Lake City
Larsen ....Lauritz Edward	Nielsen ....Karen	1864 09 15	UT, Salt Lake City
Larsen ....Marinus	Johnson ....Johanna	1869 12 20	UT, Salt Lake City
Larsen ....Neils	Anderson............Inger Marie	1848 11 11	Denmark
Larsen ....Niels Peter	Svendsen ....Karen Kirstine	1855 04 12	Denmark
Larsen ....Ole	Bentson..............Ingeborg Maria	1843 02 02	Norway
Larsen ....Oluf Christian	Pederson............Anna Maria	1863	
Larsen ....Peder	Pedersen............Sidse	1847 11 06	Denmark
Larsen ....Peder	Thomasen ....Ane	1820 05 17	Denmark
Larsen ....Soren	Bertelsen............Fredrikke C.	1864 07 02	UT, Salt Lake City
Larsen ....Soren	Fredericksen ......Maria	1854 12 10	Ocean
Larsen ....Soren C.	Sorensen............Jensine Christine	1855 09 14	Denmark
Larsen ....Svend	Hjetting..............Helsine	1858 01 11	
Larsen ....Svend	Hjetting..............Mette Marie	1861	UT
Larsen ....Tollef	Jacobsen..............Berte	1810 12 06	Norway
Larson ....Hans	Pedersen............Ane Marie	1866	Ocean
Larson ....Eric	Olafson................Sarah Britta	1860 12 31	Sweden
Larson ....John	Andersen............Else Marie	1864	
Larson ....John	Weight................Amelia	1855 10 08	
Larson ....Jons	Hansen................Anna Catharina	1838 11 30	Sweden

Male	Female	Date	Place
Larson ....Lars	Bellows................Mary Adelphia	1848	IA, Council Bluffs
Larson ....Mons	Malmstrom ....Ellen (Elna)	1852	Sweden
Larson ....Peter	Larsen ....Karen	1868 11 09	UT, Salt Lake City
Larson ....Pehr	Martenson ....Cecilia	1851 09 14	Sweden
Larson ....Thurston	Fox ....Elizabeth Mary	1859	
Larter ....Henry Neech	Armitage...............Harriet	1849 12 25	ENG
Larter ....Henry Neech	Armitage...............Harriet	1860 12 02	UT
Lasell ....James	Williams...............Harriet Cordelia	1873 06 04	
Lasson.............Ola	Jonson ....Sissa	1840 12 30	Sweden
Later ....Peter	Brown..................Elizabeth Daniels	1863 05 25	UT
Latimer ....John	Jensen ....Petrea	1884 06 19	UT, Salt Lake City
Latimer ....Thomas	Hardie ....Ann	1856 02 10	UT, Salt Lake City
Lattmann ....Hans Heinrich	Furrer ....Elisabetha	1837	
Laub ....George	Ericksen ....Anna Elizabeth	1856	UT, Salt Lake City
Laub ....George	McGinness ....Mary Jane	1846 01 06	IL, Nauvoo
Lauritzen.........Lauritz	Pedersen..............Maria	1847 05 01	Denmark
Law ....Charles	Bocock ....Elizabeth	1858 01 31	UT, Salt Lake City
Lawrence ....Francis	Garlick.................Mary Jane	1855	
Lawrenson.......William	Quick...................Ann	1824 04 19	ENG, Liverpool
Lawson ....Joseph	Greenway............Ruth Margaret	1855 09 09	UT, Salt Lake City
Lay...................William Harvey	Crosby.................Sytha	1841 12 18	MS, Aberdeen
Layne...............David	Bybee..................Lucinda	1827 09 27	KY, Barren Co.
Layton..............Charles	Bowler ....Elizabeth	1854 01 26	UT, Salt Lake City
Layton..............Christopher	Barnes.................Sarah	1852 09 26	UT, Salt Lake City
Layton..............Christopher	Golightly ....Isabella	1854 12 17	
Layton..............Christopher	Sims ....Hanna M. S.	1865 01 07	UT, Salt Lake City
Lazenby	Scott...................Elizabeth	1851	UT
Leah ....James H.	Berry ....Sarah M.		ENG
Leany...............William	Condie................Mary		UT, Salt Lake City
Leany...............William	Scearce..............Elizabeth	1845 09 07	IL, Nauvoo
Leatham ....Robert U.	Steele..................Jane	1847 12 25	Scotland
Leaver ....Samuel	Hartlett ....Mary Ann	1831 03 11	NY, Brooklyn
Leaver ....Samuel Hartlett	Spriggs................Mary Ann	1868 09 05	UT, Salt Lake City
Leavitt.............George	Brinkerhoff..........Jeanette	1852 08 29	UT, Salt Lake City
Leavitt.............George	Earl.....................Nancy Minerva	1857 07 11	UT, Salt Lake City
Leavitt.............Jeremiah	Sturdevant...........Sarah	1817 03 06	
Leavitt.............Jeremiah III	Harrover ....Eliza	1845 02 01	IL, Nauvoo
Leavitt.............Lemuel S.	Morgan................Mary Ann	1873 11 17	UT, St. George
Leavitt.............Lemuel S.	Mortensen ....Betsy Amelia	1863 10 13	UT
Leavitt.............Lemuel S.	Thompson ....Laura Melvina	1850 08 12	UT, Salt Lake City
Leavitt.............Nathaniel Jr.	Horrocks..............Mary	1857 04 04	UT, Salt Lake City
Leavitt.............Thomas Rowell	Davenport ....Antoinette	1861 03 09	UT, Salt Lake City
Leavitt.............Weare	Cowles ....Abigail		
Leavitt.............Weare	Cowles ....Phoebe		NH
LeBaron..........Alonzo	Steadwell ....Sarah (Sally)		
Lebaron ....David Tulley	Johnson ....Esther Maleta	1844 03 28	NY
Ledingham.......Alexander Morris	Griffiths...............Mary Jo	1873	
Lee ....Alfred	Laflesh ....Elizabeth		
Lee ....Alfred Gilham	Orme ....Rebecca	1857 03 10	
Lee ....Christian	Jensen ....Kirsten Marie	1854 01 26	Denmark
Lee ....Christian	Madsen ....Sophia Karen	1862 11 15	UT, Salt Lake City
Lee ....Christian	Mogensen ....Inger	1840 09 26	
Lee ....Ezekiel	Fisher.................Fannie Brittania	1857 05 12	UT, Salt Lake City
Lee ....Ezekiel	Strong ....Elizabeth	1822 01 31	

Male	Female	Date	Place
Lee ....Francis	Johnson ....Jane Vail	1835 10 24	
Lee ....John	Arrondale ....Emmeline	1830 12 05	ENG
Lee ....John	Roebuck.............Sarah	1841 11 15	ENG
Lee ....John Alma	Williams.............Mary Ann	1859 01 18	UT
Lee ....John Doyle	Bean...................Nancy	1844 11 04	
Lee ....John Doyle	Berry ....Martha Elizabeth	1846	IL, Nauvoo
Lee ....John Doyle	Gordge ....Ann	1865 06 10	UT, Salt Lake City
Lee ....John Doyle	Morse ....Teresa	1859 03 18	
Lee ....John Doyle	Shaffer ....Abigail	1845 05 03	
Lee ....John Doyle	Williams.............Mary Ann	1858	
Lee ....John Doyle	Woolsey ....Agatha Ann	1833 07 24	IL, Vandelia
Lee ....John Doyle	Young................Lavina	1847 02 27	NE
Lee ....John Doyle	Young................Mary Vance	1847 02 27	NE
Lee ....John Nelson	Rollins ....Melissa Kezia	1863 12 30	
Lee ....Joseph Hyrum	Woolsey ....Mary Elizabeth	1863 01 02	
Lee ....Lars Christian	Mogensen ....Inger	1867 11 30	
Lee ....Niels Peter	Larsen ....Marie		
Lee ....Niels Peter	Mikkelsen ....Helene	1864 04 30	Ocean
Lee ....Orin Strong	Miles..................Sarah Ann	1859 10 30	UT, Salt Lake City
Lee ....Samuel Francis	White.................Ann	1853 01 18	
Lee ....Thomas	Shields ....Primrose	1857 03 10	UT, Salt Lake City
Lee ....William Henry	Carter ....Harriet Amelia	1849 03 11	IA, Carterville
Leemaster ....Jonathan	Brown.................Caroline	1863 10 30	UT, Gunnison
Lees................John	Needham ....Martha	1853 06	ENG
Lees................Samuel	Staff...................Willoughby	1869 10 12	UT, Salt Lake City
Leetham ....John	Clarkson.............Ann	1848 08 31	ENG, Hull
LeFever ....Thomas	Steele.................Mary Campbell	1856	
LeFevre ....John	Dalton.................Ann	1829 06 21	ENG
Lefevre ....William	Banks ....Frances		
Lefevre ....William	Holyoak ....Hannah	1855 12 25	
Lehmann ....John	Gering ....Anna	1850 05 27	Switzerland
Leigh...............Samuel	Treharne ....Mary	1850 06	IA, Council Bluffs
Leishman........James A.	Thomas ....Catherine White	1857 11 30	UT, Cedar Fort
Leishman........John Allan	McCormick.........Ann	1852 01 23	Scotland
Leishman........John Campbell	Allan..................Jean (Jane)	1828 06 03	Scotland
Leithead..........James	Gardner.............Lucinda	1856 05 07	UT, Salt Lake City
Lemmon ....James A.	Nielsen ....Olevia Dorthea	1866 03 26	UT, Toquerville
Lemmon ....John	Abbott................Priscilla	1804 07 21	TN, Gallatin
Lemmon ....John	Sampson............Mary Jane	1852	
Lemmon ....Oliver Perry	Helm..................Caroline		
Lemmon ....Oliver Perry	Miller ....Mary Olsen	1886 10 13	UT, Salt Lake City
Lemmon ....Washington	Sharp ....Rachel	1856	UT
Lemmon ....Washington	Stephens............Tamer	1826 08 31	IN, Croydon
Lemmon ....Washington	Walters...............Ann	1863	UT
Lemmon ....Willis	Homer ....Anna Eliza	1859 11 01	UT, Salt Lake City
Lemons...........George	Durfee ....Marion Braidfoot		
Leonard ....Bradford	Janes ....Ann Elizabeth	1837	
Leonard ....Bradford	Madsen ....Petrea E. M	1858 02 02	
Leonard ....George Bradford	Picknell..............Sarah	1864 04 30	UT, Salt Lake City
Leonard ....George Bradford	Snider (Hillock)....Julia Ann	1857 03 15	
Leonard ....John Chatfield	Dilworth ....Maria Louisa	1855 02 22	
Leonard ....Truman	Bourne ....Margaret Evans	1857 01 06	UT, Salt Lake City
Leonard ....Truman	Meadows............Mary Ann	1857 01 06	UT, Salt Lake City
Leonard ....Truman	White.................Ortentia		

Male	Female	Date	Place
Leslie ....Andrew	Thompson ....Ann	1829 07 12	Scotland
Levi ....Abram	Wardrobe ....Mary		
Lewis ....Beason	Ryon.................Elizabeth	1846 02 06	
Lewis ....David	Carson ....Elizabeth	1852 08 04	UT, Salt Lake City
Lewis ....David	Gibson...............Mary	1850	UT, Weber Co.
Lewis ....David	Trail...................Duritha	1834 11 23	KY, Franklin
Lewis ....Elias	Roberts.............Eleanor	1856 06 04	IA, Iowa City
Lewis ....Frederick	Ferguson............Agnes Reid	1865 01 28	UT, Spanish Fork
Lewis ....Frederick	Hillman..............Adalinda	1876 10 17	UT, Salt Lake City
Lewis ....Henry	Steadwell ....Sarah (Sally)		
Lewis ....James	Cox...................Ann Marie		
Lewis ....James	Holman..............Emily Jennison	1847 05 09	MO. St. Louis
Lewis ....James	Thayne ....Ellen Jane	1870	UT, Salt Lake City
Lewis ....James Stapleton	Jones ....Nancy Hannah	1833 05 10	MO, Jackson Co.
Lewis ....James Stapleton	Svensson ....Anna Maria		
Lewis ....Jesse William	Fuller.................Mary Adelia	1855 12 27	IA, Des Moines
Lewis ....John A.	Merriman............Priscilla	1851 08 30	Wales
Lewis ....John Moss	Crismon.............Martha Jane	1848 08 10	UT, Salt Lake City
Lewis ....John Moss	Staley (widow).....		
Lewis ....John Moss	Wilde.................Sarah		
Lewis ....John Moss	Woods...............Elizabeth		
Lewis ....Joseph	Freeman.............Eliza	1844 08 11	ENG
Lewis ....Joseph	King...................Ann	1859 05 01	
Lewis ....Joseph	King...................Elizabeth Ann	1865 06 03	UT
Lewis ....Nathan	Tompkins ....Eliza	1869 10 25	
Lewis ....Neriah Jr.	Hendricks...........Rebecca	1836	KY, Simpson Co.
Lewis ....Neriah Robert	Allred.................Amanda Jane	1864 01 20	UT, Richmond
Lewis ....Orrin	Christmas............Maria	1860 07 11	UT, Salt Lake City
Lewis ....Preston King	Bowthorpe...........Virtue Ann	1857 01 04	UT, Salt Lake City
Lewis ....Preston King	Coleman.............Sarah	1869 09 13	
Lewis ....Richard	Jones ....Susannah	1869	WY, Evanston
Lewis ....Richard	Richards.............Alice Howell		
Lewis ....Rufus	Llewellyn ....Ann	1861 04 16	UT, Provo
Lewis ....Samuel	Huntsman............Sarah Jane	1854 01 01	UT, Parowan
Lewis ....Siney	Coleman.............Elizabeth	1874 01 05	UT, Salt Lake City
Lewis ....Tarleton	Carson ....Elizabeth	1856	UT, Parowan
Lewis ....Tarleton	Gimlin.................Malinda	1828 03 27	KY, Simpson Co.
Lewis ....William	Arms...................Charity	1850	
Lewis ....William S.	Jones ....Rachel		
Lewis ....William S.	Walsh.................Sarah	1868 12 01	UT, Salt Lake City
Lienhard ....Samuel	Muller ....Margaritha		
Lightner ....Adam	Rollins ....Mary Elizabeth	1835 08 11	MO, Clay Co.
Liljenquist ....Ola	Jacobsen.............Anna Christine	1848	Denmark
Liljenquist ....Ola	Nielsen ....Anne Christine	1874 08 10	UT, Salt Lake City
Lincoln ....Charles	Hoopes..............Rebecca Ann	1860 02 26	UT, Bountiful
Lind.................Jens C. A.	Nielsen ....Mary Ann	1847 04 01	Denmark
Lindahl............Sven Nilsson	Anderson............Christina Amalia	1868 05 09	UT, Salt Lake City
Lindroth ....Peter Erick	Bjorklund ....Adolphine	1850	Sweden
Lindsay ....James	Watson...............Agnes	1871 01 09	UT, Salt Lake City
Lindsay ....Robert McQueen	Geddes...............Elizabeth	1820 07 14	Scotland
Lindsay ....William	Howie ....Christina	1844 07 19	Scotland
Lindsay ....William B.	Myers ....Sarah	1819	Canada
Lindsay ....William B. Jr.	Henderson ....Sarah Elizabeth	1854 02 19	UT, Salt Lake City
Lindsay ....William B. Jr.	Parks.................Julia	1845 02 19	IL, Nauvoo

Male	Female	Date	Place
Lines.............Henry	Weech.............Emily	1869 12 10	UT, Goshen
Lines.............John	Haddon.............Jane	1838 10 30	ENG, Dunchurch
Linford.............James Henry	Crockett.............Zillah	1862 01 19	UT, Salt Lake City
Linford.............John	Christian.............Maria Bentley	1833 06 24	ENG, Gravely
Lish.............Henry Doctor	Allen.............Emily	1861 04 04	UT, Calls Fort
Lish.............William Seely Jr.	Moss.............Sarah Jane M.	1879 12 25	ID, Malad
Lisonbee.............Coker	Callaham.............Mary Ann	1825 02 01	AL, St. Clair Co.
Lisonbee.............William W.	Fullmer.............Mary Ann	1864 02 16	UT, Springville
Lister.............John Henry	Rogerson.............Sarah Ann	1860 02 03	UT, Parowan
Lister.............Richard	Ward.............Fanny		ENG
Liston.............Commodore P.	Reeves.............Elizabeth	1844 07 01	IN, Muncie
Litson.............Joseph Young	Glade.............Mary Jane	1878 05 09	UT
Litson.............Richard	Matthews.............Frances Ann	1845 02 08	
Little.............Edwin Sobieski	Decker.............Harriet Amelia	1842 03 22	
Little.............George Edwin	Taylor.............Martha	1862 01 05	UT, Salt Lake City
Little.............James	Young.............Susannah	1815	NY, Aurelius
Little.............James Amasa	Baldwin.............Hannah Matilda	1858 12	
Little.............James Amasa	Lytle.............Mary Jane	1849 12 16	UT, Salt Lake City
Little.............James Amasa	Tullidge.............Mary Elizabeth	1864 11 19	
Little.............Jesse Carter	French.............Eliza Greenwood	1840 09 29	
Little.............Jesse Carter	Hoagland.............Emily		
Little.............Jesse Carter	Holbrook.............Mary Maria	1856 01 29	
Littlefield.............Lyman O.	Hamblin.............Adeline Amarilla	1846 01 31	
Littlefield.............William David	Toomer.............Ann	1847 10 24	
Littlewood.............Martin	Parkes.............Annie	1859 05 07	
Livermore.............John	Filby.............Mary	1835 11 29	
Livingston.............Charles	Harrocks.............Ellen	1867 10 12	UT, Salt Lake City
Livingston.............Charles	Harrocks.............Jane	1861 05 25	UT, Salt Lake City
Livingston.............James	Livingston.............Christina C.	1807 10 09	
Livingston.............James Campbell	Widdison.............Agnes	1854 06 07	
Livingston.............James Campbell	Widdison.............Hannah	1862 02 15	UT, Salt Lake City
Llewellyn.............Edmund	Howells.............Mary	1834 05 10	Wales
Lloyd.............John	Goff.............Ruth	1875 11 15	UT, Salt Lake City
Lloyd.............John Heber	Jones.............Sarah Jane	1880 08 05	UT, Salt Lake City
Lloyd.............Thomas	Stone.............Susannah	1856 11 06	
Lloyd.............Thomas William	Lea.............Elizabeth Lamb	1877 02 26	UT, Farmington
Lloyd.............William	Bowen.............Ann Mariah		
Lloyd.............William John	Wilson.............Rachel	1888 09 02	
Loader.............James	Britnell.............Amy	1821 09 09	ENG
Lockhart.............John	Towery.............Margaret Maria	1834	MS, Monroe
Lofthouse.............Anthony	Lofthouse.............Ann	1827 02 01	ENG
Lofthouse.............James	Woodhead.............Charlotte E.	1856 02 19	UT, Ogden
Logan.............John	Bathgate.............Mary		
Logie.............Charles J. G.	Friedlander.............Rosa Clara	1853 05 21	Australia
London.............John	Smith.............Hannah Elizabeth	1863 10 08	UT, Coalville
Long.............Emanuel	Maddison.............Flora Louisa	1855 01 23	UT, Salt Lake City
Long.............James P.	Cocks.............Emily Ann	1847	
Long.............John	Baker.............Emma	1866 03 18	UT
Longhurst.............William Henry	Preston.............Ann	1846 01 01	ENG, Kent
Loose.............Robert	Tenney.............Betsy Jane	1844 01 24	IL, Quincy
Loosle.............Hans Casper	Faster.............Anna		
Loosle.............Hans Casper	Hundsperger.............Anna Elizabeth	1857 04 23	Switzerland
Lossee.............Abraham	Lott.............Mary Elizabeth	1848 11 12	UT, Salt Lake City
Lossee.............David Alma	Sims.............Priscilla	1905 02 01	UT

Male		Female		Date	Place
Lott	Cornelius Peter	Darrow	Permelia	1823 04 27	PA, Bridgewater
Lott	Cornelius Peter	Fausett	Narcissus R.	1846 01 22	
Lott	Peter Lyman	Snow	Sariah Hannah	1862 12 23	UT, Salt Lake City
Love	Andrew	Bigelow	Nancy Maria	1834 12 08	IL
Love	David	Hunter	Margaret	1851 07 03	MO, St. Louis
Love	Thomas	Merritt	Ellen Coil		
Love	Thomas	Thorn	Elizabeth		
Loveland	Chester	Call	Fanny	1838 02 15	OH, Madison
Loveland	Chester	Faulkner	Louisa	1868 09 05	UT, Salt Lake City
Loveland	Chester	Simmons	Celia Leonora	1854 01 21	UT, Calls Fort
Loveland	Chester	Snow	Rosetta Adaline	1866 11 17	UT, Salt Lake City
Loveland	Chester	Winters	Rosannah E.	1846 01 15	IL, Nauvoo
Loveland	Joel Chauncey	Simmons	Amanda	1857 12 13	UT, Salt Lake City
Loveless	Hyrum Smith	Wimmer	Eliza Jane	1870 04 27	
Loveless	James W.	McClellan	Matilda Elizabeth	1847 03 09	IA, Council Bluffs
Loveless	John	Anderson	Rachel Mahala	1826 01 25	
Lovell	George	Turner	Martha	1862 01 28	UT, Deseret
Lovell	John	Parsons	Ann	1835 02 15	ENG
Lovell	John	Pedersen	Ane	1857 04 04	UT
Lovell	John	Smith	Elizabeth	1852 03 10	IA, Big Bend
Loveridge	Alexander H.	Thomas	Malinda S.	1849 04 12	NE, Patanant
Loveridge	Ambrose	Marsh	Phylinda	1815 06 30	NY, Bristol
Low	Thomas	Sharp	Janet	1820 12 08	Scotland
Lowder	John	Hodgetts	Emily Teressa	1860 05 25	UT, Salt Lake City
Lowe	John	Cole	Mary Ann Gavett		
Lowe	John	Trumble	Lois Alexander	1840 11 09	MA, Salem
Lowe	Richard	Clements	Ada	1855 05 11	
Lowe	Richard Alvin	Pectol	Elizabeth	1880	UT, Springville
Lowe	Thomas	Galloway	Eliza	1849 02 03	Scotland
Lowell	William	Richards	Alice Howell		
Lowry	John	Johnston	Anna Maria	1853 02 13	UT, Manti
Lowry	John	Wilcox	Mary	1824 02 01	MO, Madison Co.
Lowry	John Jr.	Brown	Sarah Jane	1851 11 27	UT, Manti
Loynd	James	Earney	Mary Ena	1876 03 15	UT, Salt Lake City
Lucas	Hyrum John	Kjellerman	Josefina A. G.	1883 08 09	UT, Salt Lake City
Luckham	Roger	Gardner	Mary	1846	Canada
Ludvigson	Erick	Steck	Anna Louise	1862 07 19	UT, Salt Lake City
Lufkin	George W.	Townsend	Martha Ann	1854 07 09	UT, Salt Lake City
Lufkin	Samuel Henry	Johnson	Eleanor	1815	
Luke	William Jr.	Haydock	Mary	1857 01 10	UT, Salt Lake City
Lund	Paul Didrick S.	Sorensen	Anna Marie	1845 08 12	Denmark
Lund	Wilson	Nielsen	Ellen	1858 02 28	
Lundblad	Hans	Mortensen	Charste	1845 12 27	Sweden
Lunt	Henry	Gower	Ann	1863 04 11	UT, Salt Lake City
Lyman	Amasa Mason	Partridge	Caroline Ely	1844 09 06	IL, Nauvoo
Lyman	Amasa Mason	Partridge	Eliza Maria	1845 09 28	IL, Nauvoo
Lyman	Amasa Mason	Partridge	Lydia	1853 02 07	UT, Salt Lake City
Lyman	Amasa Mason	Phelps	Paulina Eliza	1843 01 15	IL, Nauvoo
Lyman	Amasa Mason	Tanner	Maria Louisa	1835 06 10	OH, Kirtland
Lyman	Amasa Mason	Walker	Diontha	1845 07	IL, Nauvoo
Lyman	Francis Marion	Taylor	Rhoda Ann	1857 11 18	CA, San Bern.
Lynch	Daniel	Kelley	Martha	1828	KY, Westerveill
Lynch	Patrick	Alley	Elizabeth Royce	1857 07 16	
Lyon	John	Holland	Caroline	1856 03 28	

Male	Female	Date	Place
Lyon............John	Thomson............Janet	1825 12 01	Scotland
Lyon............Luther Peet	Baxter............Elizabeth Harvey	1865 08 26	UT, Salt Lake City
Lyon............Thomas	Higgins............Mary Ann	1849 01 01	Scotland
Lyons............Caleb W.	Bigler............Sarah	1840 01 16	IL, Nauvoo
Lyons............Oscar Fitzallen	Marchant............Maria Louisa	1870 09 05	UT, Salt Lake City
Lythgoe............James	Heelis............Martha	1864 04 17	ENG, Manchester
Lythgoe............James	Peterson............Hannah Sophia	1892 08 16	UT, Logan
Lythgoe............Thomas	Wilcock............Esther	1825 04 04	ENG, Lancashire
Lytle............John	Witner............Christine Diana	1827 02 22	

M

Male	Female	Date	Place
Mabey............Thomas	Chalker............Hester (Esther)	1837 05 07	ENG
MacDuff............John Robertson	Hancock............Ellen	1839 09 15	ENG, Nottingham.
Mace............George	Greenhalgh............Mary Ann	1869 06 21	UT, Salt Lake City
Mace............Hiram	Armstrong............Elizabeth	1837 04 04	IL, Nauvoo
Mack............John Fredrick	Pedersen............Ane Kirstine	1866 11 28	UT, Salt Lake City
Mackelprang....Peter Mathiasen	Sorenson............Sophie M. H.	1840 12 23	Denmark
Maddox............John	Colston............Catherine E.	1829 06 08	ENG, Surrey
Madison............John	Merrick............Maria Susanna	1831	ENG
Madsen............Andrew	Archibald............Alison	1884	
Madsen............Hans Peter	Ericksen............Anne Mette	1863 12 19	UT, Salt Lake City
Madsen............Hans Peter	Pedersen............Christina	1858	Denmark
Madsen............Jacob	Hansen............Dorothea Kirstine	1838 04 16	Denmark
Madsen............James Ephraim	Jensen............Birgithe	1869 07 06	UT, Salt Lake City
Madsen............Jens	Johansen............Laurine W.	1862 11 15	UT, Salt Lake City
Madsen............Jens	Pedersen............Ane Margrethe	1850 12 27	Denmark
Madsen............Jorgen	Andersen............Johanna (Hannah)	1870 12 12	UT, Salt Lake City
Madsen............Nels	Hansen............Martha Maria	1839 10 25	Denmark
Madsen............Niels	Christensen............Mette Marie	1838 10 19	Denmark
Madsen............Ole	Anderson............Mette Johanna	1864	UT, Manti
Madsen............Peter	Johnson............Lena	1865 09 02	UT, Salt Lake City
Madsen............Peter	Jorgensen............Wilhelmina	1864 05 14	UT, Salt Lake City
Madsen............Peter	Knudsen............Caroline	1860 04 25	UT, Salt Lake City
Madsen............Peter	Madsen............Mary Ann	1847 11 12	Denmark
Madsen............Peter Jr.	Knudsen............Bertha	1881 06 02	UT, Salt Lake City
Madson............Christian A.	Lundstrom............Gustava Amalea	1864 07 03	UT, Gunnison
Maeser............Karl Gottfried	Meith............Anna H. T.	1854 06 11	Germany
Maiben............Henry	Maddison............Flora Louisa	1855 07 20	UT, Salt Lake City
Maiben............Henry	Penn............Caroline	1845 12 18	ENG
Maiben............Henry Joseph	Harrison............Louisa Eveline	1880 12 30	UT, Salt Lake City
Maiben............John	Richards............Elizabeth	1856 04 22	UT, Salt Lake City
Maiben............John Bray	Richards............Phebe Eleanor	1855 04 09	ENG, London
Mair............Allan	Murdoch............Mary	1841 06 04	Scotland
Major............William D.	Cushing............Ellen Maria	1867 10 04	UT, Salt Lake City
Major............William D.	McMaster............Virginia F.	1869 08 30	UT, Salt Lake City
Malan............John Daniel	Combe............Pauline	1825 04 28	Italy
Malan............Stephen	Chestnut............Sarah Mary	1869 12 20	UT, Logan
Mallory............Lemuel	Hayden............Flora	1846 02 06	
Malmberg............John Peter	Magnussen............Johanna Maria	1857 10 16	Sweden
Malmberg............Samuel Carlsson	Persson............Hannah	1847 12 28	Sweden
Malmgren............Sven Peter	Rosequist............Johannah	1864 04 24	UT, Ephraim
Maloy............Patrick	Billington............Rebecca Delight	1827 03 01	OH, Portagelo

Male	Female	Date	Place
Mander ....Thomas	Lishman ....Maria	1854 02 17	
Mangum ....John III	Adair..................Mary Ann	1841	AL
Mangum ....John III	Bardsley ....Ellen		
Mangum ....John III	Hamblin ....Mary		
Mangum ....William	Potter ....Delight	1853	
Manhard ....William Henry	Jones ....Lina Meniza	1853 04	UT, Kanosh
Mann ....Charles William	Busby ....Annie Maria	1863 11 04	UT, Salt Lake City
Mann ....Oscar	Cunningham.......Miriam	1860 09 06	IA
Manning..........Eli	Hollist ....Deborah	1865 03 24	UT, Salt Lake City
Manning..........Henry William	Galbraith ....Margaret	1855 03 14	UT, Salt Lake City
Manning..........Joseph George	Vowels ....Mary	1829	ENG, Bristol
Manning..........Willard Callard	Elliott ....Elizabeth	1843 06 12	ENG
Mansfield ....Matthew	...............................Margaret	1857	
Mansfield ....Matthew	Winberg..............Johanna C.	1856 06 17	UT, Mill Creek
Mansor ....Barnett	Bybee.................Lucinda	1847 11	IA, Mt. Pisgah
Marble ....Nathaniel	King....................Mary		
Marble ....William Lorenzo	Hanchett.............Sarah Marinda	1852	
Marchant ....Abraham	Johnson ....Lydia	1837 02 07	ENG, Somerset
Marchant ....Abraham Robert	Barter (Cossey)...Mary Ann	1867 01 12	UT, Peoa
Marchant ....Albert George H.	Casper ....Harriet Matilda	1873 02 17	UT, Salt Lake City
Marchant ....Edmund	Olpin..................Mary Anne	1850 10 08	ENG
Marchant ....Edmund	Pettegrew............Lucy Ann	1857 03 15	UT, Salt Lake City
Marchant ....Edmund	Underhill..............Charlotte		
Marchant ....Franklin William	Pearson...............Anna	1875 02 15	UT, Salt Lake City
Marchant ....John Alma	Maxwell...............Jane Ann	1879	
Marchant ....John Alma	Russell ....Hannah Maria	1867 11 30	UT, Salt Lake City
Marcroft ....John	Taylor ....Charlotta W.	1834	ENG
Mariner ....Charles	Grace ....Sarah	1844	
Marker ....Jens Pedersen	Hansen...............Ellen Margrethe	1849 04 07	
Markham ....Stephen	Adamson.............Eliza Jane		
Markham ....Stephen	Curtis..................Mary	1850 10 05	UT, Salt Lake City
Markham ....Stephen	Fenner................Prudence	1846 01 30	IL, Nauvoo
Markham ....Stephen	Hogeboom ....Hannah	1824 02	
Marler ....Allen	Heath ....Harriet	1832 02 02	MS, Port Gibson
Marler ....George W.	Mathews..............Mary	1863 12 06	UT, Providence
Marler ....William Norton	Gates ....Lucetta Maria	1856 10 12	UT, Lynne
Marley............William	Cutler ....Helen Mar	1886	
Marriott ....John	Burton ....Margaret	1857 12 17	UT, Kaysville
Marriott ....John	Fowkes...............Susannah H.	1842 03 18	ENG, Bedfordshire
Marriott ....John	Southwick............Teresa	1855 11 05	UT, Marriott
Marriott ....John	Stewart...............Elizabeth	1854 02 26	UT, Salt Lake City
Marrott ....William	Fowlke................Louisa	1862 02 09	UT, Pleasant Grove
Marsden ....William	Cottam ....Ellen	1865 09 02	UT, Salt Lake City
Marsden ....William	Johnson ....Sarah		
Marsh ....George J.	Andrews ....Jane Rosetta	1854 02 27	UT, Salt Lake City
Marsh ....Josiah	Powell ....Sallie Clotilda	1826 10 12	NY, Randolph
Marshall..........George Thomas	Alder..................Mary Jane	1882 11 09	UT, Salt Lake City
Marshall..........George W. B.	Haines................Rebecca Ann	1842 01 25	OH, Clinton Co.
Marshall..........Robert	Sinclair ....Ann	1849	
Marshall..........Thomas	Goode ....Sarah	1843 05 07	ENG, Herefordshire
Marshall..........William	Allen ....Martha Evins	1862	CA, San Bern.
Marsing...........Niels Larson	Bedford ....Sarah	1870 09 05	UT, Kanosh
Marsing...........Niels Larson	Harmon ....Harriet		
Mart	Mulliner ....Elizabeth Smith		

Male	Female	Date	Place
Martell............Thomas C.	Jenkins...............Elizabeth	1858 01 15	
Martensson......Jeppa	Larsson ....Arna	1834 12 12	Sweden
Martin ....Anthony	Starley.................Jane	1859 02 04	UT, Fillmore
Martin ....Edward	Salmon................Eliza	1855	ENG
Martin ....Ezra Francis	Cook...................Eliza Oliver		
Martin ....Ezra Francis	Jenkins...............Eliza G. G.		
Martin ....Ezra Francis	Packer................Sophia		
Martin ....Ezra Francis	Taberer ....Sarah Ann	1863 06 20	
Martin ....James	Stockdale ....Mary Ann	1846	
Martin ....Jesse Bigler	Clark...................Ann	1857 12 20	
Martin ....Jesse Bigler	Moore..................Sophronia	1848 12 17	UT, Salt Lake City
Martin ....John	Sargent ....Sarah Ann	1855 06 03	UT, Salt Lake City
Martin ....Josiah Fleming	Fahy...................Catherine	1859 11 03	
Martin ....Robert	Thompson...........Susannah	1863 06 30	UT, Salt Lake City
Martin ....Thomas	Bathgate.............Mary		
Martindale.......William A.	Haines................Kindness Ann	1865 06 05	UT, Salt Lake City
Martindale.......William A.	Haines................Rebecca Ann	1854 04 24	UT, Salt Lake City
Martindale.......William Clinton	McMurray ....Matilda Jane	1854 05 05	UT, Grantsville
Mason.............George Sterling	Gardner..............Hannah	1855 03 22	UT, Riverdale
Mason.............Jesse	Billington ....Rebecca Delight	1823 08 05	MA, New Ashford
Mason.............William	Price...................Ann		
Matheny..........Celly F.	Land ....Sebrina	1827	MS, Monroe
Matheny..........Sims L.	Bishop ....Vesta Lucetta		
Mather ....James H.	Ditchfield ....Mary	1840 03 03	ENG, Manchester
Mather ....John	Johnson ....Mary	1829 12 20	ENG, Duffield
Mather ....Thomas	Cantwell ....Mary Ann	1870 12 05	UT, Salt Lake City
Matheson........Alexander	Evans ....Lydia	1864 08 01	
Matheson........Daniel	Treasurer ....Catherinne	1823 11 20	Scotland
Mathews ....Allen	Meredith ....Ann	1854	UT
Mathews ....Anson	Burgess..............Elizabeth	1811 09 15	MA, Franklin Co.
Mathews ....Hopkin	Morris.................Margaret	1844 06 17	Wales
Mathews ....James	Quinney..............Mary Ann	1892 10 17	
Mathews ....Joseph Davis	Perkins...............Ruth	1868 03 07	UT, Salt Lake City
Mathis.............Isaac	Ross...................Elizabeth	1822 02 20	TN, Paris Co.
Mathis.............John Thomas	Dowdle...............Sarah Ann	1849	IA, Council Bluffs
Matlock ....Gideon Cooper	Houston..............Susanna	1848	IA, Council Bluffs
Matthews ....Abel	Broom ....Jenette	1865 02 10	UT, Salt Lake City
Matthews ....Joseph Lazarus	Carroll ....Rhoda	1832 07 14	NC, Johnston
Maud ....Mathew	Haynes...............Jane		
Maughan ....Hyrum Weston	Hibbard ....Hannah White	1875 04 05	UT, Salt Lake City
Maughan ....John Harrison	Davenport ....Sarah Mariah	1853 07 24	
Maughan ....Joseph Weston	Utley..................Mildred Caroline	1872 12 20	UT, Salt Lake City
Maughan ....Peter	Weston...............Mary Ann	1841 11 02	IL, Nauvoo
Maughan ....William Harrison	Hill.....................Elizabeth Bryce	1860 06 02	UT, Wellsville
Maughan ....William Harrison	Morgan...............Barbara	1853 12 25	UT, Tooele
Maw................Edward	Goodman ....Keziah Miles	1864 03 07	
Mawson ....Robert	Dykman..............Maria Alida	1917	
Maxfield ....Elijah Hiett	Tanner................Helen Alcy	1856 08 24	UT, So. Cotton.
Maxfield ....Jessie LeRoy	Bates.................Mary Maria	1926	UT, Stockton
Maxfield ....Robert Quorton	Cahoon ....Sarah	1864 01 07	UT, Salt Lake City
Maxham..........Charles	Russell...............Matilda	1841 01 08	
Maxwell ....Arthur	Mcauslin.............Elizabeth	1856 05 08	Ocean
Maxwell ....James	Rands.................Jessie Lavina	1879 12 25	UT, Salt Lake City
Maxwell ....John Lambert	Hird ....Jane	1860 03 06	ENG, Yorkshire

Male	Female	Date	Place
Maxwell ....Ralph	Donely ....Elizabeth	1823 07 13	ENG, Cumberland
May................James	Allen ....Martha	1856 08 24	UT, Bountiful
May................James	Lang ....Rhoda Ann	1877 11 02	UT, St. George
Mayall ....Thomas	Harford ....Elizabeth	1815 10 12	ENG, Herefordshire
Mayberry ....James	McDonald...........Mary		
Maycock ....Amos	Hurst ....Mary Jane	1875 09 01	
Maycock ....James	Webley ....Susannah	1857	
Maycock ....Thomas	Starkey...............Louisa	1859 04 11	
Mayer ....George	Yost....................Ann	1828 03 04	PA
Mayer ....John	Littlewood............Jane Lovenia	1851 01 20	UT, Fairview
Mayhew ....Elijah	Farnsworth ....Lydia	1832 10 02	
Mayhew ....Elijah	Rogers ....Ann	1868 04 18	UT, Salt Lake City
McAdams ....Bernard A.	Jones ....Martha	1871 10 23	UT, Salt Lake City
McAdams ....Samuel S.	Bickmore ....Catherine Ann	1866 05 10	
McAffee ....John Sharp	Thompson ....Ann	1841 04 25	
McAlister..........Charles H. M.	Haig....................Mary	1849	ENG
McAlister..........Robert Wesley	Walling ....Emma Smith		
McAllister........Joseph W.	Miller ....Mary Ann	1876 02 14	UT, Salt Lake City
McAllister........Richard Wesley	Bell.....................Elizabeth Eleanor	1844	PA, Philadelphia
McAllister........William J. F.	Thompson ....Elizabeth	1822 04 04	
McArthur..........Daniel D.	Bullock ....Elizabeth	1857 02 13	UT, Salt Lake City
McArthur..........Daniel D.	Hill ....Mary	1857	UT, Salt Lake City
McArthur..........Duncan	McKeen...............Susan	1818 01 01	NY, Holland
McArthur..........Duncan	Scoville...............Eliza Rebecca	1857 10 23	UT, Salt Lake City
McArthur..........John Dickson	Abbott.................Sarah Elizabeth	1865 01 13	UT, Salt Lake City
McArthur..........Washington P.	Scoville...............Eliza Rebecca	1867 11 15	UT, Mt. Pleasant
McBride ....Daniel	Mead ....Abigail	1787	NY, Albany
McBride ....George	Miller ....Ruth Ann	1855 03 27	
McBride ....James	Cheney...............Olive Mehetable	1844 03 07	IL, Nauvoo
McBride ....James	Mead ....Betsy	1818	
McBride ....James	Miller ....Ruth Ann	1859 05 13	UT, Farmington
McBride ....James Andrew	Clark...................Elizabeth	1866 02 18	UT, Santaquin
McBride ....Peter	Kerr ....Agnes Archibald	1898 09	UT
McBride ....Robert	Howard...............Margaret Ann	1833 11 25	ENG
McBride ....William	Boram ....Elizabeth H. B.	1831 09 01	OH, Randolph
McBride ....William	Murray................Helen Janet	1855	UT, Salt Lake City
McCall ....James A.	Wallace ....Ann	1822	
McCann ....Thomas R.	Johnston ....Sarah	1835 05 11	ENG, Lancashire
McCarty ....Stephen	Waite..................Martha	1878 02 02	UT, Ogden
McCauslin........Jesse	Bennett...............Mary Jane	1848	
McCauslin........Jesse	Bennett...............Nancy Ellen	1851 10	UT
McCauslin........Jesse	Durham ....Tempey		
McClellan.........James	Goldthwaite.........Lydia	1860	UT, Payson
McClellan.........James	Stewart...............Cynthia	1826 01 18	
McClellan.........Samuel Wilburn	Stewart...............Almeda	1856 12 28	UT, Payson
McClellan.........William Carroll	Day.....................Almeda	1849 07 19	IA, Pott. Co.
McClenahan ....James Kemp	Kidd...................Catherine Orthelia	1853 03 13	UT, Salt Lake City
McClenahan ....James Kemp	Pollock ....Nancy Ann	1840 04 21	IL, Stark Co.
McCombs ....Andrew	Brown.................Amelia Lavilla	1857 04 19	UT, Salt Lake City
McCowan ....Robert	Skellington ....Elizabeth	1837 09 11	ENG
McCulloch........Henry	Smith..................Mary	1857 02 27	Scotland
McCulloch........John Black	McNeil ....Margaret	1852 06	Scotland
McCulloch........William Johnson	Davidson ....Ann	1852 03 19	Scotland
McCullough .....Henry Judson	Callister ....Helen Mar	1864 05 22	UT, Fillmore

Male	Female	Date	Place
McCune .... James	Hall .... Lulu May	1894 09 14	
McCurdy .... Albert Gallatin	Bonner .... Christina	1869 09 15	UT, Midway
McDaniel .... John	Stoker .... Christina	1835 02 08	OH
McDaniel .... Samuel James	Hadden .... Duritha	1873	
McDonald .... Alexander F.	Graham .... Elizabeth	1851 05 20	Scotland
McDonald .... Duncan	Thompson .... Ann	1865 07 29	UT
McDonald .... James	Ferguson .... Sarah	1826	IRE
McDonald .... John Kilpatrick	Johnson .... Sarah	1863 12 26	UT, Salt Lake City
McDonald .... John Kilpatrick	Marsden .... Clara St. Ledger	1872 05 26	UT, Salt Lake City
McDonald .... John Kilpatrick	Marsden .... Harriet Zelnora	1869 05 31	
McDonald .... John Kilpatrick	Taaffe .... Rachel Burke	1823 04	IRE
McDonald .... Joseph Smith	Cummings .... Nancy Elizabeth	1863	UT, Heber
McDonough ..... John	Looser .... Elizbaeth	1872	
McDougal .... Isaac	Hamilton .... Susannah	1867 07 13	
McEwen .... Matthew	Smith .... Mary	1833 05 13	Scotland
McFarland .... Archibald	Mitchell .... Isabella	1854 08 03	Scotland
McFarland ...... James	Boyack .... Hannah	1855 12 06	UT, West Weber
McFarland ...... James	Pool .... Matilda	1867 06 03	UT, Salt Lake City
McFarland .... William	McCormick .... Margaret	1832 01 09	Scotland
McFarlane ...... Daniel S.	Haight .... Temperance K.	1862 02 12	UT, Cedar City
McFarlane ...... James	Smuin .... Martha Ann	1867 10 05	UT, Salt Lake City
McFerson .... Dimon Runnels	Neas .... Mary Ann	1845 11 29	IL, Nauvoo
McGary .... William Henry	Clark .... Margaret Caldwell	1868 03 07	UT, Salt Lake City
McGee .... Franklin	Dennis .... Dorothy Jane	1855 08	UT, Salt Lake City
McGhie .... James	Lindsay .... Isabella	1858 09 28	Scotland
McGhie .... William	Collins .... Elizabeth	1831 07 29	Scotland
McGhie .... William Jr.	McBlain .... Mary	1850 12 31	Scotland
McGregor .... William	Hossack .... Ann	1841 12 28	Scotland
McGregor .... William Campbell	Fish .... Sarah	1857 04 28	UT, Salt Lake City
McGuire .... John William	Stokes .... Tamar	1867 09 14	UT, Salt Lake City
McInnes .... Duncan	Davey .... Rosina		
McIntire .... Erastus William	Birch .... Annie	1874 11 23	UT, Salt Lake City
McIntosh .... John	Caldwell .... Caroline E.	1854	UT, Tooele Co.
McIntosh .... Solomon Parks	Bancroft .... Mary Elizabeth	1860 12 21	UT, Grantsville
McIntosh .... William	Caldwell .... Maria	1841 09 17	Canada
McKay .... Joseph	Anderson .... Ann		
McKay .... Thomas Sloan	Davis .... Charlotte James	1853 07 26	UT, Salt Lake City
McKay .... William	Oman .... Helen (Ellen)	1839 01 12	Scotland
McKechine ...... John	Bee .... Jane	1844 07 14	Scotland
McKee .... David Daniel	McMillen .... Mary Tweed	1816 07 11	PA, Butler Co.
McKee .... Hugh	Raymond .... Julia Sophia	1847 11 22	IA, Council Point
McKee .... Thomas	Sweat .... Persis Moore	1841 01 14	IL, Bloomfield
McKell .... Robert	Whytock .... Helen	1846 01 26	Scotland
McKenzie .... David	Crowther .... Mary Ann	1859 02 28	UT, Salt Lake City
McKenzie .... John Robert	Gunn .... Fanny		
McKenzie .... Thomas	Coolbear .... Caroline	1860 02 19	
McKinlay .... George	Hamilton .... Mary	1824 04 09	Scotland
McKinney .... Hugh	Lehman .... Sarah Ann	1832 04 30	PA, Montgomery
McKinnon .... Archibald	Brough .... Jane	1879 07 10	UT, Salt Lake City
McKinnon .... Archibald	McKay .... Mary	1861 08 09	UT, Salt Lake City
McKnight .... James	Pilch .... Lydia	1884	UT, Minersville
McKnight .... James	Stilson .... Cornelia Ann	1854 03 17	UT, Salt Lake City
McLane .... Harrison Parker	Fullmer .... Desdemona W.	1853 07 03	UT, Salt Lake City
McLatchie .... Samuel Russell	Morris .... Susan	1869 10 04	UT, Salt Lake City

Male	Female	Date	Place
McLean............Daniel	Smith.................Elizabeth	1847 04 16	Scotland
McLean............John W.	Lindsay...............Marion	1845 12 15	Scotland
McLing............James Wilford	Straw..................Emma Ruth	1865 04 19	UT, Coalville
McMasters.......William Athol	Ferguson.............Margaret D.	1842 09 02	Scotland
McMenemy......John	Cathers ....Elizabeth	1798	
McMillan ....Daniel	Murdoch ....Mary	1871 06 26	UT, Salt Lake City
McMillen ....Daniel	Davies ....Jannet	1844 12 08	ENG
McMullin ....Henry	Pierce.................Mary	1842 04 21	ME, Knox Co.
McMurdie........Samuel	Kay.....................Sarah Ann	1856 03 05	UT, Cedar City
McMurray ....John	Hutton ....Mary	1821 08 18	PA, York
McNeil ....John Corbet	Smith..................Mary Ann	1868 09 12	UT, Salt Lake City
McNeil ....Thomas	Reid....................Janet	1845 06 19	Scotland
McNiven ....James Scott	Littlefield.............Lydia	1872 01 15	UT, Salt Lake City
McNiven ....John	McNiven ....Janet	1847	Scotland
McPhail...........Archibald	McKinnon ....Jane	1849 12 04	Scotland
McPherson .....Hugh	Sutherland...........Isabella	1829 12 11	
McPherson .....James Ramsey	Ollerton ....Jane Ann	1860 07 15	UT, Nephi
McRae ....Alexander	Owens................Caroline Amelia	1855 12	UT, Salt Lake City
Mead ....Ezra	Wilcox ....Elizabeth	1811	
Mead ....Orlando Fish	Presley...............Lydia Aby	1853 06 27	UT, Salt Lake City
Meads.............Alexander M.	Hobbs................Emma Lucy	1864 10 19	UT, Salt Lake City
Mears ....George	Gibson................Sarah Ann	1828 11 08	ENG
Mecham..........Edward	Phillips...............Hannah Elizabeth	1870 01 11	UT, Salt Lake City
Mecham..........Ephraim	Derby ....Polly	1828 11 29	PA, Mercer
Mecham..........Erastus Darwin	Jones ....Martha	1849 02 04	
Mecham..........Joseph	Bovee.................Ann Elizabeth	1845 01 29	IL, Nauvoo
Mecham..........Joseph	Tuttle ....Sarah Maria	1853 01 05	UT, Salt Lake City
Mecham..........Joseph	Tyler..................Hannah Ladd	1827 02 10	
Mecham..........Joshua	Chapman ....Permelia	1793 04 05	NH, Canaan
Mecham..........Leonidas	Champlin............Margaret Emma	1851 02 25	IA, Kanesville
Mecham..........Lewis	Johnson ....Vashtia Emily	1868 08 29	UT, Salt Lake City
Mecham..........Lewis	Wells ....Lydia	1836 04 05	PA, Mercer
Mecham..........Lorenzo Dow	Clark..................Mary Ann	1865 09 09	UT, Salt Lake City
Mecham..........Moses Worthen	Derby ....Elvira	1827 11 08	
Meecham........Jeremiah Emery	Hickman.............Elizabeth Ellen	1854 04 01	
Meeks............Murfitt	Wool..................Elizabeth	1853	ENG
Meeks............William	Rhodes...............Mary Elizabeth	1837 10 05	IN, Warwick
Mefferd ....Virgil Jacob	Vallier................Mary Jane	1866 04 20	IA, Council Bluffs
Meiklejohn ......Robert	McLachlan..........Mary	1835 05 17	Scotland
Melling ....John	Knowles ....Ellen	1837	
Mellor.............James	Payne.................Mary Ann	1838 03 14	
Melville ....Alexander	Adamson.............Elizabeth		
Melville ....Alexander	Dutson................Jane Ann	1848 05 29	NE
Melville ....James Andrew	Gibbs.................Imogene J.	1869 10 12	UT, Salt Lake City
Melville ....James Andrew	Gibbs.................Medora Victoria		
Memmott ....John	Wilson ....Julia	1846 03 16	ENG, Yorkshire
Memmott ....William	Wilson ....Ann	1835 11 30	ENG, Yorkshire
Mendenhall......Louis Henry	Gay ....Mariah Henrietta	1858	
Mendenhall......Richard Lovell	Boyer.................Maria Catherine	1870 12 05	
Mendenhall......Thomas	Deal...................Mary Ellen	1864 05 15	UT, Springville
Mendenhall......Thomas	Smart ....Louisa Fleet	1863 03 31	ID, Franklin
Mendenhall......William	Lovell.................Sarah	1838 02 21	
Mercer ....John	Capstick ....Ann	1852 11 09	
Merchant ....Richard	Barnes...............Elizabeth	1827 12 30	Australia

Male	Female	Date	Place
Merkley............Christopher	Davis ....Sarah	1828 02 18	Canada
Merkley............Christopher A.	Stock ....Maria Josephine	1917 11 28	
Merkley............Nelson	Sanders..............Sarah Jane	1856 03 25	UT, Salt Lake City
Merrell ....Hosea	Saxton...............Mary Ann	1825 04 25	NY, Bridgewater
Merrell ....Joseph	Campkin.............Martha Ann	1872 05 06	UT, Salt Lake City
Merriam ....Edwin Parker	Finch ....Hannah B.	1831 11 05	
Merrick............Levi Newton	Eldredge.............Philinda	1827 11 18	VT, Addison Co.
Merril ....Jack	Smith..................Eliza Jane		
Merrill.............Albert	Richison ....Margaret Ann	1836 03 21	NY, New York City
Merrill.............Austin Shepherd	Harris ....Laura Wilder	1827 03 26	
Merrill.............Austin Shepherd	Sprague ....Martha		
Merrill.............Charles	Finley ....Sarah	1834 10 12	MO, Lewis Co.
Merrill.............Clarence	Smith..................Bathsheba	1861 01 03	UT, Salt Lake City
Merrill.............John Elwin	Davis ....Margaret	1862 04 17	
Merrill.............John Elwin	Vanleuven...........Eliza Jane	1862 04 17	UT, Paradise
Merrill.............Mariner Wood	Atkinson..............Sarah Ann	1853 11 11	UT, Bountiful
Merrill.............Marriner Wood	Standley ....Cyrene		UT, Salt Lake City
Merrill.............Philemon C.	Smith..................Mary Jane	1851 04 05	UT, Salt Lake City
Merrill.............Philemon C. II	Brown.................Lucinda Potter	1868 01 11	UT
Merrill.............Samuel	Fredriksen ....Anna Claudia	1862 11 08	
Merrill.............Samuel	Odell..................Phoebe	1802 09 10	NY, Oneida
Merritt ....Charles G.	Bunker................Rebecca Baks	1827 06 28	NY
Merritt ....Samuel Swift	Naylor.................Emma	1865 07 01	UT, Salt Lake Co.
Meservy...........Joshua	Robert ....Jeanne	1832 10 03	
Meservy...........Joshua Jr.	Brindle................Amelia Charlotte	1864 10 27	UT, Salt Lake City
Meservy...........Joshua Jr.	Brindle................Amelia Charlotte	1868 06 14	Remarried
Metcalf............Anthony	Reeder ....Mary Ann	1853 04	MO, St. Louis
Metcalf............Anthony	Sanford ....Sylvia Eliza	1862 08 27	UT, Springville
Metcalf............John Edward	Anderson............Cecelia	1869	
Metcalf............John Edward	Waslin ....Mary E.	1832 12 23	ENG
Metcalf............Levi G.	Guymon ....Melissa Jane	1850 11 03	UT, Centerville
Meyer ....Fredrick A. E.	Hannibal.............Emelie Caroline	1872 01 08	UT, Salt Lake City
Meyer ....Fredrick H. J.	Jensen ....Anna D. E.	1836 09 21	Germany
Meyrick...........John	Hutchensen.........Jamima	1861 10 28	UT, American Fork
Michelsen ....Ole	Michelsen............Maren	1842 08 16	Denmark
Michie ....Robert	Potts...................Frances	1857 03 16	ENG, Preston
Mickelsen ....Jens	Ericksen ....Karen Sophia	1857	
Mickelsen ....Niels	Ingmann..............Laura Johanna	1862 08 09	UT, Salt Lake City
Mickelsen ....Niels	Johnson ....Sena Catherine	1855 04 15	UT, Brigham City
Mickelsen ....Rasmus	Nielsen ....Ane	1848 09 03	Denmark
Mickelson ....Peter	Rath ....Maria Christina	1866 11 24	UT, Manti
Middlemas ....Edward	Jackson...............Jane	1856 08 02	
Middlemas ....Edward	Keeler.................Abigail	1835 08 15	Canada
Midgely ....Thomas	Garrett................Elizabeth Albania	1868	UT, Salt Lake City
Midgley ....Benjamin	Jackson...............Sarah Gibbons	1866 12 15	UT, Salt Lake City
Midgley ....Joshua	Hough ....Jemima R.	1853 04 08	
Midgley ....Thomas	Hinchliffe ....Ellen	1821 09 30	ENG, York
Mikesell ....Garrett W.	Cunningham........Ruth	1830 06 20	IL, Clark Co.
Mikesell ....John Aylor	Mikesell ....Catherine	1807 12 12	
Mikesell ....John C.	Porcher ....Charity Emma	1866 10 27	UT, Salt Lake City
Miles ....Albert	Daniels ....Hannah	1857 01 13	UT, Salt Lake City
Miles ....Albert	Viets ....Margaret Mariah	1833	OH, Trumbell Co.
Miles ....Benjamin A.	Lockhart ....Rachel Mahulda	1856 05 28	UT, Salt Lake City
Miles ....Edwin Ruthven	Mouritsen ....Johanne K. (Jane)	1870 05 03	UT, Salt Lake City

Male	Female	Date	Place
Miles ....Edwin Ruthven	Smith..................Annie George	1879 01 09	
Miles ....Edwin Ruthven	Wakefield ....Jane Ruth	1857 03 11	UT, Salt Lake City
Miles ....Sampson	Hickerson ....Catherine Luketis	1836 12 11	IL, Vandalia
Miller...............Alma	Hall.....................Louisa Jane	1861	NV
Miller...............Charles Dutton	Higgenbotham.....Alice	1853 01 16	
Miller...............Daniel A.	.............................Clarysa		
Miller...............Daniel A.	Bigler.................Hannah	1844 12 29	
Miller...............Daniel Arthur	Williamson...........Ellen (Eleanor)	1857 03 27	UT, Salt Lake City
Miller...............David	Fife.....................Margaret	1854 02 07	UT, Salt Lake City
Miller...............David Rudisill	Miles..................Malinda Ann	1862 10 04	
Miller...............Eleazer	Jensen ....Anna D. E.	1866 11 10	UT, Salt Lake City
Miller...............Eleazer	Van Zant ....Rebecca	1816	NY
Miller...............George	Bagley ....Martha Ann		
Miller...............Hans Koford	Norr....................Christine J.	1871	UT, Salt Lake City
Miller...............Hans Peter	Larsen ....Caroline M. K.	1861 06 22	NE, Florence
Miller...............Henry	Durfee ....Marion Braidfoot		
Miller...............Henry William	Gunn ....Fanny	1862 10 25	UT, Salt Lake City
Miller...............Henry William	Hinman...............Helen Aurelia	1858 03 02	UT, Salt Lake City
Miller...............Henry William	Pond...................Elmira	1831 06 19	IL, Quincy
Miller...............Hyrum Smith	Smithson ....Amelia Caroline	1870 05 08	UT
Miller...............Jacob	Cheney...............Helen Mar	1856 03 16	UT
Miller...............James Robison	Gardner..............Mary Jane	1859 02 20	UT, Salt Lake City
Miller...............John	Higgins ....Mary Ann	1866 04 20	UT, Salt Lake City
Miller...............John Hawkins	Shepherd ....Ann	1841 03 17	ENG
Miller...............Josiah H.	Morgan...............Amanda	1816	
Miller...............Reuben Parley	Gardner..............Margaret	1868 10 10	UT, Salt Lake City
Miller...............Robert	Fox.....................Elizabeth Mary	1889	
Miller...............Thomas	Peake.................Mary Hannah	1865	
Miller...............Thomas Rudolph	Rich....................Sarah Jane	1863 09 19	UT, Salt Lake City
Miller...............William	Neibaur ....Margaret Jane	1856 06 05	UT, Salt Lake City
Miller...............William	Wadsworth..........Lucinda Mathena	1865 11 12	UT
Miller...............William	Winter.................Ann	1854 12 25	ENG
Millet ....Artemus Jr.	Beal....................Nancy Jane	1865 10 04	UT, Glenwood
Millett ....Joseph	Glines.................Sarah Elizabeth	1854 03 26	MA, Lowell
Mills ....Charles E. T.	Bailey ....Eliza Harriet	1861 01 26	ENG
Mills ....Charles Edmond	Farr ....Frances	1832 04 17	ENG, Lancashire
Mills ....John	Hall....................Elizabeth	1836	ENG
Mills ....John	Sanford ....Jane	1827 03 13	Canada
Mills ....John Boardman	Bickmore ....Louisa Christina	1860 08 19	CA, Santa Cruz
Mills ....William	Waller.................Mary Ann		
Mills ....William Gill	Hill ....Emily	1857 06 14	UT, Salt Lake City
Mills ....William Gill	Sleater................Louisa Avalina	1856 04 25	
Milne ....David	Hess...................Anna	1871 10 09	UT, Salt Lake City
Milne ....David	Jarvis..................Ann Catherine	1870 05 03	
Milner.............John	Johnson ....Ann	1825 05 10	ENG
Milner.............John Brewitt	Yardley...............Esther (Elizabeth)	1854 03	UT, Salt Lake City
Minchel ....John	Coope ....Ann	1846 01 01	
Miner ....Albert	Durfee ....Tamma	1831 08 09	OH, Huron
Miner ....Moroni	Chase.................Nancy Elizabeth	1861 02 03	UT, Springville
Mitchell ....Benjamin T.	Houston..............Susanna	1857 03 06	UT, Salt Lake City
Mitchell ....Benjamin T.	Judd ....Lois	1848 01 01	NE
Mitchell ....David Alexander	Frost...................Christianna G.C.	1858	
Mitchell ....Hezekiah	Bowers ....Elizabeth	1856 12 31	UT, Salt Lake City
Mitchell ....Hezekiah	Mallinson...........Sarah	1832 10 07	ENG, Manchester

Male	Female	Date	Place
Mitchell ....James	Fife ....Janet	1840 01 13	Scotland
Mitchell ....James	Jensen ....Maren	1863 12 12	UT, Salt Lake City
Mitchell ....John Thomas	Newman..............Caroline	1875 06 25	UT, Salt Lake City
Mitchell ....Robert	Hunt ....Sarah	1822 01 15	ENG, London
Mitchell ....William	Legg ....Ellen	1826 05 30	Scotland
Mitchell ....William C.	Dalton..................Ann	1852 09 26	UT, Salt Lake City
Mitchell ....William C.	Moore.................Louisa	1849 07 18	IA, Kanesville
Mitchell ....William C.	Moore.................Mary	1852	
Mitton..............Edwin Crowther	Thirkell ....Caroline	1861 05 02	UT, Wellsville
Mitton..............William	Crowther ....Hannah	1832 02 12	ENG
Moesser.........Joseph Hyrum	Rushton..............Elizabeth F.	1864 08 28	UT, Salt Lake City
Moffat ....Archibald R.	Hunter ....Mary Patterson	1875 06 04	UT, Salt Lake City
Moffat ....David K.	Leishman ....Janet	1842 07 01	Scotland
Moffett ....Armstead	Emmett...............Mary Jane	1845	
Molland............James W.	Galloway ....Rebecca	1837 09 23	ENG, Liverpool
Moncur ....Robert	Jolley..................Frances Gatsey	1860 09 30	UT, Salem
Moncur ....Robert	Whytock ....Helen	1838 08 14	Scotland
Monroe	Marston ....Mary Leishman		
Monson...........Christian Hans	Mansson ....Ellen	1867 03 16	UT, Salt Lake City
Monson...........Christian Hans	Peterson.............Anna Catherine	1861 04 26	UT, Richmond
Montague ....James Shepard	Lamoreaux ....Sarah Jane	1859 01 30	UT, Payson
Montgomery ...Nathaniel	Clark...................Nancy Maria	1868 01 01	UT, North Ogden
Montgomery ....Robert	Wilson ....Mary	1830 09 06	Scotland
Montgomery ....Robert Jr.	Chadwick ....Ann	1864 03 23	UT, North Ogden
Montierth ....Alvin M.	Griffin ....Susannah	1866 03 10	UT, Salt Lake City
Moody.............John Monroe	Pool....................Elizabeth	1856 01 23	UT, Salt Lake City
Moody.............William C.	Bess ....Lola Eliza	1857 12 20	UT, Salt Lake City
Moody.............William C.	Damron ....Cinthia E.	1857 12 20	UT, Salt Lake City
Moon ....Henry	Moon ....Lydia	1841 01 30	PA, Pine Township
Moon ....Henry	Thayne ....Mary Ann	1868 01 04	
Moon ....Henry	Westwood ....Temperance	1856 03 18	UT, Salt Lake City
Moore ....David	Barker ....Sarah	1850 09 06	UT, Salt Lake City
Moore ....David	Herrick................Dianna	1854 04 07	
Moore ....David	Vorce..................Susan Mariah	1839 08 19	Canada
Moore ....Ethan Allen	Webber ....Sarah	1822 10 02	CT, Stafford
Moore ....George Sharrett	Bancroft..............Agnes Ann	1871 05 15	
Moore ....George Sharrett	Davis ....Mary Ann	1851 08 11	ENG
Moore ....Jacob	Jarman ....Catherine Lloyd	1839 08 12	Wales
Moore ....James	Young..................Alice	1838	ENG
Moore ....John Harvey	....	1856 05	
Moore ....John Harvey	....	1858 02	
Moore ....John Harvey	Drollinger.............Clarissa Jane	1841 10 06	IL, Nauvoo
Moore ....John Harvey	Sheffield ....Polly Lucina	1856 05 09	
Moore ....Joseph	Rogers ....Ann	1862	ENG
Moore ....Samuel	Bliss ....Eunice Sibley	1830 04 07	MA, Orange
Moore ....Samuel	Hawk...................Mary Caroline	1850 04 07	
Morehead ....James M.	Thomas ....Elizabeth Turner	1836 01 19	TN
Moreno ....Frank	Johnson ....Sarah Eliza V.		
Morgan ....Charles Henry	Davey..................Rosina	1870 07 02	
Morgan ....Daniel A.	Baxter.................Clarissa Adelaide	1867 11 09	UT, Salt Lake City
Morgan ....David	Turner ....Hannah	1832	
Morgan ....John Hamilton	Groesbeck...........Helen Melvina	1868 10 24	UT, Salt Lake City
Morgan ....Morgan	Lewis...................Cecelia	1833 02 16	Wales
Morgan ....Thomas	Nelson................Jean	1834 07 26	

Male	Female	Date	Place
Morgan ....William	Davis ....Elizabeth	1820 01 29	Wales
Morgan ....William	Nelson................Martha M. M.	1841 04 23	Scotland
Morgan ....William	Williams..............Martha	1855 11 13	UT, Willard
Morgan ....William Samuel	Jarman ....Catherine	1856 06 20	IA, Iowa City
Morley.............Isaac	Bache.................Nancy Ann	1846 01 22	IL, Nauvoo
Morley.............Isaac	Bradley...............Cynthia Abiah	1851 10 03	UT, Manti
Morley.............Isaac	Finch ....Hannah B.	1844	IL, Nauvoo
Morrell ....Thomas	Johnson ....Salina	1846 12 18	ENG, Middlesex
Morrell ....William Wilson	Jacobsen.............Dorthea Marie	1864 04 16	UT, Salt Lake City
Morrell ....William Wilson	Kelsey ....Matilda Elvira	1856 02 06	UT, Union Fort
Morrey ....John	Sheffield ....Polly Lucina	1864 10	UT, Payson
Morrill.............Laban	Brown.................Esther Lorraine		
Morrill.............Laban	Davis ....Lydia Ann	1854 10 17	
Morrill.............Laban	Drury ....Permelia H.	1844 02 22	IL, Nauvoo
Morris ....Charles	Ellwood ....Ann	1845 07	ENG
Morris ....Elias	Parry ....Mary	1852 05 23	IA, Council Bluffs
Morris ....Elias	Walker................Mary Lois	1856 05	UT, Salt Lake City
Morris ....George	Allen ....Maria	1858 01 15	UT, Salt Lake City
Morris ....George	Mathews.............Anne	1863 12 26	UT, Salt Lake City
Morris ....George	Newberry.............Hannah Maria	1843 08 23	IL, Nauvoo
Morris ....Isaac Conway	Williams..............Elizabeth	1852 10 16	Wales
Morris ....John	Linney ....Maria Billings	1832	ENG
Morris ....John	Ormond ....Mary	1847 10 31	Wales
Morris ....John Thomas	Walker................Mary Lois	1852 09 05	MO, St. Louis
Morris ....Joseph	Thorpe................Mary	1846	
Morris ....Richard	Alexander............Elisabeth	1827 03 20	ENG
Morris ....Samuel Abraham	Dykman...............Olive Cornelia	1876	
Morris ....William	Durham ....Sarah	1848 08 20	ENG, Lancashire
Morrison ....John	Mark...................Sarah	1834	
Morrison ....William	Cruickshank ....Mary M. F.	1843 12 22	Scotland
Morse ....John	Lewis..................Alice	1855 05 21	Wales
Morse ....Joseph Bennett	Jenkins...............Esther	1868 10	UT, Logan
Morse ....William	Evans.................Margaret	1859 10 08	
Mortensen ....Anders	Nielsen ....Karen Marie	1837 11 11	Denmark
Mortensen ....Anders Jorgen	Ipsen ....Wilhelmina C.	1865 07 15	UT, Salt Lake City
Mortensen ....Andreas Peder	Pedersen.............Ingeborg	1848 06 25	Denmark
Mortensen ....Diedrick	Christensen.........Karen Maria	1863 05 23	
Mortensen ....Hans Christian	Poulsen ....Ane Kjerstine	1866 04 22	Denmark
Mortensen ....Hans Jorgen	Alexander............Dionitia Emily	1859 05 16	UT, Parowan
Mortensen ....Jens Fredrick	Hansen...............Mette Maria	1862 05	Ocean
Mortensen ....Lars	Lee (Decker) ....Cornelia	1863 12 29	UT, Parowan
Mortensen ....Morten Peder	Jensen ....Dorthea	1859 05 10	Ocean
Mortensen ....Niels Christian	Christiansen........Marianna	1864 11 04	UT, Huntsville
Mortensen ....Niels Otto	Carson ....Elizabeth	1862	UT, Parowan
Mortensen ....Peder	Lind ....Jenzina Catherine	1871 10 30	UT, Salt Lake City
Mortensen ....Peder	Sanderson...........Helena	1827 11 09	Denmark
Mortensen ....Peter	Anderson.............Elizabeth Ann	1888 08 15	
Moses.............Julian	Neff ....Barbara Matilda	1845 03 25	IL, Nauvoo
Moss...............John	Alexander............Emma	1865 03 25	UT, Salt Lake City
Moss...............Patterson	Matthews.............Sarah	1865	
Moss...............Thomas	Goodman ....Fannie Elizabeth	1860 02 17	ENG
Moss...............William Jackson	Barrett ....Maria		
Moss...............William Jackson	McCluskey ....Ann Mitchell	1828 12 01	ENG
Mott ....John Wentworth	Lee ....Caroline Matilda	1847 01	NY

Male	Female	Date	Place
Mott ....Samuel	Dwight ....Elizabeth	1807 12 24	VT, Rutland
Mott ....Stephen	Smith..................Sarah Marinda	1861 04 07	UT, Salt Lake City
Moulton...........James Heber	Carroll ....Euphemia Ann	1874 09 28	UT, Salt Lake City
Moulton...........John Ephraim	Thacker ....Isabell Tonks	1882 03 23	UT, Salt Lake City
Moulton...........Joseph	Giles...............Mary Elizabeth	1868 12 15	UT, Salt Lake City
Moulton...........Thomas	Denton ....Sarah	1840 04 18	ENG
Mouritsen.........Lars	Sorensen............Maren	1848 09 12	Denmark
Mouritsen........Mourits	Hansen...............Karen	1885 10 22	UT, Logan
Mouritsen........Mourits	Wildman ....Susan Elizabeth	1885 10 22	UT, Logan
Mousley ....Titus	McMenemy ....Ann	1817	DE, New Castle
Mower.............Henry	...................Susan		
Mower.............Henry	Ameck................Mary		
Mower.............Henry	Burton ....Alice		
Mower.............Henry	Hall....................Elizabeth	1851 07 24	
Mower.............Henry	Hupper ....Lucretia	1847 02 05	IA, Council Bluffs
Mower.............Henry	Wheeler..............Elmera Jane	1856 09 05	
Mower.............Henry Jr.	Coon ....Lois	1863 07 11	
Mower.............John	Bidwell...............Sarah Ann	1850 04 11	IA, Council Bluffs
Mowery ....John T.	Mikesell..............Louisa Catherine	1853 12 09	
Mowrey ....Harley Jr.	Sargent ....Martha Jane	1847 07 04	WY
Moyes.............Robert	Hutchison ....Elizabeth	1836 05 22	Scotland
Moyes.............William	Eastcott ....Mary	1840 10 03	ENG
Moyes.............William	Hunt ....Zelpha		
Moyle ....James	Cannell...............Margaret Anna	1870 01 31	UT, Salt Lake City
Moyle ....James	Wood.................Elizabeth	1856 07 22	UT, Salt Lake City
Moyle ....John Rowe	Beer ....Phillipa	1834 02 23	ENG
Moyle ....John Rowe	Williams..............Mary Ann	1868 10 03	UT, Salt Lake City
Muhlestein ....Nicholas	Hauenstein..........Mary	1858 05 06	Switzerland
Muhlestein ....Nicholas	Wintch ....Anna Caroline	1868 04 13	
Muir ....George	Hannah...............Margaret	1852 04 19	Scotland
Muir ....George	Howie ....Christina	1863 06 13	UT, Heber
Muir ....James	Murray...............Mary	1836 06 11	
Muir ....Walter	Bell....................Mary	1835 11 15	Scotland
Muir ....Walter	Beveridge............Ellen	1812	Scotland
Muirbrook ....Alexander	Sutherland...........Isabella	1840 07 13	
Mulford ....Furman	Nelson................Jane	1852 10 08	UT, Salt Lake City
Mulliner...........Samuel	Capstick ....Ann		
Mulliner...........Samuel Jr.	Nisbet.................Katharine	1830 12 04	Scotland
Mumford ....Edward Thomas	Harmon ....Aseneth	1856 04 15	
Mumford ....George	Flitton ....Susan	1871 12 11	UT, Salt Lake City
Munjar ....Thomas	Ames.................Clarissa	1843	VT
Munk..............Christian Ipsen	Christensen.........Frederikka	1859 11 12	UT, Salt Lake City
Munk..............Christian Ipsen	Hansen...............Margrete		
Munk..............Christian Ipsen	Rasmussen ....Ane Marie		
Munro ....Henry	Palmer................Lovina	1834	Canada
Munson...........John	Christensen.........Maren Christine	1864 02 22	UT, Salt Lake City
Murdoch ....James	Murray...............Mary	1811 01 10	Scotland
Murdoch ....John Murray	Crawford ....Isabella	1862 08 09	UT, Salt Lake City
Murdoch ....John Murray	Steele................Anne	1848 02 15	Scotland
Murdock..........Joseph	Stacy.................Sally	1818 04 15	NY, Hamilton
Murdock..........Joseph Stacy	Hunter ....Elizabeth	1854 06 11	UT, Salt Lake City
Murdock..........Nymphus	Barney...............Sarah Melissa	1853 10 31	UT, Salt Lake City
Murdock..........Nymphus	Davies ....Esther Mariah	1857 12 06	UT, Salt Lake City
Murie ....David	Muir...................Mary	1850	

Male	Female	Date	Place
Murphy ....Emanuel Bird	Lamborn...............Eliza Ann	1876 10 16	UT, Salt Lake City
Murphy ....Emanuel Masters	Alexander...........Sarah Elizabeth	1861 05 12	UT, Salt Lake City
Murphy ....Emanuel Masters	Dennings............Margaret	1864 04	
Murphy ....Emanuel Masters	Easters...............Nancy Judd	1831 04 05	SC, Union Co.
Murphy ....Emanuel Masters	Irving ....Elizabeth	1864 08	
Murphy ....Jesse Easters	Broadbent ....Grace	1857 04 28	MO, St. Louis
Murphy ....Jesse Easters	Murphy ....Lovina Ann		
Murphy ....Jesse Easters	Sproul.................Elizabeth		
Murphy ....Jesse Easters	Sproul.................Robina	1862 02 15	
Murphy ....Mark B.	Camp ....Harriet Diannah	1858 02 09	UT, Salt Lake City
Murray ....Franklin C.	Heaton................Lovina	1873 03	UT
Murray ....Jeremiah Hatch	Ashby ....Mary	1865 03 04	
Murray ....Jeremiah Hatch	Nielsen ....Karen Maria	1863 02 06	UT, Spanish Fork
Murray ....John	Bates..................Mary Maria	1872 06 21	UT
Murray ....John	Bates..................Sarah	1833 10 28	
Murray ....John Jr.	Allred..................Rachel		
Murray ....John Jr.	Malley.................Mary Ann	1862 12 13	UT, Salt Lake City
Murray ....John T.	Davis..................Charlotte Ann	1851	UT, Centerville
Murray ....Thomas Joseph	Bathgate.............Mary		
Murray ....William Ellis	Doty....................Eliza	1846 02 03	
Musser.............Amos Milton	White..................Mary Elizabeth	1864 10 01	UT, Salt Lake City
Musser.............Samuel	Barr ....Anna	1824 01 24	PA
Myler...............James	Brownell ....Julia Ann	1843 10 05	MI, Bertrand
Myler...............Joseph Elias	Godfrey ....Emma Elizabeth	1872 10 10	UT, Salt Lake City
Myler...............Joseph Elias	Thacker ....Anna Maria	1866 07 11	UT, Clarkston

N

Male	Female	Date	Place
Naef................Johannes J. (Ira)	Frey....................Mary Aerny	1860 05 29	NE, Florence
Naegle ....Conrad	Huerni ....Maria (Mary)	1863 01 08	
Naegle ....John Conrad	Beck...................Pauline	1865 04 22	UT, Salt Lake City
Naegle ....John Conrad	Benz...................Regula	1860 10 06	UT, Salt Lake City
Nalder.............Stephen	New....................Esther	1846 11 29	ENG, Newbury
Nalder.............William New	Evans ....Emma	1869 05 03	UT, Salt Lake City
Nate................Sampson	Cornell................Elizabeth	1864 02 17	UT, Salt Lake City
Nate................Sampson	Cottrell................Mary Ann	1852 12 07	ENG
Nay ....John Jr.	Pine....................Thankful Lucy	1859	UT, Springville
Naylor ....Thomas	Sutton.................Alice	1857 09 04	UT, Salt Lake City
Naylor ....William	Ireland ....Dianah	1839 03 24	ENG
Neal ....George Augustus	Cooley................Asenath	1820 01 30	
Neal ....John	Brittingham..........Amelia	1833	PA, Allegheny Co.
Neal ....William Cooley	Dalton.................Ann Eliza	1852 06 09	
Neat................Richard	New....................Sarah	1831	ENG
Nebeker...........Ammon	Dixon..................Mary Adelma	1874 02 23	UT, Salt Lake City
Nebeker...........George	Dilworth ....Elizabeth	1851 02 13	
Nebeker...........George	Dilworth ....Maria Louisa	1863 08 29	
Nebeker...........Henry	Heaton ....Rebecca	1865 07 22	UT, Salt Lake City
Nebeker...........Henry	Van Waggoner ....Harriet Ann	1847 01 04	IA, Winter Quarters
Nebeker...........Ira	Lane...................Delia	1861 11 15	UT, Salt Lake City
Nebeker...........John	Fitzgerald ....Lurena	1835 10 25	OH, Riley
Nebeker...........John	Woodcock ....Mary	1854 09 10	UT, Salt Lake City
Nebeker...........Lewis	Gardner..............Nancy Maria	1853 11 05	UT, Salt Lake City
Nebeker...........Lewis	Thomas ....Catherine White	1851 01 05	

Male	Female	Date	Place
Nebeker..........Peter	Davis..................Elizabeth Jane	1847 02 13	
Nebeker..........Peter	Davis..................Mary Maria	1852 01 31	UT, Salt Lake City
Neddo.............Charles	Caldwell.............Caroline E.	1849 12 25	
Needham........David Stafford	Marsden............Clara St. Ledger	1898 02 17	UT, Salt Lake City
Needham........Thomas	Johnson.............Ann		
Neeley............Armenius M.	Morgan..............Susan	1856 12 08	UT, Brigham City
Neeley............Lewis	Miller..................Elizabeth	1828 04 20	IL, Vermillion Co.
Neeley............Lewis	Parsons.............Sophia	1847 06 27	IA, Council Bluffs
Neeley............William	Cravath..............Helen	1852 09 18	UT, Salt Lake City
Neeser............Rudolf	Gossauer...........Mary Magdalene	1844 01 10	Switzerland
Neff................Amos H.	Dilworth.............Martha Ann	1848 04 15	UT, Salt Lake City
Neff................Amos H.	Thomas.............Catherine E.	1864 12 17	
Neff................Benjamin Barr	Bitner.................Martha Ann	1858 02 26	
Neff................Benjamin Barr	Bowthorpe..........Maria Ann	1870 10 07	UT
Neff................Benjamin Barr	Love..................Mary Ellen	1870 10 07	UT
Neff................Franklin	Musser...............Elizabeth	1847 03 05	IA
Neff................Franklin	Stillman..............Frances Maria	1855 01 01	UT, Salt Lake City
Neff................John II	Barr....................Mary	1822 01 12	PA, Strasburg
Neff................John III	Benedict.............Ann Eliza	1863 01 31	UT, Salt Lake City
Neibaur..........Alexander	Breakell..............Ellen	1833 09 16	ENG, Preston
Neibaur..........Alexander	Wilds.................Ann	1852 11 02	
Neil................William	Robertson..........Marion	1863 12 31	Scotland
Neilson...........Lars	Mortensen..........Ann Christine	1859	UT, Ephraim
Nelson............Andrew E.	Rigtrup...............Johanna M. C.	1859 05 15	NE, Omaha
Nelson............Charles F.	Christensen........Nicolena	1875 02 01	UT, Salt Lake City
Nelson............Daniel M.	Warby................Matilda	1887 09 30	UT, Beaver
Nelson............Daniel M.	Warby................Sarah	1876 10 08	UT, Beaver
Nelson............Edmund	Taylor................Jane	1820 10 03	IL, Waterloo
Nelson............Fritz E.	Nielsen..............Caroline	1863 04 14	
Nelson............Henry	Richmond...........Sarah Ann	1848 05 16	IL, Nauvoo
Nelson............Henry Thomas	McMillen............Mary Ellen	1876	
Nelson............Isaac	Whistance..........Margaret	1854 02 23	UT, Provo
Nelson............James Horace	Pool..................Sarah Ann	1859 08 01	UT, Ogden
Nelson............Jens Christian	Bryson...............Eliza Snow	1869 11 22	UT, Salt Lake City
Nelson............Johannes	Bengtsson..........Agneta (Annetta)	1855 11 17	Sweden
Nelson............John Lowry	Cutler................Susannah	1860 11 17	
Nelson............Knud C.	Jensen...............Karen Margrette	1829 06 21	Denmark
Nelson............Lars	Paulson.............Botilda	1860	
Nelson............Peter	Netterstrom........Anna Sophia	1865 05 07	Ocean
Nelson............Price Williams	Lake..................Lydia Ann	1850 12 13	UT, Ogden
Nelson............Robert	Joseph..............Elizabeth	1842 12 12	IRE
Nelson............Soren	Larsen...............Christiana	1827 10 06	Denmark
Nelson............Soren Joseph	Purser...............Elmyra	1877 12 29	
Nelson............Swen	Jorganson..........Fredricka	1865 05	Ocean
Nelson............Thomas	Thompson..........Elizabeth D.	1805 01 20	ENG
Nelson............Thomas B.	Sorenson...........Dortha Christina		
Nelson............Thomas B.	Welker...............Mary Catherine	1853 03 27	UT, Willow Creek
Nelson............Wilford	Petersen............Matilda Hansina	1881 12 01	UT, Salt Lake City
Nelson............William G.	Vail...................Elvira	1855 11 25	
Nerdin...........Thomas	Dunn.................Elizabeth	1837 10 22	ENG
Neslen...........Robert Francis	Stevens..............Eleanor	1859 03 15	Scotland
Neslen...........Samuel	Francis...............Eunice	1829 07 13	ENG, Suffolk
Nessen...........Jens James	Jacobsen............Wilhelmina	1863 09 27	UT, Logan
Neville............Joseph Hyrum	West.................Ann Lydia	1873 05 05	UT, Salt Lake City

Male	Female	Date	Place
Newbury ....James	Brown................Nancy	1843 10 03	IL, Nauvoo
Newell.............Almon	Comstock ....Olive	1829	
Newell.............Almon	Lundy ....Rachel Bunn	1848	
Newell.............Elliot Alfred	Roberts ....Maria Louisa	1851 05 04	IA, Council Bluffs
Newman ....Henry J.	Penn...................Maria Louisa	1851 03 30	ENG
Newman ....John	Marchant ....Sarah Matilda	1859 12 26	UT, Salt Lake City
Newman ....Joseph	Hughes...............Elizabeth	1834 10 27	ENG
Newman ....Stephen James	Selley ....Hannah	1877 12 27	UT, Salt Lake City
Newman ....William	Jackson..............Mary Ann	1839 03 11	ENG
Newton ....John	Jaques ....Ann		ENG
Nibley ....James	Wilson ....Jean	1836 04 17	Scotland
Nichols............Alvin	Johnson..............Mary Ann	1857 04 08	UT, Salt Lake City
Nichols............Henry W.	Sewell ....Emily	1860 03 03	ENG, London
Nichols............John William	Everington...........Ann Reed	1863 02	UT
Nichols............Josiah	Marsh.................Ann Rachel	1853 12 25	UT, Salt Lake City
Nichols............Peter	Callaham.............Mary Ann	1849	
Nichols............William	White.................Ellen	1854 03 19	ENG, Durham
Nickerson ....Freeman	Chapman ....Hulda	1801 01 19	VT, Cavendish
Nickerson ....Levi Stillman	Neyman..............Mary Ann	1840 05 10	IL, Nauvoo
Nicol ....John	Nicholson ....Elizabeth	1823 03 23	Scotland
Nicol ....Thomas	Handberg ....Johanna C. M.	1858 03 11	UT, Salt Lake City
Nicol ....Thomas	Jensen ....Johanna Kirstine	1864 12 17	UT, Salt Lake City
Nield ....John	Broadbent ....Sarah	1863 05 23	ENG, Prestwich
Nield ....John Edward	Parker ....Jane	1877 09 19	UT, Fillmore
Nield ....Luke	Bauldry ....Anna Mary	1855 02 13	UT, Fillmore
Nield ....Luke	Green.................Elizabeth	1859 02 07	
Nield ....Luke	Wilde ....Martha	1817 06 30	ENG, Prestwich
Nield ....Luke	Wilde ....Sarah		
Nielsen ....Anders	Christensen.........Sophia	1866 06	UT
Nielsen ....Anders	Johansen ....Ane Johanne	1830 10 22	Denmark
Nielsen ....Anders	Paulsen ....Dorthea	1849	Denmark
Nielsen ....Andreas	Christensen.........Maren Sophia	1866 06 30	
Nielsen ....Andrew B.	Eriksen ....Elizabeth	1865 04 01	UT, Hyrum
Nielsen ....Augustinus	Hansen...............Ane B. E.	1854 02 05	Ocean
Nielsen ....Christian	Hansen...............Maren	1849 02 23	Denmark
Nielsen ....Christian	Jensen ....Ane Margrethe	1842 03 20	Denmark
Nielsen ....Christian	Larsen ....Karen	1829 12 05	Denmark
Nielsen ....Fredrick	Lavender ....Mary	1869	UT, Cottonwood
Nielsen ....Hans	Peterson.............Johanna	1871 06 05	UT, Salt Lake City
Nielsen ....Hans C.	Hansen...............Annie	1883 11 21	UT, St. George
Nielsen ....Hans Enoch	Osborn ....Nancy Margaret	1857 02 11	
Nielsen ....Hans I.	Allerup...............Johanne C.	1841 12 04	Denmark
Nielsen ....Hans I.	Erickson ....Josephine C.	1866 11 05	UT, Salt Lake City
Nielsen ....James	Thomsen ....Maria	1855 12 20	
Nielsen ....Jens	Andersen.............Ane Kjerstine	1858 04 16	
Nielsen ....Jens	Rasmussen ....Elsie	1850 05 18	Denmark
Nielsen ....Jens Christian	Andersen............Anna Maria	1856 10 02	UT, Big Cotton.
Nielsen ....Lars	Beckstrom ....Johanna Maria	1879 02 13	UT, Salt Lake City
Nielsen ....Lars	Pedersen............Sidsel	1853 05 18	Denmark
Nielsen ....Mads Pehr	Christensen.........Johanne	1850	
Nielsen ....Niels	Christiansen ....Christina Marie	1870 03 28	UT, Salt Lake City
Nielsen ....Niels	Hansen...............Anna	1842 10 25	Denmark
Nielsen ....Niels	Hurup ....Hartmandine N. P.	1838 09 25	Denmark
Nielsen ....Niels Christen	Ericksen ....Karen Sophia	1842 01 25	Denmark

Male	Female	Date	Place
Nielsen ....Niels H.	Hansen................Ingeborg Sophia	1847 02 26	Denmark
Nielsen ....Niels Hans	Pedersen.............Kirsten	1860 02 19	
Nielsen ....Niels Peder	Christensen.........Caroline	1868 12 13	UT, Salt Lake City
Nielsen ....Ola	Nilsson ....Elsa	1867 11 29	UT, Salt Lake City
Nielsen ....Ole	Andersen.............Sidse	1856 05 09	Denmark
Nielsen ....Ole	Mortensen...........Caroline Amelia	1841	Denmark
Nielsen ....Peder	Andersen.............Kirsten	1831 12 09	Denmark
Nielsen ....Peder	Ludvigsen............Maren	1848 09 23	Denmark
Nielsen ....Peter	Brown.................Harriet Amanda		
Nielsen ....Peter	Ditlevsen ....Mette Kirstine	1854 04 02	Denmark
Nielsen ....Peter	Larsen ....Dorthea	1868 08 09	Ocean
Nielsen ....Peter	Larsen ....Kirsten	1857 04 04	
Nielsen ....Peter	Nielsen ....Karen (Caroline)	1855 01 14	Ocean
Nielsen ....Peter	Nielsen ....Nelsina Kirstine	1872 09 22	UT, Salt Lake City
Nielsen ....Peter C.	Rasmussen.........Magdalena	1844 12 28	Denmark
Nielsen ....Rasmus	Christiansen........Hansine	1859 06 12	NE, Florence
Nielsen ....Rasmus	Jensen ....Maren Christina	1869 03 17	
Nielsen ....Thomas	Andersen.............Dorthea	1826 11 17	
Nielsen ....Thomas L.	Jensen ....Andrea	1862 04 22	Ocean
Nielson ....Ake	Anderson.............Hanna	1875 11 01	UT, Salt Lake City
Nielson ....Ake	Anderson.............Louisa		
Nielson ....Carl Henrick	Hansen................Karen Kirstine	1867 05 26	Denmark
Nielson ....Jens	Jensen ....Kirsten	1857 10 04	UT, Salt Lake City
Nielson ....Jon	Nilsson ....Ingar	1834 11 12	Sweden
Nielson ....Joseph	Butler.................Mary Elizabeth		
Nielson ....Niels Peter	Davidson.............Mary Dorothea C.	1875 03 22	UT, Mt. Pleasant
Nielson ....Niels Peter	Dutson.................Florence Virginia	1878 03 14	UT, Salt Lake City
Nielson ....Peter	Lassen ....Hulda Franziska	1862 03 08	UT, Salt Lake City
Nielsen ....Soren	Andersen.............Caroline	1867 08 24	UT, Salt Lake City
Nielson ....Soren	Jensen ....Mariane	1862 11 14	UT, Salt Lake City
Nielson ....Thomas	Jensen ....Mariane	1882 01 11	
Nilson ....Pehr	Tufveson ....Svenborg	1862 10 12	UT, Logan
Nilson ....Peter	Paulson ....Botilda	1866	UT, Mt. Pleasant
Nilsson............Nils	Tykeson ....Botilda	1837 05 26	Sweden
Nilsson............Ole	Baum..................Pernella	1844 08 04	Sweden
Nilsson............Ole	Pehrsson.............Bereta (Bertha)	1840 12 27	
Nish ....Robert	Wilson ....Agnes	1855 01 16	ENG, Liverpool
Nisonger ....Henry	Slusser ....Sarah	1836 03 03	
Nix ....James	Lane...................Sarah	1840 05 20	
Nixon ....George William	Johnson ....Elizabeth H.	1868 10 24	UT, Salt Lake City
Nixon ....James William	Fawcett ....Hannah Isabell	1876 02 21	UT, Salt Lake City
Nixon ....James William	Shultz ....Johanna Marie	1859 10 26	UT, Salt Lake City
Noakes ....John Hubbard	Childs ....Susan Amelia	1855 02 25	UT, Springville
Noakes ....Thomas	Inkpen ....Emma	1810 03 30	ENG
Noakes ....Thomas	Wilcox ....Elizabeth	1852 03 18	UT, Salt Lake City
Noall ....Simon	Squire.................Rebecca	1854 03 18	
Noble ....Joseph Bates	Hammond ....Susan	1847 02 11	IA, Winter Quarters
Nokes ....Charles M.	Hamilton.............Caroline Matilda	1879 09	UT, Salt Lake City
Normington......Thomas	Jackson..............Maria	1839 09 29	ENG
Norris..............William	Terrell.................Caroline	1844 01 18	ENG, Wicken
North...............Charles Addison	Johnson ....Albertine J.	1861 01 27	UT, Salt Lake City
North...............Hyrum Bennett	Blair....................Priscilla Jane	1869 04 05	UT, Salt Lake City
Northrup	Baldwin ....Phoebe Ann		
Northrup ....Amos	Carbine ....Mary Adelia	1844 05 02	

Male	Female	Date	Place
Norton............Alanson	Jensen ....Maren	1872 02 05	UT, Salt Lake City
Norton............Allen	Wilkinson...........Lucy	1809 12 31	NY, Granville
Norton............David Jr.	Benefield............Elizabeth	1820 02 10	IN, Fayette Co.
Norton............James Wiley	Hammer..............Nancy	1846 07 08	NE, Florence
Norton............John	Covington...........Martha Ann	1847 06	IA, Mt. Pisgah
Norwood.........Richard Smith	Norton ....Caroline Chloe	1857 12 05	UT, Salt Lake City
Norwood.........Richard Smith	Stevenson...........Elizabeth	1850 10 13	UT, Salt Lake City
Nott.................Thomas H.	Alloway..............Maria Seaborn	1837 12 25	ENG
Nowers ....Willson Gates	Anderson............Sarah	1855 06 23	
Nowlin............Jabus T.	Thomas ....Amanda	1845	IL, Nauvoo
Nuttall ....Leonard John	Clarkson.............Elizabeth	1856 12 25	UT, Provo
Nuttall ....William	Langhorn............Mary	1822 07 08	ENG, Lancaster
Nuttall ....William E.	Watson...............Rosamond	1851 08 04	ENG, Liverpool
Nybolle ....Rasmus	Sorensen............Hedvig Lucie E.	1835	
Nyman............Anders	Quarnstrom ....Sara	1839 08 23	Sweden
Nyman............Carl	Loving ....Albertina Axelina	1870 01 11	UT, Salt Lake City

O

Male	Female	Date	Place
Oakason ....Hans	Olsen..................Marie Ann	1865 09 21	UT, Salt Lake City
Oakden............William	Mills....................Elizabeth	1855 10 06	UT, Salt Lake City
Oakes ....Henry	Tremayne...........Prudence	1842 05 12	IL, Nauvoo
Oakey ....Charles	Passey ....Mary Ann	1862 01 17	UT, Lehi
Oakey ....James	Cooper ....Mary	1840 01 06	ENG, Nottingham.
Oakey ....Thomas	Collett.................Ann	1836 08	ENG
Oakley ....Ezra	Degroat ....Elizabeth	1816	NY, Gravesend
Oakley ....James D.	Palfreyman..........Fanny	1869 07 19	UT, Salt Lake City
Oaks ....David Martin	Reynolds ....Abigail Mary	1869 03 02	UT, Salt Lake City
Oaks ....Hyrum	Wood..................Sarah Ann	1846 12 06	IA, Council Bluffs
Oaks ....Hyrum Edwin	Watson...............Sarah Ann	1878 03 20	
Obray..............Samuel William	Bainbridge..........Eleanor	1852	MO, St. Louis
Obray..............Thomas L.	Brenchley...........Carolyn	1857 08 02	UT, Salt Lake City
Ogden.............Edward	Garrett...............Sarah Rooth	1834 08 11	
Ogden.............William	Vickers ....Mary	1844 08 11	ENG, Bolton
Ogilvie ....George	Hales..................Eliza Ann	1857 03 02	
Ogilvie ....George Byers	Mattatahl ....Barbara E.	1827 08 11	Canada
Ohlson.............Gustave A.	...........................Ellen		
Ohlson ....Gustave A.	Martinsson ....Anna Britta	1868 01 04	UT, Salt Lake City
Ohlsson ....Gustave	Anderson.............Johanna	1840 02 20	
Okerlund..........Ola	Carlson...............Bengta	1856 11 16	Sweden
Okey ....Edwin	Pitt.....................Mary	1840 02 26	ENG, Gloucester
Okey ....Edwin Jr.	Clark..................Mary Ellen	1874 01 19	UT, Salt Lake City
Oldfield ....John	Ditchfield ....Mary	1857 12 27	
Oldroyd...........Archibald T.	Anderson............Maria	1864 01 04	UT, Ephraim
Oldroyd...........Peter	Jolley.................Mary	1863 04 05	UT, Salt Lake City
Oldroyd...........Peter Liddle	Miecklejohn.........Catherine Mary	1850 08	Scotland
Oler................George	Lancaster ....Margaret		
Oliphant ....Richard	Young.................Susannah	1825 02	
Oliverson ....James	Roberts ....Caroline	1856 09 30	UT, Kaysville
Ollerton...........John	Dandy................Alice	1826 02 04	ENG
Olpin ....Henry	Higgenbotham.....Frances	1862 01 02	UT, Salt Lake City
Olpin ....Henry	White..................Sarah Ann	1835 10 25	ENG, Coaley
Olpin ....Joseph	Dee ....Ann	1861 10 23	UT, Salt Lake City

Male		Female		Date	Place
Olsen	Andrew Niels	Larsen	Bodel	1857	
Olsen	Andrew Niels	Mathieson	Jorgina	1876 12	
Olsen	Charles Canute	Benson	Eveline	1856	UT, Salt Lake City
Olsen	Charles John	Ockerman	Mary	1880 02 05	UT, Salt Lake City
Olsen	Christen	Pedersen	Anne	1829 09 27	Denmark
Olsen	Christian	Carlsen	Mary	1868 03 28	UT, Salt Lake City
Olsen	Christian	Ellingson	Anna	1859 05 20	Ocean
Olsen	Christian "L"	Mortensen	Maren	1865 06 17	UT, Salt Lake City
Olsen	Christoffer	Johanson	Johannah		
Olsen	Frederick	Jensen	Matilda	1869 05 31	UT, Salt Lake City
Olsen	Gideon Elias	Danielson	Johanna	1865 03 04	UT, Salt Lake City
Olsen	Hans	Christensen	Sena Katrina	1879 05 15	UT, Salt Lake City
Olsen	Iver Johannes	Christiansen	Else Marie	1843 03 03	
Olsen	Jens	Christensen	Anna Catherine	1859 10 19	
Olsen	Jes	Ebbesen	Anne Marie	1801	Denmark
Olsen	Johan	Olsen	Karen	1830 01 04	Norway
Olsen	Johannes	Christensen	Johanne	1856	
Olsen	Jorgen	Hansen	Karen Marie	1863 12 14	UT
Olsen	Lars	Nielsen	Anne Dorthea	1864 07 03	Denmark
Olsen	Lars	Olsen	Maren		
Olsen	Niels	Christiansen	Anna Marie	1854 06 25	UT, Salt Lake City
Olsen	Ole	Anderson	Karen Kirstine		
Olsen	Ole	Seversen	Gunnel	1868 05 30	UT, Salt Lake City
Olsen	Peter	Andersen	Ane	1847 07	Denmark
Olsen	Rasmus	Sorensen	Ingeborg	1836 08 04	Denmark
Olson	Christen	Fredriksen	Anna Claudia		
Olson	Clas Erick	Stark	Gustavia Sophia		
Olson	James	Pedersen	Elsie Christine	1869 06 07	UT, Ephraim
Olson	John N.	Nilson	Margaretha	1849	Sweden
Olson	Lars	Gunderson	Radine	1866 05 09	Norway
Olson	Niels	Nielsen	Ane Johanna	1855	
Olson	Sven	Persson	Anna	1841 06 17	Sweden
Olson	Swen	Christensen	Maren	1866 06 17	Ocean
Olsson	Hans	Persson	Kjerstina	1827 12 12	
Olsson	Knut	Anderson	Elin	1874 06 15	UT
Olsson	Knut	Jonsson	Elna	1834 12 29	Sweden
Oman	Aaron Gustaf	Jensen	Anna Elizabeth	1861 11 04	UT, Mt. Pleasant
Oman	Peter	Tobiasson	Anna Maria	1827 07 15	Sweden
O'Neil	Timothy	Pears	Eliza Rosannah		UT, Uintah
Openshaw	George	Ingham	Nancy	1845 02 02	ENG, Lancashire
Openshaw	Roger W.	Gledhill	Mary		
Openshaw	Roger W.	Ramsbottom	Elizabeth	1862 10 25	UT, Moroni
Openshaw	William	Greenhalgh	Ann Walmsley	1833 05 20	ENG, Lancashire
Orchard	Jacob	Harding	Susannah	1844	
Orchard	James	Harding	Susannah	1837	
Ord	Thomas	Grant	Eleanor	1856 03 04	ENG
Ordway	Stephen	Lake	Jane	1850	
Orell	Carl Fredric	Granne	Johanna Charlotta	1851 10 12	Sweden
Orison	David Franklin	Busenbark	Anna Eliza	1869	
Orme	Samuel	Kirby	Amy (Mary)	1825 12 07	ENG
Orme	Samuel W.	Cross	Sarah	1857 11 08	UT, E. T. City
Orr	James Copeland	Green	Elizabeth Jane	1863	UT
Orr	Robert	McQueen	Elizabeth	1828 04 16	Scotland
Orser	David	Allen	Martha		

Male	Female	Date	Place
Orton ....Alexander	Holmes..............Jane	1857 11 01	UT, Cedar City
Orton ....John	Ward ....Mary Ann	1840 12 24	ENG
Orton ....Joseph	Barnett ....Clara Virtue	1875 12 20	
Orton ....William	Middlefell............Elizabeth	1870	UT, Parowan
Orton ....William	Taylor ....Hannah	1834 06 09	ENG
Orton ....William Owen	Dalley ....Sarah Ann	1865 01 01	UT, Summit
Osborn............David	Butler..................Cynthia	1828 04 10	IN
Osborn............David	Standley ....Philinda	1865	UT
Osborn............David III	Thorn..................Nancy	1857 12 25	UT, Box Elder Co.
Osborn............John Wesley	Rollins ....Mary Amelia	1857 09 09	CA, San Bern.
Osborn............Thomas J.	Standley	1854	UT
Osborn............Thomas J.	Standley ....Ellen	1851 09 14	IA, Gardon Grove
Osborne..........Allen	Bryan (Brand)......Anne	1830 11 26	Scotland
Osguthorpe......John	Roper ....Lydia	1846 10 13	ENG, Sheffield
Osmond..........George	Huckvale ....Mary Georgina	1855 07	MO, St. Louis
Osterhout........John	Taylor ....Mary Ann	1862 03 08	UT, Willard
Ostler ....David	Beagley ....Anna	1861	
Ostler ....John	Gollop.................Sarah Endacott	1830 06 06	ENG
Ostler ....John C.	Howarth..............Dorothy	1873 06 09	UT, Salt Lake City
Ostler ....John C.	Prince.................Mary Ann		
Otterstrom ......Jonas	Johnson ....Maria Kaisa	1845	Sweden
Ottesen ....Christen	Andersen............Else Christine	1854	Ocean
Ottesen ....Jens	Sorensen............Johanna	1860 11 18	
Oulds ....Emanuel	Uren ....Elizabeth	1850 05 16	ENG
Ovard..............Joseph William	Heiner ....Susannah C.	1875 06 28	UT, Salt Lake City
Overson..........Christian	Jensen ....Jensine C.	1862 11 16	UT, Mt. Pleasant
Oviatt ....Henry Herman	Whitlock ....Sally Rae	1853 02 01	UT, Spring City
Owen ....James C.	Rawson ....Sariah	1851	UT, Ogden
Owen (Wragg) .Oswald	Taberer ....Sarah Ann	1859 12 21	ENG, Stafford
Owens ....Horace	Davis ....Margaret	1856 10 04	
Owens ....Horace	Layne ....Sarah		
Owens ....James C.	Burr ....Abigail Cordelia	1816	
Owens ....James C. Jr.	Robison..............Lucretia Proctor	1856 01 16	
Owens ....John Edward	Thomas ....Mary	1853 02 15	Ocean
Owens ....Owen Asa	Farnsworth ....Laura	1838	
Owens ....Robert	Allen ....Martha Evins	1850 03 07	KY, Somerset
Owens ....William John	Williams..............Ann	1868 02 29	UT, Salt Lake City

P

Male	Female	Date	Place
Pace ....Edwin	Atkinson ....Mary Jane	1855 05 01	UT, Salt Lake City
Pace ....Elisha	Baldwin ....Eliza	1827 03 25	OH, Newark
Pace ....James	Calhoun..............Margaret G.	1852 01 02	UT, Salt Lake City
Pace ....James	Strickland ....Lucinda Gibson	1831 03 21	TN
Pace ....James	Webb..................Ann	1855 12 04	UT, Payson
Pace ....William F.	Nichols ....Margaret	1828 10	TN
Pace ....William F.	Phillips................Louisa Mary	1868 11 30	UT, Salt Lake City
Pace ....Wilson Daniel	Lee ....Elizabeth	1868	
Pace ....Wilson Daniel	Redd ....Ann Moriah	1852 08 22	UT, Spanish Fork
Pack ....George	Green.................Phylotte	1790 04 01	Canada
Pack ....John	Ives ....Julia	1832 10 10	NY, Watertown
Pack ....John	Mosher...............Ruth	1846 01 21	IL, Nauvoo
Pack ....John	Sterling.............Jessie Belle	1864 01 16	

Male	Female	Date	Place
Pack ....John	Walker ....Mary Jane	1852 09 15	
Pack ....John Jr.	Scott..................Betsy Elizabeth	1865 12 20	UT, Salt Lake City
Packard ....Orren	Pine...................Thankful Lucy	1851 11 09	UT, Springville
Packer ....Isaac Hoffmire	Berry ....Lucy Charlotte	1864 11 18	UT, Salt Lake City
Packer ....James	....	1863	
Packer ....James	Mecham ....Polly Mae	1854 02 14	UT, Lehi
Packer ....Johnathan T.	Champlin............Angelina Avilda	1840	IL, Nauvoo
Packer ....Nathan W.	Taylor ....Elizabeth	1829 03 31	OH, Perry
Packer ....William Hamilton	Allen ....Sarah Briggs	1865 06 01	UT, Salt Lake City
Padrigh ....John William	Christensen........Anne	1859	UT
Page ....Daniel	Socwell...............Mary	1822 04 18	NJ, Newport
Page ....James	Graves ....Louisa	1837 10 16	ENG, Aston Parish
Page ....John	Hicks ....Lydia Ann	1838 10 11	ENG
Page ....John	Leader................Eleanor Esther	1835 07 01	ENG
Page ....John Edmond	Judd ....Lois		
Page ....Jonathan S.	Leaver ....Mary	1855 08 12	UT, Salt Lake City
Page ....William	Clark...................Mary Ann	1863 03 24	UT, Bountiful
Painter ....John Scoffins	Brooks................Mary Ann	1862 04 21	Ocean
Painter ....John Scoffins	Brooks................Sarah	1870	UT
Painter ....William	Bradshaw...........Elizabeth N.	1861 03 21	UT, Bountiful
Palfreyman ......Richard	Butler..................Hannah	1842 01 22	ENG, Denby
Palmer ....Abraham	Pierce.................Patience Delila	1825 07 10	NY, Oswegatchie
Palmer ....David Moroni	Ayers..................Lucinda Ann	1869 01 01	UT, Springdale
Palmer ....George	Draper................Phebe	1815	Canada
Palmer ....Isaac	Hodgkinson........Ann Elizabeth	1844	
Palmer ....James	Ewer...................Mary Jane	1867 08 10	UT, Salt Lake City
Palmer ....Thomas	Farr ....Frances	1865 02 09	
Palmer ....Thomas	Mills...................Louisa Harriet	1865 02 14	UT, Salt Lake City
Palmer ....William G.	Purdun ....Mary Ellen		
Palmer ....Zemira	Jaques ....Caroline	1856	
Palmer ....Zemira	Knight.................Sally	1851 12 01	UT, Provo
Panter.............William J.	Bennett...............Emma	1864 03 26	UT, Salt Lake City
Papworth ....James	Tavener..............Elizabeth	1847 12 25	ENG, Chesterton
Parish ....Samuel	Thomas ....Sarah	1861 03 01	UT, Springville
Park ....Andrew Duncan	Ellison ....Jane Ann	1868 03 14	
Park ....David	Brooks................Ann	1829	
Park ....Hamilton Gray	Steele.................Agnes	1843 04	Scotland
Park ....James Pollock	Findley ....Agnes	1849 09 21	UT, Big Cotton.
Park ....James Pollock	Pymm.................Sarah Ann		
Park ....John Miller	Stewart...............Matilda	1824 10 28	
Park ....Samuel	Gray ....Isabella		IRE
Park ....Samuel	Harvey................Jean	1849 12 31	Scotland
Park ....Samuel Wallace	Taylor ....Sarah Jane	1860 03 18	UT, Lindon
Park ....William	Duncan...............Jane	1828	
Park ....William	Findlay ....Janet McDonald	1850 04 07	UT
Park ....William	Gordon...............Mary	1854 06 11	UT, Salt Lake City
Parker.............Edwin	Cox....................Catherine	1870 10 31	UT, Salt Lake City
Parker.............Heber Thomas	Cooper ....Sarah Ann	1872 01 08	UT, Salt Lake City
Parker.............Henry Miller	Riley ....Nancy Wood	1844 01 29	IL, Nauvoo
Parker.............J. W.	Gardner..............Hannah	1846	ME
Parker.............John	Jackson...............Maria	1857 11 15	
Parker.............John Jr.	Briggs ....Ellen	1846 01 23	IL, Nauvoo
Parker.............Joseph F.	Ross...................Mary Elizabeth	1861 06 30	UT, Joseph
Parker.............Joshua	Hartley...............Drucilla Dickson	1844 08	IL, Hancock Co.

Male	Female	Date	Place
Parker............Thomas Bryant	Nelson................Martha Ann	1835 10 25	
Parker............William	Blake.................Maria	1829 04 28	ENG
Parker............William	Gibbs.................Ruth	1858 02 22	IA, Dubuque
Parker............William Cope	Edgeley..............Sarah B.	1855 05 13	UT, Salt Lake City
Parker............William George	Beal...................Nancy Jane		
Parker............Wyman Miner	Grover...............Eliza Ann	1860 01 15	UT, Farmington
Parkes............Thomas	Peake.................Mary Hannah	1850	ENG
Parkin.............Fred	Barnes...............Mary Jane	1872 10 08	
Parkin.............John	Brown................Elizabeth Wright	1839 02 28	ENG, Derbyshire
Parkin.............John Jr.	Lewis.................Mary Ann	1870 12 26	
Parkin.............Joseph H.	Cooper...............Eliza Snow	1870 02 14	UT, Salt Lake City
Parkin.............William John	Foulds................Eliza	1864 08 18	UT, Bountiful
Parkin.............William John	Thurgood............Elizabeth Selena	1884 04 24	UT, Salt Lake City
Parkinson........Charles G.	Clark..................Hannah Maria	1855 10 15	UT, Grantsville
Parkinson........Charles G.	Hill....................Sarah		
Parkinson........Henry F.	Kerr...................Agnes Archibald	1869 02 23	UT, Salt Lake City
Parkinson........Henry F.	Woodward..........Betsy Barnes	1860 01 02	UT, Wellsville
Parkinson........John	Hall...................Lulu May	1875 12 13	UT, Salt Lake City
Parkinson........Samuel R.	Chandler............Arabella Ann	1852 01 01	MO, St. Louis
Parkinson........Thomas	Bryant...............Mary Ann	1855 06 12	CA, San Bern.
Parkinson........Thomas	King..................Elizabeth	1846	ENG
Parkinson........Timothy F.	Parker...............Maria Black	1863 01 05	UT, Salt Lake City
Parkinson........Timothy G.	Harville..............Martha	1856 06 04	UT, Salt Lake City
Parkinson........Timothy G.	Nuttall...............Mary	1849 08 20	ENG, Lancashire
Parkinson........Timothy G.	Shaw.................Rebecca	1869 10 04	UT, Salt Lake City
Parkinson........Timothy H.	Williams.............Priscilla Jane	1881 03 03	
Parkis.............Stephen	Sanford..............Angeline	1865	
Parktington......	Colton................Ann		
Parrish............Samuel	Dack..................Frances	1820 02 13	Canada
Parrott............William Edward	Stevens..............Christina	1878	
Parry..............Caleb	Evans................Catherine V.	1849 02 26	ENG, Liverpool
Parry..............Edward	Haight...............Temperance K.	1919	
Parry..............John	Bartlett..............Patty	1851 12 14	
Parry..............John	Parry.................Harriet	1854 04 02	UT, Salt Lake City
Parry..............John	Williams.............Mary	1808	Wales
Parry..............John Jr.	Roberts..............Harriet Julia	1853 12 26	Wales
Parry..............Joseph	Malin.................Ann Penn	1857 01 05	UT, Salt Lake City
Parsons..........Elijah	Johnson.............Mary Christina	1869 01 11	UT, Salt Lake City
Parsons..........George	Fisher................Lydia Rebecca	1853	
Parsons..........William	Francis...............Sarah	1827 07 23	ENG
Partington.......Richard	Stafford..............Mary	1847 07 18	ENG, Oldham
Partridge.........Edward	Clisbee..............Lydia	1819 08 22	OH, Painsville
Partridge.........Edward Jr.	Buxton...............Elizabeth	1862 02 15	UT, Salt Lake City
Partridge.........Jonathan W.	Yates.................Mary Ann	1857 01 05	UT, Salt Lake City
Pass...............Thomas	Warmby.............Mary Ann	1837 05 28	ENG
Passey............John	New...................Ann	1836 04 17	ENG, St. Nicolas
Passey............John Parley	Clifton................Elizabeth Ann	1874 09 28	UT, Salt Lake City
Passey............Thomas	Theobald............Drusilla	1858 08	UT, Salt Lake City
Passey............William	New...................Sarah	1841 08 01	ENG
Paterson.........Samuel Jr.	Randall...............Elizabeth	1851 05 11	IA, Kanesville
Paterson.........William D.	Paterson.............Elizabeth Blair	1821 10 08	Scotland
Patrick............Robert	Baird.................Rachel	1859 12 29	Scotland
Patten............Charles Moroni	Patterson...........Lucinda Maria	1878 02 19	UT, Payson
Patten............George	Nelson................Mary Jane	1851 02 20	UT, Alpine

Male		Female		Date	Place
Patten	John	Ingersoll	Hannah	1824 04 25	
Patten	William Cornwall	Eddy	Wealthy	1854	UT, Payson
Patterson	Andrew	Nelson	Jean	1851	MO, St. Louis
Patterson	Edward M.	Thompson	Mary	1868 10 31	
Patterson	Edward N.	Dean	Martha Harriet	1878 02 07	
Paul	James Patten	Evans	Elizabeth	1862 10 25	UT, Salt Lake City
Paul	James Patten	Gribbon	Robina	1839	
Paul	James Patten	Hughes	Catherine	1866 03 24	UT, Salt Lake City
Paul	James Patten	Wilson	Sarah	1861	
Paul	Walter	Walker	Ann	1856 12 25	
Paxman	William	....		1875	
Paxman	William	Keys	Ann Rushen	1855 03 03	ENG, London
Pay	Richard	Goble	Mary	1859 06 26	UT, Nephi
Payne	Edward	Powell	Emma	1854 09 16	ENG
Payne	James	Morris	Mary	1864 12 25	UT, Nephi
Payne	William Lauder	Nichols	Catherine L.	1843 06 07	IL, Nauvoo
Peacock	Daniel	Noddings	Mary	1819 09 20	ENG, Yorkshire
Peacock	William	Wright	Rosetta	1847	
Pead	James	Wilkinson	Elizabeth	1845	
Pearce	Edward	Griffiths	Jean Rio	1864	
Pearce	Harrison	Cromeans	Henrietta	1836 07 25	
Pearce	Harrison	Meredith	Ann	1856 08 03	UT, Spanish Fork
Pearce	Harrison	Schneider	Magdalena	1863 10 03	
Pearce	James	Meeks	Mary Jane	1867 03 06	UT, St. George
Pearce	Robert	Brown	Sarah	1844 12 28	ENG, Somerset
Pears	John Burton	Whitehead	Rose Hannah	1822 01 30	ENG
Pearson	Benjamin A.	Curtis	Eliza Mary	1869 12 27	UT, Salt Lake City
Pearson	Jesse	Brownell	Mary Ann	1835 10 16	IN, St. Joseph Co.
Pearson	Johsua	Jeffcott	Sarah	1832	ENG
Pearson	Ola	Bengtsson	Sissa	1847 12 31	Sweden
Peart	Benjamin Loss	Ashment	Elizabeth C.	1869 08 09	UT, Salt Lake City
Peay	Francis	Baker	Eliza Jane	1853 03 05	Ocean
Peay	Francis	Blake	Mary	1820 05 13	ENG
Peay	George Thomas	Sorensen	Karen Marie	1867 03 02	UT, Salt Lake City
Peck	Lucius W.	Morris	Rosella N.	1867 09 07	
Peck	Martin Horton	Van Orden	Charlotte Amelia	1851 12 02	UT, Salt Lake City
Pectol	George	Reasor	Sarah	1828 11 02	
Pedersen		Christensen	Anne		
Pedersen	Christian	Larsen	Elsie Marie		
Pedersen	Christian	Sorensen	Jensine Kirstine	1857 06 26	Denmark
Pedersen	Hans	Pedersen	Kirsten	1855	
Pedersen	Jens	Hurup	Hartmandine N.P.	1860 01 03	Denmark
Pedersen	Jorgen Christian	Hansen	Sena		
Pedersen	Jorgen Christian	Olsen	Nicoline	1858	
Pedersen	Jorgen Christian	Sorensen	Juliane	1855 07 03	UT, Salt Lake City
Pedersen	Lars	Morgansen	Maren	1851 04 12	Denmark
Pedersen	Mikkel	Knudson	Dorthe	1832 11 13	Denmark
Pedersen	Niels	Pedersen	Sidse		Denmark
Pedersen	Peder	Hansen	Ellen Margrethe	1821 07 11	Denmark
Pedersen	Peter	Andersen	Dorthea	1837 10 20	Denmark
Pedersen	Soren Aarup	Mathiasen	Ane Kirstine	1825 05 23	
Pedersen	Soren Christian	Larsen	Elsie Marie	1861 10 22	Denmark
Pederson	Anders	Wilhelmsen	Maren		Denmark
Pederson	Hans	Christensen	Anna		

Male	Female	Date	Place
Pederson.........Simon	Sorensen..............Annie Christina	1842 12 16	Norway
Peery ....David Harold	Higginbotham......Elizabeth Letitia	1865 04 10	UT, Holiday
Pehl ....Hans Andrew	Jesperson ....Ingeborg Kristine		
Pehrson ....Eric Johan	Jonsson..............Anna Sophia	1861 05 16	Ocean
Pehrson ....Pehr	Beckstrand ....Christina	1859 12 26	
Pehrsson ....James	Nilsson ....Sissa	1876	
Pehrsson ....Ola	Nilsson ....Sissa	1856 02 10	Sweden
Peirce ....Eli	Neff ....Susanna	1850 11 21	UT, Salt Lake City
Peirson ....William	Richards.............Nancy	1819 03 04	MA
Pendleton ....Benjamin F.	Jeffery ....Alice	1861 10 26	UT, Salt Lake City
Penfold ....John	Thacker ....Elizabeth	1868 01 01	UT, Peoa
Penrod............Abraham	Durfee ....Ellen Eliza	1870 06 05	
Penrod............David	Keller...................Temperance	1831 10 14	IL, Jonesboro
Penrose ....Charles W.	Stratford ....Lucetta	1855 01 21	ENG, Essex
Perkes ....James	............................Eliza		
Perkes ....James	Gibson................Mary Ann	1854 12 09	MO
Perkins ....Absalom	Martin ....Nancy	1815	TN, Sparta
Perkins ....John	Benson................Jane	1860 03	
Perkins ....John Calvin	Perkins ....Elizabeth Jane	1852 08 20	
Perkins ....Joseph T.	Martin ....Margaret	1852 12 25	Wales
Perkins ....Thomas	Mathews..............Ann	1808 05 03	Wales
Perkins ....Ute	Warren ....Anna	1835 02	
Perkins ....Ute Warren	Laub....................Sarah	1867 09 16	
Perkins ....William Louis	Richards.............Sarah Jane	1853 10 27	
Perris ....Thomas	Spiller..................Hannah Rebecca	1835	ENG
Perrish ....George W.	York.....................Julia Ann K.	1850	
Perry...............Alexander	Shanks ....Marion Leckie	1855 12 21	UT, Salt Lake City
Perry...............Asahel	Chadwick ....Polly	1806 03 26	
Perry...............Gustavus A.	Wing....................Eunice	1816	
Perry...............Henry Elisha	Zabriskie ....Elizabeth	1848	
Perry...............John	Williams..............Grace Ann	1822 11 14	ENG
Perry...............Joseph	Lindsay...............Marion		
Perry...............Josiah Henry	Cole....................Lucinda	1845 11 30	IL, Nauvoo
Perry...............Lorenzo	Walker.................May Wray	1853 05 01	UT, Farmington
Perry...............Lyman Sylvester	Shaffer ....Nancy Ann	1855 01 22	UT, Bingham Fort
Perry...............Philander J.	Pratt ....Arvilla	1850 05 27	IA, Mt. Pisgah
Perry...............Stephen	Edwards..............Rhoby	1816 04 12	VT, Sherburne
Perry...............Stephen C.	Boggs..................Mary		
Perry...............Stephen C.	Hulet...................Anna Maria	1844 01 18	IL, Nauvoo
Perry...............Stephen C.	Stewart................Margaret Eleanor		
Perry...............Steven	Stevens ....Cynthia		
Perry...............William	Hind.....................Mary Ann	1841 07 12	ENG, Liverpool
Persson ....Peter Micias	Jacobson.............Cajsa C. C.		
Peters ....David	Davis...................Laura Jones	1840 04 11	Wales
Peters ....Lyman	Barton ....Mary Catherine	1881	
Petersen ....Christian	Anderson.............Christena	1867 01 02	UT, Mt. Pleasant
Petersen ....Hans	Lorentzen ....Anne M. D.	1851 03	Denmark
Petersen ....Hans	Sorensen.............Hedvig Lucie E.	1832	Denmark
Petersen ....Hans Peter	Christiansen ....Christina M.	1860 05 28	Denmark
Petersen ....James	Larsen ....Ansine Marie	1866 06 10	Ocean
Petersen ....Jens Peter	Backman ....Johanna Sophia	1873 02 24	UT, Salt Lake City
Petersen ....Niels	Skow ....Maren	1853 09 10	
Petersen ....Niels E.	Johnson ....Maren	1850 06 07	Denmark
Petersen ....Peder	Sorensen.............Marie	1850 10 22	Denmark

Male	Female	Date	Place
Petersen ....Peder C.	Christensen..........Ane Marie	1848 10 29	
Petersen ....Peter	Petersen.............Maren	1865 11 04	UT, Ephraim
Petersen ....Soren Lind	Lofgreen.............Kjestie	1864	Sweden
Petersen ....Soren Lind	Nielsen ....Anne Elizabeth	1861 05	Ocean
Petersen ....Thomas Christian	Mogensen ....Jacobine Kirstine		
Peterson ....Anders	Anderson.............Marna	1834	Sweden
Peterson ....Anders	Hansen...............Anne Moriah	1854 10 15	UT, Salt Lake City
Peterson ....Andrew	Pherson..............Anna Marie		Germany
Peterson ....Baltzar S.	Juulsen...............Mette Margrete	1857 05 30	Denmark
Peterson ....Canute	Nelson................Sarah Ann	1849 07 02	IA, Kanesville
Peterson ....Carl M.	Esklund ....Elizabeth	1880 11 04	
Peterson ....Charles C.	Kroll...................Christine W. C.	1861 07 03	Trail
Peterson ....Charles S.	Patten.................Ann	1849 01 21	
Peterson ....Christian	Backman..............Emma Matilda	1869 02 13	UT, Salt Lake City
Peterson ....Hans	Andersen..............Anne Martine	1849 11 03	Denmark
Peterson ....Hans	Larsen ....Anna Margrethe	1833 05 17	Denmark
Peterson ....Jens O.	Jensen ....Ane	1845 11 01	Denmark
Peterson ....Johannes	Olsson.................Anna Katrina	1834 11 26	Sweden
Peterson ....John	Roberts ....Jane Cecelia		
Peterson ....Lars Peter	Jensen ....Else Marie	1852 11 26	Denmark
Peterson ....Neils	Borsen.................Annie Bolliti		
Peterson ....Nels	Nielson ....Matilda Marie	1878 12 03	UT, Littleton
Peterson ....Niels	Nelsen.................Anne Christina	1833 10 13	Denmark
Peterson ....Niels	Shenstrom...........Bengta	1850	
Peterson ....Ole	Hansen................Maren	1846 02 05	Denmark
Peterson ....Peter	Larsen ....Maren	1878	
Peterson ....Peter	Winberg...............Johanna C.	1842 11 18	Sweden
Peterson ....Peter C.	Olsen..................Anna Marie	1850 10 15	Norway
Peterson ....Peter C.	Thompson ....Johanne	1870 05 02	UT, Salt Lake City
Peterson ....Peter O.	Andersen.............Mary	1876 02 14	UT, Salt Lake City
Peterson ....Samuel	Jensen ....Karen	1860 07 18	UT, Salt Lake City
Peterson ....Samuel	Sorensen.............Caroline E.	1856 08 24	UT, Salt Lake City
Peterson ....Solomon	Ericksen ....Albertina	1872 01 08	
Peterson ....Thomas Peter	Thygesen ....Maria	1859 09 25	UT, Salt Lake City
Peterson ....Wilhelm Sanberg	Nybolle ....Hansine Jacobine	1864 06 18	
Pettegrew ....David	Alden..................Elizabeth	1816	
Pettingill..........Alonzo	Young.................Susannah	1845	MO, St. Louis
Pettingill..........Elihu U.	Marsh.................Jane Clotilda	1849 10 26	IA, Council Bluffs
Pettit ....Brower	Abrams...............Lucinda	1854 01 17	NY, Lynbrook
Pettit ....Edwin	Hill....................Rebecca Hood	1864 10 29	
Petty ....Albert	Haggerty ....Lucinda Catherine	1853 06 05	
Petty ....Robert Cowan	Carbine ....Mary Adelia	1850 08 30	NE
Petty ....Robert Cowan	Wells ....Margaret J.	1832	TN, Nashville
Petty ....Robert Thomas	Wright.................Julia Ann	1864 01 22	UT, Salt Lake City
Pew ....Hyrum William	Weymouth..........Henrietta Druzilla	1852 03 31	UT, Salt Lake City
Pexton ....James	Parrott ....Hannah B.	1853 01 04	ENG, Yorkshire
Phelps ....William Wines	Schrader ....Harriet Henriette	1856 09 08	UT, Salt Lake City
Phillips ....Charles	Merriman.............Priscilla	1844 05 09	
Phillips ....Edward	Ivins..................Elizabeth	1833 11 26	
Phillips ....Edward	Simmonds...........Hannah	1842 08 02	IL, Camp Creek
Phillips ....John	Hancock.............Merab	1855	Wales
Phillips ....John Campbell	Hewitson ....Elizabeth Ann	1875 04 12	UT, Salt Lake City
Phillips ....Richard	Luker.................Margaret	1835 10 01	NJ, Monmouth Co.
Phillips ....Samuel	Brett ....Sarah Ann		

Male	Female	Date	Place
Phillips .... Thomas J.	Boden .... Sarah	1870 10 17	
Phillips .... William	Presdee .... Mary Ann	1793 12 03	ENG
Phillips .... William	Taylor .... Eliza	1887	UT, Salt Lake City
Phillips .... William G.	Tuckfield .... Maria Ann	1861 05 04	MA, Boston
Phillips .... William S.	Henderson .... Hannah	1834 04 21	Wales
Phippen .... Isaac	Stewart .... Adah	1818 10 15	OH, Springfield
Phippen .... James W.	Pratt .... Julia Adelia	1845 08 09	NY, Newstead
Pickett .... George	Clark .... Priscilla	1856	
Pickett .... John W.	White .... Charlotte R.	1866 12 21	UT, Salt Lake City
Pickett .... Matthew	Pocock .... Harriet	1845 11 01	ENG, Berkshire
Pickett .... Matthew	Rose .... Millicent		
Pickett .... William A.	Castle .... Mary		ENG
Pickett .... William A.	Clark .... Priscilla	1860 03 03	UT, Salt Lake City
Pickup .... George	Haws .... Eliza	1849 01 21	UT, Salt Lake City
Pickup .... George	Norton .... Caroline Chloe	1851 04 17	UT, Alpine
Pierce .... George Henry	Skinner .... Sarah	1859 04 06	
Pierce .... George Thomas	Rommrell .... Jane Nancy	1863 09 20	
Pierce .... Isaac W.	Baldwin .... Phebe	1828 01 27	
Pierce .... Robert	Baird .... Susannah	1872 11 25	UT, Salt Lake City
Pierce .... William Edward	Thacker .... Anna Maria	1873 09 29	UT, Salt Lake City
Pihl .... Henning	Madsen .... Karen Kirstine	1819 10 16	Denmark
Pihl .... Peder M.	Folkman .... Christiane	1846 11 27	
Pilling .... Edmund	Cottam .... Ellen	1845 08 31	ENG, Lancashire
Pilling .... John	Bank .... Margaret	1818 10 17	
Pilling .... John	Bedford .... Sarah	1864 10 15	UT, Salt Lake City
Pilling .... Richard	Adams .... Catherine	1856 03 10	
Pincock .... John Jr.	Douglas .... Isabella	1851 02 03	MO, St. Louis
Pine .... Joseph	Winn .... Adelia Ann S.	1814 09 27	NY
Pingree .... Job	Hooper .... Esther	1861 09 27	UT, Salt Lake City
Pingree .... Job	Morgan .... Mary	1857 09 27	UT, Ogden
Pingree .... Job	Tarrant .... Charlotte	1834 09 08	ENG
Pinkham .... Sumnar	Atwood .... Laurinda Maria		
Pitkin .... George Orrin	Frew .... Janet	1867 05 18	UT, Salt Lake City
Pitts .... Thomas	Stout .... Martha Ann	1866 07 28	UT, St. George
Pitts .... William Henry	Beeden .... Sarah Jane	1834 05 15	ENG, Quarrington
Platt .... Francis	Hester .... Eliza	1853 11 19	UT, Salt Lake City
Platt .... James	Mercer .... Elizabeth	1834 01 20	ENG, Lancashire
Platts .... John	Price .... Emily	1848	ENG
Player .... Charles Warner	Oades .... Elizabeth	1850 03 07	IA, Ferryville
Player .... William J.	Hamer .... Nancy	1850 09 24	IA, Ferryville
Player .... William Warner	Sanders .... Zillah	1821 07 22	ENG, Middlesex
Plews .... Thomas	Clough .... Mary Jane	1861 11 25	
Plumb .... Jeremiah	Shields .... Sarah Jane	1870 01 24	UT, Salt Lake City
Plunkett .... William R.	Kennedy .... Sarah Canada	1830	Scotland
Pogson .... James Walker	Moore .... Louisa	1864 05 28	
Poll .... William Flint	Long .... Charlotte	1842 11 02	ENG
Pollard .... Herbert Jonathan	Wilson .... Rachel		
Pollard .... Joseph	Bailey .... Mary Ann	1845 09 27	ENG, Surrey
Pollock	Brockbank .... Elizabeth		
Pollock .... Samuel	Meredith .... Ann	1865 10 10	UT, St. George
Pollock .... Samuel	Reeves .... Elizabeth	1847 02 05	IL, Nauvoo
Pomeroy .... Francis M.	Colburn .... Sarah Matilda	1853 04 20	UT, Salt Lake City
Pomeroy .... Francis M.	Haskell .... Irene Ursula	1844 07 13	NH
Pond .... Stillman	Thorn .... Abigail	1848 02 08	UT. Salt Lake City

Male	Female	Date	Place
Poole ....John Peter	Marshall ....Sarah	1868 03 14	
Poole ....John Rawlston	Bitton..................Harriet	1864 12 12	
Poole ....John Rawlston	Bitton..................Jane	1857 09 12	
Poole ....John Rawlston	Bleasdale ....Jennette	1848 07 06	IA, Farmington
Poole ....Peter	Berry ....Lucy Charlotte	1857	UT, Salt Lake City
Pope ....Robert	Laduc ....Sarah	1851 10 01	WI, Rosendale
Pope ....William Monroe	McBride..............Catherine	1841	IL, Nauvoo
Porritt...............Thomas	Hampton ....Sarah Elizabeth	1868 11 13	UT
Porritt...............Thomas	McCann...............Margaret	1838	ENG, Manchester
Porter...............	Hall....................Elizabeth		
Porter...............Abraham	Bisbee ....Marcia Maria	1828 10 01	NY, Allegheny
Porter...............Alma	Deuel..................Minerva Adeline	1855 11 15	UT, Centerville
Porter...............Chauncey W.	............................Amy		
Porter...............Chauncey W.	Cook...................Lydia Ann	1847 03 28	
Porter...............Chauncey W.	Strong ....Priscilla	1848 02 10	NE
Porter...............John	Bryant.................Mary Ann	1844 04 16	Australia
Porter...............John P.	Rich....................Nancy	1843 02 05	IA, Lee Co.
Porter...............Lyman Wight	Bailey ....Elizabeth	1867 10 05	UT, Salt Lake City
Porter...............Sanford	Warriner ....Nancy	1812 01 01	VT, Vershire
Potter...............David	Osborne ....Charlotte	1815	NY
Potts ....Thomas	Bailey ....Eliza	1820 08 19	
Potts ....Thomas Pullen	Jemmett ....Julie Jane	1860 05 06	ENG, Faversham
Poulsen ....Lars	Olson..................Karen	1844 10 15	Denmark
Poulsen ....Mads	Mikkelsen............Dorthea Christine	1833 10 26	Denmark
Poulsen ....Martin	Thomsen ....Maria	1851	
Poulsen ....Morten	Hansen................Karen Marie	1843 01 27	
Poulsen ....Niels Christian	Olsen..................Helge	1858 08 25	UT
Poulsen ....Paul Michael	Jorgensen ....Cecilia	1861 05 17	Ocean
Poulson ....Anders	Larson ....Bodilla Katherine	1840 11 29	
Poulson ....Niels Peter	Christensen.........Margarethe K.	1869 12 03	UT, Manti
Poulson ....Peder	Anderson.............Sidsel Catherine	1839 07 12	Denmark
Poulson ....William	Larsen ....Dorthea	1872 02 05	UT, Salt Lake City
Poulter ....George	Jackson...............Mary Elizabeth	1874 02 09	UT, Salt Lake City
Poulter ....William	Strubell................Caroline	1844 03 10	ENG
Powell ....Edward	Tongue................Ann	1846 04 27	ENG
Powell ....George	Mousley..............Maria	1837 02 26	ENG, Aldridge
Powell ....James	Wimmer..............Jemima	1833 10 06	IN, Henry Co.
Powell ....James Evans	Carter ....Elizabeth Jane	1852 09 14	WY
Powell ....James Q.	Anderson.............Ane Dorthea	1857 03 01	UT, Salt Lake City
Powell ....James Q.	Cooper ....Mary Jane	1841 09	PA, Philadelphia
Powell ....John	Blythe ....Henrietta Eaton	1864 06 18	UT, Salt Lake City
Powell ....John	Chamberlain.........Fanny	1842 11 13	ENG, London
Powell ....John	Harris ....Elizabeth	1840 11 15	Wales
Powell ....John Ammon	Shields ....Sarah Jane	1873 01 06	UT, Salt Lake City
Powell ....John Ammon	Snyder................Hannah Matilda	1863 12 13	UT, Kamas
Powell ....Joseph	Powell ....Thurza Ann	1853 06 13	ENG, Allington
Powell ....William David	Allan ....Janet (Jessie)		
Pratt...............Addison	Barnes.................Louisa	1831 04 03	Canada
Pratt...............Moroni Walker	Chugg ....Mary	1874 04 27	UT, Salt Lake City
Pratt...............Orson	Bishop.................Adelia Ann	1844 12 13	IL, Nauvoo
Pratt...............Parley P.	Frost...................Mary Ann	1837 05 09	NY
Pratt...............Parley P.	Snively ....Hannahette	1844 11 02	IL, Nauvoo
Pratt...............Parley P.	Walker................Ann Agatha	1847 04 28	NE
Pratt...............William	Mathis ....Mary Catherine		

Male	Female	Date	Place
Pratt..............William D.	Eddy...................Wealthy	1841 03 01	OH, Kirtland
Preece.............Mark	Bloomfield...........Emma	1872 11 27	
Preece.............Mark	Comish...............Eleanor	1862 11 22	UT, Salt Lake City
Preece.............Richard	Pritchard.............Susannah	1832 06 11	ENG
Prestley...........William	Holden................Margaret	1850	
Preston............Richard W.	Vine....................Susanna		ENG, Hampshire
Prestwich.........William	Langshaw............Jane	1836 05 09	ENG, Odenshaw
Price...............Charles	Andrus................Sally	1870	
Price...............Charles	Blaky..................Caroline G. W.		
Price...............Charles	Johnson..............Mary Elsa	1847 11 25	IA, Council Bluffs
Price...............Charles	Larsen................Mary	1873 02 10	
Price...............Charles	Oakey.................Ann C.		
Price...............Charles	Shelton...............Mary Jane	1841 10 09	IL, Nauvoo
Price...............Edward	Hollis..................Sophia	1864 09 26	UT, Salt Lake City
Price...............Edward Jeremiah	Bishop................Mary Jane	1852 03 30	LA, New Orleans
Price...............Ezekiel	Watkins...............Rhoda E.	1862 02 16	UT, Alpine
Price...............James	Powell.................Ann	1857 03 28	ENG, Ludlow
Price...............John Evan	Williams...............Ruth	1841 05	
Price...............John Isaac	Wingrove.............Mary Ann	1852	NY, New York City
Price...............Richard	Brown.................Frances		
Price...............Robert	Juchau................Susannah	1864 03 02	UT, Salt Lake City
Priday.............Samuel	James.................Mary	1841 12 26	ENG
Priday.............Thomas S.	Fullmer...............Sarah Ann	1869 03 11	UT, Salt Lake City
Prince.............George	Bowman..............Sarah	1837 10 10	ENG, Suffolk
Prisbrey..........Miner Jewett	Tibbits................Elizabeth	1867 07 13	UT, Salt Lake City
Priscott...........James	Gunn..................Mary	1854	ENG
Pritchett..........Samuel N. B.	Gillespie..............Mary Jane	1858	
Probert............Samuel	Memmott.............Sarah	1869 01 12	UT, Salt Lake City
Probert............William	Gibbons...............Ann	1837 06 01	ENG, Edgaston
Proctor............David	Graham...............Martha E.	1855	UT, Salt Lake City
Proctor............George William	Charles...............Mary Louise	1886 11 03	UT, Union
Prothero..........Jonathan	Reese.................Elizabeth Thomas	1869 05 31	UT, Salt Lake City
Prows.............John Thomas	Arms..................Charity	1842 12 21	IL, Nauvoo
Prows.............William Cook	....	1867	
Prows.............William Cook	Roberds..............Lodesky Ann	1850 04 14	NV, Mary's River
Prye...............John Israel	Molyneaux...........Ann	1865 12	UT, Salt Lake City
Pucell.............Samuel	Perren................Margaret	1825 08 01	ENG, Lymm
Pugh...............Edward	Kelly..................Elizabeth	1866 05 05	UT, Salt Lake City
Pugh...............Edward Jr.	Rock..................Maryann	1847 07 24	IA, Kanesville
Pugmire..........Jonathan	Benson...............Martha Kerstine	1856 03 21	
Pugmire..........Jonathan	Nielson...............Caroline	1864 04 13	UT, Salt Lake City
Pugsley...........Joseph E. F.	Harmon..............Evelyn Rosette	1875 12 23	UT, Salt Lake City
Pugsley...........Philip	Ames.................Clarissa	1855 08 24	UT, Salt Lake City
Pugsley...........Philip	Roach.................Martha	1851 06 28	ENG, Bristol
Pulsipher.........Elias	Chubbuck...........Mary	1828 01 31	
Pulsipher.........John	Huffaker.............Rozilla	1853 11 04	UT, Salt Lake City
Pulsipher.........Orson Hyde	Rasmussen.........Mette Susanne	1861 03 08	UT, Brigham City
Pulsipher.........William	Chidester............Esther	1861 10 27	UT, Salt Lake City
Pulsipher.........Zerah	Brown.................Mary	1815 08 18	PA, Susquehanna
Purnell............Shem	Driggs................Louisa	1855 09 22	UT, Kaysville
Puzey.............William Henry	Pollard................Lydia	1874 10 19	UT, Salt Lake City
Pymm.............John	Donald................Catherine	1870	
Pyper.............Alexander C.	Dollinger.............Christiana	1855 12 24	NE, Florence
Pyper.............Alexander C.	Tullidge..............Jane Puckett		

Male	Female	Date	Place

Q

Male	Female	Date	Place
Quigley ....Andrew	Fifield ....Almira	1865	
Quigley ....Andrew	Miller ....Elizabeth Ellen	1853 11 30	UT, Salt Lake City
Quigley ....Andrew	Yates..................Harriet	1856	
Quinby ....Ephraim	Pease ....Catherine Floyd	1824 08 24	

R

Male	Female	Date	Place
Raddon............James Henry	Davis ....Elizabeth	1877 05 15	
Radford...........John Whitlock	Smith..................Rachel Leah	1846 04 06	
Radford...........John Whitlock	Stevens ....Polly	1855	
Raglin	Lewis..................Elizabeth E.	1850	MO
Rainey ....David Pinkney	Dennis................Dorothy Jane	1857 02 09	UT, Provo
Ralphs ....Thomas	Johnson ....Sarah	1842 05 10	MO
Rambo............Charles D.	Jensen ....Ane Marie S.	1891 01 17	UT, Nephi
Rammell ....Charles H.	Berger ....Caroline	1862 02 14	UT, Providence
Rammell ....Charles H.	South.................Sabrin	1846 12 20	ENG
Rampton..........Henry	MacDuff.............Ada Alice	1868 11 01	
Ramsay ....Ralph	Cheshire.............Mary Ann	1869 08 02	UT, Salt Lake City
Ramsden ....Charles	Robbins ....Ellen Jane	1838 01 22	
Ranck ....Peter Jr.	Lemon ....Ann	1840 08 25	PA
Randall ....Alfred	Davis ....Emerette Louisa	1834 01 08	OH, Munson
Randall ....Alfred	Harley................Margaret	1848 01 29	NE
Randall ....Alfred	Johnson ....Mildred Eliza	1860 05 30	UT, Salt Lake City
Randall ....Alfred	Severn...............Hannah	1863 03 07	UT, Salt Lake City
Randall ....Alfred Jason	Campkin.............Ruth	1867 11 16	UT, Salt Lake City
Randall ....Brigham Young	Ross..................Sarah Darling	1877 08 04	
Randall ....Joseph Henry	Hall....................Louisa Jane	1881	UT, St. George
Randall ....Melvin Harley	Bennett..............Francis Rebecca	1875 04 15	UT, Salt Lake City
Rands ....Joseph William	Anderson...........Sarah	1847 03 29	ENG
Rankin ....Richard	Donald...............Catherine	1859 11 28	Scotland
Rappleye ....Tunis	Cutler ....Louisa E.	1836 01 17	OH, Kirtland
Rasband ....Thomas	Giles..................Elizabeth	1847 01 25	ENG, Lincoln
Rasmussen .....Andrew	Madsen ....Severine Marie	1862 10 12	UT, West Jordan
Rasmussen .....Bent	Janson ....Jensina	1871 11 13	UT, Ephraim
Rasmussen .....Christen	Mortensen ....Mette Kistena	1863 04 30	UT, Parowan
Rasmussen .....Claus	Rasmussen.........Anne Magdalene	1840 10 16	Denmark
Rasmussen .....Hans	Stephansen.........Maren	1844 06 07	Denmark
Rasmussen .....Hans P.	Ludvigsen...........Ann Kirstine	1840 12 27	Denmark
Rasmussen .....Jorgen H.	Mortensen ....Sina Marie	1869 01 25	UT, Huntsville
Rasmussen .....Lars	Sorensen............Christiana	1868 03 28	UT, Salt Lake City
Rasmussen .....Morten	Christiansen........Karen Marie	1859 04 01	UT, Ephraim
Rasmussen .....Niels	Morris ....Mary Ann	1865 12 28	UT, Parowan
Rasmussen .....Niels Peter	Thompson ....Josephine	1878 12 20	ID, Bloomington
Rasmussen .....Soren	Haagansen..........Anne	1835 08 09	Denmark
Ratz ....Christian Peter	Bolanz ....Maria Barbara	1855 08 04	
Rawlings ....Eber B.	Skinner...............Ann	1850 12 31	ENG
Rawlins ....Harvey M.	Frost..................Margaret Elzira	1846 12 03	MO, Nishnabothna
Rawlins...........James	Sharp ....Jane	1816 03 19	IN, Harrison
Rawlins...........Joseph S.	Frost..................Mary Ellen	1844 02 01	IL, Hancock Co.

Male	Female	Date	Place
Rawlinson........Charles	Smith.................Catherine	1867 08 14	
Rawson ....Daniel Berry	Boss ....Nancy	1849 11 26	UT, Salt Lake City
Rawson ....Daniel Berry	Taylor ....Mary Melvina	1866 03 10	UT, Salt Lake City
Rawson ....Horace Strong	Coffin................Elizabeth	1825 10 09	IN Wash. Co.,
Rawson ....John	Chantry ....Sarah	1844 04 08	ENG, Derbyshire
Ray ....John Alexander	Tibbits ....Elizabeth	1855 10 11	UT, Salt Lake City
Raymond	Morgan...............Hannah		
Raymond ....Charles J.	Chapman ....Hannah	1865 11 07	UT, Salt Lake City
Raymond ....Grandison	Hall.....................Celia	1849 08 12	NY
Raymond ....Samuel J.	Dean ....Elizabeth	1828	
Read................George Franklin	Pickett ....Maria Louisa	1891 06 01	
Read................John	Gregory ....Christianna	1819 02 17	PA, Philadelphia
Read................John B.	Slater.................Mary Ann	1856 05 20	
Read................Samuel George	Quilley ....Elizabeth G.	1836	ENG
Read................William M.	Brimley ....Sarah	1814 12 18	ENG
Read................William Smith	Simmons ....Elizabeth	1852 04 20	MO, St. Louis
Reber...............Samuel	Wintsch ....Anna Magdalena	1863	UT, Payson
Redd................John Hardison	Hancock.............Elizabeth	1826 03 27	NC
Redford...........Robert Patefield	Eckersall ....Lettice Brown	1841 04 12	ENG
Redford...........Robert Patefield	Vay....................Patience	1856 11 29	UT, Salt Lake City
Redington ....John	Brown................Marian	1860 12 01	ENG
Redman...........Jefferson Davis	Proctor ....Ellen		
Reece ....David	Garrett...............Elizabeth Albania	1880 07 06	
Reed...............Calvin	Curtis.................Mary	1841 07 11	IL, Nauvoo
Reed...............Charles	Doxey.................Mary	1843 03 06	ENG
Reed...............Henry	Steadwell ....Sarah (Sally)		
Reed...............John	Bearce...............Rebecca	1805	NH, Cheshire
Reed...............John	Murray................Mary	1815 04 08	
Reed...............Levi Ward	Pettit..................Matilda Eve	1852	UT, Salt Lake City
Reed...............Tillison	Byam..................Delia Deliverance	1810 12 30	NH, Jaffrey
Reeder............Robert	Flatt....................Ellen		
Reeder............Robert	Wilkinson............Lydia	1861 04 15	UT, Hyde Park
Rees ....Alfred	David..................Emma	1859 08 14	UT, Spanish Fork
Rees ....Henry Davis	Jenkins...............Margaret John	1859 03 29	UT, Spanish Fork
Rees ....Joseph A.	Hessell ....Christina Amelia	1872 06 24	UT, Salt Lake City
Rees ....Moroni	Vaughan.............Emily	1869 06 28	UT, Salt Lake City
Rees ....Thomas John	Davies ....Margaret	1836 09 10	Wales
Reese ....Charles	Griffiths..............Sarah	1856 09 06	Wales
Reese ....David	Eynon.................Martha	1855	Ocean
Reese ....John D.	Morgan...............Mary	1842 07 04	IRE
Reese ....Thomas	Jones ....Margaret	1838 12 31	Wales
Reeves ....William	Coles..................Sarah		UT
Reeves ....William	Long...................Frances		
Reeves ....William	Storer ....Mary Ann	1851	
Reid ....Edward	Shields ....Sarah	1853 08 23	IRE
Reid ....George	Whork.................Elizabeth	1817 05 14	
Reid ....Jesse Porter	Rush...................Mary B.	1840 08 23	IL, Nauvoo
Reid ....John	Davis..................Mary	1862	Trail
Reid ....John Kirkwood	Jackson..............Elizabeth	1868 01 05	UT, Salt Lake City
Reid ....John T.	Hudson...............Ann		
Reid ....John Whirk	Western..............Agnes	1865 04 24	UT, Meadow
Reid ....Thomas Hand	Macfarlane ....Ann	1854 02 09	UT, Salt Lake City
Reid ....William	Dyre ....Jane	1826	IRE
Reid ....William Taylor	Cox.....................Mary Adelaide	1869 11 23	UT, Manti

Male	Female	Date	Place
Reid ....William Taylor	McEwan ....Jane		
Reidhead ....John	....	1865	
Reidhead ....John	York....................Julia Ann K.	1863 10 24	
Remington ....Jerome N.	Badger ....Lydia Ripley	1848 01 22	
Rex ....William	Brough ....Mary Elizabeth	1874 10 06	UT, Salt Lake City
Reynolds ....John	Ramsey................Phoebe Jane	1828 01 28	
Reynolds ....Warren Ford	McNeil ....Christina	1857 06 28	
Reynolds ....Warren Ford	Merrell ....Edna Maria	1846 01 03	
Reynolds ....William F.	Hawley ....Anna	1846 02 22	
Reynolds ....William F.	Hawley ....Elizabeth		
Reynolds ....William F.	Pedersen................Ane Kirstine	1861 10 27	UT, Salt Lake City
Reynolds ....William F.	Thompson ....Neleene		
Reynolds ....William G.	Storr ....Elizabeth Maria	1872 01 06	UT, Heber
Reynolds ....William Pitt	Bardwell ....Melissa	1841 10 06	PA, Erie
Rhead.............Josiah	Lewis..................Eliza	1850 04 09	ENG, Longport
Rhees ....Charles Horatio	Budd....................Elizabeth	1863 05 21	ENG, Liverpool
Rhees ....Charles Horatio	Parratt ....Eliza	1866 12 07	UT, Salt Lake City
Rhees ....David Edward	Evans ....Alice	1853 02 13	Ocean
Rhodes ....Joseph	Clark..................Margaret Caldwell	1859	UT, Logan
Rhodes ....Joseph	Jones ....Mary Ann	1881 12 22	UT, Salt Lake City
Rice ....Ira	Harrington ....Sarah Ann	1825	NY, Ontario
Rice ....Ira	Morris ....Elizabeth Ann	1856 11 20	
Rice ....James	Oliver..................Ann	1870 03 22	UT, Salt Lake City
Rice ....Leonard Gurley	Babbitt................Elizabeth A.	1849 03 18	IA, Kanesville
Rice ....Leonard Gurley	Buckwalter ....Margaret	1853 01 02	UT, Salt Lake City
Rice ....Oscar North	Mathews.............Margaret	1869 11 15	UT, Logan
Rice ....William Kelsey	Geer...................Lucy Witter	1844 10 06	IL, Nauvoo
Rich ....Charles Coulson	Graves ....Eliza Ann	1845 01 06	IL, Nauvoo
Rich ....Charles Coulson	Grover...............Emeline	1846 02 02	IL, Nauvoo
Rich ....Charles Coulson	Pea....................Sarah D.	1837 02 11	MO, Far West
Rich ....Charles Coulson	Peck...................Sarah Jane	1845 01 09	IL, Nauvoo
Rich ....Charles Coulson	Phelps ....Mary Ann	1845 01 06	IL, Nauvoo
Rich ....Charles Coulson	Sargent ....Harriet	1847 03 28	NE
Rich ....Hyrum Smith	Stock..................Elizabeth	1867 06 29	UT, Salt Lake City
Rich ....John Henry	Pond....................Lydia	1852 12 26	ENG
Rich ....Joseph	Christian..............Maria Bentley	1857 07 26	UT, Salt Lake City
Rich ....Joseph	Howard................Elizabeth	1853 01 18	UT, Salt Lake City
Rich ....Joseph	O'Neal ....Nancy	1808 06 23	KY
Richard ....John W.	Ross....................Mary		
Richards	Campbell............Mary Ann		
Richards ....Franklin D.	Longstroth ....Nanny	1857 03 06	UT, Salt Lake City
Richards ....Franklin D.	Peirson................Susan Sanford	1853 06 26	UT, Salt Lake City
Richards ....Franklin D.	Snyder.................Jane	1842 12 18	
Richards ....Franklin D.	Thompson ....Mary	1857 03 06	
Richards ....Heber John	Johnson ....Mary Julia	1862 04 09	UT, Salt Lake City
Richards ....Hyrum T. H.	Muir....................Agnes	1876 04 18	UT, Salt Lake City
Richards ....John Kenny	Hill ....Agnes	1831	Canada
Richards ....Levi	Goodall..............Persis	1848 01 27	IL, Nauvoo
Richards ....Levi	Griffith ....Sarah	1843 12 25	IL, Nauvoo
Richards ....Levi Willard	Greene...............Louisa Lulu	1873 06 16	UT, Salt Lake City
Richards ....Levi Willard	Young..................Persis Louisa	1884	
Richards ....Morgan	Harris ....Elizabeth	1857 02 17	Wales
Richards ....Phineas	Dewey ....Wealthy	1818 02 24	MA, Richmond
Richards ....Richard S.	Stenhouse............Ida Lulu	1882	

Male	Female	Date	Place
Richards ....Samuel W.	Jones ....Ann	1857 03 19	
Richards ....Samuel W.	Mayer ....Jane Elizabeth	1856 02 16	UT, Salt Lake City
Richards ....Samuel W.	Parker ....Mary Ann	1855 02 14	UT, Salt Lake City
Richards ....Samuel W.	Parker ....Mary Haskins	1846 01 29	IL, Nauvoo
Richards ....Samuel W.	Robinson............Helena Lydia	1856 02 16	UT, Salt Lake City
Richards ....Samuel W.	Whittaker............Elizabeth	1859 01 27	UT, Salt Lake City
Richards ....Silas	Brady................Keziah Frances	1855 02 06	UT, Salt Lake City
Richards ....Silas	McClenaham.......Elizabeth	1829 11 05	OH, Sidney
Richards ....Willard	Longstroth..........Nanny	1846 01 25	IL, Nauvoo
Richards ....Willard	Thompson..........Mary	1846 01 27	IL, Nauvoo
Richards ....William	Howells ....Mary	1861 12 27	
Richardson ......Ebenezer	King...................Angeline	1833	
Richardson ......Edmund	Darrow ....Mary Ann	1840 08 02	NY, Salem
Richardson ......John	Hudson...............Ann		ENG
Richardson ......Josiah	Knight................Sarah Ann	1862 12 22	UT, Plain City
Richardson ......Shadrach	Stewart...............Lavina	1839	
Richardson ......Thomas	Stone.................Merab	1864	UT, Salt Lake City
Richardson .....William	Hone ....Sarah Jane	1879 10 16	UT, Springville
Richardson ......William A.	Knight................Violet Ellen	1867 01	UT, Salt Lake City
Riches ....John	Sufling ....Mary	1839	
Richey ....James	Mangum ....Sarah Frances	1857	
Richins............Albert Francis	Jones ....Mary Jane	1874 11 16	UT, Salt Lake City
Richins............Charles Wager	Shill ....Louisa	1851 01 27	
Richmond ....Benjamin	Vallier ....Mary Jane	1852 10 15	UT, Salt Lake City
Richmond ....Joseph B.	Orton ....Emma	1863 05 03	
Richmond ....Thomas	Green................Elizabeth		MO, St. Louis
Ricks..............Hyrum	Bitter.................Martha	1880 04 01	UT, Salt Lake City
Ricks..............Joel	Fiske ....Sarah Beriah	1852 10 26	
Ricks..............Joel	Martin ....Eleanor	1827 05 17	KY, Trigg Co.
Ricks..............Thomas Edwin	Dille ....Ruth Caroline	1863 12 06	
Ricks..............Thomas Edwin	Hendricks............Tabitha	1852 08 18	
Ricks..............Thomas Edwin	Loader................Tamar	1857 03 27	
Ricks..............Thomas Edwin	Shupe................Elizabeth Jane	1857 03 27	UT, Salt Lake City
Ricks..............Thomas Edwin	Yallop ....Ellen Maria	1866 11 29	UT, Salt Lake City
Ridd ....William James	Priscott ....Mary Catherine	1888 03 21	UT, Logan
Riddle ....Isaac	Eagles ....Mary Ann	1863 08 29	
Riddle ....Isaac	Levi ....Mary Ann	1853 03 06	UT, North Ogden
Riddle ....Isaac	Turnbaugh..........Mary Caroline		
Riddle ....John	Quantrille............Susannah Evered		
Rider...............John	McDonald...........Mary	1867 07 27	
Ridges ....Joseph H.	Gridlestone.........Emma	1858 01 31	UT, Salt Lake City
Ridges ....Joseph H.	Walker................Ann Agatha	1860 03 04	UT, Salt Lake City
Riding ....Christopher L.	Hale...................Mary Ann	1840	ENG, Burley
Riding ....Henry Hale	Blake.................Elizabeth	1870	UT, Salt Lake City
Rigby ....Aaron	Ellison ....Elizabeth	1824 07 25	
Rigby ....Barnett	Weaver...............Ann	1839 12 25	ENG, Leyland
Rigby ....Edward	Hartley...............Susanna	1811 02 26	ENG
Rigby ....George Clark	Clarke................Mary Caroline	1883 03 01	UT, Salt Lake City
Rigby ....James	Jordan ....Fanny	1870 03 21	UT, Salt Lake City
Rigby ....James	Littlewood...........Jane Lovenia	1832 10 07	ENG, Stockport
Rigby ....John	Liptrot................Grace	1860 09 16	ENG, Deane
Rigby ....John	Wright................Lucy Ann	1867 11 08	UT, Salt Lake City
Rigby ....Seth	Riding................Betsy Ann Wade	1852 01 26	UT, Salt Lake City
Rigby ....William	Haslam...............Sarah	1864 03 03	UT, Salt Lake City

Male	Female	Date	Place
Rigby ....William F.	Clark...................Mary	1852 08 09	ENG, Hatfield
Rigby ....William F.	Clarke..............Sarah Angeline	1881 04 28	UT, Salt Lake City
Rigby ....William F.	Eckersley ....Mary Ann	1871	
Rigby ....William F.	Eckersley ....Sophia	1865 06 25	
Riggs ....John	Bullock ....Jane Kilton	1843 10 08	NY, Moira
Riggs ....John	Nielsen ....Dorthe	1864 12 27	UT, Salt Lake City
Riggs ....John Ensign	Hamblin..............Adeline Amarilla	1851 12 17	UT, Tooele
Riley ....James	Emmett..............Harriet	1844	ENG, Lancaster
Riley ....John	Malley.................Mary Ann	1849 05 22	ENG, Preston
Riley ....Thomas Katen	Stoker................Susan Ann	1863 04 06	
Riley ....William W.	Lott ....Elizabeth	1849	IL
Ringrose ....Richard	Maycock.............Ann	1835 07 19	ENG, Coventry
Ringrose ....William	Anderson.............Ann	1812	ENG
Ririe ....James	Boyack ....Ann	1855 11 23	UT, Salt Lake City
Riser ....George C. Jr.	Player.................Zillah Jane	1871 12 25	UT, Salt Lake City
Ritchie ....James	Bright.................Martha	1863 07	UT, Salt Lake City
Ritchie ....Samuel	Anderson.............Ann	1837 02 05	Scotland
Roach ....William	James ....Ruth	1857 08 23	UT, Spanish Fork
Robb...............James	Turner ....Ann	1847 01 24	Scotland
Robb...............Thomas	Tattersall ....Alice	1871 02 27	UT, Salt Lake City
Robbins ....Charles B.	Allen ....Martha	1865 07 07	UT, Salt Lake City
Robbins ....Charles B.	Pitkin ....Harriet Vilate	1878	
Robbins ....Charles B.	Young.................Jane Adeline	1855 11 22	UT, Salt Lake City
Robbins ....Edward	Campbell.............Mary Ann	1797	
Robbins ....Edward Jr.	McAllister ....Agnes Nancy	1833	ENG
Robbins ....George	Oades ....Elizabeth	1848 12 09	MO, St. Louis
Robbins ....James	Childe.................Mary	1859 03 01	ENG, Coventry
Robbins ....Joseph	Arbon ....Ellen	1863 03 01	UT, Provo
Robbins ....William	Carter ....Jane	1872 07 14	UT, Hansel Spring
Robbins ....Wilson C.	Kofoed................Wilhelmine F.	1866 03 02	ID, Weston
Roberds..........Thomas R.	Bemis ....Harriet	1859 01 23	CA, San Bern.
Roberts..........Benjamin	Everington...........Ann Reed	1848 06 05	ENG, Poplar
Roberts..........Benjamin Morgan	Bullock ....Mary Ann	1856 11 23	
Roberts..........Bolivar	Benson...............Pemelia Emma	1867 11 23	UT, Salt Lake City
Roberts..........Brigham Henry	Curtis.................Margaret	1890 04	UT, Salt Lake City
Roberts..........Daniel	Lloyd ....Gwen W.	1843 01 28	Wales
Roberts..........Edward Killick	Mathews.............Emeline	1850 04 19	UT, Salt Lake City
Roberts..........Edward Killick	Rollins ....Ann Sophia	1869 04 19	UT, Salt Lake City
Roberts..........Ephraim H.	Bell ....Emma Dorothy	1861 11 02	UT, Provo
Roberts..........George	Dallimore............Maria Ann	1868 10 11	UT, Salt Lake City
Roberts..........Horace	Bigelow ....Mary Jane	1852 09 29	UT
Roberts..........Horace	Graves ....Jane Eliza	1856 12 11	UT, Salt Lake City
Roberts..........Horace	McEvers ....Harriet	1828 06 05	IL, Morgan Co.
Roberts..........Hugh	Owens.................Mary	1830 05 04	Wales
Roberts..........John T.	James ....Emily	1875 11 15	
Roberts..........Levi	Davis ....Sarah E.	1857 03 07	UT, Salt Lake City
Roberts..........Levi	Hefford ....Harriet Ann	1835 08 18	ENG, Deerhurst
Roberts..........Orville Clark	Coray ....Mary Knowlton	1868 07 24	UT, Provo
Roberts..........Robert	Hughes...............Catherine	1842 08 25	Wales
Roberts..........Robert David	Roberts ....Hannah	1870 06 06	UT, Salt Lake City
Roberts..........Samuel	Matty.................Elizabeth	1823 11 19	ENG
Roberts..........Samuel	Peat...................Mary	1852 05 18	ENG, Derby
Roberts..........Sidney	Rowell ....Sarah Ann	1830 05 26	
Roberts..........William	Evans ....Rachel Jones	1848	Wales

Male	Female	Date	Place
Roberts............William	Jones.................Jannet	1863	UT, Farmington
Roberts............William M.	Kofoed...............Wilhelmine F.	1885 10 03	ID, Montpelier
Robertson........John	Edward...............Elizabeth	1823 07 27	Scotland
Robertson........Thomas	Cordingly............Sarah Ann	1854 12 19	UT, Salt Lake City
Robins.............James	Lambert..............Elizabeth	1840	ENG
Robins.............Richard	Fullwell...............Ann	1808 12 01	ENG
Robins.............Thomas F.	Johnson.............Ann	1844 08 20	ENG, Leigh
Robins.............Thomas L. A.	Nielsen..............Maria Abelone	1876 04 28	UT, Scipio
Robinson.........Andrew	McGhie...............Agnes	1882 05 08	UT, Mill Creek
Robinson.........Henry	Townsend..........Martha Ann	1852	MO
Robinson.........Isaac Payson	Stoddard............Elsie Permelia	1863 05 29	UT, Salt Lake City
Robinson.........James	Pollard...............Mary	1849 07 28	ENG
Robinson.........John	Parsons.............Abigail	1814 07 09	ME, Cushing
Robinson.........John Jr.	Roberts.............Lucinda Victoria	1853 01 24	UT, Big Cottonwood
Robinson.........John R.	Coupe................Alice	1842 03 05	Ocean
Robinson.........John R.	Coupe................Jane	1847 08 24	IA, Pottawattamie
Robinson.........John R.	Schofield............Emma	1873 10 09	UT, Salt Lake City
Robinson.........Joseph	Parkes...............Jemima	1853 11 26	ENG, Derby
Robinson.........Joseph Lee	Atwood..............Laurinda Maria	1847 03 21	NE
Robinson.........Joseph Lee	Foster................Lydia	1853 02 16	UT, Salt Lake City
Robinson.........Joseph Lee	Taylor................Mary	1867 02 02	UT, Salt Lake City
Robinson.........Joseph Lee	Wood.................Maria	1832 07 23	NY, Booneville
Robinson.........Oliver Lee	Miller.................Lucy Maria	1854 11 26	UT, Farmington
Robinson.........Richard S.	.........................Mary Kate		
Robinson.........Richard S.	Eccles...............Mary Ann	1860	
Robinson.........Richard S.	Wootton.............Elizabeth	1853	UT, American Fork
Robison...........Alexander	Wagaman...........Nancy Ellen	1828	
Robison...........Benjamin H.	Andre.................Lillis Alvira	1853 05 12	IL, Crete
Robison...........Benjamin H.	Turner................Susannah	1864 03 26	
Robison...........Charles William	Hardy.................Lucy Adeline	1865 12 03	UT, Hooper
Robison...........David	Grover................Mary Elizabeth	1860 12 26	UT, North Morgan
Robison...........Joseph	Hancock.............Lucretia	1829 02 05	NY, Clay
Robison...........Lewis	Gheen................Louisa	1858 06 27	UT, Provo
Robison...........Lewis	Waite.................Mary Jane	1855 10 05	
Robison...........Peter	Chaffee..............Selina Hayward	1839 10 06	NY, Gilvert Mills
Robison...........William H.	Squires...............Elizabeth	1823 01 23	
Robson............James P.	Skeen................Eliza Jane	1865 05 03	
Rock................Henry	Robison.............Leannah	1858 12 17	PA, Tomstown
Rockwell..........Orrin Porter	Neff...................Mary Ann	1848	
Rockwood........Albert P.	Haven................Nancy	1827 04 03	MA, Holliston
Rockwood........Albert P.	Hodgkins............Angeline	1846 01 21	IL, Nauvoo
Rockwood........Albert P.	Olsen.................Juliane Sophia	1863 04 11	UT, Salt Lake City
Rockwood........Albert Perry	Teeples..............Elvira	1846 01 21	IL, Nauvoo
Rodeback........Charles	Morgan..............Jane	1838 10 18	PA, Newlin
Rodeback........Charles L.	Clayton..............Mary Ann	1872 10 16	
Rodeback........James	Beagle...............Phebe	1832 05 24	
Rodwell...........Edward	Parkinson...........Sarah	1850 02 12	New South Wales
Rodwell...........John	Quilley...............Elizabeth G.	1863 01 10	UT, Salt Lake City
Roe.................James	Hollis.................Elizabeth	1840 03 24	ENG
Rogers............Alexander	Brown................Janet	1864	
Rogers............Alma Denton	Collins...............Mary Jane	1861 06 15	AK, Fort Smith
Rogers............David	Meyer................Mary Ann	1853 02 20	UT, Salt Lake City
Rogers............David White	Collins...............Martha	1811 12 05	Canada
Rogers............Francis Baker	Brown................Jemima		ENG

Male	Female	Date	Place
Rogers............Henry Clay	Higbee...............Emma	1856 10 19	UT, Provo
Rogers............John	Williams..............Anne	1838 12 13	Wales
Rogers............Mark	Whitlock ....Sally Rae	1849 01 11	
Rogers............Noah	Hollister..............Eda	1819 10 08	
Rogers............Ruel Mills	Donaghe ....Diannah Lovina	1853 12 08	MO, Enterprise
Rogers............Samuel H.	Page...................Ruth	1853 02 21	UT, Lehi
Rogers............Telemachus	Case..................Martha Diana	1853 12 31	
Rogers............Telemachus	Watton...............Eliza	1843 02 05	LA, New Orleans
Rogers............Theodore	Jones ....Hannah	1852 03 06	UT, Salt Lake City
Rogers............Thomas	Evans ....Ann	1850	MO, St. Louis
Rogers............Thomas E.	Spencer.............Aurelia Read	1851 03 27	
Rogers............William	Adams...............Rebecca	1823 08 10	ENG
Rogerson.........William	Ferron ....Mary Harrison	1826 12 23	ENG, Preston
Rolfe ....Samuel Jones	Hathaway...........Elizabeth W.	1818 03 04	ME
Rollins.............Enoch Perham	Philbrook............Sophia Wing	1829 04 29	
Rollins.............James Henry	Hulme................Hanna	1851 03 03	UT, Salt Lake City
Rollins.............James Henry	Walker...............Eveline	1838 09 04	MO
Rollins.............John Porter	Van Benthuysen..Keziah K.	1815	NY, Livingston
Rollins.............Steuben	France................Amanda Melvina	1855 02 10	UT, Salt Lake City
Rolph ....M. G.	Knudsen.............Annie Johanna	1888	UT, Logan
Romney ....George	Thomas..............Margaret Ann	1863 08 29	UT, Salt Lake City
Romney ....Miles	Gaskell...............Elizabeth	1830 11 06	ENG
Romney ....Miles Park	Hill.....................Hannah Hood	1862 05 10	UT, Salt Lake City
Ronnow ....Christian P.	Clausen..............Margrethe K.	1862 02 03	
Ronnow ....Christian P.	Hansen...............Laurine Emilia	1862 11 13	UT, Ephraim
Rooker............John Bunyon	Smith.................Mary Elizabeth	1866 03 07	UT, Heber
Rooker............Samuel McRae	Wooldridge.........Permelia Emily	1835 07 27	
Rooks ....William A.	Colebrook...........Ellen Susanna	1873	
Root...............Almerin E.	Hansen...............Sidse Marie	1867 06 29	
Roper.............Henry	Grayson ....Mary Ann	1843 10 24	ENG, Sheffield
Roper.............John Henry	Mellor ....Charlotte E.	1857 02 04	UT, Provo
Roper.............John W.	Smith.................Susanna	1831 10 18	ENG, March
Rosberg..........Carl	Ericksson ....Helena	1849 04 07	Sweden
Rose ....Abraham	Sherry ....Mary Ann		
Rose ....Wesley	Nielsen ....Mary Ann	1898 06 01	
Rosenbaum .....Morris D.	Neibaur ....Alice	1858 04 02	UT, Salt Lake City
Rosenbaum .....Morris D.	Snow ....Abigail Harriet		
Rosengren.......Niels	Kay....................Josephine J.	1868 02 14	UT, Salt Lake City
Rosequist ....Pehr T.	Larson ....Ingeborg	1843 05 28	Sweden
Roskelley.........Samuel	Burton ....Sarah Maud	1885 12 25	UT, Logan
Roskelley.........Samuel	Hendricks ....Rebecca	1858 07 23	UT, Salt Lake City
Ross ....Alexander	Williams..............Diana Mary		
Ross ....Andrew Jackson	Smith.................Rachel Leah	1837 09 21	
Ross ....David	Coolbear ....Caroline		
Ross ....David James	Jackson..............Mary Ann	1857 12 13	UT, Salt Lake City
Ross ....James Darling	Smith.................Sarah Elizabeth	1857 09 08	ENG, London
Ross ....James Melvin	Nelson...............Martha Ann	1856 03 14	
Ross ....Thomas	Smith.................Rachel	1835 09 30	
Ross ....William	Ogden ....Phoebe	1810	NY
Rossiter ....Solomon	Llewellyn ....Mary		PA, Bloomsburg
Rounds ....William Carmer	Longhurst...........Amelia Ann	1868 10 17	UT, Salt Lake City
Roundy ....Jared Curtis	Drake ....Elizabeth Jefford	1879 01 17	
Roundy ....Jared Curtis	Jenne ....Lovise	1852 02 26	UT, Salt Lake City
Roundy ....Jared Curtis	Snyder...............Eliza	1856 05 09	UT, Salt Lake City

Male	Female	Date	Place
Roundy ....Lorenzo W.	Parrish...............Priscilla	1857 04 22	
Roundy ....Lorenzo W.	Wallace ....Susannah	1847 05 16	Trail
Roundy ....Myron S.	Deuel..................Mercy Ann	1864 12 03	UT, Salt Lake City
Roundy ....Shadrach	Quimby................Betsy	1814 06 22	VT, Rockingham
Rowan ....Charles H.	Flake ....Elizabeth	1867 07 15	CA, San Bernardino
Rowan ....Matthew	Martin ....Jane Ann	1853 06 06	ENG
Rowe ....David	Manning ....Hannah	1820	
Rowe ....Manning	Richards.............Elizabeth A.	1854 07 27	
Rowland ....William	Evans ....Rachel Jones		
Rowley............George	Hall.....................Elizabeth	1859	
Rowley............John	James ....Emma	1873 04 21	
Rowley............Samuel	Taylor ....Ann	1865 04 23	UT, Parowan
Rowley............William	Rowley ....Ann Jewel	1836 08 22	ENG, Worcester
Roylance ....Hyrum	Newby ....Isabella Roberts	1867 05 04	
Roylance ....James	Barnett ....Georgina Ann M.	1871 10 09	UT, Salt Lake City
Roylance ....John	Oakes.................Mary Ann	1830	ENG
Roylance ....William	Clucas ....Lucy	1864 03 27	
Roylance ....William J.	Smith..................Martha Janet	1860 10 01	
Roylance ....William J.	Yarwood.............Mary	1842	IA, Montrose
Royle ....Henry	Capstick ....Ann	1848 05 03	NE
Royle ....Henry	Ward ....Isabella	1855 05 21	
Royle ....Henry Moroni Jr.	Bahr ....Alice		
Rudd................Lorenzo Dow	Bedford ....Annis	1857 10 08	UT, Salt Lake City
Rudd................Lorenzo Dow	Bedford ....Sarah		
Rudy ....Josiah Philip	Timothy ....Martha	1891 05 26	UT, Vernal
Rumel ....John H.	Gray ....Abigail	1847 07 11	MO, St. Louis
Rush	Rush...................Mary B.		
Rushby ....George	Drabwell ....Jemima	1814 01 17	ENG
Russell............Allen	Blythe ....Henrietta Eaton	1906 10 24	UT, Manti
Russell............Alonzo H.	Foster.................Louisa Maria	1856 04 18	UT, Salt Lake City
Russell............Charles L.	Buckland ....Samantha Jane	1845 01 26	VT, Royalton
Russell............Isaac Nelson	Stillman ....Frances Maria	1850	UT, Salt Lake City
Russell............Samuel	Thorn..................Abigail	1845	IL, Nauvoo
Russell............Samuel L.	Stillman ....Frances Maria	1846 01 20	IL, Nauvoo
Ryan ....William T.	Cochrane ....Janet	1858 10 20	NY
Rydalch ....William C.	Mitton ....Jane	1848 10 07	
Rynearson ....Andrew J.	Alexander............Sarah Elizabeth	1875 01 28	
Rynearson ....Andrew J.	Herbert ....Ann	1857 03 15	

S

Male	Female	Date	Place
Sabey ....James	Bone...................Jane	1855 09 13	ENG, Northill
Sabin ....David	Dorwart ....Elizabeth	1832 02 19	PA, Lancaster
Sabin ....David	Ott ....Ann Magdalena	1879 08 07	
Sabin ....Henry Dorwart	Ericksen ....Kirsten Martena		
Sadler.............James	Evans ....Elizabeth	1857 01 25	UT, Salt Lake City
Safley ....John H.	Hillman ....Sarah	1881 12 25	
Sagers ....William H. H.	Smith..................Marion	1858 06 05	UT, Provo
Sainsbury ....John Henry	Oliphant..............Ann Maria	1871	
Sainsbury ....John Henry	Wiscombe ....Laura	1871	
Sainsbury ....John Henry	Wiscombe ....Martha Ann	1865 12 08	ENG, Portsmouth
Salisbury.........David	Madsen ....Anna	1858 09 09	UT, Nephi
Salisbury.........Francis J.	Bates..................Sarah Ann	1871 05 09	UT, Salt Lake City

Male	Female	Date	Place
Salisbury..........Joshua	Hoskin...............Elizabeth	1858 10 13	IL, Shawneetown
Salisbury..........Richard	Castle.................Hannah	1822 08 29	ENG, Packington
Salisbury..........Thomas	Knowles.............Ellen	1864 10 29	
Salmon............James	Robertson..........Margaret	1857 06 19	Scotland
Salmon............William G.	Moody...............Dorinda Melisa	1825 07 24	AL
Sampson.........Isaac	Hendryx.............Martha	1822 04 07	OH, New London
Sampson.........James K. P.	Turner................Rose Ann	1869 12 13	
Sampson.........William	Lawrensen.........Margaret	1861 03 10	UT, Santaquin
Sandell............Nils	Eklund................Maria Magdalena	1826 09 28	Sweden
Sanders...........David A.	Grover................Lucy	1868 01 04	
Sanders...........Ellis M.	Roberts..............Rachel Broom	1830 11 09	DE
Sanders...........John F.	Clement..............Mary Irene	1855 07 15	
Sanders...........Moses M.	Faucett...............Amanda A.	1826 01 12	TN, Maury
Sanders...........Moses Martin	Sparks................Mary Jane	1847 03 21	
Sanders...........William	Hunt...................Elizabeth	1837 01 08	
Sanderson.......Henry W.	Cole...................Sarah Jane		
Sanderson.......Henry W.	Sanders..............Rebecca Ann	1850 03 07	IL, Pigeon Grove
Sanderson.......James	Sparks................Mary Jane	1824 07 07	MA
Sandine...........Lars J.	Johanson............Albertina W.	1869 03 09	UT, Salt Lake City
Sanford............Cyrus	Stockwell............Sylvia Elmina	1836 10 05	
Sanford............Samuel	Mariner...............Jane	1865 01	
Sanford............William T.	Pymm.................Sarah Ann		
Sant................George	Mustard..............Margaret	1858 10 02	UT, Cedar City
Sant................John	Shaw..................Mary	1831 12 12	
Sargeant.........John H. S.	Jones.................Rhoda		
Sargent...........David Elmer	Reid...................Fanny May	1862 01 26	UT, Salt Lake City
Sargent...........William Pinkney	Snow..................Julia Marie	1877 04 08	
Saunders.........Demas A.	Barwell...............Hannah	1860 03 20	
Saunders.........George	Ashdown.............Alice B.		ENG
Saunders.........William G.	Batchelor............Amelia Ann	1866 09 22	UT, Salt Lake City
Saunders.........William G.	Merrel.................Phoebe	1839 11 11	
Saunders.........William G.	Mortensen..........Karen Marie	1864 02 14	
Saunsosee......Louis	Fausett...............Narcissus R.	1849	IA
Savage............David Leonard	Jacaway.............Susannah	1878 02 09	
Savage............Henry	Power.................Sarah	1840 10 23	ENG, Middlesex
Savage............Joseph	Hartley...............Hannah	1851 11 17	MO, St. Louis
Saville.............George	Westwood...........Caroline	1871 07 20	UT, Salt Lake City
Saville.............George	Westwood...........Ellen	1862 01 11	ENG
Saxton.............Solomon	Dexter................Matilda	1848 10 26	ENG
Scarborough....John	Brook.................Elizabeth	1850 03 07	ENG
Scharling.........Johannes	Nilsson...............Johanna		Sweden
Scheib.............John Pierre	Weinmann...........Catharina	1835 05 17	ENG, London
Schofield..........John	Banks.................Isabelle	1836 11 13	ENG, Staleybridge
Schultz.............	Kumlin.................Anna Christina		
Schwartz..........Jack	McKinnon............Jane		UT, Rich Co.
Scobey............William	Mack..................Almira	1831 08 07	
Scogings.........William B.	Page...................Susan	1862 05 10	UT, Salt Lake City
Scorup............Christian C.	Hansen...............Karen	1866 08 04	UT, Ephraim
Scott...............Andrew Hunter	Miller.................Hannah		UT, Provo
Scott...............Andrew Hunter	Roe....................Sarah Ann	1851 01 12	
Scott...............Ephraim	Smithies.............Sarah Ellen	1867 11 09	
Scott...............John	Menery...............Elizabeth	1836 04 15	Canada
Scott...............John	Pugh...................Mary	1845 03 02	IL, Nauvoo
Scott...............John	Willis..................Sarah Ann	1848 03 24	IL, Nauvoo

Male	Female	Date	Place
Scott ....John	Yeates ....Esther	1860 02 13	UT, Salt Lake City
Scott ....Robert Griffin	Stevens ....Christina	1872 08 05	UT, Salt Lake City
Scott ....Volney H.	Mikesell ....Louisa Catherine	1889 05 25	
Scoville ....Ed	Ross...................Mary	1851	
Scow...............Jens	Mikkelsen ....Anna Johanna	1864 05 28	UT, Salt Lake City
Scow...............Peter Christen	Fugl.................Kirsten Marie	1868 03 09	UT, Salt Lake City
Seabury ....Wesley H.	Keith................Louisa	1837 11 03	
Seaman ....John	Brown................Susannah S.	1855 04 04	UT, Centerville
Seaman ....John W.	Wright................Alice	1870 07 18	UT, Salt Lake City
Seamons ....George	Russell ....Fannie Royce	1860 10 21	UT, Salt Lake City
Seamons ....Henry	King..................Mary	1832 09 09	ENG
Searle ....Breed	Saxton................Rebecca Ann	1827 05 03	NY, Butler
Sears ....Isaac	Norris ....Alice Long	1889 02 14	UT, Salt Lake City
Sears ....John	Wagstaff.............Sarah	1842 12 26	ENG
Sebye ....Henry	Larsen ....Ingeborg Kristine	1856 11 17	
Secrist ....Jacob Foutz	Logan ....Ann Eliza	1842 03 14	PA, Tomstown
Seegmiller ....Charles W.	Forsyth ....Marianne	1868 02 01	UT, Salt Lake City
Seeley ....Justus Azet	Bennett..............Mehitable	1800 03 09	PA, Luzerne
Seeley ....Justus W.	Wilcox ....Clarissa Jane	1842 03 10	IA, Nashville
Seely ....Orange	Olsson................Hanna	1863 07 24	UT, Mt. Pleasant
Seely ....William	Decker................Lucy Ann	1833	
Sellers ....William Hyrum	Hutchison ....Euphemia	1871 12 11	UT, Salt Lake City
Sellew.............Chauncy	Miles..................Sarah Ann	1841 07 07	
Sellwood..........William C.	Louder...............Catherine	1853 08 01	
Selman ....Charles	Francom ....Mary Ann	1870 04 04	UT, Payson
Sessions.........Carlos Lyon	Wintle ....Elizabeth	1864 04 02	UT, Salt Lake City
Sessions.........Daniel A.	Baum..................Rachel Jenetta	1856 12 27	UT, Provo
Sessions.........David	Bartlett...............Patty	1812 06 28	ME, Newry
Sessions.........David	Teeples ....Harriet Elvira	1849	
Sessions........Perrigrine	Bryson................Sarah Ann	1866 09 29	UT, Salt Lake City
Sessions.........Perrigrine	Crossley ....Sarah		
Sessions.........Perrigrine	Mabey ....Esther	1868 11 22	UT, Salt Lake City
Sessions.........Richard	Haws.................Lucretia	1821 04 14	IL, White Co.
Sessions.........Solomon	Hargraves ....Mary	1796	
Severson ....Halvar	Evensen ....Mathie	1850 11 28	Norway
Sevey ....George W.	Butler.................Phoebe Melinda	1854 12 05	UT, Spanish Fork
Sevey ....George W.	Imlay ....Margaret N.		
Sevey ....George W.	Libby ....Hannah	1831 06 01	NY
Sevey ....George W.	Thomas ....Ann	1877	
Sevy ....John Franklin	Libby ....Sarah Ann S.	1854 07 08	PA, Ripley
Sewell.............Joseph	Stevens ....Sarah	1814 01 10	ENG, Norfolk
Shaffer............George Henry	Jessop................Esther Ann	1862 10 15	UT
Shaffer............Henry	Beard ....Eve	1816	VA, Abingdon
Shaffer............John Isaac	Hill.....................Nancy Ann	1847	
Sharp..............Brigham Young	Haynes ....Sarah Ann	1876 11 05	
Sharp..............Charles	Malin ....Ann Penn	1859 06 27	UT, Salt Lake City
Sharp..............James	Rogers ....Elizabeth		
Sharp..............John W.	Bailey ....Ann Maria	1861 03 17	ENG, Norwich
Sharp..............Jonathan	Thorpe................Elizabeth	1831 08 02	ENG, Brotherton
Sharp..............Jonathan Jr.	Jowett................Annie	1868	ENG
Sharp..............Joseph Condie	Bennett..............Jane Louise	1893 06 14	UT, Salt Lake City
Sharp..............Norman	Sargent ....Martha Jane	1845 09	IL, Nauvoo
Sharp..............William	Paterson.............Elizabeth Blair	1828 08 16	Scotland
Sharples ....Peter	Kilner..................Rachel		ENG

Male	Female	Date	Place
Shaw ....Abraham	Lawrenson ....Jane	1856 12 02	UT, Provo
Shaw ....Charles	Griffin ....Harriet Ann	1860 04 16	ENG
Shaw ....Edward Stubbs	Wrigley ....Catherine		
Shaw ....Elijah	Thomas ....Martha Ann	1850 04 06	IA, Kanesville
Shaw ....John	Fox ....Polly Maria	1812 01 01	NY, Victor
Shaw ....Myrtello	Austin ....Harriet Orilla	1839 09 17	NY, Vermontville
Shaw ....William M.	Chase................Diana Severance	1849 01 01	UT, Ogden
Shearer...........Daniel	Jacques..............Vienna		MO
Sheffield ....Anson	Mott ....Maria Howe	1832 03 11	
Shelley............James Boyer	Bathgate............Mary	1856 12 21	
Shelley............William B.	Wheeler..............Jane Dunn	1845 11 10	ENG, Bridgenorth
Shelton ....Stephen	Bonner ....Margaret	1876 09 11	UT, Salt Lake City
Shepherd........Alfren D.	Davey.................Rosina		
Shepherd........Moses T.	..........................Mary Christina		
Shepherd........Moses T.	Adamson............Eliza Jane	1840 03 22	IN, Mt. Pleasant
Shepherd........Moses T.	Bryant................Martha Amanda		
Shepherd........Moses T.	Garlic.................Hannah		
Sherman...........John	Hogeboom ....Hannah		
Sherman...........Lyman R.	Johnson ....Delcena D.	1829 01 16	NY, Pomfret
Sherwin ....Edwin	Johnson ....Sarah Eliza V.		
Shields.............John	Cunningham........Primrose	1827 08 16	
Shields.............John	Sutherland...........Isabella	1860 12 08	
Shields.............John C.	Micklejohn ....Jane	1865 12 22	UT, Tooele
Shields.............John Fenton	Howell ....Mary	1847 07 01	IL, New Lancaster
Shimmin ....Robert C.	Christensen.........Ann		
Shimmin ....Robert C.	Clucas ....Hannah	1848 11 19	Isle of Man
Shimmin ....Robert C.	Larsen ....Ana Christensen	1880 07	
Shingleton ....Stephen	Embling ....Alice		
Shingleton ....Stephen	Embling ....Maria	1866 11	UT, Salt Lake City
Shipley............John	Shugars..............Mary	1844 05 26	IL, Nauvoo
Shipley............Robert	Wright.................Harriet	1848 12 03	ENG, Hull
Shipp ....Austin	Farnsworth ....Louisa Caroline	1835 05 05	IN, Blue River
Shipp ....Milford Bard	Curtis.................Margaret	1867 12 01	UT, Salt Lake City
Shipp ....Milford Bard	Reynolds ....Ellis	1866 05 05	
Shirley ....Thomas C.	Bubb...................Martha Sarah	1857 04 08	South Africa
Shoemaker ......Jephtha	Bailey ....Ann Maria	1867 10 02	UT, Manti
Shoemaker ......Jezreel	Golden ....Nancy	1824 04 01	KY, Pendleton Co.
Shorten............James Bussey	Thacker ....Hannah		
Shreve ....Edwin A.	Wickoff ....Elizabeth Holmes	1844 05 09	
Shumway........Charles	Bird....................Henrietta	1852 01 24	UT, Salt Lake City
Shumway........Charles	Minnerly ....Louisa	1845 08	IL, Nauvoo
Shumway........Charles M.	Jardine ....Agnes		
Shumway........Charles M.	Jardine ....Sarah Wilson	1873 09 29	UT, Salt Lake City
Shumway........Stephen B.	Eddy...................Wealthy	1831 01 06	
Shupe ....Andrew J.	Creager ....Elizabeth	1837 10 12	VA, Wythe Co.
Shupe ....Brigham	Wagstaff..............Elizabeth	1871 11 25	UT, Salt Lake City
Shupe ....John W.	Thomas ....Martha Ann	1840	TN, Sullivan Co.
Shupe ....Peter	Wright.................Sarah	1814 12 22	
Shurtz.............Don C. Jr.	Barker ....Mary Alice	1878 10 15	UT, Escalante
Siddoway.........Richard	Hodson................Grace	1877 04 20	
Silcock ....Nicholas T.	Heath ....Jane	1841 04 14	ENG
Sillett..............James	Daines................Lydia		
Silver ....William John	Pile ....Mary Louise	1870 10 12	UT, Salt Lake City
Sim ....William	Eddie..................Janet	1846 06 08	Scotland

Male	Female	Date	Place
Simkins............James	Brooks................Elizabeth		
Simmons ....George	Ford....................Mary Ann	1849 12 24	
Simmons ....Henry	Davis ....Catherine	1847 09 12	ENG, St. James
Simmons ....Joseph M.	Woolley ....Henrietta	1858 07	UT, Salt Lake City
Simmons ....Joseph M.	Woolley ....Rachel Emma	1851 12 18	
Simmons ....Leven	Bradford ....Harriet	1836 02 27	IL, Carthage
Simmons ....Leven	Fisher.................Lydia Rebecca	1856 02 21	UT, Spanish Fork
Simmons ....Samuel	Hillman...............Guilieta Fidelia	1866 01 01	
Simmons ....Samuel	Shackell ....Hannah Maria	1831 10 16	ENG, St. James
Simmons ....William A.	Grover ....Eliza Ann	1856 05 09	
Simmons ....William A.	Grover ....Mary Elizabeth	1850 04 26	UT, Salt Lake City
Simmons ....William B.	Chipman.............Amanda	1825 01 17	Canada
Simmons ....William Bert	Taylor ....Mary	1857 03 15	UT, Salt Lake City
Simms ....John	Treby..................Julia	1822 10 30	CT, New London
Simons ....Edward	Simons ....Jane Meredith	1852 02 14	Ocean
Simons ....Gustavus	Fry.....................Fanny	1874 03	
Simons ....Orawell	Dixon..................Martha	1846 10 11	OH, Kirtland
Simons ....Orawell	Tenney ....Betsy Jane	1861 08 24	UT, Payson
Simper.............Thomas W.	Massey................Elizabeth	1845 10 20	ENG, Chedworth
Simpkins..........James	Kirkbride.............Jane	1844 12 25	ENG, Manchester
Simpkins..........Joseph	Lundblad ....Charlotte Elena	1867 10 18	
Simpson ....Robert M.	Watson................Allison	1862 12 26	
Simpson ....Robert Temple	Johnson ....Hilma Caroline		
Simpson ....William Henry	Smith..................Annie Lorimer	1877 10 03	UT, Randolph
Sims ....George	Gill.....................Caroline	1843 04 04	ENG
Sims ....George	McMurrin ....Isabella	1857 01 13	UT, Salt Lake City
Sinfield............Samuel	Middleton ....Hannah	1857	UT
Singleton ....Albert	Hick....................Hagar	1883 10 18	UT, Salt Lake City
Singleton ....Charles	Romeril................Fanny Mary Ann	1874 08	
Singleton ....Francis	Williams..............Amelia Ann	1840 02	ENG
Singleton ....John	Binns ....Hannah	1857 03 30	UT, American Fork
Singleton ....Robert	Webley ....Susannah	1854 02 05	
Singleton ....William	Johnston ....Anna Maria		
Singleton ....William	Webster...............Phoebe	1853 05 16	
Sirrine ....George E.	Oakey..................Sarah	1879 11 06	
Sirrine ....George W.	Crismon...............Esther Ann	1852 07 04	
Sisam ....Joseph	Payne..................Catherine	1843 07 30	ENG
Skeen ....Joseph	Dolby..................Maria Amanda	1835 09 08	PA, Lancaster Co.
Skeen ....William Dolby	Smith..................Caroline	1858 01 28	UT, Lehi
Skidmore ....Charles B.	Schrader ....Harriet Henriette	1829	
Skidmore ....Henry Brett	Elliott ....Sarah Ann	1854 06 04	PA, Philadelphia
Skinner ....Horace B.	Seace.................Eleanor	1831	OH, Cincinnati
Skinner ....Richard E.	Edds...................Mary	1844	ENG
Skougaard ....Niels M.	Christensen.........Kirsten	1850 01 05	Denmark
Skousen ....Jens Niels	Pedersen............Sidsel Marie	1856 05 06	Denmark
Slade ....Jefferson	Chestnut.............Sarah Mary	1860 11 20	
Slade ....William E.	Lacey ....Amelia	1852 06 28	ENG
Slade ....William Rufus	Moody ....Dorinda Melisa	1853 02 20	
Slater ....Albert G.	Wilde ....Mary Ann	1865 01 01	
Slater ....Richard	Corbridge ....Ann	1834 09 19	
Slater ....Thomas Tyson	Burgess ....Elizabeth	1860 09 27	MO, St. Louis
Slaughter ....Edward	Cronk ....Catherine	1832 08 09	
Slaughter ....Samuel N.	Huey...................Annie E.	1860	
Sleater ....Robert G.	Hancock ....Eliza	1869 05 03	UT, Salt Lake City

Male		Female		Date	Place
Sleater	Robert G.	Higgs	Mary Susannah	1867 09 13	UT, Salt Lake City
Slocum	Elisha	Miller	Alice Ophelia	1877	
Small	James	Hill	Alice		
Smart	Hezekiah B.	Winsor	Elizabeth	1860 06 19	ENG
Smart	Thomas	Bayliss	Elizabeth	1818 06 11	ENG
Smart	Thomas Henry	Lindroth	Hilda Josephine	1879 10 31	UT, Salt Lake City
Smart	Thomas Sharratt	Hayter	Annetta	1845 03 01	France
Smedley	Samuel	Sturton	Eliza	1863 10 26	ENG
Smith		Vockins	Sarah	1836	
Smith		Waite	Martha		
Smith	Absolom W.	Downs	Amy Emily	1840 11 05	
Smith	Absolom W.	Messam	Catherine	1855 10 31	
Smith	Adam Browning	McMurrin	Isabella	1870 05 30	UT, Tooele
Smith	Asa Downs	Draper	Amanda E. M.	1866 03 24	UT, Draper
Smith	Benjamin F.	Simmons	Mary Ann	1874 01 26	UT, Salt Lake City
Smith	Benjamin M.	Wood	Elizabeth Agnes	1855 02 28	UT, American Fork
Smith	Charles N.	Degrey	Maria	1857 12 20	UT, Salt Lake City
Smith	Conrad	Robison	Eliza	1854 07 28	
Smith	Daniel Miley	Sinfield	Emma Hannah	1863 05 10	UT, Salt Lake City
Smith	Daniel W.	Wooding	Sarah	1815 07 10	ENG, Emberton
Smith	Elias	King	Amy Jane	1856 04 15	UT, Salt Lake City
Smith	Elkanah A.	Fulcher	Mary Eade	1863 07 18	UT, Salt Lake City
Smith	George A.	Bigler	Bathsheba W.	1841 07 25	IL, Nauvoo
Smith	George A.	Clement	Nancy	1845 02 26	IL, Nauvoo
Smith	George A.	Libby	Sarah Ann	1845 11 24	IL, Nauvoo
Smith	George A.	Smith	Elizabeth B.	1868 04 11	
Smith	George W.	Wooten	Catherine	1845 12 21	ENG, Eaton Bray
Smith	George Y.	Luckie	Johann	1854 12 29	Scotland
Smith	Henry Jr.	Kershaw	Lydia Eliza	1874 08 03	UT, Salt Lake City
Smith	Henry Jr.	Snow	Ellen		
Smith	Hugh	McDowell	Agnes	1840 03 12	
Smith	Hiram Hyde	Brown	Sarah Amanda	1887 11 10	ID, Weiser
Smith	Hyrum	Fielding	Mary	1837 12 24	OH, Kirtland
Smith	Hyrum	Fielding	Mercy Rachel	1843 08 11	IL, Nauvoo
Smith	Ira	Smith	Philomela	1812 02 02	Canada
Smith	J.V.	Bennett	Emma		
Smith	James	Fovargue	Elizabeth	1853 01 09	ENG
Smith	James A.	Love	Margaret	1810 05 24	
Smith	James B.	Speirs	Lillias Thomson	1853 10 25	UT, Tooele
Smith	James T.	Hodges	Mary Anne	1858 04 06	
Smith	Jeremiah	Demont	Abigail	1817	
Smith	Jesse N.	West	Emma Seraphine	1852 05 13	UT, Parowan
Smith	Jessie W.	Van Velsor	Catherine	1855 04 01	UT, Farmingtojn
Smith	John	Aikens	Mary	1846 01 15	IL, Nauvoo
Smith	John	Foreman	Eliza Rebecca	1862 12 28	UT, Salt Lake City
Smith	John	Hills	Julia		
Smith	John	Lyman	Clarissa	1815 09 11	
Smith	John	Miller	Mary Ann	1845 10 03	Scotland
Smith	John A.	Anderson	Ann Campbell	1835 06	Canada
Smith	John Anderson	Meiklejohn	Mary	1863	
Smith	John B.	Gibson	Margaret	1851 04 15	IA, Council Bluffs
Smith	John Calvin L.	Fish	Sarah	1846 05 12	IL, Nauvoo
Smith	John F.	Vernon	Christiana V.	1863 04 27	ENG, Hull
Smith	John Glover	Ginther	Susannah	1855 10 02	UT, Draper

Male		Female		Date	Place
Smith	John Henry	Groesbeck	Josephine	1877 04 04	UT, St. George
Smith	John P.	Stratford	Eliza Ann	1878 10 10	UT, Salt Lake City
Smith	John Sivel	Wadley	Jane	1838 02 13	ENG, Gloucester
Smith	John W.	Davey	Josephine	1890 05 18	UT, Salt Lake City
Smith	John X.	Patterson	Margaret	1855 07 24	UT, Cedar City
Smith	Jonathan	Hull	Isabelle Forbes	1872 11 11	UT, Salt Lake City
Smith	Jonathan	Taylor	Nancy Jane	1847 07 11	IA, Council Bluffs
Smith	Jorgen C.	Johansen	Mattie Marie	1863 02 21	UT, Salt Lake City
Smith	Joseph J.	Coleman	Ann	1850 01 01	MO, Maryville
Smith	Joseph J.	Liddiard	Sarah Ann	1865 02 04	UT, Salt Lake City
Smith	Joseph Jr.	Dubois	Hannah Ann		
Smith	Joseph Jr.	Fullmer	Desdemona W.	1842 07	IL, Nauvoo
Smith	Joseph Jr.	Huntington	Presendia L.	1841 12 11	IL, Nauvoo
Smith	Joseph Jr.	Johnson	Delcena D.	1841	
Smith	Joseph Jr.	Kimball	Helen Mar	1843 05	IL, Nauvoo
Smith	Joseph Jr.	McBride	Martha	1842 08	IL, Nauvoo
Smith	Joseph Jr.	Partridge	Eliza Maria	1835	NY, Franklin
Smith	Joseph Jr.	Partridge	Emily Dow	1843 05 11	IL, Nauvoo
Smith	Joseph Jr.	Rollins	Mary Elizabeth	1842 02	IL, Nauvoo
Smith	Joseph Jr.	Snow	Eliza Roxey	1842 06 29	IL, Nauvoo
Smith	Joseph Jr.	Walker	Lucy	1843 05 01	
Smith	Joseph Jr.	Whitney	Sarah Ann	1842 07 27	IL, Nauvoo
Smith	Lauritz N.	Jensen	Hannah		
Smith	Lauritz N.	Mikkelsen	Maren Kirstine	1854 01 15	Ocean
Smith	Leonard I.	Benson	Eveline	1852	
Smith	Leonard I.	Stuart	Sarah	1868 11 24	UT, Salt Lake City
Smith	Lot	Walker	Jane	1852 02 14	UT, Salt Lake City
Smith	Paul	Pedersen	Mica M. C. M.	1877 01 25	UT, St. George
Smith	Paul	Willis	Jemima	1854	Ocean
Smith	Phillip L.	Frampton	Eliza	1849 03 04	IA, Mt. Pisgah
Smith	Ralph	Gridlestone	Emma	1862 12 13	UT, Salt Lake City
Smith	Rasmus	Sorensen	Juliane		Denmark
Smith	Rasmus J.	Beckman	Josephina B.	1871 08 07	
Smith	Richard	Brassel	Diana	1817 12 11	TN
Smith	Richard	Holroyd	Tabitha	1861 10 30	UT, Beaver
Smith	Robert	Humble	Francis E.		
Smith	Samuel	Daniels	Elizabeth		
Smith	Samuel	Ingram	Francis Ann	1856 07 31	
Smith	Samuel	Ingram	Sarah Ann	1853	
Smith	Samuel	Livermore	Mercy	1868 10 10	UT, Salt Lake City
Smith	Samuel	Livermore	Rosetta	1862 11 16	UT, Salt Lake City
Smith	Samuel L.	Tippets	Amanda Jane	1864 02 04	
Smith	Samuel P.	West	Mary	1814 08 17	
Smith	Samuel T.	Dean	Jane	1848 12 24	
Smith	Silas	Aikens	Mary	1828 03 04	
Smith	Silas Sanford	Ricks	Clarinda	1851 07 09	
Smith	Silas Sanford	Ricks	Sarah Ann	1853 03 17	
Smith	Sylvester	Nish	Agnes	1871	
Smith	Theodore	Baird	Susannah	1849 09 24	IL, Quincy
Smith	Thomas	Cope	Emily	1873 02 24	UT, Salt Lake City
Smith	Thomas	Galland	Mary		
Smith	Thomas	Grassing	Sarah	1835 12 25	ENG, Cheltenham
Smith	Thomas C.	Frampton	Sarah	1850 01 03	IA, Mt. Pisgah
Smith	Thomas J.	Whitaker	Elizabeth	1852 11 06	ENG, Cowpen

Male	Female	Date	Place
Smith ....Thomas Sasson	Clark....................Polly	1837 02 13	OH, Conneaut
Smith ....Thomas Sasson	Hollingshead ....Amanda Ellen	1857 07 16	UT, Salt Lake City
Smith ....Thomas X.	Gurney ....Margaret	1851 01 02	ENG
Smith ....Warren	Barnes................Amanda Melissa	1826 07 09	OH, Granville
Smith ....Warren	Barnes................Amanda Melissa	1839	
Smith ....William	Grimshaw...........Mary	1834	ENG, Lancashire
Smith ....William	Syer....................Mary Ann	1820 01 19	ENG
Smith ....William Cooper	Mole ....Mary	1869	UT, Salt Lake City
Smith ....William H. J.	Garn ....Mary Magdalene	1872 01 04	
Smith ....William J.	Hammer ....Julia Ann	1854 01	UT
Smith ....William P.	Bengtsson...........Anna	1863 12 12	UT, Salt Lake City
Smith ....William P.	Pidd....................Sarah	1867 11 26	UT, Fort Douglas
Smith ....William Read	.........................Emeline		
Smith ....William Read	Ricks ....Mary Elizabeth	1857 04 23	UT, Salt Lake City
Smithies..........James	Knowles ....Nancy Ann	1836 01 17	ENG
Smithson ....Allen F.	Taylor ....Jennett Burton	1849 12 16	
Smoot ....Abraham Owen	Eldredge.............Diana Tanner	1855 05 06	UT, Salt Lake City
Smoot ....Abraham Owen	Gibbons..............Sarah		
Smoot ....Abraham Owen	Hill.....................Emily	1846 01 09	IL, Nauvoo
Smoot ....Abraham Owen	Mauritsen ....Anne Kirstine	1856 02 17	UT, Salt Lake City
Smoot ....Abraham Owen	McMeans ....Margaret T.	1838 11 11	TN, Roane Co.
Smoot ....Abraham Owen	Rogers ....Hannah Caroline	1886 03 11	UT, Logan
Smout ....Edwin W.	Oakley................Leah	1847 02 16	ENG
Smuin ....James Blundell	Astington ....Ellen Eliza	1859 03 27	ENG
Smuin ....Thomas	Hook...................Sarah	1837 07 09	ENG
Smyth ....Richard	Looser ....Elizabeth	1877 07 09	
Snarr................James T.	Brough ....Harriet	1841 11 12	ENG
Snelgrove ....Edward	Joy ....Mary	1843 06 20	ENG
Snell ....Cyrus	Barnes................Rhoda	1832 03 13	Canada
Snell ....Rufus P.	Hillman ....Ellen Celestia	1869 02 08	UT, Salt Lake City
Snow ....Bernard	Liversedge ....Anna	1856 04 16	UT, Salt Lake City
Snow ....Don Carlos	Hallet..................Mary Elizabeth	1862 10 20	UT, Provo
Snow ....Don Carlos	Montague ....Sarah Marie		
Snow ....Erastus	Ashby ....Elizabeth R.	1847 12 19	IA, Winter Quarters
Snow ....Erastus	Beman.................Artimesia	1838 12 13	MO, Far West
Snow ....Erastus	McMenemy ....Ann	1867 10 15	UT, Salt Lake City
Snow ....Erastus	Spencer...............Julia J.	1856 04 11	UT, Salt Lake City
Snow ....Erastus	White..................Minerva	1844 04 02	IL, Nauvoo
Snow ....Gardner	Hastings ....Sarah Sawyer	1814 11 30	NH, Chesterfield
Snow ....George W.	Billings................Eunice	1857 03 27	
Snow ....George W.	Wells ....Mary		
Snow ....James C.	Carter ....Eliza Ann	1838 02 10	OH, Kirtland
Snow ....James Chauncey	Roberts ....Jane Cecelia	1856 12 02	UT, Salt Lake City
Snow ....John Chauncey	Baker..................Harriet	1859 10 06	UT, Salt Lake City
Snow ....John Chauncey	Chidester.............Esther	1883 10 26	UT, Salt Lake City
Snow ....Levi	Streeter ....Lucina	1801 11 26	
Snow ....Lorenzo	Horton ....Caroline	1853 10 09	UT, Salt Lake City
Snow ....Lorenzo	Squires...............Harriet Amelia	1846 01 17	IL, Nauvoo
Snow ....Lorenzo	Woodruff ....Phebe Amelia	1859 04 04	UT, Salt Lake City
Snow ....Warren Stone	Brown.................Mary Ann	1857 04 20	UT, Salt Lake City
Snow ....Warren Stone	Voorhees.............Mary Ann	1841 12 23	IL, Lima
Snow ....Willard L.	Bowyer...............Sarah Ann	1865 04 15	UT, Salt Lake City
Snow ....William	Adams.................Sally	1846 01 16	IL, Nauvoo
Snow ....William	Leavitt ....Lydia	1842 08	IL, Nauvoo

Male	Female	Date	Place
Snow .... William	Leavitt .... Roxanna	1853 03 12	UT, Salt Lake City
Snow .... William	Miles.................... Hannah		
Snow .... William	Rogers .... Ann	1853 03 13	UT, Salt Lake City
Snow .... William	Shearer .... Jane Maria	1850 10 13	UT, Salt Lake City
Snowball .... John	Sorensen............ Mary Bodil	1865 12 05	UT, Salt Lake City
Snowball .... Ralph	Thomas .... Jane	1865 03 18	UT, Salt Lake City
Snyder .... Ephraim S.	Fullmer .... Susannah	1861 10 27	UT, Salt Lake City
Snyder .... James C.	Forsyth .... Jane Barker	1861 09 15	UT, Salt Lake City
Snyder .... John	Mecham .... Sylvia Amaret	1855 11 03	
Snyder .... Robert A.	Livermore .... Almeda Melissa	1841 04 03	IL, Nauvoo
Snyder .... Samuel C.	Luce .... Caroline	1851 09 09	UT, Salt Lake City
Sonderbon .... Peder Jensen	Nielsen .... Mette Kirsten	1813 12 17	
Sonne .... Niels C. C.	Christiansen .... Lise	1874 11 24	UT, Salt Lake City
Soper .... Richard	Hartley................ Sarah Wells		
Sorensen .... Jeppe	Johansen .... Anna C. C.	1856 02 15	UT, Salt Lake City
Sorensen .... John	Sandersen........... Kristine	1862 12 27	UT, Salt Lake City
Sorensen .... Jorgen P.	Gyllenskog .... Eva	1872 12 24	UT, Salt Lake City
Sorensen .... Knud	Jensen .... Mette Kirstine	1849 02 25	Denmark
Sorensen .... Morton	Wicklund .... Christina	1862 07 19	UT, Salt Lake City
Sorensen .... Nicholai	Holm.................... Ane Marie	1838 05 12	Denmark
Sorensen .... Nicolai	Olsen................... Magdelena	1830 07 06	Denmark
Sorensen .... Niels	Andersen............. Anne Marie	1856 06 02	
Sorensen .... Niels	Nilsson .... Sissa	1868 12 21	UT, Salt Lake City
Sorensen .... Peder	Thompson .... Anna	1837 10 07	Denmark
Sorensen .... Peder H.	Oleson................. Annike Marie	1837 12 27	Denmark
Sorensen .... Soren	Anderson............. Martha	1863 01 31	UT, Salt Lake City
Sorenson .... Niels	Hayes.................. Sarah		
South .... John	Thurgood............. Catherine	1867 04 20	UT, Salt Lake City
Sowby.............. Isaac	Morrod................. Elizabeth	1852 04 08	
Spafford .... Horace	Roberson .... Rachel	1851 07 09	
Spahn .... Michael O.	Brown.................. Rhoda Asenath	1868 12 03	MT, Bannack
Sparks .... Alfred	Fowler .... Jane Ann	1853 01 30	Ocean
Sparks .... William	Buttars................ Bethea	1868 12 15	UT, Salt Lake City
Sparks .... William	Clarke.................. Elizabeth Jane	1881 01 27	UT, Salt Lake City
Speirs .... George	Lyon .... Janet	1848 11 15	Scotland
Speirs .... William H.	Walters................ Mary Jane	1873 03 17	UT, Salt Lake City
Spencer .... Dallas Polk	Vasquez .... Mary Ann	1866 10 07	MO, Westport
Spencer .... Daniel	Cutcliffe............... Mary Jane	1856 12 27	UT, Salt Lake City
Spencer .... George	Thompson .... Sarah Marinda	1856 04 01	UT, Washington
Spencer .... Mathias F.	Brown.................. Amelia	1826	
Spencer .... Orson	Hill .... Mary	1853	
Spens .... Nathaniel	Campbell............. Mary Jane	1869 06 21	UT, Salt Lake City
Sperry.............. John Clapp	Van Leuven......... Matilda Ann	1851 01 01	
Sperry.............. William L.	Sidwell................ Margaret Ann	1849 10 04	UT, Salt Lake City
Spilsbury.......... George	Smith................... Fanny	1842 09 05	ENG, Woster
Spooner........... David N.	Dayer .... Ann	1835	Wales
Sprague........... Alvin Henry	Olson................... Matilda Christina	1870 03 01	UT, Salt Lake City
Sprague........... Ithamer	Steadwell .... Sarah (Sally)	1848	Trail
Sprague........... Richard D.	Rose.................... Louise Maria	1832	
Sprowl .... Andrew	Alexander............ Adeline	1868 04 01	
Squire .... John P.	DeMill .... Adelia	1852 12 31	UT, Manti
Squire .... William	Morrel.................. Maria	1848 01 08	ENG, St. Paul
Squire .... William	White................... Isabelle		
Squires .... Henry A.	Catlin.................. Sarah Minnie	1846 04 27	ENG

Male	Female	Date	Place
Squires ....John Fell	Maiben ....Alice Pen	1868 08 07	UT, Salt Lake City
Squires ....John P.	Fell ....Catherine Harriet	1843 08 21	ENG, Putney
Squires ....John P.	Swain ....Emily Ellen	1868 03 21	UT, Salt Lake City
Squires ....Thomas	Smith..................Elizabeth	1855 11 04	UT, Salt Lake City
Stagnall ....Sergeant	Davis ....Anna		
Staker..............Alma	Young.................Elizabeth	1856 02 07	UT, Pleasant Grove
Staker..............Nathan	Cusworth.............Eliza	1857	UT, Pleasant Grove
Staker..............William H.	Parsons...............Catherine Maria	1851 01 01	IA, Pigeon Grove
Staley ....Daniel	Christensen.........Anna Christina	1864 10 31	UT, Logan
Stalle ....Jean Peirre	Gaudin-Moise......Jeanne Marie		Italy
Stallings...........Joseph	Barnes................Elizabeth Alice	1865 11 18	UT, Salt Lake City
Stallings...........Joseph	Hartford ....Caroline Iown	1849	
Stallings...........Joseph	Hussey ....Charlotte Jane	1856 06 01	UT, Salt Lake City
Stallings...........Joseph	Shefflin ....Margaret	1840	PA, Lancaster
Standage ....Henry	Rogers ....Henrietta	1851 04 16	UT, Salt Lake City
Standage ....William	Howard................Elizabeth	1815	
Standing ....James	Standing..............Mary	1847 06 27	MO, St. Louis
Standley ....Alexander	Upson..................Philinda	1829 03 19	OH, Suffield
Standring ....Edwin	Smith..................Rebecca	1859 06 03	
Stanfield ....Samuel	Bryan..................Elizabeth	1843 12 19	ENG
Stanford...........Alfred	Jenkins................Elizabeth	1868 10 24	UT, Salt Lake City
Stanford...........Stephen	Foreman..............Louisa	1856 05 16	ENG, Dover
Stanford...........Thomas	Barnett ....Elizabeth	1828 12 31	ENG, Southwick
Stanger............George	Etherington..........Mary	1855 02 13	ENG
Stanger............Thomas	Wilson ....Jane	1853 07 09	ENG
Stanley ....Alexander H.	Brown..................Adelia Ann	1856 10 27	UT, Bountiful
Stanley ....Thomas A.	Wellard................Eliza Mary Ann		UT, Salt Lake City
Stapley ....Charles	Bryant.................Sarah	1822 12 01	ENG
Stapley ....Charles Jr.	Parkinson.............Sarah	1854 07 24	CA, San Bern.
Stark................Daniel	Baldwin ....Elizabeth	1862 03 22	UT, Salt Lake City
Stark................Daniel	Birkenhead..........Ann Priscilla		
Stark................Daniel	Cook...................Ann	1844 12 01	MA, Boston
Stark................Soren	Petersen..............Ann Sophia	1862 04 16	Ocean
Starkie ....Edward John	Nielsen................Thora	1886 11 17	UT, Logan
Starley ....John	Jones ....Martha	1879 02 05	UT, Salt Lake City
Starr................Edward W.	Duel....................Amanda Ann	1841 10 14	IL, Quincy
Starr................Edward W.	Thomas ....Amanda	1855 07 24	
Starr................Jared	Barr ....Anna	1848 09 22	IA, Kanesville
Startup.............William D.	Hick....................Hagar	1868 11 04	UT, Salt Lake City
Stauffer............Christian	Gugger ....Anna	1854 10 13	
Stauffer............Ulrich	Schenk................Elizabeth	1859 08 26	Switzerland
Stayner............Arthur	Turner ....Emma	1857 03 27	UT, Salt Lake City
Stayner............Thomas C.	Pill ....Elizabeth	1827 09 06	ENG
Stayner............Thomas John	Orrell ....Rosa Ann	1852	ENG
Stearns ....Nathan	Frost...................Mary Ann	1831 04 01	ME, Bethel
Steed ....James	Holland................Caroline	1838 11 10	ENG
Steed ....Thomas	Bailey ....Mary Elizabeth	1857 03 27	UT, Salt Lake City
Steed ....Thomas	Reed ....Laura Lucinda	1846 12 13	IA, Keokuk
Steele ....James	Wylie ....Elizabeth	1851 08 24	ENG, Manchester
Steele ....James Inman	Smith..................Marion	1874 04 13	
Steele ....Jesse Pierce	Alexander............Francis E.	1853 10 04	UT, Salt Lake City
Steele ....John Jr.	Campbell.............Catherine	1840 01 01	IRE
Steele ....Joseph Wilson	Burridge ....Charlotte Hannah	1867 10 19	UT, Salt Lake City
Steele ....William	Brownell ....Mary Ann	1866 10 27	UT, Salt Lake City

Male	Female	Date	Place
Steele ....William	Goodwin.............Margaret Brown	1828	KY
Steers ....William	Taylor ....Eliza	1833	NY
Stenhouse ....Thomas	Warn ....Fanny	1850 02 06	ENG
Stephens ....Alexander N.	Raymond.............Amina Ann	1869 08 23	UT, Salt Lake City
Stephens ....John	Briggs.................Elizabeth	1833 05 01	IL
Stephens ....Thomas H.	Jones ....Mary	1865 12 25	UT, Henefer
Stephenson .....Anthen	Bennett...............Mary Ann	1874 03 09	UT, Salt Lake City
Stephenson .....Harris S.	Sproul.................Isabella	1862 10	UT, Salt Lake City
Stephenson .....Isaac H.	Bagley ....Martha Ann	1850	IA
Stephenson .....James J.	Bennett...............Jane	1877 12 21	UT, St. George
Stephenson .....Peter C.	Berthelsen...........Mariane	1863 05 07	Ocean
Stephenson .....Thomas C.	Christensen.........Anne Marie	1862 07 14	NE, Florence
Sterrett.............William G.	Brown.................Permelia	1850 12	UT, Salt Lake City
Stevens ....Abraham	Zimmerman.........Christina	1843 01 19	IL, Nauvoo
Stevens ....Alfred	Slater..................Mary Ann	1870 02 28	
Stevens ....Alfred Jr.	Lind ....Christiana	1837 06 21	ENG
Stevens ....Arnold	Coon ....Lois	1828 11 05	Canada
Stevens ....David Riley	Felshaw..............Caroline	1862 12 24	
Stevens ....Edward	Stephenson.........Mettie Johanna		
Stevens ....Edwin Robert	Beebe.................Lydia Ann	1882 11 02	ID, Blackfoot
Stevens ....Isaac	Dence..................Frances	1846	ENG
Stevens ....John	Hicks ....Lydia Ann	1865 10 04	UT, Provo
Stevens ....Joseph S.	King....................Abigail Marina	1865 08 12	UT, Circleville
Stevens ....Lyman	Durfee ....Martha	1836 06 21	OH, Kirtland
Stevens ....Ransom A.	Brady..................Tranquilla Ann	1863 02 17	UT, Sanpete Co.
Stevens ....Roswell	Spencer..............Sybil		NY, Stephentown
Stevens ....Sydney	Thick ....Mary Jane	1863 05 22	ENG, Liverpool
Stevens ....Walter	Holman................Abigail Elizabeth	1854 04 27	UT, Pleasant Grove
Stevens ....Walter	Mace ....Marietta	1869 10 05	UT, Salt Lake City
Stevens ....William	Seely ....Elizabeth	1854 10 12	UT, Pleasant Grove
Stevens ....William	Thomas ....Marinda	1827 09 02	Canada
Stevenson ....Edward	Dufresne ....Elizabeth Jane	1855	
Stevenson ....Edward	Porter ....Nancy Areta	1845 04 07	
Stevenson ....Edward	Williams..............Emily Electa	1857	
Stevenson ....James	Charles...............Martha	1834 06 15	ENG
Stevenson ....Joseph	Stevens...............Elizabeth	1812 06 28	
Stewart ....Andrew J.	Quimby...............Eunice Pease	1844 01 01	IA
Stewart ....Andrew J.	Riggs..................Dorothy Melissa	1868 01 25	UT, Salt Lake City
Stewart ....Andrew Jackson	Gurr....................Susanna		
Stewart ....Andrew Jackson	Nickerson ....Caroline Eliza	1851 02 21	UT, Salt Lake City
Stewart ....Archibald	Lyle ....Esther	1825 10 11	Scotland
Stewart ....Benjamin F.	Davis..................Elizabeth Jane	1850 09 07	
Stewart ....Benjamin F.	Hunter ....Rachel	1850 09 07	
Stewart ....Benjamin F.	Richardson..........Polly	1837 06 14	IL, Beardstown
Stewart ....Charles	Roberts ....Sarah Ann	1835 12 19	NY, Ogdensburg
Stewart ....George	Baker..................Ruthinda		
Stewart ....Isaac M.	White..................Elizabeth	1857 03 08	UT, Salt Lake City
Stewart ....John	Waddell ....Ann	1848 06 16	Scotland
Stewart ....John M.	Hope ....Emma Eliza	1865 06 24	UT, Salt Lake City
Stewart ....John Martin	Thompson ....Ann	1857 03 02	UT
Stewart ....Levi	Wilkerson ....Margery	1852 12 31	UT, Salt Lake City
Stewart ....Louis	Page...................Julia Ann	1873 11 20	UT, Provo
Stewart ....Matthew D.	Spiller.................Hannah Rebecca	1855 08 16	
Stewart ....Philander B.	Scott...................Sarah	1801 05 10	

Male	Female	Date	Place
Stewart ....Urban V.	Adams................Ellen	1865 07 15	UT, Salt Lake City
Stewart ....Urban V.	Jones ....Mary Ann	1860 03 17	
Stewart ....William	Cairnes...............Ruth	1857 03 04	
Stewart ....William	Jenkins...............Jane		
Stewart ....William	Marriott...............Mary Ann	1843 06 11	ENG
Stewart ....William	Murdoch ....Elizabeth	1850 11 18	Scotland
Stewart ....William J.	Gentry ....Sarah Dickens	1833 09 29	IL, Madison Co.
Stiff (Neville) ....William	Jennings.............Rachel	1826 09 27	ENG
Stillman............Charles T.	Neff ....Elizabeth	1858 01 12	UT, Salt Lake City
Stilson.............William B.	Young.................Susannah	1829	NY, Monroe Co.
Stilson.............William L.	Lytle ....Cyrena Martha	1859 05 09	UT, Salt Lake City
Stimpson ....Frederick	Davis ....Lucy Ellen		
Stimpson ....Frederick	Parker ....Sarah Jane		
Stimpson ....William	Christensen.........Ann Mary	1867 03 16	UT, Salt Lake City
Stimpson ....William	Hinchcliff ....Edna	1858 05 01	UT, Ogden
Stimpson ....William	Lubbock ....Rebecca	1848 11 17	ENG
Stinger ....John H.	Hollist ....Elizabeth	1859 10 01	NE, Florence
Stock ....John	Adams................Jane	1844 02 14	South Africa
Stock ....John	Gilson.................Francis		
Stocking..........Ensign I.	Arnold.................Elizabeth Ellen	1863 04 18	UT, Salt Lake City
Stocking..........Ensign I.	Cook...................Emma	1876 04 17	
Stocks.............Henry	Halley ....Mary	1843	ENG, Warrington
Stocks.............Moroni	Heward...............Sarah	1865 01 02	UT, Rockville
Stoddard..........Albert Leonard	Corbridge ....Mary Ann	1867 11 02	
Stoddard..........Charles H.	Duncan...............Matilda Ann	1858 03 31	
Stoddard..........John R.	Weaver...............Martha Elizabeth	1853 10 13	UT, Salt Lake City
Stoddard..........Oscar O.	Taylor ....Elizabeth	1860 10 02	UT, Salt Lake City
Stoddart..........William	Alpin ....Margaret	1836	ENG
Stoker ....David	Graybill...............Barbara	1814	
Stoker ....John	Allen ....Jane	1857 07 05	UT, Salt Lake City
Stoker ....William	Larsen ....Martha	1875 02 01	UT, Salt Lake City
Stoker ....William	Winegar..............Almira	1838 08 20	MO, Far West
Stokes ....Christopher	Nebeker ....Roselia	1868 04 25	UT, Salt Lake City
Stokes ....Jeremiah	Walker................Frances	1839 11 25	ENG
Stokes ....Jeremiah III	Olsen..................Josephine	1876 11 11	UT, Draper
Stokes ....Robert W.	Wilson................Ann	1858 05 09	MA, Boston
Stokes ....William	Batchelor............Amelia Ann	1895 01 08	
Stokes ....William	Vintiner...............Hannah Maria	1846 10 03	ENG
Stolworthy........Thomas	Jinkerson............Matilda	1849 05 13	ENG
Stolworthy........Thomas	Tuttle ....Elizabeth Ann	1880 12 08	UT, St. George
Stone ....Amos Pease	Jones ....Minerva Leantine	1846 02 01	NY, Canaan
Stone ....Amos Pease	Rawlins ....Dinah	1852	
Stone ....Amos Pease	Spencer..............Sarah	1865	
Stone ....Robert	Treby..................Julia	1826 11 27	NY, Brooklyn
Stone ....William	Cruse ....Mary	1836	
Stonebraker......Joel M.	Phelps ....Mary	1848	
Stonebraker......Joseph	Phelps ....Phebe	1849 06 16	NE
Stookey ....Enos	Child...................Jemima Elizabeth	1852 05 24	IL, Belleville
Stott ....Edwin	Paul....................Elizabeth	1876 02 18	UT, Salt Lake City
Stott ....Edwin	Sellers ....Sarah Jane H.	1861	UT, Salt Lake City
Stott ....William	Alger..................Sarah Lydia	1863 11 15	UT, Fillmore
Stott ....William	Durose ....Mary	1855 12 27	UT, Fillmore
Stott ....William H.	Nield..................Alice	1855	
Stout ....Allen J.	Fisk ....Amanda Melvina	1848 04 30	IA, Winter Quarters

Male	Female	Date	Place
Stout ....Hosea	Harmon ....Aseneth	1854 01 09	UT, Salt Lake City
Stradling ....William	Yarnell................Sarah		
Stratford..........Edwin	Crabb ....Marianna	1855 12 25	ENG, Danbury
Stratford..........Edwin A.	Coats..................Mary	1879 02 06	UT, Salt Lake City
Stratford..........George	Barwell ....Eliza	1832 05 17	ENG
Stratton ....Edward	Desaules ....Adele	1863 06 21	
Stratton ....James	Briggs................Eliza	1857 02 02	UT, Salt Lake City
Stratton ....James	Clark...................Francis		
Stratton ....James Albert	Gardner..............Emily H. A.	1864 07 03	UT, Virgin
Stratton ....Oliver	Brown.................Harriet	1841 08 22	
Straw ....James	Hill.....................Hannah	1855 02 18	ENG
Straw ....William	Hampson............Mary	1830 02 04	
Streeper...........Wilkinson	Wells ....Matilda	1834 07 10	PA, Philadelphia
Streeper...........William H.	Richards.............Mary Amelia	1867 10 16	UT, Salt Lake City
Street...............Simon	Bates.................Mary Ann	1872 03 06	
Street...............Simon	Kay.....................Ann	1884 03 15	UT, Park City
Street...............William	Kay.....................Ann	1873 01 27	WY, Almy
Stringham ....Briant	Ashby ....Harriet Maria	1852 04 20	
Stringham ....Briant	Ashby ....Susan Ann	1850 03 21	
Stringham ....Briant	Garr....................Nancy	1858 12 04	UT
Stringham ....George	Hendrickson ....Polly	1820 08 17	NY, Colesville
Stringham ....George A.	Ashby ....Mary Jane	1858 03 03	UT, Salt Lake City
Stringham ....William	Lake ....Eliza	1846 01 22	IL, Nauvoo
Strong.............Ezra	Livermore ....Almeda Melissa		
Strong.............Jacob	Bury...................Alice Fish	1857 03 05	UT, Salt Lake City
Strong.............John	Miller ....Agnes	1828 12 16	ENG
Strong.............William J.	Dyer ....Julia Maria	1852 04 04	MO, St. Louis
Stuart..............Charles	Lance ....Nancy	1840	
Stuart..............David M.	Airmet.................Susan Douglas	1867 10 26	UT, Salt Lake City
Stuart..............James M.	Glenn ....Robina	1855	
Stubbs ....Peter	Dunn ....Elizabeth	1856 10 19	UT, Salt Lake City
Stubbs ....Peter	Wride..................Ann Davis	1862 10 10	UT, Salt Lake City
Stubbs ....Richard	Ware ....Ellander	1843 06 21	IA, Lee Co.
Stucki..............John	Ruegsegger ....Katherina	1855	Switzerland
Stucki..............John U.	Butler..................Jane		
Stucki..............John U.	Huber ....Anna M.	1859 08 19	Ocean
Stucki..............John U.	Spori...................Anna Clara		
Stucki..............Samuel	Stettler................Magdalena	1846 07 14	Switzerland
Such (Search) .Joseph	Field ....Ann	1829	ENG
Sudweeks........Richard H.	Gibbs..................Hannah Eugenia	1870 11 02	
Sullivan............Archibald	Mathews..............Julia Antoinette	1850 11 06	UT, Salt Lake City
Summers ....Edwin	Hodges................Elizabeth	1862 10	
Summers ....George	Green..................Sarah Ann	1866	Trail
Summers ....George	Hodges...............Emma		
Summers ....John C.	Jones ....Mary Elizabeth	1882 02 15	
Summers ....Nicholas	Dykes.................Eliza Jane	1857 09 11	UT, Salt Lake City
Summers ....Nicholas	Pears..................Eliza Rosannah	1857 01 02	
Summers ....Thomas	Stockall ....Susanna	1826 04 09	
Sumsion ....Daniel	Spender ....Eleanor Ellen	1837 10 21	ENG
Sumsion ....William	Alleman ....Christean Mary	1858 02 03	UT, Springville
Sutherland ....Thomas	Timmings ....Mary Ann	1830 08 08	ENG
Sutton ....Henry	Ford....................Elizabeth	1846 04 23	ENG
Sutton ....John	Ellison ....Mary		
Sutton ....John A.	Woolley ....Sarah	1887 07 24	UT, Logan

Male	Female	Date	Place
Svendsen ....Jan	Knudson.............Dorthe	1874 07 06	UT, Salt Lake City
Swain..............John	Warden ....Elizabeth	1846 08 11	ENG
Swallow ....George	Day.....................Anna	1878 01 16	UT, Salt Lake City
Swan ....Ephraim	Tarrant ....Charlotte	1857	
Sweat ....Father	Long ....Frances		
Sweat ....George Hyrum	Cluff...................Lavina	1846 04 19	IL, Nauvoo
Sweat ....George Hyrum	Mecham ....Emeline	1854 03 21	UT, Salt Lake City
Sweat ....John Henry	Young.................Martha Ann	1888 09 14	UT, Wallsburg
Sweatfield.......Augustus	Bates..................Mary Ann	1863	
Sweeten ....George	Gardner..............Mary	1836 05 29	Canada
Swensen..........Lars	Christensen.........Ane Elizabeth	1862 07 19	UT, Salt Lake City
Swenson..........Johannes	Svensson ....Caroline W.	1859 05 01	
Swenson..........Knud	Hansen................Johanna Marie	1860 06 24	
Swenson..........Nils	Brock...................Lena Marie		Sweden
Swift................William	Toen...................Ann	1842	ENG, Devin
Swindlehurst....John	Rothwell ....Matilda	1852 01 17	ENG
Swinyard..........Alfred	Warn ....Elizabeth Pollow	1897 12 06	
Syddall.............Squire	Allen ....Mary	1828 12	
Sylvester..........James	Nicholson ....Rebecca	1837 02 27	ENG, Sheffield

T

Male	Female	Date	Place
Tadlock............Edwin B.	Despain...............Margaret Jane	1847 05 23	IL, Calhoun Co.
Taft ....Seth	Dykes.................Eliza Jane	1859 01 24	UT, Salt Lake City
Taft ....Stephen	Perkins ....Patience	1801	
Taggart............George Henry	McNiven ....Jessie	1870 09 26	
Taggart............George W.	Parks..................Fanny	1845 07 06	IL, Nauvoo
Taggart............George W.	Rogers ....Clarissa Marina	1857 02 08	UT, Brigham City
Tait ....William	Xavier.................Elizabeth	1850 01 21	India, Bombay
Talbot ....John J.	Hunter ....Jane		NE, Florence
Tame ....Alfred	Saville ....Mary Ann	1864 11 19	UT, Salt Lake City
Tanner ....Albert M.	Bickmore ....Lovina	1855 09 09	
Tanner ....John	Beswick..............Elizabeth	1825 11 03	NY, Bolton
Tanner ....John Joshua	Archibald ....Rebecca	1835 07	OH, Kirtland
Tanner ....Sidney	Neyman...............Rachel	1859 04 02	UT, Salt Lake City
Tanner ....Thomas	Elsey ....Susannah	1853 10 23	UT, Salt Lake City
Tanner ....Thomas	Newman.............Ann	1852 10 10	MO, St. Louis
Tanner ....Valison	Morgan...............Amanda	1887 10 15	UT, Grouse Creek
Tanner ....William Smith	Moore.................Clarissa Jane	1868 01 19	UT, Payson
Tate ....John	Seetree ....Ann	1847 10 31	ENG, Leeds
Tate ....William	Park....................Janet		
Tatton ....John C.	Brown.................Sarah	1862 07 12	UT, Salt Lake City
Tatton ....John C.	Webb..................Caroline	1839 09 22	ENG
Taylor ....Allen	Smith..................Elizabeth	1856 11 26	UT, Salt Lake City
Taylor ....Benjamin	Brown.................Ann	1839	NJ
Taylor ....Benjamin F.	Mennell ....Ann	1827	OH, Grafton
Taylor ....David	Thompson ....Mary Jane	1859 04 05	UT, Salt Lake City
Taylor ....Edward	Martin.................Margaret		
Taylor ....Edward	Nichols ....Ann	1824 10 12	ENG
Taylor ....Ernest L.	Skousen.............Johanna Marie	1884 04 11	UT. St. George
Taylor ....George	Gwyther..............Louisa	1853 10 19	ENG
Taylor ....George	Loader................Mary	1844 05 05	ENG
Taylor ....George	Smith..................Mary Franks	1836 09 05	ENG

Male	Female	Date	Place
Taylor ....George E. G.	Wickes ....Ann	1830 02	ENG
Taylor ....George Hamilton	Colebrook............Ellen Susanna	1885 10 09	UT, Logan
Taylor ....James	Taylor ....Agnes	1805 12 23	ENG
Taylor ....James W.	Rogers ....Ann	1839 10 20	
Taylor ....John	Ballantyne ....Jane	1844 02 25	IL, Nauvoo
Taylor ....John	Faulkner..............Ann	1855 09 18	ENG, Cheshire
Taylor ....John	Faulkner..............Sarah	1860 12	UT, Salt Lake City
Taylor ....John	Pummell..............Elizabeth	1832	
Taylor ....John	Young..................Margaret	1856 09 27	CT, Westport
Taylor ....John Benjamin	Fenner..................Mary Ann	1837 10 25	ENG, Worcester
Taylor ....Joseph	Collier..................Elizabeth Mary	1855 07 15	ENG
Taylor ....Joseph	Harris ....Hannah Mariah	1854	
Taylor ....Joseph	Lake ....Jane	1852	
Taylor ....Joseph	Moore..................Mary	1844 03 24	IL, Nauvoo
Taylor ....Joseph	Sidwell.................Harriet	1832 10 12	ENG
Taylor ....Joseph B.	Harvey.................Cecelia	1842 03 18	IL, Adams Co.
Taylor ....Joseph Edward	Capener ....Jane Maria	1876 07 09	UT, Salt Lake City
Taylor ....Joseph W.	Horrocks..............Mary	1869 06 15	UT, Salt Lake City
Taylor ....K. R.	Bickmore ....Lovina	1888 06 20	
Taylor ....Norman	Forbush..............Lorana	1848 04 02	
Taylor ....Norman	Forbush..............Lydia	1850 11 22	UT, Salt Lake City
Taylor ....Norman	Murray................Helen Janet	1863 07 15	UT, Salt Lake City
Taylor ....Pleasant Green	Marler..................Sarah Jane	1858 06 20	
Taylor ....Pleasant Green	Shurtliff...............Mary Eliza	1853 07 05	UT, Salt Lake City
Taylor ....Samuel	Kelsey ....Matilda Elvira	1862 04 10	UT, Smithfield
Taylor ....Stephen	King...................Mary	1870	
Taylor ....Stephen	Turner ....Martha	1832	NY
Taylor ....Steven King	Rogers ....Adelia Caroline		
Taylor ....Teancum	Hiatt....................Mary Jane	1859 05 20	UT, Salt Lake City
Taylor ....Teancum	Taylor ....Clarissa Jane	1860 08 15	UT, Salt Lake City
Taylor ....Thomas Evans	Bigler..................Sarah	1852 02 01	UT, Salt Lake City
Taylor ....William	Bancroft..............Mary Elizabeth	1851	ENG
Taylor ....William	Crane ....Mary Ann	1870	
Taylor ....William	Dean ....Mary Ann	1845 06 16	ENG
Taylor ....William	Patrick................Elizabeth	1811 03 22	KY
Taylor ....William	Postles ....Nancy	1813	ENG
Taylor ....William Pim	Sanford ....Angeline	1852 04 04	IL
Taylor ....William Robert	McCann...............Margaret	1872	
Taylor ....William W.	Blackman ....Emily Maria	1867 05 25	UT, Salt Lake City
Taylor ....William Warren	Carbine ....Mary Adelia	1862 05 17	
Taysum............Thomas	Shepherd ....Jane	1857 03 06	
Teasdale..........Martin	Cairnes...............Ruth	1834	
Teasdale..........Richard	Plane..................Francis	1816 03 26	
Teeples............George Bently	Worden ....Johanna Case	1856 02 20	
Teeples............Sidney	Gourley ....Nicholaus P.	1861 10 27	
Teeples............William R.	Cook...................Harriet Betsy	1859 08 21	
Telford ....John	Telford.................Jane	1825 03	Scotland
Telford ....John D.	Coltrin.................Sarah Matilda	1852 02 22	UT, Bountiful
Telford ....Robert	....	1852 02 22	UT, Bountiful
Tennant ....Charles	Stenhouse...........Margaret	1849	Scotland
Tennant ....James	Ayrton.................Elizabeth		
Tennant ....Thomas	Ayrton.................Jane	1851 06 25	ENG
Tenney ....Nathan C.	Jose ....Grace Tippett	1859 03 18	UT, Harmony
Tenney ....Nathan Cram	Strong ....Olive	1841 03 18	IL

Male		Female		Date	Place
Tenney	William	Webb	Eliza	1819 01 20	NY
Terry	Benjamin F.	Lay	Mary Elizabeth	1869 05 03	
Terry	Charles A.	Hammond	Sarah Loanna	1851 06 28	UT, Salt Lake City
Terry	George W.	Powell	Eliza Mary	1865 08 22	MT, Gallatin
Terry	Joel	Garner	Roemma	1863	
Terry	Joel	Pearson	Jane	1857 04 22	UT, Salt Lake City
Terry	Joshua P.	Charles	Amelia	1882 01 12	UT, Salt Lake City
Terry	Otis	Marsh	Phylinda	1847	IA, Winter Quarters
Terry	Otis L.	Hart	Jane	1851 11 18	UT, Salt Lake City
Terry	Otis L.	Judd	Levee Teressa	1851 07 06	UT, Salt Lake City
Terry	Otis L.	Vail	Sarah	1853 01 27	
Terry	Parshall	Terry	Hannah	1802 03 16	
Terry	Parshall	Williams	Anne	1857 09 13	UT, Salt Lake City
Terry	Parshall P.	Hadlock	Ester Adline	1858 03 10	UT, Salt Lake City
Terry	Thomas Sirls	Pulsipher	Eliza Jane	1855 05 06	UT, Salt Lake City
Terry	Thomas Sirls	Pulsipher	Mary Ann	1848 09 25	UT, Salt Lake City
Terry	William R.	Phillips	Mary Allen	1835 12 20	RI
Tew	Thomas	Bates	Mary	1868 11 05	UT, Salt Lake City
Tew	Thomas	Smith	Hannah	1832 01 30	ENG
Tew	Thomas Jr.	Bird	Rebecca	1856 01 22	UT, Springville
Thacker	Charles E.	Price	Maria Rawlins	1882 11 29	UT, Salt Lake City
Thacker	John Pridgen	Farrell	Mary		
Thacker	William	Tonks	Rachel	1844 06 22	ENG
Thacker	William Timothy	Tonks	Sarah R. R.	1875 12 07	UT, Salt Lake City
Thackeray	George	Condie	Helen	1855 05 12	
Thackham	William	Howard	Elizabeth	1820	
Thatcher	George	Reese	Mary	1864 11 09	UT, Provo
Thaxton	James W.	Averett	Helen Marion	1855 07 15	UT, Manti
Thaxton	Williamson	Sherry	Mary Ann	1829 05 23	KY, Allen Co.
Thayne	John J.	Boyer	Sidney	1848 10 23	PA
Theckston	John	Lavender	Alice		
Theobald	William	Lane	Martha	1841 08 01	ENG, Isle of Wight
Theobald	William	Uren	Elizabeth	1860 11 24	UT, Salt Lake City
Theurer	Frederick	Schuler	Christena	1862 02 18	UT, Providence
Thirkell	John Pinock	Brown	Mary Baynes	1836 09 21	
Thomander	Peter	Pehrsson	Ingeborg	1863	UT, Ephraim
Thomas		Riden	Hannah		
Thomas	Charles Carter	Sessions	Emeline		UT, Wasatch Co.
Thomas	Daniel C.	Gaither	Jane	1843	
Thomas	Daniel S.	Jones	Martha Paine	1826 02 03	TN, Gallatin
Thomas	Daniel Stillwell	Williams	Anne	1853 04 03	UT, Salt Lake City
Thomas	Daniel Z.	Tingle	Holly Jane	1863 04 11	UT, Salt Lake City
Thomas	Ebenezer	Jones	Elvira	1841 10 25	Wales
Thomas	Edward	Crosby	Sarah F.	1866 03 03	
Thomas	Emanuel	Ellis	Mary	1857	PA
Thomas	Frederick W.	Price	Ruth	1866 12	UT, Brigham City
Thomas	James C.	Nelson	Tena	1865 11 20	ID, Bloomington
Thomas	James Moroni	Holroyd	Mary Hebden	1862 03 30	
Thomas	James Sands	Morrow	Mary Parmelia	1830 03 16	
Thomas	James Wylie	Koyle	Mary Elizabeth	1855 01 01	UT, Salt Lake City
Thomas	Preston F.	Hadlond	Maria	1856 10 08	UT, Salt Lake City
Thomas	Richard K.	Stockdale	Caroline	1865 02 22	UT, Logan
Thomas	Samuel John	Jarman	Catherine Lloyd	1858 03 05	Wales
Thomas	Thomas R.	Richards	Catherine	1864 12 17	UT, Salt Lake City

Male	Female	Date	Place
Thomas ....Thomas S.	Anthony ....Mary Jane	1853 02 13	Ocean
Thomasen ....Niels	Johnson ....Ane Marie		
Thomasen ....Thomas N.	Anderson.............Dorthea	1826 11 17	Denmark
Thomassen......Peter O.	Petersen.............Marie Concordia	1865 05	UT
Thomassen......Peter O.	Petersen.............Petrine Rasmine	1859 04 22	Denmark
Thomassen......Peter O.	Petersen.............Wilhelmine	1866 02	UT
Thompson	Rasmussen ....Marie		
Thompson ....Charles	Barber ....Sally Maria	1841 04 06	NY, Barry
Thompson ....Daniel	Bronson...............Lorenda E.	1854 05 04	UT, Scipio
Thompson ....David	Petersen.............Maren	1855 05 09	UT, Ephraim
Thompson ....David Wilkin	Barlow ....Pemela E.	1861 09 10	
Thompson ....Ezra	Freeman..............Caroline Sophia	1854 01 23	
Thompson ......Ezra	Platt....................Ann Jane Griffin	1853 04 03	UT, Salt Lake City
Thompson ....Ezra	Powell ....Amanda Butler	1816	
Thompson ....Ezra	Trumble..............Lois Alexander	1848	Trail
Thompson ....George	Goldthorpe ....Jane	1828 10 01	ENG
Thompson ....James L.	Willis...................Matilda Delila	1837 10 05	IL, Nauvoo
Thompson ....John Crow	Clark...................Ann Broyhill	1845 03 20	IL, Quincy
Thompson ....John Crow	Fisher ....Elizabeth V.	1870	
Thompson ....John Crow	Shugars..............Mary	1852 04 06	UT, Salt Lake City
Thompson ....Joseph	Crompton ....Hannah	1862 09 28	UT, Salt Lake City
Thompson ....Joseph	Kershaw ....Annie Maria	1868 08 08	UT, Salt Lake City
Thompson ....Joseph L.	Griffin ....Caroline	1867 10 05	UT, Salt Lake City
Thompson ....Joseph L.	Griffin ....Theophenia	1873	
Thompson ....Joseph L.	Thompson ....Penelope	1835	
Thompson ....Niels	Christensen.........Johanne	1846	Denmark
Thompson ....Niels	Hjermin...............Mary Catherine	1870 05 30	UT, Salt Lake City
Thompson ....Peter	Anderson.............Dorthea	1837 10 20	Denmark
Thompson ....Peter P. S.	Hansen................Maren	1854 12 17	UT, Ephraim
Thompson ......Ralph	Skelton ....Elizabeth	1860 12 15	UT, Salt Lake City
Thompson ....Robert	Wilkin ....Elizabeth	1833 02 24	Scotland
Thompson ....Robert B.	Fielding ....Mercy Rachel	1837 06 04	OH, Kirtland
Thompson ....Thomas	Davidson.............Mary Dorothea C.		
Thompson ....William	Commander ....Matilda	1867 04 20	UT, Salt Lake City
Thompson ......William	Fenn...................Sarah	1857	UT, Provo
Thompson ....William	Hales..................Mary Ann		
Thompson ....William	Isaacson..............Mary Ellen	1868 06 01	UT, Salt Lake City
Thompson ....William H.	Cottam ....Emma	1868 11 20	UT, Salt Lake City
Thomsen ....Hans Adolph	..........................Jensine	1875 07 12	
Thomsen ....Hans Adolph	Sorensen.............Caroline	1855 11 13	Denmark
Thomson ....George	Crossley ....Hannah Mariah	1866 01 13	UT, Salt Lake City
Thomson ....George	Crossley ....Hannah Mariah	1896	
Thorley ....Thomas	Alldridge ....Ann Blunt	1861 09 21	UT, Salt Lake City
Thorn ....Richard	Armstrong ....Mary Anner	1806 09 06	NY, Clinton
Thorn ....Richard	Osborn ....Rebecca Ann	1858 12 25	UT, Uinta
Thorn ....Richard Jr.	Glines.................Harriet Anna	1846 01 13	IL, Nauvoo
Thorn ....William	Merrick ....Maria Susanna	1852 03 23	
Thorne ....Richard	Perry ....Eunice Jane	1882 02 16	UT, Salt Lake City
Thornley ....John	Stringfellow ....Margaret	1853	ENG
Thornock ....John	Bott....................Ann	1840 12 25	ENG
Thornock ....John Bott	Ward ....Emma	1865 03 10	UT, Farmington
Thornton ....Amos Griswold	Butler..................Charity A.	1862	
Thornton ....Amos Griswold	Whittaker............Mary		
Thornton ....Ezra	Goodrich ....Harriet	1814	

Male	Female	Date	Place
Thornton ....Oliver	Griswold ....Mary	1829	Canada
Thornton ....Oliver E.	Phillips................Emmaretta	1873 02 15	UT, American Fork
Thornton ....Squire	Oldfield..............Martha	1861 12 08	UT, Fairfield
Thornton ....Stephen	Curtis.................Nancy Louisa	1856 07 01	UT, Parowan
Thornton ....William	Hepworth............Mary	1834 06 22	ENG
Thorpe ....Alvin	Wilds ....Ann	1855	UT
Thorpe ....Thomas	Anthony ....Mary Jane	1875	ID, Samaria
Thorpe ....William W.	Cruse ....Charlotte	1850	MO, St. Louis
Thorsen ....Jens	Michelsen............Maren	1823 11 23	Denmark
Thorum ....Christian	Johnson ....Ane Marie	1863 10 03	UT, Salt Lake City
Thrower ....Thomas	Pilch ....Lydia	1841 01 10	ENG, Norfolk
Thueson ....John Niels	Wasden...............Alice P.	1870 06 14	
Thurber............Albert D.	Shimmin ....Eleanor Jane	1876 12 12	
Thurber............Albert King	Berry ....Thirza Malvina	1851 02 26	UT, Salt Lake City
Thurber............Albert King	Brockbank...........Agnes	1867 10 30	
Thurgood ....Thomas	Banks ....Sarah Ann	1860 02 12	ENG
Thurgood ....William	Yeates ....Elizabeth Lavinia	1863 09 15	UT, Bountiful
Thurman ....Edward	Gibson................Mary Ann	1847	ENG
Thurman ....Thomas Edward	Yardley...............Esther (Elizabeth)	1848 11 06	ENG, Dudley
Thursby ....Olaf	Christensen.........Jensine	1877 09 10	UT, Ephraim
Thurston ....Charles E.	Leonard..............Anne Jane	1878	
Thurston ....George W.	Snow ....Sarah Lucina	1858 03 28	
Thurston ....Thomas J.	Smith..................Elizabeth	1855 11 18	UT, Salt Lake City
Thurston ....Tore	Borkerson...........Anna	1858 09 28	
Thurston ....Tore	Pederson............Anne Margrethe	1855 07 24	UT, Salt Lake City
Tibbitts............John	Dand ....Sarah	1832 12 24	ENG
Tidwell ....James H.	Harvey................Elizabeth	1853 08 28	UT, Pleasant Grove
Tidwell ....James H.	Sanders..............Emma	1857 02 23	UT, Salt Lake City
Tidwell ....Jefferson	Seely ....Sarah	1860 12 16	UT, Mt. Pleasant
Tidwell ....John	Smith..................Jane	1828 12 18	IN, Marysville
Tidwell ....Peter	Allen ....Sarah Briggs	1857 08 16	UT, Salt Lake City
Tidwell ....William N.	Reynolds ....Mary Elizabeth	1857 03 01	UT, Maple Grove
Tietjen.............Johann A. H.	Kruger ....Ida Dorthea H. F.	1847 10 22	Germany
Till...................William	Bradshaw...........Sarah Ann	1824 02 22	
Timms..............William J. A.	Sisam ....Harriet	1867 04 01	UT, Salt Lake City
Timothy............John G.	Davies ....Martha	1853 09 30	Wales
Tims.................John Gardner	Marshall ....Charlotte	1852 12 22	ENG
Tindral ....Ferney Fold	Sheffield ....Polly Lucina	1853 03	UT, Payson
Tingey..............Henry	Spencer...............Hannah	1870 05 09	UT, Salt Lake City
Tingey..............Henry	Young.................Ann	1839 05 12	ENG
Tippets............Brigham L.	Tippets ....Abigail Eliza	1874 11 30	UT, Salt Lake City
Tippets............John Harvey	Wise ....Eleanor	1863 12 26	UT, Salt Lake City
Tippets............Joseph H.	Perry ....Amanda Melvina	1842 06 26	IL, Nauvoo
Tippets............Joseph M.	Tippets ....Alice Jeanette	1860 01 01	UT, Perry
Tippets............William Plummer	Mead ....Sophia Burnham	1842 01 01	
Tippetts...........Alvah L.	Beard ....Caroline	1843 09 19	IN, Clinton
Titcomb...........John	Atkins ....Mary	1830	
Titensor ....Thomas Edward	Bradbury ....Elizabeth	1867 08 03	UT, Salt Lake City
Titensor ....Thomas Edward	Robbins..............Sarah	1854 04 01	ENG, Manchester
Tobin ....John	Rich...................Sarah Jane		UT, Salt Lake City
Tobler ....John Jacob	Hafen ....Barbara	1865 10 18	
Todd ....Abraham	Tofts..................Ann	1863 05 03	ENG
Todd ....Andrew	Miecklejohn.........Catherine Mary	1846 11 13	Scotland
Todd ....George	Wride.................Jane	1869 10 18	UT, Salt Lake City

Male	Female	Date	Place
Todd ....James	Firman................Susanna	1828 06 01	
Todd ....Thomas	Murdoch ....Mary	1866 12 01	
Todd ....Thomas	Shankland ....Margaret	1850 01 25	Scotland
Tolley ....William	Bardell................Sarah	1870 10 10	
Tolley ....William F.	Gadd ....Sarah	1869	
Tolley ....William F.	Warren ....Sarah	1848 08 01	ENG
Tolman ....Benjamin H.	Angell.................Sarah Jane	1851 01 02	UT, Salt Lake City
Tolman ....Cyrus A.	Pickett ....Elizabeth	1870 10 17	
Tolman ....Cyrus A.	Pickett ....Maria Louisa	1878 12 12	
Tolman ....Cyrus Hewitt	Utley..................Margaret Eliza	1853 06 30	UT, Salt Lake City
Tolman ....Jaren T.	Briggs.................Emma	1874 06 01	UT, Salt Lake City
Tolman ....Jaren T.	Briggs.................Mary Ann	1878 12 26	UT, Salt Lake City
Tolman ....Jaren T.	Burningham........Jane A.	1886	
Tolman ....Judson	Holbrook.............Sarah Lucretia	1846 01 12	IL, Nauvoo
Tolman ....Judson	Stoker................Zebiah Jane	1869 04 05	UT, Salt Lake City
Tolman ....Judson A.	Howard...............Mary Ann	1872 12 23	UT, Salt Lake City
Tolton ....Edward	Tomlinson ....Mary Ann	1847 12 24	MO, St. Louis
Tolton ....John	Smith..................Ann	1811 11 09	ENG
Tonks...............Timothy	Jones ....Ann	1817 10 05	ENG
Toomer ....James	Cook...................Mary Jane	1854 03	ENG, Salisbury
Toone ....John	Cook...................Jemima	1857 02 22	UT, Salt Lake City
Toone ....John	Prosser...............Emma	1836 06 12	ENG
Toone ....William H.	Webb..................Hannah	1865 03 04	UT, Salt Lake City
Topham ....John	Baker..................Betsy Lucinda	1850 12 03	UT, Salt Lake City
Torbjornsen .....Niels	Madsen ....Mette Marie	1862 09 29	UT, Salt Lake City
Towler..............Daniel	Durnford ....Sarah Ann	1867 08 17	UT, Salt Lake City
Townsend........James F.	Davis ....Susan	1827 03 11	
Townsend........John W.	Walton................Ann	1847	ENG
Tracy ....Eli Alexander	Sprague ....Eliza Ann	1854 12 25	UT, Salt Lake City
Tracy ....Horace	Alexander...........Nancy Naomi	1860 04 08	
Tracy ....Joseph C.	Bemis ....Hannah	1846	
Tracy ....Moses	Alexander...........Nancy Naomi	1832 07 15	
Tremayne ....William Henry	Winter.................Ann	1870 05 30	
Trewella...........John	Stevens ....Eleanor	1853 12 25	
Trimble ....Edward	Lennox ....Elizabeth	1839 08 24	
Trimmer ....Edward W.	Leonard..............Anne Jane	1860	
Tripp ....Enoch B.	Billings................Roxanna Sophia	1846 03 29	IL, Nauvoo
Tripp ....Enoch B.	Eddins ....Jessie	1857 03 20	UT, Salt Lake City
Tristram ....George D.	Wright.................Lucy	1841 07 18	ENG
Trulock............Aquilla	Chestnut.............Sarah Mary	1865 11	
Truman ....Jacob Mica	Boyce ....Elizabeth	1849 04 19	UT, Salt Lake City
Truman ....Jacob Mica	Hales..................Julia Ardena	1857 06 14	
Truman ....Jacob Mica	Maxwell..............Catherine	1856 12 21	UT, Salt Lake City
Tryon ....Truman	Roberts ....Cyrene Elsie	1868 02 04	UT, Salt Lake City
Tucker ....George	Hurst ....Emma Jane	1868 03 07	UT, Salt Lake City
Tucker ....James	Lerwill................Betsy Valate	1860 03	ENG, Liverpool
Tucker ....William	Bonner ....Esther	1824 10 17	ENG
Tuckett............Charles	Pattenden...........Jane	1824	ENG, London
Tuckett............Henry	Frisby ....Esther	1870 11 14	UT, Salt Lake City
Tullgren ....Axel	Neilson ....Ellen	1853	Denmark
Tullgren ....Axel	Nilsson ....Ellen C.		
Tullis ....David Wilson	Eccles ....Martha	1863	UT, Pinto
Tullis ....David Wilson	Hardman ....Alice	1861	UT, Pinto
Tupper ....Silas F.	Ladd...................Hannah	1817	NY

Male	Female	Date	Place
Turley ....Isaac	Greenwood ....Sarah		
Turley ....Isaac	Tolton ....Clara Ann	1867 10 04	UT, Salt Lake City
Turnbow ....Samuel	Hart ....Silvira Caroline	1829 10 01	
Turner............Alfred	Morris ....Susan	1875 02 22	
Turner............David	Robinson............Alice	1877 01 11	UT, St. George
Turner............David Jr.	Collier...............Rose	1839	
Turner............Henry	Steed................Ann		
Turner............John	Morgan..............Lucinda		
Turner............William	Ward ....Mary Ann	1853	ENG
Turner............William A.	Boaz.................Alice Truscott	1864 10 15	UT, Salt Lake City
Turner............William A.	Nichols ....Amelia	1848 10 15	ENG
Turpin ....Jesse	Boggess ....Eliza Ann	1840 09 24	VA, Clarksburg
Turpin ....Jesse	Smith.................Jane Louisa	1846 04 16	IL, Nauvoo
Turpin ....Jesse	Wooding............Sarah	1850 01 08	UT, Salt Lake City
Tuttle ....Hubbard B.	Loomis ....Lucy	1844 05 16	
Tuttle ....Newton	Mix ....Lucinda Susanna	1847 11 24	CT, North Haven
Tuttle ....Newton	Stone................Emily Amelia	1855 04 07	
Twede............Christen F. N.	Pedersen............Christiana	1859 04 24	UT, Salt Lake City
Twitchell ....Anciel	Brown...............Margaret Melinda		
Twitchell ....Anciel	Hitchcock ....Louisa Samantha	1844 10 07	
Twitchell ....Edwin	Bishop ....Vesta Lucetta	1860 02 24	UT, Fillmore
Twitchell ....Ephraim	Knight................Phoebe Melissa	1824 03 01	OH, Pomeroy
Tye ....Jesse Askew	Tite ....Elizabeth	1856 11 09	UT, Salt Lake City
Tyler ....DeWitt C.	Pratt ....Sariah	1850 05 14	Trail
Tyler ....Lumus	Owens...............Lucinda		

U

Male	Female	Date	Place
Udall ....David	King..................Eliza	1850 12 02	ENG
Udall ....David	May ....Eliza Rebecca	1864 07 02	UT, Salt Lake City
Underwood ......Edward J.	Watson..............Janette	1866 01 01	UT, Provo
Underwood ......Joseph	Baker.................Ruth	1833 01 03	MA, Harwich
Ungermand......Henning	Rasmussen ....Anne Magdalene	1863 12 19	
Unsworth ....James	Orell ....Albertina W.	1873 03 03	
Unthank ....William	Barns.................Mary Ann	1855	
Unthank ....William	Elliker ....Margaretha		
Unthank ....William	Pucell ....Ellen	1871 05 25	
Upton..............William	Taylor ....Mary	1855 11 12	ENG, Derbyshire
Urie.................James	Swan ....Violet	1868 06 02	
Urie.................John	McMillan.............Sarah Ann	1858 01 16	
Utley ....Littlejohn	Rutledge.............Elizabeth		

V

Male	Female	Date	Place
Vail ....Gamaliel	Bartholomew ....Martha	1830 04 08	NY
Vail ....Isaac	Benson...............Suzanna	1848 06 08	
Vail ....Isaac Hawk	Bloomfield ....Emma	1861 10 26	UT, Salt Lake City
Valentine ....Hans M. K.	Loveland ....Sarah Sophia	1867 04 20	UT, Salt Lake City
Valleley...........John	Jones ....Ann	1819	
Van ....John Alfred	Smith.................Jane Louisa	1855 01 13	UT, Salt Lake City
Van Buren ....Cheney G.	Phillips...............Lucy	1831 02 17	NY, Russia
Van Cott ....John	Madsen ....Severine Marie	1876	UT, Salt Lake City

Male	Female	Date	Place
Van Cott ....John	Pratt ....Caroline Amelia	1857 02 02	
Van Cott ....Losee	Pratt ....Lovina Jemima	1812 09 05	
Van Curen ....Paul	Teeples ....Elvira	1855	
Van Etten........Elijah W.	Egbert ....Susanna	1864 06 04	UT, Salt Lake City
Van Etten........Elisha Wheat	Daley..................Abigail Jane	1850 07	
Van Leuven .....Cornelius	Draper.................Lovina	1823 05 01	Canada
Van Leuven .....Dunam	Larson................Anna Hannah	1864 11 30	
Van Leuven .....John	Pulver.................Mary Ann	1794	
Van Leuven .....Ransom	Harvey................Lucinda	1830	
Van Noy..........William Thomas	Birrell.................Agnes	1859 12 25	UT, Salt Lake City
Van Orden ......Everett C.	Harris ....Elizabeth	1857 03 12	UT, Salt Lake City
Van Orden ......William	Haight................Julia Ann	1827 03 12	NY, Green Co.
Van Orman .....Abraham	Hansen...............Anne Marie	1887 09 27	UT, Logan
Van Orman .....Abraham	Hunter ....Margaret	1867 03 06	UT, Salt Lake City
Van Tassell.....James D.	Swift ....Jane Elizabeth	1867 12 14	UT, Salt Lake City
Van Valkenburgh..Peter	Boggess ....Eliza Ann	1855	
Van Valkenburgh..Peter	Freeman.............Caroline Sophia	1850 10 17	
Van Velsor.......Stephen	Cronk ....Fanny		
Van Wagoner ..John H.	Tappen...............Clarissa	1840	
Vance ....Isaac Y.	Yeager ....Martha Eleanor	1840 11 23	
Vance ....John W.	Vail....................Angelia	1854 07 30	
Vance ....William Perkins	Hudson...............Ann	1865 03 10	
Vance ....William Perkins	Richardson..........Hannah	1874 10 19	UT
Vane ....Joseph H.	Clark..................Lucina Elmina	1881 06 23	UT, Salt Lake City
Varley ....William	Macduff ....Mary Ellen	1861 02 24	ENG
Varney ....Jacob	Shelley ....Sarah Elizabeth	1906 10 09	
Vasquez ....Pierce Louis	Land...................Narcissa B.	1851 09 25	Platte River
Vaughan ....William	Davies ....Dinah	1834 03 17	Wales
Vest ....Hyrum	Platt...................Sarah Ellen	1873 03 24	UT, Salt Lake City
Vest ....John	Potter ....Mary Ann	1820 02 24	ENG
Vest ....John Jr.	Parneby..............Elizabeth	1845 03 24	ENG
Vickers...........John	Lacey ....Ann	1847 03 09	ENG, Nottingham
Vier ....Wilhelm F. J. E.	Nielsen...............Ane Marie	1880 12 16	UT, Salt Lake City
Vilhelmsen.......Hans	Sandberg ....Annie Antionette		
Vince ....Moses Andrews	Broom ....Jenette	1854 05 30	UT, Salt Lake City
Vincent ....Daniel	Bradshaw............Sarah Ann	1857 04 09	
Vincent ....Samuel	Rogers ....Delilah Eunice		
Virgin ....George T.	Barker ....Mary Ann	1852 09 09	ENG
Vogel ....Herman A. P.	Cashmore ....Sarah Ann	1873	UT, Salt Lake City
Voorhees........Elisha	Leek ....Nancy Ann	1818 03 26	OH, Clermont
Voss ....Thomas	Haddon ....Lucy	1839	ENG
Vowles...........Samuel	Cross.................Margaret	1862 06 07	

W

Male	Female	Date	Place
Waddoups ....Thomas	Porter ....Elizabeth	1839 01 22	ENG
Waddoups ....William	Page...................Martha	1864 11 27	UT, Bountiful
Waddoups ....William	Stephenson.........Eliza Jane		
Wade ....Edward Davis	Hickenlooper ....Belinda	1849 01 21	UT, Salt Lake City
Wade ....Moses	Bundy.................Sally Mariah	1818	
Wadley ....Joseph	Dee ....Emily	1860 12 05	UT, Pleasant Grove
Wadley ....Joseph	Dorney ....Hannah	1856 11 15	UT, Pleasant Grove
Wadley ....William	McKay ....Isabella	1860 04 08	

Male	Female	Date	Place
Wadsworth ......Abiah	Hardy ....Eliza Ann	1831 02 25	ME, Lincolnville
Wadsworth ......George A.	Broadbent ....Elizabeth	1853 04 18	ENG, Sheffield
Wadsworth ......James	Hutchinson ....Elizabeth	1831 05 22	ENG, Darfield
Wadsworth ......Joseph W.	Stoddard ....Lydia	1858 03 05	UT, Salt Lake City
Wadsworth ......Thomas S.	Moore................Catherine	1864 12 02	UT, Ogden
Wadsworth ......William	Wells ....Matilda	1857	UT, Salt Lake City
Waggle ....Jacob	Vancil ....Mary		
Wagstaff ....David	Crystal................Mary	1867 03 08	UT, American Fork
Wagstaff ....Isaac	Gillians ....Mary Bathsheba	1808 10 12	
Wagstaff ....John	Humberstone ......Sarah	1844 11 25	ENG
Wagstaff ....Samuel	Webb..................Maria Lucy	1840 12 25	ENG
Waite ....John	Caldwell ....Jane		
Wakefield.........John	Wilson ....Caroline Rachel	1856 07 27	ENG
Wakefield.........Thomas	Clarke.................Mary	1837 03 25	PA, Wheatfield
Waldram ....Lorenzo	Fowlke................Louisa	1901 02 08	
Waldron ....Benjamin	Chorlton ....Harriet	1866 10 02	
Walker ....Charles L.	Middlemas..........Abigail	1861 09 28	UT, Salt Lake City
Walker ....Cyrus S.	Pearson..............Elsie	1875 12 20	UT, Salt Lake City
Walker ....Daniel C.	Slater..................Emily	1881 11 03	UT, Salt Lake City
Walker ....Edmund	Swallow..............Maria A.	1842 07 14	ENG
Walker ....Edward Marion	Sabey.................Sarah Jane	1890 08 10	
Walker ....Edward R.	Cox.....................Ann Marie	1849 09 13	IL, Green Co.
Walker ....Francis C.	Staheli ....Elizabeth	1870 04 18	UT, St. George
Walker ....George Gorril	Hopkins ....Mary	1837 03 27	ENG
Walker ....Henry	Alloway...............Maria Seaborn	1869 10 04	UT, Salt Lake City
Walker ....Henry	Dixon..................Isabella		ENG
Walker ....Henry	Preece................Ann	1825 12 19	ENG
Walker ....Henry	Pritchard.............Susannah		
Walker ....Henson	Foutz ....Elizabeth	1846 04 10	IL, Nauvoo
Walker ....Henson	Foutz ....Margaret	1857 11 09	
Walker ....Henson Jr.	Green ....Mary	1856 07 03	UT, Salt Lake City
Walker ....James	Shepherd ....Jane	1834 05 01	ENG
Walker ....Jesse H.	Hunt ....Loretta	1873 01 08	UT, Paradise
Walker ....John	Luce ....Caroline		
Walker ....John	McSkelly.............Ellen		
Walker ....John B.	Brown.................Elizabeth Ann	1835	MS
Walker ....John Smith	Pucell ....Margaret Augusta	1862 08 09	UT, Cedar City
Walker ....John William	Coleman.............Elizabeth	1834 12 08	ENG
Walker ....Joseph	Mitchell...............Ann	1828	ENG
Walker ....Joseph	Smith..................Sarah	1872	
Walker ....Joseph R.	Hudson...............Sarah Jane		
Walker ....Oliver	Cressy................Nancy	1803 02 08	
Walker ....Rufus	Mikesell ....Cynthia Ann		
Walker ....Rufus	Wilbur................Phebe Eunice	1856 01 27	UT, Salt Lake City
Walker ....Samuel F.	Dixon..................Sarah	1864 05 23	UT, Salt Lake City
Walker ....Stephen	Marchant.............Lydia Elizabeth	1866 02 12	UT
Walker ....Walter P.	Wright.................Charlotte	1864 12 17	UT, Salt Lake City
Walker ....William	Chapple...............Sarah	1863	
Walker ....William H.	Bingham.............Olive Louisa	1858 08 30	UT, Salt Lake City
Walker ....William H.	Shadden.............Mary Jane	1850 04 28	
Walker ....William J.	Ekins ....Sarah Rebecca	1855 03 26	ENG
Wall ....Robert W. W.	Bair....................Belinda Jane	1866 10 29	UT, Kaysville
Wall ....William	Sansom...............Sarah	1836 09 26	ENG, Horsley
Wall ....William M.	Gurr....................Sarah		

Male	Female	Date	Place
Wall ....William M.	Gurr..................Susanna	1859 11 12	UT, Salt Lake City
Wall ....William M.	Haws ....Nancy	1840 06 02	IL, Sangamon Co.
Wall ....William M.	Penrod ....Elizabeth	1852 08 06	UT, Provo
Wallace...........George B.	Davis ....Hannah	1852 10 15	UT, Salt Lake City
Wallace...........George B.	Davis ....Lydia	1852 10 15	UT, Salt Lake City
Wallace...........George B.	Davis ....Martha	1852 10 15	UT, Salt Lake City
Wallace...........George E.	Folsom ....Frances Emily	1873 10 16	UT, Salt Lake City
Wallace...........Hamilton M.	Butler.................Charity A.	1855 10 04	UT, Spanish Fork
Wallace...........Henry	Harper ....Elen	1863 02 07	UT, Salt Lake City
Wallace...........Thomas M.	Burnhope ....Mary Ann	1859 04 09	ENG
Wallentine........Peter C.	Caldwell ....Elizabeth	1860 08 31	UT, Salt Lake City
Waller ....Samuel	Wild ....Dianna	1819	ENG
Walsh ....Joseph C.	Moss ....Mary Sylvannus	1870 12 12	
Walsh ....Richard	Parkinson ....Mary Ann	1852 03 27	ENG
Walsh ....William	Bury...................Alice Fish	1850 07 01	
Walters ....Archer	Cross.................Harriet	1837 08 26	ENG, Rotherham
Walters ....Asa	Westcott ....Sarah Jane	1840 04 07	Isle of Jersey
Walton ....Edward	Storer ....Mary Ann	1840 03 12	ENG
Walton ....George	Hug ....Hannah	1857 06 03	UT, Salt Lake City
Walton ....Joseph	Thompson ....Ann	1854 10 29	UT, Mill Creek
Walton ....Thomas	...........................Hannah	1862	
Walton ....Thomas	Colley ....Jane	1819 05 20	ENG
Wamsley.........Thomas	Hodgkinson.........Ann Elizabeth	1826 12 25	
Wandless........Thomas	Williamson...........Ellen (Eleanor)	1847 03 28	ENG, Durham
Warburton.......Richard	Atkin ....Emily	1851 05 29	UT, Salt Lake City
Ward...............Edward	Parker ....Elizabeth	1855 05 21	UT, Parowan
Ward...............Edwin J.	Backhouse ....Mary Alice	1864 02 11	UT, Pleasant Grove
Ward...............George	Ward ....Isabella	1821 10 15	ENG, Kirby
Ward...............George P.	Nielson ....Sennie Dorothea	1866 08 18	UT, Salt Lake City
Ward...............George W.	Truelock ....Ann	1842 01 24	ENG, Bloomsburg
Ward...............James	Taylor ....Elizabeth	1838	ENG, Nottingham
Ward...............John	Hogg ....Emma	1838 05 07	ENG
Ward...............Moroni	Voss ....Eliza	1872 11 18	UT, Salt Lake City
Ward...............Samuel	Bunting ....Ann	1855 08 05	ENG, Matlock
Ward...............Thomas	Latham ....Truelove	1822 05 26	ENG, Belgrave
Ward...............Thomas	Reese.................Anne	1870	UT, Salt Lake City
Ward...............William	Cordon ....Rachel Ann	1861	UT, Willard
Ward...............William	Webster.............Susanna	1816 02 25	ENG
Wardle ....George	Fisher ....Caroline Kazia	1868 12 15	UT, Salt Lake City
Wardle ....George	Rushton..............Fanny	1842 01 24	ENG
Wardle ....James	Dixon.................Mary	1866 02 03	UT, Salt Lake City
Wardle ....Solomon	Matheson ....Ellen McKell		
Wardley ....Francis	Mills...................Hannah	1864	
Wardrobe........John	McIntosh ....Lucy	1837 09 17	Scotland
Ware...............Abisha	Rogers ....Delilah Eunice	1813 04 09	VA, Rockingham
Ware...............George	Bigg...................Naomi	1816 06 27	ENG
Wareing ....George	Gibson................Mary	1862 04 19	UT, Salt Lake City
Wark...............John	Bathgate............Mary		
Warner............Holstein M.	Dewsnup ....Ann	1866 01	
Warner............James	Benson...............Jane	1856 05 21	
Warner............James	Miller ....Ann	1855	
Warner............John Ely	Billings...............Eunice	1849 04 04	UT
Warner............Solomon	Billington ....Rebecca Delight	1830 10 07	OH, Norton
Warner............William	David.................Ann	1856	

Male	Female	Date	Place
Warner............William	Reynolds............Mary	1848 05 18	ENG
Warner............William Goodman	Goodman............Keziah Miles	1854 11 30	Ocean
Warner............William H.	Andrews............Elizabeth	1861 07 24	
Warnick ....Anders P.	Anderson............Anna Helena	1829 12 25	Sweden
Warnick ....Charles P.	Larsen ....Christine Marie	1874 03 16	UT, Salt Lake City
Warnick ....John A.	Bengtson............Maria Christena	1861 07 05	Sweden
Warr................Charles E.	Hiskey ....Clarissa Jane	1871	UT
Warr................Moses	Padfield............Eliza Ann		ENG
Warren............Elihue	Staley ....Mary	1862 04 05	UT, Salt Lake City
Warren............Zenos C.	Sweet ....Sarah	1824	
Warrick ....Thomas	Taylor................Louisa	1841 04 04	SC
Wasden ....Frederick	Esklund ....Anna Marie C.	1865 10 18	UT, Gunnison
Wasden ....Thomas	Caucom..............Mary	1841 12 06	ENG
Washburn ....Abraham	Washburn............Tamar	1824 03 16	NY
Washburn ....Abraham Daniel	Gleason..............Flora Clarinda	1849 02 11	UT, Salt Lake City
Washburn ....Daniel A.	Johnson ....Margaret Ann	1861 04 18	UT, Spring Town
Washburn ....Luther	Gilson................Clarissa Ann	1878 01 24	UT, Marysvale
Waters ....George	Beard ....Anne	1812 03 30	
Waters ....Reuben	Smith..................Mary	1852	MO, St. Louis
Watkins............John	Ackhurst ....Margaret	1851 05 04	ENG
Watkins............John	Sawyer ....Mary Ann	1863 05 01	UT, Salt Lake City
Watkins............John	Steele ....Harriet Mollet	1858	
Watkins............William	Lampard..............Hannah Maria	1820 07 09	ENG
Watkins............William L.	Hammond ....Mary Almina	1844 12 04	IL, Nauvoo
Watmough ......William	Dyas..................Mary Ann E.	1839 03 05	ENG
Watson ....Hiram Abiff	Hendricks............Rebecca	1852	UT, Salt Lake City
Watson ....James	Campbell............Janet	1845	Scotland
Watson ....James C.	Condie................Mary	1864 08 06	
Watson ....John	Mills..................Hannah	1854 05 05	ENG
Watson ....Robert	Cowan................Mary	1840 01 12	Scotland
Watson ....Thomas	Squire................Janet	1841 06 18	Scotland
Watson ....Thomas P.	Lishman ....Maria	1867 07 11	
Watson ....William	Hayball...............Ellen Jane		UT, Logan
Watt ....George Darling	Harter ....Sarah Ann	1866 08 11	UT, Salt Lake City
Watters ....Ichel	Graupe ....Augusta	1871 07 05	UT, Salt Lake City
Watterson ......William Jr.	Hobbs................Caroline	1866 12 13	
Watton ....James	Francis ....Sarah	1861 01 05	
Watton ....James	Sherry ....Mary Ann	1849 04 16	MO, St. Louis
Watts ....Baldwin H.	Levi ....Barbara Jane	1856 10 26	UT, Ogden
Watts ....Benjamin	Williamson..........Ellen	1857 01 01	UT, Paragonah
Watts ....Henry	Noble.................Louisa Rox Snow	1863 03 09	
Watts ....Henry	Whale.................Eliza	1842 04 01	ENG
Watts ....Joseph	Livingston............Mary Helen	1859 02 01	
Watts ....Robert H.	Heath ....Elizabeth	1833 12 20	
Way ....William	Simmons ....Celia Leonora	1863 10 01	
Waylett ....George D.	King....................Martha Anna	1863 01 28	UT, Salt Lake City
Wayman ....Emmanuel	Johnston ....Margaret	1856 04 10	
Wayman ....James	Golthrop ....Martha	1821 04 22	
Wayment ....Samuel J.	Chapman ....Castina F. A.	1868 03 11	ENG
Weaver ....Edward	Raymer ....Martha	1821	NY
Weaver ....Franklin	Holmes ....Sarah Elizabeth	1856 05 09	UT, Salt Lake City
Weaver ....Franklin	Read ....Christianna R.	1848 03 12	
Weaver ....Gilbert E.	Conover ....Sarah Elizabeth	1855 07 14	
Weaver ....Miles	Holmes...............Sarah Elizabeth	1855 01 01	UT, Salt Lake City

Male		Female		Date	Place
Weaver	William H.	Asper	Mary Jane	1873 08 13	UT, Grass Creek
Webb	David	Olpin	Esther	1843 08 01	ENG, Bristol
Webb	Edward Milo	Owens	Caroline Amelia	1839 12 12	IL, Nauvoo
Webb	George	Porcher	Charity Emma		
Webb	George	Ward	Mary Ann	1865 05 31	UT, Lehi
Webb	George H.	Thompson	Eliza	1853 10 27	ENG, Northill
Webb	John Stokes	Grace	Hannah	1854 02 18	
Webb	Pardon K.	Lee	Clarissa Jane	1844 01 07	MI, Comstock
Webb	William	Grace	Harriet	1864 05 09	ENG
Webb	William	Stokes	Emma	1831 04	ENG
Webley	Richard	Danby	Jane	1797 04 17	ENG
Webster	John	Wright	Mary Ann	1858 07 15	WI
Weech	Samuel	Gould	Elizabeth	1832 11 05	ENG, Somerton
Weekes	David	Riches	Hannah	1861 12 07	UT, Salt Lake City
Weekes	Robert	Bauldry	Anna Mary	1818 04 03	
Weekes	Samuel	Sawyer	Mary Eliza	1853 01 04	
Weight	Fredrick	Bocock	Elizabeth	1865 07 01	UT, Salt Lake City
Weight	Fredrick	Burgum	Charlotte	1849 08 18	
Weight	James	Foukes	Ann	1821	
Welch	Charles	Newey	Elizabeth	1856 10 05	UT, Salt Lake City
Welch	Daniel	Welch	Zipporah	1856 03 16	IL, Alton
Welch	Thomas R. G.	Cook	Mary Jane	1896	
Welchman	Arthur P.	Kershaw	Sarah Lucretia	1867 03 16	UT, Salt Lake City
Welker	James	Stoker	Elizabeth	1822 07 02	OH, Jackson Co.
Welker	James Wilburn	Pugh	Annie	1845 02 17	IA, Pottawattamie
Wellard	James Elias	Farnes	Mary Ann		Ocean
Wells	Daniel H.	Alley	Lydia Ann	1852 04 03	UT, Salt Lake City
Wells	Daniel H.	Alley	Susan Hannah	1852 04 18	UT, Salt Lake City
Wells	Daniel H.	Tupper	Hannah		
Wells	Daniel H.	Woodward	Emmeline B. B.	1852 10 18	
Wells	Henry	Hubbard	Julia Cynthia	1865	
Wells	Jonathan S.	Gardner	Margaret	1829 06 23	PA, Erie Co.
Wells	Lyman Briggs	Fordham	Bithiah	1849 04 03	NE
Wells	Samuel	Hattersley	Sarah	1842 02 06	ENG, Sheffield
Wells	Stephen R.	Lowe	Mary Ann	1851	Trail
Wells	Stephen R.	Thorne	Annie	1857 04 22	UT, Salt Lake City
Wesley	John Everett	Hunter	Elizabeth	1859 06 21	NE, Florence
West	Charles H. J.	Dangerfield	Eliza	1850 12 25	ENG, London
West	Chauncey W.	Covington	Sarah Elizabeth	1855 08 05	UT, Salt Lake City
West	David	Hadfield	Martha Ann	1881	
West	David	Hooley	Arnelia	1844 07 15	ENG
West	Ira Enos	Van Orden	Charlotte Amelia	1846 01 08	IL, Nauvoo
West	Jabez William	Hoggan	Janet	1881 01 20	UT, Salt Lake City
West	Jesse	Williams	Mary Ann	1867 08 31	UT, Salt Lake City
West	John	Keiling	Rachel	1837 11 14	ENG
West	Lewis Alvin	Baker	Elizabeth Ann	1858 11 23	UT, Ogden
West	Samuel Walker	Cooper	Margaret	1829 01 29	TN
West	Thomas	Moore	Harriet	1849 09	Ocean
West	Thomas C.	Felt	Margaret Eliza	1874 11 10	UT, Salt Lake City
West	William	Cook	Ann	1854 11 23	ENG, Borrowash
West	William Moroni	Hobbs	Tryphena Jane	1868 05 27	UT, Parowan
Westerhold	Charles	Mackelprang	Christina J.	1887 12 29	UT, Cedar City
Western	John	Pool	Matilda	1853 10 26	UT, Salt Lake City
Western	Samuel R. R.	Winsbrough	Ann	1836 03 09	ENG

Male	Female	Date	Place
Western ....Samuel W.	Wood.................Sarah Ann	1866 01 29	UT, Berryville
Westover ....Edwin L.	Erickson ....Joanna Matilda	1874 04 27	
Westwood........Richard W.	Dallin ....Catherine	1859 06 17	UT, Springville
Weymouth ....Daniel	Mead ....Sophia Burnham	1827	
Wheeler ....Henry A.	Teeples ....Elvira	1836 01 02	MI, Pontiac
Wheeler ....Joseph	Buckingham ....Mary Ann	1838 03 19	ENG
Wheeler ....Levi	Perry ....Phebe Roxy	1865 12 23	UT, Salt Lake City
Wheeler ....Samuel	Gillings ....Elizabeth	1830 12 24	ENG
Wheeler ....Simon	Stevens ....Sarah	1804 03 15	ME, Greene
Wheeler ....Thomas J.	Roberts ....Jane Cecelia		
Wheeler ....Walter	Child ....Ellen Maria	1873 07 28	UT, Salt Lake City
Wheeler ....William	Grassing.............Sarah	1854	UT, Salt Lake City
Wheelock.........Cyrus H.	Dallin ....Mary Ann	1853 12 11	UT, Salt Lake City
Wheelwright.....Matthew	Farrar ....Catherine Emma	1860 08 15	UT, Salt Lake City
Whipple ....Edson	Quinney...............Mary Ann	1857 04 26	UT, Salt Lake City
Whipple ....Edson	Yeager ....Harriet	1850 11 04	UT, Salt Lake City
Whipple ....Edson	Yeager ....Mary Ann	1850 11 04	UT, Salt Lake City
Whipple ....Nelson Wheeler	Bailey ....Susan Jane		
Whipple ....Nelson Wheeler	Gay ....Susan Ann	1857 02 09	UT, Salt Lake City
Whipple ....Nelson Wheeler	Keiling ....Rachel	1853 03 12	UT, Salt Lake City
Whitaker ....George	Robinson.............Eveline Parsons	1846 07 27	IA, Council Bluffs
Whitaker ....James	Woodland...........Nancy	1838 01 16	
Whitaker ....Thomas William	Mills...................Elizabeth	1858 03 17	UT, Salt Lake City
Whitby ....Thomas B.	Freestone...........Emma Sarah	1872 12 09	UT, Salt Lake City
White ....Alfred	Mangum ....Sarah Frances	1875	UT, Nephi
White ....Barnard	Williams...............Diana Mary	1869 03 07	UT, Salt Lake City
White ....Ernest Authenia	Thayne ....Mary Ann	1899	
White ....George	Rivers.................Mary	1845 10 13	ENG
White ....George Martin	Hill ....Margaret Ann	1863 12 19	UT, Salt Lake City
White ....Henry Harvey	Smith...................Rebecca	1808 10 09	VT, Chester
White ....James	Ellwood ....Ann	1885	UT, Salt Lake City
White ....Joel William	Thomas ....Frances Ann	1850 05 08	IA, Pottawattamie
White ....John	Brown.................Eliza	1863 11 18	
White ....John	Christmas............Maria	1821 04 09	ENG
White ....John C.	Ingram................Mary Ann	1863 03 09	UT, Spanish Fork
White ....John Griggs	Bailey ....Lucy Meranda	1808 02 17	
White ....John Stout	Everett................Ann E. A.	1849 04 05	UT, Salt Lake City
White ....Jonathan	Dodd ....Elizabeth	1835 11 03	ENG, Lincolnshire
White ....Joseph	Rogers ....Adelia Caroline		
White ....Samuel Dennis	Burton ....Mary Hannah	1841 10 24	IL, Walnut Grove
White ....Samuel Dennis	Harris ....Lydia	1866 09 08	
White ....Samuel Dennis	Thomas ....Elizabeth Turner	1852 03 24	UT, Salt Lake City
White ....Samuel O.	Woodhouse........Mary Ellen	1867 10 05	UT, Salt Lake City
White ....Samuel Steven	Foutz ....Catherine	1849 09 27	UT, Salt Lake City
White ....Stephen	McGregor ....Agnes	1859 11 01	UT, Salt Lake City
White ....Thomas Jones	Murdock ....Lorena		
White ....Thomas Jones	Reed ....Clarissa	1854 04 11	
White ....Thomas Jones	Williams..............Hannah	1847 06 20	ENG
White ....Thomas Phillip	Potts...................Alice	1857 03 16	ENG
White ....William	Syer....................Mary Ann	1837 04 17	ENG
White ....William	Warn...................Elizabeth Pollow	1852 02 16	ENG
White ....William W.	Morris ....Louisa	1880 05 20	UT, Salt Lake City
Whitehead ....Francis	Monson ....Annie Catherine	1880	
Whitehead ....Francis	Robinson.............Jacosa Jane	1868 03	UT, Richmond

Male	Female	Date	Place
Whitehead ....James Jr.	Brindle ....Amelia Charlotte	1871 10 02	UT, Salt Lake City
Whitehead ....John	Bult.................Mary	1837 09 26	ENG
Whitehead ....William	Butterworth..........Alice	1872	
Whitehead ....William	Green ....Margaret	1863 03 28	UT, Farmington
Whitehouse .....Jeremiah	Warr ....Emma Martha	1862 02 10	UT, Salt Lake City
Whitely............Joseph	Alston ....Marjorie	1891 11 01	UT, Salt Lake City
Whitesides.......Lewis	Perkins ....Susannah	1850 05 05	IA, Pleasant Valley
Whitesides.......Morris	Pierce.................Margaret	1841 07 23	IL, Nauvoo
Whiting ....Edwin	Brown.................Hannah Haines	1856 10 08	UT, Salt Lake City
Whiting ....Edwin	Cox.....................Mary Elizabeth	1846 01 27	IL, Nauvoo
Whiting ....Edwin	Tillotson..............Elizabeth P.	1833 09 21	
Whiting ....Elisha Jr.	Hulet..................Sally	1805 09 18	
Whiting ....William	Hall....................Mary Ann	1880 10 28	UT, St. George
Whitlock..........Andrew H.	Allred.................Hannah Caroline	1827 09 30	TN, Bedford
Whitlock..........Andrew H.	Overlade ....Andrear Neilson	1867 11 02	UT, Salt Lake City
Whitlock..........Charles	King...................Caroline Matilda	1853 02 01	UT, Spring City
Whitlock..........George A.	Jensen ....Mary Ann	1880 12 21	
Whitmore ....James M.	Carter ....Elizabeth	1853 02 23	TX
Whitney ....Alonzo W.	Keyes ....Henrietta	1839	
Whitney ....Francis Tuft	Alger...................Clarissa	1848	
Whitney ....Horace Kimball	Cravath ....Mary	1856 12 01	UT, Salt Lake City
Whitney ....Horace Kimball	Kimball ....Helen Mar	1846 02 04	IL, Nauvoo
Whitney ....Micah	Walker.................Diontha	1830 02 28	CT
Whitney ....New Samuel	Gurr....................Sarah Elizabeth	1872 07 29	UT, Salt Lake City
Whitney ....Newel K.	Keyes ....Henrietta	1846 01 26	IL, Nauvoo
Whitney ....Newel K.	Smith..................Elizabeth Ann	1822 10 20	OH, Kirtland
Whitney ....Newel K.	Woodward...........Emmeline B. B.	1845 01 07	IL, Nauvoo
Whitney ....Samuel Alonzo	Wall ....Fanny Maria	1863 10 18	
Whittaker ....Andrew I.	Gallant.................Betsy	1856 04 28	UT, Salt Lake City
Whittemore ......Aaron	Barnett ....Polly M. V.	1861 03 10	UT, Salt Lake City
Whittington ......George A.	Longhurst ....Mercy Marintha	1876 01 12	
Whittle ....Thomas L.	Butterfield...........Mary Jane	1853 08 07	UT, Herriman
Whittle ....Thomas L.	Fulmer................Mary Amelia	1833	
Whittle ....Zera	Pope...................Cassanda	1865 10 14	
Wickel.............Lemuel L.	Buckwalter ....Margaret	1847	MO, St. Louis
Wickel.............Richard	Weaver................Louisa	1860 07 21	MO, St. Louis
Wickham..........John	Andrews ....Sarah	1831 03 06	ENG
Wickham..........Richard	Graham ....Ellen	1863 12 10	UT, Brigham City
Widdison..........Thomas	Russell ....Janet	1821 09 21	Scotland
Widerburg........Ole	Jacobson.............Ellen	1863 09 11	
Wiggill.............Eli	Bentley ....Susannah	1832 02 20	South Africa
Wiggins...........John	Aldridge..............Ellen	1852 01 05	ENG
Wight ....Ephraim	Wight..................Sarah (Sally)		
Wight ....Joseph M.	Hurren ....Mary	1864 10 05	UT, Brigham City
Wight ....Lewis	Elliot ....Nancy Urania	1827 12 10	NY, Centerville
Wight ....Lewis William	Street ....Mary	1853 08	UT, Salt Lake City
Wight ....Stephen	Chubbuck............Mary	1853 01 30	
Wightman ....Charles B.	Dixon.................Mary Ann	1843 11 26	OH, Kirtland
Wightman ....William C.	Pepper ....Lucretia Jane	1854 08 04	UT, Payson
Wilbur ....Melvin	Dennis................Eunice	1824 02 15	RI
Wilcock ....William	Brown.................Elizabeth		
Wilcock ....William	Sharp ....Elizabeth	1851 11 05	ENG
Wilcox.............Hazard	Seeley ....Sarah	1801	NY, Albany
Wilcox.............James D.	Robinson.............Anna Maria	1854 11 26	UT

Male	Female	Date	Place
Wilcox............John H. O.	Young.................Mary	1848 03 14	UT, Salt Lake City
Wilcox..............Jonathan F.	Rice.....................Ida Ann	1880	
Wilcox.............Minard	Allred.................Julia Ann	1860 03 27	UT, Mt. Pleasant
Wilcox............Samuel Allen	Peterson.............Anna Christina	1872 10 21	UT, Salt Lake City
Wild ....Henry	Batchelor............Jane	1853 10 15	ENG
Wild ....Joseph	Binns ....Hannah	1868 01 11	
Wilder ....Austin	Barber ....Sally Maria	1829 01 18	NY, Genesee Co.
Wilding............David	Atkinson ....Alice	1828 10 23	ENG, Preston
Wilding............George	Layne ....Mary Elizabeth	1850 06 30	IA, Kanesville
Wilding............George	Winner.................Leoni Leoti	1875	
Wildman ....Edward	Baxter..................Jane	1861 03	
Wilford ....William	Clark...................Priscilla	1862 06 30	NV, Carson City
Wilkerson.........Thomas	Fallowell ....Eliza	1826	
Wilkins ....Alexander	Barney................Eliza Aribella	1857 02 07	UT, Salt Lake City
Wilkins ....Charles Jr.	Welch..................Uriah	1856	UT
Wilkins ....George W.	Lovett ....Catherine A.	1846 07 04	MA, Lowell
Wilkins ....John G.	Kennedy..............Nancy Adeline	1830	NY
Wilkins ....Oscar	Maxwell...............Elizabeth Durrah	1870 10 17	UT, Salt Lake City
Wilkinson ....Charles	Hughes................Sarah	1846 06 01	ENG
Wilkinson ....Charles	Mercer.................Sarah	1833	
Wilkinson ....Joseph	Mills....................Martha Ann	1871 05 29	UT, Salt Lake City
Wilkinson ....Nathaniel	Daines.................Lydia	1831 10 26	ENG
Wilkinson ....William C.	Brown..................Sarah Ann	1871 01 02	UT, Hoytsville
Willardson........Christian	Sorensen.............Karen	1851 04 02	Denmark
Willden............Charles W.	Turner ....Eleanor	1833 01 21	ENG
Willden............John	McEwen................Margaret	1862 06 03	UT, Beaver
Willey ....Jeremiah	Call.....................Samantha	1839 04 28	IL, Green Plains
Willi.................Ignaz	Hafen ....Barbara	1861 10 18	UT, Salt Lake City
Williams ....Bateman Haight	Jose ....Grace Tippett	1869 08 02	UT, Salt Lake City
Williams ....Benjamin	Rock...................Maryann	1837 07 04	ENG
Williams ....Benjamin	Smart ....Agnes		
Williams ....Benjamin	Watkins ....Mary	1846 11 02	Wales
Williams ....Charles	Sant....................Margaret	1861 10	UT, Smithfield
Williams ....Daniel	Jones ....Ruth	1805 04 16	Wales
Williams ....Daniel Randall	.........................Electa Caroline	1838	
Williams ....Ebenezer A.	Bowering.............Esther Ellen	1853	IA
Williams ....Ebenezer A.	Cottam ....Ellen	1857 06 21	UT, Salt Lake City
Williams ....Ebenezer A.	Riden..................Hannah		
Williams ....Elias W.	Hendricks............Lucy	1840 12 30	
Williams ....Ephraim	North ....Almira	1862 12 31	UT, Salt Lake City
Williams ....Evan Austin	Tompkins ....Eliza	1862 05 24	UT, Salt Lake City
Williams ....Ezra G.	Crombie ....Henrietta E.	1847 08 15	MO, St. Louis
Williams ....Frederick G.	Swain ....Rebecca	1815	
Williams ....George	Stevenson...........Emma Jane	1862 12 28	
Williams ....James H.	Evans ....Mary Alice	1884 06 10	UT, Salt Lake City
Williams ....John	Lucas ....Marcy Jane	1831 02 10	
Williams ....John	Parry ....Mary	1836 03 04	Wales
Williams ....John D.	Ames..................Clarissa	1850 12	
Williams ....John J.	Jones ....Mary	1857 03 06	UT, Salt Lake City
Williams ....John J.	Merrifield ....Jane Emma	1852 02 14	Wales
Williams ....John R.	Ivins...................Elizabeth	1863 07 18	UT, Salt Lake City
Williams ....Joshua	Green.................Hannah Martha	1877 01 13	UT, Ogden
Williams ....Judge	Bullock ....Mary Ann		
Williams ....Lafayette W.	Treseder.............Elizabeth	1884 12 06	UT, North Ogden

Male	Female	Date	Place
Williams ....Nathaniel	Richards ....Alice Howell	1893 05 02	UT, Beaver
Williams ....Owen	Thomas ....Ann	1836 05 14	Wales
Williams ....Robert H.	Busenbark..........Harriet	1854 02 18	UT, Salt Lake City
Williams ....Samuel H.	Harmon ....Mary Ann	1881 07 06	UT, Salt Lake City
Williams ....Thomas	Evans ....Anna	1853	
Williams ....Thomas J.	Bean....................Nancy	1842 09 04	
Williams ....Thomas P.	Fawson ....Jane	1859 06 27	
Williams ....William	Francis ....Elizabeth		ENG
Williams ....William	Jenkins...............Jane	1851 12 15	
Williams ....William	Lewis ....Cecelia	1825 11 21	Wales
Williams ....William	Williams..............Ann		
Williams ....William Francis	Johnston ....Anna Maria		
Williams ....William G.	McFate ....Aurilla	1861 03 18	UT, Virgin City
Williams ....William Jr.	Hope ....Margaret P.	1853 02 07	ENG
Williamson ....J. M.	Carmichael..........Sarah E.	1867	WY, Fort Bridger
Williamson ......James	Ray.....................Mary	1838 02 14	Scotland
Williamson ....Niels W.	Peterson.............Pernille	1844 01 05	Norway
Willie ....James Grey	Pettit..................Elizabeth Ann	1846 06 13	
Willis ....John	Bloomfield ....Mary Ann	1852 03 18	ENG
Willis ....John Henry	Reeves...............Frances	1857 03 20	UT, Salt Lake City
Willis ....Joshua Thomas	Aldridge..............Ellen	1864	UT
Willis ....Joshua Thomas	Dodge ....Sarah Melissa	1848 07 22	
Willis ....Merrill	Cherry ....Margaret	1804 12 08	
Willis ....William	Griffiths...............Mary Priscilla	1857 01 27	UT, Salt Lake City
Willis ....William T.	Wilson ....Elizabeth P.	1840	
Willis ....William W.	Long ....Frances		
Willis ....William W.	Willis..................Margaret Jane	1833 03 03	MO, Hamilton Co.
Willmore ....John Ayers	Porcher ....Charity Emma	1862 10 08	ENG
Wilson..............Bradley B.	Havens................Mary Ann	1861 12 20	UT, Payson
Wilson..............Charles	Farrow................Mary	1851 02 09	ENG, Hazelrigg
Wilson..............Elijah	Kelley ....Martha	1830 12 12	
Wilson..............George C.	Kinney ....Elizabeth	1826	
Wilson..............Hugh	Reed ....Elizabeth C.	1862 11 07	UT, Salt Lake City
Wilson..............James	Fallas ....Mary Catherine	1826 05 02	ENG
Wilson..............James	Perris.................Fanny Jane	1890 05 05	UT, Salt Lake City
Wilson..............James Thomas	Ross...................Isabella	1855 11 16	UT, Salt Lake City
Wilson..............John Marten	Bullock ....Ellen Mariah	1878 07 13	UT, Salt Lake City
Wilson..............John Ross	Evans.................Louisa	1884 07 10	UT, Salt Lake City
Wilson..............Lewis D. Jr.	Hunt ....Eliza Ellenor	1877	
Wilson..............Lewis D. Jr.	Wiggins ....Catherine	1862 12 31	
Wilson..............Sylvester	Wood...................Mary	1861 05 26	UT
Wilson..............Thomas H.	Marchant ....Caroline Ann	1859 07 17	
Wilson..............Walter	Bond....................Ann	1874 12 26	UT, Henefer
Wilson..............Wellington	McBride...............Rebecca		IL, Nauvoo
Wilson..............Wellington	Smith..................Elizabeth B.	1836 12 13	OH, Kirtland
Wimmer ....Peter	Callaham.............Mary Ann	1863 04 09	UT, Springville
Wimmer ....Peter	Shirley ....Elizabeth	1802	PA
Wimmer ....Robert	Wilkerson ....Lucretia Ann	1831 03 15	IN, Warren Co.
Wimmer ....William D.	Funnell ....Elizabeth	1864 11 12	UT, Salt Lake City
Winberg ....Sven Anders	Nilson.................Elna	1829 04 11	Sweden
Winchester ......Stephen	Case...................Nancy	1816 07 31	NY, Fort Edward
Winder ....John Rex	Parker ....Elizabeth	1857 01 11	
Windley............John	Foster.................Mary	1861 04 15	ENG, Birmingham
Winegar ....Stephen S.	Smith..................Lois	1850 08 01	UT, Salt Lake City

Male	Female	Date	Place
Wines ....Ira Doty	Shearer ....Jane Maria	1834 05 29	
Wing ....John W.	Goates ....Martha	1868 10 11	UT, Salt Lake City
Winger ....Christopher S.	Salvesen ....Ane Marie F.	1863 05 05	Ocean
Winkless ....Joseph T.	Priday................Sarah Ann	1868 07 25	UT, Salt Lake City
Winn ....John	Finch ....Christiana	1828	
Winn ....John	Pugh..................Elizabeth C.	1853	
Winn ....John	Stephenson.........Eliza Ann	1862 10 04	UT, Salt Lake City
Winn ....Thomas Griffin	Hatch..................Elizabeth	1854 12 07	UT, Lehi
Winsor ....Anson	Brower...............Emeline Zenetta	1842 03 20	
Winter ....Thomas W.	Nielsen ....Johanna	1857 02 15	UT, Salt Lake City
Winter ....Timothy J.	Collier ....Mary	1806	ENG
Winters ....Alonzo	Stone.................Hetta Amanda	1852 05 16	IA, Council Bluffs
Winters ....Hyrum	Burdick ....Rebecca		
Winters ....Oscar	Stearns...............Mary Ann	1852 08 16	WY, Deer Creek
Winters ....William	Duncan...............Matilda Ann	1876	
Wintle ....George B.	Sewell ....Elizabeth	1835 07 09	ENG
Wiser ....John McCormick	Frost...................Martha M.	1851	UT, Big Cotton.
Withers ....Isaac	Brown.................Sophia	1863 03 10	ENG
Wixey...............William	Denley ....Ann		
Wixom ....Soloman	Teeples ....Harriet Elvira	1846	IL, Nauvoo
Wood ....Andrew Patton	Plunkett..............Ellen	1857 11 03	CA, Drytown
Wood ....Charles	Horrocks.............Alice	1858 03 31	UT, Ogden
Wood ....Daniel	Cotton ....Peninah S.	1846 01 27	IL, Nauvoo
Wood ....Daniel	Grace ....Sarah	1852 01 14	
Wood ....Daniel	Snyder................Mary Elizabeth	1824 03 09	Canada
Wood ....Daniel	Sweet ....Sarah	1837 04 02	MI, Oakland Co.
Wood ....Daniel C.	Edwards ....Margaret		
Wood ....Daniel C.	Waddoups...........Elizabeth	1869 02 08	UT, Salt Lake City
Wood ....David	Crites..................Catherine	1818 03 17	Canada
Wood ....David	Wylie ....Elizabeth	1857 07 07	UT, Salt Lake City
Wood ....Edwin	Hinchcliff ....Edna		
Wood ....George	Davies ....Mary	1850 12 02	UT, Salt Lake City
Wood ....George	Shaw ....Rebecca	1838 02 25	ENG, Yorkshire
Wood ....Gideon D.	Daley..................Hannah Electa	1830 12 28	OH, Florence
Wood ....John	Cosgrove.............Sarah Ann	1849 08 26	
Wood ....John	Goble ....Fanny		
Wood ....John	Gower ....Elizabeth	1867 12 25	
Wood ....John	Smith..................Ellen	1850 01 06	ENG, Stockport
Wood ....John Peacock	Leigh ....Ann	1839 09 08	ENG
Wood ....Lyman S.	Bassett...............Semira La C. R.	1854 08 27	OH, Florence
Wood ....Samuel	Steadwell ....Sarah (Sally)	1832 07 15	OH, Norwalk
Wood ....Thomas	Watson................Rachel S.	1840	
Wood ....Wellington	Warner ....Mary Elizabeth	1873 02 04	UT, Salt Lake City
Wood ....William	Whytock ....Eliza	1888 09 26	UT, Logan
Woodard ....Charles N.	Malin ....Margaret Ann	1856 04 27	UT, Salt Lake City
Woodard ....Francis S.	Mathis ....Mary Catherine	1848 01	UT, Salt Lake City
Woodard ....Jedediah S.	Northrop ....Emily Jane		
Woodbury ....Jeremiah	Bartlett................Elizabeth	1815 06 20	MA, Montague
Woodbury ....Jeremiah	Frost...................Charlotte	1852 07 12	UT, Salt Lake City
Woodbury ....John H.	Gray ....Sarah A.	1870 05 10	UT, Salt Lake City
Woodbury ....John S.	Parker ....Martha Alice	1864 12 27	UT, Salt Lake City
Woodbury ....John Taylor	Evans.................Mary Elizabeth	1883 10 19	UT, St. George
Woodbury ....Orin N.	Cannon ....Ann	1853 02 07	UT, Salt Lake City
Woodbury ....Orin N.	Goddard ....Frances	1863 10 10	UT, Salt Lake City

Male	Female	Date	Place
Woodbury ....Orin N. Jr.	Clark..................Mary Alice	1878 03 14	UT, St. George
Woodbury ....Thomas H.	Haskell ....Catherine R.	1842 05 08	MA, New Salem
Woodcock........Samuel	Hicks ....Lydia Ann	1853	MO, St. Louis
Woodfield ....John	Roylance ....Rachel	1865 05 16	
Woodhead ......George T.	Lane....................Caroline	1853 08 14	UT, Salt Lake City
Woodhead ......William	Spencely ....Charlotte	1829 09 17	ENG
Woodhouse .....Charles C.	Kershaw ....Ida Sophia	1855 03 15	UT, Cedar City
Woodland ....John	Staplforte............Celia	1818 06 18	KY, Barren Co.
Woodland ....William W.	Peters..................Laura	1862 06 12	UT, Salt Lake City
Woodmansee ..Charles	Porter ....Harriet Eleanor	1864 09 04	
Woodmansee ..Joseph	Hill.......................Emily	1864 05 07	UT, Salt Lake City
Woodruff..........Wilford	Carter ....Phoebe W.	1837 04 13	OH, Kirtland
Woodruff..........Wilford	Jackson...............Mary Ann	1846 04 15	IL, Nauvoo
Woodruff..........Wilford	Smith...................Emma	1853 03 13	UT, Salt Lake City
Woodruff..........Wilford Jr.	Smith...................Emily Jane	1867 10 12	UT, Salt Lake City
Woods ....James	Howell ....Charlotte	1870 07 18	UT, Salt Lake City
Woodward ......James	Coon ....Lois	1854 02 16	UT, Spanish Fork
Woodward ......James	McCurdy..............Nancy	1844 01 30	
Woodward ......James Jr.	Johnston ....Maria Jane	1863 12 24	UT, Salt Lake City
Woodward ......William	Davis...................Sarah	1857 09 20	UT, Salt Lake City
Wooley ....Henry	Stretton ....Mary	1845 03 12	
Wooley ....John W.	Everington...........Ann Reed	1886	UT
Woolf ....Absolom	Hambleton...........Lucy Ann		
Woolf ....Absolom	Wood...................Harriet	1857 04 19	UT, Salt Lake City
Woolf ....James	Hurren ....Emma	1869 12 13	UT, Hyde Park
Woolf ....John A.	Devoe..................Sarah Ann	1831 04 30	NY, New York
Woolf ....John A.	Hyde....................Mary Lucretia	1866 12 21	UT, Salt Lake City
Woolfenden .....Abraham	Pearson...............Mary	1824 06 01	ENG, Ashton
Woolfit ....Joseph	Bardell................Sarah	1821 05 02	
Woolley............Edwin D.	Gordon ....Louisa Chapman		
Woolley............Edwin D.	Olpin...................Mary Ann	1850 11 10	UT, Salt Lake City
Woolley............Edwin D.	Wickersham ....Mary	1831 03 24	OH
Woolley............Edwin D.	Wilding ....Ellen	1843 12 28	IL, Nauvoo
Woolley............Franklin B.	Foss ....Olive Carl	1857 02 11	UT, Salt Lake City
Wooley ....John W.	Ensign.................Julia Searles	1851 03 20	UT, Salt Lake City
Woolley............Samuel A.	Mehring ....Catherine E.	1846 05 12	IL, Nauvoo
Woolley............Samuel A.	Phillips................Frances Ann		UT, Salt Lake City
Woolley............Thomas	Rogers ....Susannah	1860 10 08	
Woolsey...........	Pritchard.............Susannah		
Woolsey...........James	Patterson............Lovina	1846 02 05	
Woolsey...........Joseph	Shaffer ....Abigail	1808	
Woolsey...........Thomas	Hickerson ....Catherine Luketis	1859 01 22	
Woolstenhulme ....William	Evans..................Joanne	1897	
Wootton ....William	George ....Elizabeth	1862	
Worden............Nathaniel	Teeples ....Harriet Elvira	1852	UT, Provo
Workman ....Jacob L.	Reader................Nancy	1834 08 15	TN, Overton
Workman.........Jacob L.	Turner ....Rebecca Willard	1852 01 03	UT, Salt Lake City
Workman.........James T.	Grice ....Lucy	1864 01 16	UT, Salt Lake City
Works ....James M.	Jones ....Phoebe	1858 04 15	UT, Salt Lake City
Worlton ....James T.	Bourne................Elizabeth	1848 12 03	ENG
Worlton ....James T.	Dallimore............Maria Ann	1863 11 14	UT, Salt Lake City
Worsley ....John	Hamer ....Sarah	1836 11 07	ENG, Lancashire
Worthen...........Richard	Cowap.................Mary	1816 02 18	ENG
Worthen...........Samuel	..........................Jane	1865 02	

Male	Female	Date	Place
Worthen .... Samuel	Grow .... Mariah Louisa	1856 04 27	UT, Panguitch
Worthen .... Samuel	Hallam .... Sarah	1844	IL, Nauvoo
Worthington ..... Stephen S.	Eliason .... Johanna	1867 12 30	UT, Tooele Co.
Wrathall .... James	Marston .... Mary Leishman	1857 03 22	UT, Grantsville
Wright .... Abraham R.	Brockerman .... Mary Ann	1833 12 19	PA, Philadelphia
Wright .... Amos Russell	Roberts .... Catherine	1861 04 28	UT, Brigham City
Wright .... Andrew	Brett .... Sarah Ann	1849 12 16	ENG, Manchester
Wright .... James	Dusall .... Mary	1819 08 17	ENG
Wright .... James B.	Chappell .... Sarah Jane	1864 12 25	UT, Nephi
Wright .... Jefferson	Angell .... Sarah Elizabeth	1847 12 12	NE
Wright .... Jesse	Millward .... Jane	1856 06 23	ENG
Wright .... John	Smith .... Charlotte	1850 10 26	ENG
Wright .... John Fish	Gibbs .... Martha Duggan	1864 02 23	
Wright .... John P.	Fish .... Mary Hill	1825 07 31	ENG
Wright .... John P.	Syer .... Mary Ann		
Wright .... Jonathan C.	Neeley .... Mary Jane	1852 02 25	
Wright .... Jonathan C.	Olsen .... Caroline	1857 11 07	UT, Brigham City
Wright .... Jonathan C.	Wheeler .... Rebecca	1838 03 01	IL, Waynesville
Wright .... Joseph	Bowers .... Betsy Jane	1870 07 18	UT, Salt Lake City
Wright .... Joseph	Fryer .... Mary Ann		
Wright .... Lorenzo	Packer .... Levema Sonora		
Wright .... Robert R.	Beeson .... Emma		
Wright .... Thomas	Dale .... Annie	1866 01 06	ENG, Sheffield
Wright .... Thomas Brett	Clough .... Mary Jane	1871 12 04	UT, Salt Lake City
Wright .... Thomas Henry	Barrett .... Elizabeth	1846 03 09	Canada
Wright .... William	Rouse .... Charlotte	1832 04 06	ENG
Wright .... William B.	Yearsley .... Emma Smith	1860 03 15	UT, Ogden
Wright .... William H.	Taylor .... Emma	1846 09 29	
Wyatt .... Franklin H.	Archibald .... Elizabeth Watson	1885 04 29	UT, Logan
Wyatt .... John Moses	Horsecroft .... Sarah Caroline	1848 12 25	ENG
Wylie .... James W.	Morrow .... Mary Parmelia	1821 01 11	

Y

Male	Female	Date	Place
Yates .... Hyrum B.	Forsyth .... Margaret B.	1874 01 26	UT, Salt Lake City
Yates .... Thomas	Francis .... Elizabeth	1863 07 22	NE, Florence
Yates .... William	Peck .... Martha Mary Ann	1868 01 11	UT, Lehi
Yeaman .... Michael	Stevens .... Cynthia	1831 12 07	
Yeaman .... Thomas	Moore .... Martha Ann	1857 03 10	IA
Yearsley .... David D.	Dilworth .... Harriet W.		
Yearsley .... David D.	Hoopes .... Mary Ann	1829 09 11	PA, Westchester
Yearsley .... Nathan	Stewart .... Ruthinda Emma	1865 02 04	UT, Salt Lake City
Yeates .... Henry	Coleman .... Elizabeth		
Yeates .... Richard	Ellis .... Annie	1873 12 15	UT, Salt Lake City
Yorgason .... James	Johnson .... Christena	1867 12 08	UT, Moroni
Yorgason .... Soren	Nilsson .... Caroline	1833 04 23	Sweden
York .... Aaron Mereon	Carter .... Hannah	1830 12 03	ME, Newry
Youd .... Thomas	Pickles .... Elizabeth	1844 05 05	ENG, Liverpool
Young .... Adolphia	Jared .... Rhoda Bryne		TN
Young .... Alfred D.	Jared .... Rhoda Bryne		
Young .... Brigham	Alley .... Margaret Maria	1846 10 14	IL, Nauvoo
Young .... Brigham	Angell .... Mary Ann	1834 02 18	
Young .... Brigham	Bigelow .... Lucy	1847	NE

Male		Female		Date	Place
Young	Brigham	Bigelow	Mary Jane	1847 03 20	NE
Young	Brigham	Chase	Diana Severance	1844 10 10	IL, Nauvoo
Young	Brigham	Cressy	Nancy	1846 02 06	IL, Nauvoo
Young	Brigham	Decker	Clarissa	1844 05 08	
Young	Brigham	Decker	Lucy Ann	1842 06 15	IL, Nauvoo
Young	Brigham	Folsom	Harriet Amelia	1863 01 24	UT, Salt Lake City
Young	Brigham	Free	Emeline	1846 01 14	IL, Nauvoo
Young	Brigham	Pierce	Margaret	1846 01 22	IL, Nauvoo
Young	Brigham	Partridge	Emily Dow	1844 09	IL, Nauvoo
Young	Brigham	Rockwood	Ellen	1845 09 13	
Young	Brigham	Rollins	Mary Elizabeth	1846 01 17	IL, Nauvoo
Young	Brigham	Snively	Suzanna	1844 11 02	IL, Nauvoo
Young	Brigham	Snow	Eliza Roxey	1849	
Young	Brigham Jr.	Spencer	Catherine Curtis	1855 11 15	UT, Salt Lake City
Young	Ebenezer R.	Holden	Margaret	1836 05 01	CT, Westport
Young	Ebenezer R. III	Shreve	Matilda Wickoff	1866 05 01	
Young	Ernest Irving	Johnson	Sybella White		
Young	Franklin W.	Sabin	Anna Maria	1861 07 06	UT, Salt Lake City
Young	Isaac	Davis	Anna		
Young	Jacob	McCauslin	Lydia	1857 03 05	UT, Provo
Young	James	Carruth	Janet	1840 08 11	
Young	James	Seeley	Elizabeth	1828 07 20	Canada
Young	John	Gifford	Mary Ann	1850	Trail
Young	John	Smith	Catherine	1862 04 12	
Young	John	Young	Rebecca	1859 01 12	ENG, Liverpool
Young	John Ray	Knight	Lydia	1861	
Young	John W.	Young	Eathalinda M.	1850	UT, Salt Lake City
Young	Joseph	Bicknell	Jane Adeline	1834 02 18	NY
Young	Joseph	Huntley	Mary Ann	1846 02 06	IL, Nauvoo
Young	Joseph	Snow	Sarah Jane	1867 04 06	UT, Salt Lake City
Young	Joseph Angell	Stenhouse	Clara Fedarata	1867 03 04	UT, Salt Lake City
Young	Josias Richard	Canivet	Elizabeth Esther	1843	
Young	Lorenzo Dow	Goodall	Persis	1826 06 06	NY, Watertown
Young	Lorenzo Dow	Wheeler	Harriet Page	1843 03 09	IL, Nauvoo
Young	Phineas	Langdon	Clementina C. E.	1848	
Young	Phineas Howe	Clark	Phebe G.	1853 11	UT, Salt Lake City
Young	Robert	Shreve	Anne		
Young	Thomas	Campkin	Harriet	1876 12 26	UT, Salt Lake City
Young	Thomas	Webb	Martha	1857	
Young	Thomas C.	Hay	Mary	1856 10 08	UT, Salt Lake City
Young	William L.	Bunting	Helen	1850 09 30	ENG
Young	William L.	Reeves	Julia W.	1870 08 08	UT, Salt Lake City
Young	William Willis	Pearce	Harriet Ann	1876	

Z

Male		Female		Date	Place
Zimmerman	George G.	Hoke	Juliana	1816 04 04	PA, Franklin Co.
Zimmerman	John	Lamb	Harriet Laura	1850 09 21	IA, Garden Grove
Zollinger	Jacob	Loosli	Rosetta	1870 05 09	UT, Salt Lake City
Zufelt	Henry	Dillabaugh	Julia Ann	1833	
Zundel	John	Fry	Fanny	1859 11 28	
Zundel	Thomas	Hartley	Josephine	1862 05 25	UT, Mona
Zweifel	Dietrich	Baer	Katharina	1864 11 01	

MARRIAGES BY FEMALE SURNAME

	Berntson	Rasmus	1867 05 25	UT
	Davis	Nathan	1862	
	Hill	James Bennett	1865 06 10	UT
	Hogan	Eric G. M.	1858	
	Holman	John G.	1856	
	Holman	John G.	1875	
	Miller	William		
	Moore	John Harvey	1856 05	
	Moore	John Harvey	1858 02	
	Packer	James	1863	
	Paxman	William	1875	
	Prows	William Cook	1867	
	Reidhead	John	1865	
	Telford	Robert	1852 02 22	UT, Bountiful
Amy	Porter	Chauncey W.		
Ann	Bullock	Isaac		
Clarysa	Miller	Daniel A.		
Electa Caroline	Williams	Daniel Randall	1838	
Eliza	Perkes	James		
Ellen	Ohlson	Gustave A.		
Emeline	Smith	William Read		
Hannah	Walton	Thomas	1862	
Jane	Worthen	Samuel	1865 02	
Jensine	Thomsen	Hans Adolph	1875 07 12	
Kirsten	Christensen	Anders		
Louisa	Foy	Thomas Birk	1861	
Margaret	Hickman	William A.	1855 09 15	UT, Salt Lake City
Margaret	Mansfield	Matthew	1857	
Martha	Gower	Thomas		
Mary Christina	Shepherd	Moses T.		
Mary Kate	Robinson	Richard S.		
Susan	Mower	Henry		

A

Aagesen	Bertha C.	Isaacson	Neils	1850 09 18	Norway
Abbott	Ellen Elizabeth	Gardner	Elias	1852 02 09	
Abbott	Emily	Bunker	Edward	1846 02 19	IL, Nauvoo
Abbott	Priscilla	Lemmon	John	1804 07 21	TN, Gallatin
Abbott	Sarah Elizabeth	McArthur	John Dickson	1865 01 13	UT, Salt Lake City
Abrams	Lucinda	Pettit	Brower	1854 01 17	NY, Lynbrook
Ackerly	Phoebe	Ash	James	1844	ENG
Ackhurst	Margaret	Watkins	John	1851 05 04	ENG
Acomb	Elizabeth	Buttle	William	1856 11 16	UT, Salt Lake City
Adair	Mary Ann	Mangum	John III	1841	AL

Female	Male	Date	Place
Adams ....Alice	Carter ....James	1874 03 16	UT, Salt Lake City
Adams ....Betsey E.	Huff ....Thomas	1815 03 07	GA, Hancock Co.
Adams ....Catherine	Pilling ....Richard	1856 03 10	
Adams ....Ellen	Stewart................Urban V.	1865 07 15	UT, Salt Lake City
Adams ....Hannah	Harrison ....William	1856 03 24	Ocean
Adams ....Jane	Stock...................John	1844 02 14	South Africa
Adams ....Margaret	Farnsworth ....Philo T.	1857 08 24	UT, Beaver
Adams ....Mary Ann	Abel.....................Elijah	1847 02 16	OH, Hamilton
Adams ....Phoebe	Hancock..............Solomon	1836 06 28	NY
Adams ....Rebecca	Rogers ....William	1823 08 10	ENG
Adams ....Sally	Snow ....William	1846 01 16	IL, Nauvoo
Adams ....Sarah	Hone ....David	1860 09 23	ENG, Coventry
Adamson ....Agnes	Anderson.............Archibald	1826	
Adamson ....Eliza Jane	Huff ....Joseph		
Adamson ....Eliza Jane	Markham ....Stephen		
Adamson ....Eliza Jane	Shepherd ....Moses T.	1840 03 22	IN, Mt. Pleasant
Adamson ....Elizabeth	Melville ....Alexander		
Adamson ....Jannett	Grant...................Thomas T.	1913 02 01	UT, Wellsville
Adamson ....Jannett	Hutchinson..........Thomas C.	1861 06 06	Ocean
Adamson ....Johannah	Bailey ....Charles R.	1863 11 07	UT, Salt Lake City
Adamson ....Margaret	Grant...................Thomas T.	1861 10 19	
Affleck.............Jane	Kerr ....George Mercer	1863 04 16	ENG, Byker
Aikens.............Mary	Smith...................John	1846 01 15	IL, Nauvoo
Aikens.............Mary	Smith...................Silas	1828 03 04	
Ainsworth........Mary Jane	Johnson ....Jarvis	1870	
Airmet ....Susan Douglas	Stuart ....David M.	1867 10 26	UT, Salt Lake City
Aitcheson........Jennette	Bee......................George	1826	Scotland
Aitcheson........Jennette	Dobson................Joseph	1851	MO, St. Louis
Akeret ....Anna Maria	Gerber.................Johannes	1843 11 23	
Akerman ....Magdalena	Gubler ....Casper	1868 05 30	UT, Salt Lake City
Alden ....Elizabeth	Pettegrew............David	1816	
Alden ....Phebe	Kenney................John	1861 10 26	UT, Salt Lake City
Alder................Anna Barbara	Alder....................Johannes	1849 07 02	Switzerland
Alder................Jane	Bourne ....Charles	1842 06	ENG
Alder................Mary Jane	Goaslind..............John Henry Jr.	1867 05 29	
Alder................Mary Jane	Marshall ....George Thomas	1882 11 09	UT, Salt Lake City
Aldrich ....Nancy Laura	Buckland ....Alondus	1846 10 10	CA, Mission D.
Aldrich ....Nancy Laura	Buckland ....James D. Jr.	1855 07 09	UT, Bountiful
Aldridge ....Ellen	Wiggins ....John	1852 01 05	ENG
Aldridge ....Ellen	Willis...................Joshua Thomas	1864	UT
Aldridge ....Nancy Lydia	Harris ....John Smith	1850 04 04	UT, Bountiful
Aldridge ....Sariah	Harris ....Silas	1849 09 02	WY, Ind. Rock
Alexander ....Adeline	Andrus.................Milo	1852 03 27	
Alexander ....Adeline	Sprowl ....Andrew	1868 04 01	
Alexander ....Dionitia Emily	Mortensen...........Hans Jorgen	1859 05 16	UT, Parowan
Alexander ....Elisabeth	Morris ....Richard	1827 03 20	ENG
Alexander ....Emma	Moss ....John	1865 03 25	UT, Salt Lake City
Alexander ....Francis E.	Steele.................Jesse Pierce	1853 10 04	UT, Salt Lake City
Alexander ....Louisa Pool	Hatch..................Jeremiah	1842 12 26	IL, Nauvoo
Alexander ....Nancy Naomi	Tracy ....Horace	1860 04 08	
Alexander ....Nancy Naomi	Tracy ....Moses	1832 07 15	
Alexander ....Sarah Elizabeth	Murphy ....Emanuel Masters	1861 05 12	UT, Salt Lake City
Alexander ....Sarah Elizabeth	Rynearson...........Andrew J.	1875 01 28	
Alger...............Clarissa	Whitney ....Francis Tuft	1848	

Female	Male	Date	Place
Alger ....Sarah Ann	Cowley ....William E.	1863 01 11	UT, Beaver
Alger ....Sarah Lydia	Bond...................William		UT, Millard Co.
Alger ....Sarah Lydia	Stott....................William	1863 11 15	UT, Fillmore
Allan ....Janet (Jessie)	Powell ....William David		
Allan ....Jean (Jane)	Leishman ....John Campbell	1828 06 03	Scotland
Allard ....Marie Louise	Draper ....William	1849 06 03	IA
Allard ....Marie Louise	Lance ....Samuel	1815	Canada
Alldredge ....Elizabeth	Evans ....David W.	1862 06 15	UT, Salt Lake City
Alldridge ....Ann Blunt	Thorley ....Thomas	1861 09 21	UT, Salt Lake City
Alleman ....Anna Catherine	Bissell.................Joseph	1852 03 21	IA, Council Bluffs
Alleman ....Christean Mary	Sumsion ....William	1858 02 03	UT, Springville
Allen ....Eliza	Davies ....Thomas	1858 07 26	NE, Nance Co.
Allen ....Emily	Lish ....Henry Doctor	1861 04 04	UT, Calls Fort
Allen ....Jane	Blackner ....James Henry	1852 10 25	ENG, Yorkshire
Allen ....Jane	Stoker..................John	1857 07 05	UT, Salt Lake City
Allen ....Laura J.	Abbott.................Myron	1861 04 25	UT, Ogden
Allen ....Laura J.	Blake		
Allen ....Laura J.	Felt ....Marcus		
Allen ....Marcia	Allen ....Albern	1826	NY, Otsego Co.
Allen ....Margaret M. J.	Bagley ....John Grant	1861 03 27	UT, Draper
Allen ....Maria	Griffin ....Henry		
Allen ....Maria	Morris ....George	1858 01 15	UT, Salt Lake City
Allen ....Marinda	Bateman..............Samuel	1854 11 27	
Allen ....Martha	May ....James	1856 08 24	UT, Bountiful
Allen ....Martha	Orser ....David		
Allen ....Martha	Robbins...............Charles B.	1865 07 07	UT, Salt Lake City
Allen ....Martha Evins	Marshall ....William	1862	CA, San Bern.
Allen ....Martha Evins	Owens.................Robert	1850 03 07	KY, Somerset
Allen ....Mary	Barnes.................Richard	1840 02 17	ENG, Bury
Allen ....Mary	Dewey ....John Cook	1854 04 21	UT, Bountiful
Allen ....Mary	Griffith ....David	1865 11 10	UT, Salt Lake City
Allen ....Mary	Syddall ....Squire	1828 12	
Allen ....Mary Ellen	Chamberlain........William	1836 11 12	ENG, Oxford
Allen ....Sarah Briggs	James ....Reuben	1878 02 20	UT, St. George
Allen ....Sarah Briggs	Packer.................William Hamilton	1865 06 01	UT, Salt Lake City
Allen ....Sarah Briggs	Tidwell................Peter	1857 08 16	UT, Salt Lake City
Allen ....Susan	Goaslind..............John C.	1858 07 04	
Allerup ....Johanne C.	Nielsen ....Hans I.	1841 12 04	Denmark
Alley.................Elizabeth R.	Lynch ....Patrick	1857 07 16	
Alley.................Lydia Ann	Wells ....Daniel H.	1852 04 03	UT, Salt Lake City
Alley.................Margaret Maria	Young..................Brigham	1846 10 14	IL, Nauvoo
Alley.................Susan Hannah	Wells ....Daniel H.	1852 04 18	UT, Salt Lake City
Allgood ....Jane	Beech..................Thomas Lewis	1868 01 09	UT, Salt Lake City
Allison.............Matilda	Casper ....Duncan Spears	1845 05 24	IL, Nauvoo
Alloway ....Maria Seaborn	Nott ....Thomas H.	1837 12 25	ENG
Alloway ....Maria Seaborn	Walker................Henry	1869 10 04	UT, Salt Lake City
Allred ....Alice Virginia	Gifford ....Oliver D.	1873 09 11	UT, Shonesburg
Allred ....Amanda Jane	Hutchings ....William Burch	1857 03 27	
Allred ....Amanda Jane	Lewis..................Neriah Robert	1864 01 20	UT, Richmond
Allred ....Hannah C.	Whitlock ....Andrew H.	1827 09 30	TN, Bedford
Allred ....Julia Ann	Wilcox ....Minard	1860 03 27	UT, Mt. Pleasant
Allred ....Mary Carolyn	Egbert ....Joseph	1840 12 04	IL, Nauvoo
Allred ....Rachel	Murray................John Jr.		
Allred ....Sally	Hyde...................William	1850 09 01	

Female	Male	Date	Place
Alpin ....Margaret	Stoddart ....William	1836	ENG
Alston ....Marjorie	Whitely ....Joseph	1891 11 01	UT, Salt Lake City
Alton ....Salley	Hadlock ....Stephen	1816 12 05	VT
Alvord ....Charlotte	Curtis..................Lyman	1834 07 26	MO, Caldwell
Alvord ....Charlotte	Elliott ....Peter Mack	1857 02 01	UT, Salt Lake City
Ameck ....Mary	Mower ....Henry		
Ames ....Clarissa	Munjar ....Thomas	1843	VT
Ames ....Clarissa	Pugsley ....Philip	1855 08 24	UT, Salt Lake City
Ames ....Clarissa	Williams..............John D.	1850 12	
Ammann ....Anna Maria	Bonelli ....Hans George	1835 08 04	Switzerland
Amundsen ....Anna H.	Johnsen ....Olaus	1863 09 09	UT, Echo Canyon
Amundsen ....Matilda	Bills ....William Andrew	1869 03 01	UT, Salt Lake City
Amundson ....Anne Gurine	Anderson.............Christoffer	1838 07 29	Norway
Andersen ....Ane	Olsen...................Peter	1847 07	Denmark
Andersen ....Ane Kjerstine	Nielsen ....Jens	1858 04 16	
Andersen ....Anna Maria	Nielsen ....Jens Christian	1856 10 02	UT, Big Cotton.
Andersen ....Anne Marie	Sorensen.............Niels	1856 06 02	
Andersen ....Anne Martine	Peterson..............Hans	1849 11 03	Denmark
Andersen ....Bertha Christine	Larsen.................Lars Peter	1874 10 14	UT, Salt Lake City
Andersen ....Caroline	Nielson ....Soren	1867 08 24	UT, Salt Lake City
Andersen ....Dorthea	Jorgensen ....Hans	1853 07 04	IA, Council Bluffs
Andersen ....Dorthea	Nielsen ....Thomas	1826 11 17	
Andersen ....Dorthea	Pedersen.............Peter	1837 10 20	Denmark
Andersen ....Else Christine	Ottesen ....Christen	1854	Ocean
Andersen ....Else Kathrine	Christensen.........Lars M. C.	1866 04 22	Denmark
Andersen ....Else Marie	Larson.................John	1864	
Andersen ....Ingaborg	Christensen.........Jacob	1865 01 14	
Andersen ....Johanna	Madsen ....Jorgen	1870 12 12	UT, Salt Lake City
Andersen ....Johanna Marie	Frost....................Jens C. S.	1862 04 14	Ocean
Andersen ....Josephine	Jensen ....Hans R.	1871 11 06	UT, Salt Lake City
Andersen ....Karen	Hansen................Jens	1857 12 20	
Andersen ....Karen	Knudsen..............John	1857 08 21	
Andersen ....Kirsten	Jensen ....Christen	1848	Denmark
Andersen ....Kirsten	Nielsen ....Peder	1831 12 09	Denmark
Andersen ....Maren	Aagard ....Jens Pedersen	1826 10 25	Denmark
Andersen ....Maren	Jensen ....Jens	1839 07 12	Denmark
Andersen ....Maren	Jensen ....Peter Christen	1853 12 09	Denmark
Andersen ....Mary	Peterson..............Peter O.	1876 02 14	UT, Salt Lake City
Andersen ....Mary Christine	Henrie ....Joseph Ozro	1877 07 25	UT, Logan
Andersen ....Sidse	Andersen.............Thomas C.	1863 01 28	
Andersen ....Sidse	Nielsen ....Ole	1856 05 09	Denmark
Anderson ....Ane Dorthea	Powell ....James Q.	1857 03 01	UT, Salt Lake City
Anderson ....Ane Margrethe	Jennings..............Alexander	1876 04 09	UT, Levan
Anderson ....Ann	Fellows................Albert G.	1867 06 29	UT, Salt Lake City
Anderson ....Ann	McKay ....Joseph		
Anderson ....Ann	Ringrose..............William	1812	ENG
Anderson ....Ann	Ritchie ....Samuel	1837 02 05	Scotland
Anderson ....Ann Campbell	Smith...................John A.	1835 06	Canada
Anderson ....Anna	Jepson ....Martin	1862 10 11	UT
Anderson ....Anna Helena	Warnick...............Anders P.	1829 12 25	Sweden
Anderson ....Anna Marie	Hendricksen........Carl F.	1864 05	Ocean
Anderson ....Annie E.	Carlsen................Peter	1856 12 27	
Anderson ....Caroline	Andreasen...........Casper	1887	UT, Logan
Anderson ....Cecelia	Metcalf ....John Edward	1869	

Female		Male		Date	Place
Anderson	Celia	Gyllenskog	Neils N.		
Anderson	Christena	Petersen	Christian	1867 01 02	UT, Mt. Pleasant
Anderson	Christina Amalia	Beckman	Andreas	1855 10 21	Sweden
Anderson	Christina Amalia	Lindahl	Sven Nilsson	1868 05 09	UT, Salt Lake City
Anderson	Dorthea	Thomasen	Thomas N.	1826 11 17	Denmark
Anderson	Dorthea	Thompson	Peter	1837 10 20	Denmark
Anderson	Elin	Olsson	Knut	1874 06 15	UT
Anderson	Elna	Jonson	Anders Paul	1831 12 28	Sweden
Anderson	Elizabeth	Howard	William	1841	IRE
Anderson	Elizabeth Ann	Frankland	William Richard	1870 10 11	UT, Salt Lake City
Anderson	Elizabeth Ann	Mortensen	Peter	1888 08 15	
Anderson	Hanna	Nielson	Ake	1875 11 01	UT, Salt Lake City
Anderson	Helen (Ellen)	Holmes	Henry	1857 03 29	UT, Salt Lake City
Anderson	Hilda	Erickson	John A.	1882 01 23	UT, Salt Lake City
Anderson	Inger	Jensen	Lars	1852 03	Sweden
Anderson	Inger Marie	Larsen	Neils	1848 11 11	Denmark
Anderson	Johanna	Ohlsson	Gustave	1840 02 20	
Anderson	Karen Kirstine	Johnson	John	1835 08 08	Denmark
Anderson	Karen Kirstine	Olsen	Ole		
Anderson	Kristine Marie	Christiansen	Frederick J.	1856 01 13	Ocean
Anderson	Louisa	Nielson	Ake		
Anderson	Maren	Hansen	Jens	1863 09 17	UT, Salt Lake City
Anderson	Maren Annette	Christensen	Otto E. W. T.	1865 09 23	UT, Fairview
Anderson	Maria	Barnson	Christian	1853 01 08	ENG, Liverpool
Anderson	Maria	Oldroyd	Archibald T.	1864 01 04	UT, Ephraim
Anderson	Marna	Peterson	Anders	1834	Sweden
Anderson	Martha	Sorensen	Soren	1863 01 31	UT, Salt Lake City
Anderson	Mary	Christiansen	Carl F. W.	1871 07 03	UT, Salt Lake City
Anderson	Mary	Jensen	Christian	1868 05 03	UT, Salt Lake City
Anderson	Mary	Johnson	Gustav	1862	UT, Deseret
Anderson	Mette Johanna	Madsen	Ole	1864	UT, Manti
Anderson	Rachel Mahala	Loveless	John	1826 01 25	
Anderson	Sarah	Nowers	Willson Gates	1855 06 23	
Anderson	Sarah	Rands	Joseph William	1847 03 29	ENG
Anderson	Sidsel Catherine	Poulson	Peder	1839 07 12	Denmark
Andre	Lillis Alvira	Robison	Benjamin H.	1853 05 12	IL, Crete
Andrews	Delilah E. B.	Allen	Andrew Jackson	1841 04 29	KY
Andrews	Elizabeth	Warner	William H.	1861 07 24	
Andrews	Elsie	Bailey	George Brown		
Andrews	Jane Rosetta	Marsh	George J.	1854 02 27	UT, Salt Lake City
Andrews	Lovisa	Bronson	Clinton D.	1850 09 25	UT, Salt Lake City
Andrews	Sarah	Wickham	John	1831 03 06	ENG
Andrus	Adeline Brooks	Benson	Ezra Taft	1844 04 27	IL, Nauvoo
Andrus	Amanda Ann	Egan	Howard Ransom	1863 10 10	UT, Salt Lake City
Andrus	Pamelia	Benson	Ezra Taft	1832 01 01	MA, Uxbridge
Andrus	Sally	Price	Charles	1870	
Angell	Caroline Francis	Davis	David	1843 03 26	IL, Nauvoo
Angell	Caroline Francis	Holbrook	Joseph	1850 12 31	UT, Salt Lake City
Angell	Mary Ann	Young	Brigham	1834 02 18	
Angell	Sarah Elizabeth	Wright	Jefferson	1847 12 12	NE
Angell	Sarah Jane	Johnson	Jarvis	1860 09 16	UT, Salt Lake City
Angell	Sarah Jane	Tolman	Benjamin H.	1851 01 02	UT, Salt Lake City
Anglesey	Martha	Allen	Jude	1859 02 23	UT, Bountiful
Anglesey	Sarah	Allen	Jude	1866 02 03	UT, Salt Lake City

Female	Male	Date	Place
Angus ....Jane	Izatt ....Alexander S.	1870 01 29	UT, Salt Lake City
Anthony ....Mary Jane	Thomas ....Thomas S.	1853 02 13	Ocean
Anthony ....Mary Jane	Thorpe................Thomas	1875	ID, Samaria
Arbon................Ellen	Robbins................Joseph	1863 03 01	UT, Provo
Archibald ....Alison	Madsen ....Andrew	1884	
Archibald ....Elizabeth	Wyatt..................Franklin H.	1885 04 29	UT, Logan
Archibald ....Margaret	Hendry ....John Mark	1854 10 16	Scotland
Archibald ....Rebecca	Tanner................John Joshua	1835 07	OH, Kirtland
Armitage ....Harriet	Gardner..............Archibald	1857 06 21	UT, Salt Lake City
Armitage ....Harriet	Larter..................Henry Neech	1849 12 25	ENG
Armitage ....Harriet	Larter..................Henry Neech	1860 12 02	UT
Arms ....Charity	Everts..................Joshua	1830	VT
Arms ....Charity	Lewis..................William	1850	
Arms ....Charity	Prows ....John Thomas	1842 12 21	IL, Nauvoo
Armstrong........Elizabeth	Mace ....Hiram	1837 04 04	IL, Nauvoo
Armstrong........Mary Anner	Thorn..................Richard	1806 09 06	NY, Clinton
Arnesen ....Andrea	Haarby ....Niels Schaug	1839 11 15	Norway
Arneson ....Emma Caroline	Greenhalgh ....Ezekiel		
Arnold ....Elizabeth Ellen	Stocking ....Ensign I.	1863 04 18	UT, Salt Lake City
Arrondale........Emmeline	Lee ....John	1830 12 05	ENG
Arterbury..........Sarah Ann	Church ....Hayden Wells	1844 12 19	AL, Perry Co.
Ash ....Hannah	Campbell............Eli	1881 12 10	UT, Mendon
Ashby ....Elizabeth R.	Snow ....Erastus	1847 12 19	IA
Ashby ....Harriet Maria	Stringham............Briant	1852 04 20	
Ashby ....Lucy	Clark..................Edward Watkins	1843 07 25	ENG, Stafford
Ashby ....Mary	Murray ....Jeremiah Hatch	1865 03 04	
Ashby ....Mary Jane	Stringham............George A.	1858 03 03	UT, Salt Lake City
Ashby ....Susan Ann	Stringham............Briant	1850 03 21	
Ashdown..........Alice B.	Hook..................Richard	1834	ENG, Heathfield
Ashdown..........Alice B.	Saunders............George		ENG
Ashment ....Elizabeth C.	Peart ....Benjamin Loss	1869 08 09	UT, Salt Lake City
Ashton ....Sarah Ellen	Beckstead ....Thomas W.	1864	UT, Salt Lake City
Ashworth ....Martha E.	Brian..................Daniel Gross	1860 12 31	UT, Salt Lake City
Ashworth ....Sarah Ann	Chapman ....Isaac Moroni	1856 11 23	
Askew..............Hannah	Braithwaite ....Rowland	1822 03 04	ENG
Asper ....Mary Jane	Weaver................William H.	1873 08 13	UT, Grass Creek
Astington ....Ellen Eliza	Smuin..................James Blundell	1859 03 27	ENG
Astington ....Mary Ann	Krikham..............George William	1844 12 14	ENG, London
Atkin ....Emily	Warburton ....Richard	1851 05 29	UT, Salt Lake City
Atkins................Mary	Titcomb ....John	1830	
Atkinson..........Alice	Wilding ....David	1828 10 23	ENG, Preston
Atkinson..........Frances E.	Hatch..................Ransom	1854 12 18	UT, Salt Lake City
Atkinson..........Mary Jane	Pace..................Edwin	1855 05 01	UT, Salt Lake City
Atkinson..........Sarah Ann	Merrill ....Mariner Wood	1853 11 11	UT, Bountiful
Atwood ....Laurinda Maria	Pinkham ....Sumnar		
Atwood ....Laurinda Maria	Robinson............Joseph Lee	1847 03 21	NE
Aubrey ....Elizabeth Jane	Gould ....Samuel	1885 02 03	UT, Salt Lake City
Aust ....Rosina W.	Bitter..................Traugott	1859	Germany
Austin ....Harriet Orilla	Shaw ....Myrtello	1839 09 17	NY, Vermontville
Austin ....Louise Maria	Cheney................Joseph T.	1860 04 12	UT, Farmington
Averett ....Helen Marion	Thaxton..............James W.	1855 07 15	UT, Manti
Ayers ....Almira Murray	Black ....William V.	1855 02 28	UT, Salt Lake City
Ayers ....Lucinda Ann	Palmer................David Moroni	1869 01 01	UT, Springdale
Ayers ....Victoria	Black ....William V.	1857 04 04	UT, Salt Lake City

Female	Male	Date	Place
Ayrton ....Elizabeth	Tennant...............James		
Ayrton ....Jane	Tennant...............Thomas	1851 06 25	ENG

B

Female	Male	Date	Place
Babbitt ....Elizabeth A.	Rice ....Leonard Gurley	1849 03 18	IA, Kanesville
Bache ....Nancy Ann	Buchanan............John	1812 04 12	KY, Lexington
Bache ....Nancy Ann	Morley ....Isaac	1846 01 22	IL, Nauvoo
Backhouse.......Mary Alice	Ward ....Edwin J.	1864 02 11	UT
Backman ....Emma Matilda	Peterson.............Christian	1869 02 13	UT, Salt Lake City
Backman ....Johanna S.	Petersen.............Jens Peter	1873 02 24	UT, Salt Lake City
Bacon ....Elizabeth	Henry ....Robert	1865 12 17	UT, Fillmore
Badger............Lydia Ripley	Remington..........Jerome N.	1848 01 22	
Badger............Nancy Maria	Ashby ....William Hardin	1865 01 14	UT, Salt Lake City
Baer.................Katharina	Zweifel................Dietrich	1864 11 01	
Bagley ....Christina	Bickmore ....William M.	1825	IL, Madison Co.
Bagley ....Martha Ann	Miller ....George		
Bagley ....Martha Ann	Stephenson.........Isaac H.	1850	IA
Bagshaw..........Sarah	Bradshaw............Edward	1848 09 06	ENG, Derbyshire
Bahr.................Alice	Royle..................Henry Moroni Jr.		
Bailey..............Ann Maria	Sharp ....John W.	1861 03 17	ENG, Norwich
Bailey..............Ann Maria	Shoemaker..........Jephtha	1867 10 02	UT, Manti
Bailey..............Eliza	Blanchard............John Reid	1853 11 19	UT, Salt Lake City
Bailey..............Eliza	Haggie................James	1814 05 28	
Bailey..............Eliza	Potts...................Thomas	1820 08 19	
Bailey..............Eliza Harriet	Mills....................Charles E. T.	1861 01 26	ENG
Bailey..............Elizabeth	Porter ....Lyman Wight	1867 10 05	UT, Salt Lake City
Bailey..............Leah	Dunford ....Isaac	1845 11 02	ENG, Wiltshire
Bailey..............Lucy Meranda	White..................John Griggs	1808 02 17	
Bailey..............Margaret	Bullock ....James Jr.	1860 12 08	Scotland
Bailey..............Mary Ann	Adams.................John Vorley	1857 04 09	UT, Salt Lake City
Bailey..............Mary Ann	Pollard................Joseph	1845 09 27	ENG, Surrey
Bailey..............Mary Elizabeth	Steed..................Thomas	1857 03 27	UT, Salt Lake City
Bailey..............Sarah R.	Brown.................Joshua Woods	1856 04 03	UT, Salt Lake City
Bailey..............Susan Jane	Whipple ....Nelson Wheeler		
Bainbridge ....Eleanor	Obray ....Samuel William	1852	MO, St. Louis
Bainbridge ....Mary Ann	Hazen.................Robert	1853 08 29	ENG, Newcastle
Bair ....Belinda Jane	Wall ....Robert W. W.	1866 10 29	UT, Kaysville
Baird ....Agnes	Adamson.............William	1799 12 11	Scotland
Baird ....Rachel	Patrick................Robert	1859 12 29	Scotland
Baird ....Susannah	Pierce.................Robert	1872 11 25	UT, Salt Lake City
Baird ....Susannah	Smith..................Theodore	1849 09 24	IL, Quincy
Baker ....Betsy Lucinda	Topham...............John	1850 12 03	UT, Salt Lake City
Baker ....Eliza Jane	Peay...................Francis	1853 03 05	Ocean
Baker ....Elizabeth	Cripps.................Charles	1825 11 13	ENG, Surrey
Baker ....Elizabeth Ann	Jost ....Samuel Edward	1872 04 02	UT, Ogden
Baker ....Elizabeth Ann	West...................Lewis Alvin	1858 11 23	UT, Ogden
Baker ....Emma	Hillman ....Ira King	1857 02 22	UT, Salt Lake City
Baker ....Emma	Long ....John	1866 03 18	UT
Baker ....Harriet	Snow..................John Chauncey	1859 10 06	UT, Salt Lake City
Baker ....Mary Ann	Bateman.............Jeremiah		ENG
Baker ....Mary Ann	Lang ....William	1861 03 29	UT, Salt Lake City
Baker ....Ruth	Eldredge.............Elnathan	1839 09 04	

Female	Male	Date	Place
Baker ....Ruth	Underwood..........Joseph	1833 01 03	MA, Harwich
Baker ....Ruthinda	Stewart..............George		
Baldwin...........Eliza	Pace..................Elisha	1827 03 25	OH, Newark
Baldwin...........Elizabeth	Stark.................Daniel	1862 03 22	UT, Salt Lake City
Baldwin...........Hannah Matilda	Little ....James Amasa	1858 12	
Baldwin...........Phebe	Carpenter ....Daily	1842 03 13	
Baldwin...........Phebe	Pierce................Isaac W.	1828 01 27	
Baldwin...........Phoebe Ann	Hawkes ....Joseph Bryant	1837 12	
Baldwin...........Phoebe Ann	Northrup		
Bales ....Mary Ann	Dickerson ....Joseph	1858 04 14	NE, Florence
Ballam ....Elizabeth	Anderson............Enos		UT, Snowville
Ballam ....Elizabeth	Goodliffe.............Arnold		
Ballantyne........Jane	Taylor ....John	1844 02 25	IL, Nauvoo
Ballantyne........Mary	Gordon ....James P.	1843 04 04	IL, Nauvoo
Ballif................Louisa A.	Benson...............George Taft	1867 12 20	UT, Salt Lake City
Ballinger ....Nancy Eleanor	Hall....................Edward	1842 02 01	IL, Brown Co.
Ballou ....Lillis	Barney................Edson	1831 01 01	OH, Lorain Co.
Ballou ....Lillis	Comstock ....Fitch	1823 05 01	
Bancroft...........Agnes Ann	Moore.................George Sharrett	1871 05 15	
Bancroft...........Mary Elizabeth	McIntosh ....Solomon Parks	1860 12 21	UT, Grantsville
Bancroft...........Mary Elizabeth	Taylor ....William	1851	ENG
Banford...........Martha C.	Blake ....Walter	1923	
Banford...........Martha C.	Cole...................Charles Martin	1864 12 20	UT, Cherry Creek
Bank ....Margaret	Pilling ....John	1818 10 17	
Banker ....Asenath M. R.	Duncan...............Homer	1841 11 07	NY
Bankhead ....Talitha C. A.	Dennis................William T.	1836 12 08	
Banks ....Frances	Lefevre ....William		
Banks ....Isabelle	Schofield ....John	1836 11 13	ENG, Staleybridge
Banks ....Sarah Ann	Thurgood............Thomas	1860 02 12	ENG
Bannerman......Ann	Ballantyne ....David	1808 10 28	Scotland
Barber.............Almira	Daley.................Moses	1819 01 22	
Barber.............Hannah	Ellis ....John E.	1841 10 30	ENG, Sussex
Barber.............Polly	Child..................Alfred B.	1817 03 19	NY, Saratoga
Barber.............Sally Maria	Bingham.............Erastus	1853 04 07	
Barber.............Sally Maria	Thompson...........Charles	1841 04 06	NY, Barry
Barber.............Sally Maria	Wilder................Austin	1829 01 18	NY, Genesee
Barbour...........Jane	Barker ....Fredrick	1857	
Barbour...........Jane	Johnston ....James	1843	IL, LaHarpe
Barbour...........Lillias	Clark..................John	1837 12 18	Scotland
Barbour...........Lillias	Gibson................William	1856 02 17	
Bardell ....Sarah	Hunt ....John		
Bardell ....Sarah	Tolley ....William	1870 10 10	
Bardell ....Sarah	Woolfit...............Joseph	1821 05 02	
Bardsley ....Ellen	Mangum.............John III		
Bardwell..........Melissa	Reynolds.............William Pitt	1841 10 06	PA, Erie
Barentsen ....Susannah	Jewkes ....Samuel R.	1871 06 12	UT, Salt Lake City
Barker.............Harriet	Chase.................Elisha Wells	1857 02 20	UT, Salt Lake City
Barker.............Jane Isabelle	Durfee ....Henry D.	1857	UT, Ogden
Barker.............Mary Alice	Shurtz................Don C. Jr.	1878 10 15	UT, Escalante
Barker.............Mary Ann	Bond..................William	1838 08 02	ENG
Barker.............Mary Ann	Virgin.................George T.	1852 09 09	ENG
Barker.............Mercy Truth	Keetch................Charles G.	1860 12 14	NE, Florence
Barker.............Sarah	Done ....John	1852 02 15	ENG, Lancashire
Barker.............Sarah	Moore.................David	1850 09 06	UT, Salt Lake City

Female	Male	Date	Place
Barker............Sarah Elizabeth	Gurr..................William	1854 04 27	Australia
Barlow............Pamela E.	Call....................Chester	1888	
Barlow............Pemela E.	Thompson...........David Wilkin	1861 09 10	
Barnaby.........Sarah Grace	Ellis...................Edmund	1854 01 16	ENG, Wiltshire
Barnard...........Mary Ann	Coolbear.............John	1832 09 24	
Barnes............Amanda M.	Smith.................Warren	1826 07 09	OH, Granville
Barnes............Amanda M.	Smith.................Warren	1839	
Barnes............Elizabeth	Merchant............Richard	1827 12 30	Australia
Barnes............Elizabeth Alice	Stallings.............Joseph	1865 11 18	UT, Salt Lake City
Barnes............Louisa	Pratt.................Addison	1831 04 03	Canada
Barnes............Mary Jane	Parkin................Fred	1872 10 08	
Barnes............Rhoda	Snell.................Cyrus	1832 03 13	Canada
Barnes............Sarah	Layton...............Christopher	1852 09 26	UT, Salt Lake City
Barnett............Clara Virtue	Orton.................Joseph	1875 12 20	
Barnett............Elizabeth	Stanford.............Thomas	1828 12 31	ENG, Southwick
Barnett............Georgina Ann	Roylance............James	1871 10 09	UT, Salt Lake City
Barnett............Matilda	Burnham.............Luther C.	1863 11 19	UT, Salt Lake City
Barnett............Polly M. V.	Jennings.............Schuyler P.	1835	TN, Perry
Barnett............Polly M. V.	Jennings.............Schuyler P.		Remarried
Barnett............Polly M. V.	Whittemore.........Aaron	1861 03 10	UT, Salt Lake City
Barney............Eliza Aribella	Wilkins...............Alexander	1857 02 07	UT, Salt Lake City
Barney............Sarah Melissa	Murdock.............Nymphus	1853 10 31	UT, Salt Lake City
Barns..............Mary Ann	Unthank..............William	1855	
Barr.................Anna	Bitner................Abraham	1835 05 12	PA, Washington
Barr.................Anna	Musser...............Samuel	1824 01 24	PA
Barr.................Anna	Starr..................Jared	1848 09 22	IA, Kanesville
Barr.................Mary	Neff...................John II	1822 01 12	PA, Strasburg
Barrett............Eliza Ann	Foote.................Thomas	1857	NY
Barrett............Elizabeth	Wright...............Thomas Henry	1846 03 09	Canada
Barrett............Maria	Moss.................William Jackson		
Barrett............Mary Ann	Burningham.........Alfred	1865 09 09	UT, Salt Lake City
Barrow............Sarah	Blake.................William	1838 03 05	ENG, Devon
Barrow............Sarah	Cockerill.............John		
Barrow............Sarah	Hadden..............William	1870	
Barrows..........Emma Lorena	Brown................George W.	1858 08 16	UT, Salt Lake City
Barter..............Mary Ann	Marchant............Abraham Robert	1867 01 12	UT, Peoa
Bartholomew...Martha	Vail...................Gamaliel	1830 04 08	NY
Bartlett............Elizabeth	Woodbury...........Jeremiah	1815 06 20	MA, Montague
Bartlett............Patty	Parry.................John	1851 12 14	
Bartlett............Patty	Sessions.............David	1812 06 28	ME, Newry
Barton............Elizabeth	Hipwell..............William	1863 03 01	UT, West Weber
Barton............Elizabeth Ann	Ashcroft.............Henry	1861 10 26	UT, Salt Lake City
Barton............Elizabeth Ann	Bloomfield..........John	1869 01 11	UT, Salt Lake City
Barton............Martha	Hart..................John Isaac	1863 04 11	UT, West Weber
Barton............Mary Ann	Candland............David	1844 03 27	IL, Nauvoo
Barton............Mary Catherine	Ivie...................John Lehi	1852 05 16	UT, Bountiful
Barton............Mary Catherine	Peters................Lyman	1881	
Barwell............Eliza	Stratford.............George	1832 05 17	ENG
Barwell............Hannah	Saunders............Demas A.	1860 03 20	
Barzee............Mary Ann	Boice.................John	1840 05 07	
Bass..............Calista	Allen.................Ira	1834 11 28	CT
Bassett...........Semira La C.	Wood.................Lyman S.	1854 08 27	OH, Florence
Batchelor........Amelia Ann	Saunders............William G.	1866 09 22	UT, Salt Lake City
Batchelor........Amelia Ann	Stokes...............William	1895 01 08	

Female	Male	Date	Place
Batchelor ....Jane	Wild ....Henry	1853 10 15	ENG
Bates ....Emma	Hiss ....Johann Friedrich	1876 04 19	UT, Stockton
Bates ....Harriet E.	Dunn ....John	1868 08 15	UT, Salt Lake City
Bates ....Mary	Hall.....................John	1830 01 27	ENG
Bates ....Mary	Tew ....Thomas	1868 11 05	UT, Salt Lake City
Bates ....Mary Ann	Street ....Simon	1872 03 06	
Bates ....Mary Ann	Sweatfield ....Augustus	1863	
Bates ....Mary Maria	Kelley ....James H.	1876	UT
Bates ....Mary Maria	Maxfield..............Jessie LeRoy	1926	UT, Stockton
Bates ....Mary Maria	Murray ....John	1872 06 21	UT
Bates ....Orissa Angelia	Allred..................William Moore	1842 01 09	IL, Nauvoo
Bates ....Sarah	Murray ....John	1833 10 28	
Bates ....Sarah Ann	Salisbury ....Francis J.	1871 05 09	UT, Salt Lake City
Bathgate ....Mary	Hutcheson...........Thomas	1827 04 18	
Bathgate ....Mary	Logan ....John		
Bathgate ....Mary	Martin ....Thomas		
Bathgate ....Mary	Murray ....Thomas Joseph		
Bathgate ....Mary	Shelley ....James Boyer	1856 12 21	
Bathgate ....Mary	Wark...................John		
Bauer..............Fredrica E.	Beckstrom ....Hogan	1851 05 11	Sweden
Baugh ....Hannah	Humphries...........John S.	1855 02 14	UT, Salt Lake City
Bauldry ....Anna Mary	Nield...................Luke	1855 02 13	UT, Fillmore
Bauldry ....Anna Mary	Weekes ....Robert	1818 04 03	
Baum ....Elizabeth	Bean...................George W.	1853 01 06	UT, Salt Lake City
Baum ....Pernella	Nilsson ....Ole	1844 08 04	Sweden
Baum ....Rachel Jenetta	Sessions ....Daniel A.	1856 12 27	UT, Provo
Baxter ....Clarissa A.	Morgan...............Daniel A.	1867 11 09	UT, Salt Lake City
Baxter ....Elizabeth H.	Lyon ....Luther Peet	1865 08 26	UT, Salt Lake City
Baxter ....Jane	Wildman ....Edward	1861 03	
Baxter ....Jane McPhall	Gunnell...............Francis W.	1869 04 15	
Baxter ....Sarah	Balls ....John	1848 11 03	ENG, Suffolk
Bayliss ....Elizabeth	Smart ....Thomas	1818 06 11	ENG
Bayliss ....Esther	Follett ....William T.	1853 10	UT, Salt Lake City
Beagle ....Phebe	Rodeback...........James	1832 05 24	
Beagley ....Anna	Ostler ....David	1861	
Beal ....Nancy Jane	Millet..................Artemus Jr.	1865 10 04	UT, Glenwood
Beal ....Nancy Jane	Parker ....William George		
Bean ....Mary Elizabeth	Haws ....Amos W.	1855 12 27	UT, Provo
Bean ....Nancy	Decker................Zachariah B.	1849 03 06	UT, Salt Lake City
Bean ....Nancy	Lee ....John Doyle	1844 11 04	
Bean ....Nancy	Williams...............Thomas J.	1842 09 04	
Bean ....Sarah Ann	Casper ....William Wallace	1844 08 24	IL, Adams Co.
Beanland ....Sarah	Bean...................Joseph William	1842 07 25	
Bearce ....Rebecca	Reed ....John	1805	NH, Cheshire
Beard.............Anne	Waters................George	1812 03 30	
Beard.............Caroline	Barney................Benjamin F.	1849 04 27	IA, Council Bluffs
Beard.............Caroline	Tippetts ....Alvah L.	1843 09 19	IN, Clinton
Beard.............Eve	Shaffer ....Henry	1816	VA, Abingdon
Beard.............Fannie Jane	Collings ....Fredrick John	1872 12 13	
Beazer ....Ellen Ann	Barton ....Peter	1870 12 26	UT, Salt Lake City
Beck ....Elizabeth Ann	Brown.................Henry	1876 10 01	UT, Salt Lake City
Beck ....Pauline	Naegle................John Conrad	1865 04 22	UT, Salt Lake City
Beck ....Rebecca Rosina	Berry ....William Shanks	1860 11 22	UT, Spanish Fork
Beckman ....Josephina B.	Smith.................Rasmus J.	1871 08 07	

Female	Male	Date	Place
Beckstead........Emeline	Bills ....William Andrew	1852 07 04	
Beckstead.......Harriet Vernitia	Hunsaker............Abraham	1850 11 22	
Beckstead.......Margaret Mariah	Egbert ....Samuel	1839 04 18	MO, Clay Co.
Beckstead.......Sarah Ann	Elmer...................Henry	1866 03 31	UT, Salt Lake City
Beckstrand ......Christina	Pehrson...............Pehr	1859 12 26	
Beckstrom ....Johanna Maria	Nielsen ....Lars	1879 02 13	UT, Salt Lake City
Bedford............Annis	Jackson...............James Jr.	1859 11 24	UT, Lehi
Bedford............Annis	Rudd ....Lorenzo Dow	1857 10 08	UT, Salt Lake City
Bedford............Sarah	Booth...................George		
Bedford............Sarah	Marsing ....Niels Larson	1870 09 05	UT, Kanosh
Bedford............Sarah	Pilling ....John	1864 10 15	UT, Salt Lake City
Bedford............Sarah	Rudd ....Lorenzo Dow		
Bee ....Jane	Hatch...................Ira Stearns	1852 11 27	UT, Salt Lake City
Bee ....Jane	McKechine ....John	1844 07 14	Scotland
Beebe ....Eliza Ann	Cheney................Nathan C.	1834 04 22	NY, Freedom
Beebe ....Harriet Mariah	Gardner...............George B.	1852 10 16	UT, Salt Lake City
Beebe ....Lydia Ann	Howell ....William J.	1860 01 09	UT, Payson
Beebe ....Lydia Ann	Stevens ....Edwin Robert	1882 11 02	ID, Blackfoot
Beech ....Sarah	Densley ....Daniel	1851	ENG
Beecher ....Phoebe Lavina	Drake ....Richard	1864 07 24	UT, Willard
Beeden ....Sarah Jane	Pitts ....William Henry	1834 05 15	ENG
Beer.................Phillipa	Moyle ....John Rowe	1834 02 23	ENG
Beesley............Mary Ann	Halladay ....Abraham	1845 01 27	ENG, Chilvers
Beeson ....Emma	Wright..................Robert R.		
Beirdneau ....Louisa A.	Cole....................Walter Charles	1872 01 08	UT, Salt Lake City
Belcher ....Sarah	Cherrington ....John	1845 05 11	ENG, Stafford
Bell ....Agnes	Baird....................Robert	1831 01 21	Scotland
Bell ....Alice Jane	Bascom ....Joel Almon	1857 12 06	UT
Bell ....Elizabeth	Barton ....John		ENG, Lancashire
Bell ....Elizabeth	Bennett................William J.	1814 02 24	TN, Sumner Co.
Bell ....Elizabeth	Campkin..............George	1837 01 05	ENG
Bell ....Elizabeth E.	McAllister ....Richard Wesley	1844	PA, Philadelphia
Bell ....Emma Dorothy	Roberts ....Ephraim H.	1861 11 02	UT, Provo
Bell ....Mary	Bennett................Richard	1811 02 28	TN, Sumner Co.
Bell ....Mary	Heywood..............Joseph L.	1855 10 31	UT, Salt Lake City
Bell ....Mary	Muir.....................Walter	1835 11 15	Scotland
Bellows ....Mary Adelphia	Larson ....Lars	1848	IA, Council Bluffs
Beman ....Artimesia	Snow ....Erastus	1838 12 13	MO, Far West
Bemis ....Hannah	Tracy ....Joseph C.	1846	
Bemis ....Harriet	Roberds ....Thomas R.	1859 01 23	CA, San Bern.
Bemus ....Mary Judith E.	Ivory ....Mathew Hayes	1854 12 14	IL, Fulton Co.
Benbow ....Ellen	Carter..................William	1843 12 05	IL, Nauvoo
Benbow ....Isabella M.	Erekson...............Jonas	1869 08 30	
Benedict ....Ann Eliza	Neff.....................John III	1863 01 31	UT, Salt Lake City
Benefield ....Elizabeth	Norton ....David Jr.	1820 02 10	IN, Fayette Co.
Bengtson ....Anna Britta	Anderson.............Lars Jacob	1853 11 05	Sweden
Bengtson ....Maria C.	Warnick................John A.	1861 07 05	Sweden
Bengtson ....Maria Kristina	Erickson..............Swen	1853	Sweden
Bengtsson ......Agneta	Nelson.................Johannes	1855 11 17	Sweden
Bengtsson ....Anna	Cutler ....Mason Jr.	1867	
Bengtsson ....Anna	Johnson ....Alfred F. T.	1870 01 11	UT, Salt Lake City
Bengtsson ....Anna	Smith...................William P.	1863 12 12	UT, Salt Lake City
Bengtsson ....Sissa	Pearson..............Ola	1847 12 31	Sweden
Bengtsson ....Sophia	Ashdown ....Richard		

Female	Male	Date	Place
Bengtsson ....Sophia	Hanson...............Nels	1863 09 06	UT, Salt Lake City
Bennet ....Margaret	Johnston ....Andrew	1848 11 19	Scotland
Bennett ....Alice	King....................Hyrum Smith	1864 01 01	UT, Kaysville
Bennett ....Elizabeth	Hunter ....John Davidson	1863 10 27	UT, Fillmore
Bennett ....Elizabeth	Kenney...............John	1861 10 26	UT, Salt Lake City
Bennett ....Ellen	Egbert ....John Calvert	1861	
Bennett ....Emma	Collins ....Joseph Smith	1874 12	ID, Blackfoot
Bennett ....Emma	Panter ....William J.	1864 03 26	UT, Salt Lake City
Bennett ....Emma	Smith...................J.V.		
Bennett ....Francis R.	Randall...............Melvin Harley	1875 04 15	UT, Salt Lake City
Bennett ....Jane	Stephenson.........James J.	1877 12 21	UT, St. George
Bennett ....Jane Louise	Sharp ....Joseph Condie	1893 06 14	UT, Salt Lake City
Bennett ....Martha	Calkins ....William	1852 05 31	
Bennett ....Mary Ann	Burrup ....James Phillips	1855 01 26	
Bennett ....Mary Ann	Stephenson.........Anthen	1874 03 09	UT, Salt Lake City
Bennett ....Mary Jane	McCauslin ....Jesse	1848	
Bennett ....Mehitable	Seeley ....Justus Azet	1800 03 09	PA, Luzerne
Bennett ....Nancy Ellen	McCauslin ....Jesse	1851 10	UT
Bennett ....Susan Ann	Gardner..............William	1857 10	UT
Bennett ....Susan Ann	Houston..............John H.	1860 02 28	UT
Bennion ....Mary	Calder ....George	1861 04 06	UT, Taylorsville
Benson ....Christina	Anderson............Mons	1854 07 03	UT, Salt Lake City
Benson ....Cynthia E.	Allen...................Ira	1858 08 25	
Benson ....Eveline	Olsen..................Charles Canute	1856	UT, Salt Lake City
Benson ....Eveline	Smith..................Leonard I.	1852	
Benson ....Isabella	Goodwin..............William	1866 10 09	UT, Logan
Benson ....Jane	Bosnell		
Benson ....Jane	Dalton..................Edward	1855 10 09	
Benson ....Jane	Fielding ....Amos H.		
Benson ....Jane	Perkins ....John	1860 03	
Benson ....Jane	Warner ....James	1856 05 21	
Benson ....Martha K.	Bell.....................William Milton	1859 04 09	UT, Lehi
Benson ....Martha K.	Pugmire...............Jonathan	1856 03 21	
Benson ....Mary	Heelis ....Thomas B.	1863 07 27	NE, Florence
Benson ....Pemelia Emma	Roberts ....Bolivar	1867 11 23	UT, Salt Lake City
Benson ....Polly	Bartholomew ....Joseph	1843 12 10	IL, Hancock
Benson ....Suzanna	Vail.....................Isaac	1848 06 08	
Bentley ....Susannah	Wiggill ....Eli	1832 02 20	South Africa
Bentson ....Ingeborg Maria	Larsen ....Ole	1843 02 02	Norway
Bentzen ....Elina D. S.	Larsen ....Hans	1836 08 05	Denmark
Benz ....Anna	Kleinman ....Conrad	1857 02 08	UT, Salt Lake City
Benz ....Regula	Naegle.................John Conrad	1860 10 06	UT, Salt Lake City
Berg................Helena Catrine	Anderson.............Lars	1838 09 30	Sweden
Berg................Helena Catrine	Jacobson.............Franz Leonard	1869 07 12	UT, Salt Lake City
Berger.............Caroline	Rammell..............Charles H.	1862 02 14	UT, Providence
Berrett.............Ann	Barnett ....James	1822 08 22	ENG, Ashton
Berry...............Cynthia Lovina	Gardner..............Robert	1851 08 05	
Berry...............Lucy Charlotte	Packer.................Isaac Hoffmire	1864 11 18	UT, Salt Lake City
Berry...............Lucy Charlotte	Poole...................Peter	1857	UT, Salt Lake City
Berry...............Martha E.	Dorrity ....Dennis Smiling	1860	
Berry...............Martha E.	Lee ....John Doyle	1846	IL, Nauvoo
Berry...............Sarah M.	Leah ....James H.		ENG
Berry...............Thirza Malvina	Thurber ....Albert King	1851 02 26	UT, Salt Lake City
Bertelsen ....Anne Marie	Jessen.................Ebbe	1863 02 21	UT, Salt Lake City

Female	Male	Date	Place
Bertelsen ....Anne Marie	Jessen................Mads Peter	1858 09 07	
Bertelsen ....Christianna D.	Farnsworth ....Alonzo L.	1877 03 09	UT, Salt Lake City
Bertelsen ....Fredrikke C.	Larsen ....Soren	1864 07 02	UT, Salt Lake City
Bertelsen ....Johanne B.	Black ....James	1854 11	
Bertelsen ....Johanne B.	Dalley ....James	1856 10 09	UT, Salt Lake City
Bertelsen ....Kjersten	Jorgensen ....Jens	1863 02 21	UT, Salt Lake City
Bertelsen ....Maren	Larsen ....Lars Christian		Denmark
Bertelsen ....Petrina	Dalley ....James	1861 10 09	UT, Salt Lake City
Berthelsen ....Mariane	Stephenson.........Peter C.	1863 05 07	Ocean
Bess ....Lola Eliza	Moody ....William C.	1857 12 20	UT, Salt Lake City
Beswick ....Elizabeth	Tanner................John	1825 11 03	NY, Bolton
Betts ....Eliza	Bigler ....David George	1867 10 16	UT, Salt Lake City
Betts ....Elizabeth	Broadhead ....David	1868 05 04	UT, Salt Lake City
Betts ....Harriet	Broadhead ....David	1850 01 29	ENG, Coventry
Betts ....Matilda	Boswell..............Abraham	1865 07 01	UT, Salt Lake City
Beus ....Ann	Bryne (Byrne)......Moses	1857 11 30	
Bevan ....Husseler	Johnson ....Richard	1844 08 25	ENG, Stafford
Beven ....Elizabeth	Alder..................William	1814 01 14	ENG
Beveridge ....Agnes	Jardine ....John	1850 08 15	Scotland
Beveridge ....Ellen	Muir ....Walter	1812	Scotland
Beveridge ....Elizabeth	Brown.................Robert	1837 11 04	Scotland
Bewick ....Elizabeth	Collings ....James	1834	ENG
Bickmore ....Catherine Ann	McAdams ....Samuel S.	1866 05 10	
Bickmore ....Eliza Ann	Allen ....Elijah	1852 05 03	IA, Mills
Bickmore ....Fidelia	Kidd....................Alexander	1852 05 03	
Bickmore ....Louisa Christina	Mills...................John Boardman	1860 08 19	CA, Santa Cruz
Bickmore ....Lovina	Tanner................Albert M.	1855 09 09	
Bickmore ....Lovina	Taylor.................K. R.	1888 06 20	
Bickmore ....Mary Jane	Huntsman............William	1853	UT, Fillmore
Bickmore ....Sarah Elizabeth	Gunnell...............Francis W.	1859 04 04	UT, Wellsville
Bicknell ....Jane Adeline	Young..................Joseph	1834 02 18	NY
Biddle ....Mary Ann	Farmer ....James	1854 10 27	ENG
Bidwell ....Sarah Ann	Mower ....John	1850 04 11	IA, Council Bluffs
Bielby..............Esther	Heaton ....William	1851 02 10	ENG, Yorkshire
Bigelow...........Lucy	Young..................Brigham	1847	NE
Bigelow...........Mary Jane	Bair....................John	1856 04 08	
Bigelow...........Mary Jane	Bell ....Philander	1868 04 09	
Bigelow...........Mary Jane	Hunt ....Daniel Durham	1859 02 14	
Bigelow...........Mary Jane	Roberts ....Horace	1852 09 29	UT
Bigelow...........Mary Jane	Young..................Brigham	1847 03 20	NE
Bigelow...........Nancy Maria	Love ....Andrew	1834 12 08	IL
Bigg ....Naomi	Ware ....George	1816 06 27	ENG
Biggs ....Eliza Frances	Foreman.............Thomas J.	1842 08 17	NC, Careret Co.
Bigler ....Bathsheba W.	Smith ....George A.	1841 07 25	IL, Nauvoo
Bigler ....Emeline	Hess ....John W.	1845 11 02	IL, Nauvoo
Bigler ....Hannah	Miller ....Daniel A.	1844 12 29	
Bigler ....Nancy	Fleming ....Josiah W.	1828 06 05	WV
Bigler ....Sarah	Lyons ....Caleb W.	1840 01 16	IL, Nauvoo
Bigler ....Sarah	Taylor................Thomas Evans	1852 02 01	UT, Salt Lake City
Billings ....Emma	Holt....................Edward David	1865 03 10	
Billings ....Eunice	Snow ....George W.	1857 03 27	
Billings ....Eunice	Warner...............John Ely	1849 04 04	UT
Billings ....Roxanna S.	Tripp..................Enoch B.	1846 03 29	IL, Nauvoo
Billings ....Ursula	Haskell ....Ashbel Green	1822 03 03	

Female	Male	Date	Place
Billington..........Harriet	Bates..................Joseph William	1850 12 10	
Billington..........Rebecca D.	Maloy.................Patrick	1827 03 01	OH, Portagelo
Billington..........Rebecca D.	Mason................Jesse	1823 08 05	MA, New Ashford
Billington..........Rebecca D.	Warner..............Solomon	1830 10 07	OH, Norton
Bindrup...........Annie Christine	Allen..................Orin Daniel	1878 02 01	
Bingham.........Abigail	Kelley................Russel Samuel		
Bingham.........Abigail	Kelley................Russel Thomas		
Bingham.........Maria Louisa	Goodale.............Isaac N.	1849 01 17	UT, Salt Lake City
Bingham.........Olive Louisa	Walker................William H.	1858 08 30	UT, Salt Lake City
Binns...............Hannah	Singleton.............John	1857 03 30	UT, American Fork
Binns...............Hannah	Wild...................Joseph	1868 01 11	
Binns..............Sarah	Chipman.............William H.	1861 04 07	UT, Salt Lake City
Birch................Annie	McIntire..............Erastus William	1874 11 23	UT, Salt Lake City
Birch................Ellen	Jones.................John Smith	1872 12 09	UT, Salt Lake City
Birch................Esther Ann	Bennion..............John	1856 07 20	UT, Salt Lake City
Bird.................Ann	Dawson..............Meredith	1873 12 19	
Bird.................Elizabeth Ann	Bliss..................Norman Ingles	1845	IL, Hancock
Bird.................Elizabeth Ann	Gardner..............George B.	1848 05 12	IA
Bird.................Elizabeth Ann	Hardy.................Kimball	1854	
Bird.................Elizabeth W.	Howell...............Henry Nelson	1861 12 16	UT, Salt Lake City
Bird.................Henrietta	Shumway...........Charles	1852 01 24	UT, Salt Lake City
Bird.................Rebecca	Tew....................Thomas Jr.	1856 01 22	UT, Springville
Birkenhead......Ann Priscilla	Stark..................Daniel		
Birrell..............Agnes	Van Noy.............William Thomas	1859 12 25	UT, Salt Lake City
Bisbee.............Marcia Maria	Porter.................Abraham	1828 10 01	NY, Allegheny
Bisbee.............Tryphena	Crandall..............Myron Nathan	1841 01 26	IL, Nauvoo
Bishop.............Adelia Ann	Pratt..................Orson	1844 12 13	IL, Nauvoo
Bishop.............Elizabeth	Davis..................William	1831 05 31	
Bishop.............Mary Jane	Price..................Edward Jeremiah	1852 03 30	LA, New Orleans
Bishop.............Vesta Lucetta	Matheny.............Sims L.		
Bishop.............Vesta Lucetta	Twitchell.............Edwin	1860 02 24	UT, Fillmore
Bitely................Sarah Adams	Brown.................George		
Bitely................Sarah Adams	Conrad...............Charles F.	1830 02 08	NY, Ontario
Bitner..............Martha Ann	Neff....................Benjamin Barr	1858 02 26	
Bitter...............Martha	Ricks.................Hyrum	1880 04 01	UT, Salt Lake City
Bitton..............Harriet	Poole.................John Rawlston	1864 12 12	
Bitton..............Jane	Poole.................John Rawlston	1857 09 12	
Bjerregaard......Anna Christena	Beal...................Henry Allen	1863 03 28	UT, Salt Lake City
Bjork...............Anna	Bjork..................Gustave		Sweden
Bjork...............Anna Sophia	Johnson.............Andrew G.	1863 10 08	UT, Salt Lake City
Bjork...............Mary	Cederlof.............John Monson	1865	Ocean
Bjorklund.........Adolphine	Lindroth..............Peter Erick	1850	Sweden
Bjornson.........Vigdis	Holt...................William	1861 04 14	UT, Salt Lake City
Black...............Nancy	Eldredge.............Ira	1833 07 04	
Blackman........Emily Maria	Taylor.................William W.	1867 05 25	UT, Salt Lake City
Blackman........Sarah	Higgins..............Nelson	1826 12 14	OH, Fitchville
Blacknell.........Emily	Hoggard.............James	1842 02 26	ENG, Calverton
Blain...............Jane	Farmer...............James B.	1865 03 10	UT, Salt Lake City
Blair...............Priscilla Jane	North.................Hyrum Bennett	1869 04 05	UT, Salt Lake City
Blake..............Caroline Lucy	Booth..................		
Blake..............Caroline Lucy	Hardy.................Warren	1864 03 05	
Blake..............Elizabeth	Riding.................Henry Hale	1870	UT, Salt Lake City
Blake..............Emma	Carter.................John Benbow	1873 06 04	UT, Salt Lake City
Blake..............Johanna	Holladay............John D. Jr.	1867 10 20	

Female	Male	Date	Place
Blake ....Maria	Parker ....William	1829 04 28	ENG
Blake ....Mary	Peay....................Francis	1820 05 13	ENG
Blaky................Caroline G. W.	Price..................Charles		
Blanchard........Mary Ann	Brown................William P.	1854 12 24	MO, St. Louis
Bland ....Chloe	Bland..................John II	1834 11 30	MS, Carroll
Bland ....Chloe	Jones ....Peter	1854	
Bland ....Mary Lee	Ewell ....William Fletcher	1834	KY
Bland ....Mary Lee	Jones ....Peter	1854	UT, Ogden
Blanden ....Lucy Thorndyke	Hardy ....Joseph	1832 04 26	ME, Lincolnville
Bleasdale........Jennette	Poole.................John Rawlston	1848 07 06	IA, Farmington
Bligh ....Ann	Barker ....Frederick	1822 02 18	ENG, Norfolk
Bligh ....Ann	Barker ....George	1855 11 03	UT, Salt Lake City
Bliss................Elizabeth	Arnold.................Josiah	1831	NY
Bliss................Eunice Sibley	Moore.................Samuel	1830 04 07	MA, Orange
Blodgett ....Polly Emiline	Barker ....James	1851 03 02	UT, Ogden
Bloomfield........Emma	Preece...............Mark	1872 11 27	
Bloomfield........Emma	Vail ....Isaac Hawk	1861 10 26	UT, Salt Lake City
Bloomfield........Mary Ann	Chittock.............John	1835 11 14	ENG
Bloomfield........Mary Ann	Willis.................John	1852 03 18	ENG
Blythe ....Henrietta Eaton	Butler.................John Lowe	1857 09 05	UT, Salt Lake City
Blythe ....Henrietta Eaton	Powell...............John	1864 06 18	UT, Salt Lake City
Blythe ....Henrietta Eaton	Russell ....Allen	1906 10 24	UT, Manti
Boardman........Margaret	Clark..................William	1867 04 20	UT, Salt Lake City
Boaz ....Alice Truscott	Turner ....William A.	1864 10 15	UT, Salt Lake City
Bock ....Helene	Flamm ....Jacob Henry	1859 11 27	CT, Norwalk
Bocock............Elizabeth	Law ....Charles	1858 01 31	UT, Salt Lake City
Bocock............Elizabeth	Weight...............Fredrick	1865 07 01	UT, Salt Lake City
Boden ....Mary	Guymon ....James	1857 10 08	UT, Salt Lake City
Boden ....Sarah	Phillips...............Thomas J.	1870 10 17	
Boggard...........Mary	Adams...............Joshua	1862 07 26	UT, Salt Lake City
Boggess ....Eliza Ann	Turpin................Jesse	1840 09 24	VA, Clarksburg
Boggess ....Eliza Ann	Van Valkenburgh Peter	1855	
Boggs ....Mary	Perry ....Stephen C.		
Bohman...........Augusta E.	Collings ....William R.	1887 12 28	UT, St. George
Boice ....Elizabeth Ann	Clements............Albert N.	1865	
Bolanz ....Maria Barbara	Adams...............William	1864 01 16	UT, Salt Lake City
Bolanz ....Maria Barbara	Ratz...................Christian Peter	1855 08 04	
Bolton ....Fanny	Atwood...............Simeon E.	1865 09 25	UT, Salt Lake City
Bolton ....Fanny	Bennett..............Randle		
Bolton ....Sarah	Davies ....Henry	1848 08 28	ENG, Lancashire
Bond ....Ann	Cluff...................Moses	1857 02 14	UT, Salt Lake City
Bond ....Ann	Wilson ....Walter	1874 12 26	UT, Henefer
Bond ....Mary Jane	Harris ....Micah Francis	1868 01 15	UT, Coalville
Bone ....Jane	Sabey.................James	1855 09 13	ENG, Northill
Bone ....Mary Ann	Bradshaw............Richard T.	1867 07 26	UT, Lehi
Bonelli.............Louisa	Hamblin..............Jacob	1865 11 16	
Bonelli.............Suzetta	Bohn...................Adolph Joseph	1858 03 23	UT, Cedar City
Bonner............Christina	McCurdy.............Albert Gallatin	1869 09 15	UT, Midway
Bonner............Esther	Tucker................William	1824 10 17	ENG
Bonner............Margaret	Shelton...............Stephen	1876 09 11	UT, Salt Lake City
Boot ....Sarah	Birch..................Thomas Francis	1866 10 18	
Booth ....Emma	Card ....Cyrus William	1859 11 07	
Booth ....Frances Hiley	Hanson...............George	1853 09 22	ENG, Aston
Boram.............Elizabeth H. B.	McBride..............William	1831 09 01	OH, Randolph

Female	Male	Date	Place
Borjesson ....Beata Gustafva	Hansen................Peter	1863 11 16	UT, Manti
Borkerson ....Anna	Anderson................Ola	1839 02 20	Sweden
Borkerson ....Anna	Thurston..............Tore	1858 09 28	
Borsen ....Annie Bolliti	Calvert................Charles		
Borsen ....Annie Bolliti	Engberson...........Henry	1872 12 16	UT, Salt Lake City
Borsen ....Annie Bolliti	Peterson...........Neils		
Boserup ....Petrina H.	Kotter ....Herman Heinrich	1866 07 29	NE, Wyoming
Boss ....Mary	Hone ....George	1833 12 25	ENG, Banbury
Boss ....Nancy	Rawson..............Daniel Berry	1849 11 26	UT, Salt Lake City
Bosshard ....Susette	Hafen ....John George	1861 10 18	UT, Salt Lake City
Bosworth ....Mary Ann	Hubbard ....Charles W.	1832 10 30	
Bott ....Ann	Thornock............John	1840 12 25	ENG
Bott ....Elizabeth	Brough ....Samuel Richard	1858 02 01	ENG
Botting ....Ann	Atkinson ....Alfred John	1848 04 27	ENG
Boulter ....Charlotte E.	Driver ....William	1858 08 16	ENG, Middlesex
Boulter ....Elizabeth	Enniss ....John	1845 12 14	ENG
Bourne...........Elizabeth	Worlton...............James T.	1848 12 03	ENG
Bourne...........Margaret E.	Leonard ....Truman	1857 01 06	UT, Salt Lake City
Bouton ....Amanda	Dibble.................John W.	1837	
Bouton ....Sarah Louise	Felt ....Joseph Henry	1866 12 24	UT, Salt Lake City
Bovee ....Ann Elizabeth	Mecham ....Joseph	1845 01 29	IL, Nauvoo
Bovee ....Maria (Polly)	Groesbeck...........Harmon	1807	NY
Bowden ....Mary	Lang..................William	1822 02 11	ENG, Moulton
Bowen ....Ann Mariah	Call....................Anson	1851 04 16	UT, Salt Lake City
Bowen ....Ann Mariah	Lloyd ....William		
Bowen ....Elizabeth	Blackburn ....Thomas M.	1801 12 02	PA, Dunning
Bowen ....Juliette E.	Dalton................Charles W.	1847 01 13	
Bowering ....Esther Ellen	Harris ....Isaac	1833 12 25	Wales
Bowering ....Esther Ellen	Williams..............Ebenezer Albert	1853	IA
Bowers ....Betsy Jane	Wright................Joseph	1870 07 18	UT, Salt Lake City
Bowers ....Elizabeth	Mitchell..............Hezekiah	1856 12 31	UT, Salt Lake City
Bowler ....Elizabeth	Layton ....Charles	1854 01 26	UT, Salt Lake City
Bowman ....Christine	Cook..................William S.	1854 07 23	UT, Salt Lake City
Bowman ....Sarah	Prince.................George	1837 10 10	ENG, Suffolk
Bowthorpe ....Maria Ann	Baker.................Job	1859 10 06	UT, Salt Lake City
Bowthorpe ....Maria Ann	Neff ....Benjamin Barr	1870 10 07	UT
Bowthorpe ....Virtue Ann	Colebrook............Charles	1854 01 07	UT, Salt Lake City
Bowthorpe ....Virtue Ann	Lewis..................Preston King	1857 01 04	UT, Salt Lake City
Bowyer ....Sarah Ann	Snow ....Willard L.	1865 04 15	UT, Salt Lake City
Boyack.............Ann	Ririe...................James	1855 11 23	UT, Salt Lake City
Boyack.............Hannah	McFarland ....James	1855 12 06	UT, West Weber
Boyce ....Elizabeth	Truman................Jacob Mica	1849 04 19	UT, Salt Lake City
Boyce ....Margaret Ann	Andrus................Milo	1857 02 15	
Boyer..............Maria C.	Mendenhall ....Richard Lovell	1870 12 05	
Boyer..............Sidney	Thayne...............John J.	1848 10 23	PA
Bracken ....Martha Ann	Hancock.............Cyrus M.	1860 12 09	UT, Payson
Bracken ....Martha Ruth	Hampton ....James T.	1843	
Bradbury.........Elizabeth	Titensor..............Thomas Edward	1867 08 03	UT, Salt Lake City
Bradford..........Harriet	Simmons ....Leven	1836 02 27	IL, Carthage
Bradford..........Mary Ann	Gardner..............Archibald	1849 04 19	UT, Salt Lake City
Bradford..........Tryphena	Hales..................George Gillett	1864 10 15	UT, Salt Lake City
Bradley ....Amanda	Henrie ....Daniel	1849 10 29	UT, Salt Lake City
Bradley ....Cynthia Abiah	Morley ....Isaac	1851 10 03	UT, Manti
Bradley ....Sarah Jane M.	Creer.................William	1858 01 22	UT, Spanish Fork

Female	Male	Date	Place
Bradshaw ....Elizabeth N.	Painter................William	1861 03 21	UT, Bountiful
Bradshaw ....Ellen	Bench................William		
Bradshaw ....Ellen	Fowler ....William	1855 01 24	ENG
Bradshaw ....Isabelle Jane	Astle ....John	1866 12 09	UT, Hyrum
Bradshaw ....Mary	Green ....John		ENG
Bradshaw ....Sarah Ann	Jones ....Samuel	1836 08 03	ENG
Bradshaw ....Sarah Ann	Till ....William	1824 02 22	
Bradshaw ....Sarah Ann	Vincent ....Daniel	1857 04 09	
Brady ....Amelia	Gourley ....Alexander	1863 07 19	UT, Eureka
Brady ....Keziah Frances	Richards................Silas	1855 02 06	UT, Salt Lake City
Brady ....Tranquilla Ann	Jordan ....Justus Perry	1921 06 29	
Brady ....Tranquilla Ann	Stevens ....Ransom A.	1863 02 17	UT, Sanpete Co.
Braffett.............Almira Ann	Gifford ....Henry Dill	1848 11 05	IA
Braffett.............Amanda L.	Hofheins..............Jacob	1851 11 05	UT, Parowan
Braithwaite.......Elizabeth H.	Barnson..............Bernard	1881 12 28	UT, Manti
Bransford........Susanna	Delitch ....Radovan N.	1930	
Bransford........Susanna	Emery................Albion B.	1884 11 11	
Bransford........Susanna	Engalitchell..........Nicolas V.	1935	
Bransford........Susanna	Holmes ....Edward Francis	1900	
Brass ....Lucy	Bronson..............Lemon	1817 01 02	OH, Geauga
Brassel ....Diana	Smith................Richard	1817 12 11	TN
Bratt................Mary	Faulkner ....John	1828 04 29	ENG
Brazier ....Ann	Gunn ....John	1820 11 10	ENG
Brazier ....Ann	Holyoak ....George		
Brazier ....Martha	Hodges..............Richard	1830 03 26	ENG, Worcester
Breakell ....Ellen	Neibaur ....Alexander	1833 09 16	ENG, Preston
Brenchley ....Carolyn	Obray ....Thomas L.	1857 08 02	UT, Salt Lake City
Brett................Sarah Ann	Corbett ....Thomas	1857 02 23	UT, Payson
Brett................Sarah Ann	Phillips................Samuel		
Brett................Sarah Ann	Wright................Andrew	1849 12 16	ENG
Brewerton ....Elizabeth	Emery................Henry	1851 05 18	IA, Council Bluffs
Bridgeman ....Mary Young	Allred................John Jones	1852 09 23	MO, Smithville
Briggett ....Isabella Wells	Hill......................William Henry	1864 10 31	UT, Coalville
Briggs ....Eliza	Stratton ....James	1857 02 02	UT, Salt Lake City
Briggs ....Elizabeth	Stephens............John	1833 05 01	IL
Briggs ....Ellen	Douglas..............George	1823	ENG, Downham
Briggs ....Ellen	Parker ....John Jr.	1846 01 23	IL, Nauvoo
Briggs ....Emma	Tolman ....Jaren T.	1874 06 01	UT, Salt Lake City
Briggs ....Mary Ann	Tolman ....Jaren T.	1878 12 26	UT, Salt Lake City
Briggs ....Rachel	Crane ....James	1869 03 28	
Bright ....Martha	Ritchie ....James	1863 07	UT, Salt Lake City
Brimley ....Sarah	Read ....William M.	1814 12 18	ENG
Brindle ....Amelia C.	Clark...................John	1860 11 26	ENG
Brindle ....Amelia C.	Meservy ....Joshua Jr.	1864 10 27	UT, Salt Lake City
Brindle ....Amelia C.	Meservy ....Joshua Jr.	1868 06 14	Remarried
Brindle ....Amelia C.	Whitehead...........James Jr.	1871 10 02	UT, Salt Lake City
Brinkerhoff.......Jeanette	Leavitt ....George	1852 08 29	UT, Salt Lake City
Britnell ....Amy	Loader................James	1821 09 09	ENG
Brittingham ......Amelia	Galagher ....John	1848 01 11	MO, St. Louis
Brittingham ......Amelia	Gray ....John		
Brittingham .....Amelia	Neal...................John	1833	PA, Allegheny
Broadbent........Elizabeth	Wadsworth..........George A.	1853 04 18	ENG, Sheffield
Broadbent........Grace	Murphy ....Jesse Easters	1857 04 28	MO, St. Louis
Broadbent........Nancy	Folsom ....Hyrum P.	1866 12 29	UT, Salt Lake City

Female	Male	Date	Place
Broadbent.......Sarah	Nield....................John	1863 05 23	ENG, Prestwich
Broadhead.......Elizabeth	Denton ....John	1852 03	
Brock ....Lena Marie	Swenson ....Nils		Sweden
Brockbank ....Agnes	Thurber ....Albert King	1867 10 30	
Brockbank ......Elizabeth	Bushnell ....John	1854 08 15	UT, Fillmore
Brockbank ......Elizabeth	Pollock		
Brockerman .....Mary Ann	Wright................Abraham R.	1833 12 19	PA, Philadelphia
Brodin ....Augusta Matilda	Anderson............Andreas	1865 01 18	UT, Salt Lake City
Bromley ....Celesta C.	Buys ....Edward	1867 03 23	UT, Salt Lake City
Bromley ....Mary Ann	Fuller ....Sanford	1869	
Bromwich........Elizabeth	Bullock ....James	1827 11 10	
Bronson ....Lorenda E.	Thompson ....Daniel	1854 05 04	UT, Scipio
Bronson ....Mary	Ensign ....Horace	1825 09 28	
Brook ....Elizabeth	Fox.....................Charles Wilson	1862 02 02	UT, Lehi
Brook ....Elizabeth	Scarborough ....John	1850 03 07	ENG
Brooks ....Alice	Anderson............Andrew	1857 03 26	UT, Salt Lake City
Brooks ....Ann	Andrus................Milo	1855 11 22	
Brooks ....Ann	Park....................David	1829	
Brooks ....Charlotte	Hirst...................John	1837 11 05	ENG, Yorkshire
Brooks ....Elizabeth	Andrus................Milo	1855 11 22	
Brooks ....Elizabeth	Simkins ....James		
Brooks ....Eveline	Auerbach............Samuel H.	1879 12 16	UT, Salt Lake City
Brooks ....Harriet Spinks	Howard...............John Richards	1866 09	UT, Salt Lake City
Brooks ....Mariah	Degrey ....John	1827	ENG, Kingswinford
Brooks ....Mary	Fairbanks ....Joseph	1803 10 03	
Brooks ....Mary Ann	Painter................John Scoffins	1862 04 21	Ocean
Brooks ....Sarah	Painter................John Scoffins	1870	UT
Broom..............Jenette	Hill.....................Alexander	1834 10 10	
Broom..............Jenette	Matthews............Abel	1865 02 10	UT, Salt Lake City
Broom..............Jenette	Vince..................Moses Andrews	1854 05 30	UT, Salt Lake City
Broomhead......Charlotte C.	Day....................Abraham	1851 11 30	UT, Salt Lake City
Brough............Harriet	Snarr ....James T.	1841 11 12	ENG
Brough............Jane	McKinnon ....Archibald	1879 07 10	UT, Salt Lake City
Brough............Mary Elizabeth	Rex.....................William	1874 10 06	UT, Salt Lake City
Brower ....Emeline Z.	Winsor................Anson	1842 03 20	
Brown ....Adelia Ann	Stanley ....Alexander H.	1856 10 27	UT, Bountiful
Brown ....Amelia	Fordham..............Elijah	1856 04 06	
Brown ....Amelia	Spencer...............Mathias F.	1826	
Brown ....Amelia Lavilla	McCombs............Andrew	1857 04 19	UT, Salt Lake City
Brown ....Ann	Keeler.................Daniel Hutchinson	1853 01 10	UT, Salt Lake City
Brown ....Ann	Taylor ....Benjamin	1839	NJ
Brown ....Ann Kempton	Dunyon...............John	1853 10 14	UT, Salt Lake City
Brown ....Betsey Agnes	Harvey................Alfred	1869 06 27	UT
Brown ....Caroline	Leemaster ....Jonathan	1863 10 30	UT, Gunnison
Brown ....Cornelia	Clawson ....Moses	1820	NY
Brown ....Eliza	Brown.................Thomas B.	1870 05 09	
Brown ....Eliza	Dyer ....Gideon	1831 08 15	ENG
Brown ....Eliza	Houston...............Isaac	1853 04 19	
Brown ....Eliza	White..................John	1863 11 18	
Brown ....Elizabeth	Crow...................Robert	1817 09 05	MO
Brown ....Elizabeth	Wilcock...............William		
Brown ....Elizabeth Ann	Walker................John B.	1835	MS
Brown ....Elizabeth D.	Later...................Peter	1863 05 25	UT
Brown ....Elizabeth Wright	Parkin................John	1839 02 28	ENG, Derbyshire

Female	Male	Date	Place
Brown ....Esther	Brown.................Joseph G.	1857 01 18	UT, Draper
Brown ....Esther Lorraine	Morrill ....Laban		
Brown ....Evaline	Clark....................John Wesley	1841 11 18	
Brown ....Frances	Carter ....George	1868 12 14	UT, Salt Lake City
Brown ....Frances	Price....................Richard		
Brown ....Frances Sarah	Castleton.............James Joseph	1853 01 02	ENG
Brown ....Hannah	Hibbert ....James	1828 11 10	ENG
Brown ....Hannah Haines	Whiting ....Edwin	1856 10 08	UT, Salt Lake City
Brown ....Harriet	Stratton ....Oliver	1841 08 22	
Brown ....Harriet Amanda	Nielsen ....Peter		
Brown ....Jane C.	Johnson ....William D.	1848 11 29	IL, Nauvoo
Brown ....Janet	Rogers ....Alexander	1864	
Brown ....Jemima	....		ENG
Brown ....Jemima	Rogers ....Francis Baker		ENG
Brown ....Joanna Ward	Hemenway ....Jonathan	1855 03 11	
Brown ....Lucinda Potter	Merrill ....Philemon C. II	1868 01 11	UT
Brown ....Margaret	Hemsley ....Edward P.	1866 03 17	UT, Salt Lake City
Brown ....Margaret M.	Twitchell ....Anciel		
Brown ....Marian	Redington............John	1860 12 01	ENG
Brown ....Mary	Burbidge..............James R.	1836 03 21	ENG
Brown ....Mary	Duncan................William	1835 02 27	Scotland
Brown ....Mary	Pulsipher ....Zerah	1815 08 18	PA
Brown ....Mary Ann	Buchanan............Archibald W. O.	1860 01 01	UT, Manti
Brown ....Mary Ann	Snow ....Warren Stone	1857 04 20	UT, Salt Lake City
Brown ....Mary Baynes	Thirkell ....John Pinock	1836 09 21	
Brown ....Mary Eliza	Brown..................James Andrew	1851 04 12	IA, Kanesville
Brown ....Mary Eliza	Jones ....Nathaniel Vary	1857 05 31	UT, Salt Lake City
Brown ....Nancy	Critchlow ....William	1852 11 06	UT, Salt Lake City
Brown ....Nancy	Newbury...............James	1843 10 03	IL, Nauvoo
Brown ....Obedience	Boss ....Phillip	1818	NC, Rowan Co.
Brown ....Permelia	Sterrett ....William G.	1850 12	UT, Salt Lake City
Brown ....Rhoda Asenath	Spahn.................Michael O.	1868 12 03	MT, Bannack
Brown ....Sarah	Brockbank...........Isaac	1852 10 02	
Brown ....Sarah	Pearce................Robert	1844 12 28	ENG, Somerset
Brown ....Sarah	Tatton.................John C.	1862 07 12	UT, Salt Lake City
Brown ....Sarah Amanda	Smith..................Hiram Hyde	1887 11 10	ID, Weiser
Brown ....Sarah Ann	Wilkinson............William C.	1871 01 02	UT, Hoytsville
Brown ....Sarah Jane	Lowry ....John Jr.	1851 11 27	UT, Manti
Brown ....Sophia	Withers...............Isaac	1863 03 10	ENG
Brown ....Susannah S.	Seaman...............John	1855 04 04	UT, Centerville
Brownell...........Julia Ann	Myler ....James	1843 10 05	MI, Bertrand
Brownell...........Mary Ann	Harrison ....James	1870 05 04	UT, Salt Lake City
Brownell...........Mary Ann	Pearson..............Jesse	1835 10 16	IN, St. Joseph
Brownell...........Mary Ann	Steele.................William	1866 10 27	UT, Salt Lake City
Browning ....Asenath E.	Carling................Isaac V.	1854	UT, Salt Lake City
Browning ....Sarah Ann	Bunker................Edward	1852 06 26	UT, Salt Lake City
Browning ....Sarah Ann	Lang...................William T.	1847 05 29	
Bryan (Brand)..Anne	Osborne ....Allen	1830 11 26	Scotland
Bryan ....Elizabeth	Amatt..................James	1837	ENG
Bryan ....Elizabeth	Stanfield ....Samuel	1843 12 19	ENG
Bryant.............Martha Amanda	Shepherd ....Moses T.		
Bryant.............Mary	Ensign................Isaac	1803 11 03	MA, Westfield
Bryant.............Mary Ann	Parkinson............Thomas	1855 06 12	CA, San Bern.
Bryant.............Mary Ann	Porter ....John	1844 04 16	Australia

Female	Male	Date	Place
Bryant ....Sarah	Stapley ....Charles	1822 12 01	ENG
Bryant ....Sarah Jane	Gates ....Reuben	1855 11 13	UT, Logan
Bryce ....Elizabeth	Hill ....Daniel Currie		
Bryce ....Margaret	Hill ....John	1837	Canada
Bryceson ....Annie	Laker ....Lashbrook	1855 08 19	ENG
Bryson ....Eliza Snow	Nelson................Jens Christian	1869 11 22	UT, Salt Lake City
Bryson ....Sarah Ann	Sessions ....Perrigrine	1866 09 29	UT, Salt Lake City
Bubb ....Martha Sarah	Shirley ....Thomas C.	1857 04 08	South Africa
Buchanan ....Eliza Jane	Higginson ....James G.	1857 01 10	UT, Spanish Fork
Buck ....Elizabeth	Garlick................David Gaston	1816 10 01	
Buckingham.....Mary Ann	Wheeler..............Joseph	1838 03 19	ENG
Buckland.........Samantha Jane	Russell ....Charles L.	1845 01 26	VT, Royalton
Buckley ....Elmira	Day.....................Abraham	1838 06 16	VT, Windhall
Buckman ....Ruth	Gurr....................Enoch Eldredge	1838	Australia
Buckwalter......Elizabeth	Green ....Alva A.	1858 12 25	UT, American Fork
Buckwalter......Margaret	Rice....................Leonard Gurley	1853 01 02	UT, Salt Lake City
Buckwalter......Margaret	Wickel ....Lemuel L.	1847	MO, St. Louis
Budd ....Charlotte	Johnson ....Benjamin	1836 04 01	
Budd ....Elizabeth	Rhees.................Charles Horatio	1863 05 21	ENG, Liverpool
Bull ....Mary	Criddle................Henry	1837 06 22	ENG, Somerset
Bull ....Sophronia Ann	Harding ....Thomas	1875 01 17	UT, Morgan
Bullard ....Elizabeth Howe	Hyde...................William	1842 02 23	IL, Nauvoo
Bullock...........Ann Elizabeth	Brown.................James Henry	1852 02 10	ENG, Offchurch
Bullock...........Elizabeth	McArthur ....Daniel D.	1857 02 13	UT, Salt Lake City
Bullock...........Ellen Mariah	Wilson ....John Marten	1878 07 13	UT, Salt Lake City
Bullock...........Jane Kilton	Riggs..................John	1843 10 08	NY, Moira
Bullock...........Mary Ann	Hartley................Jesse Thompson		
Bullock...........Mary Ann	Roberts ....Benjamin Morgan	1856 11 23	
Bullock...........Mary Ann	Williams..............Judge		
Bullock...........Sarah	Bull ....Joseph	1812	ENG
Bult ....Mary	Whitehead...........John	1837 09 26	ENG
Bundy ....Sally Mariah	Wade..................Moses	1818	
Bunker ....Rebecca Baks	Bolton.................Curtis Edwin	1839 09 12	NY
Bunker ....Rebecca Baks	Merritt.................Charles G.	1827 06 28	NY
Bunting ....Ann	Ward ....Samuel	1855 08 05	ENG, Matlock
Bunting ....Helen	Young..................William L.	1850 09 30	ENG
Bunting ....Mary	Ashton................Samuel		
Bunting ....Sarah Ann	Bosworth.............John	1841 09 27	ENG
Burbidge ....Catherine Emma	Hoyt....................Samuel Pierce	1856 01 17	UT, Fillmore
Burchell ....Emma	Flack ....John Logan	1860 06 07	UT, Bates Creek
Burdett............Jane	Hastings ....John	1843 10 11	ENG
Burdick ....Eveline Jewell	Johnson ....George W.	1851 09 30	UT, Salt Lake City
Burdick ....Rebecca	Winters...............Hyrum		
Burgess ....Ann	Ashdown ....Richard	1841 11 10	
Burgess ....Ann	Briggs.................Thomas	1877 05 25	UT, St. George
Burgess ....Elizabeth	Bent....................Samuel	1846 01 28	IL, Nauvoo
Burgess ....Elizabeth	Mathews.............Anson	1811 09 15	MA, Franklin Co.
Burgess ....Elizabeth	Slater..................Thomas Tyson	1860 09 27	MO, St. Louis
Burgess ....Rachel	Colemere ....George	1844 11 03	IL, Nauvoo
Burgum...........Charlotte	Weight................Fredrick	1849 08 18	
Burke ....Phoebe Jane	Bingham.............Edwin	1854 12 28	
Burnett............Ellen	Brown................William Jr.	1867 07 13	
Burnham.........Harriet	Knowlton ....Sidney A.	1816 06 30	
Burnhope........Mary Ann	Wallace ....Thomas M.	1859 04 09	ENG

Female	Male	Date	Place
Burningham .....Jane A.	Tolman ....Jaren T.	1886	
Burns ....Agnes	Harvey................James	1851 12 21	Scotland
Burns ....Margaret M.	Graham ....Robert Dundas	1845 09 14	Scotland
Burr.................Abigail Cordelia	Owens ....James C.	1816	
Burridge..........Charlotte H.	Steele.................Joseph Wilson	1867 10 19	UT, Salt Lake City
Burrows ....Emma	Fisher.................James	1840 11 17	ENG, London
Burrows ....Hannah	Cook...................George	1854 01 31	ENG, Kent
Burrows ....Sarah	Davenport ....Thomas	1836 08 28	ENG, Yorkshire
Burrup.............Mary Ann	Hellewell............George E.	1878 07 24	UT, Salt Lake City
Burton.............Alice	Mower ....Henry		
Burton.............Ann	Kearl..................James	1853 09 18	ENG
Burton.............Margaret	Marriott..............John	1857 12 17	UT, Kaysville
Burton.............Mary Hannah	White.................Samuel Dennis	1841 10 24	IL, Walnut Grove
Burton.............Melissa	Coray ....William	1846 06 22	IA, Mt. Pisgah
Burton.............Melissa	Kimball ....William		
Burton.............Sarah Maud	Roskelley ....Samuel	1885 12 25	UT, Logan
Burwell............Martha	Alexander...........Horace Martin	1849	
Bury ....Alice Fish	Strong ....Jacob	1857 03 05	UT, Salt Lake City
Bury ....Alice Fish	Walsh ....William	1850 07 01	
Busby ....Annie Maria	Mann ....Charles William	1863 11 04	UT, Salt Lake City
Busenbark ....Anna Eliza	Orison ....David Franklin	1869	
Busenbark ....Harriet	Williams.............Robert H.	1854 02 18	UT, Salt Lake City
Busenbark ....Sarah Jane	Hall....................Newton D.	1843 10	
Bushell............Mary	Bennion.............Samuel	1839 04 28	ENG, Liverpool
Butcher ....Harriet	Heath ....Frederick	1855 12 02	UT, Salt Lake City
Butcher ....Matilda Caroline	Fausett..............William M.	1826 03 02	TN, Maury Co.
Butler ....Annie Harriet	Clayson ....Nathan	1868 02 24	UT, Payson
Butler ....Caroline	Johnson ....Christian	1878 05 09	UT, Salt Lake City
Butler ....Charity A.	Thornton............Amos Griswold	1862	
Butler ....Charity A.	Wallace ....Hamilton M.	1855 10 04	UT, Spanish Fork
Butler ....Cynthia	Osborn ....David	1828 04 10	IN
Butler ....Elizabeth	Campbell............David William	1866 10 11	
Butler ....Elizabeth	Gates ....Charles Henry	1858 10 24	UT, Ogden
Butler ....Hannah	Palfreyman.........Richard	1842 01 22	ENG, Denby
Butler ....Jane	Stucki ....John U.		
Butler ....Lucy Ann	Allred.................Reuben Warren	1836 12 04	TN
Butler ....Mary Elizabeth	Nielson ....Joseph		
Butler ....Phoebe M.	Sevey ....George W.	1854 12 05	UT, Spanish Fork
Buttars ....Bethea	Sparks...............William	1868 12 15	UT, Salt Lake City
Butterfield ....Mary Jane	Doty...................Benjamin	1874 05 12	
Butterfield ....Mary Jane	Hansen...............Peter		
Butterfield ....Mary Jane	Whittle ....Thomas L.	1853 08 07	UT, Herriman
Butterworth ......Alice	Whitehead..........William	1872	
Butterworth ......Ruth	Briggs.................John	1835	
Butterworth ......Ruth	Clark...................Benjamin T.	1857 06 28	
Button ....Keturah Eliza	Andrews.............Charles A. B.	1824	NY, Onondago
Buxton ....Elizabeth	Partridge ....Edward Jr.	1862 02 15	UT, Salt Lake City
Byam ....Delia D.	Curtis.................Nahum	1839 10 29	IL, Warsaw
Byam ....Delia D.	Jackman..............Levi	1850	
Byam ....Delia D.	Reed ....Tillison	1810 12 30	NH, Jaffrey
Byard ....Eliza	Kershaw ....George F. W.	1849 12 17	South Africa
Bybee ....Lucinda	Layne ....David	1827 09 27	KY, Barren Co.
Bybee ....Lucinda	Mansor ....Barnett	1847 11	IA, Mt. Pisgah
Bybee ....Polly Chapman	Hammon ....Levi	1840 09 10	IN, Clay

Female	Male	Date	Place
Bybee ....Sally Ann	Hall......................Joshua Challis	1834	

C

Female	Male	Date	Place
Cadwallader ....Abigail	Brown.................Abia William	1830 04 30	
Cadwallader ....Abigail	Brown.................Ben		
Cadwallader ....Elizabeth	Davies ....John	1831 04 17	Wales
Cady ....Maria	Campbell.............Daniel	1845	
Cady ....Maria	Helm...................Thomas	1904 12	
Cahoon...........Sarah	Maxfield..............Robert Quorton	1864 01 07	UT, Salt Lake City
Caine ....Isabelle Ann	Cowley ....James	1827 04 28	United Kingdom
Cairnes ....Ruth	Farrow.................Nicholas	1830	Scotland
Cairnes ....Ruth	Stewart...............William	1857 03 04	
Cairnes ....Ruth	Teasdale ....Martin	1834	
Caldwell..........Caroline E.	Dymock...............E. George	1868	UT
Caldwell..........Caroline E.	McIntosh ....John	1854	UT, Tooele Co.
Caldwell..........Caroline E.	Neddo.................Charles	1849 12 25	
Caldwell..........Elizabeth	Wallentine ....Peter C.	1860 08 31	UT, Salt Lake City
Caldwell..........Jane	Dunn ....Simeon Adams	1846 05	
Caldwell..........Jane	Kelsey ....Eli B.		IL, Nauvoo
Caldwell..........Jane	Kelsey ....Eli B.		Remarried
Caldwell..........Jane	Waite ....John		
Caldwell..........Margaret	Barbour ....Peter	1814 01 14	Scotland
Caldwell..........Maria	McIntosh ....William	1841 09 17	Canada
Calender..........Margaret	Gardner..............Robert	1800 05 25	Scotland
Calhoun ....Margaret G.	Hewitt.................Wilkerson		
Calhoun ....Margaret G.	Pace...................James	1852 01 02	UT, Salt Lake City
Call ....Fanny	Loveland ....Chester	1838 02 15	OH, Madison
Call ....Samantha	Willey ....Jeremiah	1839 04 28	IL, Green Plains
Callaham ....Mary Ann	Lisonbee ....Coker	1825 02 01	AL, St. Clair Co.
Callaham ....Mary Ann	Nichols ....Peter	1849	
Callaham ....Mary Ann	Wimmer...............Peter	1863 04 09	UT, Springville
Callister ....Helen Mar	McCullough ....Henry Judson	1864 05 22	UT, Fillmore
Calvert ....Mary	Allred..................Isaac	1811 02 14	
Cameron..........Eliza Jane	Brinkerhoff..........Levi	1870 04 25	
Cameron..........Helen (Ellen)	Adamson..............John	1836 12 31	Scotland
Camp...............Harriet Diannah	Greer...................Dixon Hamlin	1864 02 25	UT, Salt Lake City
Camp...............Harriet Diannah	Murphy ....Mark B.	1858 02 09	UT, Salt Lake City
Camp...............Margaret H.	Baird...................Richard A.	1870 10 03	UT, Salt Lake City
Camp...............Margaret H.	Brantley..............Thomas Berges	1866 07 01	
Campbell ....Catherine	Steele..................John Jr.	1840 01 01	IRE
Campbell ....Jane	Kinghorn.............Alexander Patrick	1859 08	
Campbell ....Janet	Watson................James	1845	Scotland
Campbell ....Lovina	Campbell.............Solomon L.	1848 12 23	MO
Campbell ....Mary Ann	Foreman..............James	1818 01 12	ENG
Campbell ....Mary Ann	Hamilton.............James Lang	1840 07 13	Canada
Campbell ....Mary Ann	Richards..............		
Campbell ....Mary Ann	Robbins..............Edward	1797	
Campbell ....Mary Jane	Spens.................Nathaniel	1869 06 21	UT, Salt Lake City
Campbell ....Phoebe	Atkinson ....William	1833 12 26	Canada
Campkin ....Harriet	Young..................Thomas	1876 12 26	UT, Salt Lake City
Campkin ....Martha Ann	Merrell................Joseph	1872 05 06	UT, Salt Lake City
Campkin ....Ruth	Randall................Alfred Jason	1867 11 16	UT, Salt Lake City

Female	Male	Date	Place
Canada............Rachel	Cummings............John	1834 03 16	TN, Gibson Co.
Candland.........Mary Catherine	Chadwick ....James	1866 01 20	UT, Salt Lake City
Canivet...........Elizabeth Esther	Young.................Josias Richard	1843	
Cannell............Margaret Anna	Moyle ....James	1870 01 31	UT, Salt Lake City
Cannon............Ann	Woodbury............Orin N.	1853 02 07	UT, Salt Lake City
Cannon............Leonora	Allred.................Reddin Alexander	1857 02 08	
Cannon............Leonora	Gardner..............Robert	1863 06 23	UT, Salt Lake City
Cannon............Mary Alice	Lambert..............Charles	1844 11 28	IL, Nauvoo
Cannon............Sarah	Jordan ....James F.	1846 04 30	ENG
Cantwell.........Mary Ann	Mather...............Thomas	1870 12 05	UT, Salt Lake City
Capener...........Jane Maria	Giles ....Thomas H.	1890 11 12	UT, Logan
Capener...........Jane Maria	Hanks.................Ehpraim K.	1856 05 26	UT
Capener...........Jane Maria	Taylor ....Joseph Edward	1876 07 09	UT, Salt Lake City
Capstick...........Ann	Mercer................John	1852 11 09	
Capstick...........Ann	Mulliner ....Samuel		
Capstick...........Ann	Royle.................Henry	1848 05 03	NE
Carbine...........Mary Adelia	Grant ....George Roberts	1857 12 17	
Carbine...........Mary Adelia	Northrup ....Amos	1844 05 02	
Carbine...........Mary Adelia	Petty..................Robert Cowan	1850 08 30	NE
Carbine...........Mary Adelia	Taylor ....William Warren	1862 05 17	
Card...............Emily	Hess ....John W.	1852 03 30	UT, Salt Lake City
Cardon............Catherine	Bryne (Byrne)......Moses	1854 11 05	UT, Salt Lake City
Carlile ....Mary	Jeffs ....Mark Walker	1865	UT, Heber
Carlsen ....Anemena C.	Hansen...............Peter Henrick	1876 06 12	UT, Salt Lake City
Carlsen ....Johanne Kristine	Averett...............Elijah	1855 07 03	UT, Salt Lake City
Carlsen ....Mary	Olsen.................Christian	1868 03 28	UT, Salt Lake City
Carlson ....Anne Marie	Jensen ....Andrew C.	1866 02 13	UT, Brigham City
Carlson ....Bengta	Okerlund ....Ola	1856 11 16	Sweden
Carmichael .....Sarah E.	Williamson...........J. M.	1867	WY, Fort Bridger
Carpenter ....Jane Mott	Bird....................James	1831	
Carr ....Mary Ann	Gardner..............Robert	1856 07 20	
Carr ....Sarah Naomi	Holt....................Jesse Payton	1856 11 30	UT, Spanish Fork
Carrier ....Rebecca	Dall....................Henry David	1839 04 29	
Carroll.............Euphemia Ann	Moulton ....James Heber	1874 09 28	UT, Salt Lake City
Carroll.............Rhoda	Matthews............Joseph Lazarus	1832 07 14	NC, Johnston
Carruth ....Janet	Cahoon ....Andrew	1848 07 16	
Carruth ....Janet	Young.................James	1840 08 11	
Carruth ....Margaret	Cahoon ....Andrew	1848 07 17	
Carson............Elizabeth	Griffith ....Patison D.	1846 04 26	IL, Nauvoo
Carson............Elizabeth	Lewis ....David	1852 08 04	UT, Salt Lake City
Carson............Elizabeth	Lewis.................Tarleton	1856	UT, Parowan
Carson............Elizabeth	Mortensen...........Niels Otto	1862	UT, Parowan
Carter ....Eliza Ann	Snow ....James C.	1838 02 10	OH, Kirtland
Carter ....Elizabeth	Casey.................John Albert	1881 03 10	
Carter ....Elizabeth	Flaherty ....Michael	1850	
Carter ....Elizabeth	Whitmore............James M.	1853 02 23	TX
Carter ....Elizabeth Jane	Powell ....James Evans	1852 09 14	WY
Carter ....Hannah	York...................Aaron Mereon	1830 12 03	ME, Newry
Carter ....Harriet Amelia	Lee ....William Henry	1849 03 11	IA, Carterville
Carter ....Jane	Harris ....William M.	1858 07 04	NY, Williamsburg
Carter ....Jane	Robbins..............William	1872 07 14	UT, Hansel
Carter ....Phoebe W.	Woodruff ....Wilford	1837 04 13	OH, Kirtland
Carter ....Ruth Clarissa	Cornia ....Peter/Pierre	1856 05 02	UT, Salt Lake City
Carter ....Sarah Bracket	Foss ....Calvin	1823 11 01	ME, Scarboro

Female	Male	Date	Place
Case ....Martha Diana	Hickman ....William	1855	
Case ....Martha Diana	Howland ....Henry	1842 12 27	IL, Ogle
Case ....Martha Diana	Rogers ....Telemachus	1853 12 31	
Case ....Nancy	Winchester ....Stephen	1816 07 31	NY, Fort Edward
Cashmore.......Sarah Ann	Kidgell ....Charles Jr.	1853 12 25	ENG, Bedford
Cashmore.......Sarah Ann	Vogel..................Herman A. P.	1873	UT, Salt Lake City
Casot ....Mary Ann	Fitzgerald ....Perry	1839 01 10	IL, Vermillion
Casper.............Harriet Matilda	Marchant.............Albert George H.	1873 02 17	UT, Salt Lake City
Casteel ....Margaret Jane	Kartchner ....William Decatur	1844 03 17	IL, Hancock Co.
Castle ....Hannah	Salisbury ....Richard	1822 08 29	ENG, Packington
Castle ....Mary	Pickett ....William A.		ENG
Cathers...........Elizabeth	McMenemy ....John	1798	
Catlin ....Marinda	Bartholomew ....Noah Willis		
Catlin ....Mary Altaina	Bartholomew.......Noah Willis	1848 06 17	UT
Catlin ....Sarah Minnie	Squires................Henry A.	1846 04 27	ENG
Cattle ....Betsy	Klingensmith ....Phillip	1855 10 09	UT, Salt Lake City
Caucom ....Mary	Wasden...............Thomas	1841 12 06	ENG
Chadwick.........Ann	Montgomery ....Robert Jr.	1864 03 23	UT, North Ogden
Chadwick.........Mary Ann	Hull.....................Robert McClellan	1863 06 01	ID, Franklin
Chadwick.........Polly	Perry ....Asahel	1806 03 26	
Chaffee............Selina Hayward	Robison...............Peter	1839 10 06	NY, Gilvert Mills
Chalker ....Hester (Esther)	Mabey ....Thomas	1837 05 07	ENG
Chamberlain ....Catherine	Burgess...............William	1859	
Chamberlain ....Fanny	Powell ....John	1842 11 13	ENG, London
Chambers........Dorothy	Birch...................Joseph	1851 05 27	ENG, Lancashire
Champlin ....Angelina Avilda	Packer.................Johnathan T.	1840	IL, Nauvoo
Champlin ....Margaret Emma	Mecham ....Leonidas	1851 02 25	IA, Kanesville
Champlin ....Mary Jane	Dickson ....Stuart	1849 08 27	IA
Chandler..........Arabella Ann	Parkinson ....Samuel R.	1852 01 01	MO, St. Louis
Chandler..........Elizabeth	Hollist ....Henry	1837 12 25	ENG
Chandler..........Rebecca	Ford....................John	1833 06 23	ENG, Cambridge
Chandler..........Roseline	Harmon ....Ansel P.	1862 11 29	UT, Salt Lake City
Chantry............Hannah	Buck...................Charles	1859 12 22	ENG, Nottingham
Chantry............Sarah	Rawson ....John	1844 04 08	ENG, Derbyshire
Chapin ....Harriet	Clinger................James	1845 12 07	IL
Chapman.........Castina F. A.	Wayment.............Samuel J.	1868 03 11	ENG
Chapman.........Fanny Ridsdale	Jones ....John Pidding	1882	
Chapman.........Frances C.	Bosworth.............James B.	1874	UT, Croyden
Chapman.........Frances F.	Barnes................William Jeffries	1841 02 07	ENG, Bedfordshire
Chapman.........Hannah	Babcock ....Adolphus	1858 05 25	UT, Spanish Fork
Chapman.........Hannah	Chester ....Thomas	1833 01 28	ENG
Chapman.........Hannah	Goodworth ....Joseph	1845 10 29	ENG, Yorkshire
Chapman.........Hannah	Raymond.............Charles J.	1865 11 07	UT, Salt Lake City
Chapman.........Hulda	Nickerson ....Freeman	1801 01 19	VT, Cavendish
Chapman.........Jane	Fisher ....Vardis J.	1832 07 02	
Chapman.........Lucy	Cook...................William	1805 12 19	
Chapman.........Martha Ann	Fackrell ....James Jr.	1850 01 13	UT, Salt Lake City
Chapman.........Permelia	Mecham ....Joshua	1793 04 05	NH, Canaan
Chappel ....Parna	Harris ....Emer	1826 05 29	PA
Chappell ....Naomi	Gillett..................Samuel	1865 12 12	
Chappell ....Sarah Jane	Wright.................James B.	1864 12 25	UT, Nephi
Chapple ....Sarah	Bennett...............William B.	1866 10 27	UT, Salt Lake City
Chapple ....Sarah	Walker ....William	1863	
Charles ....Amelia	Terry...................Joshua P.	1882 01 12	UT, Salt Lake City

Female	Male	Date	Place
Charles ....Martha	Stevenson ....James	1834 06 15	ENG
Charles ....Mary Louise	Proctor ....George William	1886 11 03	UT, Union
Chase ....Desdemona	Gleason...............John S.	1839 11 08	NY, Livingston
Chase ....Diana S.	Shaw ....William M.	1849 01 01	UT, Ogden
Chase ....Diana S.	Young..................Brigham	1844 10 10	IL, Nauvoo
Chase ....Hannah Gove	Adams.................Barnabas L.	1856 11 16	UT, Salt Lake City
Chase ....Hannah Gove	Blair....................Edward	1873 05 13	UT, Salt Lake City
Chase ....Harriet Louise	Browning ....James Green	1855 07 20	
Chase ....Lurancy	Hill.....................Heamon Alison	1860 11 25	UT, Salt Lake City
Chase ....Nancy Bailey	Farr ....Lorin	1845 01 01	IL, Nauvoo
Chase ....Nancy E.	Miner ....Moroni	1861 02 03	UT, Springville
Chatterly ....Sarah	Kay ....John Rushton	1840 05 31	ENG, Prestwich
Chatters..........Ann Marie	Hookway ....Thomas	1815 11 09	ENG
Cheney ....Helen Mar	Miller ....Jacob	1856 03 16	UT
Cheney ....Malinda	Higley ....Clark	1837 09 17	
Cheney ....Olive M.	McBride ....James	1844 03 07	IL, Nauvoo
Cherrington......Elizabeth	Berry ....John Francis	1862 03 26	UT, Salt Lake City
Cherrington......Elizabeth	Chesnut..............Henry	1876 07 05	UT, Salt Lake City
Cherrington......Elizabeth	Golding...............Johnathon E.	1869	UT, Salt Lake City
Cherry.............Margaret	Willis..................Merrill	1804 12 08	
Cherry.............Mary Margaret	Brandon ....Thomas J.	1856 05 09	UT, Salt Lake City
Cheshire ....Mary Ann	Ramsay ....Ralph	1869 08 02	UT, Salt Lake City
Chester...........Ann	Ashby ....Benjamin	1857	
Chestnut..........Sarah Mary	Foy ....John Moroni	1862 12 13	UT, Salt Lake City
Chestnut..........Sarah Mary	Malan ....Stephen	1869 12 20	UT, Logan
Chestnut..........Sarah Mary	Slade..................Jefferson	1860 11 20	
Chestnut..........Sarah Mary	Trulock ....Aquilla	1865 11	
Chevalier ....Marie	De La Mare ....Philippe	1852 03 10	MO, St. Louis
Chidester.........Esther	Pulsipher............William	1861 10 27	UT, Salt Lake City
Chidester.........Esther	Snow ....John Chauncey	1883 10 26	UT, Salt Lake City
Chidester.........Eunice	Harmon ....Levi N.	1854 11 08	UT, Salt Lake City
Child ....Ellen Maria	Wheeler..............Walter	1873 07 28	UT, Salt Lake City
Child ....Jemima E.	Stookey ....Enos	1852 05 24	IL, Belleville
Childe ....Mary	Robbins..............James	1859 03 01	ENG, Coventry
Childs ....Patience Dolly	Holt....................William	1853 07 28	UT, Salt Lake City
Childs ....Susan Amelia	Noakes...............John Hubbard	1855 02 25	UT, Springville
Chipman ....Amanda	Simmons ....William B.	1825 01 17	Canada
Chipman ....Sinah Ceneth	Eldridge..............John S.	1849 03 24	
Chorlton..........Harriet	Jones ....Levinas Jr.	1856 03 02	ENG
Chorlton..........Harriet	Waldron..............Benjamin	1866 10 02	
Christensen .....Ane	Christensen.........Jens	1818 10 04	Denmark
Christensen .....Ane Elizabeth	Swensen ....Lars	1862 07 19	UT, Salt Lake City
Christensen .....Ane Kerstine	Johansen ....Peter	1858 11 21	UT
Christensen .....Ane Marie	Petersen.............Peder C.	1848 10 29	
Christensen .....Ann	Shimmin ....Robert C.		
Christensen .....Ann Mary	Stimpson ....William	1867 03 16	UT, Salt Lake City
Christensen .....Anna	Anderson............Anders Christian	1857 12 27	
Christensen .....Anna	Jensen ....Morten	1826 03 27	Denmark
Christensen .....Anna	Pederson............Hans		
Christensen .....Anna Catherine	Olsen..................Jens	1859 10 19	
Christensen .....Anna Christina	Staley ....Daniel	1864 10 31	UT, Logan
Christensen .....Anne	Jensen ....Anders	1844 08 31	Denmark
Christensen .....Anne	Padrigh...............John William	1859	UT
Christensen .....Anne	Pedersen...........		

Female	Male	Date	Place
Christensen .....Anne Marie	Christiansen ....Christian	1814 12 29	Denmark
Christensen .....Anne Marie	Stephenson ....Thomas C.	1862 07 14	NE, Florence
Christensen .....Annie	Anderson............Christian	1871 04 17	UT, Salt Lake City
Christensen .....Annie	Anderson............Joseph Smith	1878	
Christensen .....Ansine K.	Hansen...............Michael A.	1857	Denmark
Christensen .....Ansine K.	Howard...............George Jr.	1866 02 16	UT, Salt Lake City
Christensen .....Barbara	Jensen ....Christian	1850 10 29	Denmark
Christensen .....Brita K. B.	Esklund ....Lars P. H.	1847 11 05	Sweden
Christensen .....Caroline	Nielsen ....Niels Peder	1868 12 13	UT, Salt Lake City
Christensen .....Christene	Guymon ....James	1870 08 01	UT, Salt Lake City
Christensen .....Christina	Aagard ....Andrew James	1921 03 23	UT, Moroni
Christensen .....Christina	Jensen ....Andrew L.	1872 05 18	UT, Salt Lake City
Christensen .....Dorthea	Ahrens...............Claus Johann	1859 11 15	Denmark
Christensen .....Else Marie	Frost..................Anders S.	1827 03 17	Denmark
Christensen .....Frederikka	Munk ....Christian Ipsen	1859 11 12	UT, Salt Lake City
Christensen .....Jensine	Thursby ....Olaf	1877 09 10	UT, Ephraim
Christensen .....Johanna	Christensen ....Hans	1832 06 06	Denmark
Christensen .....Johanna Kristine	Bastholm ....Niels P.	1855 01 30	Denmark
Christensen .....Johanne	Nielsen ....Mads Pehr	1850	
Christensen .....Johanne	Olsen..................Johannes	1856	
Christensen .....Johanne	Thompson ....Niels	1846	Denmark
Christensen .....Karen Caroline	Christensen ....James	1862 05 17	Denmark
Christensen .....Karen Maria	Mortensen ....Diedrick	1863 05 23	
Christensen .....Karen Marie	Jensen ....Jens Christian	1840 12 01	Denmark
Christensen .....Karen Marie	Kofoed...............Hans Ancher		
Christensen .....Kersten	Ericksen ....Marcus	1833	Denmark
Christensen .....Kirsten	Skougaard...........Niels M.	1850 01 05	Denmark
Christensen .....Kirstine	Jensen ....Gregers	1832 11 02	Denmark
Christensen .....Maren	Jensen ....Soren Peter	1866 11 08	UT, Salt Lake City
Christensen .....Maren	Olson..................Swen	1866 06 17	Ocean
Christensen .....Maren Christine	Munson ....John	1864 02 22	UT, Salt Lake City
Christensen .....Maren Sophia	Nielsen ....Andreas	1866 06 30	
Christensen .....Margarethe K.	Poulson ....Niels Peter	1869 12 03	UT, Manti
Christensen .....Mary Elizabeth	Ayling ....Christian	1881 12 01	UT, Salt Lake City
Christensen .....Mette Marie	Kjar....................Lars Christian	1843 12 01	Denmark
Christensen .....Mette Marie	Madsen ....Niels	1838 10 19	Denmark
Christensen .....Nelsina Maria	Anderson............Andrew R.	1871	
Christensen .....Nicolena	Nelson................Charles F.	1875 02 01	UT, Salt Lake City
Christensen .....Sara Kristine	Forrester ....Robert		
Christensen .....Sara Kristine	Fredricksen ....Carl Antone	1873 05 26	UT, Ephraim
Christensen .....Sena Katrina	Olsen..................Hans	1879 05 15	UT, Salt Lake City
Christensen .....Sophia	Nielsen ....Anders	1866 06	UT
Christian ....Maria Bentley	Linford ....John	1833 06 24	ENG, Gravely
Christian ....Maria Bentley	Rich...................Joseph	1857 07 26	UT, Salt Lake City
Christiansen ...Anna Marie	Larsen ....Christian Greis	1860 01 15	UT, Salt Lake City
Christiansen ...Anna Marie	Olsen.................Niels	1854 06 25	UT, Salt Lake City
Christiansen ...Christina M.	Petersen.............Hans Peter	1860 05 28	Denmark
Christiansen ...Christina Marie	Nielsen ....Niels	1870 03 28	UT, Salt Lake City
Christiansen ....Else Marie	Jensen ....Christian G.	1853 04 03	MO, St. Louis
Christiansen ....Else Marie	Olsen.................Iver Johannes	1843 03 03	
Christiansen ....Hansine	Nielsen ....Rasmus	1859 06 12	NE, Florence
Christiansen ....Johanna	Anderson............John Larsen	1860 12 10	UT, Salt Lake City
Christiansen ....Karen Marie	Rasmussen ....Morten	1859 04 01	UT, Ephraim
Christiansen ....Lise	Sonne................Niels C. C.	1874 11 24	UT, Salt Lake City

Female	Male	Date	Place
Christiansen ....Marianna	Mortensen ....Niels Christian	1864 11 04	UT, Huntsville
Christiansen ....Severene	Christensen.........Jens Peter	1869 06 08	UT, Salt Lake City
Christmas ....Maria	Lewis..................Orrin	1860 07 11	UT, Salt Lake City
Christmas ....Maria	White..................John	1821 04 09	ENG
Christofferson ..Johanna	Denison..............Hans	1846 11 22	Denmark
Christophersen Johanne M. K.	Halling.................Lars	1862 12 24	UT, Brigham City
Christton ....Jane	Fisher ....Thomas F.	1834 01 25	ENG, Camberwell
Chubbuck ....Mary	Pulsipher............Elias	1828 01 31	
Chubbuck ....Mary	Wight..................Stephen	1853 01 30	
Chugg..............Mary	Pratt ....Moroni Walker	1874 04 27	UT, Salt Lake City
Churchill ....Elizabeth	Bowden..............William	1830 09 20	ENG, Bristol
Churchill ....Elizabeth	Cassity ....Edward Penale		
Clare...............Edith Ann	Byrne..................John Phillip	1884 02 17	WY, Uinta
Clark ....Ann	Martin ....Jesse Bigler	1857 12 20	
Clark ....Ann Broyhill	Thompson ....John Crow	1845 03 20	IL, Quincy
Clark ....Catherine	Chatterley............Joseph	1852 02 21	UT, Salt Lake City
Clark ....Catherine	Corlett ....James	1837 05 23	
Clark ....Eliza Ann	Horrocks..............Edward		MA, Boston
Clark ....Elizabeth	Bracken...............Levi	1810	OH
Clark ....Elizabeth	McBride...............James Andrew	1866 02 18	UT, Santaquin
Clark ....Ellen Victoria	Hale....................Alma Helaman	1865 08 19	UT, Salt Lake City
Clark ....Francis	Stratton ....James		
Clark ....Hannah Maria	Parkinson............Charles G.	1855 10 15	UT, Grantsville
Clark ....Huldah Meriah	Ballantyne ....Richard	1847 02 17	
Clark ....Jane	Hacking...............John S.	1856 05 16	MO, St. Louis
Clark ....Julia Ann	Clark...................Wheeler		
Clark ....Julia Ann	Harrington ....Jonathan	1824 10 16	PA, Bucks Co.
Clark ....Kate Arabel	Carothers ....John Thomas	1866 01 11	CA, Sacramento
Clark ....Lucina Elmina	Vane...................Joseph H.	1881 06 23	UT, Salt Lake City
Clark ....Lucy Jane	Barkdull...............Solomon M.	1848 08 20	IA, Council Bluffs
Clark ....Margaret C.	McGary ....William Henry	1868 03 07	UT, Salt Lake City
Clark ....Margaret C.	Rhodes...............Joseph	1859	UT, Logan
Clark ....Margaretta U.	Call....................Anson	1857 02 07	
Clark ....Marion Wallace	Dodge ....Augustas E.	1850 09 05	UT, Salt Lake City
Clark ....Mary	Rigby..................William F.	1852 08 09	ENG, Hatfield
Clark ....Mary Alice	Boulton...............Martin Cook	1870 11 14	UT, Salt Lake City
Clark ....Mary Alice	Woodbury............Orin N. Jr.	1878 03 14	UT, St. George
Clark ....Mary Ann	Mecham ....Lorenzo Dow	1865 09 09	UT, Salt Lake City
Clark ....Mary Ann	Page..................William	1863 03 24	UT, Bountiful
Clark ....Mary Ellen	Okey...................Edwin Jr.	1874 01 19	UT, Salt Lake City
Clark ....Nancy	Holman................John G.	1849 08 23	IA, Kanesville
Clark ....Nancy Maria	Montgomery ....Nathaniel	1868 01 01	UT, North Ogden
Clark ....Phebe G.	Young..................Phineas Howe	1853 11	UT, Salt Lake City
Clark ....Polly	Forbush...............Rufus	1811 11 05	MA, Royalston
Clark ....Polly	Smith..................Thomas Sasson	1837 02 13	OH, Conneaut
Clark ....Priscilla	Pickett ....George	1856	
Clark ....Priscilla	Pickett ....William A.	1860 03 03	UT, Salt Lake City
Clark ....Priscilla	Wilford................William	1862 06 30	NV, Carson City
Clark ....Sabina	Adams.................Azra Matson	1831 03 23	Canada
Clark ....Sarah Ann	Bond...................Stephen A.	1860 12 06	UT, Lehi
Clark ....Sarah Ann	Hale....................Alma Helaman	1861 12 24	UT, Grantsville
Clark ....Zerviah Eliza	Folsom ....William H.	1837 08 21	NY, Pembroke
Clarke ....Elizabeth Jane	Griffin ....William Hyrum		
Clarke ....Elizabeth Jane	Sparks................William	1881 01 27	UT, Salt Lake City

Female	Male	Date	Place
Clarke ....Mary	Ainscough ....William	1843	IL, Nauvoo
Clarke ....Mary	Wakefield ....Thomas	1837 03 25	PA, Wheatfield
Clarke ....Mary Caroline	Rigby ....George Clark	1883 03 01	UT, Salt Lake City
Clarke ....Sarah Angeline	Rigby ....William F.	1881 04 28	UT, Salt Lake City
Clarkson ....Ann	Leetham ....John	1848 08 31	ENG, Hull
Clarkson ....Elizabeth	Nuttall................Leonard John	1856 12 25	UT, Provo
Clausen ....Margrethe K.	Hansen...............Carl C.	1847 06 14	
Clausen ....Margrethe K.	Ronnow..............Christian P.	1862 02 03	
Clawson...........Helen Cordelia	Beatie.................Hampden S.	1855 12 02	UT, Salt Lake City
Clawson...........Lola Ann	Allen...................Elihu M.	1827	NY
Clayton ....Martha	Dorton ....Joseph A.	1858 04	
Clayton ....Mary Ann	Rodeback............Charles L.	1872 10 16	
Clegg ....Alice	Broadhead ....Robert	1861 01 15	UT, Heber
Clegg ....Catherine	Beardshall...........William		
Clegg ....Margaret Ellen	Barnes................William Henry	1873 12 28	UT, Salt Lake City
Clegg ....Mary	Beardshall...........William		
Clegg ....Mary	Henthorn		ENG
Clement ....Mary Irene	Sanders..............John F.	1855 07 15	
Clement ....Nancy	Smith..................George A.	1845 02 26	IL, Nauvoo
Clements ....Ada	Lowe ....Richard	1855 05 11	
Clements ....Elizabeth	Kendall...............Levi Newell	1852 11 29	UT, Salt Lake City
Clemmensen ...Martha Kristina	Isaacson.............Peter	1857 04 21	UT, Salt Lake City
Clifton ....Elizabeth Ann	Passey ....John Parley	1874 09 28	UT, Salt Lake City
Clisbee ....Lydia	Hunting...............William	1841	IL, Nauvoo
Clisbee ....Lydia	Partridge ....Edward	1819 08 22	OH, Painsville
Clotworthy ....Jane	Frew...................John	1846 05 01	Scotland
Clough ....Mary Jane	Plews ....Thomas	1861 11 25	
Clough ....Mary Jane	Wright.................Thomas Brett	1871 12 04	UT, Salt Lake City
Cloward ....Charlotte R.	Harmer...............Elias	1845	PA, Chester
Clucas ....Hannah	Shimmin ....Robert C.	1848 11 19	Isle of Man
Clucas ....Lucy	Roylance ....William	1864 03 27	
Cluff...............Lavina	Sweat ....George Hyrum	1846 04 19	IL, Nauvoo
Cluley ....Sarah Priscilla	Greaves ....Joseph	1853 02 22	ENG, Liverpool
Coates ....Jane	Hunt ....John Jr.	1810 02 01	
Coats ....Mary	Stratford ....Edwin A.	1879 02 06	UT, Salt Lake City
Cochrane.........Janet	Hamilton.............John Jr.	1901 05 15	UT, Salt Lake City
Cochrane.........Janet	Ryan...................William T.	1858 10 20	NY
Cocker ....Mary	Burrup ....James	1867 02 09	UT, Salt Lake City
Cocker ....Mary	Clegg..................William	1853 12 19	ENG
Cocks ....Emily Ann	Davis		
Cocks ....Emily Ann	Hillman ....Silas	1850 02 16	IA
Cocks ....Emily Ann	Long...................James P.	1847	
Code................Eliza	Broadbent ....Levi	1848 06 15	ENG
Coffin ....Elizabeth	Rawson ....Horace Strong	1825 10 09	IN, Wash. Co.
Coffman...........Susan Elmina	Bramall...............Samuel	1875 11 01	UT, Salt Lake City
Colburn ....Sarah Matilda	Pomeroy.............Francis M.	1853 04 20	UT, Salt Lake City
Cole ....Elizabeth Ann	Baldwin ....David	1825 02 01	ENG, Birmingham
Cole ....Elizabeth Ann	Cutler ....Isaac	1849 11 15	
Cole ....Esther Celestia	Baker..................William Evans	1865 03 08	UT, Riverdale
Cole ....Lucinda	Perry ....Josiah Henry	1845 11 30	IL, Nauvoo
Cole ....Mary Ann	Lowe ....John		
Cole ....Sarah Jane	Sanderson...........Henry W.		
Cole ....Susan Ann	Davis ....Joshua	1840 11 12	IL, Madison Co.
Colebrook ....Ellen Susanna	Rooks.................William A.	1873	

Female	Male	Date	Place
Colebrook ....Ellen Susanna	Taylor ....George Hamilton	1885 10 09	UT, Logan
Coleman ....Ann	Smith ....Joseph J.	1850 01 01	MO, Maryville
Coleman ....Annora	Boden ....James	1847 03 10	Wales
Coleman ....Elizabeth	Birch ....William	1856	
Coleman ....Elizabeth	Gillions ....John	1860	
Coleman ....Elizabeth	Jacobs ....John	1853 10 27	UT, Salt Lake City
Coleman ....Elizabeth	Lewis ....Siney	1874 01 05	UT, Salt Lake City
Coleman ....Elizabeth	Walker ....John William	1834 12 08	ENG
Coleman ....Elizabeth	Yeates ....Henry		
Coleman ....Elizabeth Glenn	Crosby ....John P.	1804 12 18	
Coleman ....Rebecca	Evans ....David		
Coleman ....Sarah	Lewis ....Preston King	1869 09 13	
Coles ....Sarah	Reeves ....William		UT
Collard ....Mercie Hunt	Ivory ....George W.	1879 10 02	
Collett ....Ann	Oakey ....Thomas	1836 08	ENG
Colley ....Jane	Walton ....Thomas	1819 05 20	ENG
Collier ....Elizabeth Mary	Taylor ....Joseph	1855 07 15	ENG
Collier ....Mary	Fry ....William	1844	
Collier ....Mary	Hughes ....Robert	1862	
Collier ....Mary	Winter ....Timothy J.	1806	ENG
Collier ....Rose	Turner ....David Jr.	1839	
Collin ....Elizabeth	Gillins ....John T.	1826 06 26	ENG
Collins.............Eliza	Hunsaker............Abraham	1833 01 03	IL, Quincy
Collins.............Elizabeth	McGhie...............William	1831 07 29	Scotland
Collins.............Martha	Rogers ....David White	1811 12 05	Canada
Collins.............Mary Hicks	Crapo ....Joseph G.	1826 06 18	
Collins.............Mary Jane	Rogers ....Alma Denton	1861 06 15	AK, Fort Smith
Collins.............Sarah Adaline	Freeman.............John W.		
Colston ....Catherine E.	Brett ....James	1879 03 27	UT, Salt Lake City
Colston ....Catherine E.	Maddox ....John	1829 06 08	ENG, Surrey
Colton ....Ann	Fryer..................William	1833 06 18	
Colton ....Ann	Parktington..........		
Coltrin ....Sarah Matilda	Telford...............John D.	1852 02 22	UT, Bountiful
Coman.............Harriet	Dye.....................Robert	1841 08 12	ENG, Wymondham
Combe.............Marianne	Beus...................Michael	1836 11 14	Italy
Combe.............Pauline	Malan ....John Daniel	1825 04 28	Italy
Comish ....Eleanor	Preece................Mark	1862 11 22	UT, Salt Lake City
Commander.....Matilda	Evans ....Thomas	1859 05 03	ENG, Birmingham
Commander.....Matilda	Thompson ....William	1867 04 20	UT, Salt Lake City
Comstock ....Olive	Newell ....Almon	1829	
Condie ....Helen	Thackeray ....George	1855 05 12	
Condie ....Mary	Leany ....William		UT, Salt Lake City
Condie ....Mary	Watson................James C.	1864 08 06	
Connery...........Sarah Ann	Bryson................Samuel	1839	IRE, Downs
Conover...........Sarah Elizabeth	Weaver................Gilbert E.	1855 07 14	
Conrad.............Sarah Helen	Bunnell ....David Edwin	1830 04 15	NY, Fayette
Cook ....Ann	Stark...................Daniel	1844 12 01	MA, Boston
Cook ....Ann	West ....William	1854 11 23	ENG, Borrowash
Cook ....Eliza Oliver	Martin ....Ezra Francis		
Cook ....Emma	Butterfield...........George	1870 02 14	
Cook ....Emma	Stocking ....Ensign I.	1876 04 17	
Cook ....Hannah E.	Hoyt...................Israel	1855 11 25	UT, Nephi
Cook ....Harriet Agnes	Green ....Benjamin	1862 02 22	
Cook ....Harriet Agnes	Howsley ....Charles D.	1831 10 21	

Female	Male	Date	Place
Cook ....Harriet Betsy	Teeples ....William R.	1859 08 21	
Cook ....Jemima	Toone.................John	1857 02 22	UT, Salt Lake City
Cook ....Lydia	Gallup.................Luke William	1850 04 30	MO, Linden
Cook ....Lydia Ann	Porter ....Chauncey W.	1847 03 28	
Cook ....Mary Jane	Toomer.................James	1854 03	ENG, Salisbury
Cook ....Mary Jane	Welch ....Thomas R. G.	1896	
Cook ....Rachel	Drollinger.............Samuel	1819 12 21	OH, Bulter Co.
Cook ....Sarah Harris	Boulton.................Thomas	1849 03 26	ENG, Worchester
Cooke ....Charlotte	Hale.................Aroet	1865 03 18	
Coolbear.........Caroline	Ager ....John	1861 01 05	
Coolbear.........Caroline	Durrant.................James		
Coolbear.........Caroline	McKenzie ....Thomas	1860 02 19	
Coolbear.........Caroline	Ross.................David		
Cooley ....Asenath	Neal.................George Augustus	1820 01 30	
Coon.............Frances Ann	Hardman ....Lehi Nephi	1860 06 15	UT, Salt Lake City
Coon.............Lois	Jordan ....Nathaniel	1847 11 27	IA, Pott. Co.
Coon.............Lois	Mower ....Henry Jr.	1863 07 11	
Coon.............Lois	Stevens ....Arnold	1828 11 05	Canada
Coon.............Lois	Woodward...........James	1854 02 16	UT, Spanish Fork
Coon.............Rachel	Cooley.................Andrew Wood	1868 02 22	UT, Salt Lake City
Coons ....Adaline	Buchanan...........John	1851 02 23	IA, Coonsville
Coons ....Laura Elizabeth	Cutler ....Thomas R.	1870 12 26	UT, Salt Lake City
Coope.............Ann	Harvey.................John	1854	UT, Salt Lake City
Coope.............Ann	Minchel.................John	1846 01 01	
Cooper.............Catherine	Holbrook.............Joseph H. A.	1878 01 13	UT, Salt Lake City
Cooper.............Eliza Snow	Parkin.................Joseph H.	1870 02 14	UT, Salt Lake City
Cooper.............Margaret	West.................Samuel Walker	1829 01 29	TN
Cooper.............Mary	Oakey.................James	1840 01 06	ENG
Cooper.............Mary Jane	Powell ....James Q.	1841 09	PA, Philadelphia
Cooper.............Rachel Russell	Kempton...........Nathan	1837	TX
Cooper.............Sarah Ann	Parker ....Heber Thomas	1872 01 08	UT, Salt Lake City
Cooper.............Sariah	Hartley.................Charles R.	1874 01 04	UT, Salt Lake City
Cope.............Emily	Cutler ....Ransom	1885 12 03	
Cope.............Emily	Smith.................Thomas	1873 02 24	UT, Salt Lake City
Coray ....Aurilla	Dusenberry ....Mahlon	1831 05 21	PA, Easton
Coray ....Mary Knowlton	Roberts ....Orville Clark	1868 07 24	UT, Provo
Corbett.............Mary	Harris ....Martin Jr.		
Corbridge.........Ann	Slater.................Richard	1834 09 19	
Corbridge.........Mary Ann	Hamblin.............Oscar	1854 02 18	UT, Salt Lake City
Corbridge.........Mary Ann	Stoddard ....Albert Leonard	1867 11 02	
Cordingly ....Sarah Ann	Robertson ....Thomas	1854 12 19	UT, Salt Lake City
Cordon.............Rachel Ann	Brandow.............Alfred H.	1888 11 04	UT, Willard
Cordon.............Rachel Ann	Herold ....Robert William	1879	
Cordon.............Rachel Ann	Ward ....William	1861	UT, Willard
Cornelius ....Mary Ann	Cable.................John		
Cornell ....Elizabeth	Nate ....Sampson	1864 02 17	UT, Salt Lake City
Cosgrove ....Sarah Ann	Auger ....Jabez	1855 01 01	PA, Philadelphia
Cosgrove ....Sarah Ann	Bowering ....George Kirkham	1869 09 20	UT, Salt Lake City
Cosgrove ....Sarah Ann	Wood.................John	1849 08 26	
Cottam.............Ellen	Marsden...........William	1865 09 02	UT, Salt Lake City
Cottam.............Ellen	Pilling ....Edmund	1845 08 31	ENG, Lancashire
Cottam.............Ellen	Williams.............Ebenezer Albert	1857 06 21	UT, Salt Lake City
Cottam.............Emma	Thompson ....William H.	1868 11 20	UT, Salt Lake City
Cotton.............Peninah S.	Wood.................Daniel	1846 01 27	IL, Nauvoo

Female		Male		Date	Place
Cottrell	Elizabeth	Day	Henry Eastman	1862 11 01	UT, Salt Lake City
Cottrell	Mary Ann	Nate	Sampson	1852 12 07	ENG
Couch	Mary Ann	Guymon	James Neils	1839 10 02	
Coupe	Alice	Robinson	John R.	1842 03 05	Ocean
Coupe	Jane	Robinson	John R.	1847 08 24	IA
Court	Emmeline	Lake	William	1832 02 12	ENG, North Molton
Cousin	Elizabeth	Crystal	Andrew	1850 05 30	Scotland
Cousins	Sarah	Brown	Jonathan	1838 10 31	ENG, Berkshire
Coutts	Christina	Hunter	James Forbes	1846 07 27	
Covert	Betsy	Knight	Joseph Jr.	1832 03 22	OH, Kirtland
Covert	Mary Emma	Andrus	Milo	1858 02 28	
Covert	Mary Emma	Holden	John Wyley		
Covington	Emily Jane	Farr	Winslow Jr.	1858 10 17	UT, Washington
Covington	Martha Ann	Gay	Alexander	1841 08 24	NC
Covington	Martha Ann	Gibson	Benjamin		
Covington	Martha Ann	Norton	John	1847 06	IA, Mt. Pisgah
Covington	Sarah Elizabeth	West	Chauncey W.	1855 08 05	UT, Salt Lake City
Cowan	Margaret	Bryson	John	1815 06 15	IRE
Cowan	Margaret	Dunlap	Joseph	1860 10 09	UT, Salt Lake City
Cowan	Mary	Watson	Robert	1840 01 12	Scotland
Cowap	Mary	Worthen	Richard	1816 02 18	ENG
Cowles	Abigail	Leavitt	Weare		
Cowles	Elvira Annie	Holmes	Jonathan H.	1844 12 01	IL, Nauvoo
Cowles	Phoebe	Leavitt	Weare		NH
Cowley	Elizabeth Jane	Dutson	John William	1850 08 10	MO, St. Louis
Cowling	Hannah S.	Hepworth	Edmund	1862 09 17	ENG
Cowper	Elizabeth	Jeffery	Thomas Alfred	1862 02 22	UT, Salt Lake City
Cox	Ann Marie	Lewis	James		
Cox	Ann Marie	Walker	Edward R.	1849 09 13	IL, Green Co.
Cox	Catherine	Parker	Edwin	1870 10 31	UT, Salt Lake City
Cox	Emma	Jones	Jacob	1861 05 14	UT, Fairview
Cox	Jemima	Jex	William	1865 01	UT, Salt Lake City
Cox	Mary Adelaide	Reid	William Taylor	1869 11 23	UT, Manti
Cox	Mary Elizabeth	Whiting	Edwin	1846 01 27	IL, Nauvoo
Cox	Sarah S.	Hutchings	Elias	1816 12 29	OH, Avery
Cox	Therissa E.	Clark	John Haslem	1867 05 01	UT, Manti
Crabb	Georgina Calder	Barton	Hyrum	1880 01 01	UT, Salt Lake City
Crabb	Marianna	Stratford	Edwin	1855 12 25	ENG, Danbury
Cracroft	Sarah	Debenham	Henry W.	1870 10 03	UT, Salt Lake City
Craddock	Catherine	Armstrong	William	1838 10 22	
Cram	Charlesetta P.	Johnson	William Derby Jr.	1879 05 29	UT, St. George
Crandall	Eliza	Deal	John Wesley	1842 10 28	IL, Adams Co.
Crandall	Emeline	Bird	Richard	1845 03 07	NY
Crandall	Julia Ann	Boyer	John Sell	1866 02 08	
Crandall	Laura	Bird	Richard	1855 03 06	UT, Salt Lake City
Crandall	Laura	Johnson	Willis Kelsey	1849 12 27	IA
Crane	Mary Ann	Taylor	William	1870	
Craner	Harriet Ann	Harris	Alexander	1855 06 21	UT, Salt Lake City
Crapo	Clarissa D.	Davenport	Edward W.	1848 08 10	
Cravath	Eliza Doty	Kimball	Heber Chase	1856 04 11	UT
Cravath	Helen	Neeley	William	1852 09 18	UT, Salt Lake City
Cravath	Mary	Whitney	Horace Kimball	1856 12 01	UT, Salt Lake City
Crawford	Isabella	Murdoch	John Murray	1862 08 09	UT, Salt Lake City
Creager	Elizabeth	Shupe	Andrew J.	1837 10 12	VA, Wythe Co.

Female	Male	Date	Place
Cree..............Jane	John ....David	1865 10 08	UT, Salt Lake City
Creemar ....Hannah	Klingensmith ....Phillip		
Creer ....Alice Ann	Jones ....Llewellyn	1868 03 28	UT, Salt Lake City
Cresswell........Eliza	Cliff....................Edward	1863 04 27	ENG, Staffordshire
Cressy ....Nancy	Walker................Oliver	1803 02 08	
Cressy ....Nancy	Young................Brigham	1846 02 06	IL, Nauvoo
Criddle ....Charlotte	Gull.....................John	1867 01 12	UT, Salt Lake City
Cripps ....Sarah Ann	Hayward.............Gammon	1850 06 01	ENG
Crismon ....Esther Ann	Sirrine.................George W.	1852 07 04	
Crismon ....Martha Jane	Lewis..................John Moss	1848 08 10	UT, Salt Lake City
Crisp ....Matilda	Goodman ....William	1839 11 11	ENG, Bedfordshire
Crites ....Catherine	Wood..................David	1818 03 17	Canada
Crockett ....Zillah	Linford ....James Henry	1862 01 19	UT, Salt Lake City
Croft................Elizabeth	Knowles ....William H.	1851 08 10	ENG, Preston
Crombie...........Henrietta E.	Williams..............Ezra G.	1847 08 15	MO, St. Louis
Cromeans........Henrietta	Pearce................Harrison	1836 07 25	
Crompton.........Alice	Jackson..............Thomas	1842 08 14	ENG
Crompton.........Hannah	Thompson ....Joseph	1862 09 28	UT, Salt Lake City
Crompton.........Harriet Maria	Hocking ....William H.	1862 11 08	UT, Salt Lake City
Crompton.........Virtue Leah	Blackburn ....Elias Hicks	1862 01 31	UT, Salt Lake City
Cronk...............Catherine	Slaughter............Edward	1832 08 09	
Cronk...............Fanny	Van Velsor ....Stephen		
Crook...............Mary	Eagle..................Elias	1844 02 23	
Crook...............Mary	Knell...................Robert	1855 02 23	UT, Kaysville
Crooks ....Sarah Ann	Brewerton...........Thomas W.	1850 12 25	ENG, Nottingham
Crosby ....Elizabeth	Brown.................John	1844 05 21	
Crosby ....Martha Vilate	Flake ....Green	1854	NC
Crosby ....Sarah F.	Thomas ....Edward	1866 03 03	
Crosby ....Sytha	Lay ....William Harvey	1841 12 18	MS, Aberdeen
Cross ....Agnes	Douglass.............William	1842 10 14	IRE
Cross ....Ann	Eardley...............John	1846 08 03	ENG, Derbyshire
Cross ....Harriet	Walters...............Archer	1837 08 26	ENG, Rotherham
Cross ....Margaret	Bate....................Peter	1837	ENG
Cross ....Margaret	Vowles ....Samuel	1862 06 07	
Cross ....Sarah	Orme ....Samuel W.	1857 11 08	UT, E. T. City
Crossgrove ......Josephine L.	Cannon ....David Henry	1867 10 19	UT, Salt Lake City
Crossley ....Hannah Mariah	Cooper ....David	1870	UT, Richmond
Crossley ....Hannah Mariah	Thomson ....George	1866 01 13	UT, Salt Lake City
Crossley ....Hannah Mariah	Thomson ....George	1896	
Crossley ....Sarah	Sessions ....Perrigrine		
Crowther.........Hannah	Doddis................Harry		
Crowther.........Hannah	Mitton ....William	1832 02 12	ENG
Crowther.........Mary Ann	McKenzie ....David	1859 02 28	UT, Salt Lake City
Cruickshank.....Mary M. F.	Morrison ....William	1843 12 22	Scotland
Crumb..............Amy	Fackrell ....James	1819	VT
Cruse ....Charlotte	Thorpe................William W.	1850	MO, St. Louis
Cruse ....Julia	Howe..................Amos	1851 06 09	MO, St. Louis
Cruse ....Mary	Stone..................William	1836	
Crystal ....Mary	Howard...............Lockwood A.	1876 03 20	UT, Salt Lake City
Crystal ....Mary	Wagstaff.............David	1867 03 08	UT, American Fork
Cullumber ....Martha	Bickmore ....Thomas	1866 05 10	
Cumming ....Jane	Baird...................Robert II	1853 06 08	Scotland
Cummings ....Nancy E.	McDonald............Joseph Smith	1863	UT, Heber
Cunningham ....Elizabeth	Kelly ....William Edward	1858 07 19	UT, American Fork

Female	Male	Date	Place
Cunningham....Miriam	Mann..................Oscar	1860 09 06	IA
Cunningham....Primrose	Shields ....John	1827 08 16	
Cunningham....Ruth	Mikesell..............Garrett W.	1830 06 20	IL, Clark Co.
Cunningham....Seviah	Egbert ....Robert Cowden	1846 04 01	IL, Nauvoo
Cunningham....Seviah	Huntsman...........Isaiah	1868	
Currie.............Christina	Garrett...............Levi Clutcher	1863 01 10	UT, Salt Lake City
Currie.............Elizabeth	Hill ....Alexander	1806 05 30	Scotland
Curtis ....Celestia	Durfee ....Jabez	1850 12 25	UT, Salt Lake City
Curtis ....Eliza Mary	Pearson..............Benjamin A.	1869 12 27	UT, Salt Lake City
Curtis ....Margaret	Roberts ....Brigham Henry	1890 04	UT, Salt Lake City
Curtis ....Margaret	Shipp.................Milford Bard	1867 12 01	UT, Salt Lake City
Curtis ....Mary	Houghton ....Ornon	1845 07	IA, Montrose
Curtis ....Mary	Markham............Stephen	1850 10 05	UT, Salt Lake City
Curtis ....Mary	Reed ....Calvin	1841 07 11	IL, Nauvoo
Curtis ....Nancy Louisa	Thornton.............Stephen	1856 07 01	UT, Parowan
Curtis ....Sabrina	Harward ....Thomas	1851 04 06	
Curtis ....Sabrina	King...................George	1846	
Curtis ....Serepta L.	Jolley.................William J.	1850 04 25	IA, Council Bluffs
Curtis ....Ursula	Durfee ....Abraham	1846	
Curtis ....Ursula	Gifford ....Samuel K.	1870	
Cushing ....Ellen Maria	Cushing..............Arthur John	1869 12 24	UT, Salt Lake City
Cushing ....Ellen Maria	Major ....William D.	1867 10 04	UT, Salt Lake City
Cusworth ....Eliza	Burton ....Joseph	1846 06 08	ENG
Cusworth ....Eliza	Staker.................Nathan	1857	UT
Cutcliffe ....Mary Jane	Aver...................Ulrich	1873 02 18	UT, Salt Lake City
Cutcliffe ....Mary Jane	Spencer..............Daniel	1856 12 27	UT, Salt Lake City
Cutler..............Anna	Galloway ....Charles Wesley	1849	
Cutler..............Helen Mar	Henderson ....Samuel Goforth	1855 05 06	UT, Salt Lake City
Cutler..............Helen Mar	Marley ....William	1886	
Cutler..............Louisa E.	Rappleye............Tunis	1836 01 17	OH, Kirtland
Cutler..............Susannah	Nelson................John Lowry	1860 11 17	

D

Female	Male	Date	Place
Dack ....Frances	Parrish................Samuel	1820 02 13	Canada
Daggett............Hannah	Aiken ....Samuel Ruggles	1851 09 13	
Daggett............Hannah	Boice..................John	1862 11 15	
Daggett............Hannah	Buckland ....Joseph	1823 02 16	VT, Orange
Daggett............Hannah	Collins ....Nathan N.	1847	
Daines ....Lydia	Sillett ....James		
Daines ....Lydia	Wilkinson............Nathaniel	1831 10 26	ENG
Dale.................Annie	Wright.................Thomas	1866 01 06	ENG, Sheffield
Daley ....Abigail Jane	Andrus................Milo	1833 02 21	OH, Huron
Daley ....Abigail Jane	Andrus................Milo	1886 03 17	ID, Oxford
Daley ....Abigail Jane	Van Etten ....Elisha Wheat	1850 07	
Daley ....Hannah Electa	Wood..................Gideon D.	1830 12 28	OH, Florence
Dall ....Rebecca	Holladay ....John D. III	1870 01 01	UT, Santaquin
Dalley ....Sarah Ann	Orton ....William Owen	1865 01 01	UT, Summit
Dalley ....Susannah	Clark..................George Sheffer	1850 03 23	IA, Council Bluffs
Dallimore ....Maria Ann	Roberts ....George	1868 10 11	UT, Salt Lake City
Dallimore ....Maria Ann	Worlton..............James T.	1863 11 14	UT, Salt Lake City
Dallin ....Catherine	Westwood ....Richard W.	1859 06 17	UT, Springville
Dallin ....Mary Ann	Wheelock ....Cyrus H.	1853 12 11	UT, Salt Lake City

Female	Male	Date	Place
Dalton ....Ann	LeFevre...............John	1829 06 21	ENG
Dalton ....Ann	Mitchell................William C.	1852 09 26	UT, Salt Lake City
Dalton ....Ann Eliza	Neal....................William Cooley	1852 06 09	
Damron............Cinthia E.	Moody ....William C.	1857 12 20	UT, Salt Lake City
Damron............Susan Emaline	Allphin.................Israel	1858 03 17	UT, Salt Lake City
Damron............Susan Emaline	Coldiron..............William H.	1850 12 02	
Dana................Elizabeth	Gibbs..................William	1844 04 16	NY, Lockport
Danby ....Jane	Webley ....Richard	1797 04 17	ENG
Dand................Sarah	Tibbitts ....John	1832 12 24	ENG
Dandy ....Alice	Ollerton...............John	1826 02 04	ENG
Dangerfield ......Eliza	West....................Charles H. J.	1850 12 25	ENG, London
Daniels ....Elizabeth	Casto..................Mathew Gailand	1846 02 07	IL, Nauvoo
Daniels ....Elizabeth	Smith...................Samuel		
Daniels ....Hannah	Job ....Thomas	1848 05 02	Wales
Daniels ....Hannah	Miles...................Albert	1857 01 13	UT, Salt Lake City
Daniels ....Phebe	Hulme..................William	1860 11 04	UT, Payson
Danielson ....Hanna	Faux....................Jabez	1862 12 24	UT, Moroni
Danielson ....Johanna	Olsen..................Gideon Elias	1865 03 04	UT, Salt Lake City
Dansie ....Sarah Ann	Crane ....James S.	1878 10 11	UT, Salt Lake City
Darrow.............Mary Ann	Cox.....................Frederick Walter	1858 01 09	UT, Manti
Darrow.............Mary Ann	Richardson..........Edmund	1840 08 02	NY, Salem
Darrow.............Permelia	Lott.....................Cornelius Peter	1823 04 27	PA, Bridgewater
Dart..................Mary Minerva	Judd ....Zadok Knapp	1852 11 14	UT, Parowan
Davenport........Antoinette	Leavitt ....Thomas Rowell	1861 03 09	UT, Salt Lake City
Davenport........Sarah Ann	Adams.................Charles	1863 03 31	UT, Parowan
Davenport........Sarah Mariah	Maughan.............John Harrison	1853 07 24	
Davey ....Eliza Louisa	Crockwell ....George	1871 10 23	UT, Salt Lake City
Davey ....Josephine	Kimball ....Jeremiah H.		UT, Salt Lake City
Davey ....Josephine	Smith...................John W.	1890 05 18	UT, Salt Lake City
Davey ....Rosina	Lamb		
Davey ....Rosina	McInnes ....Duncan		
Davey ....Rosina	Morgan................Charles Henry	1870 07 02	
Davey ....Rosina	Shepherd ....Alfren D.		
David ....Ann	Harris ....David	1851 08 23	
David ....Ann	Warner ....William	1856	
David ....Emma	Rees....................Alfred	1859 08 14	UT, Spanish Fork
Davidson ....Ann	McCulloch ....William Johnson	1852 03 19	Scotland
Davidson ....Eleanor	Alexander............John	1863 03 27	
Davidson ....Eleanor	Ellett...................John James	1840 04 22	
Davidson ....Mary Dorothea	Nielson ....Niels Peter	1875 03 22	UT, Mt. Pleasant
Davidson ....Mary Dorothea	Thompson ....Thomas		
Davies ....Ann	Dalley.................William	1818	ENG, Leominster
Davies ....Charlotte	Dearden ....Thomas	1867 03 10	ENG
Davies ....Dinah	Jones ....William Ellis	1856 02 03	MO, St. Joseph
Davies ....Dinah	Vaughan..............William	1834 03 17	Wales
Davies ....Elinor	Beckstead ....George W.	1859 04 28	UT, Provo
Davies ....Elizabeth	Job ....Thomas	1855 08 18	
Davies ....Ellen	Hughes................Francis David	1869 05 03	UT, Salt Lake City
Davies ....Esther Mariah	Murdock ....Nymphus	1857 12 06	UT, Salt Lake City
Davies ....Harriet	Hughes................Francis David	1864 04 24	Wales
Davies ....Jannet	McMillen..............Daniel	1844 12 08	ENG
Davies ....Margaret	Rees....................Thomas John	1836 09 10	Wales
Davies ....Martha	Timothy ....John G.	1853 09 30	Wales
Davies ....Mary	Brown..................Robert	1872 09 21	UT, Beaver

Female		Male		Date	Place
Davies	Mary	Wood	George	1850 12 02	UT, Salt Lake City
Davies	Mary Emiah	Dodds	George	1873 04 16	UT, New Harmony
Davis	Alice	Crane	James	1858 04 05	IA, Iowa City
Davis	Ann H.	Davis	David	1853 12 25	Wales
Davis	Ann H.	Davis	David W.	1859 06 10	UT, Logan
Davis	Anna	Stagnall	Sergeant		
Davis	Anna	Young	Isaac		
Davis	Catherine	Simmons	Henry	1847 09 12	ENG, St. James
Davis	Charlotte Ann	Davis	Daniel C.	1859 02 10	
Davis	Charlotte Ann	Murray	John T.	1851	UT, Centerville
Davis	Charlotte James	McKay	Thomas Sloan	1853 07 26	UT, Salt Lake City
Davis	Comfort	Boulter	Thomas	1822 05 07	ENG
Davis	Cynthia	Clyde	George W.	1824 10 30	NY, Ogdensburg
Davis	Elizabeth	Ayrton	William	1878 08 22	UT, Salt Lake City
Davis	Elizabeth	Day	David	1857 04 03	UT, Salt Lake City
Davis	Elizabeth	Jenkins	James	1842 05 09	Wales
Davis	Elizabeth	Morgan	William	1820 01 29	Wales
Davis	Elizabeth	Raddon	James Henry	1877 05 15	
Davis	Elizabeth Jane	Nebeker	Peter	1847 02 13	
Davis	Elizabeth Jane	Stewart	Benjamin F.	1850 09 07	
Davis	Emerette L.	Randall	Alfred	1834 01 08	OH, Munson
Davis	Hannah	Huntsman	James W.	1831 12 28	MI, White Pidgeon
Davis	Hannah	Wallace	George B.	1852 10 15	UT, Salt Lake City
Davis	Laura Jones	Peters	David	1840 04 11	Wales
Davis	Lucretia	Gay	Moses B.	1830 12 02	
Davis	Lucy Ellen	Stimpson	Frederick		
Davis	Lydia	Wallace	George B.	1852 10 15	UT, Salt Lake City
Davis	Lydia Ann	Morrill	Laban	1854 10 17	
Davis	Lydia Rebecca	Hardy	Joseph	1868 10 03	UT, Salt Lake City
Davis	Margaret	Merrill	John Elwin	1862 04 17	
Davis	Margaret	Owens	Horace	1856 10 04	
Davis	Margaret Ann	Harman	Charles M.	1882 03 30	UT, Salt Lake City
Davis	Maria	Giles	Thomas	1807 12 18	Wales
Davis	Martha	Wallace	George B.	1852 10 15	UT, Salt Lake City
Davis	Mary	Biddlecome	George R.	1873 06 14	UT, Tooele
Davis	Mary	Dorney	William	1816	ENG
Davis	Mary	Evans	Abram	1832 12 17	Wales
Davis	Mary	Reid	John	1862	Trail
Davis	Mary Ann	Moore	George Sharrett	1851 08 11	ENG
Davis	Mary Maria	Nebeker	Peter	1852 01 31	UT, Salt Lake City
Davis	Roxanna	Davis	James Duane	1831 01 16	
Davis	Sarah	Hawkins	Thomas S.		
Davis	Sarah	Jones	William Edward	1871 10 03	UT, Salt Lake City
Davis	Sarah	Merkley	Christopher	1828 02 18	Canada
Davis	Sarah	Woodward	William	1857 09 20	UT, Salt Lake City
Davis	Sarah Agnes	Karren	Charles Hopkins	1871 12 25	UT, Lehi
Davis	Sarah E.	Carter	Samuel	1861	UT, Salt Lake City
Davis	Sarah E.	Roberts	Levi	1857 03 07	UT, Salt Lake City
Davis	Sarah Rebecca	Garner	David E.	1870	UT, Salt Lake City
Davis	Susan	Townsend	James F.	1827 03 11	
Davis	Susan Keziah	Ellis	Frederick W.	1869 09 06	UT, Salt Lake City
Dawtry	Mary Ann	Buckley	Samuel	1837	ENG
Dawtry	Mary Ann	Cocker	Joseph	1832 12 10	ENG
Dawtry	Mary Ann	Fielding	James H.	1861 04 27	UT, Salt Lake City

Female	Male	Date	Place
Day .... Almeda	McClellan .... William Carroll	1849 07 19	IA, Pott. Co.
Day .... Anna	Swallow .... George	1878 01 16	UT, Salt Lake City
Day .... Elizabeth	Gammon .... Thomas	1840 10 27	ENG, Devon
Day .... Mary Ann	Fluiett .... William	1855 07 15	
Day .... Mary Ann	Handy .... William	1866 11 11	
Daybell .... Sarah	Giles .... George Thomas	1867 01 28	UT, Heber
Dayer .... Ann	Spooner .... David N.	1835	Wales
Deacon .... Mary Ann	Beal .... John	1822 03 04	
Deal .... Mary Ellen	Mendenhall .... Thomas	1864 05 15	UT, Springville
Dean .... Elizabeth	Raymond .... Samuel J.	1828	
Dean .... Jane	Smith .... Samuel T.	1848 12 24	
Dean .... Martha Harriet	Patterson .... Edward N.	1878 02 07	
Dean .... Mary Ann	Taylor .... William	1845 06 16	ENG
Dean .... Rosetta	Glazier .... Shepherd	1841 10 13	IL, LaHarpe
Decker .... Clarissa	Young .... Brigham	1844 05 08	
Decker .... Harriet Amelia	Hanks .... Ephraim K.	1848 09 22	
Decker .... Harriet Amelia	Little .... Edwin Sobieski	1842 03 22	
Decker .... Lucy Ann	Seely .... William	1833	
Decker .... Lucy Ann	Young .... Brigham	1842 06 15	IL, Nauvoo
Dee .... Ann	Olpin .... Joseph	1861 10 23	UT, Salt Lake City
Dee .... Emily	Wadley .... Joseph	1860 12 05	UT
Degen .... Elizabeth	Bushman .... Martin	1827 05 20	PA, Lancaster
DeGrey .... Charlotte	Baddley .... George	1861 10 04	UT, Salt Lake City
Degrey .... Keziah	Hall .... John Charles	1857 09 25	UT, Salt Lake City
Degrey .... Maria	Smith .... Charles N.	1857 12 20	UT, Salt Lake City
Degrey .... Sarah	Dixon .... Henry A.	1865 01 21	
Degrey .... Selina	Hall .... John Charles	1853 04 26	ENG, Dudley
Degroat .... Elizabeth	Oakley .... Ezra	1816	NY, Gravesend
Dellow .... Sara	Badcock (Web) ... William	1866 05 21	ENG, Litlington
DeMill .... Adelia	Squire .... John P.	1852 12 31	UT, Manti
Demill .... Mariah	Funk .... Daniel B.	1841 04 22	IL, Adams Co.
Demille .... Lora Ann	Gifford .... Samuel K.	1848 10 01	IA
Demont .... Abigail	Smith .... Jeremiah	1817	
Dempsey .... Clarissa	Fackrell .... Joseph C.	1845 08 28	MI, Bertrand
Dence .... Frances	Stevens .... Isaac	1846	ENG
Denley .... Ann	Cook .... John	1836	ENG, Compton
Denley .... Ann	Wixey .... William		
Dennings .... Margaret	Murphy .... Emanuel Masters	1864 04	
Dennis .... Delia C. C.	Beers .... William	1868 08 08	UT, Salt Lake City
Dennis .... Dorothy Jane	McGee .... Franklin	1855 08	UT, Salt Lake City
Dennis .... Dorothy Jane	Rainey .... David Pinkney	1857 02 09	UT, Provo
Dennis .... Eunice	Wilbur .... Melvin	1824 02 15	RI
Densley .... Ann	Bowen .... John Morris	1872 02 26	UT, Salt Lake City
Densley .... Mary	Bowen .... John Morris	1883 09 13	UT, Salt Lake City
Denton .... Sarah	Moulton .... Thomas	1840 04 18	ENG
Derby .... Elvira	Mecham .... Moses Worthen	1827 11 08	
Derby .... Polly	Mecham .... Ephraim	1828 11 29	PA, Mercer
Dermott .... Susan Ann	Barker .... John Henry	1862 06 28	NE, Florence
Derrick .... Mary Ann S.	Gale .... James	1854 01 01	UT, Salt Lake City
Desaules .... Adele	Blair .... Isaac	1899 12 13	
Desaules .... Adele	Stratton .... Edward	1863 06 21	
Despain .... Ella Eugenia	Boyce .... John	1879 01 30	
Despain .... Margaret Jane	Tadlock .... Edwin B.	1847 05 23	IL, Calhoun Co.
Dessoulavy ...... Marie Elizabeth	DeSaules .... Daniel H.	1818 02 17	Switzerland

Female	Male	Date	Place
Deuel ....Mercy Ann	Roundy...............Myron S.	1864 12 03	UT, Salt Lake City
Deuel ....Minerva A.	Porter ....Alma	1855 11 15	UT, Centerville
Devoe ....Sarah Ann	Woolf...................John A.	1831 04 30	NY, New York
Dewey ....Wealthy	Richards..............Phineas	1818 02 24	MA, Richmond
Dewsnup ....Ann	Campbell............Orson Grant	1871 05 21	
Dewsnup ....Ann	Warner ....Holstein M.	1866 01	
Dexter..............Matilda	Saxton.................Solomon	1848 10 26	ENG
Dibble ....Ida Elizabeth	Hatch...................Orson Samuel	1870 12 12	UT, Salt Lake City
Dibble ....Julia Frances	Atwood ....Walter Henry	1865 07 08	UT, Salt Lake City
Dick ....Janet	Frame...................Archibald	1864 09 23	Scotland
Dickey..............Margaret	Bickmore ....David	1793 08 31	ME, Knox Co.
Dietschweiler ...Anna Maria	Gubler ....Heinrich	1861 10 18	
Dietschweiler ...Anna Maria	Hess....................Johannes	1850 01 17	
Dietzel ....Adelgunda	Heiner ....Johann Martin	1838 01 06	
Dillabaugh ....Julia Ann	Zufelt ....Henry	1833	
Dille ....Ruth Caroline	Ricks ....Thomas Edwin	1863 12 06	
Dilworth ....Elizabeth	Nebeker ....George	1851 02 13	
Dilworth ....Harriet W.	Brinton.................David	1848 01 14	NE
Dilworth ....Harriet W.	Yearsley ....David D.		
Dilworth ....Lavina W.	Harper.................Charles Alfred	1839 12 19	PA
Dilworth ....Maria Louisa	Leonard...............John Chatfield	1855 02 22	
Dilworth ....Maria Louisa	Nebeker ....George	1863 08 29	
Dilworth ....Martha Ann	Neff ....Amos H.	1848 04 15	UT, Salt Lake City
Dilworth ....Mary Jane	Hammond ....Francis A.	1848 11 17	UT, Salt Lake City
Ditchfield..........Mary	Hopkins ....Ezekiel	1861 11 16	
Ditchfield..........Mary	Mather.................James H.	1840 03 03	ENG
Ditchfield..........Mary	Oldfield...............John	1857 12 27	
Ditlevsen..........Mette Kirstine	Nielsen ....Peter	1854 04 02	Denmark
Dixon ....Emma Jane	Douglass ....Samuel	1874 10 26	UT, Salt Lake City
Dixon ....Isabella	Walker.................Henry		ENG
Dixon ....Martha	Simons................Orawell	1846 10 11	OH, Kirtland
Dixon ....Mary	Wardle.................James	1866 02 03	UT, Salt Lake City
Dixon ....Mary Adelma	Nebeker ....Ammon	1874 02 23	UT, Salt Lake City
Dixon ....Mary Ann	Wightman............Charles B.	1843 11 26	OH, Kirtland
Dixon ....Sarah	Walker.................Samuel F.	1864 05 23	UT, Salt Lake City
Dodd ....Elizabeth	Clegg...................Benjamin	1850	UT, Salt Lake City
Dodd ....Elizabeth	White...................Jonathan	1835 11 03	ENG
Dodge..............Sarah Melissa	Willis...................Joshua Thomas	1848 07 22	
Doidge ....Mary Ann	Barker ....Joseph	1860 06 11	ENG
Doidge ....Mary Ann	Dunton ....James Harvey	1878 06 14	UT, St. George
Dolby ....Maria Amanda	Skeen..................Joseph	1835 09 08	PA, Lancaster
Dollinger ....Christiana	Pyper...................Alexander C.	1855 12 24	NE, Florence
Donaghe...........Diannah Lovina	Rogers ....Ruel Mills	1853 12 08	MO, Enterprise
Donald ....Catherine	Pymm..................John	1870	
Donald ....Catherine	Rankin.................Richard	1859 11 28	Scotland
Donald ....Isabella	Forsyth ....Thomas R.	1839 04 01	Scotland
Donely ....Elizabeth	Maxwell ....Ralph	1823 07 13	ENG
Dorney.............Hannah	Wadley ....Joseph	1856 11 15	UT
Dorris...............Drusilla	Hendricks ....James	1827 05 31	
Dorsey ....Eliza	Ashworth.............Benjamin	1839 06 02	ENG, Yorkshire
Dorwart ....Elizabeth	Sabin ....David	1832 02 19	PA, Lancaster
Doty ....Eliza	Brown..................Alfred	1848 04 30	
Doty ....Eliza	Cravath ....Austin	1828 12 25	NY, Gainsville
Doty ....Eliza	Kimball ....Heber Chase	1856 04 11	

Female	Male	Date	Place
Doty ....Eliza	Murray ....William Ellis	1846 02 03	
Douglas ....Isabella	Pincock ....John Jr.	1851 02 03	MO, St. Louis
Dowding ....Elizabeth	Gardner..............Archibald	1867 03 02	UT, Salt Lake City
Dowding ....Elizabeth	Hall.....................Allen	1875 01 29	UT, Salt Lake City
Dowdle ....Sarah Ann	Mathis ....John Thomas	1849	IA, Council Bluffs
Downer ....Lydia	Gates ....Samuel Jr.	1830 02 04	
Downs ....Amy Emily	Smith.................Absolom W.	1840 11 05	
Doxey ....Mary	Bunting ....John Slater	1865 10 20	UT, Salt Lake City
Doxey ....Mary	Reed ....Charles	1843 03 06	ENG
Drabble...........Sarah	Davis ....Edward W.	1822 01 13	ENG, London
Drabwell ....Jemima	Hough ....William	1833 05	ENG
Drabwell ....Jemima	Rushby..............George	1814 01 17	ENG
Drake..............Elizabeth J.	Ballam ....Henry R.	1852 07 13	ENG, London
Drake..............Elizabeth J.	Davis ....Daniel George	1860 04 29	
Drake..............Elizabeth J.	Roundy...............Jared Curtis	1879 01 17	
Drake..............Lucy	Aldous ....Charles	1860 11 26	UT, Ogden
Draper ....Amanda E. M.	Smith.................Asa Downs	1866 03 24	UT, Draper
Draper ....Jane	Bulkley ....Newman	1844 01 07	IL, Nauvoo
Draper ....Lovina	Van Leuven.........Cornelius	1823 05 01	Canada
Draper ....Mary	Daybell ....Finity	1841 03 09	ENG, Falkingham
Draper ....Phebe	Brown................Ebenezer	1842 08 26	IL, Pike
Draper ....Phebe	Palmer...............George	1815	Canada
Draycott ....Hannah	Bates.................John	1837 05 16	ENG, Stapenhill
Drayson ....Ann	Bramall..............William	1849 11 26	ENG
Driggs ....Jane	Hyde..................Rosel James	1865 03 10	UT, Salt Lake City
Driggs ....Louisa	Purnell...............Shem	1855 09 22	UT, Kaysville
Driggs ....Maria	Bennett..............Thomas	1862 01 14	UT, Kaysville
Driver..............Mary Ann E.	Burton ....Joseph F.	1886 03 30	UT, Logan
Drollinger ....Clarissa Jane	Moore.................John Harvey	1841 10 06	IL, Nauvoo
Druce..............Lilly Harriet A.	Lambert..............Charles John	1867 10 26	UT, Salt Lake City
Drummond.......Margaret	Hoggan ....George W.	1843 10 30	Scotland
Drury...............Permelia H.	Morrill ....Laban	1844 02 22	IL, Nauvoo
Dubois ....Elizabeth	Grant..................George D.	1851 02 02	UT, Salt Lake City
Dubois ....Elizabeth	Lamb..................Benjamin Rush	1842 09 26	PA, Philadelphia
Dubois ....Hannah Ann	Dibble.................Philo		
Dubois ....Hannah Ann	Ells		
Dubois ....Hannah Ann	Smith.................Joseph Jr.		
Duel ....Amanda Ann	Starr ....Edward W.	1841 10 14	IL, Quincy
Duff.................Helen	Dick...................David	1867 06	Scotland
Duff.................Helen	Frame.................Archibald	1882 03 13	UT, Salt Lake City
Duffin ....Martha Ann	Bardsley ....William	1868 06 08	UT, Gunnison
Dufresne ....Elizabeth Jane	Stevenson ....Edward	1855	
Dugard............Sarah Ann	Crowther ....George	1833	ENG
Duncan ....Jane	Park....................William	1828	
Duncan ....Matilda Ann	Coltrin................Henry Clay	1906 05 02	
Duncan ....Matilda Ann	Stoddard ....Charles H.	1858 03 31	
Duncan ....Matilda Ann	Winters...............William	1876	
Duncan ....Susan	Henrie ....Joseph	1852 01 29	UT, Salt Lake City
Duncombe ....Sarah	Cook...................Melvin Darwin	1870 12 19	UT, Salt Lake City
Dunford............Lydia	Alder..................George Alfred	1864 04 01	MO, St. Louis
Dunkley ....Frances	Dickerson ....William	1820 01 05	ENG, Bedford
Dunn...............Elizabeth	Nerdin ....Thomas	1837 10 22	ENG
Dunn...............Elizabeth	Stubbs...............Peter	1856 10 19	UT, Salt Lake City
Dunn...............Maria	Curtis.................Benjamin G.	1825 03 24	OH, Brown Co.,

Female	Male	Date	Place
Dunn..............Mary	Ensign................Martin Luther	1852 01 08	UT, Salt Lake City
Dunning..........Eunice	Holbrook.............Chandler	1831 06 22	NY, Wethersfield
Dunsdon..........Sarah Ann	Bird.....................Charles	1853 02 03	
Durbin.............Avarilla	Casper................William	1809 05 06	OH, Knox Co.
Durfee.............Delana	Dudley................William Davis	1838 10 28	MO, Far West
Durfee.............Delana	Ford....................William	1845 08 03	IL, Nauvoo
Durfee.............Dolly	Garner................David	1842 10 18	IL, Lima
Durfee.............Ellen Eliza	Penrod................Abraham	1870 06 05	
Durfee.............Emma	Bassett................Loren Elias	1865 12 24	
Durfee.............Marion B.	Lemons................George		
Durfee.............Marion B.	Miller..................Henry		
Durfee.............Martha	Stevens..............Lyman	1836 06 21	OH, Kirtland
Durfee.............Melinda	Hatch..................Josephus	1822 12 06	
Durfee.............Tamma	Curtis..................Enos	1850 10 20	UT, Salt Lake City
Durfee.............Tamma	Curtis..................John White	1857 04 07	UT, Salt Lake City
Durfee.............Tamma	Miner..................Albert	1831 08 09	OH, Huron
Durham............Charlotte L.	Bowen................Israel	1825	NY
Durham............Charlotte L.	Dalton.................Simon C.	1872	
Durham............Charlotte L.	Hawkes..............Joseph Bryant	1850	
Durham............Charlotte L.	Haws..................Peter	1852	
Durham............Sarah	Morris.................William	1848 08 20	ENG, Lancashire
Durham............Tempey	McCauslin..........Jesse		
Durnford..........Sarah Ann	Towler................Daniel	1867 08 17	UT, Salt Lake City
Durose.............Mary	Stott...................William	1855 12 27	UT, Fillmore
Durrant............Jane	Adams................Thomas	1868 12 18	UT, Porterville
Dusall..............Mary	Wright.................James	1819 08 17	ENG
Dusenberry......Martha Jane	Glazier................Charles Dean	1864 10 04	UT, Provo
Dutson.............Florence V.	Nielson...............Niels Peter	1878 03 14	UT, Salt Lake City
Dutson.............Jane Ann	Melville..............Alexander	1848 05 29	NE
Dutson.............Rebecca D.	Jacobson............Ole Hans	1878 03 14	UT, Salt Lake City
Dutson.............Susanna	Burrup................Edward	1798 03 28	ENG, St. Clement
Dutton.............Sophia	Boren.................Willis	1857 12 10	
Dutton.............Sophia	DeGraw..............Jacob	1833 08 24	
Dwight............Elizabeth	Mott...................Samuel	1807 12 24	VT, Rutland
Dyas................Mary Ann E.	Watmough..........William	1839 03 05	ENG
Dye.................Harriet	Bunting..............James Lovett	1859 05 15	
Dyer................Julia Maria	Strong................William J.	1852 04 04	MO, St. Louis
Dyer................Mary	Glade.................James	1855 12 25	
Dykes.............Eliza Jane	Burgess..............Hyrum	1852	
Dykes.............Eliza Jane	Summers.............Nicholas	1857 09 11	UT, Salt Lake City
Dykes.............Eliza Jane	Taft.....................Seth	1859 01 24	UT, Salt Lake City
Dykman..........Maria Alida	Bess...................James L.	1870 03 14	UT, Salt Lake City
Dykman..........Maria Alida	Mawson..............Robert	1917	
Dykman..........Olive Cornelia	Morris.................Samuel Abraham	1876	
Dyre................Jane	Reid....................William	1826	IRE

E

Female	Male	Date	Place
Eagles.............Hannah Maria	Harris.................Robert	1825 09 28	ENG
Eagles.............Mary Ann	Riddle.................Isaac	1863 08 29	
Eames.............Juletta	Hancock.............Alvah B.	1823	
Eames.............Mary Ann	Carver................John	1850 03 10	Ocean
Eames.............Sarah Ann	Carver................John	1871 01 09	UT, Salt Lake City

Female	Male	Date	Place
Earl ....Nancy Minerva	Leavitt ....George	1857 07 11	UT, Salt Lake City
Earney ....Mary Ena	Loynd ....James	1876 03 15	UT, Salt Lake City
Eastcott ....Mary	Moyes ....William	1840 10 03	ENG
Easters ....Nancy Judd	Murphy ....Emanuel Masters	1831 04 05	SC, Union Co.
Eastman ....Sylvia Savonia	Hatch..................Lorenzo Hill	1851 02 28	UT, Salt Lake City
Ebbesen ....Anne Marie	Olsen..................Jes	1801	Denmark
Eberson ....Priscilla	Higley ....Myron Spencer	1826 06	
Eccles ....Martha	Tullis..................David Wilson	1863	UT, Pinto
Eccles ....Mary Ann	Robinson............Richard S.	1860	
Eckersall..........Lettice Brown	Crossley ....William	1835	ENG, Pilkington
Eckersall..........Lettice Brown	Redford ....Robert Patefield	1841 04 12	ENG
Eckersley.........Fannie	Brown..................John Weaver	1859 11	
Eckersley.........Fannie	Draper.................William Lathrop	1864	
Eckersley.........Mary Ann	Rigby..................William F.	1871	
Eckersley.........Sophia	Rigby..................William F.	1865 06 25	
Eddie ....Janet	Sim.....................William	1846 06 08	Scotland
Eddins ....Jessie	Tripp...................Enoch B.	1857 03 20	UT, Salt Lake City
Eddins ....Louisa Ann	Hales..................George	1852 10 17	UT, Salt Lake City
Edds ....Mary	Hopkins..............Charles	1852 10 11	UT, Salt Lake City
Edds ....Mary	Skinner...............Richard E.	1844	ENG
Eddy ....Wealthy	Patten................William Cornwall	1854	UT, Payson
Eddy ....Wealthy	Pratt ....William D.	1841 03 01	OH, Kirtland
Eddy ....Wealthy	Shumway ....Stephen B.	1831 01 06	
Edge ....Elsie	Booth..................Richard T.	1846 08 13	ENG, Bedford
Edgeley ....Sarah B.	Parker.................William Cope	1855 05 13	UT, Salt Lake City
Edmonds ....Mary Jane	Harrison ....George R.	1846 08 30	ENG, London
Edmundston ....Margaret	Bonner ....George Jr.	1849 10 22	Scotland
Edward ....Elizabeth	Robertson ....John	1823 07 27	Scotland
Edwards ....Elizabeth	Hanks.................George William	1865 07 23	UT, Paragonah
Edwards ....Margaret	Wood..................Daniel C.		
Edwards ....Margaret J.	Haskell ....Thales	1857	UT, Salt Lake City
Edwards ....Mary	Hubbard ....Charles W.	1856 02	UT, Salt Lake City
Edwards ....Rhoby	Perry ....Stephen	1816 04 12	VT, Sherburne
Egbert..............Susanna	Jerman...............Daniel Smith	1877 12 17	UT, Salt Lake City
Egbert..............Susanna	Van Etten ....Elijah W.	1864 06 04	UT, Salt Lake City
Eggler..............Margaretha	Abplanalp ....Peter	1856 11 30	Switzerland
Egli ....Anna Katherina	Bosshard............Johannes	1840 10 12	Switzerland
Ekins................Sarah Rebecca	Walker................William J.	1855 03 26	ENG
Eklund ....Maria M.	Sandell...............Nils	1826 09 28	Sweden
Eldredge ....Diana Tanner	Smoot................Abraham Owen	1855 05 06	UT, Salt Lake City
Eldredge ....Esther Ann	Garn ....Thomas	1868 03 14	UT, Salt Lake City
Eldredge ....Philinda	Keeler................Daniel Hutchinson	1843 02 06	IL, Nauvoo
Eldredge ....Philinda	Merrick ....Levi Newton	1827 11 18	VT, Addison Co.
Eldridge ....Ellen Eliza	Harrison ....John Heber	1870 10 24	UT, Salt Lake City
Eliason.............Johanna	Worthington.........Stephen S.	1867 12 30	UT, Tooele Co.
Eliasson...........Anna Christina	Dayley ....Jacob	1879 01 09	UT, Salt Lake City
Elliker..............Margaretha	Klingensmith ....Phillip		
Elliker..............Margaretha	Unthank..............William		
Ellingson..........Anna	Olsen..................Christian	1859 05 20	Ocean
Elliot...............Nancy Urania	Wight..................Lewis	1827 12 10	NY, Centerville
Elliott..............Eliza Anne	Baker.................Henry Walker	1851 01 05	ENG, London
Elliott..............Elizabeth	Manning ....Willard Callard	1843 06 12	ENG
Elliott..............Roxcy Lucina	Keller.................Alva	1833 07 23	
Elliott..............Sarah Ann	Skidmore...........Henry Brett	1854 06 04	PA, Philadelphia

Female	Male	Date	Place
Ellis................Annie	Yeates................Richard	1873 12 15	UT, Salt Lake City
Ellis................Hannah Louise	Harrison.............William	1836 07 24	ENG
Ellis................Martha	Harvey................James		
Ellis................Mary	Thomas.............Emanuel	1857	PA
Ellis................Mary Ann	Cragun.............Wilford Elisha	1871 01 02	UT, Salt Lake City
Ellis................Mary Ann	Hatch................Meltiar	1856 05 06	UT, Salt Lake City
Ellison.............Elizabeth	Rigby................Aaron	1824 07 25	
Ellison.............Jane Ann	Park................Andrew Duncan	1868 03 14	
Ellison.............Mary	Evans................John Jr.	1854 12 25	MO, St. Louis
Ellison.............Mary	Sutton................John		
Ellwood...........Ann	Morris................Charles	1845 07	ENG
Ellwood...........Ann	White................James	1885	UT, Salt Lake City
Ellwood...........Ellen	Goff................Heber	1874 05 03	UT, Salt Lake City
Ellyer..............Lucy	Fullmer.............Junius Sextus	1866 09 16	UT, Salt Lake City
Elsey...............Mary Ann	Bradshaw...........Samuel	1852	UT, Salt Lake City
Elsey...............Susannah	Tanner................Thomas	1853 10 23	UT, Salt Lake City
Elsmore..........Maria	Ellis................Alexander G.	1863 05 14	ENG
Elston.............Nancy Jane	Hammer.............Austin	1826 12 26	IN, Wayne Co.
Elwood...........Mahala	Bell................Thomas	1854	UT, Salt Lake City
Embling..........Alice	Shingleton...........Stephen		
Embling..........Maria	Shingleton...........Stephen	1866 11	UT, Salt Lake City
Emmett...........Harriet	Riley................James	1844	ENG, Lancaster
Emmett...........Mary Jane	Holden................Willey H.	1843 05 11	IL, Nauvoo
Emmett...........Mary Jane	Moffett................Armstead	1845	
Emms.............Mary Ann	Hobbs................Charles W.	1854 08 28	ENG
Enderby..........Louisa Carritt	Halls................William	1861 04 15	ENG
Ennis..............Elizabeth	Daley................John	1809	
Ensign............Julia Searles	Woolley.............John W.	1851 03 20	UT, Salt Lake City
Epperson........Martha Jane	Busenbark..........Henry D.	1852 06	IA, Honey Creek
Eramusson......Gudney	Bjarnson.............Manus	1862 12 13	
Erasmuson......Gudney	Hafledasson........Arna	1828 10 04	Iceland
Ericksen..........Albertina	Peterson.............Solomon	1872 01 08	
Ericksen..........Anna Elizabeth	Laub................George	1856	UT, Salt Lake City
Ericksen..........Anne Mette	Madsen.............Hans Peter	1863 12 19	UT, Salt Lake City
Ericksen..........Karen Sophia	Mickelsen...........Jens	1857	
Ericksen..........Karen Sophia	Nielsen.............Niels Christen	1842 01 25	Denmark
Ericksen..........Kirsten M.	Benson.............Jens Peter	1857 10 16	UT, Lehi
Ericksen..........Kirsten M.	Sabin................Henry Dorwart		
Ericksen..........Mette Christina	Benson.............Jens Peter	1855 04 15	UT, Salt Lake City
Erickson..........Christina	Heder................Johannes O.	1845	Sweden
Erickson..........Elsie	Anderson...........William O.	1866 03 30	UT, Salt Lake City
Erickson..........Joanna Matilda	Despain.............Henry Waters	1879 05 24	
Erickson..........Joanna Matilda	Westover...........Edwin L.	1874 04 27	
Erickson..........Josephine	Halverson...........Oliver H.	1881 02 17	UT, Gunnison
Erickson..........Josephine C.	Nielsen.............Hans I.	1866 11 05	UT, Salt Lake City
Ericksson........Anna Marie	Eliason.............Andreas P.	1863 09 12	UT, Salt Lake City
Ericksson........Helena	Rosberg.............Carl	1849 04 07	Sweden
Eriksen...........Elizabeth	Hansen................Christian	1850 11 01	Denmark
Eriksen...........Elizabeth	Nielsen.............Andrew B.	1865 04 01	UT, Hyrum
Eriksen...........Nicoline	Jensen................Hans Peter	1859 11 06	UT, Salt Lake City
Erskine...........Jessie	Hunter................William	1880 11 04	UT, Salt Lake City
Esbjornsson.....Anna	Anderson...........Gustave	1858 03 22	UT, Salt Lake City
Eskelson.........Johanna Maria	Adams................Samuel Ferry	1878 11 28	UT, Richmond
Eskelson.........Johanna Maria	Allsop................John	1867 03 16	UT, Salt Lake City

Female	Male	Date	Place
Eskildsen.........Maren Katrina	Bowman..............Hyrum W.	1867 05 25	UT, Salt Lake City
Eskland............Emma J.	Hansen................Hans Petrus A.	1884 01 14	UT, Scipio
Esklund............Anna Marie C.	Wasden...............Frederick	1865 10 18	UT, Gunnison
Esklund............Elizabeth	Peterson.............Carl M.	1880 11 04	
Essom ....Frances	Clayson..............Thomas	1835 11 02	
Etherington ......Mary	Stanger..............George	1855 02 13	ENG
Evans ....Alice	Anthony..............John	1835 02 23	Wales
Evans ....Alice	Davies................David	1826 04 10	Wales
Evans ....Alice	Rhees.................David Edward	1853 02 13	Ocean
Evans ....Amelia	Camp ....Richard	1857	UT, Salt Lake City
Evans ....Amelia	Davis ....William	1864 12	UT, Salt Lake City
Evans ....Ann	Brown.................Robert	1852 11 18	ENG, Bristol
Evans ....Ann	Jones ....John Rodderick	1857 01 05	ENG, Tredegar
Evans ....Ann	Rogers ....Thomas	1850	MO, St. Louis
Evans ....Anna	Jenkins................David	1842 11 19	Wales
Evans ....Anna	Williams..............Thomas	1853	
Evans ....Catherine V.	Parry ....Caleb	1849 02 26	ENG, Liverpool
Evans ....Elizabeth	Hollingshead.......Nelson	1861 06 29	UT, Salt Lake City
Evans ....Elizabeth	Hughes...............Peter	1854 03 04	Wales
Evans ....Elizabeth	Paul....................James Patten	1862 10 25	UT, Salt Lake City
Evans ....Elizabeth	Sadler.................James	1857 01 25	UT, Salt Lake City
Evans ....Emma	Nalder ....William New	1869 05 03	UT, Salt Lake City
Evans ....Hannah	Bowen.................Thomas	1834	Wales
Evans ....Hannah	Giles...................Thomas Davis		
Evans ....Joanne	Goodworth ....Richard	1866	
Evans ....Joanne	Woolstenhulme ...William	1897	
Evans ....Louisa	Wilson ....John Ross	1884 07 10	UT, Salt Lake City
Evans ....Lydia	Matheson ....Alexander	1864 08 01	
Evans ....Margaret	Morse.................William	1859 10 08	
Evans ....Mary	Baker..................Thomas	1817 10 13	ENG, Warwick
Evans ....Mary Alice	Williams..............James H.	1884 06 10	UT, Salt Lake City
Evans ....Mary Elizabeth	Woodbury............John Taylor	1883 10 19	UT, St. George
Evans ....Rachel Jones	Harris ....John	1855 08 12	
Evans ....Rachel Jones	Roberts ....William	1848	Wales
Evans ....Rachel Jones	Rowland..............William		
Evans ....Sarah	Jeremy ....Thomas Evans	1838 03 16	Wales
Evensen ....Anniken J.	Borresen ....Niels H.	1864 02	
Evensen ....Ingeborg R.	Gardner..............Neil	1863 01 10	UT, Salt Lake City
Evensen ....Mathie	Severson.............Halvar	1850 11 28	Norway
Everett ....Ann E. A.	White..................John Stout	1849 04 05	UT, Salt Lake City
Everington ....Ann Reed	Dustin.................Seth	1870	
Everington ....Ann Reed	Nichols ....John William	1863 02	UT
Everington ....Ann Reed	Roberts ....Benjamin	1848 06 05	ENG, Poplar
Everington ....Ann Reed	Wooley................John W.	1886	UT
Ewell...............Barbara Ann	Evans ....David	1841 11 23	IL
Ewell...............Pirene Brown	Jameson ....Alexander	1853 08 07	UT, Provo
Ewer ....Mary Jane	Palmer................James	1867 08 10	UT, Salt Lake City
Eynon ....Martha	Reese.................David	1855	Ocean

F

| Faasch............Maria | Germer...............Johann M. J. T. | 1834 04 01 | |
| Fackrell..........Juliette | Howard..............James | 1869 04 19 | UT, Salt Lake City |

Female	Male	Date	Place
Fahy ....Catherine	Martin ....Josiah Fleming	1859 11 03	
Fairchild ....Polly Tryphena	Bryson ....Samuel	1867 05 25	UT, Salt Lake City
Fall....................Ann	Freestone............Thomas	1837 08 01	Canada
Fall....................Ann	Hodnett ....Andrew	1861 08 05	UT, Alpine
Fallas ....Mary Catherine	Wilson ....James	1826 05 02	ENG
Fallowell ....Eliza	Wilkerson ....Thomas	1826	
Farmer.............Elizabeth Ann	Butterfield...........Almon	1866 01 27	UT, Salt Lake City
Farnes ....Mary Ann	Wellard................James Elias		Ocean
Farnsworth ......Laura	Frampton............Nathaniel	1824 05 27	OH, Burlington
Farnsworth ......Laura	Owens ....Owen Asa	1838	
Farnsworth ......Louisa Caroline	Shipp..................Austin	1835 05 05	IN, Blue River
Farnsworth ......Lydia	Mayhew..............Elijah	1832 10 02	
Farr..................Frances	Mills...................Charles Edmond	1832 04 17	ENG, Lancashire
Farr..................Frances	Palmer................Thomas	1865 02 09	
Farrar...............Catherine E.	Wheelwright ....Matthew	1860 08 15	UT, Salt Lake City
Farrell ....Mary	Thacker ....John Pridgen		
Farrell ....Teresa Ann	Duncan...............John C.	1872 05 27	UT, Cedar City
Farrow ....Mary	Dodds.................Thomas	1868 02 29	UT, Salt Lake City
Farrow ....Mary	Wilson ....Charles	1851 02 09	ENG, Hazelrigg
Faster ....Anna	Loosle ....Hans Casper		
Faucett ....Amanda A.	Sanders..............Moses M.	1826 01 12	TN, Maury
Faucett ....Eliza McKee	Ivie ....James R.	1824 06	TN, Maury Co.
Faulkner ....Ann	Taylor.................John	1855 09 18	ENG, Cheshire
Faulkner ....Louisa	Babcock ....William Lorenzo	1889 06 18	
Faulkner ....Louisa	Loveland ....Chester	1868 09 05	UT, Salt Lake City
Faulkner ....Sarah	Taylor.................John	1860 12	UT, Salt Lake City
Faulkner ....Susann	Harper ....Richard	1849 08 16	ENG, Anwick
Fausett ....Harriet C.	Bean...................James Addison	1853 02 10	UT, Provo
Fausett ....Narcissus R.	Barkdull.............Isaiah Jones		
Fausett ....Narcissus R.	Lott....................Cornelius Peter	1846 01 22	
Fausett ....Narcissus R.	Saunsosee ....Louis	1849	IA
Fawcett............Hannah Isabell	Nixon..................James William	1876 02 21	UT, Salt Lake City
Fawson............Ann Marie	Cooke.................Charles M.	1865 12 24	
Fawson............Jane	Williams..............Thomas P.	1859 06 27	
Fell...................Catherine H.	Squires ....John P.	1843 08 21	ENG, Putney
Fellows ....Phoebe Louisa	Hunt ....Emanuel	1857 03	UT, Salt Lake City
Fellows ....Phoebe Louisa	Hunt ....Levi	1863 04 01	UT, Gunnison
Felshaw...........Caroline	Stevens ....David Riley	1862 12 24	
Felt ....Margaret Eliza	West...................Thomas C.	1874 11 10	UT, Salt Lake City
Feltman...........Anna Barbara	Johnson ....John Peter	1863 11 21	UT, Salt Lake City
Fenn ....Sarah	Thompson...........William	1857	UT, Provo
Fenner.............Mary Ann	Taylor.................John Benjamin	1837 10 25	ENG, Worcester
Fenner.............Prudence	Fairchild ....Joshua Jr.	1827	OH, Marion
Fenner.............Prudence	Kinyon ....Aldric		
Fenner.............Prudence	Markham............Stephen	1846 01 30	IL, Nauvoo
Ferguson ....Agnes Reid	Lewis..................Frederick	1865 01 28	UT, Spanish Fork
Ferguson ....Elizbaeth Ann	Holyoak..............George Jr.	1866 10 09	UT, Salt Lake City
Ferguson ....Jane	Jenkins...............David	1807	
Ferguson ....Margaret D.	McMasters ....William Athol	1842 09 02	Scotland
Ferguson ....Sarah	McDonald...........James	1826	IRE
Ferron..............Mary Harrison	Rogerson ....William	1826 12 23	ENG, Preston
Fewkes ....Catherine	Hicken ....Thomas	1845 06 30	
Field................Ann	Jakeman ....James	1833 11 13	ENG
Field................Ann	Such (Search).....Joseph	1829	ENG

Female		Male		Date	Place
Field	Hannah	Hinchcliff	Elijah	1812 11 02	ENG
Field	Mary	Garner	William Jr.	1856 11 01	UT, Slaterville
Field	Susan	Alder	Alfred	1848 03 26	MO, St. Louis
Fielding	Ellen	Burton	William W.	1861 09 02	UT, Salt Lake City
Fielding	Hannah	Dunn	James	1861 01 10	UT, Salt Lake City
Fielding	Mary	Duffin	Isaac	1849 06 03	PA, Philadelphia
Fielding	Mary	Kimball	Heber Chase	1844 09 14	
Fielding	Mary	Smith	Hyrum	1837 12 24	OH, Kirtland
Fielding	Mercy Rachel	Smith	Hyrum	1843 08 11	IL, Nauvoo
Fielding	Mercy Rachel	Thompson	Robert B.	1837 06 04	OH, Kirtland
Fielding	Rachel	Burton	William W.	1856 03 28	UT, Salt Lake City
Fife	Agnes (Ann)	Bingham	Sanford	1863 10 10	UT, Salt Lake City
Fife	Janet	Johnson	Joel Hills	1845 10 25	OH, Kirtland
Fife	Janet	Mitchell	James	1840 01 13	Scotland
Fife	Margaret	Easton	John	1850	MO, Grovie
Fife	Margaret	Miller	David	1854 02 07	UT, Salt Lake City
Fifield	Almira	Quigley	Andrew	1865	
Filby	Mary	Barrett	John	1869 04 05	
Filby	Mary	Livermore	John	1835 11 29	
Filcher	Eliza	Chipman	William H.	1859	
Fillmore	Antha Elmira	Huish	Lorenzo Snow	1875 06 22	
Fillmore	Mary Jane	Lamb	James Orrin	1854 02 22	NY, Rochester
Fillmore	Miranda Ann	Cushing	William Ellis	1872 08 18	
Fillmore	Thankful R.	Johnson	Joseph E.	1869	UT, Spring Lake
Finch	Christiana	Winn	John	1828	
Finch	Hannah B.	Merriam	Edwin Parker	1831 11 05	
Finch	Hannah B.	Morley	Isaac	1844	IL, Nauvoo
Finch	Rebecca Jane	Argyle	Joseph	1840 12 24	ENG, Birmingham
Findlay	Janet	Park	William	1850 04 07	UT
Findley	Agnes	Park	James Pollock	1849 09 21	UT, Big Cotton.
Fink	Catherine R.	Foy	Thomas Birk		
Finley	Sarah	Hardy	Samuel B.	1854 07 02	UT, Salt Lake City
Finley	Sarah	Merrill	Charles	1834 10 12	MO, Lewis Co.
Firman	Susanna	Todd	James	1828 06 01	
Firth	Emily Mary	Firth	Arthur	1869 11 25	UT, South Weber
Firth	Mary Ann	Dorius	Lewis Olsen	1862 10 04	UT, Salt Lake City
Fish	Ann	Bell	John Watson	1834 10	ENG
Fish	Mary Hill	Wright	John P.	1825 07 31	ENG
Fish	Sarah	McGregor	William Campbell	1857 04 28	UT, Salt Lake City
Fish	Sarah	Smith	John Calvin L.	1846 05 12	IL, Nauvoo
Fisher	Caroline Kazia	Wardle	George	1868 12 15	UT, Salt Lake City
Fisher	Elizabeth V.	Thompson	John Crow	1870	
Fisher	Fannie Brittania	Lee	Ezekiel	1857 05 12	UT, Salt Lake City
Fisher	Lydia Rebecca	Babcock	Nathaniel	1880	UT, Spanish Fork
Fisher	Lydia Rebecca	Parsons	George	1853	
Fisher	Lydia Rebecca	Simmons	Leven	1856 02 21	UT, Spanish Fork
Fisher	Mary Ann	Andrew	Frederick C.	1854 11 19	
Fisher	Verena	Hofheins	Peter	1855	UT
Fisk	Amanda M.	Stout	Allen J.	1848 04 30	IA
Fiske	Sarah Beriah	Allen	Ezra Hale	1837 12 25	
Fiske	Sarah Beriah	Ricks	Joel	1852 10 26	
Fitzgerald	Lurena	Nebeker	John	1835 10 25	OH, Riley
Flake	Elizabeth	Rowan	Charles H.	1867 07 15	CA
Flatt	Ellen	Reeder	Robert		

Female	Male	Date	Place
Fleming............Elizabeth	Dunn ....William G.	1837 10 02	ENG, Lancashire
Fleming............Sarah Ann	Cluff.....................David Jr.	1851 03 19	UT, Salt Lake City
Fletcher ....Mary	Hepworth............Thomas	1848 08 27	ENG, Liverpool
Flint.................Hannah	Beesley ....William	1857 04 11	UT, Salt Lake City
Flint.................Hannah	Holbrook............Joseph	1843 01 01	IL, Nauvoo
Flint.................Mary	Call....................Anson	1833 10 03	OH, Lake Co.
Flitton..............Susan	Mumford.............George	1871 12 11	UT, Salt Lake City
Fluskey ....Charlotte	Curtis.................Theodore		
Folkman...........Christiane	Pihl ....Peder M.	1846 11 27	
Follett..............Sarah Ann	Fullmer ....Almon L.	1843 12 17	
Folsom.............Frances Emily	Wallace ....George E.	1873 10 16	UT, Salt Lake City
Folsom.............Harriet Amelia	Young.................Brigham	1863 01 24	UT, Salt Lake City
Forbush ....Lorana	Taylor ....Norman	1848 04 02	
Forbush ....Louisa Maria	Graham ....John Duren	1860 02 28	UT, Salt Lake City
Forbush ....Lydia	Taylor ....Norman	1850 11 22	UT, Salt Lake City
Ford ....Elizabeth	Sutton................Henry	1846 04 23	ENG
Ford ....Emma	Hatch.................Ransom Osborn	1863 05 15	
Ford ....Margaret Jane	Finley ....David		
Ford ....Margaret Jane	Johnson ....Aaron	1855 05 08	UT, Springville
Ford ....Mary Ann	Joyce.................Thomas	1838 02 13	ENG
Ford ....Mary Ann	Simmons ....George	1849 12 24	
Fordham ....Bithiah	Wells ....Lyman Briggs	1849 04 03	NE
Foreman ....Eliza Rebecca	Smith.................John	1862 12 28	UT, Salt Lake City
Foreman ....Louisa	Stanford ....Stephen	1856 05 16	ENG, Dover
Forrester..........Phoebe	Benson...............Richard	1844 06 30	
Forsyth ....Hannah H.	Beck ....Joseph Ellison	1835 12 17	PA, Philadelphia
Forsyth ....Jane Barker	Snyder...............James C.	1861 09 15	UT, Salt Lake City
Forsyth ....Margaret B.	Yates.................Hyrum B.	1874 01 26	UT, Salt Lake City
Forsyth ....Marianne	Seegmiller...........Charles W.	1868 02 01	UT, Salt Lake City
Foss.................Olive Carl	Woolley ....Franklin B.	1857 02 11	UT, Salt Lake City
Foss.................Sarah Elizabeth	Cowley ....Matthias	1857 10 17	
Foss.................Sarah Elizabeth	Fox....................Jesse Williams	1871 03 13	UT, Salt Lake City
Foster ....Eliza Arnette	Cluff...................Benjamin	1856 02 20	UT, Salt Lake City
Foster ....Elizabeth	Evans ....James R.	1851 04 15	ENG, Birmingham
Foster ....Emma E.	Floyd ....Leonard	1873 08 27	ID, St. Charles
Foster ....Louisa Maria	Russell ....Alonzo H.	1856 04 18	UT, Salt Lake City
Foster ....Lydia	Robinson............Joseph Lee	1853 02 16	UT, Salt Lake City
Foster ....Maria	Bennett..............Richard	1863	ENG, Birmingham
Foster ....Mary	Windley ....John	1861 04 15	ENG, Birmingham
Foster ....Sarah	Barton ....William Bell	1867 06 08	UT, Salt Lake City
Foster ....Sophia Minerva	Burgess..............Harrison	1835 07 01	OH, Kirtland
Foukes............Ann	Weight................James	1821	
Foulds.............Eliza	Parkin................William John	1864 08 18	UT, Bountiful
Foutz ....Catherine	White.................Samuel Steven	1849 09 27	UT, Salt Lake City
Foutz ....Elizabeth	Hess..................Jacob	1816	PA, Franklin Co.
Foutz ....Elizabeth	Walker................Henson	1846 04 10	IL, Nauvoo
Foutz ....Margaret	Walker................Henson	1857 11 09	
Fovargue ....Elizabeth	Smith.................James	1853 01 09	ENG
Fowkes ....Susannah H.	Marriott..............John	1842 03 18	ENG, Bedfordshire
Fowle..............Elizabeth Jane	Dawson.............Alexander	1860 02 22	South Africa
Fowler.............Jane Ann	Sparks...............Alfred	1853 01 30	Ocean
Fowler.............Keziah	Brandon ....George W.	1831 10 06	
Fowler.............Mary Caroline	King...................Eleazer Jr.	1853 04 27	UT, Salt Lake City
Fowlke ....Clara	Cullimore............James	1864 02 10	UT, Lindon

Female	Male	Date	Place
Fowlke ....Louisa	Marrott................William	1862 02 09	UT
Fowlke ....Louisa	Waldram................Lorenzo	1901 02 08	
Fox ....Elizabeth Mary	Graham ....George	1877 05 12	
Fox ....Elizabeth Mary	Larson ....Thurston	1859	
Fox ....Elizabeth Mary	Miller ....Robert	1889	
Fox ....Polly Maria	Shaw ....John	1812 01 01	NY, Victor
Foxall ....Mary	Chadwick ....Abraham	1850 12	
Foy ....Susannah	Chidester............John Peck	1851 10 23	UT, Salt Lake City
Frampton ....Eliza	Smith..................Phillip L.	1849 03 04	IA, Mt. Pisgah
Frampton ....Sarah	Smith..................Thomas C.	1850 01 03	IA, Mt. Pisgah
France ....Amanda M.	Rollins ....Steuben	1855 02 10	UT, Salt Lake City
Francis............Ann	Haynes................John	1863	
Francis............Elizabeth	Williams..............William		ENG
Francis............Elizabeth	Yates..................Thomas	1863 07 22	NE, Florence
Francis............Eunice	Neslen................Samuel	1829 07 13	ENG, Suffolk
Francis............Mary Ann	Green..................Charles	1862 11 24	
Francis............Sarah	Parsons..............William	1827 07 23	ENG
Francis............Sarah	Watton................James	1861 01 05	
Francom ....Mary Ann	Selman...............Charles	1870 04 04	UT, Payson
Frandson ....Johanne Marie	Halls..................William	1871	
Franklin...........Elizabeth	Betts..................Peter	1822 04 28	ENG, Middlesex
Franklin...........Ruth	Curtis..................Enos	1805 12 15	NY, New York
Frantzen ....Karen	Dorius.................John F. F.	1857 04 25	
Fredericksen....Maria	Larsen ....Soren	1854 12 10	Ocean
Fredricksen......Martine	Anderson............Charles A.	1865 11 02	UT, Salt Lake City
Fredriksen ....Anna Claudia	Merrill ....Samuel	1862 11 08	
Fredriksen ....Anna Claudia	Olson..................Christen		
Free ....Emeline	Young..................Brigham	1846 01 14	IL, Nauvoo
Freeman ....Caroline S.	Cutler ....Perley	1828 02 28	
Freeman ....Caroline S.	Hawkins ....Benjamin	1857 04 07	
Freeman ....Caroline S.	Thompson ....Ezra	1854 01 23	
Freeman ....Caroline S.	Van Valkenburg ..Peter	1850 10 17	
Freeman ....Eliza	Lewis..................Joseph	1844 08 11	ENG
Freeman ....Hannah	Heath ....Nicholas	1828 05 13	
Freeman ....Olive Hovey	Bingham..............Erastus Jr.	1843 10 29	IL, Nauvoo
Freeman ....Olive Hovey	Farr ....Winslow	1816 12 05	VT, Waterford
Freestone ....Elizabeth Ann	Jensen ....Lars Rove	1864 08 27	UT, Salt Lake City
Freestone ....Elizabeth Ann	Langston ....John	1857 03 07	
Freestone ....Emma Sarah	Whitby ....Thomas B.	1872 12 09	UT, Salt Lake City
French ....Eliza G.	Little ....Jesse Carter	1840 09 29	
Fretwell...........Mary Elizabeth	Davis..................Henry Tames	1864 04 23	UT, Salt Lake City
Frew ....Janet	Pitkin..................George Orrin	1867 05 18	UT, Salt Lake City
Frey ....Mary Aerny	Naef ....Johannes J. (Ira)	1860 05 29	NE, Florence
Friedlander ......Rosa Clara	Logie ....Charles J. G.	1853 05 21	Australia
Frisby..............Esther	Tuckett ....Henry	1870 11 14	UT, Salt Lake City
Frith ....Elizabeth	Clifton................Charles	1864 03 26	UT, Salt Lake City
Frith ....Elizabeth	Cook...................John	1839 03 01	ENG, Derbyshire
Frost ....Charlotte	Woodbury...........Jeremiah	1852 07 12	UT, Salt Lake City
Frost ....Christianna	Mitchell..............David Alexander	1858	
Frost ....Isabella P.	Hilton..................Hugh	1852 04 09	
Frost ....Margaret Elzira	Rawlins ....Harvey M.	1846 12 03	MO, Nishnabothna
Frost ....Martha M.	Akes ....Harmon J.	1839 03 14	IA, Jefferson Co.
Frost ....Martha M.	Langley ....George W.	1846 01 20	IL, Nauvoo
Frost ....Martha M.	Wiser..................John McCormick	1851	UT, Big Cotton.

Female	Male	Date	Place
Frost .... Mary Angeline	Adams .... Jerome J.	1854 01 29	IA, Freemont
Frost .... Mary Ann	Pratt .... Parley P.	1837 05 09	NY
Frost .... Mary Ann	Stearns .... Nathan	1831 04 01	ME, Bethel
Frost .... Mary Ellen	Rawlins .... Joseph S.	1844 02 01	IL, Hancock Co.
Frost .... Rachael	Hellewell .... Robert	1844 07 04	ENG
Fry .... Fanny	Simons .... Gustavus	1874 03	
Fry .... Fanny	Zundel .... John	1859 11 28	
Fryer .... Jane	Harrison .... Richard	1855 02 25	UT, Salt Lake City
Fryer .... Jane	Jorden .... Frank	1842	ENG
Fryer .... Mary Ann	Wright .... Joseph		
Fugl .... Kirsten Marie	Scow .... Peter Christen	1868 03 09	UT, Salt Lake City
Fulcher .... Mary Eade	Smith .... Elkanah A.	1863 07 18	UT, Salt Lake City
Fuller .... Lisania	Judd .... Hyrum	1844 06 27	IL, Warsaw
Fuller .... Martha Jane	Ellis .... John E.	1879	
Fuller .... Martha Jane	Jackson .... William	1846 11 19	
Fuller .... Mary Adelia	Lewis .... Jesse William	1855 12 27	IA, Des Moines
Fuller .... Mary Maria	Cook .... Daniel	1820	Canada
Fuller .... Zurviah Gleason	Eardley .... James	1852 03 15	MO, St. Louis
Fullmer .... Ann Adelaide	Dennis .... William T.	1857 09 06	UT, Salt Lake City
Fullmer .... Desdemona W.	Benson .... Ezra Taft	1846 01 21	IL, Nauvoo
Fullmer .... Desdemona W.	McLane .... Harrison Parker	1853 07 03	UT, Salt Lake City
Fullmer .... Desdemona W.	Smith .... Joseph Jr.	1842 07	IL, Nauvoo
Fullmer .... Elvira Martha	Hickenlooper ...... John T.	1856 11 16	UT, Salt Lake City
Fullmer .... Joanna Price	Bess .... James L.	1854	
Fullmer .... Joanna Price	Curtis .... Erastus	1860 02 14	UT, Spanish Fork
Fullmer .... Lavinia E.	Ashcraft .... James Eli	1859 01 23	UT, Springville
Fullmer .... Lavinia E.	Coates .... William B.	1855	
Fullmer .... Lavinia E.	Coltrin .... Zebedee	1857 02 25	
Fullmer .... Mary Ann	Lisonbee .... William W.	1864 02 16	UT, Springville
Fullmer .... Rhoda Ann	Chapman .... Hyrum	1871 04 10	UT, Salt Lake City
Fullmer .... Sarah Ann	Priday .... Thomas S.	1869 03 11	UT, Salt Lake City
Fullmer .... Susannah	Snyder .... Ephraim S.	1861 10 27	UT, Salt Lake City
Fullwell .... Ann	Robins .... Richard	1808 12 01	ENG
Fulmer .... Mary Amelia	Whittle .... Thomas L.	1833	
Funk .... Diddrikke H.	Harris .... George W.	1862 02 07	UT, Richmond
Funk .... Matilda K.	Folkman .... Jens Peter	1857 03 31	Denmark
Funnell .... Elizabeth	Wimmer .... William D.	1864 11 12	UT, Salt Lake City
Furrer .... Anna Regula	Cardon .... John	1856 10	
Furrer .... Elisabetha	Lattmann .... Hans Heinrich	1837	

G

Female	Male	Date	Place
Gabbitas .... Emma	Beardall .... Francis	1853 06 25	ENG, Yorkshire
Gadd .... Sarah	Tolley .... William F.	1869	
Gahrson .... Tarjer Serine	Evensen .... Henrik	1843 09 22	Norway
Gahrson .... Tarjer Serine	Gardner .... Archibald	1856 11 10	
Gailey .... Charlotte	Clark .... Thomas Henry	1825 11 28	
Gaither .... Jane	Thomas .... Daniel C.	1843	
Galbraith .... Margaret	Manning .... Henry William	1855 03 14	UT, Salt Lake City
Gallafent .... Elizabeth	Adamson .... William	1868 07 25	UT, Salt Lake City
Gallaher .... Elizabeth	Benson .... Ezra Taft	1853 06 04	UT, Salt Lake City
Galland .... Mary	Casto .... Abel	1812 06 03	
Galland .... Mary	Smith .... Thomas		

Female	Male	Date	Place
Gallant ....Betsy	Whittaker ....Andrew I.	1856 04 28	UT, Salt Lake City
Galloway ....Eliza	Lowe ....Thomas	1849 02 03	Scotland
Galloway ....Rebecca	Molland ....James W.	1837 09 23	ENG, Liverpool
Gardner ....Agnes	Gardner ....William		
Gardner ....Alice Ann	Barney................Alma	1871 09 22	UT, Kanarraville
Gardner ....Elizabeth	Higginson ....George B.		
Gardner ....Emily H. A.	Stratton ....James Albert	1864 07 03	UT, Virgin
Gardner ....Hannah	Mason ....George Sterling	1855 03 22	UT, Riverdale
Gardner ....Hannah	Parker ....J. W.	1846	ME
Gardner ....Jessie	Freckleton ....John O.	1860 07 05	Scotland
Gardner ....Lucinda	Leithead ....James	1856 05 07	UT, Salt Lake City
Gardner ....Margaret	Miller ....Reuben Parley	1868 10 10	UT, Salt Lake City
Gardner ....Margaret	Wells ....Jonathan S.	1829 06 23	PA, Erie Co.
Gardner ....Mary	Luckham ....Roger	1846	Canada
Gardner ....Mary	Sweeten ....George	1836 05 29	Canada
Gardner ....Mary Amelia	Cloward..............Thomas P.	1853 09 01	UT, Provo
Gardner ....Mary Jane	Miller ....James Robison	1859 02 20	UT, Salt Lake City
Gardner ....Nancy Maria	Nebeker ....Lewis	1853 11 05	UT, Salt Lake City
Gardner ....Penelope R.	Goodrich ....Benjamin F.	1823 04 01	
Garlic ....Hannah	Shepherd ....Moses T.		
Garlick ....Mary Jane	Hatch..................Isaac Burres	1845 09 10	IA, Charleston
Garlick ....Mary Jane	Hatch..................William	1858	UT, Payson
Garlick ....Mary Jane	Lawrence ....Francis	1855	
Garlick ....Talitha Cumi	Avery..................William H.	1845 03 12	IL, Nauvoo
Garlick ....Talitha Cumi	Cheney................Elam	1854 02 13	
Garn ....Mary Magdalene	Smith..................William H. J.	1872 01 04	
Garner ....Elizabeth Jane	Browning ....David H.	1854 05 28	
Garner ....Martha Ann	Critchlow ....Benjamin	1861 01 01	UT, Ogden
Garner ....Mary Marinda	Chadwick ....Abraham	1866 12 13	UT, North Ogden
Garner ....Rebecca	Clark...................Samuel	1827 07 18	OH, Clark
Garner ....Roemma	Harbertson ....James		
Garner ....Roemma	Terry...................Joel	1863	
Garr ....Mary Virginia	Ashby ....Nathaniel	1858 02 13	UT, Salt Lake City
Garr ....Nancy	Badger ....Rodney	1845 03 09	IL, LaHarpe
Garr ....Nancy	Stringham............Briant	1858 12 04	UT
Garrard ....Sarah S.	Blodgett..............Greenleaf	1871 12 25	
Garrard ....Sarah S.	Campbell.............Isaiah	1854 01 21	UT, Salt Lake City
Garrett ....Ann Priscilla	Davis ....Daniel Kelley	1888 01 12	UT, Bountiful
Garrett ....Elizabeth A.	Midgely...............Thomas	1868	UT, Salt Lake City
Garrett ....Elizabeth A.	Reece..................David	1880 07 06	
Garrett ....Sarah Rooth	Ogden ....Edward	1834 08 11	
Gascoigne ....Catherine	Clark...................George	1850 10 21	
Gaskell ....Elizabeth	Romney...............Miles	1830 11 06	ENG
Gates ....Genet	Bingham..............Willard	1853 04 24	UT, Salt Lake City
Gates ....Lucetta Maria	Marler..................William Norton	1856 10 12	UT, Lynne
Gates ....Lucinda	Bingham..............Erastus	1820 03 21	VT, Essex Co.
Gates ....Mary Ann A.	Humble................George	1828 07 27	
Gates ....Mary Anne	Dimick ....Thomas J.	1827 02	NY, Monroe
Gaudin-Moise ..Jeanne Marie	Cardon ....Philippe	1863 03 21	UT, Hyrum
Gaudin-Moise ..Jeanne Marie	Stalle..................Jean Peirre		Italy
Gay ....Mariah H.	Hales ....George Gillett	1873 05 05	
Gay ....Mariah H.	Mendenhall ....Louis Henry	1858	
Gay ....Susan Ann	Whipple ....Nelson Wheeler	1857 02 09	UT, Salt Lake City
Gaylord ....Mary S.	Forbush..............Sanford	1844 05 27	IL, Hancock Co.

Female	Male	Date	Place
Geddes............Elizabeth	Lindsay................Robert McQueen	1820 07 14	Scotland
Geer ....Lucy Witter	Rice.....................William Kelsey	1844 10 06	IL, Nauvoo
Geldard...........Ann	Boyce..................George		ENG
Gentle..............Charlotte	Fotheringham......John	1819 04 18	Scotland
Gentry..............Sarah Dickens	Stewart..............William J.	1833 09 29	IL, Madison Co.
George ....Ann T.	Doney.................John	1853 01 22	ENG, Cornwall
George ....Elizabeth	Cornwall.............William		
George ....Elizabeth	James ....Thomas	1855	
George ....Elizabeth	Labrum...............Thomas	1837 11 12	ENG
George ....Elizabeth	Wootton..............William	1862	
Gering..............Anna	Lehmann.............John	1850 05 27	Switzerland
Germer.............Henrietta C. C.	Hawkins ....William C.	1860 02 09	
Germer ....Mary Ann	Kleinman............Conrad	1857 04 08	UT, Salt Lake City
Gheen..............Amanda Trimble	Kimball ....Heber Chase	1845 12 01	IL, Nauvoo
Gheen..............Ann Alice	Kimball ....Heber Chase	1844 09 10	IL, Nauvoo
Gheen..............Louisa	Kirk.....................William	1886	
Gheen..............Louisa	Robison..............Lewis	1858 06 27	UT, Provo
Gibbons ....Ann	Probert ....William	1837 06 01	ENG, Edgaston
Gibbons ....Laura Caroline	Green ....Silas Sprague	1872 10 21	UT, Salt Lake City
Gibbons ....Sarah	Smoot.................Abraham Owen		
Gibbs ....Eliza Jerusha	Fox ....Jesse Williams	1849 06 02	IA, Council Bluffs
Gibbs ....Hannah E.	Sudweeks ....Richard H.	1870 11 02	
Gibbs ....Imogene J.	Melville ....James Andrew	1869 10 12	UT, Salt Lake City
Gibbs ....Martha Duggan	Wright.................John Fish	1864 02 23	
Gibbs ....Mary	Bigelow ....Nahum	1826 12 12	IL, Laurenceville
Gibbs ....Mary Amanda	Bishop ....Mahonri M.	1868 07 18	UT, Salt Lake City
Gibbs ....Mary Amanda	Hellebrant...........Oliver Lastie	1894 04 09	
Gibbs ....Medora Victoria	Melville ....James Andrew		
Gibbs ....Ruth	Adshed...............William		
Gibbs ....Ruth	Parker ....William	1858 02 22	IA, Dubuque
Gibbs ....Sarah Waterous	Eldredge.............Horace S.	1851 04 21	UT, Salt Lake City
Gibson ....Almira Jane	Fifield ....Matthew P.	1852 04 05	UT, Bountiful
Gibson ....Bianca Jane	Johnston ....James	1862 09 01	UT, Salt Lake City
Gibson ....Francis Abigail	Green ....Alvin Greely	1850 12 27	UT, Salt Lake City
Gibson ....Lydia Ardilca	Hunt ....Gilbert	1847 03	CO, Pueblo
Gibson ....Margaret	Smith..................John B.	1851 04 15	IA, Council Bluffs
Gibson ....Marion	Geddes ....Robert	1793	
Gibson ....Mary	Lewis..................David	1850	UT, Weber Co.
Gibson ....Mary	Wareing..............George	1862 04 19	UT, Salt Lake City
Gibson ....Mary Ann	Perkes................James	1854 12 09	MO
Gibson ....Mary Ann	Thurman..............Edward	1847	ENG
Gibson ....Sarah Ann	Mears ....George	1828 11 08	ENG
Gifford.............Mary Ann	Chidester............John P.	1806	
Gifford.............Mary Ann	Darrow ....George		
Gifford.............Mary Ann	Young..................John	1850	Trail
Gifford.............Priscilla	Hoops.................Warner	1839 10 18	
Gilbert..............Mary Harriet	Felshaw...............William	1827 02 01	NY
Giles ....Elizabeth	Rasband..............Thomas	1847 01 25	ENG, Lincoln
Giles ....Laura Ann	Carlile.................George	1856 11 25	
Giles ....Louisa	Bulkley ....Samuel	1872 03 04	UT, Salt Lake City
Giles ....Mary Elizabeth	Moulton...............Joseph	1868 12 15	UT, Salt Lake City
Giles ....Sarah	Farr ....Lorin	1851 07 26	
Gill ....Caroline	Cochrane ....John		
Gill ....Caroline	Sims ....George	1843 04 04	ENG

Female	Male	Date	Place
Gill ....Eliza	Couche...............Sam		
Gill ....Eliza	Hartley................S. John	1836 01 31	ENG
Gill ....Louisa	Clark...................Raymond	1827 09 16	
Gill ....Maria	Clayfield ....Richard	1825	
Gillespie...........Mary Jane	Garlick...............Joseph	1872 02 13	UT, Fairview
Gillespie...........Mary Jane	Pritchett.............Samuel N. B.	1858	
Gillians.............Mary B.	Wagstaff.............Isaac	1808 10 12	
Gillings............Elizabeth	Wheeler..............Samuel	1830 12 24	ENG
Gilmore...........Mary Elizabeth	Harris ....John	1812	Wales
Gilson ....Clarissa Ann	Beckstead ....Alexander	1856 02 03	
Gilson ....Clarissa Ann	Washburn...........Luther	1878 01 24	UT, Marysvale
Gilson ....Francis	Stock ....John		
Gimlin ....Malinda	Lewis..................Tarleton	1828 03 27	KY, Simpson Co.
Gingell ....Charlotte E.	Adams................Orson Bennett	1859 07 21	UT, Parowan
Gingell ....Charlotte E.	Edminson ....Stokley	1866	
Ginther.............Susannah	Bright.................John	1796	
Ginther.............Susannah	Smith..................John Glover	1855 10 02	UT, Draper
Givens ....Mary (Polly)	Harris ....McGee	1826 12 29	TN, Wilson Co.
Glade..............Mary Jane	Litson ....Joseph Young	1878 05 09	UT
Gleason ....Flora Clarinda	Johnson ....Benjamin F.	1846 01 23	IL, Nauvoo
Gleason ....Flora Clarinda	Washburn...........Abraham Daniel	1849 02 11	UT, Salt Lake City
Gledhill ....Amelia Jane	Gottfredson ....Peter	1872 04 22	UT, Salt Lake City
Gledhill ....Mary	Openshaw...........Roger W.		
Glenn..............Robina	Stuart ....James M.	1855	
Glines ....Harriet Anna	Thorn.................Richard Jr.	1846 01 13	IL, Nauvoo
Glines ....Sarah Elizabeth	Millett.................Joseph	1854 03 26	MA, Lowell
Gloyd ....Abigail	Hyde..................William	1860 01 01	UT, Salt Lake City
Goates............Martha	Wing..................John W.	1868 10 11	UT, Salt Lake City
Goble..............Fanny	Wood..................John		
Goble..............Frances	Howell ....Henry	1855 03 10	ENG
Goble..............Harriet	Bird.......................		
Goble..............Mary	Pay.....................Richard	1859 06 26	UT, Nephi
Goddard ....Frances	Woodbury............Orin N.	1863 10 10	UT, Salt Lake City
Goddard ....Hannah Maria	Johnson ....John Ellis	1849 12	IA, Kanesville
Goddard ....Mary	Collins ....John	1863	
Goddard ....Mary	Davis ....William	1865 04 10	UT, Salt Lake City
Godfrey...........Emma E.	Myler ....Joseph Elias	1872 10 10	UT, Salt Lake City
Godfrey...........Sarah	Clark...................William Henry	1877 10 10	UT, Salt Lake City
Goff................Naomi	Hardcastle...........William	1890 03 20	UT, Sandy
Goff................Ruth	Lloyd ....John	1875 11 15	UT, Salt Lake City
Goheen............Fredonia M.	Forsyth ....Thomas R.	1863 04 05	
Gold...............Sarah Ann	Denney...............Charles	1872 12 02	UT, Salt Lake City
Golden............Christeen	Kimball ....Heber Chase	1846 02 03	IL, Nauvoo
Golden............Nancy	Shoemaker..........Jezreel	1824 04 01	KY, Pendleton
Golding ....Sarah	Broadhead ....William	1830	
Goldthorpe.......Jane	Thompson ....George	1828 10 01	ENG
Goldthrope.......Susannah	Heaps.................Thomas	1854 07 30	ENG
Goldthwaite .....Lydia	Bailey ....Calvin	1828	
Goldthwaite .....Lydia	Dalton.................John	1851 09 18	
Goldthwaite .....Lydia	Knight.................Newel	1835 11 23	OH, Kirtland
Goldthwaite .....Lydia	McClellan ....James	1860	UT, Payson
Golightly ....Isabella	Layton ....Christopher	1854 12 17	
Gollop.............Sarah Endacott	Ostler ....John	1830 06 06	ENG
Golthrop..........Martha	Wayman..............James	1821 04 22	

Female	Male	Date	Place
Goodall ....Persis	Richards..............Levi	1848 01 27	IL, Nauvoo
Goodall ....Persis	Young..................Lorenzo Dow	1826 06 06	NY, Watertown
Goode..............Sarah	Chadwick ....Joseph	1857	
Goode..............Sarah	Marshall ....Thomas	1843 05 07	ENG
Goodman.........Fannie E.	Moss ....Thomas	1860 02 17	ENG
Goodman.........Keziah Miles	Maw ....Edward	1864 03 07	
Goodman.........Keziah Miles	Warner ....William Goodman	1854 11 30	Ocean
Goodrich..........Harriet	Thornton..............Ezra	1814	
Goodridge.......Lusannah E.	Hovey ....Joseph Grafton	1852 01 14	
Goodridge.......Mary Jane	Flint ....William	1850 12 24	UT, Salt Lake City
Goodridge.......Sophia Lois	Hardy ....Leonard W.	1850 11 28	UT, Salt Lake City
Goodson.........Eliza	Jex ....Richard	1847 10 12	ENG, Crostwick
Goodson.........Eliza	Jex ....William	1854 02 22	
Goodwin ....Margaret	Steele..................William	1828	KY
Gordge ....Ann	Kennedy..............Frank		
Gordge ....Ann	Lee ....John Doyle	1865 06 10	UT, Salt Lake City
Gordon ....Louisa C.	Woolley ....Edwin D.		
Gordon ....Mary	Park.....................William	1854 06 11	UT, Salt Lake City
Gordon ....Mary Everett	Ensign ....Samuel	1832 11 29	MA
Gordon ....Sarah	Guymon ....Thomas	1809 02 23	NC, Stokes
Gore ....Ellen	Dinwoodey ....Henry	1846 02 08	
Gosnold ....Caroline B.	Bleak ....James G.	1860 11 24	UT, Salt Lake City
Gossauer........Mary M.	Neeser ....Rudolf	1844 01 10	Switzerland
Goudin............Susanna	Cardon ....Jean Paul	1857 03 16	UT, Ogden
Gould..............Elizabeth	Weech.................Samuel	1832 11 05	ENG, Somerton
Gourlay...........Elizabeth	Anderson............William	1823 11 28	Scotland
Gourley...........Nicholaus P.	Teeples ....Sidney	1861 10 27	
Gove...............Miriam	Chase.................Sisson A. D.	1832 05 16	
Gowans ....Betsy	Gowans..............Hugh S.	1854 08 11	Scotland
Gowens ....Barbara	Bowen ....Benjamin L.	1876 07 24	UT, Salt Lake City
Gower..............Ann	Lunt ....Henry	1863 04 11	UT, Salt Lake City
Gower..............Elizabeth	Clark...................Daniel	1839 10 27	ENG
Gower..............Elizabeth	Wood..................John	1867 12 25	
Grace..............Hannah	Webb..................John Stokes	1854 02 18	
Grace..............Harriet	Webb..................William	1864 05 09	ENG
Grace..............Sarah	Mariner...............Charles	1844	
Grace..............Sarah	Wood..................Daniel	1852 01 14	
Graham ....Christina Burns	Ericson ....John M.	1887 08 17	UT, Salt Lake City
Graham ....Elizabeth	McDonald...........Alexander F.	1851 05 20	Scotland
Graham ....Ellen	Wickham ....Richard	1863 12 10	UT, Brigham City
Graham ....Isabell	Blain ....John	1838 12 25	ENG
Graham ....Martha E.	Proctor ....David	1855	UT, Salt Lake City
Graham ....Mary Ann	Daley..................William	1834 03 12	
Graham ....Mary Elizabeth	Allen ....Elihu Moroni	1853	UT
Graitus............Ann	Gillies ....Ebenezer	1853 02	ENG
Granger ....Ann	Higbee................John S.	1852 03	
Granne ....Johanna	Orell ....Carl Fredric	1851 10 12	Sweden
Grant ....Eleanor	Ord ....Thomas	1856 03 04	ENG
Grant ....Thankful Ann	Fillmore ....Daniel B.	1839 09 22	WI, Muskego
Granteer ....Electa	Kilbourn..............Ozias Jr.	1832 11 28	CT, Canton
Grassing ....Ann	Bryant.................Edwin	1826	ENG, Gloucester
Grassing ....Sarah	Smith..................Thomas	1835 12 25	ENG
Grassing ....Sarah	Wheeler..............William	1854	UT, Salt Lake City
Graupe ....Augusta	Watters...............Ichel	1871 07 05	UT, Salt Lake City

Female	Male	Date	Place
Graves............Eliza Ann	Rich...................Charles Coulson	1845 01 06	IL, Nauvoo
Graves............Jane Eliza	Roberts ....Horace	1856 12 11	UT, Salt Lake City
Graves............Louisa	Page...................James	1837 10 16	ENG, Aston Parish
Gray...............Abigail	Rumel.................John H.	1847 07 11	MO, St. Louis
Gray...............Isabella	Park...................Samuel		IRE
Gray...............Sarah A.	Woodbury............John H.	1870 05 10	UT, Salt Lake City
Graybill ....Barbara	Stoker.................David	1814	
Grayson..........Mary Ann	Roper ....Henry	1843 10 24	ENG, Sheffield
Greathouse......Mary Ann	Downs ....James	1847 03 03	IA, Council Bluffs
Greaves...........Ann	Gailey ....John	1843 06 27	IL, Nauvoo
Green	Chipman...............James	1858 12 25	UT, American Fork
Green ....Alice Elisabeth	Carter ....Erastus Francis	1870 11 21	
Green ....Ann	Carling................John	1844 06 10	IL, Nauvoo
Green ....Ann	Dutson................John	1826 02 07	ENG
Green ....Eliza	Blake ....Fredrick		
Green ....Elizabeth	Arnold.................Henry	1857 02 20	UT, Salt Lake City
Green ....Elizabeth	Hamilton..............Eli		
Green ....Elizabeth	Nield...................Luke	1859 02 07	
Green ....Elizabeth	Richmond............Thomas		MO, St. Louis
Green ....Elizabeth Jane	Orr.....................James Copeland	1863	UT
Green ....Emily	Blake ....Fredrick	1868 09 12	UT, Salt Lake City
Green ....Hannah Martha	Williams...............Joshua	1877 01 13	UT, Ogden
Green ....Harriet Ann	Earnshaw ....Mark	1864 10 01	UT, Salt Lake City
Green ....Margaret	Whitehead...........William	1863 03 28	UT, Farmington
Green ....Margaret F.	Fox ....Thomas James	1875 11 27	UT, Union
Green ....Mary	Boardman ....Robert	1844 06 18	ENG
Green ....Mary	King...................Daniel	1855 10 29	UT, Salt Lake City
Green ....Mary	Walker................Henson Jr.	1856 07 03	UT, Salt Lake City
Green ....Phylotte	Jacob ....Udney Hay	1856 03 11	UT, Salt Lake City
Green ....Phylotte	Pack...................George	1790 04 01	Canada
Green ....Sarah	Holyoak ....George	1825 01 17	ENG
Green ....Sarah Ann	Summers.............George	1866	Trail
Green ....Susannah	Gillins ....Henry	1866 11 10	IA, Council Bluffs
Greene ....Louisa Lulu	Richards..............Levi Willard	1873 06 16	UT, Salt Lake City
Greenfield........Ann	Lambert..............William	1839	ENG
Greenhalgh......Ann Walmsley	Openshaw...........William	1833 05 20	ENG, Lancashire
Greenhalgh......Margaret Alice	Billings................William W.	1882 01 19	UT, Manti
Greenhalgh......Mary Ann	Mace ....George	1869 06 21	UT, Salt Lake City
Greenhalgh......Ruth Elizabeth	Cram ....Charles S. Jr.	1888 01 17	
Greenhalgh......Sarah Ellen	Bennett...............Hyrum Bell	1866 10 04	UT, Salt Lake City
Greensmith......Zillah	Birkinshaw...........William	1863 03 28	UT, Salt Lake City
Greenway ....Ruth Margaret	Lawson...............Joseph	1855 09 09	UT, Salt Lake City
Greenwood......Hannah	Fielding ....Joseph	1838 06 11	ENG, Preston
Greenwood......Mary	Broadbent ....James W.	1835	ENG
Greenwood......Sarah	Turley ....Isaac		
Greer ....Diannah	Camp ....Williams W.	1822 01 18	
Gregersen ....Dorthea	Jensen ....Jens P.	1866 10 23	UT, Salt Lake City
Gregory ....Christianna	Graham ....James		
Gregory ....Christianna	Read ....John	1819 02 17	PA, Philadelphia
Gribble............Mary Ann	Lamoreaux ....David Burlock	1838 05 31	OH, Chardon
Gribbon...........Robina	Paul...................James Patten	1839	
Grice..............Lucy	Workman.............James T.	1864 01 16	UT, Salt Lake City
Gridlestone ......Emma	Ridges................Joseph H.	1858 01 31	UT, Salt Lake City
Gridlestone ......Emma	Smith.................Ralph	1862 12 13	UT, Salt Lake City

Female	Male	Date	Place
Griffeth............Phoebe Ann	Hyde..................Herman	1884	ID, Fairview
Griffeth............Phoebe Ann	Hyde..................William	1867 08 31	UT, Salt Lake City
Griffin.............Caroline	Thompson..........Joseph L.	1867 10 05	UT, Salt Lake City
Griffin.............Elizabeth	King..................John	1868 11 01	UT, Salt Lake City
Griffin.............Harriet Ann	Shaw.................Charles	1860 04 16	ENG
Griffin.............Lydia	Deaken..............John	1868 10 24	UT
Griffin.............Lydia	James................David	1871 11 07	UT, Salt Lake City
Griffin.............Sarah	Bullock..............Henry	1859 04 21	ENG, Stafford
Griffin.............Susannah	Clifford..............Benjamin Rush	1875 09 14	
Griffin.............Susannah	Montierth............Alvin M.	1866 03 10	UT, Salt Lake City
Griffin.............Theophenia	Griffiths..............John Bishop	1863 11 22	
Griffin.............Theophenia	Thompson..........Joseph L.	1873	
Griffith............Sarah	Richards.............Levi	1843 12 25	IL, Nauvoo
Griffiths..........Jane Ellenor	Fullmer..............Almon L. II	1864 07 31	UT, Salt Lake City
Griffiths..........Jean Rio	Baker.................Henry	1832 09 24	ENG
Griffiths..........Jean Rio	Pearce...............Edward	1864	
Griffiths..........Margaret Ann	Clegg.................Henry		
Griffiths..........Mary Jo	Ledingham..........Alexander Morris	1873	
Griffiths..........Mary Priscilla	Farnsworth..........Philo T.	1860 06 15	UT, Salt Lake City
Griffiths..........Mary Priscilla	Willis.................William	1857 01 27	UT, Salt Lake City
Griffiths..........Sarah	Reese................Charles	1856 09 06	Wales
Grimes............Cherrizade	Averett...............Elijah	1830 02 09	IL, Hamilton
Grimethsson....Hanne Laurine	Hansen..............Peder	1862 10 18	
Grimshaw........Mary	Smith.................William	1834	ENG, Lancashire
Grinnel............Jane	Brewer...............William	1806 04 07	
Griswold..........Mary	Thornton.............Oliver	1829	Canada
Groesbeck.......Adelia	Lambert..............John	1846 02 06	IL, Nauvoo
Groesbeck.......Helen Melvina	Morgan...............John Hamilton	1868 10 24	UT, Salt Lake City
Groesbeck.......Josephine	Smith.................John Henry	1877 04 04	UT, St. George
Grover............Adeline	Daley.................Phineas	1853 01 27	CA, San Bern.
Grover............Eliza Ann	Parker................Wyman Miner	1860 01 15	UT, Farmington
Grover............Eliza Ann	Simmons............William A.	1856 05 09	
Grover............Emeline	Rich...................Charles Coulson	1846 02 02	IL, Nauvoo
Grover............Hannah	Gutteridge..........Robert	1841 01 09	ENG
Grover............Lucy	Sanders..............David A.	1868 01 04	
Grover............Mary Elizabeth	Robison..............David	1860 12 26	UT, North Morgan
Grover............Mary Elizabeth	Simmons............William A.	1850 04 26	UT, Salt Lake City
Grover............Percia C.	Bunnell..............Stephen	1856 09 19	UT, Provo
Grow..............Mariah Louisa	Worthen.............Samuel	1856 04 27	UT, Panguitch
Gubler............Anna Katherina	Gubler................Casper	1861 11 09	UT, Salt Lake City
Guest.............Elizabeth C.	Cooper...............James		
Gugger...........Anna	Stauffer..............Christian	1854 10 13	
Gunderson.......Radine	Olson.................Lars	1866 05 09	Norway
Gunn..............Fanny	McKenzie...........John Robert		
Gunn..............Fanny	Miller................Henry William	1862 10 25	UT, Salt Lake City
Gunn..............Mary	Priscott..............James	1854	ENG
Gurney...........Margaret	Smith.................Thomas X.	1851 01 02	ENG
Gurnsey..........Jerusha	Bemis................Alvin	1824	NY, Jefferson Co.
Gurr..............Sarah	Wall..................William M.		
Gurr..............Sarah Elizabeth	Whitney.............New Samuel	1872 07 29	UT, Salt Lake City
Gurr..............Susanna	Stewart..............Andrew Jackson		
Gurr..............Susanna	Wall..................William M.	1859 11 12	UT, Salt Lake City
Gutteridge.......Mary Ann	Clare.................Richard	1861 08 26	ENG, Lancaster
Gutteridge.......Mary Ann	Ingersoll............Jonas	1867 03 12	UT, Salt Lake City

Female	Male	Date	Place
Guymon..........Barzilla	Caldwell ....Matthew	1843 10 17	IL, Carthage
Guymon...........Harriet	Crandall...............Hyrum O.		
Guymon..........Lucinda Harris	Hurst ....Phillip	1857 01 01	UT
Guymon..........Margaret E.	Crandall...............Hyrum O.	1864 03 06	UT, Springville
Guymon..........Melissa Jane	Johnson ....Robert L.	1862 08 16	UT, Salt Lake City
Guymon..........Melissa Jane	Metcalf ....Levi G.	1850 11 03	UT, Centerville
Guymon..........Polly Ann	Johnson ....Robert L.	1846 04 30	IL, Nauvoo
Gwyther ....Louisa	Taylor ....George	1853 10 19	ENG
Gylenskog ....Christina	Henrichson..........Soren P.	1866 11 16	
Gyllenskog.......Eva	Sorensen............Jorgen P.	1872 12 24	UT, Salt Lake City

H

Female	Male	Date	Place
Haagansen ......Anne	Rasmussen.........Soren	1835 08 09	Denmark
Hadden...........Duritha	Dodge ....Nathaniel Morgan	1862	
Hadden...........Duritha	Hofheins.............Jacob	1859 01 04	
Hadden...........Duritha	McDaniel.............Samuel James	1873	
Haddon...........Jane	Lines ....John	1838 10 30	ENG, Dunchurch
Haddon...........Lucy	Voss...................Thomas	1839	ENG
Hadfield ....Martha Ann	West...................David	1881	
Hadley ....Jane	Baird...................Robert Erwin		
Hadley ....Mary	Baird...................Robert Erwin	1858 08 12	UT, Salt Lake City
Hadlock ....Chastina	Allen ....Alanson David	1850 11 10	UT
Hadlock ....Ester Adline	Terry...................Parshall P.	1858 03 10	UT, Salt Lake City
Hadlock ....Henrietta	Hill.....................William James	1867 09 21	UT
Hadlock ....Sally Cilicia	Hill.....................William James	1855 02 25	
Hadlond ....Maria	Thomas...............Preston F.	1856 10 08	UT, Salt Lake City
Hafen...............Anna Katharina	Fechser ....Johann F.	1867 09 14	UT, Salt Lake City
Hafen...............Barbara	Tobler.................John Jacob	1865 10 18	
Hafen...............Barbara	Willi ....Ignaz	1861 10 18	UT, Salt Lake City
Haggerty..........Lucinda	Ayers..................Caleb	1832 01 11	NJ, Stanhope
Haggerty..........Lucinda	Petty...................Albert	1853 06 05	
Hague ....Betty	Gledhill ....Edward		ENG
Hahn................Susannah	Egbert ....John	1809 11 11	KY, Nelson Co.
Haidon ....Sarah	Davis..................William	1842 12 19	ENG
Haig.................Mary	McAlister ....Charles H. M.	1849	ENG
Haight..............Caroline Eliza	Arthur ....Christopher J.	1854 12 30	
Haight..............Elizabeth	Hatch..................Jeremiah	1789 11 23	VT, Addison Co.
Haight..............Julia Ann	Bernhisel.............John Milton	1846 01 20	IL, Nauvoo
Haight..............Julia Ann	Van Orden...........William	1827 03 12	NY, Green Co.
Haight..............Temperance K.	McFarlane ....Daniel S.	1862 02 12	UT, Cedar City
Haight..............Temperance K.	Parry ....Edward	1919	
Haines ....Kindness Ann	Badger ....John C.	1855	UT, Grantsville
Haines ....Kindness Ann	Johnson ....Thomas Smith	1849 02 04	
Haines ....Kindness Ann	Martindale ....William A.	1865 06 05	UT, Salt Lake City
Haines ....Rebecca Ann	Marshall ....George W. B.	1842 01 25	OH, Clinton Co.
Haines ....Rebecca Ann	Martindale ....William A.	1854 04 24	UT, Salt Lake City
Haines ....Sarah Ann	Crook ....Samuel Lane	1856 05 29	Ocean
Hakansson ......Kjerstena	Anderson............Paul	1846	Sweden
Hakes ....Sarah Melissa	Clark...................Daniel Porter	1845 08 31	
Hald................Trine Marie	Frantzen..............Anders	1864 10 29	UT, Salt Lake City
Hale ....Mary Ann	Birch..................James	1847 04 12	ENG, Staffordshire
Hale ....Mary Ann	Birch..................Richard	1858	

Female		Male		Date	Place
Hale	Mary Ann	Riding	Christopher L.	1840	ENG, Burley
Hale	Rachel J. S.	Hoagland	Lucas	1848 12 24	UT, Salt Lake City
Hales	Eliza Ann	Ogilvie	George	1857 03 02	
Hales	Harriet	Ellis	John	1839 10 31	IL, Adams Co.
Hales	Julia Ardena	Truman	Jacob Mica	1857 06 14	
Hales	Mary Ann	Hales	Stephen	1816 08 31	ENG
Hales	Mary Ann	Thompson	William		
Hales	Mary Isabella	Horne	Joseph	1836 05 09	Canada
Hall	Ann	Hardcastle	William	1830 04 22	ENG
Hall	Celia	Raymond	Grandison	1849 08 12	NY
Hall	Charlotte Maria	Foulger	Herbert John	1881 10 11	UT, Salt Lake City
Hall	Elizabeth	Bills	John	1848 01 06	IL, Nauvoo
Hall	Elizabeth	Blackner	Richard	1820 05 29	ENG, Heckington
Hall	Elizabeth	Butler	John	1834 06 18	ENG
Hall	Elizabeth	Jenkins	Morgan	1867 10 26	UT, Salt Lake City
Hall	Elizabeth	Mills	John	1836	ENG
Hall	Elizabeth	Mower	Henry	1851 07 24	
Hall	Elizabeth	Porter			
Hall	Elizabeth	Rowley	George	1859	
Hall	Harriet	Ingram	John	1862 03 30	ENG, Warwick
Hall	Louisa Jane	Miller	Alma	1861	NV
Hall	Louisa Jane	Randall	Joseph Henry	1881	UT, St. George
Hall	Louisa Maria	Harris	Charles	1855 04 20	UT, Ogden
Hall	Lulu May	King	Franklin Ernest	1896 07 03	
Hall	Lulu May	McCune	James	1894 09 14	
Hall	Lulu May	Parkinson	John	1875 12 13	UT, Salt Lake City
Hall	Mary Ann	Johnson	Lorenzo	1857 03 01	UT, Salt Lake City
Hall	Mary Ann	Whiting	William	1880 10 28	UT, St. George
Hall	Mary Maria	Kempton	Nathan		
Hall	Sarah Jane	Houtz	Phillip	1864 05 01	UT, Springville
Hall	Sarah Jane	Johnson	Marion Maroni	1897 12 08	UT, Springville
Hallam	Sarah	Worthen	Samuel	1844	IL, Nauvoo
Hallet	Mary Elizabeth	Snow	Don Carlos	1862 10 20	UT, Provo
Halley	Mary	Stocks	Henry	1843	ENG, Warrington
Halliday	Elizabeth	Archibald	William R.	1857 09 08	Scotland
Halliday	Mary	Dade	John		
Halliday	Mary	Gale	Henry	1865 03 18	
Halliday	Mary	Holroyd	Seth	1828 12 24	ENG
Halliwell	Alice	Ellison	James	1842 06 01	ENG, Lancashire
Halstensen	Hilda Mathilda	Brinton	David	1867 10 19	UT, Salt Lake City
Halstensen	Hilda Mathilda	Halsett	Antone Ludwig	1879	UT, Salt Lake City
Halvorson	Marie	Amundsen	Ole	1845 04 29	Norway
Ham	Ann	Hickenlooper	William		
Hambleton	Gerusha L.	Boswell	Abraham	1853 06 13	
Hambleton	Lucy Ann	Woolf	Absolom		
Hamblin	Adeline Amarilla	Littlefield	Lyman O.	1846 01 31	
Hamblin	Adeline Amarilla	Riggs	John Ensign	1851 12 17	UT, Tooele
Hamblin	Mary	Mangum	John III		
Hamer	Elizabeth C.	Cantwell	James Sherlock	1838 04 27	ENG, Lancashire
Hamer	Nancy	Player	William J.	1850 09 24	IA, Ferryville
Hamer	Sarah	Brown	Cornelius	1852	IA
Hamer	Sarah	Worsley	John	1836 11 07	ENG, Lancashire
Hamilton	Caroline Matilda	Nokes	Charles M.	1879 09	UT, Salt Lake City
Hamilton	Margaret	Buys	Edward	1876	

Female	Male	Date	Place
Hamilton ....Mary	McKinlay ....George	1824 04 09	Scotland
Hamilton ....Mary Ann	Alder....................George		ENG
Hamilton ....Sarah Jane	Gardner................Archibald	1857 06 21	UT, Salt Lake City
Hamilton ....Sarah Jane	Howard................Samuel Lorenzo	1865 04 01	UT, Salt Lake City
Hamilton ....Susannah	Grant...................Robert Collier	1823 03 23	Scotland
Hamilton ....Susannah	McDougal.............Isaac	1867 07 13	
Hammer..........Johanna C.	Carlson................Swen	1865 12 01	UT, Salt Lake City
Hammer..........Julia Ann	Smith...................William J.	1854 01	UT
Hammer..........Nancy	Norton ....James Wiley	1846 07 08	NE, Florence
Hammond.......Amanda M.	Burgess...............Harrison	1846 02 06	IL, Nauvoo
Hammond.......Mary Almina	Watkins...............William L.	1844 12 04	IL, Nauvoo
Hammond.......Sarah Loanna	Terry...................Charles A.	1851 06 28	UT, Salt Lake City
Hammond.......Susan	Ashby..................Nathaniel	1826 11 30	MA, Salem
Hammond.......Susan	Noble...................Joseph Bates	1847 02 11	IA
Hampson ....Mary	Straw...................William	1830 02 04	
Hampton...........Sarah Elizabeth	Porritt ....Thomas	1868 11 13	UT
Hanchett ....Sarah Marinda	Marble ....William Lorenzo	1852	
Hancock ....Alta	Davis...................Jonathan G.	1858 01 28	UT, Springville
Hancock ....Amy	Hancock..............George W.	1852 04 04	UT, Salt Lake City
Hancock ....Ann	Done ....Abraham	1825	
Hancock ....Clarissa	Alger...................Samuel		
Hancock ....Eliza	Sleater.................Robert G.	1869 05 03	UT, Salt Lake City
Hancock ....Elizabeth	Redd ....John Hardison	1826 03 27	NC
Hancock ....Ellen	Burns...................Joseph	1831 03 20	ENG, Brampton
Hancock ....Ellen	MacDuff...............John Robertson	1839 09 15	ENG
Hancock ....Louisa	Hayball...............George S.	1850 09 20	ENG
Hancock ....Lucretia	Robison...............Joseph	1829 02 05	NY, Clay
Hancock ....Merab	Gordge ....Samuel	1847 11 14	
Hancock ....Merab	Phillips.................John	1855	Wales
Hand................Rachel	Allen....................Gideon	1799 10 03	CT, Litchfield
Handberg.........Johanna C. M.	Nicol....................Thomas	1858 03 11	UT, Salt Lake City
Handley ....Elizabeth	Gledhill ....John E.	1860 12 31	ENG, Oldham
Hanks ....Elizabeth	Gribble ....John	1852	ENG
Hanks ....Elizabeth	Hanks..................William	1829	
Hannah...........Margaret	Muir.....................George	1852 04 19	Scotland
Hannibal ....Emelie Caroline	Meyer ....Fredrick A. E.	1872 01 08	UT, Salt Lake City
Hansen ....Amy	Draper.................Almon	1866 12 11	UT, Rockville
Hansen ....Ane B. E.	Nielsen................Augustinus	1854 02 05	Ocean
Hansen ....Ane Kjerstine	Jensen ....Hans	1837	Denmark
Hansen ....Ane Margaret	Carlsen................Ole	1845 08 09	Denmark
Hansen ....Ane Marie	Christiansen........Peter	1867 05 24	UT, Salt Lake City
Hansen ....Anna	Nielsen................Niels	1842 10 25	Denmark
Hansen ....Anna Catharina	Larson ....Jons	1838 11 30	Sweden
Hansen ....Anna Christine	Burnham ....Wallace C.	1878 10 12	UT, Salt Lake City
Hansen ....Anna Marie	Black ....William Morley	1859 10 26	UT, Manti
Hansen ....Anne Marie	Jensen ....Peter Madsen	1859 03 09	Denmark
Hansen ....Anne Marie	Van Orman..........Abraham	1887 09 27	UT, Logan
Hansen ....Anne Moriah	Peterson.............Anders	1854 10 15	UT, Salt Lake City
Hansen ....Annie	Nielsen................Hans C.	1883 11 21	UT, St. George
Hansen ....Annie Marie	Fitt ....William	1868 07 31	UT, Salt Lake City
Hansen ....Bendicta C.	Hansen................James Peter	1855	Denmark
Hansen ....Christiane	Breinholt.............Jens Christian	1874 03 30	
Hansen ....Christine	Funk....................Diderick	1825 11 12	
Hansen ....Dorothea K.	Madsen ....Jacob	1838 04 16	Denmark

Female	Male	Date	Place
Hansen ....Dorthea	Hjorth ....Niels Peder	1844 07 08	Denmark
Hansen ....Eliza Marie	Hunsaker.............Isaac	1868 11 01	UT, Salt Lake City
Hansen ....Ellen Margrethe	Marker..................Jens Pedersen	1849 04 07	
Hansen ....Ellen Margrethe	Pedersen.............Peder	1821 07 11	Denmark
Hansen ....Elsie Sophie	Carstensen..........Peter Cornelius		
Hansen ....Gunnell Marie	Jeppson ....Jeppa H.	1854 10 11	
Hansen ....Hannah Jane	Jennings..............Cyrus M.	1874 02 05	UT, Rockville
Hansen ....Ingeborg S.	Nielsen ....Niels H.	1847 02 26	Denmark
Hansen ....Johanna	Jensen ....Jens	1852 10 22	Denmark
Hansen ....Johanna Marie	Swenson ....Knud	1860 06 24	
Hansen ....Johanne M.	Hansen.................Peder	1835 05 29	Denmark
Hansen ....Julia Elzina	Hall.......................Alfred Lorenzo	1882 01 18	UT, St. George
Hansen ....Karen	Mouritsen ....Mourits	1885 10 22	UT, Logan
Hansen ....Karen	Scorup..................Christian C.	1866 08 04	UT, Ephraim
Hansen ....Karen C.	Green ....Cornelius	1859 10 16	UT, Salt Lake City
Hansen ....Karen Kirstine	Heiselt ....Niels Christian	1859 04 17	Ocean
Hansen ....Karen Kirstine	Larsen ....Hans	1849 11 14	Denmark
Hansen ....Karen Kirstine	Nielson ....Carl Henrick	1867 05 26	Denmark
Hansen ....Karen M.	Christiansen ....Lars Nielsen	1869 04 26	UT, Salt Lake City
Hansen ....Karen Maria	Allen ....Joseph Stewart	1854 01 28	UT
Hansen ....Karen Marie	Andersen.............Christen	1817 03 14	Denmark
Hansen ....Karen Marie	Hansen.................Niels Miller	1868 06 20	Ocean
Hansen ....Karen Marie	Jensen ....Ole	1843 11 18	Denmark
Hansen ....Karen Marie	Olsen....................Jorgen	1863 12 14	UT
Hansen ....Karen Marie	Poulsen ....Morten	1843 01 27	
Hansen ....Kirsten	Bastian ....Jacob	1861 02 07	UT, Moroni
Hansen ....Laurentze	Jensen ....Christen	1870 07 11	UT, Salt Lake City
Hansen ....Laurine Emilia	Ronnow................Christian P.	1862 11 13	UT, Ephraim
Hansen ....Maren	Jacobson.............Hans	1840 07 04	Denmark
Hansen ....Maren	Jensen ....Mads Christian	1845 06 10	Denmark
Hansen ....Maren	Nielsen ....Christian	1849 02 23	Denmark
Hansen ....Maren	Peterson.............Ole	1846 02 05	Denmark
Hansen ....Maren	Thompson ....Peter P. S.	1854 12 17	UT, Ephraim
Hansen ....Margrete	Munk ....Christian Ipsen		
Hansen ....Martha Kirstine	Beers...................Phillip Zend		
Hansen ....Martha Kirstine	Hawkins ....Jonah W.	1864 12 10	UT, Salt Lake City
Hansen ....Martha Maria	Madsen ....Nels	1839 10 25	Denmark
Hansen ....Mary	....	1874	
Hansen ....Mette Maria	Mortensen ....Jens Fredrick	1862 05	Ocean
Hansen ....Mettie Marie	Hansen.................Jens	1868 01 23	UT, Salt Lake City
Hansen ....Petrea	Brown...................James Polly	1855	
Hansen ....Sena	Pedersen.............Jorgen Christian		
Hansen ....Sidse Marie	Gardner................Archibald	1869 12 20	
Hansen ....Sidse Marie	Root ....Almerin E.	1867 06 29	
Hanson ....Alice	Hatch...................Lorenzo Hill	1860 01 02	
Hanson ....Ellen Elna	Butler...................Pehr Larson	1811	Sweden
Harbell ....Margaret Ann	Friel ....Edward	1855 11 16	UT, Salt Lake City
Harbert ....Sarah B.	Harvey.................Jonathan L.	1819 01 31	WV, Harrison
Hardcastle ....Elizabeth	Evans ....John	1858 07 24	NY, Oneida
Hardie..............Ann	Latimer ....Thomas	1856 02 10	UT, Salt Lake City
Harding............Amy	Francom..............William	1837 09 03	ENG, Somerset
Harding ....Ellen Sarah	Aland...................John Sparrow	1832 11 12	ENG
Harding............Mary	Enslow ....Elza	1848 03	
Harding..........Female Mary	Field ....William	1825 02 14	ENG, Rosebury

Female	Male	Date	Place
Harding...........Susannah	Orchard...............Jacob	1844	
Harding...........Susannah	Orchard...............James	1837	
Hardman.........Alice	Eccles................Thomas	1843 08 06	ENG
Hardman.........Alice	Tullis..................David Wilson	1861	UT, Pinto
Hardwick.........Ann	Cartwright...........John	1859 01 30	ENG, Derbyshire
Hardy..............Eliza Ann	Wadsworth.........Abiah	1831 02 25	ME, Lincolnville
Hardy..............Hannah	Crompton..........John	1850 03 01	IA, Council Bluffs
Hardy..............Hannah	Eckersley...........William	1833 10 21	ENG, Middleton
Hardy..............Lucy Adeline	Robison..............Charles William	1865 12 03	UT, Hooper
Hardy..............Mary Adelia	Gheen................Stephen H.	1856 11 06	
Hardy..............Pamelia Anne	Kempton.............Nathan	1856	UT
Hardy..............Sarah Ann	Allen..................James D.	1825 03 02	NJ, Salem
Harford...........Elizabeth	Mayall................Thomas	1815 10 12	ENG
Hargraves........Mary	Sessions............Solomon	1796	
Harley.............Margaret	Randall...............Alfred	1848 01 29	NE
Harmon...........Aseneth	Gheen................William	1841	
Harmon...........Aseneth	Mumford............Edward Thomas	1856 04 15	
Harmon...........Aseneth	Stout..................Hosea	1854 01 09	UT, Salt Lake City
Harmon...........Evelyn Rosette	Pugsley..............Joseph E. F.	1875 12 23	UT, Salt Lake City
Harmon...........Harriet	Marsing.............Niels Larson		
Harmon...........Lucinda	Jackman.............Levi	1849 11 18	UT, Salt Lake City
Harmon...........Mary Ann	Williams.............Samuel H.	1881 07 06	UT, Salt Lake City
Harmon...........Sarah	Cheney...............Elijah	1846 06	
Harmon...........Sarah	Harmon..............Oliver	1810	
Harmon...........Susan	Dixon..................Harvey	1876	
Haroldsen........Maren	Anderson............Gustave	1861 09 28	UT
Harper.............Elen	Wallace..............Henry	1863 02 07	UT, Salt Lake City
Harper.............Emma Louisa	Hillyard..............William	1884 10 15	UT, Logan
Harrington........Lydia	Alden..................Briggs	1841 05 09	NY, Henderson
Harrington........Lydia	Bates..................Cyrus	1813 02 18	
Harrington........Mary Miranda	Avery..................Charles Edward	1843 12 30	IA, Lee
Harrington........Sarah Ann	Rice....................Ira	1825	NY, Ontario
Harris..............Agnes Nancy	Baum..................Jacob	1826 10 12	PA, Manor
Harris..............Anaretta	Brimhall..............John	1850 06	UT, Woods Cross
Harris..............Elizabeth	Browett...............Daniel	1834 06 02	ENG
Harris..............Elizabeth	Butler..................James	1858	
Harris..............Elizabeth	Johnston.............William James	1867 07 20	
Harris..............Elizabeth	Powell.................John	1840 11 15	Wales
Harris..............Elizabeth	Richards.............Morgan	1857 02 17	Wales
Harris..............Elizabeth	Van Orden..........Everett C.	1857 03 12	UT, Salt Lake City
Harris..............Elizabeth Rose	Adams................Elias	1863 11 29	UT, Kaysville
Harris..............Hannah Mariah	Taylor.................Joseph	1854	
Harris..............Laura Wilder	Merrill.................Austin Shepherd	1827 03 26	
Harris..............Lydia	Harris.................Daniel	1853 10 05	CA, San Bern.
Harris..............Lydia	White..................Samuel Dennis	1866 09 08	
Harris..............Mary Ann	Aston..................John	1886 11 02	
Harris..............Mary Ann	Bowen................Lewis	1836 09 28	Wales
Harris..............Naomi	Bent....................Samuel		
Harris..............Naomi	Duel...................Benjamin	1823	NY, Palmyra
Harris..............Naomi	Kellogg...............Ezekiel	1826 10	NY, Palmyra
Harrison..........Alice	Cast...................Eric Magnus	1864 12 25	
Harrison..........Alice	Catlin..................Richard		
Harrison..........Ann	Holt....................Matthew	1851 05 09	ENG
Harrison..........Annie Hester	Frost..................Allen	1861 11 20	UT, Bountiful

Female	Male	Date	Place
Harrison..........Edith Frances	Hoggan ....George D.	1877 11 29	UT, Salt Lake City
Harrison..........Eliza Ann	Jenkins................Lewis	1870 05 22	UT, Salt Lake City
Harrison..........Louisa Eveline	Maiben ....Henry Joseph	1880 12 30	UT, Salt Lake City
Harrison..........Mary Ann	Janes ....Jacob	1869 01 11	UT, Salt Lake City
Harrison..........Sarah Ann	Farnes................Thomas S.	1861 03 02	ENG, London
Harrocks ....Elizabeth	Coulam................George	1869 12 27	
Harrocks ....Ellen	Livingston...........Charles	1867 10 12	UT, Salt Lake City
Harrocks ....Jane	Livingston...........Charles	1861 05 25	UT, Salt Lake City
Harrod ....Ellen	France................Joseph	1856 10 12	UT, Salt Lake City
Harrop ....Mary Jane	Judd ....James	1866 11 04	UT, Coalville
Harrover ....Eliza	Leavitt ....Jeremiah III	1845 02 01	IL, Nauvoo
Hart.................Jane	Terry..................Otis L.	1851 11 18	UT, Salt Lake City
Hart.................Silvira Caroline	Turnbow ....Samuel	1829 10 01	
Harter ....Sarah Ann	Watt...................George Darling	1866 08 11	UT, Salt Lake City
Hartford ....Caroline Iown	Hussey ....Elijah	1834 08 28	
Hartford ....Caroline Iown	Stallings ....Joseph	1849	
Hartlett............Mary Ann	Leaver ....Samuel	1831 03 11	NY, Brooklyn
Hartley ....Ann	Greenwood ....William	1839 11 24	ENG, Burnley
Hartley ....Drucilla Dickson	Parker ....Joshua	1844 08	IL, Hancock Co.
Hartley ....Hannah	Hall....................Joseph	1837 10 29	ENG, Wakefield
Hartley ....Hannah	Savage...............Joseph	1851 11 17	MO, St. Louis
Hartley ....Josephine	Zundel ....Thomas	1862 05 25	UT, Mona
Hartley ....Sarah Wells	Curtis.................Lyman	1862 07 26	UT, Salt Lake City
Hartley ....Sarah Wells	Soper ....Richard		
Hartley ....Susanna	Rigby ....Edward	1811 02 26	ENG
Harvey ....Ann	Day....................Joseph	1839 01 28	ENG, Essex
Harvey ....Cecelia	Driggs.................Shadrach F.		
Harvey ....Cecelia	Taylor ....Joseph B.	1842 03 18	IL, Adams Co.
Harvey ....Elizabeth	Baxter.................Isaac	1825 07 25	ENG, Chester
Harvey ....Elizabeth	Cloggie ....William		
Harvey ....Elizabeth	Tidwell...............James H.	1853 08 28	UT
Harvey ....Emma	Butler..................William	1856 01 23	ENG
Harvey ....Jean	Park...................Samuel	1849 12 31	Scotland
Harvey ....Lucinda	Van Leuven.........Ransom	1830	
Harville ....Martha	Bickmore ....Isaac M.	1829 03 01	ME, Friendship
Harville ....Martha	Parkinson ....Timothy G.	1856 06 04	UT, Salt Lake City
Harwood ....Anna	Goodwin..............Edwin Abijah	1860 10	
Haskell.............Catherine R.	Woodbury...........Thomas H.	1842 05 08	MA, New Salem
Haskell.............Irene Ursula	Pomeroy.............Francis M.	1844 07 13	NH
Haslam ....Sarah	Rigby ....William	1864 03 03	UT, Salt Lake City
Hastings ....Mary Elizabeth	Farley ....Winthrop	1863 01 24	UT, Salt Lake City
Hastings ....Sarah Sawyer	Snow ....Gardner	1814 11 30	NH, Chesterfield
Hastings ....Teresa	Judd ....Thomas Alfred	1830 12 27	Canada
Hatch ....Adeline	Barber ....George	1852 02 05	
Hatch ....Elizabeth	Winn..................Thomas Griffin	1854 12 07	UT, Lehi
Hatch ....Wealtha Rhoana	Henrie ....James	1850 12 28	UT, Bountiful
Hatchard..........Mary Ann	Jeffs ....William Yem	1847	ENG, Gloucester
Hathaway ....Elizabeth W.	Rolfe..................Samuel Jones	1818 03 04	ME
Hattersley ....Sarah	Wells ....Samuel	1842 02 06	ENG, Sheffield
Hauenstein ......Mary	Muhlestein..........Nicholas	1858 05 06	Switzerland
Haven ....Elizabeth	Barlow ....Israel	1840 02 23	IL, Quincy
Haven ....Nancy	Rockwood ....Albert P.	1827 04 03	MA, Holliston
Havens ....Mary Ann	Wilson ....Bradley B.	1861 12 20	UT, Payson
Hawk ....Mary Caroline	Moore.................Samuel	1850 04 07	

Female	Male	Date	Place
Hawker ....Sarah Ann	Green ....Austin G.	1870 05 16	UT, Salt Lake City
Hawkins ....Harriet	Critchlow ....William	1832 02 14	PA, Butler
Hawkins ....Sarah	Byington ....Hiram N.	1828 01 27	NY, Oneida Co.
Hawkins ....Sarah	Hickenlooper ....William	1829 08 29	
Hawkins ....Susannah	Bailey ....Charles R.	1863 11 07	UT, Salt Lake City
Hawley............Anna	Reynolds ....William F.	1846 02 22	
Hawley............Elizabeth	Reynolds ....William F.		
Haws ....Eliza	Holdaway ....Shadrack	1853 01 06	UT, Provo
Haws ....Eliza	Pickup ....George	1849 01 21	UT, Salt Lake City
Haws ....Lucinda	Holdaway ....Shadrack	1848 12 24	UT, Salt Lake City
Haws ....Lucretia	Sessions ....Richard	1821 04 14	IL, White Co.
Haws ....Lydia Catherine	Curtis..................Hyrum	1884 08 06	
Haws ....Lydia Catherine	Haskell ....Chester K.	1853 03 12	UT, Provo
Haws ....Mary Eliza	Curtis..................Hyrum	1859 10 04	UT, Provo
Haws ....Nancy	Wall ....William M.	1840 06 02	IL, Sangamon Co.
Hay ....Mary	Young..................Thomas C.	1856 10 08	UT, Salt Lake City
Hayball ....Ellen Jane	England ....Thomas	1885 04 26	
Hayball ....Ellen Jane	Watson...............William		UT, Logan
Hayden ....Flora	Drake ....Jacob	1834 07 01	NY, Pompey
Hayden ....Flora	Mallory ....Lemuel	1846 02 06	
Haydock ....Ellen	Langton ....James	1826 04 09	ENG
Haydock ....Mary	Luke ....William Jr.	1857 01 10	UT, Salt Lake City
Hayes ....Clara W. T.	Huey...................Robert French	1844 05 20	South Africa
Hayes ....Sarah	Butterfield............Jacob K.	1855 02 28	UT, Salt Lake City
Hayes ....Sarah	Sorenson.............Niels		
Haynes ....Daphne	Hamblin...............Isaiah	1812 11 30	
Haynes ....Elizabeth	Box.....................John Henry	1837 11 30	IN, Lawrence Co.
Haynes ....Jane	James ....William	1835 06 15	ENG, Pinvin
Haynes ....Jane	Maud ....Mathew		
Haynes ....Sarah Ann	Sharp ....Brigham Young	1876 11 05	
Hays ....Rebecca Ann	Henefer ....William	1850 01 01	NJ, Trenton
Hayter............Annetta	Fleet ....Henry	1841 10 24	ENG
Hayter............Annetta	Smart ....Thomas Sharratt	1845 03 01	France
Hazen ....Ann	Cooley................Andrew Wood	1870 02 14	UT, Salt Lake City
Heaps ....Mary Ann	Hillyard ....Thomas	1852 01 28	ENG
Heath.............Elizabeth	Watts..................Robert H.	1833 12 20	
Heath.............Harriet	Marler.................Allen	1832 02 02	MS, Port Gibson
Heath.............Jane	Silcock................Nicholas T.	1841 04 14	ENG
Heaton............Hannah	Hansen................Niels Peter	1870 03 27	NV, Overton
Heaton............Lovina	Murray................Franklin C.	1873 03	UT
Heaton............Rebecca	Nebeker ....Henry	1865 07 22	UT, Salt Lake City
Heaver............Elizabeth	Clarke.................John Henry	1854 01 08	ENG, London
Hedrick ....Mary	Garner.................Philip	1830 04 04	IL, Carthage
Heelis ....Martha	Lythgoe ....James	1864 04 17	ENG
Hefford............Harriet Ann	Roberts ....Levi	1835 08 18	ENG, Deerhurst
Hegglund ....Anna Sophia	Beckstrand ....Elias A.	1862 01 24	
Heiner.............Elizabeth	Grover ....Thomas	1865 02 10	UT, Salt Lake City
Heiner.............Susannah C.	Jackman..............Parmeno	1892 02 14	UT, Salt Lake City
Heiner.............Susannah C.	Ovard ....Joseph William	1875 06 28	UT, Salt Lake City
Heinrich ....Eda Henrietta	Farnsworth ....Alonzo L.	1875 04 08	UT, Salt Lake City
Helgesen ....Marta Karena	Dahle..................Johannes	1862	
Helm ....Caroline	Lemmon ....Oliver Perry		
Hemingway......Ada Cemantha	Davidson ....Robert	1861 11 08	UT, Salt Lake City
Hemsley ....Elizabeth	Etherington.........John	1818 03 29	

Female	Male	Date	Place
Henderson.......Eliza Jane	Brinkerhoff...........James	1854 06 11	UT, Salt Lake City
Henderson.......Hannah	Phillips................William S.	1834 04 21	Wales
Henderson.......Janet	Andersen............Andrew	1875 10 11	UT, Salt Lake City
Henderson.......Mary	Allred.................Isaac	1846 01 15	
Henderson.......Mary	Heiner ....George	1866 12 22	UT, Salt Lake City
Henderson.......Sarah Elizabeth	Lindsay...............William B. Jr.	1854 02 19	UT, Salt Lake City
Hendricks ....Lucy	Williams..............Elias W.	1840 12 30	
Hendricks ....Rebecca	Lewis..................Neriah Jr.	1836	KY, Simpson Co.
Hendricks ....Rebecca	Roskelley ....Samuel	1858 07 23	UT, Salt Lake City
Hendricks ....Rebecca	Watson................Hiram Abiff	1852	UT, Salt Lake City
Hendricks ....Tabitha	Ricks ....Thomas Edwin	1852 08 18	
Hendrickson ....Elizabeth Ann	Brady..................Lindsay A.	1831 10 18	KY, Washington
Hendrickson ....Frances Anna	Hopkins ....Ezekiel Jr.	1865 01 21	UT, Salt Lake City
Hendrickson ....Polly	Stringham............George	1820 08 17	NY, Colesville
Hendryx ....Martha	Sampson..............Isaac	1822 04 07	OH, New London
Henricksen ......Karen Marie	Jorgensen ....Hans	1864	Denmark
Henriksen ....Anna Maria	Jensen ....Jes	1851 01 29	Denmark
Henwood ....Elizabeth T.	Gailey.................John	1858 08 25	UT, Salt Lake City
Hepworth ....Mary	Thornton.............William	1834 06 22	ENG
Herbert ....Ann	Rynearson...........Andrew J.	1857 03 15	
Herns................Martha Jane	Boice..................John	1835	Canada
Herrick ....Dianna	Clark...................Isaac	1851 06 10	UT, Ogden
Herrick ....Dianna	Moore.................David	1854 04 07	
Herrick ....Eliza Ann	Keyes ....William Henry H.	1834 04 12	MO, Clay Co.
Hess ....Anna	Milne ....David	1871 10 09	UT, Salt Lake City
Hessell.............Christina Amelia	Crismon...............Charles	1867 10 12	UT, Salt Lake City
Hessell.............Christina Amelia	Rees...................Joseph A.	1872 06 24	UT, Salt Lake City
Hester..............Eliza	Platt...................Francis	1853 11 19	UT, Salt Lake City
Heward ....Sarah	Stocks ....Moroni	1865 01 02	UT, Rockville
Hewitson..........Elizabeth Ann	Phillips................John Campbell	1875 04 12	UT, Salt Lake City
Hiatt ....Mary Jane	Taylor ....Teancum	1859 05 20	UT, Salt Lake City
Hibbard............Hannah White	Maughan............Hyrum Weston	1875 04 05	UT, Salt Lake City
Hibbitt ....Mary Ann	Jeffery ....Thomas Alfred	1853 12 29	ENG, Birmingham
Hick ....Hagar	Singleton ....Albert	1883 10 18	UT, Salt Lake City
Hick ....Hagar	Startup ....William D.	1868 11 04	UT, Salt Lake City
Hickenlooper ...Belinda	Wade..................Edward Davis	1849 01 21	UT, Salt Lake City
Hickerson ....Catherine	Miles..................Sampson	1836 12 11	IL, Vandalia
Hickerson ....Catherine	Woolsey ....Thomas	1859 01 22	
Hickman ....Elizabeth Ellen	Meecham ....Jeremiah Emery	1854 04 01	
Hickman ....Harriet	Coltrin................Graham		
Hicks...............Anna Hannah	King...................David A.	1866	
Hicks...............Annie	Free...................Absalom P.	1857 03 05	UT, Salt Lake City
Hicks...............Lydia Ann	Page..................John	1838 10 11	ENG
Hicks...............Lydia Ann	Stevens ....John	1865 10 04	UT, Provo
Hicks...............Lydia Ann	Woodcock ....Samuel	1853	MO, St. Louis
Higbee ....Emma	Rogers ....Henry Clay	1856 10 19	UT, Provo
Higgenbotham .Alice	Ashton................Richard	1837 12 17	ENG
Higgenbotham .Alice	Miller ....Charles Dutton	1853 01 16	
Higgenbotham .Frances	Clayton...............Albert	1851 07 10	ENG
Higgenbotham .Frances	Olpin..................Henry	1862 01 02	UT, Salt Lake City
Higginbotham ..Elizabeth Letitia	Peery..................David Harold	1865 04 10	UT, Holiday
Higgins ....Almira	Chase.................John Darwin	1847 02 17	CO, Pueblo
Higgins ....Catherine B.	Holladay ....John D.	1822 04 16	SC, Kershaw
Higgins ....Catherine B.	Jones ....Benjamin		

Female	Male	Date	Place
Higgins ....Mary Ann	Lyon ....Thomas	1849 01 01	Scotland
Higgins ....Mary Ann	Miller ....John	1866 04 20	UT, Salt Lake City
Higgs ....Annie Elizabeth	Clayton...............William	1870 12 30	UT, Salt Lake City
Higgs ....Annie Elizabeth	Jensen ....Michael	1881 05 11	UT, Manti
Higgs ....Mary Susannah	Sleater................Robert G.	1867 09 13	UT, Salt Lake City
Higley ....Lucretia	Higley ....Oliver	1801 06 20	VT, Marlboro
Hill ....Agnes	Richards.............John Kenny	1831	Canada
Hill ....Alice	Bright.................Gilbert	1869 12 06	
Hill ....Alice	Small..................James		
Hill ....Ann	Dobson...............William Frain	1868 12 28	UT, Salt Lake City
Hill ....Elizabeth B.	Greenwell............Ambrose	1854 09 25	ENG
Hill ....Elizabeth Bryce	Gardner..............John	1856 01	
Hill ....Elizabeth Bryce	Maughan ....William Harrison	1860 06 02	UT, Wellsville
Hill ....Emily	Harris ....Zachariah	1834	IL, Macoupin Co.
Hill ....Emily	Mills..................William Gill	1857 06 14	UT, Salt Lake City
Hill ....Emily	Smoot.................Abraham Owen	1846 01 09	IL, Nauvoo
Hill ....Emily	Woodmansee......Joseph	1864 05 07	UT, Salt Lake City
Hill ....Hannah	Straw.................James	1855 02 18	ENG
Hill ....Hannah Hood	Romney.............Miles Park	1862 05 10	UT, Salt Lake City
Hill ....Isabella Hood	Hamilton............James C.	1870 11 28	UT, Salt Lake City
Hill ....Julia	Ivins..................Israel	1857 02 13	UT, Salt Lake City
Hill ....Margaret	Hall...................Joseph Smith	1865 01 20	
Hill ....Margaret Ann	Caldwell ....Robert C.	1854	
Hill ....Margaret Ann	White.................George Martin	1863 12 19	UT, Salt Lake City
Hill ....Mary	Bullock ....James	1836 03 28	Canada
Hill ....Mary	Crismon.............Charles	1830 05 06	
Hill ....Mary	McArthur ....Daniel D.	1857	UT, Salt Lake City
Hill ....Mary	Spencer.............Orson	1853	
Hill ....Nancy Ann	Shaffer ....John Isaac	1847	
Hill ....Rebecca Hood	Pettit..................Edwin	1864 10 29	
Hill ....Sarah	Parkinson ....Charles G.		
Hillier ....Lemira	Collins ....Aquilla	1860 07 04	ENG, Wiltshire
Hillman ....Adalinda	Koyle ....John Hyrum	1861 11 25	UT, Spanish Fork
Hillman ....Adalinda	Lewis.................Frederick	1876 10 17	UT, Salt Lake City
Hillman ....Ellen Celestia	Snell..................Rufus P.	1869 02 08	UT, Salt Lake City
Hillman ....Guilieta Fidelia	Simmons ....Samuel	1866 01 01	
Hillman ....Mandana	Dalley ....William	1846 09 04	IA, Trading Point
Hillman ....Sarah	Haws ....Jason	1851 09 07	IA, Coonville
Hillman ....Sarah	Safley ....John H.	1881 12 25	
Hills................Julia	Johnson ....Ezekiel	1801 01 12	MA, Grafton
Hills................Julia	Smith ....John		
Hills................Olive	Browning ....James Green	1852 03 22	UT, Salt Lake City
Hills................Olive	Chase.................Eli	1840 07 25	NY
Hillyer ....Ann	Hooper ....John	1812 05 17	ENG
Hinchcliff..........Edna	Evans.................David	1854 11 03	
Hinchcliff..........Edna	Stimpson ....William	1858 05 01	UT, Ogden
Hinchcliff..........Edna	Wood..................Edwin		
Hinchliffe..........Ellen	Midgley...............Thomas	1821 09 30	ENG, York
Hind ....Mary Ann	Dand ....Thomas	1807 01 26	ENG, Harrington
Hind ....Mary Ann	Perry ....William	1841 07 12	ENG, Liverpool
Hinkle ....Mary Rhodes	Foster................Charles Allan	1851	UT, Ogden
Hinman ....Helen Aurelia	Miller ....Henry William	1858 03 02	UT, Salt Lake City
Hird................Jane	Maxwell..............John Lambert	1860 03 06	ENG, Yorkshire
Hirst................Charlotte	Coon ....John Abraham	1881 01 06	UT, Salt Lake City

Female	Male	Date	Place
Hirst ....Mary	Hepworth............Joseph	1837 04 09	ENG, Yorkshire
Hiskey..............Clarissa Jane	Warr ....Charles E.	1871	UT
Hislop ....Isabelle	Allen ....Ammon	1881 11 03	UT, Huntsville
Hitchcock........Louisa S.	Twitchell..............Anciel	1844 10 07	
Hjermin ....Mary Catherine	Thompson ....Niels	1870 05 30	UT, Salt Lake City
Hjetting ....Helsine	Bohn..................Magnus Carl F.	1843 01 29	Denmark
Hjetting ....Helsine	Larsen ....Svend	1858 01 11	
Hjetting ....Mette Marie	Larsen ....Svend	1861	UT
Hjorth ....Johanne D. A.	Hulse..................Hyrum Smith	1873 04 01	UT, Salt Lake City
Hoagland ....Emily	Little ....Jesse Carter		
Hobbs ....Alice Lavina	Banks ....William Ellis	1877 04 11	UT, St. George
Hobbs ....Caroline	Watterson............William Jr.	1866 12 13	
Hobbs ....Ellen Agnes	Fielding ....Amos H.	1871	UT, Parowan
Hobbs ....Emma Lucy	Meads ....Alexander M.	1864 10 19	UT, Salt Lake City
Hobbs ....Mary Ann	Gadd ....Alfred	1864 01 10	UT, Nephi
Hobbs ....Sarah Elizabeth	Harriman ....Henry H.	1871 09 23	UT, St. George
Hobbs ....Tryphena Jane	West..................William Moroni	1868 05 27	UT, Parowan
Hobson ....Mary	Hewitson ....George	1843 08 26	ENG, York
Hocquard.........Elizabeth	Carlisle ....John	1857 02 08	UT, Salt Lake City
Hocquard.........Fanny Sophia	Carlisle ....Thomas Fields	1854 01 22	UT
Hodges ....Elizabeth	Covington ....Berrill	1812 11 08	ENG, Bedford
Hodges ....Elizabeth	Summers............Edwin	1862 10	
Hodges ....Emma	Summers............George		
Hodges ....Hannah	Beazer................Mark	1849 01 14	ENG
Hodges ....Mary Anne	Smith..................James T.	1858 04 06	
Hodgetts ....Emily Teressa	Lowder ....John	1860 05 25	UT, Salt Lake City
Hodgkins ....Angeline	Horne ....Moses	1835 11 08	ME, Friendship
Hodgkins ....Angeline	Rockwood ....Albert P.	1846 01 21	IL, Nauvoo
Hodgkinson .....Ann Elizabeth	Palmer................Isaac	1844	
Hodgkinson .....Ann Elizabeth	Wamsley ....Thomas	1826 12 25	
Hodierne..........Ann	Fawson ....Abraham	1838 05 06	ENG, Foleshill
Hodson ....Grace	Siddoway ....Richard	1877 04 20	
Hofhine ....Mary Jane	Doty...................Benjamin	1856 12 01	UT, Salt Lake City
Hogan..............Caroline	Hyer ....Christian Larsen	1850 11 23	UT, Bountiful
Hogan..............Lovina	Hyer ....Christian Larsen		
Hogeboom.......Hannah	Markham..............Stephen	1824 02	
Hogeboom.......Hannah	Sherman ....John		
Hogg................Emma	Ward ....John	1838 05 07	ENG
Hoggan............Janet	West..................Jabez William	1881 01 20	UT, Salt Lake City
Hoggan............Margaret	Hoggan ....Thomas A.	1872 12 16	UT, Salt Lake City
Hoke ....Juliana	Zimmerman.........George G.	1816 04 04	PA, Franklin Co.
Holbrook ....Alice Matilda	Crapo ....Leonides L.	1867 02 24	UT, Paradise
Holbrook ....Charlotte	Call....................Anson Vasco	1853 01 28	
Holbrook ....Mary Maria	Little ....Jesse Carter	1856 01 29	
Holbrook ....Phebe	Harding ....Dwight	1833 02 12	NY
Holbrook ....Sarah Lucretia	Tolman ....Judson	1846 01 12	IL, Nauvoo
Holden ....Jane Eliza	Knight.................William Thomas R.	1868 03 21	UT, Salt Lake City
Holden ....Margaret	Hardman ....Richard	1828 01 07	ENG, Brindle
Holden ....Margaret	Prestley ....William	1850	
Holden ....Margaret	Young.................Ebenezer R.	1836 05 01	CT, Westport
Holden ....Mary Ann	Cook...................David	1852 12 15	UT, Provo
Holdsworth ......Martha	Dean ....John	1832 01 06	ENG, Pendle
Holladay ....Caron Happoch	Bingham..............Thomas	1849 09 06	UT, Salt Lake City
Holland ....Caroline	Dalrymple ....Andrew	1861 01 05	UT, Salt Lake City

Female	Male	Date	Place
Holland ....Caroline	Lyon ....John	1856 03 28	
Holland ....Caroline	Steed...................James	1838 11 10	ENG
Hollingshead....Amanda Ellen	Smith.................Thomas Sasson	1857 07 16	UT, Salt Lake City
Hollis..............Elizabeth	Roe ....James	1840 03 24	ENG
Hollis..............Harriet	Blake ....Benjamin F.	1841 05 31	ENG
Hollis..............Sophia	Connell..............William Michael	1859	ENG
Hollis..............Sophia	Hill ....Samuel	1847 05 10	ENG, Birmingham
Hollis..............Sophia	Price...................Edward	1864 09 26	UT, Salt Lake City
Hollist.............Deborah	Manning ....Eli	1865 03 24	UT, Salt Lake City
Hollist.............Elizabeth	Stinger................John H.	1859 10 01	NE, Florence
Hollister ....Eda	Rogers ....Noah	1819 10 08	
Holm ....Ane Marie	Jensen ....Niels	1857 08 07	UT, Salt Lake City
Holm ....Ane Marie	Sorensen............Nicholai	1838 05 12	Denmark
Holm ....Margrethe K.	Evans ....David	1861 05 04	UT, Salt Lake City
Holman ....Abigail Elizabeth	Stevens ....Walter	1854 04 27	UT
Holman ....Emily Jennison	Lewis ....James	1847 05 09	MO. St. Louis
Holmes ....Ann	Burton ....Robert Lamb	1849	ENG
Holmes ....Emma	Allen ....Marshall F.	1859 02 27	UT, Ogden
Holmes ....Jane	Benbow..............John	1826 10 16	ENG, Worcester
Holmes ....Jane	Orton ....Alexander	1857 11 01	UT, Cedar City
Holmes ....Mary Ann	Hunt ....William	1816 02 13	ENG
Holmes ....Sarah	Benbow..............Thomas	1845 02 10	IL, Nauvoo
Holmes ....Sarah Elizabeth	Weaver...............Franklin	1856 05 09	UT, Salt Lake City
Holmes ....Sarah Elizabeth	Weaver...............Miles	1855 01 01	UT, Salt Lake City
Holroyd ....Ellen Taylor	Argyle.................Joseph Jr.	1867 09 28	UT, Salt Lake City
Holroyd ....Mary Hebden	Thomas ....James Moroni	1862 03 30	
Holroyd ....Tabitha	Smith..................Richard	1861 10 30	UT, Beaver
Holt ....Mary	Beard ....William	1854 08 27	ENG, Wochester
Holt ....Mary	Finch ....William	1863 12 31	UT, Salt Lake City
Holt ....Mary	Hughes...............Robert		
Holt ....Mary	Hulet..................Orin Sylvester		
Holt ....Mary Ann	Barker ....William	1855 10 05	UT, Salt Lake City
Holyoak ....Hannah	Lefevre ....William	1855 12 25	
Holyoak ....Sarah	James ....Joseph	1854 10 02	UT, Salt Lake City
Homer...............Anna Eliza	Lemmon ....Willis	1859 11 01	UT Salt Lake City
Homer...............Mary Ann	Boram ....Alfred	1890 07 04	ID, Rigby
Homer...............Nancy Ann	Harris ....Martin Jr.	1859 11 01	UT, Salt Lake City
Hone................Emma	Evans ....George	1867 03 31	UT, Salt Lake City
Hone................Sarah Jane	Richardson..........William	1879 10 16	UT, Springville
Hook ....Ellen	Burningham.........Thomas	1861 08	UT, Salt Lake City
Hook ....Sarah	Smuin.................Thomas	1837 07 09	ENG
Hookway..........Eliza	Berrett ....John Watts	1865 12 16	UT, Mill Creek
Hooley ....Arnelia	West...................David	1844 07 15	ENG
Hooper.............Esther	Pingree...............Job	1861 09 27	UT, Salt Lake City
Hooper.............Jane Wilkie	Blood.................William	1861 09	
Hoopes ....Mary Ann	Allen ....Albern		
Hoopes ....Mary Ann	Yearsley ....David D.	1829 09 11	PA, Westchester
Hoopes ....Rebecca Ann	Fifield ....Matthew P.	1862 03 03	UT, Richmond
Hoopes ....Rebecca Ann	Lincoln...............Charles	1860 02 26	UT, Bountiful
Hope................Emma Eliza	England..............John	1920 10 20	UT, Logan
Hope................Emma Eliza	Geddes ....William	1870 02 21	UT, Salt Lake City
Hope................Emma Eliza	Stewart..............John M.	1865 06 24	UT, Salt Lake City
Hope................Margaret P.	Williams..............William Jr.	1853 02 07	ENG
Hopkin ....Mary	Beck...................John Forsyth	1868 02 15	UT, Salt Lake City

Female	Male	Date	Place
Hopkin ....Rebekah	Eyre.....................George	1861 04 17	ENG, Sheffield
Hopkins ....Caroline	Clark....................John	1852 05 31	
Hopkins ....Mary	Walker................George Gorril	1837 03 27	ENG
Horne..............Eliza	Hartley................Charles	1840 11 01	ENG
Horrocks ....Alice	Wood.................Charles	1858 03 31	UT, Ogden
Horrocks ....Elizabeth	Jackson..............Aaron	1848 05 28	ENG, Cheshire
Horrocks ....Elizabeth	Kingsford.............William	1857 07 06	
Horrocks ....Mary	Cook....................William	1876	UT, Heber City
Horrocks ....Mary	Leavitt ....Nathaniel Jr.	1857 04 04	UT, Salt Lake City
Horrocks ....Mary	Taylor ....Joseph W.	1869 06 15	UT, Salt Lake City
Horrocks ....Rachel	Duke...................Robert Stone	1872 11 11	UT, Salt Lake City
Horsecroft.......Sarah Caroline	Wyatt..................John Moses	1848 12 25	ENG
Horspool ....Martha Jane	Hellewell.............Joseph H.	1879 11 27	UT, Salt Lake City
Horton.............Caroline	Snow ....Lorenzo	1853 10 09	UT, Salt Lake City
Hoskin ....Elizabeth	Hoskin ....Benjamin H.	1848 08 25	
Hoskin ....Elizabeth	Salisbury ....Joshua	1858 10 13	IL, Shawneetown
Hossack...........Ann	McGregor ....William	1841 12 28	Scotland
Hough..............Ann	Carson ....George	1817	PA, Mifflin Co.
Hough..............Elizabeth	Frampton.............David	1829 03 26	IL, Nauvoo
Hough..............Jemima R.	Midgley...............Joshua	1853 04 08	
Houghton.........Ann	Gunn ....Thomas	1855 02 28	ENG, London
Houston ....Catherine	Alexander............Horace Martin	1849	
Houston ....Phoebe	Alexander............Alvah	1822 05 09	NH, Acworth
Houston ....Susanna	Matlock...............Gideon Cooper	1848	IA, Council Bluffs
Houston ....Susanna	Mitchell...............Benjamin T.	1857 03 06	UT, Salt Lake City
Houtz ....Catharine	Boyer..................Augustus Sell	1839	PA
Howard ....Eleanor	Halls ....William	1880 01 08	
Howard ....Elizabeth	Isom ....Owen	1835 03 11	ENG
Howard ....Elizabeth	Rich....................Joseph	1853 01 18	UT, Salt Lake City
Howard ....Elizabeth	Standage.............William	1815	
Howard ....Elizabeth	Thackham ....William	1820	
Howard ....Emma	Corbridge ....William	1870 04 14	UT, Salt Lake City
Howard ....Jane	Barnes................George	1836 05 01	ENG
Howard ....Jane	Barnes................William	1857 03 12	
Howard ....Katherine Alice	Brockbank...........Isaac Jr.	1860 06 25	
Howard ....Margaret Ann	Ferrin..................Samuel	1857 05 03	UT, Ogden
Howard ....Margaret Ann	McBride...............Robert	1833 11 25	ENG
Howard ....Mary Ann	Tolman................Judson A.	1872 12 23	UT, Salt Lake City
Howard ....Mary Elizabeth	Carter ....William F.	1854 09 10	UT, Salt Lake City
Howard ....Sarah Freelove	Bawden ....Henry	1857 03 18	UT
Howarth ....Dorothy	Beagley ....John	1868 12 24	
Howarth ....Dorothy	Ostler ....John C.	1873 06 09	UT, Salt Lake City
Howarth ....Mary	Kay....................Joseph	1855	ENG
Howe ....Ann	Crane ....George	1868 02 01	ENG, London
Howell..............Ann	Burt ....John Davidson	1875 08 09	
Howell..............Ann	Jones ....Ricy Davis	1854 07 01	
Howell..............Charlotte	Woods................James	1870 07 18	UT, Salt Lake City
Howell..............Harriet Jane	Crook ....William Joshua	1880 10 14	UT, Salt Lake City
Howell..............Mary	Shields ....John Fenton	1847 07 01	IL, New Lancaster
Howell..............Mary Lavina	Brady..................Jordan	1861 12 10	UT, Fairview
Howells ....Mary	Llewellyn ....Edmund	1834 05 10	Wales
Howells ....Mary	Richards.............William	1861 12 27	
Howells ....Mary Price	Adams................John	1857 09 14	UT, Tooele
Howie ....Christina	Lindsay...............William	1844 07 19	Scotland

Female	Male	Date	Place
Howie ....Christina	Muir.....................George	1863 06 13	UT, Heber
Howland ....Ann Eliza	Cook...................Phineas W.	1840 01 01	MI
Hoy ....Susannah	Foy ....Martin W.	1872 05 27	UT, Salt Lake City
Hubbard...........Julia Cynthia	Barker ....Byron	1867 12 07	UT, Salt Lake City
Hubbard...........Julia Cynthia	Wells ....Henry	1865	
Huber...............Anna M.	Stucki ....John U.	1859 08 19	Ocean
Huckvale..........Mary Georgina	Osmond ....George	1855 07	MO, St. Louis
Hudson ....Ann	Burton ....Joseph	1843 04 30	ENG
Hudson ....Ann	Reid....................John T.		
Hudson ....Ann	Richardson..........John		ENG
Hudson ....Ann	Vance..................William Perkins	1865 03 10	
Hudson ....Deseret McBride	Kelley ....Russel Thomas		
Hudson ....Sarah Jane	Walker.................Joseph R.		
Huerni..............Maria (Mary)	Naegle................Conrad	1863 01 08	
Huey ....Annie E.	Slaughter............Samuel N.	1860	
Huffaker...........Rozilla	Pulsipher ....John	1853 11 04	UT, Salt Lake City
Huffman...........Mary	Elmer.................Hyrum K.	1845 06 09	IA, Lee Co.
Hug ....Hannah	Walton................George	1857 06 03	UT, Salt Lake City
Hughes ....Ann	Hall....................Thomas	1839 12 30	Wales
Hughes ....Ann Melsome	Hancock ....James	1846	ENG
Hughes ....Catherine	Paul...................James Patten	1866 03 24	UT, Salt Lake City
Hughes ....Catherine	Roberts ....Robert	1842 08 25	Wales
Hughes ....Elizabeth	Jones ....William	1825	NY, New York
Hughes ....Elizabeth	Newman..............Joseph	1834 10 27	ENG
Hughes ....Elizabeth A.	Cotterell.............William	1871 07 03	UT, Salt Lake City
Hughes ....Martha Maria	Cannon ....Angus Munn	1884 10 06	UT, Salt Lake City
Hughes ....Mary	Hunter ....David P.	1867 08 09	UT, Farmington
Hughes ....Sarah	Wilkinson.............Charles	1846 06 01	ENG
Hulet ....Anna Maria	Perry ....Stephen C.	1844 01 18	IL, Nauvoo
Hulet ....Electa Fidelia	Hillman...............Silas	1842 09 10	IL, Nauvoo
Hulet ....Sally	Whiting ....Elisha Jr.	1805 09 18	
Hulks ....Sarah Ann	Henefer ....James	1846 08 30	
Hull ....Isabelle Forbes	Davis..................William C.	1867 11 08	UT, Salt Lake City
Hull ....Isabelle Forbes	Smith..................Jonathan	1872 11 11	UT, Salt Lake City
Hulme ....Alice	Eckersley ....Joseph	1845 05 23	
Hulme ....Alice	Haslam................John	1834	
Hulme ....Ann	Barlow................Thomas	1847 11 05	
Hulme ....Barbara	Heath ....John	1825	ENG
Hulme ....Hanna	Rollins ....James Henry	1851 03 03	UT, Salt Lake City
Humberstone...Sarah	Wagstaff.............John	1844 11 25	ENG
Humble ....Francis E.	Ferguson............Jacob S.	1851 08 31	ENG
Humble ....Francis E.	Smith..................Robert		
Humphrey........Elizabeth	Dixon..................Charles	1799 10 13	Canada
Humphrey........Mary Jane	Brower................Ariah Coats	1854 03 05	UT, Salt Lake City
Humphreys .....Sarah Jane	Burbidge.............James W.	1858 07 05	UT, Salt Lake City
Humphris ....Elizabeth	Hill ....William John	1863 05 03	UT, North Ogden
Hundsperger....Anna Elizabeth	Loosle ....Hans Casper	1857 04 23	Switzerland
Hunt................Ann Elizabeth	Doxey.................Thomas	1853 07 10	IA, Council Bluffs
Hunt................Eliza Ellenor	Wilson ....Lewis D. Jr.	1877	
Hunt................Elizabeth	Sanders..............William	1837 01 08	
Hunt................Hannah	Collard................James E.	1865 10 01	
Hunt................Loretta	Walker.................Jesse H.	1873 01 08	UT, Paradise
Hunt................Mary	Clark...................Lorenzo		UT, Salt Lake City
Hunt................Sarah	Booth..................William	1833	

Female	Male	Date	Place
Hunt............Sarah	Mitchell............Robert	1822 01 15	ENG, London
Hunt............Zelpha	Moyes ....William		
Hunter............Agnes Ann	Hunter ....Robert	1835 04 21	Scotland
Hunter............Elizabeth	Cook............David Patterson	1859 02 04	UT, Salt Lake City
Hunter............Elizabeth	Murdock............Joseph Stacy	1854 06 11	UT, Salt Lake City
Hunter............Elizabeth	Wesley ....John Everett	1859 06 21	NE, Florence
Hunter............Jane	Talbot ....John J.		NE, Florence
Hunter............Janet	Cook............David S.	1852 09 24	UT, Salt Lake City
Hunter............Margaret	Love ....David	1851 07 03	MO, St. Louis
Hunter............Margaret	Van Orman............Abraham	1867 03 06	UT, Salt Lake City
Hunter............Mary Patterson	Moffat ....Archibald R.	1875 06 04	UT, Salt Lake City
Hunter............Rachel	Adair............Samuel	1853 05 09	UT, Payson
Hunter............Rachel	Davis............Henry	1825 11 14	
Hunter............Rachel	Stewart............Benjamin F.	1850 09 07	
Huntington ......Mary Asenath	Cooley............Andrew Wood	1866 02 17	UT, Grantsville
Huntington ......Presendia L.	Buell............Norman	1827 01 08	NY, Jefferson
Huntington ......Presendia L.	Kimball ....Heber Chase	1846 11 07	
Huntington ......Presendia L.	Smith............Joseph Jr.	1841 12 11	IL, Nauvoo
Huntley ....Mary Ann	Burnham ....James L.	1834 12 01	VT, Waitsfield
Huntley ....Mary Ann	Young............Joseph	1846 02 06	IL, Nauvoo
Huntsman ....Catharine J.	Bickmore............Gilbert M.	1849 03 13	IA, Council Bluffs
Huntsman ....Salena	Chipman............James	1863 08 01	
Huntsman ....Sarah Jane	Lewis............Samuel	1854 01 01	UT, Parowan
Hupper............Lucretia	Mower ....Henry	1847 02 05	IA, Council Bluffs
Hurren ....Emma	Woolf............James	1869 12 13	UT, Hyde Park
Hurren ....Mary	Wight............Joseph M.	1864 10 05	UT, Brigham City
Hurst............Emma Jane	Tucker ....George	1868 03 07	UT, Salt Lake City
Hurst............Mary Jane	Crandall............Martin Pardon	1862 10 04	UT, Springville
Hurst............Mary Jane	Crandall............Myron Nathan	1857 03 13	UT, Salt Lake City
Hurst............Mary Jane	Maycock............Amos	1875 09 01	
Hurup............Hartmandine N.	Nielsen ....Niels	1838 09 25	Denmark
Hurup............Hartmandine N.	Pedersen............Jens	1860 01 03	Denmark
Huskinson........Sarah	Giles............William		ENG
Hussey ....Charlotte Jane	Stallings ....Joseph	1856 06 01	UT, Salt Lake City
Hussey ....Margaret E.	Brower............Ariah Coats	1838 09 06	IL
Hutchensen .....Jamima	Meyrick............John	1861 10 28	UT, American Fork
Hutchinson ......Elizabeth	Wadsworth ....James	1831 05 22	ENG, Darfield
Hutchison ....Annie	Graham ....Robert D.	1876 10 28	UT, Salt Lake City
Hutchison ....Elizabeth	Moyes ....Robert	1836 05 22	Scotland
Hutchison ....Euphemia	Dale............James Robert	1867 11 16	UT, Salt Lake City
Hutchison ....Euphemia	Sellers ....William Hyrum	1871 12 11	UT, Salt Lake City
Hutchison ....Margaret S.	Armstrong ....Thomas K.	1869 01 19	UT, Salt Lake City
Hutton............Mary	McMurray ....John	1821 08 18	PA, York
Hyde ....Abbie	Cowley ....Matthias		
Hyde ....Martha Ann	Hunter ....Edward	1856 03 30	
Hyde ....Mary Lucretia	Woolf............John A.	1866 12 21	UT, Salt Lake City
Hyder............Charlotte J.	Evans............William M.	1852 07 15	UT, Salt Lake City

I

Female	Male	Date	Place
Imlay............Margaret N.	Sevey ....George W.		
Ingersoll..........Hannah	Patten............John	1824 04 25	
Ingham ....Nancy	Openshaw..........George	1845 02 02	ENG, Lancashire

Female	Male	Date	Place
Ingmann ....Laura Johanna	Mickelsen ....Niels	1862 08 09	UT, Salt Lake City
Ingram ....Francis Ann	Smith.................Samuel	1856 07 31	
Ingram ....Harriet	Gardner..............Henry Bone	1845 11 22	ENG, Sussex
Ingram ....Harriet	Hoyt....................Silas	1854 11 21	UT, Parowan
Ingram ....Lucy Jane	Holley.................James	1852 05 10	ENG
Ingram ....Mary Ann	White..................John C.	1863 03 09	UT, Spanish Fork
Ingram ....Sarah Ann	Smith..................Samuel	1853	
Inkley ....Sarah Ann	Clawson ....Moses	1853 09 25	UT, Salt Lake City
Inkley ....Sarah Ann	Lamb..................Brigham Young	1883	UT
Inkpen..............Emma	Noakes...............Thomas	1810 03 30	ENG
Ipsen................Andrea Hansine	Hansen...............Hans Peter		
Ipsen................Andrea Hansine	Hansen...............John Johannes	1861 05 16	Ocean
Ipsen................Margaret C.	Holm...................Jens Neilson	1842 04 30	Denmark
Ipsen................Wilhelmina C.	Mortensen ....Anders Jorgen	1865 07 15	UT, Salt Lake City
Ireland ....Ann	Bawden..............Henry	1844 03 17	ENG, Barnstable
Ireland ....Dianah	Naylor.................William	1839 03 24	ENG
Irvin..................Jennet	Cufley................William	1857	UT, Salt Lake City
Irvin..................Jennet	Jenkins...............Thomas	1884 05	
Irving...............Elizabeth	Murphy...............Emanuel Masters	1864 08	
Isaacson ....Mary Ellen	Thompson ....William	1868 06 01	UT, Salt Lake City
Iversen.............Ane Marie	Christiansen........Christian		UT
Iversen.............Ane Marie	Johansen ....Ole	1805 06 28	
Iverson.............Ane Christena	Hegsted..............Hans C. S.	1866 01 20	UT, Salt Lake City
Iverson.............Karen Marie	Jensen ....Thomas C.	1841 10 28	Denmark
Ives.................Julia	Pack...................John	1832 10 10	NY, Watertown
Ives.................Roxana	Jones ....Merlin	1820 08 17	CT, Wellingford
Ivins ....Anna Laurie	Ivins...................Israel	1844 03 19	NJ, Horrerstown
Ivins ....Elizabeth	Phillips................Edward	1833 11 26	
Ivins ....Elizabeth	Williams..............John R.	1863 07 18	UT, Salt Lake City
Ivins ....Rachel R.	Grant..................Jedediah M.	1855 11 29	UT, Salt Lake City
Izatt.................Jane	Campbell.............David	1832	

J

Female	Male	Date	Place
Jacaway ....Susannah	Black ....George	1850 04 06	MO, St. Louis
Jacaway ....Susannah	Savage...............David Leonard	1878 02 09	
Jackson ....Abigail Mindwell	Lamb..................Erastus	1829	NY
Jackson ....Almira Lucinda	Adams................Samuel Lorenzo	1885 10 25	
Jackson ....Anne	Cooper ....William H.	1861 12 07	ENG, Yorkshire
Jackson ....Elizabeth	Kirkman..............John	1856 12 13	UT, Salt Lake City
Jackson ....Elizabeth	Reid....................John Kirkwood	1868 01 05	UT, Salt Lake City
Jackson ....Emma	Adams................Samuel Lorenzo	1852 02 05	ENG, Liverpool
Jackson ....Hannah	Allen ....William L. N.	1848 08 14	
Jackson ....Hester Ann	Johnson ....Jarvis	1849 08 05	NE
Jackson ....Jane	Middlemas...........Edward	1856 08 02	
Jackson ....Maria	Jakeman ....Henry	1859 06 02	UT, Moroni
Jackson ....Maria	Normington ....Thomas	1839 09 29	ENG
Jackson ....Maria	Parker ....John	1857 11 15	
Jackson ....Mary Ann	Newman..............William	1839 03 11	ENG
Jackson ....Mary Ann	Ross...................David James	1857 12 13	UT, Salt Lake City
Jackson ....Mary Ann	Woodruff ....Wilford	1846 04 15	IL, Nauvoo
Jackson ....Mary Elizabeth	Poulter................George	1874 02 09	UT, Salt Lake City
Jackson ....Sarah Ann	Chidester............Myron Alphonzo	1881 03 31	

Female	Male	Date	Place
Jackson ....Sarah Gibbons	Midgley...............Benjamin	1866 12 15	UT, Salt Lake City
Jackson ....Sophronia Ann	Ellis ....David Moroni	1879 06 19	
Jacobsen ....Anna Christine	Liljenquist............Ola	1848	Denmark
Jacobsen ....Berte	Larsen ....Tollef	1810 12 06	Norway
Jacobsen ....Cammilla D.	Corbett ....Samuel	1860 10 02	
Jacobsen ....Christine Marie	Christensen.........Soren C.	1862 05 31	UT, Mt. Pleasant
Jacobsen ....Christine Marie	Larsen ....Jens	1836 09 02	Denmark
Jacobsen ....Dorthea Marie	Morrell ....William Wilson	1864 04 16	UT, Salt Lake City
Jacobsen ....Inger Kerstine	Beck....................Stephen	1847	Denmark
Jacobsen ....Maria Christina	Housley...............George F.	1859 07 24	UT, Draper
Jacobsen ....Sidse Marie	Jensen ....Hans	1840 11 09	Denmark
Jacobsen ....Wilhelmina	Nessen ....Jens James	1863 09 27	UT, Logan
Jacobson ....Cajsa C. C.	Christensen.........Bothel	1820 10 18	Sweden
Jacobson ....Cajsa C. C.	Persson...............Peter Micias		
Jacobson ....Ellen	Widerburg ....Ole	1863 09 11	
Jacques ....Vienna	Shearer ....Daniel		MO
James...............Emily	Roberts ....John T.	1875 11 15	
James...............Emma	Johnson ....Lorenzo	1857 03 01	UT, St. George
James...............Emma	Rowley ....John	1873 04 21	
James...............Margaret	Crump ....William Charles	1853	
James...............Mary	Priday.................Samuel	1841 12 26	ENG
James...............Ruth	Roach..................William	1857 08 23	UT, Spanish Fork
James...............Sarah	Carter ....Samuel	1879	
James...............Sarah	Johnson ....Aaron	1857 03 01	UT, Salt Lake City
Jamison ....Agnes	Hoggan ....Walter	1851 07 18	
Janes................Ann Elizabeth	Leonard...............Bradford	1837	
Janson..............Jensina	Rasmussen ....Bent	1871 11 13	UT, Ephraim
Jansson ....Caisa Lisa	Engstrom.............Magnus	1863 10	UT
Jansson ....Maria Katerina	Jansson...............Jan Peter	1832 02 03	Sweden
Japp.................Ellison	Gourley ....Paul	1853 06 03	Scotland
Jaques ....Ann	Newton................John		ENG
Jaques ....Caroline	Gifford ....Levi Jr.	1859	UT
Jaques ....Caroline	Palmer.................Zemira	1856	
Jardine.............Agnes	Shumway ....Charles M.		
Jardine.............Sarah Wilson	Shumway ....Charles M.	1873 09 29	UT, Salt Lake City
Jared ....Rhoda Bryne	Young..................Adolphia		TN
Jared ....Rhoda Bryne	Young..................Alfred D.		
Jarman ....Catherine	Morgan................William Samuel	1856 06 20	IA, Iowa City
Jarman ....Catherine Lloyd	Moore.................Jacob	1839 08 12	Wales
Jarman ....Catherine Lloyd	Thomas...............Samuel John	1858 03 05	Wales
Jarman ....Marie	Degrey ....Samuel	1888 03 20	UT, Salt Lake City
Jarrold ....Sarah	Hyder ....Richard Hugh	1828 04	ENG, London
Jarvis ....Amelia	Badcock (Webb) .William	1869 09 15	UT, Salt Lake City
Jarvis ....Ann Catherine	Milne ....David	1870 05 03	
Jasper..............Elizabeth	Davies ....Edward	1827 11 17	ENG, Kinnerly
Jeffcott............Sarah	Jones ....Richard George	1860 07 11	UT, Salt Lake City
Jeffcott............Sarah	Pearson...............Johsua	1832	ENG
Jeffery.............Alice	Pendleton............Benjamin F.	1861 10 26	UT, Salt Lake City
Jeffries ....Elizabeth	Barnes................William	1816 11 04	ENG, Bedfordshire
Jeffs................Emma	Gunnell...............Francis W.	1869 04 05	UT, Salt Lake City
Jelly ....Adelaide	Fuller..................Edmund B.	1851 06 26	MO, St. Louis
Jemmett...........Julie Jane	Potts...................Thomas Pullen	1860 05 06	ENG, Faversham
Jenkins ....Caroline G.	Dutson................John W.	1858 09 07	UT, Fillmore
Jenkins ....Charlotte	Cole....................John	1843 08 25	IL, Nauvoo

Female	Male	Date	Place
Jenkins ....Eliza G. G.	Martin ....Ezra Francis		
Jenkins ....Elizabeth	Martell ....Thomas C.	1858 01 15	
Jenkins ....Elizabeth	Stanford ....Alfred	1868 10 24	UT, Salt Lake City
Jenkins ....Esther	Morse ....Joseph Bennett	1868 10	UT, Logan
Jenkins ....Jane	Davis ....David Evan	1867 06 22	
Jenkins ....Jane	Howe..................William	1833 05 07	Wales
Jenkins ....Jane	Stewart...............William		
Jenkins ....Jane	Williams..............William	1851 12 15	
Jenkins ....Margaret John	Rees...................Henry Davis	1859 03 29	UT, Spanish Fork
Jenkins ....Mary Jane	Cooley................Andrew Wood	1868 02 22	UT, Salt Lake City
Jenkins ....Sarah	James ....William Bowen	1854 10 22	Wales
Jenne................Lovise	Roundy................Jared Curtis	1852 02 26	UT, Salt Lake City
Jennings ....Martha	Adams................William Henry	1839 11 03	ENG, Dover
Jennings ....Rachel	Stiff (Neville)........William	1826 09 27	ENG
Jennings ....Sarah	Butterfield...........Jacob Kemp	1850 10 20	UT, Salt Lake City
Jennings ....Sarah	Hayes.................William W.	1838 04 16	ENG
Jensen.............Andrea	Nielsen ....Thomas L.	1862 04 22	Ocean
Jensen.............Ane	Peterson..............Jens O.	1845 11 01	Denmark
Jensen.............Ane Katrina	Anderson.............Hans	1885 02 25	
Jensen.............Ane Margrethe	Nielsen ....Christian	1842 03 20	Denmark
Jensen.............Ane Marie S.	Bristol.................William		
Jensen.............Ane Marie S.	Cambron ....Joseph	1875	UT, Nephi
Jensen.............Ane Marie S.	Gulbransen ....Hans	1867 07 06	
Jensen.............Ane Marie S.	Rambo ....Charles D.	1891 01 17	UT, Nephi
Jensen.............Anna	Larsen ....Johannes	1866 11 25	UT, Salt Lake City
Jensen.............Anna D. E.	Meyer.................Fredrick H. J.	1836 09 21	Germany
Jensen.............Anna D. E.	Miller ....Eleazer	1866 11 10	UT, Salt Lake City
Jensen.............Anna Elizabeth	Oman ....Aaron Gustaf	1861 11 04	UT, Mt. Pleasant
Jensen.............Anna Johanna	Jensen ....Peter George	1882 11 30	UT, Salt Lake City
Jensen.............Anna Katherine	Hansen...............James	1851 04 06	
Jensen.............Anna Maria	Davidson ....Hans Christian	1852 11 02	Denmark
Jensen.............Anna Marie	Barnhurst ....Samuel	1857 11 29	UT, Salt Lake City
Jensen.............Anne	Aagard ....Anders Jensen	1865 03 14	UT, Moroni
Jensen.............Anne C. C.	Fransen..............Christian A.	1878 11 14	UT, Salt Lake City
Jensen.............Annie Edith	Kjar....................Louis Christian	1884 11 14	UT, Logan
Jensen.............Annie Katrina	Bartlett...............Charles C.	1868 09 12	UT, Salt Lake City
Jensen.............Birgithe	Madsen ....James Ephraim	1869 07 06	UT, Salt Lake City
Jensen.............Carolina	Andersen.............Peder Christian	1866 11 04	UT, Salt Lake City
Jensen.............Caroline	Carlson...............James	1870 02 14	UT, Salt Lake City
Jensen.............Caroline	Godfrey ....Thomas	1880 06 17	UT, Salt Lake City
Jensen.............Caroline Maria	Dorius.................Lewis Olsen	1867 05 11	UT, Salt Lake City
Jensen.............Christina	Forbush..............Sanford	1871 03 27	
Jensen.............Clara Christine	Andersen.............Lars C.	1864 11 06	
Jensen.............Dorthea	Bayles ....Herman D.	1858 12 28	UT, Parowan
Jensen.............Dorthea	Mortensen ....Morten Peder	1859 05 10	Ocean
Jensen.............Elizabeth	Hansen...............Niels	1843 05 28	Denmark
Jensen.............Else Marie	Peterson..............Lars Peter	1852 11 26	Denmark
Jensen.............Frederickka A.	Brotherson ....Hans	1869 10 18	UT, Salt Lake City
Jensen.............Hannah	Smith..................Lauritz N.		
Jensen.............Helvig Maria	Eldredge..............Ira	1861 11 22	
Jensen.............Jensine C.	Jensen ....Peter Y.	1868 05 30	UT, Salt Lake City
Jensen.............Jensine C.	Overson ....Christian	1862 11 16	UT, Mt. Pleasant
Jensen.............Jensine S. P.	Anderson.............Anders	1827 10 02	Denmark
Jensen.............Jensine S. P.	Anderson.............Rasmus Peter	1857 10	Denmark

Female	Male	Date	Place
Jensen..............Johanna K.	Nicol....................Thomas	1864 12 17	UT, Salt Lake City
Jensen..............Karen	Andersen.............Christen	1829 05 08	Denmark
Jensen..............Karen	Peterson..............Samuel	1860 07 18	UT, Salt Lake City
Jensen..............Karen M.	Nelson.................Knud C.	1829 06 21	Denmark
Jensen..............Karen Marie	Godfrey ....Thomas	1867 04 01	UT, Clarkston
Jensen..............Kirsten	Nielson.................Jens	1857 10 04	UT, Salt Lake City
Jensen..............Kirsten Marie	Christensen.........Anders C.	1857 03 03	Denmark
Jensen..............Kirsten Marie	Engstrom.............Carl Gustaf	1871 12 04	UT
Jensen..............Kirsten Marie	Lee......................Christian	1854 01 26	Denmark
Jensen..............Kjirste	Jensen ....Peter Christen		
Jensen..............Maren	Anderson.............Hans	1845 10 17	Denmark
Jensen..............Maren	Cutler ....Sheldon Bela	1861 03 02	UT, Salt Lake City
Jensen..............Maren	Jorgensen ....Jasper	1845 07 16	Denmark
Jensen..............Maren	Larsen ....Anders	1841 05 21	Denmark
Jensen..............Maren	Mitchell...............James	1863 12 12	UT, Salt Lake City
Jensen..............Maren	Norton.................Alanson	1872 02 05	UT, Salt Lake City
Jensen..............Maren Christina	Nielsen ....Rasmus	1869 03 17	
Jensen..............Maren Johanne	Christensen.........Mads	1854 11 24	Denmark
Jensen..............Mariane	Christensen.........Jens	1846 01 01	
Jensen..............Mariane	Hanson................Niels C.	1863 05 05	Denmark
Jensen..............Mariane	Nielson ....Soren	1862 11 14	UT, Salt Lake City
Jensen..............Mariane	Nielson ....Thomas	1882 01 11	
Jensen..............Marie	Hansen................Peder Niels	1862 10 06	UT, Fairview
Jensen..............Mary Ann	Whitlock ....George A.	1880 12 21	
Jensen..............Matilda	Justesen..............Lars A.	1862 10 25	
Jensen..............Matilda	Olsen...................Frederick	1869 05 31	UT, Salt Lake City
Jensen..............Mette	Johnson ....Rasmus	1857 02 13	UT, Salt Lake City
Jensen..............Mette Kirstine	Sorensen.............Knud	1849 02 25	Denmark
Jensen..............Petrea	Latimer ....John	1884 06 19	UT, Salt Lake City
Jenson..............Sophia E.	Johnson ....Robert	1862 12 09	
Jensson ....Annie	Anderson.............Anders Christian	1874 02 17	
Jensson ....Annie	Hjorth ....Peter Herman	1868 12 07	UT, Salt Lake City
Jensson ....Annie	Jessop.................Thomas	1879 04 10	UT, Salt Lake City
Jeremy.............Esther	Davis ....David Lazarus	1866 11 29	UT, Salt Lake City
Jespersen........Mariane	Anderson.............Anders J.	1833 10 08	Denmark
Jesperson........Ingeborg K.	Allen ....Joseph Stewart	1857 09 11	
Jesperson........Ingeborg K.	Hansen................Mourtis	1834 11 08	Denmark
Jesperson........Ingeborg K.	Pehl.....................Hans Andrew		
Jessen ....Anne	Bertelsen.............Jens	1827 11 11	Denmark
Jessop ....Elizabeth	Connelly ....John		
Jessop ....Elizabeth	Golightly ....Richard	1855 01 20	UT, Salt Lake City
Jessop ....Esther Ann	Shaffer ....George Henry	1862 10 15	UT
Jeune...............Elizabeth H.	Hocquard ....Francis	1819	Channel Isle
Jewell ....Martha Amelia	Bemus.................Linus	1827 02 25	IL, Fulton
Jex..................Sarah Ann T.	Brockbank ....Joshua	1868 03 07	UT, Salt Lake City
Jinkerson.........Matilda	Stolworthy ....Thomas	1849 05 13	ENG
Jinks ....Harriet	Druce ....Henry	1845 05 04	ENG, Stratford
Jinks ....Julia Ann	Druce ....John	1842 06 19	ENG
Johannas.........Engelina	Backman ....Olaus A.	1847	Sweden
Johannesen.....Caroline M.	Arneson...............Augustinus	1855 04 26	Norway
Johansen.........Ane Johanne	Nielsen ....Anders	1830 10 22	Denmark
Johansen.........Anna	Dahle..................Hans Hansen	1822 07 06	Norway
Johansen.........Anna C. C.	Sorensen.............Jeppe	1856 02 15	UT, Salt Lake City
Johansen.........Annie	Hansen................Hans	1851 12 12	

Female	Male	Date	Place
Johansen.........Julia Teoa	Hanson................Ole	1866 05 16	UT, Salt Lake City
Johansen.........Kirstina	Halversen............Jonas	1865	UT, Hyrum
Johansen.........Kirstina	Hansen................Jens	1855 05 06	Denmark
Johansen.........Laurine W.	Knudsen.............Neils	1869 05 30	UT, Deweyville
Johansen.........Laurine W.	Madsen ....Jens	1862 11 15	UT, Salt Lake City
Johansen.........Mattie Marie	Smith...................Jorgen C.	1863 02 21	UT, Salt Lake City
Johanson.........Albertina W.	Sandine.............Lars J.	1869 03 09	UT, Salt Lake City
Johanson.........Anna Cajia	Angell.................Solomon	1863 10 31	UT, Salt Lake City
Johanson.........Johannah	Bengtsson...........Nils	1830 07 04	Sweden
Johanson.........Johannah	Olsen..................Christoffer		
John................Marie Jeanette	Jones ....Llewellyn G.	1840 07 11	Wales
John................Martha	Jenkins...............Henry	1843 07 09	
Johnson..........Albertine J.	North ....Charles Addison	1861 01 27	UT, Salt Lake City
Johnson..........Ane Marie	Thomasen ....Niels		
Johnson..........Ane Marie	Thorum...............Christian	1863 10 03	UT, Salt Lake City
Johnson..........Ann	Milner ....John	1825 05 10	ENG
Johnson..........Ann	Needham ....Thomas		
Johnson..........Ann	Robins................Thomas F.	1844 08 20	ENG, Leigh
Johnson..........Anna Dorthea	Kempe................Christopher J.	1866 03 10	UT, Salt Lake City
Johnson..........Annetta	Larsen ....Christian Greis	1864 04 09	UT, Salt Lake City
Johnson..........Boletta Marie	Allen...................Simeon F.	1863 12 05	UT, Salt Lake City
Johnson..........Caroline Cecelia	Gunderson ....Erick		
Johnson..........Charlotte E.	Draper ....Nephi	1870 11 15	UT, Rush Valley
Johnson..........Christena	Yorgason............James	1867 12 08	UT, Moroni
Johnson..........Cynthia Parker	Drake ....Daniel N.	1844 01 04	IL, Hancock Co.
Johnson..........Delcena D.	Babbitt................Almon W.	1846 01 24	IL, Nauvoo
Johnson..........Delcena D.	Sherman ....Lyman R.	1829 01 16	NY, Pomfret
Johnson..........Delcena D.	Smith..................Joseph Jr.	1841	
Johnson..........Eleanor	Lufkin ....Samuel Henry	1815	
Johnson..........Elizabeth Ann	Johnson ....William	1818 03 03	ENG
Johnson..........Elizabeth H.	Nixon..................George William	1868 10 24	UT, Salt Lake City
Johnson..........Emma Ida	Jesperson ....James Peter	1880 09 19	UT, Richfield
Johnson..........Esther A.	Cram ....Victor Doe P.	1879 12 17	UT, St. George
Johnson..........Esther Maleta	Lebaron..............David Tulley	1844 03 28	NY
Johnson..........Fanny C.	Caldwell ....David Henry	1856 01 24	UT, Taylorsville
Johnson..........Hannah Edith	Adcock ....Charles	1869	
Johnson..........Hannah Edith	Aston..................William Henry		
Johnson..........Hilma Caroline	Hales..................Stephen F.	1878 11 14	UT, Salt Lake City
Johnson..........Hilma Caroline	Simpson ....Robert Temple		
Johnson..........Inger K.	Homer ....Henry	1874 10 01	UT, Salt Lake City
Johnson..........Jane Vail	Lee ....Francis	1835 10 24	
Johnson..........Johanna	Larsen ....Marinus	1869 12 20	UT, Salt Lake City
Johnson..........Josephine C. M.	Johnson ....Niels Peter	1869 05 03	UT, Salt Lake City
Johnson..........Julia Ann	Babbitt................Almon W.	1833 11 23	OH
Johnson..........Lena	Madsen ....Peter	1865 09 02	UT, Salt Lake City
Johnson..........Lydia	Marchant.............Abraham	1837 02 07	ENG, Somerset
Johnson..........Maren	Petersen.............Niels E.	1850 06 07	Denmark
Johnson..........Margaret	Guymon ....Noah T.	1845 11 25	IL, Nauvoo
Johnson..........Margaret Ann	Washburn............Daniel A.	1861 04 18	UT, Spring Town
Johnson..........Margaret Jane	Cluff...................Moses	1857 04 22	
Johnson..........Maria Kaisa	Otterstrom...........Jonas	1845	Sweden
Johnson..........Mary	Mather................John	1829 12 20	ENG, Duffield
Johnson..........Mary Ann	Farnsworth..........Albert S.	1874 01 12	UT, Salt Lake City
Johnson..........Mary Ann	Jarvis.................Joshua	1861 04 20	ENG, Bethnel

Female	Male	Date	Place
Johnson..........Mary Ann	Nichols ....Alvin	1857 04 08	UT, Salt Lake City
Johnson..........Mary Charlotte	Cahoon ....Rais Bell C. R.	1867 11 16	UT, Salt Lake City
Johnson..........Mary Christina	Parsons.............Elijah	1869 01 11	UT, Salt Lake City
Johnson..........Mary Elsa	Price.................Charles	1847 11 25	IA, Council Bluffs
Johnson..........Mary Julia	Richards............Heber John	1862 04 09	UT, Salt Lake City
Johnson..........Melissa Almera	Babbitt...............Don Carlos	1864 01 24	
Johnson..........Mildred Eliza	Randall..............Alfred	1860 05 30	UT, Salt Lake City
Johnson..........Polly Ann	Angell ....Truman O.	1832 10 07	NY, Genesee
Johnson..........Salina	Morrell ....Thomas	1846 12 18	ENG, Middlesex
Johnson..........Sarah	Allsop ....Thomas	1863 02	
Johnson..........Sarah	Coleman...........Henry	1892	
Johnson..........Sarah	Fowers ....Jesse	1841 11	ENG
Johnson..........Sarah	Marsden ....William		
Johnson..........Sarah	McDonald...........John Kilpatrick	1863 12 26	UT, Salt Lake City
Johnson..........Sarah	Ralphs...............Thomas	1842 05 10	MO
Johnson..........Sarah Eliza V.	Hickman.............William A.	1855 09 15	UT, Salt Lake City
Johnson..........Sarah Eliza V.	Moreno...............Frank		
Johnson..........Sarah Eliza V.	Sherwin.............Edwin		
Johnson..........Sarah Ellen	Hall....................Miles	1850	IA, Leon
Johnson..........Sena Catherine	Mickelsen..........Niels	1855 04 15	UT, Brigham City
Johnson..........Sybella White	Clayton..............Nephi Willard	1884 06 26	
Johnson..........Sybella White	Young................Ernest Irving		
Johnson..........Vashtia Emily	Mecham ....Lewis	1868 08 29	UT, Salt Lake City
Johnston.........Anna Maria	Lowry ....John	1853 02 13	UT, Manti
Johnston.........Anna Maria	Singleton ....William		
Johnston.........Anna Maria	Williams.............William Francis		
Johnston.........Elizabeth	Johnson ....Robert	1845 01 12	ENG, Lancaster
Johnston.........Jane	Black ....William	1822 07 31	IRE, Antrim
Johnston.........Janet	Hamilton.............Henry	1857 11 07	
Johnston.........Margaret	Finlayson............David	1850 02 26	
Johnston.........Margaret	Wayman.............Emmanuel	1856 04 10	
Johnston.........Maria Jane	Johnson ....George W.	1844 04 14	IL, Macedonia
Johnston.........Maria Jane	Woodward..........James Jr.	1863 12 24	UT, Salt Lake City
Johnston.........Sarah	McCann..............Thomas R.	1835 05 11	ENG, Lancashire
Johnstone........Ann	Clarke................Amos	1853 11 13	Wales
Jolley ....Caroline C.	Donelson............Charles M.	1850 05 01	IA, Harris Grove
Jolley ....Diana Louisa	Dorrity ....Dennis	1835	TN, Dresden
Jolley ....Diana Louisa	Jones ....Calvin T.	1832	TN, Dresden
Jolley ....Frances G.	Moncur..............Robert	1860 09 30	UT, Salem
Jolley ....Mary	Oldroyd ....Peter	1863 04 05	UT, Salt Lake City
Jolly ....Margaret Ann	Jensen ....Ole	1868 02 29	UT, Clarkston
Jonason..........Anna	Johnson ....John	1850 10 26	Sweden
Jonassen.........Magla	Ericksen ....Henrik S.	1822 06 12	Norway
Jones.............Amy Amillia	Garlick...............Joseph G.	1851 10 31	UT, Salt Lake City
Jones.............Ann	Cash.................James		
Jones.............Ann	Haslam..............Henry H.	1865 01 20	UT, Salt Lake City
Jones.............Ann	Richards............Samuel W.	1857 03 19	
Jones.............Ann	Tonks ....Timothy	1817 10 05	ENG
Jones.............Ann	Valleley ....John	1819	
Jones.............Anne	Farr ....Franklin R.	1866 12 22	UT, Salt Lake City
Jones.............Catherine	Bennett..............Benjamin	1818 12 31	Wales
Jones.............Charlotte E.	Berrett ....Charles Henry	1872 04 10	UT
Jones.............Eliza	Howls ....Thomas	1842 04 11	ENG, Worcester
Jones.............Elizabeth	Knight................James Philander	1860 08 08	

Female	Male	Date	Place
Jones...............Elizabeth Ann	Guymon ....Noah T.	1847 02 12	NE
Jones...............Elvira	Thomas ....Ebenezer	1841 10 25	Wales
Jones...............Esther	Collett.................Daniel	1833 04 14	ENG
Jones...............Hannah	Rogers ....Theodore	1852 03 06	UT, Salt Lake City
Jones...............Hannah Jane	Harper................Thomas	1854 10 29	UT, Salt Lake City
Jones...............Jane	Bradford ....Pleasant S.	1864 10 15	UT, Salt Lake City
Jones...............Jane	Edmunds.............Nathaniel	1851 12 06	Wales
Jones...............Jannet	Roberts ....William	1863	UT, Farmington
Jones...............Lina Meniza	Manhard..............William Henry	1853 04	UT, Kanosh
Jones...............Margaret	Beemus...............George M.	1865 08	UT, Salt Lake City
Jones...............Margaret	Reese.................Thomas	1838 12 31	Wales
Jones...............Margaret Ann	Harding ....Alma	1867 11 02	UT, Salt Lake City
Jones...............Martha	McAdams ....Bernard A.	1871 10 23	UT, Salt Lake City
Jones...............Martha	Mecham ....Erastus Darwin	1849 02 04	
Jones...............Martha	Starley................John	1879 02 05	UT, Salt Lake City
Jones...............Martha Paine	Thomas ....Daniel S.	1826 02 03	TN, Gallatin
Jones...............Mary	Chilton................Isaac	1878	
Jones...............Mary	Davies ....Thomas T.	1843 01 06	Wales
Jones...............Mary	Evans ....Abel	1850 05 05	LA, New Orleans
Jones...............Mary	Harding ....George	1864 07 02	UT, Salt Lake City
Jones...............Mary	Stephens.............Thomas H.	1865 12 25	UT, Henefer
Jones...............Mary	Williams..............John J.	1857 03 06	UT, Salt Lake City
Jones...............Mary Ann	James ....Howell	1837 03 27	Wales
Jones...............Mary Ann	Rhodes...............Joseph	1881 12 22	UT, Salt Lake City
Jones...............Mary Ann	Stewart...............Urban V.	1860 03 17	
Jones...............Mary Elizabeth	Fox.....................George Sellman	1842 02 21	ENG, Aston
Jones...............Mary Elizabeth	Hall....................Job Pitcher	1848 02 25	IA
Jones...............Mary Elizabeth	Summers.............John C.	1882 02 15	
Jones...............Mary Jane	Richins ....Albert Francis	1874 11 16	UT, Salt Lake City
Jones...............Minerva L.	Stone.................Amos Pease	1846 02 01	NY, Canaan
Jones...............Nancy Hannah	Lewis.................James Stapleton	1833 05 10	MO, Jackson Co.
Jones...............Phoebe	Works.................James M.	1858 04 15	UT, Salt Lake City
Jones...............Rachel	Lewis.................William S.		
Jones...............Rhoda	Bennion..............Samuel	1868 10 25	UT, Salt Lake City
Jones...............Rhoda	Sargeant ....John H. S.		
Jones...............Ruth	Williams..............Daniel	1805 04 16	Wales
Jones...............Sarah Jane	Lloyd ....John Heber	1880 08 05	UT, Salt Lake City
Jones...............Sarah Rebecca	Avery.................Vernile Thomas	1872 02 05	UT, Salt Lake City
Jones...............Sarah Rebecca	Bird...................William F. II		
Jones...............Susannah	Lewis.................Richard	1869	WY, Evanston
Jonson...............Anna Cecelia	Borgquist............Rasmus	1866 11 05	UT, Salt Lake City
Jonson...............Anna Cecelia	Kellman ....Johannes	1860	
Jonson...............Johanna	Aasen.................Svend Jakobsen	1822 07 21	
Jonson...............Johanna	Dahl...................Endre (Andrew)	1832	
Jonson...............Sissa	Hjorth ....Niels Peter	1879	UT, Fairview
Jonson...............Sissa	Lasson ....Ola	1840 12 30	Sweden
Jonsson..........Anna Sophia	Pehrson..............Eric Johan	1861 05 16	Ocean
Jonsson..........Elna	Olsson................Knut	1834 12 29	Sweden
Jonsson..........Ingar	Borg ....Pehr	1830 12 17	Sweden
Jordan ....Fanny	Rigby.................James	1870 03 21	UT, Salt Lake City
Jordan ....Mary	Evans ....William	1864 05 22	Ocean
Jorganson........Fredricka	Nelson................Swen	1865 05	Ocean
Jorgensen........Anna	Larsen ....Johannes	1850	Denmark
Jorgensen........Anne Catherine	Anderson............Mons	1850	Denmark

Female	Male	Date	Place
Jorgensen........Anne Catherine	Babcock ....George	1862 10 20	UT, Spanish Fork
Jorgensen........Cecilia	Poulsen ....Paul Michael	1861 05 17	Ocean
Jorgensen........Maren Kirstine	Christiansen ....Lars Nielsen	1850 12 29	
Jorgensen........Maren Kirstine	Jorgensen ....Lars	1841 04 02	
Jorgensen........Sophia P.	Andreasen..........Andrew Carl	1880 12 02	UT, Salt Lake City
Jorgensen........Wilhelmina	Madsen ....Peter	1864 05 14	UT, Salt Lake City
Jose................Grace Tippett	Tenney ....Nathan C.	1859 03 18	UT, Harmony
Jose................Grace Tippett	Williams..............Bateman Haight	1869 08 02	UT, Salt Lake City
Joseph.............Elizabeth	Nelson................Robert	1842 12 12	IRE
Jowett..............Annie	Sharp ....Jonathan Jr.	1868	ENG
Joy...................Mary	Snelgrove...........Edward	1843 06 20	ENG
Juchau..............Susannah	Price..................Robert	1864 03 02	UT, Salt Lake City
Judd................Hannah	Bolton................John	1878 03	
Judd................Hannah	Court ....William Lee	1853 06 27	ENG, Coventry
Judd................Jane Lucinda	Call....................Israel	1880 06 11	UT, St. George
Judd................Jane Lucinda	Knight................Joseph	1863 02 17	
Judd................Levee Teressa	Terry..................Otis L.	1851 07 06	UT, Salt Lake City
Judd................Lois	Mitchell..............Benjamin T.	1848 01 01	NE
Judd................Lois	Page..................John Edmond		
Judd................Margaret Gay	Clawson ....Hiram B.	1852 08 21	UT, Salt Lake City
Judd................Susannah C.	Boyce................Benjamin	1836 02 08	Canada
Judd................Susannah C.	Day....................Hugh	1847 09 07	NE, Florence
Judson.............Mary Jane	Hanson...............William L.	1857 08 21	UT, Salt Lake City
Juulsen ....Mette Margrete	Peterson.............Baltzar S.	1857 05 30	Denmark

K

Female	Male	Date	Place
Karren.............Catherine	Hatch.................Lorenzo Hill	1854 11 11	UT, Lehi
Kay ....Ann	Street ....Simon	1884 03 15	UT, Park City
Kay ....Ann	Street ....William	1873 01 27	WY, Almy
Kay ....Elizabeth	Howarth..............John	1853 02 27	ENG
Kay ....Josephine J.	Rosengren ....Niels	1868 02 14	UT, Salt Lake City
Kay ....Nancy	Barton ....William	1840 04 08	ENG, Lancashire
Kay ....Sarah Ann	McMurdie ....Samuel	1856 03 05	UT, Cedar City
Keeler ....Abigail	Middlemas...........Edward	1835 08 15	Canada
Keeling ....Dorcas	Burgess..............William	1854 12 17	UT, Salt Lake City
Keeling ....Dorcas	Dykes ....George Parker	1837	MO
Keep ....Ann	Davies ....Morgan	1865 03 01	UT, Lehi
Keep ....Ruth	Griffin ....John	1870 02 21	
Keep ....Sarah	Buttars...............David	1866 12 16	UT, Lehi
Keep ....Sarah	Francis ....Thomas R.	1865	
Kegg ....Elizabeth	Comish..............William	1831 02 12	Isle of Man
Keiling.............Rachel	West..................John	1837 11 14	ENG
Keiling.............Rachel	Whipple ....Nelson Wheeler	1853 03 12	UT, Salt Lake City
Keith ....Louisa	Seabury..............Wesley H.	1837 11 03	
Keller ....Melinda	Boren ....Coleman	1830 03 07	IL, Union Co.
Keller ....Nancy Ann	Bigler................Jacob G.	1855 11 25	UT, Nephi
Keller ....Nancy Ann	Lambson ....Alfred B.	1852 04 18	
Keller ....Temperance	Penrod ....David	1831 10 14	IL, Jonesboro
Kelley..............Martha	Lynch ....Daniel	1828	KY, Westerveill
Kelley..............Martha	Wilson ....Elijah	1830 12 12	
Kellogg ....Rhoda	Gardner..............Charles	1855 08 12	
Kelly................Elizabeth	Pugh..................Edward	1866 05 05	UT, Salt Lake City

Female	Male	Date	Place
Kelly..............Emily	Adamson............Peter	1894 07 17	
Kelly..............Emily	Koepernick..........Charles Robert	1862 11 06	UT, Salt Lake City
Kelsey.............Cecelia	Burlingame.........Orson	1854	UT, Union Fort
Kelsey.............Matilda Elvira	Morrell................William Wilson	1856 02 06	UT, Union Fort
Kelsey.............Matilda Elvira	Taylor................Samuel	1862 04 10	UT, Smithfield
Kelsey.............Polly Zehviah	Johnson ....Aaron	1827 09 13	CT, New Haven
Kempton ....Hannah	Deournso ....Lewis	1875	
Kempton ....Hannah	Drake ....Daniel N.	1849	UT
Kendell ....Jane	Firth....................John	1845 05 12	ENG, Yorkshire
Kennan ....Ruth	Davis ....Charles A.	1839 04 11	MA, Worcester
Kennedy ....Mary Ann	Bird....................Charles	1826 03 22	PA, Tioga Co.
Kennedy ....Nancy Adeline	Wilkins...............John G.	1830	NY
Kennedy ....Sarah Canada	Plunkett ....William R.	1830	Scotland
Kent................Susan	Greene ....Evan M.	1835 08 29	
Kerr..................Agnes	McBride.............Peter	1898 09	UT
Kerr..................Agnes	Parkinson ....Henry F.	1869 02 23	UT, Salt Lake City
Kerr..................Mary	Hendry ....John Mark	1875	
Kershaw ....Annie Maria	Thompson ....Joseph	1868 08 08	UT, Salt Lake City
Kershaw ....Ida Sophia	Woodhouse.........Charles C.	1855 03 15	UT, Cedar City
Kershaw ....Lydia Eliza	Smith..................Henry Jr.	1874 08 03	UT, Salt Lake City
Kershaw ....Sarah Lucretia	Welchman ....Arthur P.	1867 03 16	UT, Salt Lake City
Keyes ....Henrietta	Hales..................Stephen	1851 12 23	UT, Salt Lake City
Keyes ....Henrietta	Whitney ....Alonzo W.	1839	
Keyes ....Henrietta	Whitney ....Newel K.	1846 01 26	IL, Nauvoo
Keys ....Ann Rushen	Paxman................William	1855 03 03	ENG, London
Keys ....Elizabeth P.	Cheshire.............George	1841 06 11	ENG
Kidd ....Catherine	McClenahan........James Kemp	1853 03 13	UT, Salt Lake City
Killip...............Ann	Cowley ....Charles	1833 12 26	Isle of Man
Kilner ....Rachel	Harrop................James	1836 10 29	ENG, Eccles
Kilner ....Rachel	Sharples.............Peter		ENG
Kilpack............Louisa	Fawson ....Abraham	1862 12 15	ENG
Kimball............Dorothy	Bullock ....Benjamin III	1818 01 24	NH, Grafton
Kimball............Helen Mar	Smith..................Joseph Jr.	1843 05	IL, Nauvoo
Kimball............Helen Mar	Whitney ....Horace Kimball	1846 02 04	IL, Nauvoo
King ....Abigail Marina	Stevens ....Joseph S.	1865 08 12	UT, Circleville
King ....Amy Jane	Smith..................Elias	1856 04 15	UT, Salt Lake City
King ....Angeline	Richardson..........Ebenezer	1833	
King ....Ann	Lewis..................Joseph	1859 05 01	
King ....Caroline Matilda	Whitlock ....Charles	1853 02 01	UT, Spring City
King ....Eliza	Udall..................David	1850 12 02	ENG
King ....Elizabeth	Parkinson ....Thomas	1846	ENG
King ....Elizabeth Ann	Lewis..................Joseph	1865 06 03	UT
King ....Martha Anna	Waylett ....George D.	1863 01 28	UT, Salt Lake City
King ....Mary	Clutton................George	1826	
King ....Mary	Marble ....Nathaniel		
King ....Mary	Seamons.............Henry	1832 09 09	ENG
King ....Mary	Taylor ....Stephen	1870	
King ....Sarah	Coons.................Libbeus T.	1846 01 24	IL, Nauvoo
King ....Sarah	Hillman...............Mayhew	1807	NY, Cambridge
Kinnersley.......Sarah Emily	Dinwoodey ....Henry	1864 09 24	UT, Salt Lake City
Kinney ....Elizabeth	Wilson ....George C.	1826	
Kirby ....Amy (Mary)	Orme ....Samuel	1825 12 07	ENG
Kirkbride ....Jane	Simpkins ....James	1844 12 25	ENG
Kirkham ....Mariah	Giles..................Thomas	1832 05 30	ENG

Female	Male	Date	Place
Kirkman ....Margaret M.	Green ....John	1835 12 23	South Africa
Kjellerman ....Josefina A. G.	Lucas ....Hyrum John	1883 08 09	UT, Salt Lake City
Klemmetson ....Hannah	Jeppeson ....Jacob	1837 03 20	Sweden
Knapp ....Clarinda	Allen ....Andrew Lee	1824 12 11	NY, Allegany
Knight ....Adaline	Belnap ....Gilbert	1845 12 21	IL, Nauvoo
Knight ....Anna	Demill ....Freeborn	1819 03 11	
Knight ....Elizabeth	Johnson ....Joseph W.	1842 02 03	IL, Nauvoo
Knight ....Lydia	Young.................John Ray	1861	
Knight ....Mary Elizabeth	Bassett ....Charles Henry	1853 03 05	UT, Salt Lake City
Knight ....Mary Jane	Allred ....John Allen	1856 04	UT, Slaterville
Knight ....Olive Mary	Benson ....Ezra Taft	1858 03 19	UT, Salt Lake City
Knight ....Phoebe M.	Twitchell ....Ephraim	1824 03 01	OH, Pomeroy
Knight ....Sally	Palmer.................Zemira	1851 12 01	UT, Provo
Knight ....Sarah Ann	Richardson..........Josiah	1862 12 22	UT, Plain City
Knight ....Violet Ellen	Richardson..........William A.	1867 01	UT, Salt Lake City
Knoppel ....Amelia F. J.	Hansen...............Frederick Emil	1869 05 14	
Knoppel ....Amelia F. J.	Jorgensen ....Jorgen C.	1859 10 23	NY, New York City
Knowles..........Ellen	Melling................John	1837	
Knowles..........Ellen	Salisbury ....Thomas	1864 10 29	
Knowles..........Nancy Ann	Smithies ....James	1836 01 17	ENG
Knowlton..........Martha Jane	Coray ....Howard	1841 02 06	IL, Hancock
Knox ....Ann	Gardner..............Alexander	1832 10 06	Scotland
Knox ....Ann	Gillespie ....Peter	1856 11 07	UT
Knox ....Dorothy	Corless...............John	1862 02 11	UT, Salt Lake City
Knox ....Mary Ann	Corless...............John	1872 07 22	UT, Salt Lake City
Knudsen ....Abelone	Hansen...............Anders	1839 07 25	Denmark
Knudsen ....Anna Maria	Jensen ....Jens	1861 05 04	UT, Salt Lake City
Knudsen ....Annie Johanna	Rolph..................M. G.	1888	UT, Logan
Knudsen ....Bertha	Madsen ....Peter Jr.	1881 06 02	UT, Salt Lake City
Knudsen ....Caroline	Madsen ....Peter	1860 04 25	UT, Salt Lake City
Knudsen ....Else Marie	Bybee.................Byram	1856 08 15	UT, Salt Lake City
Knudsen ....Helge	Hogan ....Eric G. M.	1829 03 26	Norway
Knudsen ....Johanne	Christensen........Johan	1824	
Knudson ....Dorthe	Pedersen.............Mikkel	1832 11 13	Denmark
Knudson ....Dorthe	Svendsen............Jan	1874 07 06	UT, Salt Lake City
Koefoed ....Maren K.	Benson...............Yeppa	1819 06 03	Denmark
Kofoed ....Wilhelmine F.	Robbins..............Wilson C.	1866 03 02	ID, Weston
Kofoed ....Wilhelmine F.	Roberts ....William M.	1885 10 03	ID, Montpelier
Koyle ....Mary Elizabeth	Thomas ....James Wylie	1855 01 01	UT, Salt Lake City
Kristensen ......Mette	Bagg...................Thomas Vognsen		
Kristensen ......Mette	Jensen ....Jens	1835 10 23	Denmark
Kristensen ......Mette	Jensen ....Lars Christian		
Kroll ....Christine W. C.	Peterson.............Charles C.	1861 07 03	Trail
Kroll ....Elizabeth	Bradley...............George W.	1835 03 02	NY
Kroll ....Elizabeth	Bradley...............Thomas J.	1828	NY, Clarence
Kruger.............Ida Dorthea H.	Tietjen ....Johann A. H.	1847 10 22	Germany
Kuder..............Mary Eleanor	France................Joseph	1850 01 01	UT, Salt Lake City
Kumlin ....Anna Christina	Schultz		

L

Labrum ....Jane Elizabeth	Butler..................Alva	1867 03 16	UT, Salt Lake City
Lacey...............Amelia	Dean ....Joseph	1865 01 05	UT, Salt Lake City

Female	Male	Date	Place
Lacey .... Amelia	Slade .... William E.	1852 06 28	ENG
Lacey .... Ann	Bennett .... Thomas	1839 12 25	ENG
Lacey .... Ann	Vickers .... John	1847 03 09	ENG, Nottingham
Ladd .... Hannah	Tupper .... Silas F.	1817	NY
Laduc .... Sarah	Pope .... Robert	1851 10 01	WI, Rosendale
Laflesh .... Elizabeth	Lee .... Alfred		
Laird .... Janet	Jenkins .... James Hardie	1842 10 22	Scotland
Lake .... Eliza	Stringham .... William	1846 01 22	IL, Nauvoo
Lake .... Hannah	Chappell .... William E.	1859 01 08	ENG, Devonshire
Lake .... Jane	Ordway .... Stephen	1850	
Lake .... Jane	Taylor .... Joseph	1852	
Lake .... Lydia Ann	Nelson .... Price Williams	1850 12 13	UT, Ogden
Lake .... Sabra	Dixon .... William W.	1842 08 16	IL, Scott Co.
Lakeman .... Rebecca	Farley .... James		
Laker .... Amy Ellen	Cook .... Alonzo H.	1878 11 14	UT, Salt Lake City
Lamb .... Almyra	Hardy .... Samuel P.	1856 12 04	UT, Salt Lake City
Lamb .... Harriet Laura	Zimmerman .... John	1850 09 21	IA, Garden Grove
Lambert .... Elizabeth	Robins .... James	1840	ENG
Lambert .... Isabella	Ayrton .... John	1824 11 27	ENG, Yorkshire
Lamborn .... Eliza Ann	Murphy .... Emanuel Bird	1876 10 16	UT, Salt Lake City
Lambson .... Melissa Jane	Davis .... Albert Westly	1865 11 25	UT, Salt Lake City
Lamoreaux ...... Sarah Jane	Montague .... James Shepard	1859 01 30	UT, Payson
Lampard .... Hannah Maria	Watkins .... William	1820 07 09	ENG
Lampitt .... Elizabeth	Knight .... Charles	1840	ENG, Worcester.
Lamport .... Electa	Gardner .... Benjamin	1822 05 29	
Lancaster .... Margaret	Oler .... George		
Lance .... Nancy	Cooper .... Isaac	1852 05 01	
Lance .... Nancy	Dayton .... Hiram	1846 02 24	IA
Lance .... Nancy	Stuart .... Charles	1840	
Land .... Narcissa B.	Ashcraft .... Joseph	1840	
Land .... Narcissa B.	Buchanan .... James	1879 01 27	CO, Huerfano
Land .... Narcissa B.	Coldwell .... John	1837 05 22	MO, Jackson Co.
Land .... Narcissa B.	Greflo .... Julius	1869 08 26	MO, Jackson Co.
Land .... Narcissa B.	Vasquez .... Pierce Louis	1851 09 25	Platte River
Land .... Sebrina	Croft .... Jacob	1854 01	OK
Land .... Sebrina	Cropper .... George Waters	1841	TX, Harris Co.
Land .... Sebrina	Matheny .... Celly F.	1827	MS, Monroe
Landrum .... Henrietta	Dotson .... William	1853 07 03	AL
Lane .... Caroline	Woodhead .... George T.	1853 08 14	UT, Salt Lake City
Lane .... Delia	Nebeker .... Ira	1861 11 15	UT, Salt Lake City
Lane .... Elizabeth Ann	Bybee .... Byram	1820 01 05	KY, Barren Co.
Lane .... Martha	Theobald .... William	1841 08 01	ENG
Lane .... Nancy Phipps	Blackburn .... Elias Hicks	1852 04 12	UT, Salt Lake City
Lane .... Sarah	Elsey .... Joseph	1827 01 08	ENG
Lane .... Sarah	Nix .... James	1840 05 20	
Lang .... Rhoda Ann	May .... James	1877 11 02	UT, St. George
Lang .... Sarah	Hamilton .... John	1806 03 05	IRE
Langdon .... Clementina C.	Hutchinson .... Jacob F.	1837	
Langdon .... Clementina C.	Young .... Phineas	1848	
Langfield .... Ann	Brown .... Jonathan	1856 11	UT
Langgaard .... Marie Kirstine	Hemmert .... Mathias	1863	
Langgaard .... Marie Kirstine	Jensen .... Niels	1849 01 30	
Langhorn .... Mary	Nuttall .... William	1822 07 08	ENG, Lancaster
Langman .... Rebecca C.	Cluff .... Moses	1856 12 25	UT, Salt Lake City

228 |

Female	Male	Date	Place
Langshaw ....Jane	Prestwich ....William	1836 05 09	ENG, Odenshaw
Langshaw ....Mary	Goble ....Edwin	1868 10 24	UT, Salt Lake City
Langton ....Mary Catherine	Gibbs..................John	1852 12 24	
Larkin...............Susan	Goates ....William	1844 06 07	ENG
Larnder ....Sarah	Cole...................William George	1837 02 12	ENG, London
Larsen ....Ana Christensen	Shimmin ....Robert C.	1880 07	
Larsen ....Andrea Marie	Hansen................Paul	1868 06 06	UT, Salt Lake City
Larsen ....Anna Christena	Keller..................James Morgan	1860 01 05	UT, Salt Lake City
Larsen ....Anna Christina	Brown..................Hans Jorgen	1867 04 20	UT, Salt Lake City
Larsen ....Anna Christine	Jensen ....Jens Christian	1870	UT, Logan
Larsen ....Anna Christine	Hansen................Paul	1885 08 17	UT, Providence
Larsen ....Anna Kirstine	Humble................Henry	1866 05 17	
Larsen ....Anna Margrethe	Peterson..............Hans	1833 05 17	Denmark
Larsen ....Anne Kristine	Hansen................Peter	1862 09 24	Denmark
Larsen ....Ansine Marie	Hall....................William	1881 08 09	UT, Salt Lake City
Larsen ....Ansine Marie	Petersen..............James	1866 06 10	Ocean
Larsen ....Bergitte	Johnson ....John	1843 04 26	Norway
Larsen ....Bergitte	Knudsen..............Hans	1850 04 16	Norway
Larsen ....Bodel	Olsen...................Andrew Niels	1857	
Larsen ....Bodil Marie	Jensen ....Jens	1856 02 22	Denmark
Larsen ....Caroline M. K.	Miller ....Hans Peter	1861 06 22	NE, Florence
Larsen ....Christena	Jensen ....Peter	1886 12 29	UT, Logan
Larsen ....Christiana	Nelson.................Soren	1827 10 06	Denmark
Larsen ....Christine Marie	Warnick..............Charles P.	1874 03 16	UT, Salt Lake City
Larsen ....Dorothea	Blanch................Wealthy		
Larsen ....Dorthea	Nielsen................Peter	1868 08 09	Ocean
Larsen ....Dorthea	Poulson..............William	1872 02 05	UT, Salt Lake City
Larsen ....Elena Hancena	Lambert...............John	1855 06 10	UT, Salt Lake City
Larsen ....Elsie Marie	Christiansen ....Soren		
Larsen ....Elsie Marie	Pedersen..............Christian		
Larsen ....Elsie Marie	Pedersen..............Soren Christian	1861 10 22	Denmark
Larsen ....Helena	Eliason ....Johannes L.	1867 03 04	UT, Salt Lake City
Larsen ....Ingeborg K.	Alexanderson ......Knud	1836 02 29	
Larsen ....Ingeborg K.	Sebye.................Henry	1856 11 17	
Larsen ....Karen	Larson ....Peter	1868 11 09	UT, Salt Lake City
Larsen ....Karen	Nielsen................Christian	1829 12 05	Denmark
Larsen ....Kirsten	Nielsen................Peter	1857 04 04	
Larsen ....Maren	Andersen..............Peder	1836 04 08	Denmark
Larsen ....Maren	Benson................Ezra Taft	1866 09 15	UT, Salt Lake City
Larsen ....Maren	Bertelsen.............Niels	1831 12 01	Denmark
Larsen ....Maren	Peterson..............Peter	1878	
Larsen ....Marianne	Larsen ....Christian	1868 12 21	UT, Salt Lake City
Larsen ....Marie	Lee ....Niels Peter		
Larsen ....Martha	Stoker.................William	1875 02 01	UT, Salt Lake City
Larsen ....Mary	Anderson.............Gustave	1874 11 23	UT, Clover
Larsen ....Mary (Marie)	Johnson ....James	1850 11 29	
Larsen ....Mary	Price...................Charles	1873 02 10	
Larsen ....Mette Maria	Eskildsen.............Niels C.	1846 05 23	Denmark
Larsen ....Sarah	Clawson ....James	1873 01 29	UT, Spring City
Larsen ....Winka	Harris ....Martin Lot	1879 12 18	UT, St. George
Larson ....Anna Hannah	Van Leuven........Dunam	1864 11 30	
Larson ....Bodilla K.	Poulson ....Anders	1840 11 29	
Larson ....Hannah	Jensen ....James	1875 01 01	UT, Hyrum
Larson ....Ingeborg	Jonson ....Truls	1852	Sweden

Female	Male	Date	Place
Larson ....Ingeborg	Rosequist ....Pehr T.	1843 05 28	Sweden
Larson ....Kjersti	Jorganson ....Lars	1858	
Larson ....Kjersti	Larsen ....John Niels	1869 09 15	
Larsson............Anna Christina	Cramer ....John Charles	1883 12 06	UT, Salt Lake City
Larsson............Arna	Anderson............Nils	1844 01 28	Sweden
Larsson............Arna	Martensson ....Jeppa	1834 12 12	Sweden
Larsson............Bengta	Carlson...............Swen	1852 12 17	Sweden
Larsson............Kjarsta P.	Anderson............Peter N.	1854 11 03	Sweden
Lashbrook.......Annie	Hillier ....George C.	1861 11 25	ENG, Croyden
Lassen.............Hulda Franziska	Nielson ....Peter	1862 03 08	UT, Salt Lake City
Last...................Hannah	Cornaby ....Samuel	1851 01 30	ENG, Norfolk
Latham ....Truelove	Ward ....Thomas	1822 05 26	ENG, Belgrave
Lattmann ....Barbara	Germer...............John M.	1858 03 12	UT, Plain City
Laub ....Sarah	Perkins ....Ute Warren	1867 09 16	
Lauritzen.........Maria	Jensen ....Andreas	1868 01 30	UT, Salt Lake City
Lausten............Johanna K.	Larsen ....Johane	1836 10 07	Denmark
Lavender ....Alice	Field ....John	1862 04 05	UT, Salt Lake City
Lavender ....Alice	Hocklippe ....James	1853	
Lavender ....Alice	Theckston ....John		
Lavender ....Mary	Bateman.............Thomas Jr.	1861 09 18	UT, West Jordan
Lavender ....Mary	Nielsen ....Fredrick	1869	UT, Cottonwood
Lawrence.........Emma Hannah	Collings ....Richard	1844 05 26	ENG, London
Lawrensen.......Margaret	Sampson.............William	1861 03 10	UT, Santaquin
Lawrenson.......Jane	Shaw..................Abraham	1856 12 02	UT, Provo
Lawson ....Mary	Cook..................Joseph Wood	1864 03 12	UT, Salt Lake City
Lawson ....Mary	Hulet..................Charles	1857 03 23	UT, Salt Lake City
Lawson ....Mary	Kirkman.............Robert L.	1845 01 01	
Lay...................Maria	Bowers ....James	1831 04 01	ENG, Stafford
Lay...................Mary Elizabeth	Terry..................Benjamin F.	1869 05 03	
Lay...................Rhoda E.	Hamblin..............Francis M.	1861 10 21	UT, Santa Clara
Layne...............Mary Elizabeth	Wilding ....George	1850 06 30	IA, Kanesville
Layne...............Sarah	Owens.................Horace		
Lea ....Elizabeth Lamb	Lloyd ....Thomas William	1877 02 26	UT, Farmington
Leach...............Harriet J.	Barnard ....Ezra J.	1856 04 15	
Leach...............Rosannah	Binnall................Charles	1856 02 06	UT, Salt Lake City
Leach...............Rosannah	Bowers ....John	1835 11 08	ENG, Oldbury
Leader ....Eleanor Esther	Page...................John	1835 07 01	ENG
Leah ....Sarah Ann	Hart ....Samuel Cornelius	1849 03 31	ENG
Leaver ....Mary	Page...................Jonathan S.	1855 08 12	UT, Salt Lake City
Leavitt.............Betsy	Hamblin..............William H.	1854 05 01	UT, Tooele
Leavitt.............Hannah	Fish ....Horace	1824 05 18	Canada
Leavitt.............Lucinda	Brown.................Benjamin F.	1848 02 12	MI, Hillsdale
Leavitt.............Lydia	Snow..................William	1842 08	IL, Nauvoo
Leavitt.............Mary	Hamblin..............William H.		
Leavitt.............Roxanna	Fletcher ....Benjamin	1838 04 12	IL
Leavitt.............Roxanna	Huntsman............John	1841 06 23	
Leavitt.............Roxanna	Snow..................William	1853 03 12	UT, Salt Lake City
LeBaron...........Melissa B.	Johnson ....Benjamin F.	1841 12 25	OH, Kirtland
Lebaron ....Naomi Roxanna	Holman...............James Sawyer	1833 03 24	
Lecoultre..........Elsie Marie	Ballif..................Serge Louis	1849 04 27	
Ledingham.......Janet F.	Christopherson....Martin	1874 12 27	UT, Salt Lake City
Lee ....Caroline Matilda	Mott...................John Wentworth	1847 01	NY
Lee ....Clarissa Jane	Webb..................Pardon K.	1844 01 07	MI, Comstock
Lee (Decker)....Cornelia	Mortensen ....Lars	1863 12 29	UT, Parowan

Female	Male	Date	Place
Lee ....Eliza Ann	Hale.................Aroet L.	1869 09 11	UT, Grantsville
Lee ....Elizabeth	Pace.................Wilson Daniel	1868	
Lee ....Elizabeth Ann	Kennington..........William Henry	1874	UT
Lee ....Fanny	Carlile.................James	1863 04 18	
Lee ....Fanny	Chatwin ....Henry	1869 06 07	UT, Heber
Lee ....Margaret	Jones ....John Pidding	1839 09 23	ENG
Leech...............Mary Ann	Adams ....William	1842 10 10	IRE, Down
Leek................Nancy Ann	Voorhees............Elisha	1818 03 26	OH, Clermont
Legg ....Ellen	Mitchell...............William	1826 05 30	Scotland
Leggett ....Charlotte E.	Burgess...............William	1853	
Leggett ....Elizabeth	Gardner...............Matthew A.	1838 06 24	
Leggett ....Susan	Clark.................Ezra Thompson	1861 11 08	UT, Salt Lake City
Lehman ....Sarah Ann	Ewings ....Alexander	1820	
Lehman ....Sarah Ann	McKinney ....Hugh	1832 04 30	PA, Montgomery
Leigh................Ann	Wood.................John Peacock	1839 09 08	ENG
Leishman.........Ann McGregor	Greer ....John Black	1853 05 19	UT, Salt Lake City
Leishman.........Isabella	Ames ....Samuel	1864 01 13	UT, Salt Lake City
Leishman.........Jane	Hill ....Daniel Brice	1865 01 20	UT, Salt Lake City
Leishman.........Janet	Moffat ....David K.	1842 07 01	Scotland
Lemmons.........Mary	Clark.................Isaac		
Lemon ....Ann	Ranck.................Peter Jr.	1840 08 25	PA
Lennox.............Elizabeth	Trimble ....Edward	1839 08 24	
Lense...............Catherine	Beckstead ....Alexander	1823 01 25	Canada
Leonard ....Anne Jane	Thurston.............Charles E.	1878	
Leonard ....Anne Jane	Trimmer..............Edward W.	1860	
Leonard ....Catherine	King...................Solomon	1876 01 17	
Lerwill ....Betsy Valate	Tucker ....James	1860 03	ENG, Liverpool
Leuba ....Charlotte L.	Graehl ....George L.	1841	
Levi.................Barbara Jane	Watts.................Baldwin H.	1856 10 26	UT, Ogden
Levi.................Mary Ann	Riddle................Isaac	1853 03 06	UT, North Ogden
Lewis ....Alice	Morse ....John	1855 05 21	Wales
Lewis ....Ann	Clegg.................Henry Jr.	1855 12 03	UT, Salt Lake City
Lewis ....Annie Elizabeth	Fuller ....Cornelius	1865 01 01	UT, Harrisburg
Lewis ....Aurelia	Hinman...............Lyman	1819 08 16	NY
Lewis ....Cecelia	Morgan...............Morgan	1833 02 16	Wales
Lewis ....Cecelia	Williams..............William	1825 11 21	Wales
Lewis ....Eliza	Beech.................John	1842 12 25	ENG, Longport
Lewis ....Eliza	Farnsworth..........Stephen M.	1854 05 30	UT, Salt Lake City
Lewis ....Eliza	Rhead ....Josiah	1850 04 09	ENG, Longport
Lewis ....Eliza Jane	Fish ....Joseph	1869	UT, Salt Lake City
Lewis ....Elizabeth	Bean..................James	1824 07 27	MO, Lincoln
Lewis ....Elizabeth E.	Gardner..............Archibald	1851 04 20	UT, Salt Lake City
Lewis ....Elizabeth E.	Raglin................	1850	MO
Lewis ....Esther	Gunnell...............Francis W.	1864 07 02	UT, Salt Lake City
Lewis ....Martha Ann	Bingham.............Sanford	1847 07 18	NE, Platte River
Lewis ....Mary Ann	Parkin................John Jr.	1870 12 26	
Lewis ....Rachel Stapleton	Harper ....Thomas		
Libby................Hannah	Sevey ....George W.	1831 06 01	NY
Libby................Hannah Knight	Carter ....John	1805 03 02	ME, Cumberland
Libby................Sarah Ann	Smith ....George A.	1845 11 24	IL, Nauvoo
Libby................Sarah Ann S.	Sevy ....John Franklin	1854 07 08	PA, Ripley
Liddiard...........Sarah Ann	Smith ....Joseph J.	1865 02 04	UT, Salt Lake City
Liljenquist ....Clara J. J.	Johnson ....Julius	1871 10 22	UT, Salt Lake City
Lind.................Christiana	Stevens ....Alfred Jr.	1837 06 21	ENG

Female	Male	Date	Place
Lind..................Jenny	Freestone............George	1872 08 12	UT, Salt Lake City
Lind..................Jenzina C.	Mortensen............Peder	1871 10 30	UT, Salt Lake City
Lind..................Maria M.	Freestone............James F.	1869 04 12	UT, Salt Lake City
Lindau..............Christina S. M.	Foremaster............Fredrick W.	1859 08 24	Prussia
Lindroth ....Hilda Josephine	Smart ....Thomas Henry	1879 10 31	UT, Salt Lake City
Lindsay ....Isabella	McGhie................James	1858 09 28	Scotland
Lindsay ....Marion	Camp ....Williams W.	1865	UT, Salt Lake City
Lindsay ....Marion	McLean ....John W.	1845 12 15	Scotland
Lindsay ....Marion	Perry ....Joseph		
Lindvall ....Maximiliana M.	Folkman ....Christopher O.	1869 04 26	UT, Salt Lake City
Linney..............Maria Billings	Morris ....John	1832	ENG
Lint..................Jane Francis	Cameron ....William	1837 11 23	
Liptrot ....Grace	Rigby..................John	1860 09 16	ENG, Deane
Lishman..........Maria	Bickley................Thomas	1850 01 11	
Lishman..........Maria	Mander..............Thomas	1854 02 17	
Lishman..........Maria	Watson................Thomas P.	1867 07 11	
Litson ....Eliza Mary	Glade ....James	1863 10	UT
Littlefield ....Lydia	McNiven..............James Scott	1872 01 15	UT, Salt Lake City
Littlewood ....Elizabeth Tyrene	Juchau ....James Joseph	1860 08	UT, Salt Lake City
Littlewood ....Jane Lovenia	Mayer..................John	1851 01 20	UT, Fairview
Littlewood ....Jane Lovenia	Rigby..................James	1832 10 07	ENG, Stockport
Livermore ....Almeda Melissa	Hawkins		
Livermore ....Almeda Melissa	Snyder..................Robert A.	1841 04 03	IL, Nauvoo
Livermore ....Almeda Melissa	Strong ....Ezra		
Livermore ....Mercy	Smith..................Samuel	1868 10 10	UT, Salt Lake City
Livermore ....Rosetta	Smith..................Samuel	1862 11 16	UT, Salt Lake City
Liversedge.......Anna	Snow ....Bernard	1856 04 16	UT, Salt Lake City
Livesay ....Catherine	Cottam ....John	1816	
Livingston ....Christina C.	Livingston............James	1807 10 09	
Livingston ....Isabella	Aiken ....Samuel Ruggles	1857 04 22	UT, Salt Lake City
Livingston ....Margaret	Gardner..............Archibald	1839 02 19	Canada
Livingston ....Mary Helen	Watts..................Joseph	1859 02 01	
Llewellyn..........Ann	Lewis..................Rufus	1861 04 16	UT, Provo
Llewellyn..........Elizabeth	Davis..................William B.	1876 04 16	UT, Goshen
Llewellyn..........Mary	Burchell ....Joseph	1839 07 18	ENG, Birmingham
Llewellyn..........Mary	Rossiter..............Solomon		PA, Bloomsburg
Lloyd................Elizabeth Ann	Evans ....John Thomas	1855 11 25	
Lloyd................Gwen W.	Evans ....David Rees	1853 07 08	UT, Brigham City
Lloyd................Gwen W.	Roberts ....Daniel	1843 01 28	Wales
Loader ....Mary	Hart ....James	1873 01 20	UT, Salt Lake City
Loader ....Mary	Taylor..................George	1844 05 05	ENG
Loader ....Sarah	Harris ....George H. A.	1862 05 30	UT
Loader ....Sarah	Holman................John G.	1875 12 22	
Loader ....Tamar	Ricks ....Thomas Edwin	1857 03 27	
Lockhart..........Rachel	Miles..................Benjamin A.	1856 05 28	UT, Salt Lake City
Lockwood ....Julie Ann	Hales..................Charles Henry	1852 10 31	IL, Quincy
Lofdahl............Oliva Maria	Andelin ....Olof A.	1866 02 10	
Lofgreen ....Kjestie	Petersen..............Soren Lind	1864	Sweden
Lofthouse........Ann	Cranshaw............Richard	1852 07 18	ENG
Lofthouse........Ann	Lofthouse ....Anthony	1827 02 01	ENG
Logan ....Ann Eliza	Secrist................Jacob Foutz	1842 03 14	PA, Tomstown
Logan ....Mary Bathgate	Adams................Joshua	1859 12 22	
Logan ....Ruth Bailey	Cloward..............Daniel	1840 10 15	PA, Unionville
Logan ....Ruth Bailey	Fausett................William M.		

Female	Male	Date	Place
Long ....Charlotte	Poll ....William Flint	1842 11 02	ENG
Long ....Eliza	Kelly ....John Phillip	1838 12 25	ENG, Bromyard
Long ....Frances	Reeves...............William		
Long ....Frances	Sweat.................Father		
Long ....Frances	Willis..................William Wesley		
Long ....Maria	Cushing...............James	1850 10 13	ENG, Norfolk
Longhurst ....Amelia Ann	Hewlett...............Thomas	1865 04 22	UT, Salt Lake City
Longhurst ....Amelia Ann	Rounds...............William Carmer	1868 10 17	UT, Salt Lake City
Longhurst ....Mercy Marintha	Whittington ....George A.	1876 01 12	
Longman ....Ann	Bench.................William	1836 10 14	ENG
Longstroth ....Nanny	Richards..............Franklin D.	1857 03 06	UT, Salt Lake City
Longstroth ....Nanny	Richards..............Willard	1846 01 25	IL, Nauvoo
Loomis.............Lucy	Andrus................Milo	1851 06 01	UT
Loomis.............Lucy	Tuttle ....Hubbard B.	1844 05 16	
Looser ....Elizabeth	Smyth.................Richard	1877 07 09	
Looser ....Elizbaeth	McDonough.........John	1872	
Loosli ....Rosetta	Zollinger ....Jacob	1870 05 09	UT, Salt Lake City
Lorentzen ....Anne M. D.	Petersen..............Hans	1851 03	Denmark
Losee..............Jemimah	Cox.....................Fredrick W.	1844 01 27	IL, Nauvoo
Losee..............Mary Jane	Huff ....Joseph	1836 11 10	Canada
Lott ....Elizabeth	Riley...................William W.	1849	IL
Lott ....Mary Elizabeth	Lossee ....Abraham	1848 11 12	UT, Salt Lake City
Louder ....Catherine	Burrows...............William Creeland	1857 01 01	
Louder ....Catherine	Sellwood ....William C.	1853 08 01	
Love................Elizabeth A.	Bradley...............George Henry	1857 03 10	UT, Nephi
Love................Isabell	Glade ....James	1869 06 28	
Love................Jane	Baxter.................Robert Wright	1848 03 27	Scotland
Love................Margaret	Smith..................James A.	1810 05 24	
Love................Mary Ellen	Neff ....Benjamin Barr	1870 10 07	UT
Loveland.........Sarah Sophia	Valentine ....Hans M. K.	1867 04 20	UT, Salt Lake City
Lovell..............Martha Ann	Anderson.............Anders P.	1873 04 14	UT, Salt Lake City
Lovell..............Sarah	Mendenhall ....William	1838 02 21	
Lovett..............Catherine A.	Wilkins................George W.	1846 07 04	MA, Lowell
Loving.............Albertina A.	Nyman.................Carl	1870 01 11	UT, Salt Lake City
Lowe...............Betsy	Allen ....James Carson	1883 03 01	UT, Salt Lake City
Lowe...............Ellen	Allen ....James Carson	1884	UT
Lowe...............Mary Ann	Wells ....Stephen R.	1851	Trail
Lowe...............Mary Dudley	Howard................Thomas	1864 12 25	UT
Lowe...............Sarah Louisa	Bridges...............Henry M.	1824	ENG
Lubbock..........Rebecca	Stimpson ....William	1848 11 17	ENG
Lublin..............Kate	Alexander............Thomas Murphy	1864 07 26	UT
Lucas..............Marcy Jane	Barney................Henry	1846	
Lucas..............Marcy Jane	Williams..............John	1831 02 10	
Luce...............Caroline	Chatwin ....William	1865 08	
Luce...............Caroline	Snyder.................Samuel C.	1851 09 09	UT, Salt Lake City
Luce...............Caroline	Walker.................John		
Luckie.............Johann	Smith..................George Y.	1854 12 29	Scotland
Luddington.......Angeline A.	Bush...................William James	1864 09 12	UT, Pleasant Grove
Ludvigsen........Ann Kirstine	Bilby ....John	1861 05 10	UT, Salt Lake City
Ludvigsen........Ann Kirstine	Rasmussen..........Hans P.	1840 12 27	Denmark
Ludvigsen........Maren	Halling................Jorgen (John)	1861 11 02	UT, Brigham City
Ludvigsen........Maren	Nielsen...............Peder	1848 09 23	Denmark
Luker ....Margaret	Phillips................Richard	1835 10 01	NJ, Monmouth
Lundberg ....Laura	Berntson.............Rasmus	1861 12 22	Sweden

Female	Male	Date	Place
Lundblad..........Charlotte Elena	Simpkins ....Joseph	1867 10 18	
Lundblad..........Mary Christina	Ash.....................Joseph	1876	
Lundblad..........Mary Christina	Barton ....Joseph Alma	1870	
Lundquist.........Henrietta E.	Bell.....................Thomas	1865 11 07	UT, Salt Lake City
Lundstrom ....Gustava A.	Madson ....Christian A.	1864 07 03	UT, Gunnison
Lundstrom ....Gustava A.	Capsson.............Nils	1854 02 05	Ocean
Lundy..............Rachel Bunn	Jerman ....James A.	1843	
Lundy..............Rachel Bunn	Newell ....Almon	1848	
Lunn ....Keturah Ann	Broadbent ....Enoch	1842 07 05	ENG
Lyle.................Esther	Stewart...............Archibald	1825 10 11	Scotland
Lyman.............Clarissa	Smith..................John	1815 09 11	
Lyman.............Lelia Deseret	Bartholomew.......Edwin	1871 12 25	UT, Fillmore
Lyon................Janet	Speirs.................George	1848 11 15	Scotland
Lyon................Sophia M.	Fogelburg...........Wilhelm	1885 08 20	UT, Logan
Lyon................Sophia M.	Hyde...................Orson	1865 10 10	
Lythgoe...........Ann	Booth..................John	1856 04	ENG, Eccles
Lytle ....Cyrena Martha	Stilson ....William L.	1859 05 09	UT, Salt Lake City
Lytle ....Mary Jane	Little ....James Amasa	1849 12 16	UT, Salt Lake City

M

Female	Male	Date	Place
Mabey.............Esther	Dofflemeyer.........George	1902	
Mabey.............Esther	Sessions ....Perrigrine	1868 11 22	UT, Salt Lake City
Mabey.............Jane	Holt.....................William	1862 05 04	ENG
MacDuff..........Ada Alice	Rampton ....Henry	1868 11 01	
Macduff..........Mary Ellen	Varley................William	1861 02 24	ENG
Mace..............Marietta	Stevens ....Walter	1869 10 05	UT, Salt Lake City
Macfarlane.......Ann	Reid....................Thomas Hand	1854 02 09	UT, Salt Lake City
Mack..............Almira	Covey.................Benjamin	1836 10 23	
Mack..............Almira	Scobey ....William	1831 08 07	
Mackelprang....Annie Eva A.	Bailey ....Nephi	1873 12 11	UT, Cedar City
Mackelprang....Christina J.	Chatterly............Morton	1866 02 01	UT, Cedar City
Mackelprang....Christina J.	Westerhold.........Charles	1887 12 29	UT, Cedar City
Mackey ....Ann	Chapman ....Welcome	1855 10 05	UT, Manti
Maddison.........Flora Louisa	Long...................Emanuel	1855 01 23	UT, Salt Lake City
Maddison.........Flora Louisa	Maiben ....Henry	1855 07 20	UT, Salt Lake City
Maddox...........Louisa	Davey.................Charles B.	1860 01 20	UT, Salt Lake City
Maddox...........Susanna M. A.	Davey.................Charles B.	1851 08 24	ENG, London
Madsen...........Ane	Hansen...............Jorgen L.	1848 10 14	Denmark
Madsen...........Anna	Salisbury ....David	1858 09 09	UT, Nephi
Madsen...........Christina	Christensen.........James	1859 12	
Madsen...........Christine Marie	Hansen...............Lars (Lewis)	1871 03 06	UT, Salt Lake City
Madsen...........Inger Kerstine	Ipson ....Niels Peter	1864 10 10	UT, Salt Lake City
Madsen...........Karen Kirstine	Pihl....................Henning	1819 10 16	Denmark
Madsen...........Marie	Jensen ....James	1873	UT
Madsen...........Mary Ann	Madsen ....Peter	1847 11 12	Denmark
Madsen...........Mary Christina	Hendrickson........Henry	1873 11 01	UT, Glenwood
Madsen...........Mette Marie	Johnson ....John	1868 04 18	UT, Salt Lake City
Madsen...........Mette Marie	Torbjornsen.........Niels	1862 09 29	UT, Salt Lake City
Madsen...........Petrea E. M	Leonard..............Bradford	1858 02 02	
Madsen...........Severine Marie	Rasmussen.........Andrew	1862 10 12	UT, West Jordan
Madsen...........Severine Marie	Van Cott ....John	1876	UT, Salt Lake City
Madsen...........Sophia Karen	Lee ....Christian	1862 11 15	UT, Salt Lake City

Female	Male	Date	Place
Magnussen......Johanna Maria	Malmberg............John Peter	1857 10 16	Sweden
Magnusson......Carolina W.	Johnson ....Augustus	1859 03 13	Sweden
Maguire ....Juley Ann	Dunn ....John Barker	1853 02 11	UT, North Ogden
Maiben............Alice Pen	Squires..............John Fell	1868 08 07	UT, Salt Lake City
Mailes ....Mary Ann	Jones ....Thomas English	1842 01 16	IL, Nauvoo
Mainwaring ......Elizabeth	Brockbank...........Isaac	1835	ENG, Liverpool
Malan..............Jane Dinah	Hatch.................William Edson	1865 03 03	UT, Salt Lake City
Malan..............Madeleine	Farley................Isaac Robeson	1855 03 11	UT, Salt Lake City
Malan..............Mary Catherine	Barker ....James	1856 06 06	UT, Ogden
Malan..............Mary Catherine	Gaydou...............Anthony	1850 09 10	
Malan..............Pauline Amelia	Farley................Isaac Robeson	1855 03 11	UT, Salt Lake City
Malholm..........Elizabeth	Kleinman............Conrad	1839 04	
Malin...............Ann Penn	Parry ....Joseph	1857 01 05	UT, Salt Lake City
Malin...............Ann Penn	Sharp ....Charles	1859 06 27	UT, Salt Lake City
Malin...............Margaret Ann	Woodard............Charles N.	1856 04 27	UT, Salt Lake City
Mallarnee........Sarah Ann	Jones ....James Naylor	1829 10 17	OH, Steubenville
Mallett............Mary Thorne	Henriod ....Eugene A.	1854 11 05	UT, Salt Lake City
Malley.............Mary Ann	Murray...............John Jr.	1862 12 13	UT, Salt Lake City
Malley.............Mary Ann	Riley..................John	1849 05 22	ENG, Preston
Mallinson ....Sarah	Mitchell..............Hezekiah	1832 10 07	ENG
Malmberg ....Johanna C.	Dahle.................Johannes	1872 03 04	
Malmstrom.......Ellen (Elna)	Larson ....Mons	1852	Sweden
Mander ....Sarah Ann	Green.................Henry T.	1879 10 22	UT, Salt Lake City
Mandeville ......Susan	Fairbanks ....David	1838 11 26	NJ
Mangum ....Sarah Frances	Cazier................David C.	1857 06 07	UT, Nephi
Mangum ....Sarah Frances	Richey ....James	1857	
Mangum ....Sarah Frances	White.................Alfred	1875	UT, Nephi
Manhard ....Lovina	Brown.................Joseph G.	1857	
Mann ....Lydia Catherine	Adams...............David Barclay	1849 05 30	IA
Mann ....Margaret	Foutz.................Jacob	1822 07 22	
Manning..........Abigail	Busenbark...........Isaac	1824	NY, Seneca Co.
Manning..........Anna Eliza	Evans ....Samuel L.	1846 09 07	ENG, Bristol
Manning..........Hannah	Rowe.................David	1820	
Manning..........Jane Elizabeth	James ....Isaac	1845	IL, Nauvoo
Mansson..........Ellen	Monson ....Christian Hans	1867 03 16	UT, Salt Lake City
Marchant ....Caroline Ann	Wilson ....Thomas H.	1859 07 17	
Marchant ....Lydia Elizabeth	Walker...............Stephen	1866 02 12	UT
Marchant ....Maria Louisa	Lyons ....Oscar Fitzallen	1870 09 05	UT, Salt Lake City
Marchant ....Mary Ann	Green.................Austin G.	1856 09 06	UT, Salt Lake City
Marchant ....Sarah Matilda	Newman..............John	1859 12 26	UT, Salt Lake City
Mariner ....Jane	Sanford ....Samuel	1865 01	
Mark ....Janel	Archibald ....James R.	1866 12 01	UT
Mark ....Mary	Archibald ....James R.	1857 01 07	NY, New York
Mark ....Sarah	Morrison.............John	1834	
Markham ....Ruth	Abbott................Joshua	1834	
Markham ....Ruth	Gardner..............Elias		
Markland..........Elizabeth	Jones ....Edward	1826 11 06	ENG
Marler ....Sarah Jane	Lake ....Bailey		
Marler ....Sarah Jane	Lake ....William B.	1850 12 26	
Marler ....Sarah Jane	Taylor................Pleasant Green	1858 06 20	
Marler ....Susan	Harmon ....Henry Martin	1856	UT, Ogden
Marriott ....Elizabeth	Burton ....Robert Walton	1845 02 06	IL, Nauvoo
Marriott ....Mary Ann	Stewart...............William	1843 06 11	ENG
Marsden ....Clara St. Ledger	McDonald...........John Kilpatrick	1872 05 26	UT, Salt Lake City

Female	Male	Date	Place
Marsden ....Clara St. Ledger	Needham ....David Stafford	1898 02 17	UT, Salt Lake City
Marsden ....Emma	Beckstead ....Henry	1862 04 01	UT, Salt Lake City
Marsden ....Harriet Zelnora	Chapman ....Welcome	1876	
Marsden ....Harriet Zelnora	McDonald...........John Kilpatrick	1869 05 31	
Marsh ....Ann	Abbott................Lewis	1829 06 22	MA, Wayland
Marsh ....Ann Rachel	Nichols ....Josiah	1853 12 25	UT, Salt Lake City
Marsh ....Jane Clotilda	Pettingill ....Elihu U.	1849 10 26	IA, Council Bluffs
Marsh ....Mary Jane	Ford....................William	1857 03 05	
Marsh ....Phylinda	Loveridge ....Ambrose	1815 06 30	NY, Bristol
Marsh ....Phylinda	Terry...................Otis	1847	IA
Marshall...........Charlotte	Tims ....John Gardner	1852 12 22	ENG
Marshall...........Ellen	Jones ....Frederick W.	1864 08 17	
Marshall...........Joanna	Jenkins...............Thomas	1838 04 19	
Marshall...........Louisa	Boyce ....Martin Calvin	1865 05 07	
Marshall...........Lovinia	Adams.................John N.	1866 05 29	UT, Franklin
Marshall...........Mary Jane	Burton ....William Hudson	1876 10 23	
Marshall...........Sarah	Callan.................Stephen J. P.	1888 07 18	
Marshall...........Sarah	Poole..................John Peter	1868 03 14	
Marshall...........Selina	Gregory ....Robert	1863 01 02	ID, Franklin
Marshall...........Tryphena	Hunt ....Bethuel Howard	1864 11 09	ID, Franklin
Marston ....Mary Leishman	Monroe		
Marston ....Mary Leishman	Wrathall..............James	1857 03 22	UT, Grantsville
Martenson ....Cecilia	Larson ....Pehr	1851 09 14	Sweden
Martin ....Eleanor	Ricks ....Joel	1827 05 17	KY, Trigg Co.
Martin ....Eveline	Boggs.................Francis	1832	
Martin ....Jane Ann	Rowan.................Matthew	1853 06 06	ENG
Martin ....Margaret	Perkins ....Joseph T.	1852 12 25	Wales
Martin ....Margaret	Taylor.................Edward		
Martin ....Nancy	Perkins ....Absalom	1815	TN, Sparta
Martinsson.......Anna Britta	Ohlson.................Gustave A.	1868 01 04	UT, Salt Lake City
Marvin.............Rhoda Ann	Fullmer ....David	1831 09 18	PA, Union
Maslen.............Elizabeth	Cooper ....William	1858 05 08	NE, Monroe
Mason.............Sophia	Crook ....James	1811	
Masser............Ellen	Carter.................Samuel	1860 03 08	ENG, Stafford.
Massey............Elizabeth	Simper................Thomas W.	1845 10 20	ENG, Chedworth
Mather ....Sarah Ann	Hall.....................Newton D.	1856 02 07	UT, Ogden
Matheson.........Ellen McKell	Wardle................Solomon		
Mathews ....Ann	Perkins ....Thomas	1808 05 03	Wales
Mathews ....Anne	Morris ....George	1863 12 26	UT, Salt Lake City
Mathews ....Elizabeth	Campbell.............Joseph H.	1861 01 01	UT, Providence
Mathews ....Emeline	Roberts ....Edward Killick	1850 04 19	UT, Salt Lake City
Mathews ....Harriet Eliza	Bates..................Cyrus W.	1846 12 13	
Mathews ....Joan	Johnson ....Charles M.	1871 11 27	UT, Providence
Mathews ....Julia Antoinette	Sullivan ....Archibald	1850 11 06	UT, Salt Lake City
Mathews ....Margaret	Rice....................Oscar North	1869 11 15	UT, Logan
Mathews ....Mary	Marler.................George W.	1863 12 06	UT, Providence
Mathews ....Mary Ann	Barnett ....George	1850 09 17	ENG, Ashton
Mathias...........Ada	Clifford................Leander H.	1854	UT, Fort Brigham
Mathiasen........Ane Kirstine	Pedersen............Soren Aarup	1825 05 23	
Mathiason........Anna Emilie	Klemmensen.......Peter Ankjar	1869	UT, Salt Lake City
Mathiesen........Karen Sophia	Larsen................Lars	1864	UT, Cottonwood
Mathieson........Jorgina	Olsen..................Andrew Niels	1876 12	
Mathieson........Margaret	Fife.....................James	1824 09 19	Scotland
Mathis.............Anna Maria D.	Bryner ....Hans Ulrich Jr.	1849	Switzerland

Female	Male	Date	Place
Mathis............Mary Catherine	Pratt ....William		
Mathis............Mary Catherine	Woodard ....Francis S.	1848 01	UT, Salt Lake City
Mathis............Sarah Ann	Holman...............James Alonzo	1855 11 30	UT, Payson
Matisen...........Suzannah S. A.	Jeppersen ....Niels Jacob	1847 11	
Mattatahl.........Barbara E.	Campbell............Alexander	1817	
Mattatahl.........Barbara E.	Ogilvie ....George Byers	1827 08 11	Canada
Matthews ....Aurelia	Hollingshead ....Thomas	1823 02 06	Canada
Matthews ....Frances Ann	Litson ....Richard	1845 02 08	
Matthews ....Mahala Ann R.	Holladay ....John D. Jr.	1848 11 02	UT, Holladay
Matthews ....Sarah	Moss ....Patterson	1865	
Matty..............Elizabeth	Harrod................Charles	1855 10 20	ENG
Matty..............Elizabeth	Roberts ....Samuel	1823 11 19	ENG
Maughan ....Mary Ann	Atkin ....Thomas Jr.	1856 05 20	UT, Salt Lake City
Mauritsen........Anne Kirstine	Smoot.................Abraham Owen	1856 02 17	UT, Salt Lake City
Maxham..........Cynthia Sildona	Dack...................Philip	1859 05 15	
Maxwell ....Catherine	Truman...............Jacob Mica	1856 12 21	UT, Salt Lake City
Maxwell ....Elizabeth Durrah	Wilkins...............Oscar	1870 10 17	UT, Salt Lake City
Maxwell ....Jane Ann	Marchant............John Alma	1879	
May................Eliza Rebecca	Udall..................David	1864 07 02	UT, Salt Lake City
May................Harriet	Dewey................John Cook	1857 02 11	
May................Ruth	Fox ....Jesse W. Jr.	1873 05 08	UT, Salt Lake City
Mayall ....Myra	Henrie ....William	1824 11 17	OH, Cincinnati
Maycock ....Ann	Ringrose.............Richard	1835 07 19	ENG, Coventry
Maycock ....Maria	Garrett................William	1841 04 04	ENG, Coventry
Mayer ....Jane Elizabeth	Richards..............Samuel W.	1856 02 16	UT, Salt Lake City
Mayer ....Rachel Ann	Brimhall..............George W.	1852 02 02	UT, Salt Lake City
Mayhew ....Caroline Abigail	Chipman..............Washburn	1868 05 30	UT, Salt Lake City
Mayo...............Brittanna	Jolley..................Henry B. M.	1833 10 31	TN, Dresden
McAllister........Agnes Nancy	Robbins..............Edward Jr.	1833	ENG
McAuslin.........Ann	Adamson.............Dougal	1855 11	UT, Murray
Mcauslin ....Elizabeth	Maxwell..............Arthur	1856 05 08	Ocean
McBlain...........Mary	McGhie...............William Jr.	1850 12 31	Scotland
McBride ....Catherine	Pope...................William Monroe	1841	IL, Nauvoo
McBride ....Henrietta	Belnap................Gilbert	1852 06 26	UT, Salt Lake City
McBride ....Isabelle	Dayley ....James	1834 03 18	OH
McBride ....Jane	Bullock ....Thomas Henry		
McBride ....Janetta Ann	Ferrin..................Jacob S.	1857 03 29	UT, Ogden
McBride ....Martha	Kimball ....Heber Chase	1846 01 26	IL, Nauvoo
McBride ....Martha	Knight.................Vinson	1826 07 26	NY
McBride ....Martha	Smith..................Joseph Jr.	1842 08	IL, Nauvoo
McBride ....Rebecca	Wilson ....Wellington		IL, Nauvoo
McCann ....Margaret	Porritt ....Thomas	1838	ENG
McCann ....Margaret	Taylor.................William Robert	1872	
McCauslin........Lydia	Young..................Jacob	1857 03 05	UT, Provo
McClellan........Louisa Jane	Bell ....Eli	1858 08 16	UT, Payson
McClellan........Matilda E.	Loveless.............James W.	1847 03 09	IA, Council Bluffs
McClenaham ...Elizabeth	Richards.............Silas	1829 11 05	OH, Sidney
McCluskey.......Ann Mitchell	Moss ....William Jackson	1828 12 01	ENG
McCormick .....Ann	Leishman ....John Allan	1852 01 23	Scotland
McCormick .....Margaret	McFarland...........William	1832 01 09	Scotland
McCoy ....Catherine	Clarkson.............Thomas	1821 10 21	ENG
McCrary ....Sarah Ann	Graham ....Thomas B.	1825 06 27	AL, Green Co.
McCullough .....Nancy Eleanor	Keele..................Richard John	1808 09 18	TN, Bedford
McCurdy ....Nancy	Koyle ....Hyrum	1838	

Female	Male	Date	Place
McCurdy ....Nancy	Woodward...........James	1844 01 30	
McDonald ....Eliza	Clyde.................William M.	1851 01 24	UT, Alpine
McDonald ....Jane	Clyde.................George W. Jr.	1851 09 30	
McDonald ....Mary	Mayberry ....James		
McDonald ....Mary	Rider ....John	1867 07 27	
McDowell........Agnes	Smith.................Hugh	1840 03 12	
McEvers ....Harriet	Roberts ....Horace	1828 06 05	IL, Morgan Co.
McEwan...........Jane	Reid...................William Taylor		
McEwen...........Margaret	Willden ....John	1862 06 03	UT, Beaver
McFarland ....Sarah Jean	Casper ....James Moroni	1876 02 14	UT, Salt Lake City
McFarlane ....Ann	Erskine..............Archibald	1851 06 03	Scotland
McFate ....Aurilla	Williams.............William G.	1861 03 18	UT, Virgin City
McFate ....Martha	Jackson.............James Jr.	1863	
McGhie ....Agnes	Robinson............Andrew	1882 05 08	UT, Mill Creek
McGhie ....Annie Rebecca	Egbert ....Hyrum Smith	1890 09 25	UT, Salt Lake City
McGhie ....Elizabeth	Boam..................Thomas	1854 05	MO, St. Louis
McGill ....Helen Adams	Hunter ....George F.	1870 01 17	UT, Salt Lake City
McGinness ......Mary Jane	Laub..................George	1846 01 06	IL, Nauvoo
McGregor ....Agnes	Cooper ....Frederick A.	1870 06 13	
McGregor ....Agnes	Cutler ....Harmon	1859 12 19	UT, Salt Lake City
McGregor ......Agnes	White.................Stephen	1859 11 01	UT, Salt Lake City
McGregor ....Annie Louisa	Bell....................James	1858 02 15	UT, Salt Lake City
McIntire...........Margaret	Burgess..............Melanchton	1855 04 10	
McIntosh..........Lucy	Wardrobe ....John	1837 09 17	Scotland
McIntyre...........Agnes	Austin................William	1853 07 15	UT
McKay ....Catherine	Grow ....John Wood	1869 11 08	UT, Salt Lake City
McKay ....Isabella	Wadley ....William	1860 04 08	
McKay ....Mary	McKinnon ....Archibald	1861 08 09	UT, Salt Lake City
McKee ....Harriet Persis	Babcock ....John	1867 02 26	UT, Salt Lake City
McKeen ....Susan	McArthur ....Duncan	1818 01 01	NY, Holland
McKenzie..........Catherine	Anderson............Alexander	1836 08 14	Scotland
McKenzie.........Catherine	Dye....................William	1869 04 12	UT, Salt Lake City
McKenzie.........Christina P.	Graham ....John	1820 05 12	Scotland
McKenzie.........Jane T.	Allred..................James Franklin	1860 07 01	
McKeown.........Jane	Gardner.............Robert	1841 03 17	Canada
McKinley ....Marion	Gillespie ....Alexander	1849 02 11	Scotland
McKinney.........Sarah Jane	Hales.................Henry William	1857 01 11	UT, Salt Lake City
McKinnon ....Jane	Baxter................Robert Wright	1856 12 28	UT, Salt Lake City
McKinnon ....Jane	McPhail ....Archibald	1849 12 04	Scotland
McKinnon ....Jane	Schwartz ....Jack		UT, Rich Co.
McLachlan ....Mary	Meiklejohn...........Robert	1835 05 17	Scotland
McLean............Elizabeth	Aird....................William	1853 02	Scotland
McLiesh ....Ann	Gowans..............Andrew	1823 06 20	Scotland
McMaster.........Virginia F.	Major.................William D.	1869 08 30	UT, Salt Lake City
McMeans........Margaret T.	Adkinson ....Charles	1826 12 28	
McMeans........Margaret T.	Smoot.................Abraham Owen	1838 11 11	TN, Roane Co.
McMenemy.....Ann	Mousley..............Titus	1817	DE, New Castle
McMenemy.....Ann	Snow..................Erastus	1867 10 15	UT, Salt Lake City
McMillan ....Sarah Ann	Farrell.................John		
McMillan ....Sarah Ann	Heyborne ....John	1842 09 14	ENG
McMillan ....Sarah Ann	Urie ....John	1858 01 16	
McMillen ....Mary Ellen	Nelson................Henry Thomas	1876	
McMillen ....Mary Tweed	McKee................David Daniel	1816 07 11	PA, Butler Co.
McMillian ....Phebe Hannah	Bethers..............William S.	1866 09 14	UT, Heber

Female	Male	Date	Place
McMurray ....Harriet Lucinda	Fairchild ....Moroni F.	1855 01 18	UT, Grantsville
McMurray ....Matilda Jane	Martindale ....William Clinton	1854 05 05	UT, Grantsville
McMurrin ....Isabella	Sims ....George	1857 01 13	UT, Salt Lake City
McMurrin ....Isabella	Smith..................Adam Browning	1870 05 30	UT, Tooele
McNeil ....Christina	Reynolds ....Warren Ford	1857 06 28	
McNeil ....Emily Reid	Ballard................Henry	1867 10 04	
McNeil ....Janet Jane	Davidson ....Robert	1880 06 10	
McNeil ....Margaret	McCulloch ....John Black	1852 06	Scotland
McNeil ....Margaret Reid	Ballard................Henry	1861 05 05	UT, Logan
McNiven ....Janet	Hogg ....Robert	1862 11 26	UT, Salt Lake City
McNiven ....Janet	McNiven ....John	1847	Scotland
McNiven ....Jessie	Taggart................George Henry	1870 09 26	
McNutt ....Mary Ann	Blair....................Harrison	1852	IL, Adams Co.
McPhail............Henrietta	Eckersell ....James B.	1861 04 21	
McPherson ......Isabella	Bevan..................James	1859 11 03	UT, Salt Lake City
McQuarrie.......Agnes	Herrick................Lester James	1867 06 12	UT, Salt Lake City
McQuarrie.......Mary M.	Bunker................Edward	1861 04 20	UT, Salt Lake City
McQueen.........Elizabeth	Orr......................Robert	1828 04 16	Scotland
McRee ....Mary	Black ....George	1838	MS, Copiah
McRee ....Mary	Brown.................James	1846 07 16	IL, Nauvoo
McSkelly ....Ellen	Walker.................John		
Mead ....Abigail	McBride...............Daniel	1787	NY, Albany
Mead ....Betsy	McBride...............James	1818	
Mead ....Maria	Hortin ....Edmund	1834 12 07	ENG
Mead ....Sophia B.	Tippets ....William Plummer	1842 01 01	
Mead ....Sophia B.	Weymouth..........Daniel	1827	
Meadows ....Maria	Busby ....William	1846 10 23	ENG, Lancaster
Meadows ....Mary Ann	Leonard..............Truman	1857 01 06	UT, Salt Lake City
Mealmaker.......Elizabeth	Boyack ....James	1827 11 14	Scotland
Mecham...........Elizabeth L.	Ford....................William	1853	
Mecham...........Emeline	Sweat ....George Hyrum	1854 03 21	UT, Salt Lake City
Mecham...........Lucina	Boren ....William Jasper	1859 07 03	UT, Provo
Mecham...........Mary Henrietta	Batty...................Miles	1864 07 24	UT, Salt Lake City
Mecham...........Permelia	Bigelow ....Daniel	1865 07 23	UT, Silver Creek
Mecham...........Polly Mae	Packer.................James	1854 02 14	UT, Lehi
Mecham...........Roxena	Carter ....William F.	1847 03 13	NE
Mecham...........Sally Ann	Carter ....William F.	1857 12 02	
Mecham...........Sylvia Amaret	Carter ....Dominicus	1839 03 28	MO, Far West
Mecham...........Sylvia Amaret	Snyder.................John	1855 11 03	
Medler ....Mary Ann	England...............Daniel	1828 02 11	ENG
Meears ....Salina	Blunt...................Joseph	1863 05 24	ENG, Whiton
Meeks.............Mary Jane	Pearce................James	1867 03 06	UT, St. George
Mehring ....Catherine E.	Woolley ....Samuel A.	1846 05 12	IL, Nauvoo
Meiklejohn ....Mary	Hill.....................Alexander	1857 01 28	
Meiklejohn ....Mary	Smith..................John Anderson	1863	
Meith...............Anna H. T.	Maeser ....Karl Gottfried	1854 06 11	Germany
Meith...............Camilla Clara	Cobb ....James T.	1864 11 14	
Mellor..............	Clark...................Edward Watkins	1857 02 03	
Mellor.............Charlotte E.	Roper ....John Henry	1857 02 04	UT, Provo
Mellor.............Clara Althera	Hill.....................James Allen	1873 11 03	UT, Salt Lake City
Memmott ....Martha Ann	Ivie ....Benjamin M.	1864 07 21	UT, Mt. Pleasant
Memmott ....Sarah	Probert ....Samuel	1869 01 12	UT, Salt Lake City
Mendenhall......Elizabeth Wells	Bird....................Richard Leroy	1871 09 18	UT, Salt Lake City
Mendenhall......Susannah	Cloward..............Jacob Jr.	1848 12 05	IA, Council Bluffs

Female	Male	Date	Place
Menery ....Elizabeth	Scott.....................John	1836 04 15	Canada
Mennell............Ann	Taylor ....Benjamin F.	1827	OH, Grafton
Mercer ....Elizabeth	Platt.....................James	1834 01 20	ENG, Lancashire
Mercer ....Sarah	Wilkinson............Charles	1833	
Meredith ....Ann	Mathews............Allen	1854	UT
Meredith ....Ann	Pearce................Harrison	1856 08 03	UT, Spanish Fork
Meredith ....Ann	Pollock ....Samuel	1865 10 10	UT, St. George
Meredith ....Mary	Cook....................Thomas		
Merrel ....Phoebe	Saunders............William G.	1839 11 11	
Merrell ....Edna Maria	Reynolds ....Warren Ford	1846 01 03	
Merrick............Fanny	Keeler.................Daniel A.	1846 02 06	
Merrick............Fanny	Kofford ....Paul Ernest	1849 07 29	MO, St. Louis
Merrick............Maria Susanna	Madison ....John	1831	ENG
Merrick............Maria Susanna	Thorn..................William	1852 03 23	
Merrifield.........Jane Emma	Williams.............John J.	1852 02 14	Wales
Merrifield.........Sarah	Denning..............James	1849 07 08	Wales
Merrill..............Almira	Lamb ....Abel	1826	
Merrill..............Elthura R.	Collett.................Reuben	1861 01 17	UT, Smithfield
Merrill..............Laura Cordelia	Cox.....................Jehu Jr.	1854 12 24	UT, Salt Lake City
Merrill..............Polly Matilda	Colton.................Philander	1833 07 13	MI, Macomb
Merriman ....Priscilla	Evans ....Thomas David	1856 04 03	Wales
Merriman ....Priscilla	Lewis..................John A.	1851 08 30	Wales
Merriman ....Priscilla	Phillips................Charles	1844 05 09	
Merritt ....Ellen Coil	Bolton.................Curtis Edwin	1846 02 06	IL, Nauvoo
Merritt ....Ellen Coil	Love ....Thomas		
Messam...........Catherine	Cottrell................George	1841 12 14	ENG
Messam...........Catherine	Smith..................Absolom W.	1855 10 31	
Messenger.......Keziah	Benson................Benjamin	1795 12 15	NY, Ramslea Co.
Metcalf............Eliza Roxie	Bartholomew ....John	1868 10 11	UT, Manti
Meyer ....Marie Theresa	Christensen.........Jacob	1855 07 29	Denmark
Meyer ....Mary Ann	Rogers ....David	1853 02 20	UT, Salt Lake City
Michael ....Mary Ann	Hatch..................Isaac Burres Jr.	1880 01 29	UT, Salt Lake City
Michelsen ....Maren	Michelsen............Ole	1842 08 16	Denmark
Michelsen ....Maren	Thorsen..............Jens	1823 11 23	Denmark
Mickelson ....Maren	Jorgensen ....Jorgen	1838 05 04	Denmark
Micklejohn ....Jane	Shields ....John C.	1865 12 22	UT, Tooele
Middlefell ....Elizabeth	Bentley ....John	1831	
Middlefell ....Elizabeth	Orton ....William	1870	UT, Parowan
Middlemas ....Abigail	Walker.................Charles L.	1861 09 28	UT, Salt Lake City
Middleton ....Hannah	Hawkey ....Foster	1847 12 06	ENG
Middleton ....Hannah	Sinfield ....Samuel	1857	UT
Middleton ....Sarah	Holding...............Daniel	1844 03 02	ENG, Chester
Mieeklejohn .....Catherine Mary	Oldroyd ....Peter Liddle	1850 08	Scotland
Mieeklejohn .....Catherine Mary	Todd....................Andrew	1846 11 13	Scotland
Mikesell ....Catherine	Mikesell ....John Aylor	1807 12 12	
Mikesell ....Cynthia Ann	Green ....William	1856	IA, Pott. Co.
Mikesell ....Cynthia Ann	Walker.................Rufus		
Mikesell ....Louisa C.	Mowery ....John T.	1853 12 09	
Mikesell ....Louisa C.	Scott...................Volney H.	1889 05 25	
Mikkelsen ....Anna Johanna	Jensen ....Christen	1848 05 03	Denmark
Mikkelsen ....Anna Johanna	Scow ....Jens	1864 05 28	UT, Salt Lake City
Mikkelsen ....Dorthea C.	Poulsen..............Mads	1833 10 26	Denmark
Mikkelsen ....Fredrikka	Christensen.........Peter Christian	1869 05 17	
Mikkelsen ....Helene	Lee.....................Niels Peter	1864 04 30	Ocean

Female	Male	Date	Place
Mikkelsen ....Inger Marie	Blanch ....Wealthy	1865 03 19	
Mikkelsen ....Jensine D.	Larsen ....Hans	1862	UT, Salt Lake City
Mikkelsen ....Maren Kirstine	Smith....................Lauritz N.	1854 01 15	Ocean
Miles ....Belinda	Edwards ....Esaias	1847 10 24	IA, Council Bluffs
Miles ....Hannah	Snow ....William		
Miles ....Malinda Ann	Chalmers.............Horace S.		UT, Salt Lake City
Miles ....Malinda Ann	Miller ....David Rudisill	1862 10 04	
Miles ....Sarah Ann	Andrus.................Milo	1848 01 01	NE
Miles ....Sarah Ann	Lee ....Orin Strong	1859 10 30	UT, Salt Lake City
Miles ....Sarah Ann	Sellew ....Chauncy	1841 07 07	
Miller...............Agnes	Strong ....John	1828 12 16	ENG
Miller...............Alice Ophelia	Dalton..................Matthew W.	1868 04 05	
Miller...............Alice Ophelia	Slocum ....Elisha	1877	
Miller...............Amy	Howe...................Amos	1876	UT
Miller...............Ann	Bradley...............Thomas		
Miller...............Ann	Keep....................James Joseph	1836 07 24	ENG, Reading
Miller...............Ann	Warner ....James	1855	
Miller.............Clarissa A.	Hoyt....................Israel	1848 11 25	UT, Salt Lake City
Miller...............Elizabeth	Neeley.................Lewis	1828 04 20	IL, Vermillion Co.
Miller...............Elizabeth Ellen	Quigley...............Andrew	1853 11 30	UT, Salt Lake City
Miller...............Freelove	Hammond ....Milton Datus	1864 01 29	
Miller...............Hannah	Clark...................Raymond	1847 05 02	MO, Platte Co.
Miller...............Hannah	Scott...................Andrew Hunter		UT, Provo
Miller...............Isabella C.	Bigler..................Adam C.	1867 04 04	UT, Farmington
Miller...............Lovisa	Hammond ....Milton Datus	1853 12 11	UT, Farmington
Miller...............Lucy Maria	Robinson.............Oliver Lee	1854 11 26	UT, Farmington
Miller...............Martha	Hill ....Isaac	1852 10 27	UT, Salt Lake City
Miller...............Mary	Barron ....Alexander F.	1848 01 04	TX, Harris Co.
Miller...............Mary Ann	McAllister ....Joseph W.	1876 02 14	UT, Salt Lake City
Miller...............Mary Ann	Smith...................John	1845 10 03	Scotland
Miller...............Mary Elmira	Compton ....John Allen	1865 12 09	UT, Salt Lake City
Miller...............Mary Elmira	Hess....................Alma	1862 05 10	UT, Salt Lake City
Miller...............Mary Jane	Blazzard..............John H.	1846 03 30	NE
Miller...............Mary Jane	Hill ....Isaac	1852 10 27	UT, Salt Lake City
Miller...............Mary Olsen	Lemmon ....Oliver Perry	1886 10 13	UT, Salt Lake City
Miller...............Ruth Ann	McBride...............George	1855 03 27	
Miller...............Ruth Ann	McBride...............James	1859 05 13	UT, Farmington
Miller...............Sarah Jane	Carbine ....William V.	1879 05 30	UT, Salt Lake City
Mills ....Barbara B.	Haws ....William W.	1853 12 01	UT, Provo
Mills ....Elizabeth	Oakden ....William	1855 10 06	UT, Salt Lake City
Mills ....Elizabeth	Whitaker..............Thomas William	1858 03 17	UT, Salt Lake City
Mills ....Elvira Pamela	Cox......................Orville S.	1839 10 03	IL, Adams Co.
Mills ....Hannah	Greenwell.............Ambrose	1861	
Mills ....Hannah	Wardley...............Francis	1864	
Mills ....Hannah	Watson................John	1854 05 05	ENG
Mills ....Jane	Hone ....George Jr.	1864 04 26	ENG
Mills ....Louisa Harriet	Palmer.................Thomas	1865 02 14	UT, Salt Lake City
Mills ....Martha Ann	Wilkinson.............Joseph	1871 05 29	UT, Salt Lake City
Mills ....Mary	Hibbert ....Benjamin	1862 01 01	
Mills ....Sarah Ellen	Gunn ....William B.	1872 01 27	UT, Enterprise
Millward ....Jane	Wright.................Jesse	1856 06 23	ENG
Milnes ....Tabitha	Child...................Thomas	1847 03 28	ENG, Bradford
Minchell ....Esther	Coons.................Libbeus T.	1867	
Mineer ....Elizabeth	Felt ....Joseph Henry		

Female	Male	Date	Place
Miner ....Eunice	Allen ....Andrew	1806 01 03	VT, Montpelier
Miner ....Matilda	Curtis.................John White	1855 10 21	UT, Salt Lake City
Minnerly..........Louisa	Shumway ....Charles	1845 08	IL, Nauvoo
Mitchell ....Ann	Walker.................Joseph	1828	ENG
Mitchell ....Elizabeth	Barnett ....Henry W.	1862 03 25	ENG, Tyne
Mitchell ....Elizabeth	Horrocks.............Edward G.	1864 06 04	UT, Salt Lake City
Mitchell ....Euphemia	Bain....................Robert Angus	1857 01	
Mitchell ....Isabella	McFarland ....Archibald	1854 08 03	Scotland
Mitchell ....Jane	Cowan.................Alexander	1860 01 22	UT, Salt Lake City
Mitchell ....Marian Elizabeth	Hand ....George Edward	1877 12 25	UT, Payson
Mitchell ....Mary Ann	Davis..................Elisha H.	1846 12 25	ENG, London
Mitchell ....Priscilla V.	Christensen.........Rasmus	1857 01 28	UT, Tooele
Mitchell ....Sarah Jane	Fullmer...............Eugene B.	1854 03 20	UT, Salt Lake City
Mitton...............Jane	Rydalch ....William C.	1848 10 07	
Mix....................Lucinda S.	Tuttle ....Newton	1847 11 24	CT, North Haven
Mode ....Caroline	Grouard...............Benjamin F.	1839 05 30	PA
Mode ....Sarah Ann	Hofheins.............Peter	1835 11 25	PA, Philadelphia
Mogensen........Inger	Lee ....Christian	1840 09 26	
Mogensen........Inger	Lee ....Lars Christian	1867 11 30	
Mogensen........Jacobine K.	Jensen ....Christen	1854 06 02	
Mogensen........Jacobine K.	Jorgensen ....Rasmus	1861 05 20	Ocean
Mogensen........Jacobine K.	Petersen.............Thomas Christian		
Mogensen........Kristine	Boserup..............Christian R.	1835 05 24	Denmark
Mole................Mary	Cullen.................Martin	1875 06 26	UT, Morgan
Mole................Mary	Smith..................William Cooper	1869	UT, Salt Lake City
Molland............Hannah	Byington.............Joseph H.	1864 02 27	UT, Salt Lake City
Molyneaux ....Ann	Alston.................James	1852 11 08	ENG
Molyneaux ....Ann	Prye....................John Israel	1865 12	UT, Salt Lake City
Monson............Annie C.	Whitehead..........Francis	1880	
Montague ....Sarah Marie	Snow...................Don Carlos		
Montgomery ....Margaret	Gardner...............Milo Van Dusen	1859 09 29	UT, North Ogden
Montgomery ....Martha Louisa	Bell.....................Alfred	1832 09 08	IL, Shelby Co.
Montgomery ....Martha Louisa	Elder...................David	1825 11 07	
Montgomery ....Mary Elizabeth	Bailey ....William	1864 03 01	UT, Ogden
Moody..............Dorinda Melisa	Goheen ....Michael Roup	1837 04 25	TX, Bastrop
Moody..............Dorinda Melisa	Salmon ....William G.	1825 07 24	AL
Moody..............Dorinda Melisa	Slade..................William Rufus	1853 02 20	
Moon ....Hannah	Hunt ....Thomas	1847 12 27	ENG
Moon ....Lydia	Moon ....Henry	1841 01 30	PA, Pine Township
Moon ....Margaret	Clayton...............William	1843 04 27	IL, Nauvoo
Moon ....Ruth	Clayton...............William	1836 10 09	ENG, Lancashire
Moore ....Almira	Duke...................James	1851 10 10	UT, Wallsburg
Moore ....Catherine	Wadsworth..........Thomas S.	1864 12 02	UT, Ogden
Moore ....Clarissa Jane	Tanner................William Smith	1868 01 19	UT, Payson
Moore ....Dorcas Adelia	Kingsbury ....Joseph C.	1845 03 04	
Moore ....Elizabeth	Bleak..................James Godson	1849 10 14	ENG, London
Moore ....Elizabeth S.	Giles...................Thomas H.	1845 02 13	ENG
Moore ....Harriet	Allen...................Samuel	1854 04 10	UT, Salt Lake City
Moore ....Harriet	Kelley ....Russel Thomas	1858 01 31	UT, Salt Lake City
Moore ....Harriet	West...................Thomas	1849 09	Ocean
Moore ....Louisa	Mitchell..............William C.	1849 07 18	IA, Kanesville
Moore ....Louisa	Pogson...............James Walker	1864 05 28	
Moore ....Martha Ann	Yeaman..............Thomas	1857 03 10	IA, Montgomery
Moore ....Mary	Farley ....Edward	1821 08 09	VA, Greenbriar

Female	Male	Date	Place
Moore ....Mary	Mitchell...............William C.	1852	
Moore ....Mary	Taylor ....Joseph	1844 03 24	IL, Nauvoo
Moore ....Olivia Sophia	Bancroft..............William N.	1871 05 15	
Moore ....Sophronia	Martin ....Jesse Bigler	1848 12 17	UT, Salt Lake City
Morgan ....Amanda	Barlow ....Joseph Smith	1867 11 30	UT, Cedar Fort
Morgan ....Amanda	Miller ....Josiah H.	1816	
Morgan ....Amanda	Tanner...............Valison	1887 10 15	UT
Morgan ....Ann	Jennings.............Henry	1848 05 14	MO, St. Louis
Morgan ....Barbara	Maughan ....William Harrison	1853 12 25	UT, Tooele
Morgan ....Hannah	Evans ....Edward	1804 12 09	Wales
Morgan ....Hannah	Raymond..............		
Morgan ....Jane	Rodeback...........Charles	1838 10 18	PA, Newlin
Morgan ....Lucinda	Howd ....Simeon Fuller	1847 03 16	IA, Council Bluffs
Morgan ....Lucinda	Turner ....John		
Morgan ....Margaret	Curtis.................Theodore	1846 01 17	IL, Nauvoo
Morgan ....Mary	Jones ....Thomas	1840 07 13	ENG, Aberystruth
Morgan ....Mary	Pingree..............Job	1857 09 27	UT, Ogden
Morgan ....Mary	Reese.................John D.	1842 07 04	IRE
Morgan ....Mary Ann	Adams................Samuel Lorenzo	1863 10 10	UT, Salt Lake City
Morgan ....Mary Ann	Leavitt ....Lemuel S.	1873 11 17	UT, St. George
Morgan ....Rebecca	Davis ....Richard J.	1849 07 22	Wales
Morgan ....Sarah Ann	Edwards ....David	1839 06 22	Wales
Morgan ....Susan	Neeley ....Armenius M.	1856 12 08	UT, Brigham City
Morgansen ......Maren	Anderson.............Ove C.	1838 10 19	Denmark
Morgansen ......Maren	Hancock..............Levi W.	1868 08 09	
Morgansen ......Maren	Pedersen.............Lars	1851 04 12	Denmark
Morley..............Cordella C.	Cox.....................Fredrick W.	1846 01 27	IL, Nauvoo
Morley..............Diantha	Billings................Titus	1817 02 16	
Morley..............Lucy Diantha	Allen ....Joseph Stewart	1835 09 02	MO, Clay Co.
Morley..............Mary	Atkin ....Thomas	1826 02 13	ENG
Morrel ....Maria	Squire.................William	1848 01 08	ENG, St. Paul
Morrell ....Sarah	Curtis.................Joseph H.	1835 06 21	ENG, Middlesex
Morris ....Ann	Creer ....Edward	1835 06 20	ENG, Lancashire
Morris ....Ann	Foster................William Jr.	1830	ENG
Morris ....Elizabeth	Farmer ....Richard	1810	ENG
Morris ....Elizabeth Ann	Butler..................Richard	1841 09 20	Wales
Morris ....Elizabeth Ann	Rice....................Ira	1856 11 20	
Morris ....Harriet	Bishop ....William Evans	1863 09 28	UT, Salt Lake City
Morris ....Jane	Evans ....David	1811 08 01	ENG, Prestwich
Morris ....Jane	Jones ....David	1837	Wales
Morris ....Louisa	White..................William W.	1880 05 20	UT, Salt Lake City
Morris ....Margaret	Mathews..............Hopkin	1844 06 17	Wales
Morris ....Martha	Cooke..................Henry	1832 06 03	ENG, Sussex
Morris ....Mary	Broadhead ....David	1856 02 17	UT, Salt Lake City
Morris ....Mary	Payne..................James	1864 12 25	UT, Nephi
Morris ....Mary Ann	Rasmussen.........Niels	1865 12 28	UT, Parowan
Morris ....Rachel	Davies ....William R.	1824	Wales
Morris ....Rosella N.	Jenkins................John	1870 11 25	UT, Salt Lake City
Morris ....Rosella N.	Peck ....Lucius W.	1867 09 07	
Morris ....Susan	Buckwalter ....John E.	1863 07 23	UT, American Fork
Morris ....Susan	Guilliford.............		
Morris ....Susan	McLatchie............Samuel Russell	1869 10 04	UT, Salt Lake City
Morris ....Susan	Turner ....Alfred	1875 02 22	
Morrison ....Ellen	Clayton...............Edward	1867 01 08	ID, Franklin

Female	Male	Date	Place
Morrod ....Elizabeth	Sowby ....Isaac	1852 04 08	
Morrow ....Jane McCune	Asper....................Elias	1849 03 07	
Morrow ....Mary Parmelia	Cook....................Washington N.	1845	
Morrow ....Mary Parmelia	Thomas ....James Sands	1830 03 16	
Morrow ....Mary Parmelia	Wylie ....James W.	1821 01 11	
Morse ....Margaret	Jones ....Ricy Davis	1868 10 18	UT, Salt Lake City
Morse ....Teresa	Bridges................William Erskine	1831	
Morse ....Teresa	Chamberlain........Solomon	1848	UT, Salt Lake City
Morse ....Teresa	Lee ....John Doyle	1859 03 18	
Mortensen ....Ane K.	Hansen................Mads L.	1874 12	
Mortensen ....Ann Christine	Clapp....................Benjamin L.	1856 10 12	UT, Salt Lake City
Mortensen ....Ann Christine	Neilson ....Lars	1859	UT, Ephraim
Mortensen ....Anna Margaret	Guymon ....Lafayette	1861 02 20	UT, Parowan
Mortensen ....Betsy Amelia	Leavitt ....Lemuel S.	1863 10 13	UT
Mortensen ....Boldid (Boletta)	Christensen.........Christen	1837	Denmark
Mortensen ....Caroline	Durham ....Thomas	1867 10 14	UT, Salt Lake City
Mortensen ....Caroline Amelia	Nielsen ....Ole	1841	Denmark
Mortensen ....Catherine	Christiansen........Neils Christian	1845 10 28	
Mortensen ....Charste	Lundblad ....Hans	1845 12 27	Sweden
Mortensen ....Inger Katherine	Johnson ....John James	1870 07 11	
Mortensen ....Karen Marie	Saunders.............William G.	1864 02 14	
Mortensen ....Maren	Knowlton ....Sidney A.	1863 01 17	
Mortensen ....Maren	Olsen....................Christian "L"	1865 06 17	UT, Salt Lake City
Mortensen ....Mary	Jensen ....Peter (Peder)	1867 12 06	
Mortensen ....Mette Kistena	Rasmussen.........Christen	1863 04 30	UT, Parowan
Mortensen ....Mette Marie	Frost....................Jens C. S.	1866 12 15	UT, Ephraim
Mortensen ....Sarah	Larsen ....John Christian	1872 09 30	UT, Salt Lake City
Mortensen ....Sina Marie	Rasmussen.........Jorgen H.	1869 01 25	UT, Huntsville
Morton ....Eliza	Anderson.............James Pace	1857 03 10	UT, Parowan
Morton ....Phoebe Ann	Angell....................James William	1804	
Moses ....Fidelia	Benedict ....Joshua Northrop	1843 11 30	
Mosher ....Ruth	Pack....................John	1846 01 21	IL, Nauvoo
Mosier..............Mary	Draper................Thomas Jr.	1805	
Mosier..............Mary	Draper................William		
Moss................Margaret	Bleasdale ....William	1820 09 27	ENG
Moss................Mary S.	Walsh..................Joseph C.	1870 12 12	
Moss................Sarah Jane M.	Lish ....William Seely Jr.	1879 12 25	ID, Malad
Mott ....Maria Howe	Sheffield ....Anson	1832 03 11	
Mott ....Mary	Coltrin..................Zebedee	1843 02 05	IL, Nauvoo
Moulton............Charlotte	Carroll ....Willard	1869 03 16	UT, Salt Lake City
Moulton............Sarah	Hawkins ....John Bennett	1856 12 05	UT, Salt Lake City
Moulton............Sophia E.	Hicken ....Addison	1873 12 22	UT, Salt Lake City
Mounts.............Celia	Hunt ....Jefferson	1823 12 01	IL
Mouritsen.........Johanne K.	Miles...................Edwin Ruthven	1870 05 03	UT, Salt Lake City
Mouritsen.........Maren	Jensen ....Anton C.	1865 11 20	UT, Smithfield
Mousley ....Ann Amanda	Cannon ....Angus Munn	1858 07 18	UT, Salt Lake City
Mousley ....Maria	Powell ....George	1837 02 26	ENG, Aldridge
Mousley ....Sarah Maria	Cannon ....Angus Munn	1858 07 18	UT, Salt Lake City
Mower..............Susan	Cragun ....Simeon	1849	IA, Kanesville
Moyer ....Mary	Grow ....Henry	1834 01 24	PA
Moyes.............Mary Jane	Grimshaw...........Duckworth	1867 04 04	UT, Beaver
Mudd ....Sarah Esther	Davis.................Edward G.	1847 07 25	ENG, Middlesex
Muir ....Agnes	Findlay ....Williams	1868 12 14	
Muir ....Agnes	Richards.............Hyrum T. H.	1876 04 18	UT, Salt Lake City

Female	Male	Date	Place
Muir ....Mary	Bunnell ....Daniel Kimball	1874 02 01	UT, Salt Lake City
Muir ....Mary	Hughes..............Ross Burton	1871 01 23	UT, Salt Lake City
Muir ....Mary	Hunter ....George	1858 12 23	UT, Cedar City
Muir ....Mary	Murie ....David	1850	
Muller..............Margaritha	Hochstrasser.......Rudolf	1839 01 25	Switzerland
Muller..............Margaritha	Lienhard ....Samuel		
Mulliner...........Elizabeth Smith	Jones ....John Markland	1853 07 23	UT, Salt Lake City
Mulliner...........Elizabeth Smith	Mart.....................		
Munch..............Cecillia	Kofoed...............Hans A.	1838 11 17	Denmark
Munday...........Jane	Andrus................Milo	1855 11 22	
Munday...........Jane	Brown................Samuel	1853 04 19	
Munk...............Amelia	Christensen........Jens	1858	
Munk...............Amelia	Jensen ....Lars Christian	1874 07 08	UT, Salt Lake City
Munro ....Ester Ann	Boulter................John	1855 01 29	UT, Draper
Munz..............Maria M.	Huber ....Johannes	1863 10 18	UT, Payson
Murdoch ....Elizabeth	Stewart...............William	1850 11 18	Scotland
Murdoch ....Mary	Mair ....Allan	1841 06 04	Scotland
Murdoch ....Mary	McMillan.............Daniel	1871 06 26	UT, Salt Lake City
Murdoch ....Mary	Todd...................Thomas	1866 12 01	
Murdock..........Betsey Bonney	Green ....Alphonso	1838 12 29	NY, Madison Co.
Murdock..........Lorena	White..................Thomas Jones		
Murphy ....Lovina Ann	Murphy ....Jesse Easters		
Murray ....Helen Janet	Cushing..............Hosea	1847 02 04	IA
Murray ....Helen Janet	McBride..............William	1855	UT, Salt Lake City
Murray ....Helen Janet	Taylor................Norman	1863 07 15	UT, Salt Lake City
Murray ....Mary	Muir ....James	1836 06 11	
Murray ....Mary	Murdoch.............James	1811 01 10	Scotland
Murray ....Mary	Reed ....John	1815 04 08	
Murray ....Vilate	Kimball ....Heber Chase	1822 11 07	NY, Mendon
Musser............Elizabeth	Neff ....Franklin	1847 03 05	IA
Mustard ....Margaret	Sant....................George	1858 10 02	UT, Cedar City
Myers..............Sarah	Lindsay...............William B.	1819	Canada

N

Female	Male	Date	Place
Naser..............Caroline	Christiansen........Christian Peter	1865 07 08	UT, Salt Lake City
Nash ....Anna	Gifford ....Alpheus	1817 04 27	NY, Butternuts
Nash ....Mary	Adams.................John	1816	ENG, Kent
Naylor.............Eliza	Cazier..................David C.		
Naylor.............Emma	Merritt..................Samuel Swift	1865 07 01	UT, Salt Lake
Naylor.............Mary Ann	Goff ....Isaac	1833 08 26	ENG
Neal ....Mary Ann	Browning ....James Green	1827 11 20	TN, Sumner
Neal ....Mary Melissa	Huntington...........Oliver B.	1845 08 17	NY, Cambria
Neal ....Sarah Charlotte	Clark....................Thomas B.	1853 11 15	UT, Salt Lake City
Neal ....Sarah Charlotte	Gallagher ....John		
Neas ....Mary Ann	McFerson............Dimon Runnels	1845 11 29	IL, Nauvoo
Nease ....Rhoda Leech	Guymon ....James	1847 03 13	
Nebeker..........Roselia	Stokes ....Christopher	1868 04 25	UT, Salt Lake City
Needham.........Martha	Lees ....John	1853 06	ENG
Neeley ....Mary Jane	Wright.................Jonathan C.	1852 02 25	
Neese ....Matilda Jane	Hunt ....Jefferson		
Neff.................Barbara Matilda	Moses ....Julian	1845 03 25	IL, Nauvoo
Neff.................Elizabeth	Stillman ....Charles T.	1858 01 12	UT, Salt Lake City

Female	Male	Date	Place
Neff..............Martha E.	Eldredge.............Alanson	1870 05 09	UT, East Mill Creek
Neff..............Mary Ann	Rockwell.............Orrin Porter	1848	
Neff..............Susanna	Boothe...............Willis Henry	1860 03 08	
Neff..............Susanna	Peirce................Eli	1850 11 21	UT, Salt Lake City
Neibaur..........Alice	Rosenbaum.........Morris D.	1858 04 02	UT, Salt Lake City
Neibaur..........Margaret Jane	Miller ....William	1856 06 05	UT, Salt Lake City
Neilson ....Ellen	Tullgren ....Axel	1853	Denmark
Neilson ....Mette Marie	Hansen...............Hans Godfred	1845 11 07	Denmark
Neilson ....Mette Marie	Jensen ....Hans Severin	1837 03 17	Denmark
Nelsen ....Anne Christina	Peterson............Niels	1833 10 13	Denmark
Nelson ....Ann	Hogan ....Goudy		
Nelson ....Anne	Butler................Peter	1845	Sweden
Nelson ....Bergetta	Hogan ....Goudy	1853 12 24	UT, Salt Lake City
Nelson ....Charlotte Amelia	Krogue ....Jens Peter	1857	UT, Salt Lake City
Nelson ....Christiana	Hogan ....Goudy	1853 12 24	UT, Salt Lake City
Nelson ....Ellen	Hayball ....Hyrum	1872 05 06	UT, Salt Lake City
Nelson ....Jane	Jones ....Thomas English	1857 07 05	UT, Salt Lake City
Nelson ....Jane	Mulford ....Furman	1852 10 08	UT, Salt Lake City
Nelson ....Jean	Morgan...............Thomas	1834 07 26	
Nelson ....Jean	Patterson............Andrew	1851	MO, St. Louis
Nelson ....Katherine	Jensen ....Jes		
Nelson ....Martha Ann	Parker ....Thomas Bryant	1835 10 25	
Nelson ....Martha Ann	Ross..................James Melvin	1856 03 14	
Nelson ....Martha M. M.	Morgan...............William	1841 04 23	Scotland
Nelson ....Mary Elizabeth	Hatch.................Alvah A.	1868 12 07	UT, Salt Lake City
Nelson ....Mary Eunice	Griffin ....Herbert Loyal	1880 07 24	UT, Salt Lake City
Nelson ....Mary Eunice	Kay.....................William	1853 04 07	
Nelson ....Mary Jane	Patten.................George	1851 02 20	UT, Alpine
Nelson ....Samantha	Johnson ....Warren M.	1872 10 28	UT, Salt Lake City
Nelson ....Sarah Ann	Peterson.............Canute	1849 07 02	IA, Kanesville
Nelson ....Tena	Thomas ....James C.	1865 11 20	ID, Bloomington
Nerdin............Harriet	Holland...............Thomas	1866 02 17	
Nerdin............Harriet	Hooley................Thomas	1858	UT
Netterstrom......Anna Sophia	Nelson................Peter	1865 05 07	Ocean
New ....Ann	Passey ....John	1836 04 17	ENG, St. Nicolas
New ....Esther	Nalder ....Stephen	1846 11 29	ENG, Newbury
New ....Sarah	Neat ....Richard	1831	ENG
New ....Sarah	Passey ....William	1841 08 01	ENG
Newberry ....Hannah Maria	Morris ....George	1843 08 23	IL, Nauvoo
Newby ....Isabella Roberts	Roylance ....Hyrum	1867 05 04	
Newell............Ruth Amelia	Despain..............Solomon J.	1842 06 30	
Newey ....Elizabeth	Welch.................Charles	1856 10 05	UT, Salt Lake City
Newham ....Mary	Bancroft..............William C.	1849 03 02	
Newling...........Ann	Hunt ....Isaac	1854 03 27	UT, Salt Lake City
Newman ....Ann	Tanner................Thomas	1852 10 10	MO, St. Louis
Newman ....Caroline	Mitchell...............John Thomas	1875 06 25	UT, Salt Lake City
Newman ....Eliza	Jones ....William Edward	1857 08 12	UT, Paragonah
Newman ....Mary	Graves ....Daniel	1840 06 07	ENG, London
Newman ....Nancy Ann	Bulkley ....Noah	1807	NY, Tioga
Newton ....Elizabeth	James ....Thomas John	1864 11 18	UT, Salt Lake City
Newton ....Louisa	Beebe.................William Albert	1835	NY
Newton ....Ruth Hannah	Draper................William Jr.	1854 04 17	UT, Draper
Neyman..........Mary Ann	Nickerson............Levi Stillman	1840 05 10	IL, Nauvoo
Neyman..........Rachel	Fullmer...............Almon L.	1852 01 10	UT, Salt Lake City

Female	Male	Date	Place
Neyman..........Rachel	Tanner...............Sidney	1859 04 02	UT, Salt Lake City
Niblet ....Helen	Huish..................James William	1842 02 14	ENG, Avening
Nicholas..........Mary Ann	Allen ....Jude	1837	
Nichols............Amelia	Turner ....William A.	1848 10 15	ENG
Nichols............Ann	Taylor ....Edward	1824 10 12	ENG
Nichols............Catherine L.	Payne.................William Lauder	1843 06 07	IL, Nauvoo
Nichols............Margaret	Pace...................William F.	1828 10	TN
Nicholson........Elizabeth	Cunningham........James	1834 02 15	
Nicholson........Elizabeth	Nicol ....John	1823 03 23	Scotland
Nicholson........Rebecca	Sylvester ....James	1837 02 27	ENG, Sheffield
Nickerson ....Carolina Eliza	Grover ....Thomas	1841 02 20	IL, Nauvoo
Nickerson ....Caroline Eliza	Hubbard ....Marshall M.	1827 09 18	NY, Perrysburg
Nickerson ....Caroline Eliza	Stewart...............Andrew Jackson	1851 02 21	UT, Salt Lake City
Nickerson ....Huldah Abigail	Barrus ....Emery	1833 12 19	
Nield ....Alice	Stott...................William H.	1855	
Nielsen ....Ane	Hansen...............Hendrick	1857 04	Denmark
Nielsen ....Ane	Mickelsen ....Rasmus	1848 09 03	Denmark
Nielsen ....Ane Johanna	Jensen ....Christian G.	1857 09 27	
Nielsen ....Ane Johanna	Olson..................Niels	1855	
Nielsen ....Ane Marie	Vier....................Wilhelm F. J. E.	1880 12 16	UT, Salt Lake City
Nielsen ....Ane Sophia	Breinholt.............Lars J.		
Neilsen ....Anna Amelia	Brown.................Hans Jorgen	1862 04 13	Ocean
Nielsen ....Anna Marie	Jacobsen.............Lars	1854 04 08	Denmark
Nielsen ....Anna Marie	Johnson ....John	1865 12 01	UT, Salt Lake City
Nielsen ....Anna Sophia	Knudsen..............Jorgen	1855 01 13	UT, Salt Lake City
Nielsen ....Anne Christine	Liljenquist............Ola	1874 08 10	UT, Salt Lake City
Nielsen ....Anne Dorthea	Olsen..................Lars	1864 07 03	Denmark
Nielsen ....Anne Elizabeth	Petersen..............Soren Lind	1861 05	Ocean
Nielsen ....Ansine E.	Jensen ....Johannes C.	1855 11 16	Denmark
Nielsen ....Brigitte	Iversen ....Hans	1870 12 05	UT, Salt Lake City
Nielsen ....Caroline	Nelson.................Fritz E.	1863 04 14	
Nielsen ....Caroline J. K. S.	Anderson.............Jens	1863 04 06	Denmark
Nielsen ....Dorthe	Riggs..................John	1864 12 27	UT, Salt Lake City
Nielsen ....Ellen	Lund ....Wilson	1858 02 28	
Nielsen ....Else Kirstine	Domgaard ....Niels P.	1845 10 12	Denmark
Nilesen ....Henrietta C.	Beckstrand..........Elias A.	1869 06 07	UT, Salt Lake City
Nielsen ....Inger	Jensen ....Jens Iver	1867 05 24	
Nielsen ....Inger	Jensen ....Jens Peter	1861 10 22	
Nielsen ....Inger Christine	Johnson ....Hans Jorge J.	1844 05	Norway
Nielsen ....Johanna	Winter.................Thomas W.	1857 02 15	UT, Salt Lake City
Nielsen ....Johanne Marie	Borresen ....Niels H.	1851 11 01	Denmark
Nielsen ....Karen	Fredricksen ....Anders	1848 02 12	Denmark
Nielsen ....Karen	Larsen................Lauritz Edward	1864 09 15	UT, Salt Lake City
Nielsen ....Karen	Nielsen...............Peter	1855 01 14	Ocean
Nielsen ....Karen C.	Jensen ....Jens Peter	1878 06 05	UT, St. George
Nielsen ....Karen Maria	Murray................Jeremiah Hatch	1863 02 06	UT, Spanish Fork
Nielsen ....Karen Marie	Bohn...................Adolph Joseph	1846	Denmark
Nielsen ....Karen Marie	Mortensen...........Anders	1837 11 11	Denmark
Nielsen ....Karen Petra	Hoogensen..........Christen	1859 05 06	Ocean
Nielsen ....Kersten	Andersen.............Christian	1852 05 04	Denmark
Nielsen ....Kirsten	Christensen.........Andrew	1864 01 18	UT, Mt. Pleasant
Nielsen ....Kirsten	Christensen.........Jens	1855 11 01	UT, Salt Lake City
Nielsen ....Kirstine Marie	Christensen.........John Nicolai	1869 06 28	UT, Salt Lake City
Nielsen ....Kirstine Marie	Clemensen...........Niels	1863 10 24	UT, Salt Lake City

Female	Male	Date	Place
Nielsen ....Margrethe	Jensen ....Lars Christian	1857 03 31	UT, Salt Lake City
Nielsen ....Margrethe	Larsen ....Anders	1827 10 23	Denmark
Nielsen ....Maria Abelone	Robins................Thomas L. A.	1876 04 28	UT, Scipio
Nielsen ....Marthine N. M.	Hjort ....William Lauritz	1868 11 07	UT, Salt Lake City
Nielsen ....Marianne	Beal....................Henry Allen	1868 04 28	UT, Salt Lake City
Nielsen ....Mary Ann	Lind ....Jens C. A.	1847 04 01	Denmark
Nielsen ....Mary Ann	Rose...................Wesley	1898 06 01	
Nielsen ....Mette Kirsten	Andersen.............Christen	1806 07 13	Denmark
Nielsen ....Mette Kirsten	Sonderbon ....Peder Jensen	1813 12 17	
Nielsen ....Nelsina Kirstine	Nielsen ....Peter	1872 09 22	UT, Salt Lake City
Nielsen ....Olevia Dorthea	Durfee ....Abraham A.	1884 02 08	
Nielsen ....Olevia Dorthea	Lemmon ....James A.	1866 03 26	UT, Toquerville
Nielsen ....Petrasanne C.	Casto...................William W.	1867 11 16	UT, Salt Lake City
Nielsen ....Teralina F.	Hartvigsen...........Peter A.	1864 07 18	NE, Florence
Nielsen ....Thora	Jacobsen..............Christian L.	1882 01 12	UT, Salt Lake City
Nielsen ....Thora	Starkie.................Edward John	1886 11 17	UT, Logan
Nielson ....Anne Margreth	Anderson.............Joseph S.	1875 12 06	UT, Salt Lake City
Nielson ....Caroline	Pugmire...............Jonathan	1864 04 13	UT, Salt Lake City
Nielson ....Matilda Marie	Peterson..............Nels	1878 12 03	UT, Littleton
Nielson ....Sennie D.	Ward ....George P.	1866 08 18	UT, Salt Lake City
Nightingale ......Jemima	Davis ....Edward W. Jr.	1857 02 26	UT, Salt Lake City
Nightingale ......Margaret	Cain.....................John T.	1850 10 22	
Nilson ....Elna	Winberg...............Sven Anders	1829 04 11	Sweden
Nilson ....Hannah	Hogan ....Eric G. M.	1862 12 20	UT, Bountiful
Nilson ....Margaretha	Olson...................John N.	1849	Sweden
Nilson ....Maria Sophie	Amundson............Dyre	1865 10 29	UT, Salt Lake City
Nilsson............Caroline	Yorgason..............Soren	1833 04 23	Sweden
Nilsson............Ellen C.	Tullgren ....Axel		
Nilsson............Elsa	Jonson ....Jons	1842 07 15	Sweden
Nilsson............Elsa	Nielsen ....Ola	1867 11 29	UT, Salt Lake City
Nilsson............Ingar	Nielson ....Jon	1834 11 12	Sweden
Nilsson............Johanna	Johnson ....Jens	1845 07 04	Sweden
Nilsson............Johanna	Scharling ....Johannes		Sweden
Nilsson............Sissa	Pehrsson..............James	1876	
Nilsson............Sissa	Pehrsson..............Ola	1856 02 10	Sweden
Nilsson............Sissa	Sorensen..............Niels	1868 12 21	UT, Salt Lake City
Nisbet ....Katharine	Mulliner ....Samuel Jr.	1830 12 04	Scotland
Nish ....Agnes	Hutchison ....David	1840 12 30	Scotland
Nish ....Agnes	Smith...................Sylvester	1871	
Nisonger ....Pheobe	Cushing...............Phillip Hosea	1871 09 07	UT, Santaquin
Noah ....Margaret	Hulet...................Charles	1816 10 10	OH, Ravenna
Noble ....Angeline Wilcox	Hinckley ....Ira Nathaniel	1855 07 22	UT, Salt Lake City
Noble ....Louisa Rox	Watts...................Henry	1863 03 09	
Noble ....Susan F.	Grant...................George D.	1858 01 01	UT, Bountiful
Noble ....Susan F.	Grant...................Jedediah M.	1849 02 11	
Noddings ....Mary	Clark....................John	1832	
Noddings ....Mary	Peacock ....Daniel	1819 09 20	ENG, Yorkshire
Norr ....Christine J.	Miller ....Hans Koford	1871	UT, Salt Lake City
Norris..............Alice Long	Sears...................Isaac	1889 02 14	UT, Salt Lake City
Norris..............Emily	Bowden ....Joseph	1872 01 08	UT, Salt Lake City
Norris..............Mary	Evans ....Thomas	1854 03 09	Wales
Norris..............Mary	Forbes.................James	1860 09 21	
North...............Almira	Williams...............Ephraim	1862 12 31	UT, Salt Lake City
Northrop ....Emily Jane	Woodard ....Jedediah S.		

Female	Male	Date	Place
Norton..............Caroline Chloe	Norwood..............Richard Smith	1857 12 05	UT, Salt Lake City
Norton..............Caroline Chloe	Pickup ....George	1851 04 17	UT, Alpine
Norton..............Isabelle	Judd ....William Riley	1854 03 23	UT, Salt Lake City
Norton..............Melissa Isabel	Allred.................Paulinus H.	1848 02 03	IA, Council Bluffs
Nott..................Maria Seaburn	Hamilton..............John C.	1866 08 18	UT, Salt Lake City
Nowell..............Alice	Earnshaw ....Thomas	1804 06 16	ENG, Yorkshire
Nuns ....Mary Ann	Berrett ....Richard T.	1860 01 01	UT, Ogden
Nutman............Elizabeth Jane	Graham ....Alexander	1859 06 26	MO, St. Louis
Nuttall ....Mary	Haslam................Robert	1828 10 19	ENG, Prestwich
Nuttall ....Mary	Parkinson ....Timothy G.	1849 08 20	ENG, Lancashire
Nuttall ....Mary Jane	Broadbent ....Thomas	1863 04 11	UT, Salt Lake City
Nybolle ....Hansine J.	Huff ....James	1858	UT, Manti
Nybolle ....Hansine J.	Kjar....................Sixtus	1863 09 03	
Nybolle ....Hansine J.	Peterson.............Wilhelm Sanberg	1864 06 18	

O

Female	Male	Date	Place
Oades..............Elizabeth	Player......_.......Charles Warner	1850 03 07	IA, Ferryville
Oades..............Elizabeth	Robbins..............George	1848 12 09	MO, St. Louis
Oakes ....Mary Ann	Roylance............John	1830	ENG
Oakey ....Ann C.	Price...................Charles		
Oakey ....Sarah	Sirrine.................George E.	1879 11 06	
Oakley ....Leah	Smout.................Edwin W.	1847 02 16	ENG
Ockerman........Mary	Olsen..................Charles John	1880 02 05	UT, Salt Lake City
Odell ....Phoebe	Merrill ....Samuel	1802 09 10	NY, Oneida
O'Dwyer...........Frances	Heaton................Jonathan	1822	ENG
Ogden..............Lucy Ann	King....................Thomas Franklin	1863 01 01	UT, Salt Lake City
Ogden..............Phoebe	Chase.................Isaac	1818 08	NY
Ogden..............Phoebe	Ross...................William	1810	NY
Ohlsen ....Margrethe	Englested............Rasmus Madsen	1858 03 25	UT, Emery
Ohlsen ....Margrethe	Hansen...............Embreth		
Ohlsen ....Margrethe	Jacobsen............Lars		
Olafson ....Sarah Britta	Anderson.............Anders		
Olafson ....Sarah Britta	Larson ....Eric	1860 12 31	Sweden
Oldfield ....Martha	Herman ....Henry		ENG
Oldfield ....Martha	Thornton..............Squire	1861 12 08	UT, Fairfield
Oler..................Margaretta	Baldwin ....Nathan Bennett		
Oleson ....Annike Marie	Sorensen.............Peder H.	1837 12 27	Denmark
Olin ....Rebecca E.	King....................Thomas J.	1827 07 08	VT, Shaftsbury
Oliphant ....Ann Maria	Sainsbury ....John Henry	1871	
Oliver ....Ann	Rice....................James	1870 03 22	UT, Salt Lake City
Ollerton............Jane Ann	McPherson..........James Ramsey	1860 07 15	UT, Nephi
Ollerton............Sarah	Eatough...............George	1874	
Ollerton............Sarah	Gullies ....Martin		
Olpin ....Dorcas	Gibby..................John	1867 11 23	UT, Salt Lake City
Olpin ....Ellen	Gibby..................John	1860 06 17	
Olpin ....Esther	Webb..................David	1843 08 01	ENG, Bristol
Olpin ....Julia	Bluemel..............Oswald Karl	1871 05 22	UT, Morgan
Olpin ....Mary Ann	Woolley ....Edwin D.	1850 11 10	UT, Salt Lake City
Olpin ....Mary Anne	Marchant............Edmund	1850 10 08	ENG
Olpin ....Sarah Ann W.	Cooper ....William	1865 11 09	UT, Salt Lake City
Olsen ....Anna	Daniels ....Thomas E.	1864 06 04	UT, Salt Lake City
Olsen ....Anna Marie	Peterson.............Peter C.	1850 10 15	Norway

Female	Male	Date	Place
Olsen ....Barbara J. D.	Larsen ....Christian Jens	1853 10 30	Denmark
Olsen ....Bodil	Jensen ....Knud	1834 04 28	Denmark
Olsen ....Caroline	Wright.................Jonathan C.	1857 11 07	UT, Brigham City
Olsen ....Gjertrude Marie	Amundsen..........Dyre	1833 11 10	Norway
Olsen ....Gjertrude Marie	Jakobsen.............Peder S.	1828 09 20	Norway
Olsen ....Hedvig Marie	Jensen ....Hans Christian	1846 06 05	Denmark
Olsen ....Helge	Kingsford............Edward	1861 12 25	
Olsen ....Helge	Poulsen ....Niels Christian	1858 08 25	UT
Olsen ....Josephine	Stokes ....Jeremiah III	1876 11 11	UT, Draper
Olsen ....Juliane Sophia	Rockwood ....Albert P.	1863 04 11	UT, Salt Lake City
Olsen ....Karen	Olsen...................Johan	1830 01 04	Norway
Olsen ....Magdelena	Sorensen............Nicolai	1830 07 06	Denmark
Olsen ....Maren	Olsen...................Lars		
Olsen ....Marie Ann	Oakason.............Hans	1865 09 21	UT, Salt Lake City
Olsen ....Mette Christina	Jensen ....Paul Martines	1851 04 15	Denmark
Olsen ....Nicoline	Pedersen.............Jorgen Christian	1858	
Olsen ....Olena	Bertelsen.............Andreas	1886	
Olsen ....Olena	Erickson ....Engebret	1849	
Olsen ....Olena	Hendrickson........Niels	1868	
Olsen ....Olena	Kempe.................Christopher J.	1866 03 10	UT, Salt Lake City
Olson ....Anna	Hunt ....John Cook	1866 11 19	UT, Salt Lake City
Olson ....Johanna	Anderson.............Johannes	1852 12 18	Sweden
Olson ....Karen	Poulsen ....Lars	1844 10 15	Denmark
Olson ....Matilda Christina	Sprague ....Alvin Henry	1870 03 01	UT, Salt Lake City
Olsson ....Anna Katrina	Peterson..............Johannes	1834 11 26	Sweden
Olsson ....Hanna	Eliason ....Lars A.	1836 12 02	Sweden
Olsson ....Hanna	Seely ....Orange	1863 07 24	UT, Mt. Pleasant
Olsson ....Matta	Johnson ....Peter (Pehr)	1845 07 05	Sweden
Oman...............Christina C.	Jensen ....Peter Jens	1863 09 13	UT, Mt. Pleasant
Oman...............Helen (Ellen)	McKay ....William	1839 01 12	Scotland
O'Neal..............Nancy	Rich.....................Joseph	1808 06 23	KY
O'Neil..............Rachel Ellis	Coleman...............Louis	1876 03 20	UT, Salt Lake City
Orchard ....Ruth	Fausett................Nephi R.	1868 09 26	UT, Salt Lake City
Orell.................Albertina W.	Unsworth.............James	1873 03 03	
Orgill ....Sarah	Hart ....Stephen James	1876 09 25	UT, Salt Lake City
Orme ....Rebecca	Lee ....Alfred Gilham	1857 03 10	
Ormond ....Mary	George ....William	1852 10 31	UT, Salt Lake City
Ormond ....Mary	Morris..................John	1847 10 31	Wales
Orrell................Rosa Ann	Stayner................Thomas John	1852	ENG
Orton ....Emma	Richmond.............Joseph B.	1863 05 03	
Osborn.............Nancy M.	Nielsen ....Hans Enoch	1857 02 11	
Osborn.............Rebecca Ann	Thorn...................Richard	1858 12 25	UT, Uinta
Osborne...........Annie	Clark....................James	1869 03 01	UT, Salt Lake City
Osborne...........Charlotte	Hammond ....John	1853 01 19	UT, Salt Lake City
Osborne...........Charlotte	Potter ....David	1815	NY
Osguthorpe......Lydia	Bolton..................Charles G.		
Osguthorpe......Priscilla M.	Bolton..................Charles G.	1873 02 05	UT, Salt Lake City
Ostler ....Sarah Ann	Furner ....William Jr.	1862 12 22	UT, Nephi
Ostler ....Sarah Ann	Jenkins................Richard	1870 03 14	UT, Salt Lake City
Ott...................Ann Magdalena	Sabin ....David	1879 08 07	
Otten...............Frances Ann	Adams.................William Henry	1858	
Otten...............Frances Ann	Crossland............Junius	1841 05 29	ENG, London
Otterstrom ....Josephine	Cramer................Christopher	1879 01 23	UT, Salt Lake City
Overlade..........Andrear Neilson	Whitlock ....Andrew H.	1867 11 02	UT, Salt Lake City

Female	Male	Date	Place
Overton...........Parthenia	Holt....................James	1845 02 11	
Owen ....Ann	Conover ....Abram Golden	1857 02 26	UT, Provo
Owens ....Caroline Amelia	McRae................Alexander	1855 12	UT, Salt Lake City
Owens ....Caroline Amelia	Webb.................Edward Milo	1839 12 12	IL, Nauvoo
Owens ....Lucinda	Bair....................John	1843 10 19	
Owens ....Lucinda	Tyler...................Lumus		
Owens ....Mary	Roberts ....Hugh	1830 05 04	Wales
Oysterbanks ....Sarah S.	Fullmer..............David	1845 12 07	IL, Nauvoo

P

Female	Male	Date	Place
Pace ....Nancy	Anderson............Miles	1821 08 09	TN, Rutherford
Pack ....Lucy Amelia	Baker..................Joseph	1859 07 10	UT, Salt Lake City
Pack ....Lucy Amelia	Kimball ....William Henry	1857 02 12	
Packer ....Levema	Wright................Lorenzo		
Packer ....Sophia	Martin ....Ezra Francis		
Padfield ....Eliza Ann	Warr ....Moses		ENG
Page ....Julia Ann	Stewart..............Louis	1873 11 20	UT, Provo
Page ....Martha	Waddoups..........William	1864 11 27	UT, Bountiful
Page ....Ruth	Rogers ....Samuel H.	1853 02 21	UT, Lehi
Page ....Susan	Scogings ....William B.	1862 05 10	UT, Salt Lake City
Palfreyman ......Fanny	Oakley................James D.	1869 07 19	UT, Salt Lake City
Palmer ....Lovina	Brandon ....Thomas J.	1847	IA
Palmer ....Lovina	Bulkley ....Newman	1857	
Palmer ....Lovina	Munro.................Henry	1834	Canada
Park ....Jane	Gardner..............Archibald	1852 08 24	UT, Salt Lake City
Park ....Jane	Hill ....Alexander Hood	1857 01 19	
Park ....Janet	Tate....................William		
Park ....Marion Ellen	Gordon...............James P.	1854 02 07	UT, Salt Lake City
Park ....Martha Jane	Guymon ....James	1866 11 24	UT, Salt Lake City
Park ....Mary Ann	Brockbank...........Isaac Jr.	1865 01	
Park ....Mary Ann	Bryce.................Ebenezer	1854 04 16	UT, Salt Lake City
Parker..............Alice	Corbridge ....Edward	1843 07 17	ENG
Parker..............Eliza	Baddley ....George	1845 11 02	ENG, Staffordshire
Parker..............Elizabeth	Ward ....Edward	1855 05 21	UT, Parowan
Parker..............Elizabeth	Winder................John Rex	1857 01 11	
Parker..............Emeline	Kesler.................Frederick	1836 05 19	IA, Augusta
Parker..............Emma	Cordon ....Alfred	1836 12 19	ENG
Parker..............Exile Liberty	Ewing ....Anderson	1865	UT, Provo
Parker..............Jane	Nield...................John Edward	1877 09 19	UT, Fillmore
Parker..............Maria Black	Parkinson ....Timothy F.	1863 01 05	UT, Salt Lake City
Parker..............Martha Alice	Woodbury............John S.	1864 12 27	UT, Salt Lake City
Parker..............Mary Ann	Richards.............Samuel W.	1855 02 14	UT, Salt Lake City
Parker..............Mary Haskins	Richards.............Samuel W.	1846 01 29	IL, Nauvoo
Parker..............Mary Jane	Butterfield...........Thomas J.	1835 02 15	ME, Farmington
Parker..............Mary Josephine	Chidester............John Madison	1836 12 28	
Parker..............Mary Lovisa	Hammond ....John	1819 12 15	NY, Malone
Parker..............Sarah Jane	Stimpson ....Frederick		
Parkes ....Annie	Littlewood............Martin	1859 05 07	
Parkes ....Jemima	Robinson............Joseph	1853 11 26	ENG, Derby
Parkes ....Mary Ann	Cazier................Adelbert	1880 10 12	
Parkin ....Mary Anne	Aldous ....Robert F.	1835 12 24	ENG, London
Parkinson ....Ellen	Covey.................Hyrum	1867 07 19	UT, Salt Lake City

Female	Male	Date	Place
Parkinson ....Mary Ann	Walsh ....Richard	1852 03 27	ENG
Parkinson ....Sarah	Rodwell ....Edward	1850 02 12	New South Wales
Parkinson ....Sarah	Stapley ....Charles Jr.	1854 07 24	CA, San Bern.
Parks ....Fanny	Taggart..............George W.	1845 07 06	IL, Nauvoo
Parks ....Julia	Lindsay..............William B. Jr.	1845 02 19	IL, Nauvoo
Parneby ....Elizabeth	Calkins ....William	1875 02 20	
Parneby ....Elizabeth	Vest....................John Jr.	1845 03 24	ENG
Parratt..............Eliza	Rhees.................Charles Horatio	1866 12 07	UT, Salt Lake City
Parrish ....Nancy Sarepta	Cole....................William Riley	1840 03 19	IL, Quincy
Parrish ....Priscilla	Roundy................Lorenzo W.	1857 04 22	
Parrott..............Hannah B.	Pexton................James	1853 01 04	ENG, Yorkshire
Parry ....Harriet	Parry ....John	1854 04 02	UT, Salt Lak City
Parry ....Jane	Jones ....Joseph	1847	Wales
Parry ....Mary	Morris ....Elias	1852 05 23	IA, Council Bluffs
Parry ....Mary	Williams..............John	1836 03 04	Wales
Parshley ....Tamson	Egan...................Howard	1838 12 01	MA, Essex
Parsons ....Abigail	Robinson.............John	1814 07 09	ME, Cushing
Parsons ....Ann	Lovell..................John	1835 02 15	ENG
Parsons ....Catherine M.	Staker.................William H.	1851 01 01	IA, Pigeon Grove
Parsons ....Naomi	Jones ....Richard	1849 11 19	ENG, Middlesex
Parsons ....Sophia	Neeley................Lewis	1847 06 27	IA, Council Bluffs
Partington ....Catherine Ann	Findlay ....Hugh	1856 03 25	UT, Salt Lake City
Partridge..........Caroline Ely	Lyman ....Amasa Mason	1844 09 06	IL, Nauvoo
Partridge..........Eliza Maria	Lyman ....Amasa Mason	1845 09 28	IL, Nauvoo
Partridge..........Eliza Maria	Smith..................Joseph Jr.	1835	NY, Franklin
Partridge..........Emily Dow	Smith..................Joseph Jr.	1843 05 11	IL, Nauvoo
Partridge..........Emily Dow	Young..................Brigham	1844 09	IL, Nauvoo
Partridge..........Lydia	Lyman ....Amasa Mason	1853 02 07	UT, Salt Lake City
Paskett ....Jane Belbin	Judd ....George	1869 12 06	UT, Salt Lake City
Pass ....Rachel	Davenport ....James B.	1872 10 07	UT, Salt Lake City
Passey..............Mary Ann	Oakey.................Charles	1862 01 17	UT, Lehi
Paterson ....Elizabeth Blair	Paterson..............William D.	1821 10 08	Scotland
Paterson ....Elizabeth Blair	Sharp ....William	1828 08 16	Scotland
Paterson ....Jane	Brough ....Thomas	1851 11 09	ENG, Staffordshire
Patrick ....Elizabeth	Allred..................James	1846 02 03	IL, Nauvoo
Patrick ....Elizabeth	Taylor ....William	1811 03 22	KY
Patten ....Ann	Peterson..............Charles S.	1849 01 21	
Patten ....Deborah	Billings.................Alfred Nelson	1851 12 09	UT, Salt Lake City
Pattenden ....Jane	Tuckett ....Charles	1824	ENG, London
Patterson ....Agnes Ann	Farnsworth ....Philo T.	1858 12 10	
Patterson ....Elizabeth	Hunter ....Adam P.	1842 04 25	Scotland
Patterson ....Lovina	Busenbark...........Isaac	1853	
Patterson ....Lovina	Woolsey ....James	1846 02 05	
Patterson ....Lucinda Maria	Patten.................Charles Moroni	1878 02 19	UT, Payson
Patterson ....Margaret	Smith..................John X.	1855 07 24	UT, Cedar City
Paul ....Elizabeth	Stott...................Edwin	1876 02 18	UT, Salt Lake City
Pauling ....Susanna	Houtz..................John Christian	1830	PA
Paulsen ....Dorthea	Nielsen ....Anders	1849	Denmark
Paulsen ....Ingaborg	Anderson.............Niels	1857 11 15	UT, Ephraim
Paulson ....Botilda	Nelson.................Lars	1860	
Paulson ....Botilda	Nilson.................Peter	1866	UT, Mt. Pleasant
Paxton ....Jane	Black..................John	1864 08 15	UT, Parowan
Payne ....Catherine	Sisam.................Joseph	1843 07 30	ENG
Payne ....Mary Ann	Mellor.................James	1838 03 14	

Female	Male	Date	Place
Payne ....Priscilla	Jacobs................John	1862	UT, Grantsville
Pea ....Sarah D.	Rich.....................Charles Coulson	1837 02 11	MO, Far West
Pead ....Mary	Howard...............William	1868 12 21	UT, Salt Lake City
Peake ....Mary Hannah	Miller ....Thomas	1865	
Peake ....Mary Hannah	Parkes................Thomas	1850	ENG
Pearce ....Harriet Ann	Young..................William Willis	1876	
Pearce ....Mary	Ballantyne ....Richard	1855 11 25	
Pears ....Eliza Rosannah	O'Neil ....Timothy		UT, Uintah
Pears ....Eliza Rosannah	Summers.............Nicholas	1857 01 02	
Pearson ....Anna	Marchant ....Franklin William	1875 02 15	UT, Salt Lake City
Pearson ....Elizabeth	Clark...................James		ENG
Pearson ....Elsie	Walker.................Cyrus S.	1875 12 20	UT, Salt Lake City
Pearson ....Emily Jane	Clark...................Israel Justes	1853	
Pearson ....Frances E.	Bridges................Charles Henry	1859 06 20	UT, Salt Lake City
Pearson ....Jane	Fisher ....John	1841 05 31	ENG
Pearson ....Jane	Hacking ....James	1827 01 27	ENG
Pearson ....Jane	Terry...................Joel	1857 04 22	UT, Salt Lake City
Pearson ....Julia Helena	Hess....................John W.	1856 11 16	
Pearson ....Mary	Woolfenden..........Abraham	1824 06 01	ENG, Ashton
Pease ....Catherine Floyd	Haws ....Elijah	1829 06	
Pease ....Catherine Floyd	Quinby.................Ephraim	1824 08 24	
Peasnall...........Love	James ....Daniel	1877 10 22	UT, Tooele
Peat ....Mary	Roberts ....Samuel	1852 05 18	ENG, Derby
Peck ....Martha Mary A.	Yates..................William	1868 01 11	UT, Lehi
Peck ....Sarah Jane	Rich....................Charles Coulson	1845 01 09	IL, Nauvoo
Pectol ....Eliza Ann	Hutchings ....Shepherd P.	1850 01 01	UT, Salt Lake City
Pectol ....Elizabeth	Case...................Solomon Cowles	1851 09 06	UT, Springville
Pectol ....Elizabeth	Lowe ....Richard Alvin	1880	UT, Springville
Pectol ....Jemima Bell	Beal....................John		
Pectol ....Jemima Bell	Brown..................Neuman	1857 05	
Pedersen ....Ane	Andersen.............Jens	1846 12 01	Denmark
Pedersen ....Ane	Lovell..................John	1857 04 04	UT
Pedersen ....Ane Kirstine	Hansen...............Rasmus	1849 11 11	Denmark
Pedersen ....Ane Kirstine	Jensen ....Peter Christian	1854 12 05	Denmark
Pedersen ....Ane Kirstine	Mack ....John Fredrick	1866 11 28	UT, Salt Lake City
Pedersen ....Ane Kirstine	Reynolds ....William F.	1861 10 27	UT, Salt Lake City
Pedersen ....Ane Marie	Larson ....Hans	1866	Ocean
Pedersen ....Ane Margrethe	Eliason ....Johan	1847 04 24	Denmark
Pedersen ....Ane Margrethe	Madsen ....Jens	1850 12 27	Denmark
Pedersen ....Ane T. M.	Cornum ....Jens C.	1862 06 17	NE, Florence
Pedersen ....Anna Lena	Jensen ....Michael	1868 01 01	UT, Manti
Pedersen ....Anne	Olsen..................Christen	1829 09 27	Denmark
Pedersen ....Caroline	Hansen...............Andrew Janus	1878 07 25	UT, Salt Lake City
Pedersen ....Caroline	Jensen ....Jorgen C.	1851 05 21	Denmark
Pedersen ....Christiana	Twede ....Christen F. N.	1859 04 24	UT, Salt Lake City
Pedersen ....Christina	Madsen ....Hans Peter	1858	Denmark
Pedersen ....Ellen Bendixen	Jensen ....Andrew	1866	UT, Moroni
Pedersen ....Else Marie	Andersen.............Hans Frederik	1836 10 21	Denmark
Pedersen ....Elsie Christine	Christensen.........Anders C.	1889	UT, Ephraim
Pedersen ....Elsie Christine	Olson..................James	1869 06 07	UT, Ephraim
Pedersen ....Gertrude Marie	Jensen ....Mads Christian	1855 01 27	UT, Salt Lake City
Pedersen ....Gertrude Marie	Kjaer..................Christian N.	1847 08 31	Denmark
Pedersen ....Ingeborg	Mortensen...........Andreas Peder	1848 06 25	Denmark
Pedersen ....Inger	Jeppesen ....Rasmus	1867 01 05	UT, Salt Lake City

Female	Male	Date	Place
Pedersen ....Inger	Larsen ....Lars	1857 11 13	Denmark
Pedersen ....Johanne K.	Christensen...........Jens Christian	1859 10	
Pedersen ....Johanne Marie	Jensen ....Fredrick C.	1842 11 26	Denmark
Pedersen ....Karen Marie	Gottfredson ....Jens	1856 08 12	
Pedersen ....Kirsten	Larsen ....Lars	1856 11 16	UT, Brigham City
Pedersen ....Kirsten	Nielsen ....Niels Hans	1860 02 19	
Pedersen ....Kirsten	Pedersen.............Hans	1855	
Pedersen ....Maren	Andersen..............Lars	1842	Denmark
Pedersen ....Maren	Christensen.........Berthel		
Pedersen ....Maren	Jensen ....Anders	1856 05 25	Denmark
Pedersen ....Maria	Lauritzen ....Lauritz	1847 05 01	Denmark
Pedersen ....Maria Petrea	Anderson..............Neils	1876 05 08	UT, Salt Lake City
Pedersen ....Mette Marie	Christensen.........Niels Thomas		
Pedersen ....Mica M. C. M.	Elder..................Claybourne	1858 01 31	
Pedersen ....Mica M. C. M.	Gibbs.................Carl F. W. C.	1852 05 31	Denmark
Pedersen ....Mica M. C. M.	Smith.................Paul	1877 01 25	UT, St. George
Pedersen ....Nilla	Christensen.........Anders		UT, Salt Lake City
Pedersen ....Sidse	Ericksen ....Jorgen	1846 07 31	Denmark
Pedersen ....Sidse	Larsen ....Peder	1847 11 06	Denmark
Pedersen ....Sidse	Pedersen.............Niels		Denmark
Pedersen ....Sidsel	Nielsen ....Lars	1853 05 18	Denmark
Pedersen ....Sidsel Marie	Skousen ....Jens Niels	1856 05 06	Denmark
Pedersen ....Sophia	Jensen ....Jens	1866	UT, Salt Lake City
Pederson ....Anna Maria	Larsen ....Oluf Christian	1863	
Pederson ....Anne Margrethe	Thurston ....Tore	1855 07 24	UT, Salt Lake City
Pederson ....Anne Marie	Christensen.........Niels	1840 09 20	Denmark
Pederson ....Laurssine	Heiselt ....Hans C.	1860	
Peek ....Joanna	Kendall ....William	1853 12 07	ENG, Sohom
Pehrson ....Elena	Hakansson ....Johannes	1817 08 02	Sweden
Pehrson ....Elna Petronella	Johnson ....Andrew John	1855 12 22	Sweden
Pehrsson ....Bereta (Bertha)	Nilsson ....Ole	1840 12 27	
Pehrsson ....Ingeborg	Thomander...........Peter	1863	UT, Ephraim
Peirson ....Susan Sanford	Richards..............Franklin D.	1853 06 26	UT, Salt Lake City
Pendleton ....Sarah E.	Connell...............James	1869 10 04	UT, Salt Lake City
Penfold ....Mary	Goble ....William	1841 01 12	ENG, Brighton
Penmen ....Jane (Jean)	Hutchison ....William	1845 10	Scotland
Penn ....Caroline	Maiben ....Henry	1845 12 18	ENG
Penn ....Maria Louisa	Newman.............Henry J.	1851 03 30	ENG
Penrod ....Elizabeth	Wall..................William M.	1852 08 06	UT, Provo
Penrod ....Mary Elizabeth	Bybee ....David Bowman	1857 02 28	UT, Salt Lake City
Penrose ....Jessie Lucetta	Jones ....William Richard	1883 12 16	UT, Salt Lake City
Pepper...........Lucretia Jane	Wightman...........William C.	1854 08 04	UT, Payson
Perkins ....Elizabeth Jane	Belcher...............Edward Everett	1863 12 02	NV, Washoe
Perkins ....Elizabeth Jane	Perkins ....John Calvin	1852 08 20	
Perkins ....Patience	Bingham.............Erastus	1852 04 04	
Perkins ....Patience	Drake ....Daniel	1813 12 02	
Perkins ....Patience	Taft...................Stephen	1801	
Perkins ....Ruth	Mathews.............Joseph Davis	1868 03 07	UT, Salt Lake City
Perkins ....Susannah	Whitesides ....Lewis	1850 05 05	IA, Pleasant Valley
Perks ....Ellen	Johnston ....William J.	1863 01 26	
Perren............Margaret	Pucell ....Samuel	1825 08 01	ENG, Lymm
Perris ....Fanny Jane	Jennings.............Mansfield C.	1857 12 29	NV, Las Vegas
Perris ....Fanny Jane	Wilson ....James	1890 05 05	UT, Salt Lake City
Perry.............Amanda M.	Tippets ....Joseph H.	1842 06 26	IL, Nauvoo

Female	Male	Date	Place
Perry...............Elizabeth M.	Hatch..................Orin	1855 11 10	UT, Salt Lake City
Perry...............Eunice Jane	Thorne................Richard	1882 02 16	UT, Salt Lake City
Perry...............Phebe Roxy	Cutler	1889 03 20	UT
Perry...............Phebe Roxy	Wheeler..............Levi	1865 12 23	UT, Salt Lake City
Persson ....Anna	Olson..................Sven	1841 06 17	Sweden
Persson ....Hannah	Malmberg...........Samuel Carlsson	1847 12 28	Sweden
Persson ....Kjerstina	Olsson................Hans	1827 12 12	
Persson ....Martha	Anderson.............Johannes	1844 05 10	Sweden
Peters ....Laura	Woodland............William W.	1862 06 12	UT, Salt Lake City
Petersen ....Ann Sophia	Stark...................Soren	1862 04 16	Ocean
Petersen ....Josephine M.	Larsen ....Lars Kervin	1870 05 10	UT, Logan
Petersen ....Julia K.	Jensen ....David	1868 11 18	
Petersen ....Karen	Carstensen..........Peter Cornelius	1864 04 27	Ocean
Petersen ....Karen	Hansen................James	1856 02 03	UT, Salt Lake City
Petersen ....Karen	Hansen................Peter	1851 04 24	Denmark
Petersen ....Maren	Petersen..............Peter	1865 11 04	UT, Ephraim
Petersen ....Maren	Thompson ....David	1855 05 09	UT, Ephraim
Petersen ....Marie Concordia	Thomassen ....Peter O.	1865 05	UT
Petersen ....Martena Arup	Binderup.............Christen C.	1854 06 22	Denmark
Petersen ....Matilda H.	Nelson................Wilford	1881 12 01	UT, Salt Lake City
Petersen ....Petrine	Jorgensen ....Christian	1878 09 26	UT, Salt Lake City
Petersen ....Petrine Rasmine	Thomassen ....Peter O.	1859 04 22	Denmark
Petersen ....Sena	Frost...................Jens C. S.	1872 04 10	
Petersen ....Wilhelmine	Thomassen ....Peter O.	1866 02	UT
Peterson ....Anna Catherine	Monson ....Christian Hans	1861 04 26	UT, Richmond
Peterson ....Anna Christina	Wilcox ....Samuel Allen	1872 10 21	UT, Salt Lake City
Peterson ....Annie Christine	Anderson.............James	1876 11 19	UT, Spring City
Peterson ....Bertha Kirstine	Jacobsen.............Jorgen	1843 04 02	Denmark
Peterson ....Carren	Beckstrand ....Karl J.	1862 02 28	UT, Salt Lake City
Peterson ....Christina	Jeppson ....Jeppa H.	1865 01 27	UT, Salt Lake City
Peterson ....Elsa	Bengtsson...........Jons	1820 12 19	Sweden
Peterson ....Hannah Sophia	Johnson ....John	1879 01 02	UT, Salt Lake City
Peterson ....Hannah Sophia	Lythgoe ....James	1892 08 16	UT, Logan
Peterson ....Johanna	Haag		NE
Peterson ....Johanna	Johnson ....Nils Toman	1848 10 22	Sweden
Peterson ....Johanna	Larsen ....Christian	1866 02	UT, Spanish Fork
Peterson ....Johanna	Nielsen................Hans	1871 06 05	UT, Salt Lake City
Peterson ....Johanna M.	Atkinson ....Alfred Henry	1871 07 10	UT, Salt Lake City
Peterson ....Maren F.	Christensen.........Carl C. A.	1868 11 30	UT, Salt Lake City
Peterson ....Mary	Fisher ....Moroni	1875 09 27	UT, Salt Lake City
Peterson ....Pernille	Williamson...........Niels W.	1844 01 05	Norway
Peterson ....Stina Kajsa	Felt.....................John Johnson	1862 06 21	UT, Salt Lake City
Pettegrew ....Lucy Ann	Cutler ....Harmon	1842 08 29	IA, Zarahemla
Pettegrew ....Lucy Ann	Marchant............Edmund	1857 03 15	UT, Salt Lake City
Pettit ....Elizabeth Ann	Willie ....James Grey	1846 06 13	
Pettit ....Matilda Eve	Reed ....Levi Ward	1852	UT, Salt Lake City
Petty ....Mary Prianna	Hillman...............Ira King	1851 06 08	UT, Salt Lake City
Petty ....Mary Prianna	Homer ....Russell King	1867 11 23	UT, Clarkston
Petty ....Sarah G.	Brown.................Neuman	1851 05 08	
Phelps ....Almira	Davenport ....James	1822 09 04	NY, Olean
Phelps ....Martha	Abraham ....James	1852 11 08	ENG
Phelps ....Mary	Allen ....Rufus	1861 06 03	
Phelps ....Mary	Stonebraker ....Joel M.	1848	
Phelps ....Mary Ann	Rich...................Charles Coulson	1845 01 06	IL, Nauvoo

Female	Male	Date	Place
Phelps ....Paulina Eliza	Lyman ....Amasa Mason	1843 01 15	IL, Nauvoo
Phelps ....Phebe	Stonebraker ....Joseph	1849 06 16	NE
Pherson ....Anna Marie	Anderson.............Andrew		Germany
Philbrook ....Elizabeth Ann	Hardy ....Zachariah	1822 07 17	ME, Belfast
Philbrook ....Sophia Wing	Lambert...............Abial	1823	
Philbrook ....Sophia Wing	Rollins ....Enoch Perham	1829 04 29	
Phillips ....Almira	Allman ....Thomas	1863 02 21	UT, Salt Lake City
Phillips ....Ann	Ellis ....James	1845 05 11	Wales
Phillips ....Emmaretta	Thornton.............Oliver E.	1873 02 15	UT, American Fork
Phillips ....Frances Ann	Woolley ....Samuel A.		UT, Salt Lake City
Phillips ....Hannah E.	Freshwater..........William	1877 08 14	UT, St. George
Phillips ....Hannah E.	Jacques..............Thomas	1855 03 08	UT, Provo
Phillips ....Hannah E.	Mecham ....Edward	1870 01 11	UT, Salt Lake City
Phillips ....Louisa Mary	Pace...................William F.	1868 11 30	UT, Salt Lake City
Phillips ....Lucy	Van Buren ....Cheney G.	1831 02 17	NY, Russia
Phillips ....Mary Allen	Terry...................William R.	1835 12 20	RI
Philpot ....Martha Eliza	Boice ....Benjamin	1859 06 09	UT, Salt Lake City
Phippen ....Julia Ann	Eldredge.............Hyrum	1866 07 28	UT, Coalville
Phippen ....Julia Ann	Evans ....Benjamin Bowen	1886 10 22	UT, Logan
Pickett.............Elizabeth	Tolman ....Cyrus A.	1870 10 17	
Pickett.............Jane	Barker ....John T.	1870 06 20	UT, Salt Lake City
Pickett.............Maria Louisa	Read ....George Franklin	1891 06 01	
Pickett.............Maria Louisa	Tolman ....Cyrus A.	1878 12 12	
Pickle..............Magdelena	Durfee ....Edmund	1809 10 18	RI, Tiverton
Pickle..............Magdelena	Durfee ....Jabez	1846 01 21	IL, Nauvoo
Pickles ....Elizabeth	Youd...................Thomas	1844 05 05	ENG, Liverpool
Picknell ....Sarah	Leonard..............George Bradford	1864 04 30	UT, Salt Lake City
Picton ....Mary Ann	Cook...................Fredrick	1863 01 13	UT, Salt Lake City
Pidd ....Sarah	Griffiths...............Joseph	1854 03 27	UT, Salt Lake City
Pidd ....Sarah	Smith..................William P.	1867 11 26	UT, Fort Douglas
Pierce ....Helen (Ellen)	Conder ....Edward	1846	MO, St. Louis
Pierce ....Jane Ann	Jones ....Elisha Warren	1871 03 06	UT, Heber
Pierce ....Margaret	Whitesides ....Morris	1841 07 23	IL, Nauvoo
Pierce ....Margaret	Young.................Brigham	1846 01 22	IL, Nauvoo
Pierce ....Mary	McMullin.............Henry	1842 04 21	ME, Knox Co.
Pierce ....Patience Delila	Palmer................Abraham	1825 07 10	NY, Oswegatchie
Pierson ....Hannah	Anderson.............Niel	1862 10 25	UT, West Jordan
Pierson ....Polly Ann	Gardner..............Moses Isaac	1815 02 02	NY, Seneca Co.
Pilch...............Lydia	Blackburn............Jehu		
Pilch...............Lydia	McKnight.............James	1884	UT, Minersville
Pilch...............Lydia	Thrower...............Thomas	1841 01 10	ENG, Norfolk
Pile ....Mary Louise	Felt.....................Nathaniel Henry	1857 12 07	UT, Salt Lake City
Pile ....Mary Louise	Silver..................William John	1870 10 12	UT, Salt Lake City
Pilgrim ....Rececca	Goates ....William	1857 04 07	UT, Salt Lake City
Pill..................Caroline	Farnham..............Augustus A.	1858 02 07	UT, Salt Lake City
Pill..................Elizabeth	Stayner...............Thomas C.	1827 09 06	ENG
Pilley..............Ann	Brewerton............George	1822 08 06	ENG
Pillings ....Elizabeth	Cole....................Martin Richard	1840	ENG
Pillings ....Elizabeth	Hellewell.............Robert	1854 05 24	
Pincock............Ellen	Bennett...............James	1833 06 30	ENG, Lancashire
Pine ....Thankful Lucy	Kelley ....Joseph	1856 04 22	UT
Pine ....Thankful Lucy	Nay.....................John Jr.	1859	UT, Springville
Pine ....Thankful Lucy	Packard..............Orren	1851 11 09	UT, Springville
Pippen ....Sarah	Jolley..................Reuben M.	1829 01 13	TN, Weekly Co.

Female		Male		Date	Place
Pitkin	Harriet Vilate	Robbins	Charles B.	1878	
Pitt	Mary	Okey	Edwin	1840 02 26	ENG, Gloucester
Pittam	Jane	Bodily	Robert	1840 12 27	ENG
Pittaway	Mary	Godfrey	John	1845 09 15	ENG, Dodderhill
Pitts	Annie Elizabeth	Kesler	Joseph	1864 02 04	UT, Salt Lake City
Pitts	Mary	Griffin	William	1839 08 19	ENG, Worcester
Plane	Francis	Teasdale	Richard	1816 03 26	
Platt	Ann Jane Griffin	Goodridge	William	1839 06 02	MA
Platt	Ann Jane Griffin	Thompson	Ezra	1853 04 03	UT, Salt Lake City
Platt	Nancy Ellen	Harrison	John William	1854 09 27	ENG, Lancashire
Platt	Sarah Ellen	Vest	Hyrum	1873 03 24	UT, Salt Lake City
Platte	Susie	Greene	Evan M.	1869 04 12	UT, Salt Lake City
Player	Sarah Ann	Harvey	J. Frederick	1886 01 01	
Player	Zillah	Allen	Joseph	1844 09 16	IL, Nauvoo
Player	Zillah Jane	Riser	George C. Jr.	1871 12 25	UT, Salt Lake City
Plitcroft	Mary	Birch	Thomas	1814 05 02	ENG
Pluck	Catherine Ann	Cloward	Jacob	1815 02 17	PA, Bucks Co.
Plummer	Dorothy E.	Bissell	Henry	1816	MA, Boston
Plunkett	Ellen	Wood	Andrew Patton	1857 11 03	CA, Drytown
Plunkett	Mary Melinda	Adams	Nathan W.	1855 02 15	UT, American Fork
Pocock	Harriet	Pickett	Matthew	1845 11 01	ENG, Berkshire
Pollard	Louisa	Evans	Moses	1866 03 09	
Pollard	Lydia	Puzey	William Henry	1874 10 19	UT, Salt Lake City
Pollard	Mary	Robinson	James	1849 07 28	ENG
Pollard	Mary Ann	Allred	James A.	1866 01 06	UT, Spring City
Pollard	Sophia	Hubbard	Charles W.	1856 06 04	UT, Salt Lake City
Pollock	Nancy Ann	McClenahan	James Kemp	1840 04 21	IL, Stark Co.
Pond	Elmira	Miller	Henry William	1831 06 19	IL, Quincy
Pond	Loenza	Kingsbury	Joseph C.	1846 01 27	IL, Nauvoo
Pond	Lydia	Rich	John Henry	1852 12 26	ENG
Pons	Lydia	Farley	Winthrop	1857 03 08	CO, Manasa
Ponton	Huldah	Budge	Thomas Scott	1862 05	
Pool	Elizabeth	Moody	John Monroe	1856 01 23	UT, Salt Lake City
Pool	Matilda	McFarland	James	1867 06 03	UT, Salt Lake City
Pool	Matilda	Western	John	1853 10 26	UT, Salt Lake City
Pool	Sarah Ann	Nelson	James Horace	1859 08 01	UT, Ogden
Pope	Cassanda	Whittle	Zera	1865 10 14	
Pope	Mary Ann	Hobbs	Willon Down	1835 11 09	ENG, Brighton
Porcher	Charity Emma	Mikesell	John C.	1866 10 27	UT, Salt Lake City
Porcher	Charity Emma	Webb	George		
Porcher	Charity Emma	Willmore	John Ayers	1862 10 08	ENG
Porter	Elizabeth	Waddoups	Thomas	1839 01 22	ENG
Porter	Harriet Eleanor	Woodmansee	Charles	1864 09 04	
Porter	Nancy Areta	Stevenson	Edward	1845 04 07	
Post	Annie	Hansen	Peder	1853 03 23	Denmark
Postles	Nancy	Taylor	William	1813	ENG
Potter	Delight	Mangum	William	1853	
Potter	Mary Ann	Vest	John	1820 02 24	ENG
Potts	Alice	White	Thomas Phillip	1857 03 16	ENG
Potts	Frances	Michie	Robert	1857 03 16	ENG, Preston
Potts	Sarah	Blanchard	John Reid	1854 03 08	
Potts	Sarah	Hendricks	Josiah	1869 10 05	
Poulsen	Ane Kjerstine	Mortensen	Hans Christian	1866 04 22	Denmark
Poulsen	Antonette	Jorgensen			

Female		Male		Date	Place
Poulsen	Antonette	Larsen	Gunder	1840 04 04	Denmark
Poulsen	Else Margretha	Anderson	Peter L.	1865 04 25	UT, Ephraim
Poulsen	Pauline Kerstine	Freestone	James F.	1868 02 15	UT, Salt Lake City
Pouney	Sarah	Brindle	Benjamin W.	1839 12 25	ENG
Powell	Amanda Butler	Thompson	Ezra	1816	
Powell	Ann	Price	James	1857 03 28	ENG, Ludlow
Powell	Eliza Mary	Bridges	Robert Albert	1880	
Powell	Eliza Mary	Carter	John Russell	1856	UT, Parowan
Powell	Eliza Mary	Terry	George W.	1865 08 22	MT, Gallatin
Powell	Emma	Payne	Edward	1854 09 16	ENG
Powell	Fanny Louisa	Cropper	Leigh Richmond	1864 09 17	UT, Deseret
Powell	Margaret	Betts	James	1867 04 03	UT, Payson
Powell	Margaret	Hicken	Thomas	1865 08 15	UT, Salt Lake City
Powell	Mary J.	Erekson	Jonas	1852 12 31	UT, Salt Lake City
Powell	Sallie Clotilda	Ferrin	Samuel	1833 01 21	PA
Powell	Sallie Clotilda	Marsh	Josiah	1826 10 12	NY, Randolph
Powell	Thurza Ann	Powell	Joseph	1853 06 13	ENG, Allington
Power	Sarah	Savage	Henry	1840 10 23	ENG, Middlesex
Prater	Elizabeth A.	Holdaway	David Oscar	1855	UT, Provo
Prater	Elizabeth A.	Huntsman	John	1846 06 07	OH, Perry
Pratt	Arvilla	Perry	Philander J.	1850 05 27	IA, Mt. Pisgah
Pratt	Caroline Amelia	Van Cott	John	1857 02 02	
Pratt	Eliza	Bishop	William Henry	1841 03 21	IN, La Port
Pratt	Jane Elizabeth	Kesler	Frederick	1854 03 20	UT, Salt Lake City
Pratt	Julia Adelia	Phippen	James W.	1845 08 09	NY, Newstead
Pratt	Lois	Hunt	John	1857 07 04	
Pratt	Lovina Jemima	Van Cott	Losee	1812 09 05	
Pratt	Olivia Thankful	Driggs	Benjamin W.	1857 02 16	UT
Pratt	Sariah	Tyler	DeWitt C.	1850 05 14	Trail
Preator	Mary Salome	Egan	William Hyrum	1872 01 30	UT, Deep Creek
Preece	Ann	Walker	Henry	1825 12 19	ENG
Prescott	Eliza Jane	Cram	Charles S.	1846 11 10	NY, New York
Presdee	Mary Ann	Phillips	William	1793 12 03	ENG
Presley	Lydia Aby	Mead	Orlando Fish	1853 06 27	UT, Salt Lake City
Preston	Ann	Longhurst	William Henry	1846 01 01	ENG, Kent
Preston	Eliza Ann	Felt	Nathaniel Henry	1839 10 03	MA, Salem
Price	Ann	Mason	William		
Price	Annie	Daybell	William	1877 11 12	UT, Heber
Price	Eliza Ann	Haight	Isaac C.	1853 10 10	
Price	Elizabeth	Bentley	Richard	1843 09 09	IL, Nauvoo
Price	Emily	Platts	John	1848	ENG
Price	Maria Rawlins	Thacker	Charles E.	1882 11 29	UT, Salt Lake City
Price	Mary Ann	Fullmer	John S.	1837 05 24	TN, Nashville
Price	Mary Ann	Hyde	Orson		IL, Nauvoo
Price	Mary Jane	Hill	William Brown	1859 08 31	UT, Salt Lake City
Price	Ruth	Thomas	Frederick W.	1866 12	UT, Brigham City
Priday	Sarah Ann	Winkless	Joseph T.	1868 07 25	UT, Salt Lake City
Pridmore	Emily Maria	Cordon	Alfred	1856 10 09	UT, Salt Lake City
Prince	Mary Ann	Ostler	John C.		
Prior	Ann	Jarvis	George Franklin	1846 09 17	ENG, Southwark
Priscott	Mary Catherine	Ridd	William James	1888 03 21	UT, Logan
Pritchard	Elizabeth	Jenkins	John	1852 01 17	UT, Salt Lake City
Pritchard	Susannah	Preece	Richard	1832 06 11	ENG
Pritchard	Susannah	Walker	Henry		

Female	Male	Date	Place
Pritchard ....Susannah	Woolsey		
Pritchett ....Kittie Evelyn	Dixon..................Harvey	1870 03 07	UT, Salt Lake City
Proctor.............Ellen	Brewer.................Myron	1854 03	UT, Salt Lake City
Proctor.............Ellen	Ivers ....William D.	1868	
Proctor.............Ellen	Redman ....Jefferson Davis		
Prosser.............Emma	Toone..................John	1836 06 12	ENG
Prudum............Frances Jane	Hamblin..............Frederick	1859 05	
Pucell...............Ellen	Unthank...............William	1871 05 25	
Pucell..............Margaret A.	Butt.....................Uriah R.	1857 02 18	
Pucell..............Margaret A.	Walker................John Smith	1862 08 09	UT, Cedar City
Pugh ....Annie	Welker................James Wilburn	1845 02 17	IA
Pugh ....Elizabeth C.	Winn....................John	1853	
Pugh ....Mary	Scott...................John	1845 03 02	IL, Nauvoo
Pugh ....Susan	Bright.................John Jr.	1835 08 13	TN
Puglsey...........Mary	Lang ....William	1851 07 04	IL, Troy
Pullen ....Caroline	Batchelor............Edward	1841 01 26	
Pulsipher ....Eliza Jane	Terry...................Thomas Sirls	1855 05 06	UT, Salt Lake City
Pulsipher ....Mariah	Burgess..............William	1840 09 14	
Pulsipher ....Mary	Burrell................John Battish	1850	IA, Council Bluffs
Pulsipher ....Mary Ann	Terry...................Thomas Sirls	1848 09 25	UT, Salt Lake City
Pulsipher ....Sarah	Alger..................John	1842 01 11	IL, Nauvoo
Pulver ....Mary Ann	Van Leuven........John	1794	
Pummell ....Elizabeth	Taylor ....John	1832	
Purdun............Mary Ellen	Palmer................William G.		
Purser.............Elmyra	Nelson................Soren Joseph	1877 12 29	
Purser.............Maria	Colebrook...........Charles	1846 03 10	ENG, Worcester
Pyle ....Sarah Riddle	Cox.....................Jehu	1824 01 13	IN, Monroe
Pymm ....Sarah Ann	Park....................James Pollock		
Pymm ....Sarah Ann	Sanford ....William T.		

Q

Female	Male	Date	Place
Quantrille ....Susannah E.	Garrard...............Timothy	1827	
Quantrille ....Susannah E.	Riddle.................John		
Quarnstrom .....Sara	Nyman.................Anders	1839 08 23	Sweden
Quick ....Ann	Lawrenson ....William	1824 04 19	ENG, Liverpool
Quilley ....Elizabeth G.	Read ....Samuel George	1836	ENG
Quilley ....Elizabeth G.	Rodwell ....John	1863 01 10	UT, Salt Lake City
Quimby ....Betsy	Roundy................Shadrach	1814 06 22	VT, Rockingham
Quimby ....Eunice Pease	Stewart...............Andrew J.	1844 01 01	IA
Quinney ....Mary Ann	Mathews.............James	1892 10 17	
Quinney ....Mary Ann	Whipple ....Edson	1857 04 26	UT, Salt Lake City

R

Female	Male	Date	Place
Radburn...........Eliza	Eldridge..............Joseph	1847 04 20	ENG
Radmall ....Elizabeth Ann	Hunting...............Nathan	1861 04 17	UT, Gunnison
Raikes ....Ellen	Gaisford ....Isaac	1851 06 13	ENG, Wiltshire
Railey ....Malinda Jane	Adams................Elias	1837 06 01	IL, Quincy
Ramsbottom ....Elizabeth	Openshaw...........Roger W.	1862 10 25	UT, Moroni
Ramsey ....Phoebe Jane	Reynolds............John	1828 01 28	
Ranck ....Sarah Jane	Capson...............Charles	1852 08 12	

Female	Male	Date	Place
Randall ....Elizabeth	Paterson..............Samuel Jr.	1851 05 11	IA, Kanesville
Rands ....Jessie Lavina	Maxwell ....James	1879 12 25	UT, Salt Lake City
Rasmussen .....Ane Marie	Munk ....Christian Ipsen		
Rasmussen .....Anne	Jacobson..............James	1865 05 10	Ocean
Rasmussen .....Anne M.	Christiansen........Christian		
Rasmussen .....Anne M.	Rasmussen..........Claus	1840 10 16	Denmark
Rasmussen .....Anne M.	Ungermand ....Henning	1863 12 19	
Rasmussen .....Anne Maria	Jensen ....Olof	1841 06 23	Denmark
Rasmussen .....Caroline	Fillerup ....Anders P.	1867 06 30	Ocean
Rasmussen .....Elsie	Nielsen ....Jens	1850 05 18	Denmark
Rasmussen .....Karen (Caroline)	Justesen..............Lars Alexander	1841 11 10	Denmark
Rasmussen .....Kjerstine	Jensen ....Soren	1867 03 09	UT, Salt Lake City
Rasmussen .....Magdalena	Nielsen ....Peter C.	1844 12 28	Denmark
Rasmussen .....Maren Johanna	Christensen.........Martin	1866 10 28	UT, Salt Lake City
Rasmussen .....Marie	Christiansen........Peter	1841 11 12	
Rasmussen .....Marie	Thompson		
Rasmussen .....Matilda	Ford....................Alfred Charles	1863 12 26	UT, Salt Lake City
Rasmussen .....Mette Susanne	Pulsipher ....Orson Hyde	1861 03 08	UT, Brigham City
Rasmussen .....Sophia C.	Christensen.........Mads F. T.	1861 06 03	
Ratcliff ....Ann	Karren ....Thomas	1832 05 04	ENG, Liverpool
Rath................Maria Christina	Jensen ....Lars (Louis)	1858	Denmark
Rath................Maria Christina	Mickelson ....Peter	1866 11 24	UT, Manti
Rawle ....Ann Blackmore	Fry......................Richard	1860 03 25	ENG, Liverpool
Rawlins...........Dinah	Stone..................Amos Pease	1852	
Rawlins...........Elzira	Kerr ....Robert Marion		
Rawlins...........Lucinda	Cunningham........Andrew	1841 04 22	IL, Adams Co.
Rawlins...........Nancy Jane	Kerr ....Robert Marion	1860 01 01	UT, Draper
Rawson ....Sariah	Owen...................James C.	1851	UT, Ogden
Ray ....Mary	Williamson...........James	1838 02 14	Scotland
Raybold ....Anna Maria	Degrey................Alfred	1853 09 20	ENG, Dudley
Raymer...........Martha	Draper ....William Jr.	1846 01 28	IL, Nauvoo
Raymer...........Martha	Weaver................Edward	1821	NY
Raymond ....Amina Ann	Stephens.............Alexander N.	1869 08 23	UT, Salt Lake City
Raymond ....Julia Sophia	McKee.................Hugh	1847 11 22	IA, Council Point
Raymond ....Martha	Hart ....Samuel Walter	1880 02 20	UT, Woodruff
Raymond ....Theresa	Crossgrove..........Charles	1830 09 01	PA, Peansbury
Raynor............Felicia	Astle ....Francis	1836 03 21	ENG
Read...............Alicia Quilley	Arnold..................Orson Pratt	1860 11 04	UT, Salt Lake City
Read...............Amelia	Bailey ....William Henry	1837	
Read...............Christianna R.	Weaver................Franklin	1848 03 12	
Read...............Hannah	Graham ....James		
Read...............Naomi	Cowan.................Robert	1875 05 01	UT, Slaterville
Read...............Thisbe Quilley	Hanks..................Ephraim K.	1862 04 05	UT, Salt Lake City
Reader............Nancy	Workman..............Jacob L.	1834 08 15	TN, Overton
Reasor............Eunice	Brown..................James Polly	1836 04 13	IN, Floyd Co.
Reasor............Sarah	Pectol ....George	1828 11 02	
Redd...............Ann Moriah	Pace....................Wilson Daniel	1852 08 22	UT, Spanish Fork
Redd...............Marinda	Bankhead............Alexander	1862	UT, Spanish Fork
Redd...............Mary	Holt.....................John	1814 11	NC, Onslow Co.
Redding ....Ann	Judd ....Thomas	1841 05 31	ENG
Redding ....Maria	Bates..................Joseph	1847 01 04	ENG, Warwick
Redford...........Ann Eckersall	Haslam................James Holt	1869 04 05	UT, Salt Lake City
Reed...............Clarissa	Hancock..............Levi W.	1831 03 29	
Reed...............Clarissa	White..................Thomas Jones	1854 04 11	

Female	Male	Date	Place
Reed...............Elizabeth C.	Wilson ....Hugh	1862 11 07	UT, Salt Lake City
Reed...............Laura Lucinda	Steed.................Thomas	1846 12 13	IA, Keokuk
Reed...............Mary Mahala	Crockett..............Wilford W.	1860 07 29	UT, Payson
Reed...............Mary Sophia	Crockett..............Alvin	1852 06 29	UT, Payson
Reeder............Eliza	Hurren ....James David	1850 09 22	
Reeder............Mary Ann	Metcalf ....Anthony	1853 04	MO, St. Louis
Rees ....Phoebe	Evans ....David	1825 07 16	Wales
Rees ....Sarah Jane	Anderson............Archibald A.	1859 08 23	UT, Spanish Fork
Reese ....Anne	Ward ....Thomas	1870	UT, Salt Lake City
Reese ....Catherine	Clawson ....Zephaniah	1824 01 08	NY
Reese ....Elizabeth	Prothero ....Jonathan	1869 05 31	UT, Salt Lake City
Reese ....Mary	Thatcher.............George	1864 11 09	UT, Provo
Reeves ....Ann Eliza	Godfrey ....Joseph	1840	NJ
Reeves ....Elizabeth	Liston ....Commodore P.	1844 07 01	IN, Muncie
Reeves ....Elizabeth	Pollock ....Samuel	1847 02 05	IL, Nauvoo
Reeves ....Frances	Willis.................John Henry	1857 03 20	UT, Salt Lake City
Reeves ....Julia W.	Young................William L.	1870 08 08	UT, Salt Lake City
Reeves ....Mary	Coleman.............George	1840	NY, Niagra
Reeves ....Mary	Godfrey ....Joseph	1857 03 07	UT, Salt Lake City
Reid ....Anna Jane	Judd ....William Riley	1856 11 26	UT, Salt Lake City
Reid ....Fanny May	Sargent ....David Elmer	1862 01 26	UT, Salt Lake City
Reid ....Janet	McNeil ....Thomas	1845 06 19	Scotland
Renny ....Mary	Laird ....James	1847 08 20	Scotland
Reynolds ....Abigail Mary	Oaks.................David Martin	1869 03 02	UT, Salt Lake City
Reynolds ....Celia Ann	Despain ....James H.	1846 11 10	
Reynolds ....Celia Ann	Garrity ....Pat	1886 01 13	
Reynolds ....Ellis	Shipp.................Milford Bard	1866 05 05	
Reynolds ....Mary	Warner ....William	1848 05 18	ENG
Reynolds ....Mary Elizabeth	Tidwell...............William N.	1857 03 01	UT, Maple Grove
Rhees ....Ellen	Dredge ....Jesse R.	1854 04 29	Wales
Rhodes ....Mary	Benson...............Jerome M.	1830 10	
Rhodes ....Mary Elizabeth	Meeks ....William	1837 10 05	IN, Warwick
Rice ....Ida Ann	Wilcox ....Jonathan F.	1880	
Rich ....Caroline Whiting	Humphreys..........Hyrum T.	1873 10 07	
Rich ....Jane Ann	Green ....Hervey	1837 11 14	OH, Huron Co.
Rich ....Nancy	Porter ....John P.	1843 02 05	IA, Lee Co.
Rich ....Sarah Jane	Miller ....Thomas Rudolph	1863 09 19	UT, Salt Lake City
Rich ....Sarah Jane	Tobin ....John		UT, Salt Lake City
Richards ....Alice Howell	Kite.....................		
Richards ....Alice Howell	Lewis.................Richard		
Richards ....Alice Howell	Lowell................William		
Richards ....Alice Howell	Williams..............Nathaniel	1893 05 02	UT, Beaver
Richards ....Catherine	Thomas ....Thomas R.	1864 12 17	UT, Salt Lake City
Richards ....Elizabeth A.	Rowe.................Manning	1854 07 27	
Richards ....Elizabeth	Maiben ....John	1856 04 22	UT, Salt Lake City
Richards ....Frances	Brady.................Marion H.	1855 02 06	UT
Richards ....Lucy Ann	Brady.................Marion H.	1858 03 22	UT, Salt Lake City
Richards ....Mary	James ....James	1854 02 14	UT, Salt Lake City
Richards ....Mary Amelia	Streeper ....William H.	1867 10 16	UT, Salt Lake City
Richards ....Nancy	Peirson...............William	1819 03 04	MA
Richards ....Phebe Eleanor	Maiben ....John Bray	1855 04 09	ENG, London
Richards ....Rhoda Ann J.	Knowlton ....Benjamin Franklin	1863 10 13	UT, Salt Lake City
Richards ....Sarah Jane	Perkins ....William Louis	1853 10 27	
Richardson ......Elizabeth M.	Huffaker ....Simpson D.	1846 01 18	IL, Nauvoo

Female	Male	Date	Place
Richardson ......Hannah	Vance.................William Perkins	1874 10 19	UT
Richardson ......Isabella	Golightly ....Richard	1828	ENG
Richardson ......Jerusha Ann	Bair.....................John	1846 01 27	IL, Nauvoo
Richardson ......Jerusha Ann	Card ....Amasa	1842 01 08	
Richardson ......Laura	Bess ....Joel	1830	NY, Steuben Co.
Richardson ......Polly	Stewart...............Benjamin F.	1837 06 14	IL, Beardstown
Riches ....Hannah	Weekes ....David	1861 12 07	UT, Salt Lake City
Riches ....Martha	Bloomfield ....John	1822 10 28	ENG, Bungay
Richey ....Emily	Case...................Solomon Cowles		
Richison...........Margaret Ann	Merrill ....Albert	1836 03 21	NY, New York City
Richmond ....Sarah Ann	Nelson................Henry	1848 05 16	IL, Nauvoo
Ricks...............Clarinda	Smith..................Silas Sanford	1851 07 09	
Ricks...............Mary Elizabeth	Smith..................William Read	1857 04 23	UT, Salt Lake City
Ricks...............Sarah Ann	Smith..................Silas Sanford	1853 03 17	
Riden ....Hannah	Barnett ....James		
Riden ....Hannah	Bowering ....Isaac	1812 01 22	Wales
Riden ....Hannah	Thomas		
Riden ....Hannah	Williams..............Ebenezer A.		
Rider..............Adelia	Carbine ....Edmund Zebulon	1823 02 15	
Riding ....Betsy Ann W.	Rigby..................Seth	1852 01 26	UT, Salt Lake City
Rigby ....Ellen	Capener ....William	1861 03 23	
Rigby ....Susannah	Gardner..............Charles	1867 01 11	UT, Salt Lake City
Riggs ....Dorothy M.	Stewart...............Andrew J.	1868 01 25	UT, Salt Lake City
Rigtrup............Johanna M. C.	Nelson................Andrew E.	1859 05 15	NE, Omaha
Riley ....Nancy Wood	Parker ....Henry Miller	1844 01 29	IL, Nauvoo
Ringrose ....Mary Ann	Hastings ....John Jr.	1870 06 20	UT, Salt Lake City
Risley..............Susan Amelia	Chapman ....Welcome	1831	NY, Madison
Ritchie ....Betsy	Crawley ....Thomas	1863 03 21	Ocean
Rivers ....Mary	Elvers ....Carl	1864	UT, Salt Lake City
Rivers ....Mary	White..................George	1845 10 13	ENG
Roach ....Martha	Pugsley ....Philip	1851 06 28	ENG, Bristol
Robb...............Isabella	Duncan...............Adam	1869 06 21	UT, Salt Lake City
Robbins ....Ellen Jane	Bailey ....John Cook	1827	ENG
Robbins ....Ellen Jane	Ramsden............Charles	1838 01 22	
Robbins ....Margaret Burtis	Beck...................Joseph Ellison	1862 12 13	UT, Salt Lake City
Robbins ....Sarah	Titensor ....Thomas Edward	1854 04 01	ENG
Roberds...........Lodesky Ann	Prows ....William Cook	1850 04 14	NV, Mary's River
Roberson........Rachel	Ford....................Jonathan	1826 04 16	IN, Bartholomew
Roberson........Rachel	Spafford ....Horace	1851 07 09	
Robert.............Jeanne	Meservy ....Joshua	1832 10 03	
Roberts...........Ann	Griffiths...............Joseph	1843 01 03	ENG, Liverpool
Roberts...........Caroline	Oliverson.............James	1856 09 30	UT, Kaysville
Roberts...........Catherine	Wright.................Amos Russell	1861 04 28	UT, Brigham City
Roberts...........Cyrene Elsie	Hicks ....William B.	1837	IL, Carlton
Roberts...........Cyrene Elsie	Knapp..................John Claus	1860	
Roberts...........Cyrene Elsie	Tryon..................Truman	1868 02 04	UT, Salt Lake City
Roberts...........Eleanor	Lewis..................Elias	1856 06 04	IA, Iowa City
Roberts...........Hannah	Roberts ....Robert David	1870 06 06	UT, Salt Lake City
Roberts...........Harriet Ann	Bodily ....Robert Jr.	1869 02 02	UT, Salt Lake City
Roberts...........Harriet Julia	Parry ....John Jr.	1853 12 26	Wales
Roberts...........Jane	Bennett...............John	1843 10 22	
Roberts...........Jane Cecelia	Peterson.............John		
Roberts...........Jane Cecelia	Snow..................James Chauncey	1856 12 02	UT, Salt Lake City
Roberts...........Jane Cecelia	Wheeler..............Thomas J.		

Female	Male	Date	Place
Roberts............Lucina	Cahoon ....Reynolds	1842	
Roberts............Lucina	Johnson ....Peter Henry	1824 11 24	VT, Addison Co.
Roberts............Lucinda Victoria	Robinson..............John Jr.	1853 01 24	UT
Roberts............Lucy Ann	Dart ....John	1831 11 24	
Roberts............Maria Louisa	Newell ....Elliot Alfred	1851 05 04	IA, Council Bluffs
Roberts............Mary Ann	Beard ....Stephen	1863 06 22	UT, Henefer
Roberts............Mary Ann M.	Day.....................James	1867 03 23	UT, Salt Lake City
Roberts............Nancy Ann T.	Greer..................Nathaniel Hunt	1821	GA
Roberts............Rachel Broom	Sanders...............Ellis M.	1830 11 09	DE
Roberts............Sarah Ann	Stewart...............Charles	1835 12 19	NY, Ogdensburg
Roberts............Sarah Elizabeth	Griffith ....Patison D.	1863 02 07	UT, Salt Lake City
Robertson.......Margaret	Salmon................James	1857 06 19	Scotland
Robertson........Marion	Neil......................William	1863 12 31	Scotland
Robey ....Mary Jane	Epperson............Sidney Hiram	1853 11 07	UT, Provo
Robinson ....Alice	Jackson................John	1861 06 16	ENG
Robinson ....Alice	Jackson................Jonathan	1869 01 11	
Robinson ....Alice	Turner ....David	1877 01 11	UT, St. George
Robinson ....Anna Maria	Wilcox ....James D.	1854 11 26	UT
Robinson ....Elizabeth	Condie.................Gibson	1857 02 24	UT, Salt Lake City
Robinson ....Eveline P.	Whitaker..............George	1846 07 27	IA, Council Bluffs
Robinson ....Helena Lydia	Richards..............Samuel W.	1856 02 16	UT, Salt Lake City
Robinson ....Jacosa Jane	Whitehead..........Francis	1868 03	UT, Richmond
Robinson ....Margaret E.	Carroll ....Patrick	1854	Canada
Robinson ....Martha	Blackham ....Samuel	1826	ENG
Robinson ....Millizzer	Cooper................William	1843 07 21	ENG, Eastwood
Robinson ....Sarah Ann	Dowdle ....Robert	1818 05 27	SC
Robinson ....Sarah Ann	Holyoak ....Henry	1865 01 02	UT, Paragonah
Robison ....Eliza	Smith...................Conrad	1854 07 28	
Robison ....Leannah	Rock....................Henry	1858 12 17	PA, Tomstown
Robison ....Lucretia Proctor	Owens.................James C. Jr.	1856 01 16	
Robison ....Matilda	King....................Thomas Rice	1831 12 25	NY, Cicero
Rochester ....Lydia Ellen	Cooper ....William Darby	1846 10 13	
Rock ....Elizabeth	Hinckley ....Ira Nathaniel	1878 05 23	UT, Salt Lake City
Rock ....Maryann	Pugh...................Edward Jr.	1847 07 24	IA, Kanesville
Rock ....Maryann	Williams..............Benjamin	1837 07 04	ENG
Rockwood........Ellen	Young.................Brigham	1845 09 13	
Rodeback ....Rebecca H.	Cook...................William	1875 10 25	UT, Salt Lake City
Roe.................Isabella Jane	Boyd...................George Albert	1866 11 10	UT, Salt Lake City
Roe.................Sarah Ann	Scott...................Andrew Hunter	1851 01 12	
Roebuck ....Sarah	Lee ....John	1841 11 15	ENG
Rogers............Adelia Caroline	Taylor ....Steven King		
Rogers............Adelia Caroline	White..................Joseph		
Rogers............Ann	Mayhew..............Elijah	1868 04 18	UT, Salt Lake City
Rogers............Ann	Moore.................Joseph	1862	ENG
Rogers............Ann	Snow ....William	1853 03 13	UT, Salt Lake City
Rogers............Ann	Taylor ....James W.	1839 10 20	
Rogers............Caroline Bacon	Hardy ....Samuel B.	1826 01 17	MA, Georgetown
Rogers............Clarissa Marina	Taggart...............George W.	1857 02 08	UT, Brigham City
Rogers............Delilah Eunice	Vincent................Samuel		
Rogers............Delilah Eunice	Ware ....Abisha	1813 04 09	VA, Rockingham
Rogers............Eliza	Gardner..............James	1860 12	
Rogers............Elizabeth	Sharp ....James		
Rogers............Francis	Adair...................Thomas Jefferson		
Rogers............Hannah C.	Daniels ....Aaron	1845 12 14	

Female	Male	Date	Place
Rogers............Hannah C.	Smoot................Abraham Owen	1886 03 11	UT, Logan
Rogers............Henrietta	Standage.............Henry	1851 04 16	UT, Salt Lake City
Rogers............Mary	Fryer....................Thomas C.	1857	
Rogers............Sarah	Crockett..............Edward Hall	1832	ENG
Rogers............Susannah	Woolley ....Thomas	1860 10 08	
Rogerson........Sarah Ann	Lister ....John Henry	1860 02 03	UT, Parowan
Rogo...............Anne M.	Halling ....Peder J.	1823 02 08	Denmark
Rollins............Ann Sophia	Beckstead ....Sidney M.	1850 06 11	NE, Bellevue
Rollins............Ann Sophia	Roberts ....Edward Killick	1869 04 19	UT, Salt Lake City
Rollins............Mary Amelia	Hakes.................Collins Rowe	1909 11 19	UT, Salt Lake City
Rollins............Mary Amelia	Osborn ....John Wesley	1857 09 09	CA, San Bern.
Rollins............Mary Elizabeth	Lightner ....Adam	1835 08 11	MO, Clay Co.
Rollins............Mary Elizabeth	Smith..................Joseph Jr.	1842 02	IL, Nauvoo
Rollins............Mary Elizabeth	Young.................Brigham	1846 01 17	IL, Nauvoo
Rollins............Melissa Kezia	Heybourne ....Charles M.	1921 10 31	
Rollins............Melissa Kezia	Lee.....................John Nelson	1863 12 30	
Romeril ....Fanny Mary	Decloux ....Maurice	1859 08 19	UT, Salt Lake City
Romeril ....Fanny Mary	Singleton ....Charles	1874 08	
Rommrell ....Jane Nancy	Hammond ....Joseph	1858	
Rommrell ....Jane Nancy	Pierce.................George Thomas	1863 09 20	
Romney............Sarah	Cahoon ....Mahonri M.	1853 11 02	
Roper...............Lydia	Osguthorpe ....John	1846 10 13	ENG, Sheffield
Rose ....Andrea Petrea	Gronemann.........George	1851 11 07	Denmark
Rose ....Louise Maria	Sprague ....Richard D.	1832	
Rose ....Millicent	Pickett ....Matthew		
Roseberg.........Emma Caroline	Jenson ....Jens	1874 01 02	
Rosengren........Kjersti Lovisa	Beckstrom ....Andrew J.	1863 10 28	UT, Mt. Pleasant
Rosequist ....Johannah	Malmgren ....Sven Peter	1864 04 24	UT, Ephraim
Ross ....Catherine	Gillespie ....John Scott	1852 11 16	UT, Salt Lake City
Ross ....Elizabeth	Mathis ....Isaac	1822 02 20	TN, Paris Co.
Ross ....Isabella	Wilson ....James Thomas	1855 11 16	UT, Salt Lake City
Ross ....Jane Duncan	Fisher.................James	1869 10 11	UT, Salt Lake City
Ross ....Jane Duncan	Graham ....William	1848 01	Scotland
Ross ....Margaret	Cutler ....Royal James	1857 12 08	UT, Salt Lake City
Ross ....Mary	Henderson ....Robert	1846 09 26	Scotland
Ross ....Mary	Richard...............John W.		
Ross ....Mary	Scoville...............Ed	1851	
Ross ....Mary Elizabeth	Parker ....Joseph F.	1861 06 30	UT, Joseph
Ross ....Sarah Darling	Randall...............Brigham Young	1877 08 04	
Ross ....Sarah Elizabeth	Lamb..................James Jackson	1863 03 21	UT, Salt Lake City
Rosser.............Elizabeth	Jenkins..............William	1845 12 13	Wales
Rostron...........Sarah	Cook...................John	1858 03 17	UT, Salt Lake City
Rostron...........Sarah	Holt....................James Cooper	1847 03 24	ENG
Rothwell..........Ellen	Crofts ....John	1854 01 01	ENG
Rothwell..........Matilda	Swindlehurst ....John	1852 01 17	ENG
Round.............Flora Jane	Bull ....Charles	1861 12 08	
Rouse ....Charlotte	Wright................William	1832 04 06	ENG
Rowberry........Mary Parry	Jenkins..............William	1840 07 01	ENG
Rowe ....Margaret	Kerr ....Joseph		
Rowe ....Orryanna	Chase.................Stephen	1799 05 12	NY
Rowe ....Ruth	Kerr ....Joseph	1852	
Rowell.............Sarah Ann	Roberts ....Sidney	1830 05 26	
Rowley............Ann Jewel	Baston................Andrew	1857	UT, Parowan
Rowley............Ann Jewel	Ford...................Luke	1857 10 14	

Female	Male	Date	Place
Rowley..........Ann Jewel	Rowley..............William	1836 08 22	ENG, Worcester
Rowley............Louisa	Guymon.............Noah T.	1857 03 02	UT, Salt Lake City
Roylance.........Rachel	Woodfield.............John	1865 05 16	
Rudland.........Charlotte	Dansie................Robert	1849 04 08	
Ruegsegger.....Katherina	Stucki.................John	1855	Switzerland
Runnels.........Sarah Elizabeth	Haskell..............George Niles	1816	VT, Dixon
Runyon...........Sarah Ann	Hunt..................Marshall	1851 03 15	UT, Holladay
Rupp...............Anna Marie	Gerber................John T.	1864 08 28	WY
Rupp...............Mary Ann	Hirschi................Gottlieb	1861 09 14	UT, Salt Lake City
Rush...............Mary B.	Reid..................Jesse Porter	1840 08 23	IL, Nauvoo
Rush...............Mary B.	Rush...................		
Rushton..........Elizabeth F.	Moesser.............Joseph Hyrum	1864 08 28	UT, Salt Lake City
Rushton..........Fanny	Wardle................George	1842 01 24	ENG
Rushton..........Henrietta	Bullock...............Thomas	1838 06 25	
Rusk..............Hannah Mariah	Kinder................John Henry	1857 04 12	ENG, Dunkinfield
Russ...............Sarah	Farr...................Elbridge	1828 07 03	MA, Hunsdale
Russell............Elizabeth	Archibald............Thomas	1835 04 18	Scotland
Russell............Fannie Royce	Seamons.............George	1860 10 21	UT, Salt Lake City
Russell............Frances Maria	Huff...................Thaddeus W.	1864 12 17	UT, Salt Lake City
Russell............Hannah	Ballard...............William	1820 10 16	ENG, Hampshire
Russell............Hannah Maria	Marchant............John Alma	1867 11 30	UT, Salt Lake City
Russell............Janet	Widdison............Thomas	1821 09 21	Scotland
Russell............Matilda	Maxham..............Charles	1841 01 08	
Russell............Sarah	Crouch...............Ebenezer	1846 10 20	ENG, Sussex
Russon...........Ann	Bird...................John	1830	
Rutledge.........Elizabeth	Utley..................Littlejohn		
Rutledge.........Matilda	Baird..................Samuel		
Rutledge.........Matilda	Church...............Hayden Wells	1870 10 15	
Rutledge.........Matilda	Greer..................William F.	1854 06 27	
Rutter..............Ann	Harrocks.............Daniel	1840 09 07	ENG
Ruxton............Isabella	Burnett...............David R.	1831 10 19	Scotland
Ryan...............Alice	Jones.................Hyrum	1888 07 02	UT, Heber
Ryon...............Elizabeth	Lewis.................Beason	1846 02 06	

S

Female	Male	Date	Place
Sabey.............Sarah Jane	Jacobs................John	1874 08 10	UT, Salt Lake City
Sabey.............Sarah Jane	Walker................Edward Marion	1890 08 10	
Sabin..............Anna Maria	Young.................Franklin W.	1861 07 06	UT, Salt Lake City
Sabin..............Beulah	Hoyt...................James	1807	NY, Boonville
Sabin..............Elizabeth	Froerer...............Frederick G.	1851 07 19	UT, Salt Lake City
Sabin..............Sarah Ann	Card...................William Fuller	1811 12 28	NY, Dutchess
Sainsbury........Elizabeth Alice	Fullmer...............William P.	1884 06 19	UT, Salt Lake City
Salisbury..........Sarah Ann	Davis..................Isaac	1815	
Salmon...........Eliza	Martin.................Edward	1855	ENG
Salmon...........Margaret	Calderwood.........Alexander	1862 12 28	
Salthouse........Elizabeth	Daniels...............James E.	1816 10 13	ENG
Salvesen..........Ane Marie F.	Winger................Christopher S.	1863 05 05	Ocean
Sampson.........Mary Jane	Lemmon.............John	1852	
Sampson.........Sarah	Case..................Solomon Cowles	1855 12 04	
Sampson.........Sarah	Goff...................James	1852 04 12	UT, Salt Lake City
Sampson.........Sarah	Hancock.............Benjamin		
Sandall.........Martha	Elsmore..............Thomas	1845 06 01	ENG, Glou.

Female	Male	Date	Place
Sandberg..........Annie Antionette	Vilhelmsen ....Hans		
Sandell ....Anna Caroline	Edman.................Hans Odahl	1856 12 19	Sweden
Sanders ....Ellen	Kimball ....Heber Chase	1846 01 07	IL, Nauvoo
Sanders ....Emma	Tidwell................James H.	1857 02 23	UT, Salt Lake City
Sanders ....Hannah M.	Huntington..........Oliver B.	1852 11 25	UT, Salt Lake City
Sanders ....Harriet	Kimball ....Heber Chase	1846 01 07	IL, Nauvoo
Sanders ....Marian	Jenkins...............James Hardie	1880	UT
Sanders ....Matta Marie	Bastian ....Jacob	1867 10 28	UT, Salt Lake City
Sanders ....Rebecca Ann	Sanderson...........Henry W.	1850 03 07	IL, Pigeon Grove
Sanders ....Sarah Jane	Merkley ....Nelson	1856 03 25	UT, Salt Lake City
Sanders ....Zillah	Brown..................Charles		
Sanders ....Zillah	Player.................William Warner	1821 07 22	ENG, Middlesex
Sandersen ....Kristine	Sorensen.............John	1862 12 27	UT, Salt Lake City
Sanderson ....Caroline A.	Ballantyne ....Richard	1857 03 16	
Sanderson ....Helena	Mortensen..........Peder	1827 11 09	Denmark
Sanford...........Angeline	Parkis.................Stephen	1865	
Sanford...........Angeline	Taylor.................William Pim	1852 04 04	IL
Sanford...........Cecilla Elmina	Johnson ....Aaron	1857 03 01	
Sanford...........Jane	Mills...................John	1827 03 13	Canada
Sanford...........Sylvia Eliza	Metcalf ....Anthony	1862 08 27	UT, Springville
Sanger..............Irene	Alton..................Abel	1794 11 27	CT
Sansom ....Sarah	Wall ....William	1836 09 26	ENG, Horsley
Sant ....Margaret	Williams..............Charles	1861 10	UT, Smithfield
Santifer...........Eliza Branch	Clark...................John Norman	1816 04 24	VA, Patrick Co.
Sargent...........Harriet	Rich....................Charles Coulson	1847 03 28	NE
Sargent...........Louisa	Harris ....Martin H.	1859 04 03	UT, Ogden
Sargent...........Martha Jane	Mowrey ....Harley Jr.	1847 07 04	WY
Sargent...........Martha Jane	Sharp ....Norman	1845 09	IL, Nauvoo
Sargent...........Sarah Ann	Martin.................John	1855 06 03	UT, Salt Lake City
Saunders ....Eliza	Fowles................Timothy	1839 08 13	ENG
Saunders ....Eliza	Green ....William	1867 10 26	UT, Salt Lake City
Saunders ....Eliza	Keller..................Alva	1854 07	UT, Salt Lake City
Savage ....Hannah Maria	Eldredge.............Ira	1852 02 28	
Saville.............Mary Ann	Tame..................Alfred	1864 11 19	UT, Salt Lake City
Sawyer ....Mary Ann	Halbom...............John		
Sawyer ....Mary Ann	Watkins ....John	1863 05 01	UT, Salt Lake City
Sawyer ....Mary Eliza	Weekes ....Samuel	1853 01 04	
Saxey ....Lucy Ann S.	Bennett...............George A.		UT
Saxton ....Frances	Brown.................William	1814 04 18	ENG, Warwick
Saxton ....Mary Ann	Merrell ....Hosea	1825 04 25	NY, Bridgewater
Saxton ....Rebecca Ann	Searle.................Breed	1827 05 03	NY, Butler
Scarborough....Annie	Hatch..................Lorenzo L.	1873 12 01	UT, Salt Lake City
Scearce ....Elizabeth	Leany ....William	1845 09 07	IL, Nauvoo
Scheel ....Elise R. S.	Christensen.........Carl C. A.	1857 04 24	
Scheib ....Sabina	Hart ....James Henry	1861 05 04	UT, Salt Lake City
Schenk ....Elizabeth	Stauffer ....Ulrich	1859 08 26	Switzerland
Scherlin ....Johanna C.	Chlarson..............Hans Nadrian	1861 09 20	
Schneider ....Anna Marie	Gali....................Peter	1864 10 22	
Schneider ....Magdalena	Itten ....John	1861 10 18	UT, Salt Lake City
Schneider ....Magdalena	Pearce................Harrison	1863 10 03	
Schofield.........Elizabeth	Broadbent ....Joseph		
Schofield.........Emma	Robinson.............John R.	1873 10 09	UT, Salt Lake City
Schow.............Christena R.	Henrie ....James	1861 12 06	UT, Salt Lake City
Schrader.........Harriet Henriette	Phelps ....William Wines	1856 09 08	UT, Salt Lake City

Female	Male	Date	Place
Schrader..........Harriet Henriette	Skidmore.............Charles B.	1829	
Schuebel ....Eva	Gerber................John T.	1865 11 22	UT, Salt Lake City
Schuler ....Christena	Theurer ....Frederick	1862 02 18	UT, Providence
Scorey ....Elizabeth	Gilchrist..............Neil II	1866 06 02	UT, Salt Lake City
Scott ....Amy	Chase................Abner	1808 11 02	VT, Addison Co.
Scott ....Betsy Elizabeth	Pack..................John Jr.	1865 12 20	UT, Salt Lake City
Scott ....Elizabeth	Bills ....John	1834 01 07	PA, Allegheny
Scott ....Elizabeth	Lazenby	1851	UT
Scott ....Sarah	Stewart...............Philander B.	1801 05 10	
Scoville ....Eliza Rebecca	Haws·................George W.	1892 01	
Scoville ....Eliza Rebecca	McArthur ....Duncan	1857 10 23	UT, Salt Lake City
Scoville ....Eliza Rebecca	McArthur ....Washington P.	1867 11 15	UT, Mt. Pleasant
Seabury ....Ruth Ann	Ercanbrack..........William T.	1864 11 11	
Seace ....Eleanor	Skinner...............Horace B.	1831	OH, Cincinnati
Seamons ....Eliza	England..............William	1860 06 05	IA, Council Bluffs
Seamons ....Jemima	Daines................Robert	1859 05 01	
Seamons ....Lydia	Crowther ....Edwin Dugard	1861 06 09	UT, Salt Lake City
Seamons ....Rachel	Hancy.................James	1855 10 11	ENG, Rumburg
Searle ....Rebecca Ann	Cloward..............William	1848	
Seavey ....Eunice	Baxter................Zimri Harford	1832 05 02	ME, Milton
Seddon ....Ester	Forbes................Henry Clay	1860	UT
Seeley ....Elizabeth	Young.................James	1828 07 20	Canada
Seeley ....Sarah	Wilcox ....Hazard	1801	NY, Albany
Seely ....Elizabeth	Stevens..............William	1854 10 12	UT
Seely ....Sarah	Tidwell...............Jefferson	1860 12 16	UT, Mt. Pleasant
Seetree...........Ann	Tate...................John	1847 10 31	ENG, Leeds
Sellers ....Sarah Jane H.	Stott..................Edwin	1861	UT, Salt Lake City
Selley..............Hannah	Newman..............Stephen James	1877 12 27	UT, Salt Lake City
Selston ....Susanna	Hall...................John	1830 01 24	
Selwood...........Caroline	Kimber...............Charles	1841 08 02	ENG, Thatcham
Senior ....Mary Elizabeth	Bennett..............John Bell	1863 02 02	
Serman...........Eliza Hannah	King..................John	1861 11 15	UT, Salt Lake City
Sessions.........Emeline	Thomas ....Charles Carter		UT, Wasatch Co.
Settle ....Hannah	Lapish ....Joseph	1853 07 03	ENG
Severn ....Hannah	Randall...............Alfred	1863 03 07	UT, Salt Lake City
Seversen ....Gunnel	Olsen.................Ole	1868 05 30	UT, Salt Lake City
Seward ....Annie Rebecca	Kennington..........William Henry	1865 04 01	UT, Salt Lake City
Sewell.............Ann	Hawkins ....James R. A.	1843 05 01	ENG
Sewell.............Elizabeth	Wintle................George B.	1835 07 09	ENG
Sewell.............Emily	Nichols...............Henry W.	1860 03 03	ENG, London
Shackell..........Hannah Maria	Simmons.............Samuel	1831 10 16	ENG, St. James
Shadden ....Mary Jane	Walker................William H.	1850 04 28	
Shaffer............Abigail	Lee ....John Doyle	1845 05 03	
Shaffer............Abigail	Woolsey ....Joseph	1808	
Shaffer............Nancy Ann	Perry ....Lyman Sylvester	1855 01 22	UT, Bingham Fort
Shankland ......Margaret	Todd..................Thomas	1850 01 25	Scotland
Shanks ....Armelia	Berry ....Jesse Woods	1820 02 08	TN, Wilson Co.
Shanks ....Marion Leckie	Perry ....Alexander	1855 12 21	UT, Salt Lake City
Sharp..............Cecelia	Crawford ....John	1853 04 06	UT, Salt Lake City
Sharp..............Elizabeth	Wilcock..............William	1851 11 05	ENG
Sharp..............Helen (Ellen)	Fife ....Adam	1825	Scotland
Sharp..............Jane	Rawlins ....James	1816 03 19	IN, Harrison
Sharp..............Janet	Low ....Thomas	1820 12 08	Scotland
Sharp..............Mary	Cox...................Levi Ashton	1853 10 02	

Female	Male	Date	Place
Sharp...............Rachel	Lemmon..............Washington	1856	UT
Shaw ....Clemina	Evans..................David		
Shaw ....Elizabeth	Jones..................William Parsons	1858 02 25	UT, Kaysville
Shaw ....Hannah Jane	Burridge.............George W.	1847 11 18	Scotland
Shaw ....Mary	Donald................Malcolm	1822 09 27	Scotland
Shaw ....Mary	Hodgson..............Henry W. S.	1845 04 10	ENG, Yorkshire
Shaw ....Mary	Sant....................John	1831 12 12	
Shaw ....Rebecca	Green.................Thomas	1862 05 03	
Shaw ....Rebecca	Parkinson............Timothy G.	1869 10 04	UT, Salt Lake City
Shaw ....Rebecca	Wood..................George	1838 02 25	ENG, Yorkshire
Shearer...........Jane Maria	Snow..................William	1850 10 13	UT, Salt Lake City
Shearer...........Jane Maria	Wines.................Ira Doty	1834 05 29	
Sheen..............Ann Eliza	Adams................George Pilling	1876 12 30	
Sheffield ....Jane Ann	Daniels...............Thomas E.	1855 11 25	UT, Payson
Sheffield ....Polly Lucina	Moore.................John Harvey	1856 05 09	
Sheffield ....Polly Lucina	Morrey................John	1864 10	UT, Payson
Sheffield ....Polly Lucina	Tindral...............Ferney Fold	1853 03	UT, Payson
Shefflin ....Margaret	Stallings ....Joseph	1840	PA, Lancaster
Shefford..........Priscilla	Collins ....John	1824 11 06	ENG
Sheldon ....Harriet	Brown.................Abraham	1834 03 26	VT, Simonsville
Shelley............Ellen Gibson	Green.................Alva A.		
Shelley............Sarah Elizabeth	Conder ....Edward	1854 11 19	
Shelley............Sarah Elizabeth	Varney................Jacob	1906 10 09	
Shelton ....Ann	Howard...............Joseph	1842 11 24	ENG
Shelton ....Emily	Barnes................John Richard	1853 03 23	ENG, Lancashire
Shelton ....Mary Ann	Fausett...............John McKee	1852 07 28	UT, Salt Lake City
Shelton ....Mary Jane	Price...................Charles	1841 10 09	IL, Nauvoo
Shenstrom ....Bengta	Anderson.............Ola	1856 12 06	
Shenstrom ....Bengta	Peterson..............Niels	1850	
Shepard...........Rozina	Francis................Frederic Nelson	1862 11 01	
Shepard...........Rozina	Hyer ....Christian Larsen	1869 02 15	UT, Salt Lake City
Shepard...........Rozina	Knapp.................Albert	1849 01 07	UT, Salt Lake City
Shephard.........Cynthia	Edwards.............Caleb G.	1846 02 05	
Shepherd.........Ann	Miller ....John Hawkins	1841 03 17	ENG
Shepherd.........Jane	Taysum ....Thomas	1857 03 06	
Shepherd.........Jane	Walker................James	1834 05 01	ENG
Shepherd.........Mary	Derrick................Zachariah W.	1836 04 16	ENG
Shepherd.........Mary Park	Horne ....Joseph	1856 11 30	UT, Salt Lake City
Sheriff.............Frances	Kilpack ....John		
Sherry.............Mary Ann	Rose...................Abraham		
Sherry.............Mary Ann	Thaxton..............Williamson	1829 05 23	KY, Allen Co.
Sherry.............Mary Ann	Watton................James	1849 04 16	MO, St. Louis
Shields............Mary	Bevan.................James	1850 05 09	IA, Council Bluffs
Shields............Primrose	Lee ....Thomas	1857 03 10	UT, Salt Lake City
Shields............Sarah	Reid....................Edward	1853 08 23	IRE
Shields............Sarah Jane	Plumb.................Jeremiah	1870 01 24	UT, Salt Lake City
Shields............Sarah Jane	Powell ....John Ammon	1873 01 06	UT, Salt Lake City
Shill.................Ann	Bird....................Andrew		
Shill.................Louisa	Richins ....Charles Wager	1851 01 27	
Shimmin ....Eleanor Jane	Thurber ....Albert D.	1876 12 12	
Shipley............Hannah	Burton................Samuel Jr.	1804 01 11	ENG, Yorkshire
Shirley ....Elizabeth	Wimmer..............Peter	1802	PA
Shomaker.......Jerusha Lois	Billings................George Pierce	1856 04 27	UT, Provo
Shooter...........Mary	Hadley................Richard D.	1826 04 04	ENG

Female	Male	Date	Place
Showell............Ellen Louisa	Farnsworth..........Stephen M.	1856 02 26	UT, Salt Lake City
Shreve.............Anne	Young.................Robert		
Shreve.............Matilda Wickoff	Young.................Ebenezer R. III	1866 05 01	
Shugars..........Mary	Shipley...............John	1844 05 26	IL, Nauvoo
Shugars..........Mary	Thompson..........John Crow	1852 04 06	UT, Salt Lake City
Shuler.............Sarah	Buckwalter..........John	1828 02 21	PA
Shuler.............Sarah	Kimball...............Heber Chase	1846 02 07	IL, Nauvoo
Shultz.............Johanna Marie	Nixon.................James William	1859 10 26	UT, Salt Lake City
Shupe.............Elizabeth Jane	Ricks.................Thomas Edwin	1857 03 27	UT, Salt Lake City
Shupe.............Sarah Ann	Alvord................Gideon W.	1860 09 16	UT, North Ogden
Shurtliff..........Mary Eliza	Taylor...............Pleasant Green	1853 07 05	UT, Salt Lake City
Siddoway.........Isabella	Armstrong..........Francis	1864 12 10	
Sidwell.............Harriet	Taylor.................Joseph	1832 10 12	ENG
Sidwell.............Margaret Ann	Sperry...............William L.	1849 10 04	UT, Salt Lake City
Siebenaller......Anna	Chadwick...........Abraham	1899	
Sigrist.............Elizabeth	Fischer..............Hans Jacob	1862 12 06	UT, Salt Lake City
Simkins..........Rachel	Jones................John Lee	1862 01 07	UT, Cedar City
Simmonds.......Hannah	Phillips...............Edward	1842 08 02	IL, Camp Creek
Simmons........Amanda	Loveland.............Joel Chauncey	1857 12 13	UT, Salt Lake City
Simmons........Catherine S.	Fox....................Isaac W.	1869 05 31	UT, Salt Lake City
Simmons........Celia Leonora	Loveland.............Chester	1854 01 21	UT, Calls Fort
Simmons........Celia Leonora	Way...................William	1863 10 01	
Simmons........Elizabeth	Read.................William Smith	1852 04 20	MO, St. Louis
Simmons........Hannah	Gibb..................John Lye	1878 01 31	UT, Salt Lake City
Simmons........Hannah Maria	Hyde..................Rosel	1862 02 22	UT, Salt Lake City
Simmons........Lucy (Sally)	Groves...............Elisha Hurd	1836 01 16	OH, Kirtland
Simmons........Margaret	Beck..................George	1910 11 23	
Simmons........Margaret	Bennett..............Eli	1868 07 11	UT, Salt Lake City
Simmons........Mary	Edwards.............Philip	1860 02 19	ENG, Sussex
Simmons........Mary Ann	Baker.................John	1832 10 25	ENG
Simmons........Mary Ann	Harris................McGee		UT, Salt Lake City
Simmons........Mary Ann	Smith.................Benjamin F.	1874 01 26	UT, Salt Lake City
Simmons........Sarah	Ballou................Richard		
Simons...........Jane Meredith	Beddo................George	1845 10 21	Wales
Simons...........Jane Meredith	Simons...............Edward	1852 02 14	Ocean
Simonsen.......Bertha Serina	Jensen...............David	1859 08 20	Norway
Simonsen.......Julia	Jensen...............David		
Simpson.........Elizabeth	Bradshaw...........Richard	1844 03 11	
Simpson.........Elizabeth	Haigh.................William	1834 10 10	
Simpson.........Euphemia	Hamilton.............Henry		
Simpson.........Joan	Gould................Robert	1855 01 08	PA, Philadelphia
Sims..............Hannah Maria	Layton...............Christopher	1865 01 07	UT, Salt Lake City
Sims..............Priscilla	Clayson.............Thomas Jr.	1868 02 24	UT, Payson
Sims..............Priscilla	Lossee...............David Alma	1905 02 01	UT
Sinclair...........Ann	Marshall.............Robert	1849	
Sinfield...........Emma Hannah	Smith.................Daniel Miley	1863 05 10	UT, Salt Lake City
Singleton........Mary	Cowell................John	1841 01 21	ENG, Lancashire
Singleton........Mary	Dean..................John		
Singleton........Mary	Gregory..............John	1869 10 04	
Sisam............Harriet	Timms...............William J. A.	1867 04 01	UT, Salt Lake City
Sission...........Celestia Falinda	Bacon................Chauncy	1841 03 17	IL, Nauvoo
Siversen.........Sophia Maria	Hannibal............Peter C.	1845 02 08	
Skeen.............Caroline F.	Butler.................John Lowe	1831 02 03	KY, Simpson Co.
Skeen.............Eliza Jane	Robson..............James P.	1865 05 03	

Female	Male	Date	Place
Skellington.......Elizabeth	Chapman...........Robert		
Skellington.......Elizabeth	McCowan...........Robert	1837 09 11	ENG
Skelton...........Elizabeth	Thompson..........Ralph	1860 12 15	UT, Salt Lake City
Skinner...........Ann	Rawlings...........Eber B.	1850 12 31	ENG
Skinner...........Sarah	Pierce..............George Henry	1859 04 06	
Skousen.........Johanna Marie	Taylor..............Ernest L.	1884 04 11	UT. St. George
Skow.............Maren	Petersen...........Niels	1853 09 10	
Skriggins.........Mary Ellen	Kelley..............Russel Thomas		
Slade.............Amelia Eliza	Bennion...........Alfred	1882 08 28	UT, Salt Lake City
Slade.............Martha	Dickson...........William H.	1872 03 22	UT, Richville
Slade.............Rhoda	Goodrich...........George A.	1879 10 09	UT, Salt Lake City
Slafter...........Asenath	Bent...............Samuel	1845 12	IL, Nauvoo
Slafter...........Asenath	Janes..............Josiah	1832 12 06	CT, Mansfield
Slater............Ann	Bunting...........James	1819 03 15	ENG, Derbyshire
Slater............Emily	Walker.............Daniel C.	1881 11 03	UT, Salt Lake City
Slater............Hannah	Bone..............John	1860 08 28	UT, Salt Lake City
Slater............Mary Ann	Kelly..............George		
Slater............Mary Ann	Read..............John B.	1856 05 20	
Slater............Mary Ann	Stevens...........Alfred	1870 02 28	
Slawson.........Catherine	Ames..............Ira	1857 09 11	UT, Salt Lake City
Slawson.........Catherine	Brown.............Ezekiel	1825 03 20	PA, Erie
Sleater...........Louisa Avalina	Mills..............William Gill	1856 04 25	
Slusser...........Sarah	Nisonger..........Henry	1836 03 03	
Smart............Agnes	Williams...........Benjamin		
Smart............Louisa Fleet	Mendenhall.........Thomas	1863 03 31	ID, Franklin
Smart............Mary Ann Maria	Barker.............John Newman	1849 02 19	ENG
Smith.............Abigail	Abbott..............Stephen J.	1825 12 11	NY, Steuben
Smith.............Abigail	Brown..............James	1846 02 08	IL, Nauvoo
Smith.............Agnes	Burgess...........Hyrum	1872 03 06	
Smith.............Alice	Done...............George	1858 09 09	UT, Cottonwood
Smith.............Alma Janette	Abbott..............Thomas Marsh	1859 04 25	UT, Salt Lake City
Smith.............Alvira Lavona	Hendricks.........William D.	1851	
Smith.............Ann	Atkinson...........Charles John	1814 11 20	ENG, Surrey
Smith.............Ann	Bailey.............Joseph	1818 07 13	
Smith.............Ann	Huish..............Walter Henry	1848 06 12	
Smith.............Ann	Hulse..............Charles Wesley	1845 06 26	ENG
Smith.............Ann	Ingram.............Edward Jr.	1838 08 12	ENG
Smith.............Ann	Tolton.............John	1811 11 09	ENG
Smith.............Annie	Brown..............Norman	1858 12 01	
Smith.............Annie George	Miles..............Edwin Ruthven	1879 01 09	
Smith.............Annie Lorimer	Kennedy...........John	1907 04 04	UT, Salt Lake City
Smith.............Annie Lorimer	Simpson...........William Henry	1877 10 03	UT, Randolph
Smith.............Bathsheba	Merrill.............Clarence	1861 01 03	UT, Salt Lake City
Smith.............Caroline	Charman...........George	1844	ENG, Nottingham
Smith.............Caroline	Cottam.............Thomas	1847 10 09	
Smith.............Caroline	Skeen..............William Dolby	1858 01 28	UT, Lehi
Smith.............Caroline Clara	Callister...........Thomas	1845 08 31	
Smith.............Catherine	Crosland...........Benjamin	1852 06 14	UT, Salt Lake City
Smith.............Catherine	Rawlinson..........Charles	1867 08 14	
Smith.............Catherine	Young..............John	1862 04 12	
Smith.............Charlotte	Wright.............John	1850 10 26	ENG
Smith.............Eliza Jane	Ivie...............James Thomas	1871 01 08	UT, Scipio
Smith.............Eliza Jane	Merril.............Jack		
Smith.............Elizabeth	Bedford...........James	1844 10 20	ENG

Female	Male	Date	Place
Smith ....Elizabeth	Crane ....Elias	1857 06 13	NE, Florence
Smith ....Elizabeth	Day....................Richard	1846 02 23	ENG, Elkstone
Smith ....Elizabeth	Hill ....James Bennett	1839 09 01	ENG, Cheshire
Smith ....Elizabeth	Lovell.................John	1852 03 10	IA, Big Bend
Smith ....Elizabeth	McLean ....Daniel	1847 04 16	Scotland
Smith ....Elizabeth	Squires...............Thomas	1855 11 04	UT, Salt Lake City
Smith ....Elizabeth	Taylor ....Allen	1856 11 26	UT, Salt Lake City
Smith ....Elizabeth	Thurston.............Thomas J.	1855 11 18	UT, Salt Lake City
Smith ....Elizabeth Ann	Whitney ....Newel K.	1822 10 20	OH, Kirtland
Smith ....Elizabeth B.	Smith..................George A.	1868 04 11	
Smith ....Elizabeth B.	Wilson ....Wellington	1836 12 13	OH, Kirtland
Smith ....Ellen	Wood..................John	1850 01 06	ENG, Stockport
Smith ....Elsa Ellis	Hawley ....William John	1821	Canada
Smith ....Emily	Hoyt....................Samuel Pierce	1832 04 17	
Smith ....Emily Jane	Woodruff ....Wilford Jr.	1867 10 12	UT, Salt Lake City
Smith ....Emma	Woodruff ....Wilford	1853 03 13	UT, Salt Lake City
Smith ....Esther	Fuller ....Amos B.	1832 03 08	
Smith ....Fanny	Spilsbury ....George	1842 09 05	ENG, Woster
Smith ....Francis	Harris ....Moses	1824 01 01	IN, Cork Co.
Smith ....Hannah	Arrowsmith ....Josiah Thomas	1854 11 15	UT, Salt Lake City
Smith ....Hannah	Tew ....Thomas	1832 01 30	ENG
Smith ....Hannah E.	London ....John	1863 10 08	UT, Coalville
Smith ....Harriet	Goff ....Thomas	1856 05 11	ENG
Smith ....Jane	Coleman..............George	1857 01 28	UT, Lehi
Smith ....Jane	Tidwell................John	1828 12 18	IN, Marysville
Smith ....Jane Corner	Fawcett ....William	1837 08 03	
Smith ....Jane Louisa	Crawford ....Samuel Sinclair	1862 10 03	UT, Salt Lake City
Smith ....Jane Louisa	Turpin.................Jesse	1846 04 16	IL, Nauvoo
Smith ....Jane Louisa	Van....................John Alfred	1855 01 13	UT, Salt Lake City
Smith ....Lois	Winegar...............Stephen S.	1850 08 01	UT, Salt Lake City
Smith ....Lucy Maria	Cox....................Daniel William	1847 06 17	IL, Green Co.
Smith ....Lucy Maria	Dawson ....William	1863 01 20	UT, Lehi
Smith ....Marion	Sagers................William H. H.	1858 06 05	UT, Provo
Smith ....Marion	Steele.................James Inman	1874 04 13	
Smith ....Martha	Bennett...............Hyrum Bell	1845 08 17	IA, Lee Co.
Smith ....Martha Ann	Harris ....William Jasper	1857 04 24	UT, Provo
Smith ....Martha Janet	Roylance ....William J.	1860 10 01	
Smith ....Mary	McCulloch ....Henry	1857 02 27	Scotland
Smith ....Mary	McEwen ....Matthew	1833 05 13	Scotland
Smith ....Mary	Waters................Reuben	1852	MO, St. Louis
Smith ....Mary Ann	Dixon.................Henry A.	1869 04 13	UT, Salt Lake City
Smith ....Mary Ann	McNeil ....John Corbet	1868 09 12	UT, Salt Lake City
Smith ....Mary Elizabeth	Rooker ....John Bunyon	1866 03 07	UT, Heber
Smith ....Mary Franks	Taylor ....George	1836 09 05	ENG
Smith ....Mary Jane	Merrill ....Philemon C.	1851 04 05	UT, Salt Lake City
Smith ....Olive Amanda	Cook...................Milton		
Smith ....Olive Amanda	Fullmer ....John S.	1846 01 21	IL, Nauvoo
Smith ....Peninah	Frost...................McCaslin	1809 11 28	NC
Smith ....Philomela	Lake ....James Jr.	1823 09 03	
Smith ....Philomela	Smith..................Ira	1812 02 02	Canada
Smith ....Rachel	Ross ....Thomas	1835 09 30	
Smith ....Rachel Leah	Radford ....John Whitlock	1846 04 06	
Smith ....Rachel Leah	Ross ....Andrew Jackson	1837 09 21	
Smith ....Rebecca	Standring...........Edwin	1859 06 03	

Female	Male	Date	Place
Smith ....Rebecca	White.................Henry Harvey	1808 10 09	VT, Chester
Smith ....Sarah	Griffin ....Charles E.	1854 01 16	UT, Salt Lake City
Smith ....Sarah	Walker................Joseph	1872	
Smith ....Sarah Ann	Busenbark..........Elias M.	1876 10 15	
Smith ....Sarah Ann	Fisher................Thomas F.	1857 04 10	UT, Salt Lake City
Smith ....Sarah Elizabeth	Ross.................James Darling	1857 09 08	ENG, London
Smith ....Sarah Isabel	Gardner.............Fredrick	1853	
Smith ....Sarah Jane	Hastings ....William	1859 04 16	MA, Boston
Smith ....Sarah Marinda	Burnham ....George Franklin	1862 11 07	UT, Richmond
Smith ....Sarah Marinda	Mott....................Stephen	1861 04 07	UT, Salt Lake City
Smith ....Sobrina	Lamb..................Lisbon	1866 02 03	UT, Salt Lake City
Smith ....Susanna	Ewing.................Samuel	1853 07 16	
Smith ....Susanna	Fotheringham......John	1862 06 24	
Smith ....Susanna	Johnson ....Theodore	1849 04 30	
Smith ....Susanna	Roper ....John W.	1831 10 18	ENG, March
Smithies...........Mary	Kimball ....Heber Chase	1857 01 25	UT, Salt Lake City
Smithies...........Sarah Ellen	Scott...................Ephraim	1867 11 09	
Smithson ....Amelia Caroline	Miller ....Hyrum Smith	1870 05 08	UT
Smithson ....Mary Ann B.	Harmon ....James	1828	SC, Pendleton
Smoot.............Nancy Beal	Freeman.............John	1826 02 09	KY, Calloway Co.
Smuin ....Eliza	Clark...................Michael	1861 10 28	UT, Salt Lake City
Smuin ....Harriet	Clark...................Michael	1859 09 24	UT, Salt Lake City
Smuin ....Martha Ann	McFarlane ....James	1867 10 05	UT, Salt Lake City
Smuin ....Rachel	Dittmore ....Henry	1864 03 01	UT, Salt Lake City
Snadon ....Mary	Hunter ....James William	1813 05 13	Scotland
Snarr................Mary Ann	Arnold.................John	1869 01 11	UT, Salt Lake City
Snedden ....Jennet	Duncan...............James	1851	PA
Sneddon..........Agnes	Adamson.............Thomas C.	1869 11 15	UT, Salt Lake City
Sneddon..........Agnes	Allen...................Peter	1857	MO, St. Louis
Sneddon..........Margaret	Bowman.............William	1820 10 28	Scotland
Snider ....Sally Ann	Brinkerhoff..........James	1836 01 01	NY, Cayuga
Snider ....Julia Ann	Leonard..............George Bradford	1857 03 15	
Snively............Hannahette	Pratt ....Parley P.	1844 11 02	IL, Nauvoo
Snively............Suzanna	Young.................Brigham	1844 11 02	IL, Nauvoo
Snow ....Abigail Dow	Kesler.................Frederick	1857 04 21	UT, Salt Lake City
Snow ....Abigail Harriet	Rosenbaum.........Morris D.		
Snow ....Eliza Roxey	Smith.................Joseph Jr.	1842 06 29	IL, Nauvoo
Snow ....Eliza Roxey	Young.................Brigham	1849	
Snow ....Elizabeth C.	Crawford ....John	1856 02 02	UT, Manti
Snow ....Ellen	Smith.................Henry Jr.		
Snow ....Julia Marie	Cox....................Jacob	1871 01 23	
Snow ....Julia Marie	Cox....................Joseph Daniel	1865 12 31	
Snow ....Julia Marie	Jones ....Frederick W.	1887 09 02	
Snow ....Julia Marie	Sargent ....William Pinkney	1877 04 08	
Snow ....Martha Jane	Edmiston ....John Jr.	1842	IL, Hancock
Snow ....Rosetta Adaline	Loveland ....Chester	1866 11 17	UT, Salt Lake City
Snow ....Sarah Jane	Kinsman.............Marshall C.	1853 12 05	UT, Provo
Snow ....Sarah Jane	Young.................Joseph	1867 04 06	UT, Salt Lake City
Snow ....Sarah Lucina	Thurston.............George W.	1858 03 28	
Snow ....Sariah Hannah	Lott....................Peter Lyman	1862 12 23	UT, Salt Lake City
Snyder ....Amy	Brown.................John	1854 02 22	
Snyder ....Eliza	Johnson ....William Henry	1858 04 16	UT, Springville
Snyder ....Eliza	Roundy...............Jared Curtis	1856 05 09	UT, Salt Lake City
Snyder ....Eliza Ann	Haight.................Isaac C.	1836 12 31	NY, Cayuga Co.

Female	Male	Date	Place
Snyder ....Hannah Matilda	Powell ....John Ammon	1863 12 13	UT, Kamas
Snyder ....Harriet	Johnson ....Joseph Ellis	1840 10 01	IL, Nauvoo
Snyder ....Jane	Richards.............Franklin D.	1842 12 18	
Snyder ....Mary Elizabeth	Wood..................Daniel	1824 03 09	Canada
Snyder ....Permelia	Hatch.................Meltiar	1845 01 01	
Socwell ....Mary	Page...................Daniel	1822 04 18	NJ, Newport
Soderstrom ......Maria Christiana	Bohman..............John W.	1857 02 25	
Sorensen ....Anna Margrethe	Johansen ....Lars	1816 08 25	Denmark
Sorensen ....Anna Marie	Hjorring ....Nicolai	1836 06 14	Denmark
Sorensen ....Anna Marie	Lund ....Paul Didrick S.	1845 08 12	Denmark
Sorensen ....Annie Christina	Pederson............Simon	1842 12 16	Norway
Sorensen ....Caroline	Thomsen ....Hans Adolph	1855 11 13	Denmark
Sorensen ....Caroline E.	Peterson.............Samuel	1856 08 24	UT, Salt Lake City
Sorensen ....Christiana	Coons.................Sidney	1877 05 20	
Sorensen ....Christiana	Rasmussen ....Lars	1868 03 28	UT, Salt Lake City
Sorensen ....Ellen	Christensen........Jeppe	1858	UT, Salt Lake City
Sorensen ....Elsie	Christensen........Jeppe	1858 08 15	UT, Salt Lake City
Sorensen ....Hedvig Lucie E.	Nybolle ....Rasmus	1835	
Sorensen ....Hedvig Lucie E.	Petersen............Hans	1832	Denmark
Sorensen ....Ingeborg	Larsen ....Jens	1829 11 11	Denmark
Sorensen ....Ingeborg	Olsen.................Rasmus	1836 08 04	Denmark
Sorensen ....Jensine C.	Jensen ....Niels	1861 11 16	UT, Salt Lake City
Sorensen ....Jensine C.	Larsen ....Soren C.	1855 09 14	Denmark
Sorensen ....Jensine Helene	Christensen........Lays	1847 12 07	
Sorensen ....Jensine Kirstine	Pedersen............Christian	1857 06 26	Denmark
Sorensen ....Johanna	Ottesen ....Jens	1860 11 18	
Sorensen ....Juliane	Pedersen............Jorgen Christian	1855 07 03	UT, Salt Lake City
Sorensen ....Juliane	Smith..................Rasmus		Denmark
Sorensen ....Julianna Marie	Larsen ....Bent Rolfson	1873 06 30	UT, Salt Lake City
Sorensen ....Karen	Christensen........Anders	1831	Denmark
Sorensen ....Karen	Jacobsen............David	1828 11 14	Denmark
Sorensen ....Karen	Jensen ....Peder	1850 04 18	Denmark
Sorensen ....Karen	Willardson ....Christian	1851 04 02	Denmark
Sorensen ....Karen Marie	Larsen ....Christian Greis	1857 04 01	Denmark
Sorensen ....Karen Marie	Peay...................George Thomas	1867 03 02	UT, Salt Lake City
Sorensen ....Karen Sophie	Jensen ....Jens		
Sorensen ....Maren	Mouritsen ....Lars	1848 09 12	Denmark
Sorensen ....Marie	Petersen............Peder	1850 10 22	Denmark
Sorensen ....Mary Bodil	Snowball ....John	1865 12 05	UT, Salt Lake City
Sorensen ....Mette J. P.	Jensen ....James	1865 09 21	UT, Salt Lake City
Sorenson ....Dortha Christina	Nelson................Thomas B.		
Sorenson ....Sophie M. H.	Mackelprang ....Peter Mathiasen	1840 12 23	Denmark
South ....Sabrin	Rammell..............Charles H.	1846 12 20	ENG
Southwick ....Teresa	Marriott...............John	1855 11 05	UT, Marriott
Southworth ......Sarah Zurviah	Burbank..............Daniel M.	1864 07 18	UT, Salt Lake City
Spafford...........Martha Jane	Fuller ....Sanford	1853 03 10	
Sparks ....Mary Jane	Sanders..............Moses Martin	1847 03 21	
Sparks ....Mary Jane	Sanderson..........James	1824 07 07	MA
Spaulding ....Margaret	Buttars................David	1848 12 14	Scotland
Speirs ....Lillias Thomson	Smith..................James B.	1853 10 25	UT, Tooele
Spencely.........Charlotte	Woodhead..........William	1829 09 17	ENG
Spencer ....Aurelia Read	Rogers ....Thomas E.	1851 03 27	
Spencer ....Catherine Curtis	Young.................Brigham Jr.	1855 11 15	UT, Salt Lake City
Spencer ....Hannah	Tingey ....Henry	1870 05 09	UT, Salt Lake City

Female	Male	Date	Place
Spencer ....Henrietta	Barker ....William	1871 07	
Spencer ....Henrietta	Hunter ....Edward	1856 05 20	UT, Salt Lake City
Spencer ....Julia J.	Snow ....Erastus	1856 04 11	UT, Salt Lake City
Spencer ....Martha	Cahoon ....Daniel Stiles	1846 01 16	
Spencer ....Mary	Flint ....John	1838 12 05	ENG
Spencer ....Sarah	Stone................Amos Pease	1865	
Spencer ....Sybil	Stevens ....Roswell		NY, Stephentown
Spender...........Eleanor Ellen	Sumsion ....Daniel	1837 10 21	ENG
Spendlove ....Emma	Hinton.................John Nocks	1861 05 19	Ocean
Sperry ....Charlotte Ellen	Davenport ....Joseph C.	1871 02 05	
Spiller ....Hannah R.	Perris...................Thomas	1835	ENG
Spiller ....Hannah R.	Stewart...............Matthew D.	1855 08 16	
Spooner...........Sarah Jane	Johnson ....Benjamin F.	1857 04 05	UT, Salt Lake City
Spori ....Anna Clara	Stucki ....John U.		
Spouncer ....Christiana	Carlile.................Robert		ENG
Sprague...........Abigail	Bradford ....Jehial Lee	1830 08 21	
Sprague...........Abigail	Gardner...............Archibald	1849 04 19	
Sprague...........Eliza Ann	Tracy ....Eli Alexander	1854 12 25	UT, Salt Lake City
Sprague...........Martha	Merrill ....Austin Shepherd		
Spriggs ....Mary Ann	Leaver ....Samuel Hartlett	1868 09 05	UT, Salt Lake City
Sproul ....Elizabeth	Murphy ....Jesse Easters		
Sproul ....Isabella	Stephenson.........Harris S.	1862 10	UT, Salt Lake City
Sproul ....Robina	Murphy...............Jesse Easters	1862 02 15	
Squire ....Janet	Don ....William		
Squire ....Janet	Watson................Thomas	1841 06 18	Scotland
Squire ....Rebecca	Noall...................Simon	1854 03 18	
Squires ....Elizabeth	Robison...............William H.	1823 01 23	
Squires ....Harriet Amelia	Snow ....Lorenzo	1846 01 17	IL, Nauvoo
Stacy ....Sally	Murdock ....Joseph	1818 04 15	NY, Hamilton
Staff................Willoughby	Green ....William	1822 07 15	ENG, Norwich
Staff................Willoughby	Lees ....Samuel	1869 10 12	UT, Salt Lake City
Stafford...........Mary	Green ....John	1857 12 25	UT, Provo
Stafford...........Mary	Partington............Richard	1847 07 18	ENG, Oldham
Staheli ....Elizabeth	Walker.................Francis C.	1870 04 18	UT, St. George
Staker ....Elizabeth	Draper.................William	1827 06 11	Canada
Staker ....Mary Ann	Farnsworth ....Alonzo L.	1866 09 08	UT, Salt Lake City
Staley ....Mary	Warren ....Elihue	1862 04 05	UT, Salt Lake City
Staley (widow) .	Lewis..................John Moss		
Standing ....Mary	Standing.............James	1847 06 27	MO, St. Louis
Standley	Osborn ....Thomas J.	1854	UT
Standley ....Cyrene	Merrill ....Marriner Wood		UT, Salt Lake City
Standley ....Ellen	Osborn ....Thomas J.	1851 09 14	IA, Gardon Grove
Standley ....Lydia	Burnham ....Wallace K.	1865 04 11	UT, Salt Lake City
Standley ....Sarah Jane	Barnes................Daniel Hays	1842 05 17	MO, Randolph
Standley ....Sarah Jane	Dopp ....Peter	1850 07 02	IA, Kanesville
Standley ....Sarah Jane	Kent....................Samuel	1828 02 05	CT, Hartford
Stanfield ....Elizabeth	Lang ....John	1867 10 10	UT, Salt Lake City
Stanfield ....Emily Hill	Jenkins...............Henry Laird	1819 05 01	UT, Goshen
Stanford...........Esther E.	Comish...............John	1862 11 22	UT, Salt Lake City
Stanger...........Ann	Hogge ....Charles	1852 06 26	ENG, Yorkshire
Stanley ....Ann	Harris ....John	1846 01 29	
Stannard.........Sarah	Crane ....John L.	1849 11 16	
Stanton ....Lucy Celesta	Bassett ....Oliver H.		
Staples ....Joyce	Jackson...............Thomas	1836 08 21	ENG, Westerham

Female	Male	Date	Place
Stapley ....Sarah Ann	Jackson..............James Jr.	1863	
Staplforte ....Celia	Woodland............John	1818 06 18	KY, Barren Co.
Starbuck ....Abigail	Coffin..................William B.	1833 09 21	IN
Stark ....Gustavia Sophia	Chandler ....Frank	1866 06 29	UT, Coalville
Stark ....Gustavia Sophia	Olson.................Clas Erick		
Starkey ....Louisa	Maycock.............Thomas	1859 04 11	
Starkey ....Sarah Ann	Duerden ....Richard	1866 02 17	ENG
Starley ....Jane	Martin ....Anthony	1859 02 04	UT, Fillmore
Starr...............Eunice Ann	Bird....................Jasper Thomas		UT, Salt Lake City
Statham ....Martha	Kinnersley ....Henry	1836 05 17	
Stead ....Ann	Firth...................William	1818 08 08	ENG
Stead ....Mary	Evans ....John	1817 12 11	ENG
Stead ....Mary	Griffith ....David	1802 03 28	
Steadwell........Sarah (Sally)	Brown.................James	1845 01 10	IL, Nauvoo
Steadwell........Sarah (Sally)	Kelly		
Steadwell........Sarah (Sally)	LeBaron ....Alonzo		
Steadwell........Sarah (Sally)	Lewis ....Henry		
Steadwell........Sarah (Sally)	Reed ....Henry		
Steadwell........Sarah (Sally)	Sprague ....Ithamer	1848	Trail
Steadwell........Sarah (Sally)	Wood..................Samuel	1832 07 15	OH, Norwalk
Stearns ....Mary Ann	Winters...............Oscar	1852 08 16	WY, Deer Creek
Steck ....Anna Louise	Ludvigson............Erick	1862 07 19	UT, Salt Lake City
Steed ....Ann	Turner ....Henry		
Steed ....Mary Ann	Hess...................John W.	1857 03 27	UT, Salt Lake City
Steele ....Agnes	Baker..................Amenzo White	1864 11 19	
Steele ....Agnes	Hill ....John	1859 11 26	
Steele ....Agnes	Park...................Hamilton Gray	1843 04	Scotland
Steele ....America Ann	Beirdneau............Nehemiah	1846 04 30	IA
Steele ....Anne	Murdoch..............John Murray	1848 02 15	Scotland
Steele ....Betsy	Alsop ....Thomas Hill		IA
Steele ....Harriet Mollet	Watkins ....John	1858	
Steele ....Jane	Leatham ....Robert U.	1847 12 25	Scotland
Steele ....Lovina Ann	Barrus ....Benjamin F.	1861	
Steele ....Mary Campbell	Fish ....Joseph	1859 03 22	
Steele ....Mary Campbell	LeFever..............Thomas	1856	
Steers ....Sarah Frances	Broadbent ....Francis G.	1860 12 24	UT, Salt Lake City
Stenhouse ....Clara Fedarata	Agramonte ....Clarence H. M.	1879 06	UT, Richfield
Stenhouse ....Clara Fedarata	Young.................Joseph Angell	1867 03 04	UT, Salt Lake City
Stenhouse ....Emelia Eliza	Godbe ....Antoine Peter	1873 06 07	UT, Salt Lake City
Stenhouse ....Ida Lulu	Richards.............Richard S.	1882	
Stenhouse ....Margaret	Grier ....John	1859 01 13	Scotland
Stenhouse ....Margaret	Tennant..............Charles	1849	Scotland
Stentz ....Christiana	Alleman ....John	1832 12 11	PA, Middletown
Stephansen .....Maren	Rasmussen.........Hans	1844 06 07	Denmark
Stephens ....Tamer	Lemmon ....Washington	1826 08 31	IN, Croydon
Stephenson .....Catherine	Corless ....Edward	1829 08 21	ENG
Stephenson .....Eliza Ann	Case...................George W.		
Stephenson .....Eliza Ann	Winn ....John	1862 10 04	UT, Salt Lake City
Stephenson .....Eliza Jane	Waddoups...........William		
Stephenson .....Mettie Johanna	Stevens ....Edward		
Sterling ....Jessie Belle	Pack...................John	1864 01 16	
Stettler ....Magdalena	Stucki ....Samuel	1846 07 14	Switzerland
Stevens ....Christina	Parrott ....William Edward	1878	
Stevens ....Christina	Scott..................Robert Griffin	1872 08 05	UT, Salt Lake City

Female	Male	Date	Place
Stevens ....Cynthia	Perry ....Steven		
Stevens ....Cynthia	Yeaman..............Michael	1831 12 07	
Stevens ....Eleanor	Neslen................Robert Francis	1859 03 15	Scotland
Stevens ....Eleanor	Trewella ....John	1853 12 25	
Stevens ....Elizabeth	Stevenson ....Joseph	1812 06 28	
Stevens ....Polly	Radford ....John Whitlock	1855	
Stevens ....Sarah	Sewell ....Joseph	1814 01 10	ENG, Norfolk
Stevens ....Sarah	Wheeler..............Simon	1804 03 15	ME, Greene
Stevenson ....Catherine	Gibby..................William D.	1857 05 26	UT, Salt Lake City
Stevenson ......Elizabeth	Bailey ....Job T.	1845 06 24	IA, Charleston
Stevenson ......Elizabeth	Norwood..............Richard Smith	1850 10 13	UT, Salt Lake City
Stevenson ....Emma Jane	Williams..............George	1862 12 28	
Stevenson ....Esther	Grange ....Samuel	1864 02 11	UT, Salt Lake City
Stevenson ....Mary	Clark...................Ezra Thompson	1845 05 18	IA, Lee Co.
Stevenson ......Sarah Ann	Fullmer ....John S.	1856	UT, Salt Lake City
Stewart ....Adah	Phippen...............Isaac	1818 10 15	OH, Springfield
Stewart ....Almeda	McClellan ....Samuel Wilburn	1856 12 28	UT, Payson
Stewart ....Annie T.	Heggie.................Andrew W.	1865 02 03	UT, Salt Lake City
Stewart ....Cynthia	McClellan ....James	1826 01 18	
Stewart ....Cynthia Utley	Hill.....................George W.	1845 09 18	
Stewart ....Eliza Jane	Ensign ....Horace D.	1850 01	UT, Ogden
Stewart ....Elizabeth	Crane ....James	1864 09 20	UT, Salt Lake City
Stewart ....Elizabeth	Geddes ....William	1855 06 03	UT, Salt Lake City
Stewart ....Elizabeth	Marriott...............John	1854 02 26	UT, Salt Lake City
Stewart ....Jane Ann	Hatch..................Ira Stearns	1857 03 20	UT, Salt Lake City
Stewart ....Lavina	Richardson..........Shadrach	1839	
Stewart ....Margaret	Perry ....Stephen C.		
Stewart ....Martha	Geddes ....William	1856 07 10	UT, Plain City
Stewart ....Mary Lucinda	Burnham ....Luther C.	1875	
Stewart ....Mary Priscilla	Burriston..............John	1858 11 09	
Stewart ....Mary Priscilla	Hawley ....Asa Smith	1866 04 11	
Stewart ....Matilda	Allred..................Isaac	1852 11 05	
Stewart ....Matilda	Park....................John Miller	1824 10 28	
Stewart ....Ruthinda Emma	Yearsley ....Nathan	1865 02 04	UT, Salt Lake City
Stewart ....Sarah Ellen	Davis ....Elisha H.	1871 01 30	UT, Salt Lake City
Stiff ....Hannah	Cox.....................John Jr.	1858 08 22	ENG, Hampshire
Stiles................Thirza	Cahoon ....Reynolds	1810 12 11	NY, Herkimer
Stillman............Frances Maria	Neff ....Franklin	1855 01 01	UT, Salt Lake City
Stillman............Frances Maria	Russell ....Isaac Nelson	1850	UT, Salt Lake City
Stillman............Frances Maria	Russell ....Samuel L.	1846 01 20	IL, Nauvoo
Stilson..............Cornelia Ann	McKnight ....James	1854 03 17	UT, Salt Lake City
Stock ....Elizabeth	Rich....................Hyrum Smith	1867 06 29	UT, Salt Lake City
Stock ....Maria J.	Allred..................Medwin Newton	1875 05 31	UT, Salt Lake City
Stock ....Maria J.	Merkley ....Christopher A.	1917 11 28	
Stockall............Susanna	Summers.............Thomas	1826 04 09	
Stockdale.........Caroline	Thomas ....Richard K.	1865 02 22	UT, Logan
Stockdale.........Mary Ann	Carter ....Edwin J.	1830	ENG, Devonshire
Stockdale.........Mary Ann	Martin.................James	1846	
Stockwell ....Sylvia Elmina	Sanford ....Cyrus	1836 10 05	
Stockwell ....Vilate	Burgess..............William	1813 05 01	NH, Chesterfield
Stoddard.........Elsie Permelia	Robinson.............Isaac Payson	1863 05 29	UT, Salt Lake City
Stoddard.........Lydia	Wadsworth ....Joseph W.	1858 03 05	UT, Salt Lake City
Stoddard.........Mary Ann	Dickson ....Billa	1837 04 10	
Stoddart..........Hannah	Allred..................Thomas Butler	1885	

Female	Male	Date	Place
Stoddart..........Hannah	Barney................William Street	1864	
Stoker.............Catherine	Hulet..................Sylvanus Cyrus	1850 05 19	IA, Mt. Pisgah
Stoker.............Christina	McDaniel.............John	1835 02 08	OH
Stoker.............Elizabeth	Welker................James	1822 07 02	OH, Jackson Co.
Stoker.............Susan Ann	Riley...................Thomas Katen	1863 04 06	
Stoker.............Zebiah Jane	Tolman................Judson	1869 04 05	UT, Salt Lake City
Stoker.............Zebiah Mariba	Ford...................William M.	1852 11	IA, Trader's Point
Stokes............Emma	Webb..................William	1831 04	ENG
Stokes............Tamar	McGuire.............John William	1867 09 14	UT, Salt Lake City
Stone.............Eliza	Hutchings...........William Burch	1857 03 27	
Stone.............Emily Amelia	Tuttle.................Newton	1855 04 07	
Stone.............Hetta Amanda	Winters..............Alonzo	1852 05 16	IA, Council Bluffs
Stone.............Mary	Duke..................Jonathan O.	1828 12 30	ENG, Derby
Stone.............Mary Eliza	Hutchens...........William B.	1854 11 02	UT, Salt Lake City
Stone.............Merab	Richardson..........Thomas	1864	UT, Salt Lake City
Stone.............Susannah	Lloyd.................Thomas	1856 11 06	
Storer.............Mary Ann	Reeves...............William	1851	
Storer.............Mary Ann	Walton...............Edward	1840 03 12	ENG
Storr...............Elizabeth Maria	Reynolds............William G.	1872 01 06	UT, Heber
Stott...............Emma	Bullock..............Isaac	1856 12 14	
Stott...............Hannah Lees	Fisher................James	1844 11 17	ENG
Stout..............Lydia M. F.	Bliss..................Norman Ingles	1871 04 30	
Stout..............Lydia M. F.	Griffin................Charles E.	1866 09 22	
Stout..............Lydia M. F.	Jennings.............Cyrus M.	1884	
Stout..............Martha Ann	Pitts..................Thomas	1866 07 28	UT, St. George
Stowe.............Elizabeth	Higgs.................Thomas	1844 05 21	NY, Utica
Strait..............Elizabeth	Free...................Absalom P.	1823 08 02	
Strait..............Sarah	Hill....................Richard	1816 03 31	OH, Washington
Stratford..........Eliza Ann	Smith.................John P.	1878 10 10	UT, Salt Lake City
Stratford..........Julia	Budge.................William	1856 11 24	ENG, Baxex
Stratford..........Lucetta	Penrose..............Charles W.	1855 01 21	ENG, Essex
Straw..............Emma Ruth	McLing................James Wilford	1865 04 19	UT, Coalville
Straw..............Prudence	Cherrington.........Joseph	1877 02 01	UT, Springville
Street.............Mary	Bateman.............Thomas	1829 08 18	ENG
Street.............Mary	Wight.................Lewis William	1853 08	UT, Salt Lake City
Streeter...........Lucina	Snow..................Levi	1801 11 26	
Stretton...........Mary	Blood.................William	1836 02 16	ENG
Stretton...........Mary	Wooley...............Henry	1845 03 12	
Strickland.........Lucinda Gibson	Pace..................James	1831 03 21	TN
Stringfellow......Lucy	Day...................James Henry	1874 11	UT, Draper
Stringfellow......Margaret	Thornley.............John	1853	ENG
Stringham........Elemeda	Harmon..............Appleton M.	1846 01 01	IL, Nauvoo
Strobridge........Sophronia	Cook..................Henry F.	1837 04 09	
Stromberg........Kajsa Lisa	Felt...................John Johnson	1863 09 12	UT, Salt Lake City
Stromberg........Maria Kristina	Felt...................John Johnson		
Strong.............Elizabeth	Lee...................Ezekiel	1822 01 31	
Strong.............Elizabeth Ann	Boardman...........Robert Jr.	1868 06 12	UT, Salt Lake City
Strong.............Olive	Tenney...............Nathan Cram	1841 03 18	IL
Strong.............Priscilla	Porter................Chauncey W.	1848 02 10	NE
Strubell...........Caroline	Poulter...............William	1844 03 10	ENG
Stuart.............Marion	Baxter................Robert Wright	1868 10 11	UT, Wellsville
Stuart.............Mary Elizabeth	Cooper..............Isaac	1857 03 18	
Stuart.............Sarah	Howell...............Thomas C. D.	1835 07 05	TN, Gibson Co.
Stuart.............Sarah	Smith.................Leonard I.	1868 11 24	UT, Salt Lake City

Female	Male	Date	Place
Stucki............Rosena	Blickenstorfer ......Gottleib	1873 08 04	UT, Salt Lake City
Stucki............Rosena	Hafen ....John George	1885 02 28	
Stucki............Rosetta	Atkin ....William	1879 10 02	UT, St. George
Stucki............Rosetta	Hunt ....Jefferson	1900 12 21	UT, St. George
Sturdevant ......Sarah	Leavitt ....Jeremiah	1817 03 06	
Sturton............Eliza	Smedley ....Samuel	1863 10 26	ENG
Sudbury ....Mary	Humphreys..........Thomas	1831 12 26	ENG, Mansfield
Suddery ....Ruth	Blair....................Isaac	1850 04 20	ENG, Middlesex
Sufling ....Mary	Riches ....John	1839	
Summers ....Emma	Bennett...............David Van Horn	1864	UT, Manti
Summers ....Emma	Call....................Anson	1857 02 27	UT, Salt Lake City
Summers ....Emma	Jeffs ....William W.	1851 08 25	ENG
Sumner...........Perselia	Hunt ....Wilson	1840 12 27	KY, Belton
Sumner...........Susannah	Fackrell ....David B.	1855 11 10	UT, Bountiful
Sutherland ......Eliza	Dallin ....William	1862 10 18	
Sutherland ......Isabella	McPherson..........Hugh	1829 12 11	
Sutherland ......Isabella	Muirbrook ....Alexander	1840 07 13	
Sutherland ......Isabella	Shields ....John	1860 12 08	
Sutherland ....Mary Ann	Gleason...............John S.	1864 07 16	UT, Salt Lake City
Sutter..............Maria	Hochstrasser.......Rudolf	1859 09 10	Ocean
Sutton ....Alice	Naylor.................Thomas	1857 09 04	UT, Salt Lake City
Svendsen ....Karen Kirstine	Larsen ....Niels Peter	1855 04 12	Denmark
Svenson ....Anna M.	Hessel ....Peter	1840 12 26	
Svensson.........Anna Maria	Lewis..................James Stapleton		
Svensson.........Caroline W.	Anderson............Gustave	1868 09 19	UT, Salt Lake City
Svensson.........Caroline W.	Swenson ....Johannes	1859 05 01	
Swain..............Emily Ellen	Squires ....John P.	1868 03 21	UT, Salt Lake City
Swain..............Rebecca	Kimball ....Heber Chase		
Swain..............Rebecca	Williams..............Frederick G.	1815	
Swallow ....Maria A.	Walker................Edmund	1842 07 14	ENG
Swan ....Violet	Urie ....James	1868 06 02	
Sward ....Inger	Johnson ....John	1870 06 13	UT, Salt Lake City
Sweat ....Persis Moore	McKee................Thomas	1841 01 14	IL, Bloomfield
Sweet ....Sarah	Warren ....Zenos C.	1824	
Sweet ....Sarah	Wood.................Daniel	1837 04 02	MI, Oakland Co.
Swenson..........Johanna	Eliason ....Andrew	1867 11 16	UT, Salt Lake City
Swenson..........Louisa	Johnson ....John	1858 07 27	Sweden
Swift................Jane Elizabeth	Van Tassell ....James D.	1867 12 14	UT, Salt Lake City
Swindlehurst....Sophia	Dean ....Heber C.	1879 04 02	UT, St. George
Syer ....Mary Ann	Hill ....William		
Syer ....Mary Ann	Smith.................William	1820 01 19	ENG
Syer ....Mary Ann	White.................William	1837 04 17	ENG
Syer ....Mary Ann	Wright................John P.		
Sykes..............Eleanor	Ekins ....George	1851 02 04	ENG, Brampton
Sylvester.........Mary Elizabeth	Birch.................Joseph	1861 11 17	UT, Salt Lake City
Symonds ....Mary	Alley ....George	1822 09 15	MA
Syverson ....Paulina	Johnson ....Olaus	1867 01 13	UT, Salt Lake City

T

Female	Male	Date	Place
Taaffe ....Rachel Burke	McDonald............John Kilpatrick	1823 04	IRE
Taberer...........Sarah Ann	Martin.................Ezra Francis	1863 06 20	
Taberer...........Sarah Ann	Owen (Wragg).....Oswald	1859 12 21	ENG, Stafford

Female		Male		Date	Place
Taft	Karen Marie	Johnson	John P. R.	1845	Denmark
Taggart	Eliza Ann	Goodrich	George A.	1862 11 10	
Taggart	Harriet Maria	Goodrich	George A.	1866 05 05	UT, Salt Lake City
Talbott	Margaret	Jones	Elisha	1831 09 03	OH, Smithfield
Tally	Mary	Holden	Joshua	1819 09 23	TN
Tanner	Helen Alcy	Maxfield	Elijah Hiett	1856 08 24	UT, So. Cotton.
Tanner	Maria Louisa	Lyman	Amasa Mason	1835 06 10	OH, Kirtland
Tanner	Thankful Loretta	Harmon	Norton	1843 01 04	
Tantam	Elizabeth	Bull	Daniel Berry	1840 10 25	ENG, Warwick
Tappen	Clarissa	Van Wagoner	John H.	1840	
Tarrant	Charlotte	Banford	Samuel	1845 06 12	ENG, Warwick
Tarrant	Charlotte	Etherington	Thomas	1869	
Tarrant	Charlotte	Pingree	Job	1834 09 08	ENG
Tarrant	Charlotte	Swan	Ephraim	1857	
Tattersall	Alice	Robb	Thomas	1871 02 27	UT, Salt Lake City
Tatton	Frances Ann	Bench	William	1862 12 25	UT, Salt Lake City
Tavener	Elizabeth	Papworth	James	1847 12 25	ENG, Chesterton
Taylor	Agnes	Gange	Thomas E. Jr.	1873 09 20	UT, Salt Lake City
Taylor	Agnes	Taylor	James	1805 12 23	ENG
Taylor	Ann	Rowley	Samuel	1865 04 23	UT, Parowan
Taylor	Annie	Dee	Thomas D.	1871 04 10	UT, Salt Lake City
Taylor	Charlotta W.	Marcroft	John	1834	ENG
Taylor	Clarissa Jane	Taylor	Teancum	1860 08 15	UT, Salt Lake City
Taylor	Eliza	Gallian	Jesse	1854 04 02	MO, St. Louis
Taylor	Eliza	Howell	William John	1859 10 03	UT, Salt Lake City
Taylor	Eliza	Phillips	William	1887	UT, Salt Lake City
Taylor	Eliza	Steers	William	1833	NY
Taylor	Elizabeth	Arrowsmith	William	1840	
Taylor	Elizabeth	Boyce	George	1847 07 16	Trail
Taylor	Elizabeth	Packer	Nathan W.	1829 03 31	OH, Perry
Taylor	Elizabeth	Stoddard	Oscar O.	1860 10 02	UT, Salt Lake City
Taylor	Elizabeth	Ward	James	1838	ENG, Nottingham
Taylor	Elizabeth Agnes	Barney	Royal Alonzo	1881 05 19	UT, Salt Lake City
Taylor	Elizabeth Ann	Criddle	John	1854 06	UT, Salt Lake City
Taylor	Elizabeth Ann	Driggs	Samuel	1840 10 04	IL, Nauvoo
Taylor	Emma	Wright	William H.	1846 09 29	
Taylor	Hannah	Orton	William	1834 06 09	ENG
Taylor	Harriet	Harper	Charles Alfred	1855 12 02	UT, Salt Lake City
Taylor	Hattie Jane	Higginson	William T.	1873 02 10	
Taylor	Henrietta	Holladay	David Hollis	1852 02 01	CA, San Bern.
Taylor	Jane	Faulkner	Edward	1838 11 11	
Taylor	Jane	Nelson	Edmund	1820 10 03	IL, Waterloo
Taylor	Jennett Burton	Smithson	Allen F.	1849 12 16	
Taylor	Julia Ann	Allred	Isaac	1832 10 11	TN, Bedford
Taylor	Lora Ann	Brown	Neuman	1852 06 18	UT, Manti
Taylor	Louisa	Egbert	Joseph	1852 06 17	
Taylor	Louisa	Warrick	Thomas	1841 04 04	SC
Taylor	Martha	Little	George Edwin	1862 01 05	UT, Salt Lake City
Taylor	Mary	Robinson	Joseph Lee	1867 02 02	UT, Salt Lake City
Taylor	Mary	Simmons	William Bert	1857 03 15	UT, Salt Lake City
Taylor	Mary	Upton	William	1855 11 12	ENG, Derbyshire
Taylor	Mary Ann	Osterhout	John	1862 03 08	UT, Willard
Taylor	Mary Melvina	Rawson	Daniel Berry	1866 03 10	UT, Salt Lake City
Taylor	Nancy Jane	Smith	Jonathan	1847 07 11	IA, Council Bluffs

Female	Male	Date	Place
Taylor ....Rhoda Ann	Lyman ....Francis Marion	1857 11 18	CA, San Bern.
Taylor ....Sarah Jane	Florence ....Henry	1861 11 13	UT
Taylor ....Sarah Jane	Harwood.............James T.	1858 06 30	UT, Lehi
Taylor ....Sarah Jane	Park.....................Samuel Wallace	1860 03 18	UT, Lindon
Teeples...........Elvira	Rockwood ....Albert Perry	1846 01 21	IL, Nauvoo
Teeples...........Elvira	Van Curen...........Paul	1855	
Teeples...........Elvira	Wheeler..............Henry A.	1836 01 02	MI, Pontiac
Teeples...........Harriet Elvira	Clarke.................Francis	1867 01 28	UT, Eden
Teeples...........Harriet Elvira	Sessions ....David	1849	
Teeples...........Harriet Elvira	Wixom.................Soloman	1846	IL, Nauvoo
Teeples...........Harriet Elvira	Worden ....Nathaniel	1852	UT, Provo
Tegan ....Methine	Connell................Samuel	1883 10 03	UT, St. George
Tegan ....Methine	Ford.....................Alford	1870 01 17	
Telford ....Anna	....	1852 02 22	UT, Bountiful
Telford ....Jane	Telford.................John	1825 03	Scotland
Telle.................Martha	Cannon ....George Q.	1868	UT, Salt Lake City
Tellefsen..........Rachel	Carver ....John	1864 12 10	UT, Salt Lake City
Tenney ....Betsy Jane	Loose ....Robert	1844 01 24	IL, Quincy
Tenney ....Betsy Jane	Simons ....Orawell	1861 08 24	UT, Payson
Tenney ....Eliza L.	Cannon ....George Q.	1865 07 29	UT, Salt Lake City
Terrell ....Caroline	Norris ....William	1844 01 18	ENG, Wicken
Terry ....Amy	Draper.................Zemira	1842 01 31	IL, Pleasant Vale
Terry ....Elizabeth	Heward................John	1844 05 20	IL, Nauvoo
Terry ....Elizabeth	Kirby...................Francis	1833 07 18	
Terry ....Hannah	Terry....................Parshall	1802 03 16	
Terry ....Marilla	Crawford ....John	1841 01 20	IL
Terry ....Marilla	Hansen.................Nils	1846 01 28	
Terry ....Mary Abby	Frampton.............William M.	1855 05 27	UT, Draper
Thacker ....Anna Maria	Givens.................James	1885 11 12	UT, Wallsburg
Thacker ....Anna Maria	Harper.................James	1893 03 12	UT, Wallsburg
Thacker ....Anna Maria	Ivie ....Hyrum Lewis	1894 12 29	UT, Provo
Thacker ....Anna Maria	Myler ....Joseph Elias	1866 07 11	UT, Clarkston
Thacker ....Anna Maria	Pierce.................William Edward	1873 09 29	UT, Salt Lake City
Thacker ....Elizabeth	Penfold...............John	1868 01 01	UT, Peoa
Thacker ....Hannah	Shorten ....James Bussey		
Thacker ....Isabell Tonks	Moulton ....John Ephraim	1882 03 23	UT, Salt Lake City
Thayne ....Ellen Jane	Lewis..................James	1870	UT, Salt Lake City
Thayne ....Mary Ann	Moon ....Henry	1868 01 04	
Thayne ....Mary Ann	White..................Ernest Authenia	1899	
Theobald ....Drusilla	Passey ....Thomas	1858 08	UT, Salt Lake City
Thick...............Mary Jane	Stevens ....Sydney	1863 05 22	ENG, Liverpool
Thirkell............Caroline	Mitton ....Edwin Crowther	1861 05 02	UT, Wellsville
Thirkell............Jemima Brown	Darley.................William F.	1857 03 22	
Thomas ....Amanda	Durfee ....Nephi	1857	UT, Springville
Thomas ....Amanda	Nowlin ....Jabus T.	1845	IL, Nauvoo
Thomas ....Amanda	Starr ....Edward W.	1855 07 24	
Thomas ....Ann	Sevey..................George W.	1877	
Thomas ....Ann	Williams..............Owen	1836 05 14	Wales
Thomas ....Ann Bingham	Collins ....Albert W.	1851 03 03	
Thomas ....Catherine E.	Neff ....Amos H.	1864 12 17	
Thomas ....Catherine W.	Leishman ....James A.	1857 11 30	UT, Cedar Fort
Thomas ....Catherine W.	Nebeker ....Lewis	1851 01 05	
Thomas ....Elizabeth T.	Morehead............James M.	1836 01 19	TN
Thomas ....Elizabeth T.	White..................Samuel Dennis	1852 03 24	UT, Salt Lake City

Female	Male	Date	Place
Thomas ....Frances Ann	White.................Joel William	1850 05 08	IA
Thomas ....Jane	Snowball ....Ralph	1865 03 18	UT, Salt Lake City
Thomas ....Jane Elizabeth	Berry ....John Williams	1851 05 08	UT, Salt Lake City
Thomas ....Malinda S.	Loveridge ....Alexander H.	1849 04 12	NE, Patanant
Thomas ....Margaret	Beck...................Alfred R. M.	1867 12 14	UT, Salt Lake City
Thomas ....Margaret Ann	Romney...............George	1863 08 29	UT, Salt Lake City
Thomas ....Marinda	Stevens..............William	1827 09 02	Canada
Thomas ....Martha Ann	Shaw..................Elijah	1850 04 06	IA, Kanesville
Thomas ....Martha Ann	Shupe.................John W.	1840	TN, Sullivan Co.
Thomas ....Mary	Owens.................John Edward	1853 02 15	Ocean
Thomas ....Ruth	Jones ....Thomas	1827 03 07	Wales
Thomas ....Sarah	Jones ....Robert		Wales
Thomas ....Sarah	Parish.................Samuel	1861 03 01	UT, Springville
Thomas ....Susan Newman	Collins ....Albert W.	1841 03 03	GA
Thomasen ....Ane	Larsen ....Peder	1820 05 17	Denmark
Thomasen ....Maren	Andersen.............Jans	1839 11	Denmark
Thomasen ....Maren C.	Folkman ....Jens Peter	1865 09 02	UT, Salt Lake City
Thompson ....Ann	Leslie.................Andrew	1829 07 12	Scotland
Thompson ....Ann	McAffee..............John Sharp	1841 04 25	
Thompson ....Ann	McDonald............Duncan	1865 07 29	UT
Thompson ....Ann	Stewart...............John Martin	1857 03 02	UT
Thompson ....Ann	Walton................Joseph	1854 10 29	UT, Mill Creek
Thompson ....Anna	Sorensen.............Peder	1837 10 07	Denmark
Thompson ....Eliza	Webb..................George H.	1853 10 27	ENG, Northill
Thompson ......Elizabeth	Groesbeck...........Nicholas	1841 03 25	IL, Springfield
Thompson ......Elizabeth	McAllister ....William J. F.	1822 04 04	
Thompson ......Elizabeth D.	Nelson................Thomas	1805 01 20	ENG
Thompson ....Harriet Ann	Baker..................Phillip Jr.	1860 03 02	
Thompson ....Jane	Bleak..................James Godson	1861 10 26	UT, Salt Lake City
Thompson ......Johanne	Peterson..............Peter C.	1870 05 02	UT, Salt Lake City
Thompson ....Josephine	Rasmussen ....Niels Peter	1878 12 20	ID, Bloomington
Thompson ......Laura Althea	Gardner..............Archibald	1852	
Thompson ......Laura Melvina	Leavitt ....Lemuel S.	1850 08 12	UT, Salt Lake City
Thompson ......Margaret	Brower................Ariah Coats	1853 02 06	UT, Salt Lake City
Thompson ......Maria	Hatch..................Orin	1856 05 02	UT, Salt Lake City
Thompson ....Marial	Bent...................Samuel	1846 01 14	IL, Nauvoo
Thompson ....Marial	Crosby................David B.	1834 09 21	
Thompson ....Marial	Draper ....William	1848 05 06	NE
Thompson ....Martha	Boulton...............Thomas		
Thompson ....Martha	Duke...................Jonathan O.	1855 12 03	
Thompson ....Mary	Patterson.............Edward M.	1868 10 31	
Thompson ....Mary	Richards.............Franklin D.	1857 03 06	
Thompson ....Mary	Richards.............Willard	1846 01 27	IL, Nauvoo
Thompson ......Mary Ann L.	Butler..................John Ockford	1868 06 06	UT, Salt Lake City
Thompson ......Mary Jane	Taylor ....David	1859 04 05	UT, Salt Lake City
Thompson ....Neleene	Reynolds.............William F.		
Thompson ....Penelope	Thompson...........Joseph L.	1835	
Thompson ....Rachel	Atkin...................William	1854 12 18	ENG
Thompson ....Rhoda Ann	Baker..................George	1840 10 05	
Thompson ......Sarah Ann	Duke...................Jonathan O.	1855 10 19	UT, Provo
Thompson ......Sarah Ann	Emmons.............Charles Henry	1870 11 14	UT, Salt Lake City
Thompson ......Sarah Marinda	Black ....William Morley	1874 05 10	UT, Glendale
Thompson ......Sarah Marinda	Spencer..............George	1856 04 01	UT, Washington
Thompson ......Susannah	Martin ....Robert	1863 06 30	UT, Salt Lake City

Female	Male	Date	Place
Thomsen ....Christine	Christensen.........Niels Christian		
Thomsen ....Johanne Marie	Christensen.........Christen	1867 02 17	
Thomsen ....Johanne Marie	Christensen.........Niels Christian	1868 02 05	
Thomsen ....Maria	Nielsen ....James	1855 12 20	
Thomsen ....Maria	Poulsen ....Martin	1851	
Thomson ....Caroline	Jensen ....Jens Martinus	1863 03 12	UT
Thomson ....Janet	Lyon ....John	1825 12 01	Scotland
Thorn ....Abigail	Pond..................Stillman	1848 02 08	UT. Salt Lake City
Thorn ....Abigail	Russell ....Samuel	1845	IL, Nauvoo
Thorn ....Elizabeth	Giles ....George	1868 03 16	
Thorn ....Elizabeth	Hall...................Timothy	1865 03	UT, Salt Lake City
Thorn ....Elizabeth	Love ....Thomas		
Thorn ....Lydia Ann	Chase.................Solomon Drake	1840 04 19	NY, Sparta
Thorn ....Mary Ann	Anderson.............George	1860 02 15	UT, Salt Lake City
Thorn ....Mary Ann	Deuel.................Osmyn M.	1855 11 26	UT, Salt Lake City
Thorn ....Nancy	Osborn ....David III	1857 12 25	UT, Box Elder
Thorn ....Sarah	Bingham ....Alonzo	1854 03 04	UT
Thorn ....Sarah	Case...................George W.	1866 02 04	UT, Salt Lake City
Thorne ....Annie	Wells ....Stephen R.	1857 04 22	UT, Salt Lake City
Thorne ....Sarah Ann	Foutz ....Jacob Jr.	1866 01 07	
Thorning ....Marie	Bohn..................Jacob J. M.	1849 04 10	Denmark
Thornton ....Eliza	Homer ....Russell King	1861 03 29	UT, Salt Lake City
Thornton ....Sarah	Coleman..............Prime	1826 08 28	ENG, Bedfordshire
Thorpe ....Elizabeth	Sharp ....Jonathan	1831 08 02	ENG, Brotherton
Thorpe ....Mary	Beal...................Henry Allen	1854 07 04	UT, Ephraim
Thorpe ....Mary	Morris ....Joseph	1846	
Threlfall...........Jane	Gardner...............James	1855 03 03	
Thurgood ....Catherine	South..................John	1867 04 20	UT, Salt Lake City
Thurgood ....Elizabeth S.	Parkin.................William John	1884 04 24	UT, Salt Lake City
Thurman ....Mary Elizabeth	Griffith ....G. Andrew	1869 12 13	
Thurston ....Christiane M.	Aldous ....George Parkin	1865 12 24	
Thygesen.........Maria	Peterson..............Thomas Peter	1859 09 25	UT, Salt Lake City
Tibbits ....Elizabeth	Prisbrey ....Miner Jewett	1867 07 13	UT, Salt Lake City
Tibbits ....Elizabeth	Ray....................John Alexander	1855 10 11	UT, Salt Lake City
Tice................Polly	Campbell..............Jared LeRoy	1842 03 13	NY, Steuben Co.
Tidwell ....Mary Jane	Johnson ....Benjamin Henry	1852 08 06	
Tiffany.............Sarah (Sally)	Call....................Cyril	1806 04 06	VT, Franklin Co.
Tillotson ....Elizabeth P.	Whiting ....Edwin	1833 09 21	
Tilton...............Polly Wyman	Hyde..................Herman	1810 12 05	
Timmings.........Mary Ann	Sutherland...........Thomas	1830 08 08	ENG
Timms..............Hannah A. A.	Devey ....John	1868 06 20	ENG, Liverpool
Timothy...........Martha	Gardner...............Charles A.	1878 12 05	UT, Salt Lake City
Timothy...........Martha	Rudy..................Josiah Philip	1891 05 26	UT, Vernal
Tingle..............Holly Jane	Averett................Jeduthan	1835 08 11	AL, Marion Co.
Tingle..............Holly Jane	Edwards ....Samuel James	1857 03 15	UT, Salt Lake City
Tingle..............Holly Jane	Thomas ....Daniel Zarababel	1863 04 11	UT, Salt Lake City
Tippets ....Abigail Eliza	Tippets ....Brigham L.	1874 11 30	UT, Salt Lake City
Tippets ....Alice Jeanette	Tippets ....Joseph M.	1860 01 01	UT, Perry
Tippets............Amanda Jane	Smith.................Samuel L.	1864 02 04	
Titcomb...........Mary Jane A.	Free...................Preston Strait	1855 08 22	UT, Salt Lake City
Tite ....Elizabeth	Tye....................Jesse Askew	1856 11 09	UT, Salt Lake City
Tittensor ....Mary Ellen	Larsen ....John Christian	1877 02 07	UT, Logan
Tittensor ....Susannah	Larsen ....John Christian	1877 02 07	UT, Logan
Titus...............Melissa	Berrett ....Charles Henry	1861 12 25	UT, Ogden

Female	Male	Date	Place
Tobiasson........Anna Maria	Oman ....Peter	1827 07 15	Sweden
Todd ....Emily	Brown................William Albert	1890 01 15	UT, Taylorsville
Toen ....Ann	Swift ....William	1842	ENG, Devin
Tofts ....Ann	Todd................Abraham	1863 05 03	ENG
Tokelove..........Mary	Chesson.............John	1822 07	ENG, London
Tolton ....Clara Ann	Turley ....Isaac	1867 10 04	UT, Salt Lake City
Tomlinson........Mary Ann	Tolton ....Edward	1847 12 24	MO, St. Louis
Tomlinson........Temperance	Lance ....Lewis	1861 05 21	TX
Tompkins........Eliza	Bailey ....John	1850 02 26	ENG
Tompkins........Eliza	Lewis................Nathan	1869 10 25	
Tompkins........Eliza	Williams..............Evan Austin	1862 05 24	UT, Salt Lake City
Tompkins........Julia Ann	Gibbs................John Duggan	1840	ENG
Tongue ....Ann	Powell ....Edward	1846 04 27	ENG
Tonks..............Elizabeth	Clayton..............John	1874 08 13	UT, Morgan
Tonks..............Rachel	Thacker..............William	1844 06 22	ENG
Tonks..............Sarah R. R.	Deuel.................Osmyn M.	1868 08 22	UT, Salt Lake City
Tonks..............Sarah R. R.	Thacker.............William Timothy	1875 12 07	UT, Salt Lake City
Toomer............Ann	Fry.....................John J.	1837 07 03	
Toomer............Ann	Littlefield..............William David	1847 10 24	
Topham ....Jemima	Dewsnup............John D.	1836 03 13	ENG, Lancashire
Topham ....Sarah	Clark.................Joseph	1849 10 17	UT, Provo
Torstensen ......Maren	Anderson............Gustave	1842 12 27	Norway
Tourn ....Martha Marie	Cardon ....Philippe	1821 02 01	Italy
Towery............Margaret Maria	Lockhart ....John	1834	MS, Monroe
Townsend.......Martha Ann	Lufkin ....George W.	1854 07 09	UT, Salt Lake City
Townsend........Martha Ann	Robinson............Henry	1852	MO
Tracy ....Marie Evaline	Keyes ....Alma	1861 04 27	OR, Clackamas
Trail ....Duritha	Lewis.................David	1834 11 23	KY, Franklin
Tranum ....Dorthea C.	Christensen.........Mads	1831 03 31	Denmark
Treasurer........Catherinne	Matheson ....Daniel	1823 11 20	Scotland
Treby ....Julia	Simms ....John	1822 10 30	CT, New London
Treby ....Julia	Stone.................Robert	1826 11 27	NY, Brooklyn
Tregale ....Hannah	Burton ....William G.	1852 05 09	ENG, Devonshire
Treharne..........Jane	Ashton................Edward	1854 02 05	UT, Salt Lake City
Treharne..........Mary	Leigh ....Samuel	1850 06	IA, Council Bluffs
Tremayne ....Prudence	Barkdull ....Michael	1824 05 06	OH, Akron
Tremayne ....Prudence	Oakes.................Henry	1842 05 12	IL, Nauvoo
Treseder ....Elizabeth	Chandler ....Calvin H.	1874 05 25	UT, Salt Lake City
Treseder ....Elizabeth	Williams..............Lafayette W.	1884 12 06	UT, North Ogden
Trimble ....Susan	Finlinson............George	1866	UT, Fillmore
Trippess..........Sarah	Duncan..............Homer	1863 07 11	
Tristram ....Lucy	Lake ....Joseph	1872 11	UT, Henefer
Trower ....Sarah	Chandler ....Frank	1857 11 07	ENG, Sussex
Truedsson ....Hannah Pernilla	Gyllenskog ....Neils N.	1846	
Truelock..........Ann	Ward ....George W.	1842 01 24	ENG
Trumble ....Lois Alexander	Lowe ....John	1840 11 09	MA, Salem
Trumble ....Lois Alexander	Thompson ....Ezra	1848	Trail
Tucker ....Harriet	Blackham ....James	1853 11 20	UT, Salt Lake City
Tucker ....Mary Ann	Bailey ....James	1846	IL, Nauvoo
Tucker ....Mary Ann	Chaney...............		
Tucker ....Mary Ann	Cook.................James Benjamin	1860	
Tucker ....Mary Ann	Kinney ....Loren	1851 10 05	UT, Salt Lake City
Tucker ....Mary Ann	Kinney ....Loren		Remarried
Tucker ....Sarah	Gover ....Morris	1848 06 11	ENG

Female	Male	Date	Place
Tuckfield..........Maria Ann	Phillips...............William G.	1861 05 04	MA, Boston
Tufveson..........Svenborg	Nilson ....Pehr	1862 10 12	UT, Logan
Tull.................Ann	Bentley ....Joseph	1877	UT
Tull.................Ann	Lang..................Benjamin	1856 02 18	ENG
Tullidge...........Jane Puckett	Pyper.................Alexander C.		
Tullidge...........Mary Elizabeth	Little ....James Amasa	1864 11 19	
Tupper ....Hannah	Grover ....Thomas	1844 12 17	IL, Nauvoo
Tupper ....Hannah	Wells ....Daniel H.		
Tupper ....Luduska S.	Grover ....Thomas	1846	IL, Nauvoo
Turnbaugh ......Mary Caroline	Langford.............James H.	1856 09 14	
Turnbaugh ......Mary Caroline	Riddle................Isaac		
Turnbeaugh .....Nancy Ann	Averett...............George W. G.	1853 02 24	IL, Pike
Turnbow ....Sophronia E. L.	Carter.................William	1857 02 08	
Turner..............Ann	Howe..................Richard	1862	
Turner..............Ann	Robb ....James	1847 01 24	Scotland
Turner..............Eleanor	Willden ....Charles W.	1833 01 21	ENG
Turner..............Elizabeth	Jarvis.................Henry	1837 08 04	ENG, Essex
Turner..............Emma	Alley ....Stephen Webb	1868 10 03	UT, Salt Lake City
Turner..............Emma	Stayner...............Arthur	1857 03 27	UT, Salt Lake City
Turner..............Hannah	Morgan...............David	1832	
Turner..............Louise	Haight................William V. O.	1861 07 04	UT, Farmington
Turner..............Martha	Lovell.................George	1862 01 28	UT, Deseret
Turner..............Martha	Taylor ....Stephen	1832	NY
Turner..............Mary	Clarkson.............John	1857 07 04	UT, Fillmore
Turner..............Mary	Ellett ....John James	1861 11 11	
Turner..............Rebecca Willard	Workman.............Jacob L.	1852 01 03	UT, Salt Lake City
Turner..............Rose Ann	Sampson.............James K. P.	1869 12 13	
Turner..............Selina	Cromar...............William T.	1861 04 15	ENG, Sheffield
Turner..............Susannah	Robison..............Benjamin H.	1864 03 26	
Turpin..............Mary	Bennion..............John	1857 04 19	UT, Salt Lake City
Turple..............Susan Ann E.	Brady.................Charles	1841	
Turple ....Susan Ann E.	Cook..................Henry Lyman	1852 09 28	UT, Goshen
Turrell ....Melissa	Atwood...............Simeon E.	1834 09 30	NY, Chautauqua
Tuttle ....Elizabeth Ann	Brown.................Robert H.	1861 04 16	UT, Manti
Tuttle ....Elizabeth Ann	Stolworthy ....Thomas	1880 12 08	UT, St. George
Tuttle ....Mary Ann	Billings...............Titus	1854 01 20	
Tuttle ....Mary Ann	Egan..................Howard	1849	
Tuttle ....Mary Ann	Gardner..............Walter Elias	1866 11 28	
Tuttle ....Sarah Maria	Mecham ....Joseph	1853 01 05	UT, Salt Lake City
Tweddle..........Elizabeth	Knox..................William	1842 08 01	ENG, Durham
Tykeson...........Botilda	Nilsson ....Nils	1837 05 26	Sweden
Tyler ....Hannah Ladd	Mecham ....Joseph	1827 02 10	

U

Female	Male	Date	Place
Underhill ....Charlotte	Clark..................William	1853	ENG
Underhill ....Charlotte	Gibbs.................Horace Dewitt	1855 01 10	UT, Salt Lake City
Underhill ....Charlotte	Marchant............Edmund		
Underwood ......Elizabeth	Ellwood ....Robert	1849 12 24	ENG
Upson ....Philinda	Osborn ....David	1865	UT
Upson ....Philinda	Standley ....Alexander	1829 03 19	OH, Suffield
Uren................Elizabeth	Oulds.................Emanuel	1850 05 16	ENG
Uren................Elizabeth	Theobald ....William	1860 11 24	UT, Salt Lake City

Female	Male	Date	Place
Utley ....Harriet T.	Carter ....William	1853 11 23	UT, Salt Lake City
Utley ....Margaret Eliza	Tolman ....Cyrus Hewitt	1853 06 30	UT, Salt Lake City
Utley ....Mildred Caroline	Maughan ....Joseph Weston	1872 12 20	UT, Salt Lake City

V

Female	Male	Date	Place
Vail ....Angelia	Vance................John W.	1854 07 30	
Vail ....Cynthia	Benson...............Alva	1820 08 11	
Vail ....Elvira	Nelson...............William G.	1855 11 25	
Vail ....Sarah	Howell ....Edmond W.	1836 10 05	
Vail ....Sarah	Terry..................Otis L.	1853 01 27	
Vallier ....Mary Jane	Caldwell ....Robert	1860	Trail
Vallier ....Mary Jane	Caldwell ....Robert	1909 11 23	IA, Logan
Vallier ....Mary Jane	Mefferd ....Virgil Jacob	1866 04 20	IA, Council Bluffs
Vallier ....Mary Jane	Richmond............Benjamin	1852 10 15	UT, Salt Lake City
Van Alstyne .....Phoebe	Cole...................Barnet	1820 12 15	OH, Sheffield
Van Benthuysen...Elizabeth	Gilbert ....Algernon S.	1823 09 21	OH, Cuyahoga
Van Benthuysen...Keziah K.	Bunnell ....Zuriel		
Van Benthuysen...Keziah K.	Burke.................John Matthias	1832	MO
Van Benthuysen...Keziah K.	Rollins ....John Porter	1815	NY, Livingston
Van Buren ......Mary Francis	Callaway ....Levi H.	1850 11 17	IA, Garden Grove
Van Dyke.........Caroline	Grant ....Jedediah M.	1844 07 02	
Van Leuven .....Eliza Jane	Merrill ....John Elwin	1862 04 17	UT, Paradise
Van Leuven .....Matilda Ann	Sperry ....John Clapp	1851 01 01	
Van Orden ....Charlotte A.	Peck...................Martin Horton	1851 12 02	UT, Salt Lake City
Van Orden ....Charlotte A.	West...................Ira Enos	1846 01 08	IL, Nauvoo
Van Orden ....Julia	Haight.................Hector Caleb	1829 12 18	NY, Greene Co.
Van Velsor.......Catherine	Smith..................Jessie W.	1855 04 01	UT, Farmingtojn
Van Waggoner Harriet Ann	Havens...............John	1839 02 13	NJ
Van Waggoner Harriet Ann	Nebeker ....Henry	1847 01 04	IA
Van Wagoner ..Sarah	Fairbanks ....John B.	1844 08 31	
Van Zant.........Rebecca	Miller ....Eleazer	1816	NY
Vance ....Mary Francis	Allred.................James Martin	1860 03 21	UT, Mt. Pleasant
Vancil..............Mary	Adair..................Thomas Jefferson		
Vancil..............Mary	Waggle...............Jacob		
Varney ....Abigail	Griffin ....Albert B.		
Vasquez ....Mary Ann	Spencer..............Dallas Polk	1866 10 07	MO, Westport
Vaughan ....Elizabeth	Hunt ....James Wilson	1865 03 23	UT
Vaughan ....Emily	Rees...................Moroni	1869 06 28	UT, Salt Lake City
Vaughan ....Martha	Jones ....William Ellis	1859 06	
Vaughan ....Mary Ann	Caldwell ....David	1813 05 14	Scotland
Vaughn ....Hulda Dimeras	Bassett ....Loren Elias	1844	IL
Vaughn ....Hulda Dimeras	Harmon ....Alpheus	1823 02 01	PA, Erie Co.
Vay ....Patience	Lambert..............Richard	1811 10 06	ENG
Vay ....Patience	Redford ....Robert Patefield	1856 11 29	UT, Salt Lake City
Vernon............Christiana V.	Smith..................John F.	1863 04 27	ENG, Hull
Very ....Lucy Ann N.	Angell.................Solomon		
Very ....Lucy Ann N.	Dennett ....Daniel Quinby		
Very ....Lucy Ann N.	Flanigan ....Thomas	1842 10 08	MA, Salem
Vest ....Margaret Ann	Harrison ....John	1881 06 19	UT, Mona
Vest ....Margaret Ann	Kay....................John Thomas	1864 04 15	UT, Mona
Vickers............Mary	Ogden ....William	1844 08 11	ENG, Bolton
Vickery............Sophia C.	Davis ....Thomas William	1861	OH

Female	Male	Date	Place
Viets ....Margaret Mariah	Miles...................Albert	1833	OH, Trumbell Co.
Vilhelmsen.......Annie J.	Davis..................William C.	1869 11 22	UT, Salt Lake City
Vine ....Susanna	Briggs.................Hugh L.		
Vine ....Susanna	Collyer................Samuel	1881 05 02	
Vine ....Susanna	Preston..............Richard W.		ENG, Hampshire
Vintiner ....Hannah Maria	Stokes ....William	1846 10 03	ENG
Vockins............Sarah	Bradfield.............George	1840 10 25	
Vockins............Sarah	Smith..................	1836	
Voorhees.........Mary Ann	Snow ....Warren Stone	1841 12 23	IL, Lima
Vorce ....Susan Mariah	Moore.................David	1839 08 19	Canada
Voss ....Eliza	Ward ....Moroni	1872 11 18	UT, Salt Lake City
Voss ....Mary Ann	Cole...................John	1873	UT, Willard
Voss ....Mary Ann	Cordon ....Alfred	1865 04 22	UT, Salt Lake City
Voss ....Phebe	Ford...................Joseph	1875	UT
Voss ....Phebe	Ford...................Thomas	1867 12 07	UT, Salt Lake City
Voss ....Sarah	Cordon ....Edwin P.	1867 12 14	UT, Salt Lake City
Vowels.............Mary	Manning ....Joseph George	1829	ENG, Bristol

W

Female	Male	Date	Place
Waddell ....Ann	Dugdale..............Edmund	1869	
Waddell ....Ann	Stewart...............John	1848 06 16	Scotland
Waddoups ....Elizabeth	Wood..................Daniel C.	1869 02 08	UT, Salt Lake City
Wade ....Laura	Atwood ....William Turrell	1867 11 30	
Wade ....Minerva	Hickman.............William A.	1849 05 01	IA, Council Bluffs
Wade ....Sarah Jane	Atwood ....William Turrell	1868 10 31	UT, Salt Lake City
Wadley ....Jane	Smith..................John Sivel	1838 02 13	ENG, Gloucester
Wadsworth ......Lucinda M.	Miller ....William	1865 11 12	UT
Wadsworth ......Susan Aroline	Arave..................Nelson	1855 02 18	UT, Salt Lake City
Wagaman........Nancy Ellen	Robison..............Alexander	1828	
Waggle ....Hannah	Carson ....Valentine	1862	UT, Nephi
Wagle ....Cynthia	Bradley...............George W.	1854 03 14	
Wagle ....Cynthia	Downs ....Reuben John	1861 05 19	UT, Nephi
Wagstaff ....Elizabeth	Shupe..................Brigham	1871 11 25	UT, Salt Lake City
Wagstaff ....Fanny	Bone...................William	1867 07 26	UT, Lehi
Wagstaff ....Mary	Bone...................William	1833 12 05	ENG, Bedfordshire
Wagstaff ....Mary Ann	Bullock ....Thomas Henry	1864 06 25	UT
Wagstaff ....Rachel Eleanor	Hayes.................John J.	1853 02 23	Ocean
Wagstaff ....Sarah	Sears..................John	1842 12 26	ENG
Wainwright.......Esther	Bennion..............John	1842 02 15	ENG, Liverpool
Waite ....Martha	Colvin.................Alvin	1856	UT, North Ogden
Waite ....Martha	Gates.................Samuel	1858 01 08	UT, Salt Lake City
Waite ....Martha	McCarty..............Stephen	1878 02 02	UT, Ogden
Waite ....Martha	Smith..................		
Waite ....Mary Jane	Robison..............Lewis	1855 10 05	
Wakefield........Caroline R.	Fitt.....................George	1877 11 14	UT, Salt Lake City
Wakefield........Jane Ruth	Miles..................Edwin Ruthven	1857 03 11	UT, Salt Lake City
Walker ....Ann	Paul...................Walter	1856 12 25	
Walker ....Ann Agatha	Pratt ....Parley P.	1847 04 28	NE
Walker ....Ann Agatha	Ridges................Joseph H.	1860 03 04	UT, Salt Lake City
Walker ....Diontha	Lyman ....Amasa Mason	1845 07	IL, Nauvoo
Walker ....Diontha	Whitney ....Micah	1830 02 28	CT
Walker ....Elizabeth	Grover...............Thomas	1857 03 27	UT, Salt Lake City

Female	Male	Date	Place
Walker ....Emma	Grover ....Thomas	1856 10 29	UT, Salt Lake City
Walker ....Eveline	Rollins ....James Henry	1838 09 04	MO
Walker ....Frances	Stokes ....Jeremiah	1839 11 25	ENG
Walker ....Harriet (Alice)	Fuller ....Elijah K.	1866 11 17	UT, Salt Lake City
Walker ....Jane	Smith ....Lot	1852 02 14	UT, Salt Lake City
Walker ....Jerusha C.	Blanchard............William C.	1867 10 12	UT, Salt Lake City
Walker ....Louisa	Barney................Edson	1847 05 10	
Walker ....Lucy	Kimball ....Heber Chase	1845 02 08	
Walker ....Lucy	Smith ....Joseph Jr.	1843 05 01	
Walker ....Margaret Ann	Kay.....................Joseph Chatterly	1869 02 15	UT, Salt Lake City
Walker ....Mary Jane	Pack ....John	1852 09 15	
Walker ....Mary Lois	Morris ....Elias	1856 05	UT, Salt Lake City
Walker ....Mary Lois	Morris ....John Thomas	1852 09 05	MO, St. Louis
Walker ....May Wray	Perry ....Lorenzo	1853 05 01	UT, Farmington
Walker ....Nancy Reeder	Alexander............Horace Martin	1834 09 14	
Walker ....Sarah	Gough ....Joseph Hollings	1853 04 06	Ocean
Wall ....Fanny Maria	Chandler ....Henry	1903 09 01	UT, Millville
Wall ....Fanny Maria	Whitney ....Samuel Alonzo	1863 10 18	
Wall ....Sarah Emily	Cowley ....William M.	1860 02 22	UT, Salt Lake City
Wallace............Ann	McCall ....James A.	1822	
Wallace............Susannah	Roundy................Lorenzo W.	1847 05 16	Trail
Waller ....Margaret	Howlett ....William Titus	1855 10 29	
Waller ....Mary Ann	Mills...................William		
Walling............Emma Smith	McAlister ....Robert Wesley		
Walmsley.........Ellen	Clegg..................Jonathan	1836	
Walsh ....Mary Ann	Bridge.................Joseph	1865 07 08	UT, Salt Lake City
Walsh ....Sarah	Lewis..................William S.	1868 12 01	UT, Salt Lake City
Walsom ....Mary Ann	Gee ....William	1866 07 17	UT, Fayette
Walters ....Ann	Lemmon..............Washington	1863	UT
Walters ....Louisa	Davis ....Mormon	1876 10 16	UT, Salt Lake City
Walters ....Martha	Hardman ....Abraham W.	1860 09 09	UT
Walters ....Mary Jane	Speirs.................William H.	1873 03 17	UT, Salt Lake City
Walters ....Sarah	Clayton................William	1856 11 30	UT, Salt Lake City
Walton ....Ann	Townsend ....John W.	1847	ENG
Walton ....Isabella	Burton ....James	1825 03 05	ENG, Yorkshire
Walton ....Jane	Bickley................William Green	1867 03 21	UT, Pine Valley
Walton ....Jane	Hale....................Job	1861 09 20	UT, Salt Lake City
Wann ....Susanna	Hunter ....Edward	1846 01 29	
Warby ....Matilda	Nelson................Daniel M.	1887 09 30	UT, Beaver
Warby ....Sarah	Nelson................Daniel M.	1876 10 08	UT, Beaver
Ward...............Emma	Thornock ....John Bott	1865 03 10	UT, Farmington
Ward...............Emma Ellen	Chapman ....William	1875 08	UT, Salt Lake City
Ward...............Fanny	Gould ....Samuel	1850	IA, Council Bluffs
Ward...............Fanny	Lister ....Richard		ENG
Ward...............Hannah	Ashby ....Samuel	1847 04 15	ENG, Thornby
Ward...............Isabella	Royle..................Henry	1855 05 21	
Ward...............Isabella	Ward ....George	1821 10 15	ENG, Kirby
Ward...............Louisa	Higginbotham......William Elliott	1831 09 08	
Ward...............Lucy	Cole....................James Barnet	1856 11 02	WY, Fort Bridger
Ward...............Mary	Briscoe ....George	1862	ENG
Ward...............Mary Ann	Horsely...............Robert	1868 07	ENG
Ward...............Mary Ann	Orton..................John	1840 12 24	ENG
Ward...............Mary Ann	Turner ....William	1853	ENG
Ward...............Mary Ann	Webb..................George	1865 05 31	UT, Lehi

Female	Male	Date	Place
Ward..............Susannah	Allen...................Orville Morgan	1848 06 20	IA
Ward..............Susannah	Brady..................Lindsay A.	1852 06 11	UT, Salt Lake City
Warden..........Elizabeth	Swain ....John	1846 08 11	ENG
Wardrobe........Mary	Fotheringham......William	1857 01 25	UT, Salt Lake City
Wardrobe........Mary	Levi ....Abram		
Ware.............Ellander	Stubbs...............Richard	1843 06 21	IA, Lee Co.
Ware.............Mary	Gates ....Jacob	1862 10 25	UT, Provo
Ware.............Mary Bigg	Igguldin ....John	1834	ENG
Ware.............Mary Bigg	King...................Enoch Marvin	1841 03 30	IL, Nauvoo
Wareing ....Elizabeth	Crittenden ....Chauncey S.	1865 02 01	
Warmby ....Mary Ann	Pass ....Thomas	1837 05 28	ENG
Warn..............Elizabeth Pollow	Camp ....Reuben		
Warn..............Elizabeth Pollow	Swinyard ....Alfred	1897 12 06	
Warn..............Elizabeth Pollow	White..................William	1852 02 16	ENG
Warn..............Fanny	Stenhouse..........Thomas	1850 02 06	ENG
Warner............Mary Elizabeth	Wood.................Wellington	1873 02 04	UT, Salt Lake City
Warr...............Emma Martha	Whitehouse ....Jeremiah	1862 02 10	UT, Salt Lake City
Warren............Abigail	Daniels ....Sheffield		
Warren............Anna	Perkins ....Ute	1835 02	
Warren............Elizabeth	Allred.................James	1803 11 17	NC, Randolph
Warren............Sarah	Tolley ....William F.	1848 08 01	ENG
Warriner..........Nancy	Porter ....Sanford	1812 01 01	VT, Vershire
Wasden ....Alice P.	Hutchinson..........Jacob F.	1861 06 09	UT, Gunnison
Wasden ....Alice P.	Thueson.............John Niels	1870 06 14	
Washburn ....Amanda	Chipman.............Stephen	1826	Canada
Washburn ....Amanda	Currie ....John	1855	UT
Washburn ....Emma Jane	Black ....William Morley	1851 02 02	UT, Manti
Washburn ....Tamar	Washburn............Abraham	1824 03 16	NY
Waslin.............Mary E.	Metcalf ....John Edward	1832 12 23	ENG
Watkins...........Elizabeth	Allan ....Charles Edward	1869 07 24	UT, Salt Lake City
Watkins...........Mary	Williams..............Benjamin	1846 11 02	Wales
Watkins...........Rhoda E.	Price..................Ezekiel	1862 02 16	UT, Alpine
Watmough ....Amanda S.	Chamberlain........John Allen	1864 12 29	UT, Salt Lake City
Watson ....Agnes	Lindsay...............James	1871 01 09	UT, Salt Lake City
Watson ....Allison	Simpson..............Robert M.	1862 12 26	
Watson ....Janette	Underwood...........Edward J.	1866 01 01	UT, Provo
Watson ....Margaret Miller	Dewitt.................Abel A.	1860 03 15	
Watson ....Mary Amelia	Knight.................John	1835	ENG
Watson ....Rachel S.	Chapman ....William	1848 09 12	
Watson ....Rachel S.	Wood.................Thomas	1840	
Watson ....Rosamond	Nuttall................William E.	1851 08 04	ENG, Liverpool
Watson ....Sarah Ann	Oaks..................Hyrum Edwin	1878 03 20	
Wattis ....Mary T.	Bennett...............Thomas	1836 06 30	ENG
Wattis ....Mary T.	Kay.....................William	1844 02 07	IL, Nauvoo
Watton ....Eliza	Rogers................Telemachus	1843 02 05	LA, New Orleans
Watts ....Hannah	Handy.................Samuel	1842 10 25	ENG
Watts ....Rebecca	Hoops.................Jonathan	1812	
Weaver............Ann	Rigby..................Barnett	1839 12 25	ENG, Leyland
Weaver...........Christiana M.	Henrie ....Joseph Ozro		
Weaver...........Julia Cecelia	Armstrong ....David	1862	UT
Weaver...........Louisa	Wickel................Richard	1860 07 21	MO, St. Louis
Weaver...........Martha E.	Stoddard ....John R.	1853 10 13	UT, Salt Lake City
Weaver...........Miranda Bridget	Casteel...............James Nolan	1855	CA, San Bern.
Webb ....Amelia Emily	Bowles ....Enoch	1865 12 08	UT, Nephi

Female	Male	Date	Place
Webb ....Ann	Pace ....James	1855 12 04	UT, Payson
Webb ....Caroline	Tatton ....John C.	1839 09 22	ENG
Webb ....Eliza	Tenney ....William	1819 01 20	NY
Webb ....Fannie	James ....David Jenkins	1875 11 15	UT, Salt Lake City
Webb ....Hannah	Toone..................William H.	1865 03 04	UT, Salt Lake City
Webb ....Maria Lucy	Wagstaff.............Samuel	1840 12 25	ENG
Webb ....Martha	Campkin..............Isaac	1847 02 13	ENG
Webb ....Martha	Young..................Thomas	1857	
Webb ....Mary	Badcock ....Moses	1842 07 14	ENG, Littlington
Webb ....Mary	Jarvis..................George	1878 04 04	UT, St. George
Webber ....Sarah	Braffitt.................George W.	1852 12 02	
Webber ....Sarah	Moore ....Ethan Allen	1822 10 02	CT, Stafford
Webley ....Susannah	Hurst ....William	1830 07 11	ENG
Webley ....Susannah	Maycock..............James	1857	
Webley ....Susannah	Singleton ....Robert	1854 02 05	
Webster ....Margaret	Esplin ....John	1853 11 10	UT, Salt Lake City
Webster ....Mary Ann	Andrus................Milo	1852 12 23	
Webster ....Phoebe	Singleton ....William	1853 05 16	
Webster ....Susanna	Ward ....William	1816 02 25	ENG
Weech ....Emily	Lines ....Henry	1869 12 10	UT, Goshen
Weeks ....Mary Ann	Jones ....Charles	1846 09 20	ENG
Weight ....Amelia	George ....John	1875	
Weight ....Amelia	Larson ....John	1855 10 08	
Weinmann ....Catharina	Scheib ....John Pierre	1835 05 17	ENG, London
Weisbrodt ....Esther C. E.	Francis ....Samuel	1857 07 01	Switzerland
Welborne ....Nancy Garrett	Hunt ....Amos	1840 12 21	KY, Greenville
Welch ....Ann	Crookston...........Robert	1847 06 20	NE
Welch ....Ann	Guppy ....John		
Welch ....Ann	Jones ....David	1869 12 27	UT
Welch ....Uriah	Wilkins...............Charles Jr.	1856	UT
Welch ....Zipporah	Welch ....Daniel	1856 03 16	IL, Alton
Welker ....Mary Catherine	Nelson................Thomas B.	1853 03 27	UT, Willow Creek
Wellard ....Eliza Mary Ann	Stanley ....Thomas A.		UT, Salt Lake City
Wells...............Isabella	Davis ....Nathan Cutler	1840 11 11	NY, Warren Co.
Wells...............Lydia	Mecham ....Lewis	1836 04 05	PA, Mercer
Wells...............Margaret J.	Petty ....Robert Cowan	1832	TN, Nashville
Wells...............Mary	Snow ....George W.		
Wells...............Matilda	Streeper ....Wilkinson	1834 07 10	PA, Philadelphia
Wells...............Matilda	Wadsworth ....William	1857	UT, Salt Lake City
Wells...............Mehetable	Cheney...............Aaron	1813	
Wells...............Tirzah	Chase..................Ezra	1818 08 22	MA, Franklin Co.
Wernham.........Martha	Lambourne..........William Jr.	1868 02 29	UT, Salt Lake City
West ....Ann Lydia	Neville ....Joseph Hyrum	1873 05 05	UT, Salt Lake City
West ....Emma S.	Smith..................Jesse N.	1852 05 13	UT, Parowan
West ....Mary	Smith..................Samuel P.	1814 08 17	
Westcott ....Sarah Jane	Walters................Asa	1840 04 07	Isle of Jersey
Western ....Agnes	Reid....................John Whirk	1865 04 24	UT, Meadow
Weston ....Anna	Hodges...............Nathaniel M.	1873	UT
Weston ....Louisa	Hodges...............Nathaniel M.	1869 10 11	UT, Salt Lake City
Weston ....Mary Ann	Davis..................John	1840 12 23	
Weston ....Mary Ann	Maughan ....Peter	1841 11 02	IL, Nauvoo
Westwood.......Caroline	Saville ....George	1871 07 20	UT, Salt Lake City
Westwood........Ellen	Saville ....George	1862 01 11	ENG
Westwood.......Temperance	Moon ....Henry	1856 03 18	UT, Salt Lake City

Female	Male	Date	Place
Weymouth ....Henrietta D.	Pew ....Hyrum William	1852 03 31	UT, Salt Lake City
Whale ....Eliza	Watts ....Henry	1842 04 01	ENG
Wheeler ....Elizabeth	Brownell ....Gideon	1814	MA, Dartmouth
Wheeler ....Elmera Jane	Mower ....Henry	1856 09 05	
Wheeler ....Harriet Page	Decker.................Isaac Perry	1821	NY, Phelps
Wheeler ....Harriet Page	Young..................Lorenzo Dow	1843 03 09	IL, Nauvoo
Wheeler ....Jane Dunn	Shelley ....William B.	1845 11 10	ENG, Bridgenorth
Wheeler ....Mary	Chadwick ....Abraham	1853 05 22	
Wheeler ....Phoebe Marietta	Hatch..................Wilder	1872 10 03	
Wheeler ....Rebecca	Wright.................Jonathan C.	1838 03 01	IL, Waynesville
Wheeler ....Rhoda	Hill ....Return Richard	1841	
Wheeler ....Sarah	Etherington..........Thomas	1858 03 09	UT, Salt Lake City
Wheeler ....Sylvia Desire	Beecher...............Ransom Asa	1838 11 22	KS
Whimlett ....Elizabeth	Godfrey ....Thomas	1821 04 26	ENG, Hanbury
Whistance.......Margaret	Nelson.................Isaac	1854 02 23	UT, Provo
Whitaker ....Elizabeth	Smith...................Thomas J.	1852 11 06	ENG, Cowpen
Whitaker ....Mary Ann	Harrison ....Richard	1836 09 10	
Whitaker ....Rozilla	Dalton..................Matthew W.	1850 12 15	
Whitcomb ....Hannah	Haws ....Gilberth	1822 06 02	
White ....Agnes M. M. J.	Hawks ....Amos	1859 01 23	UT, Spanish Fork
White ....Ann	Bradshaw ....John	1817 08 27	ENG, Derbyshire
White ....Ann	Lee ....Samuel Francis	1853 01 18	
White ....Charlotte R.	Pickett ....John W.	1866 12 21	UT, Salt Lake City
White ....Eliza Elizabeth	Driggs..................Shadrach F.	1836 06	Ohio
White ....Elizabeth	Stewart................Isaac M.	1857 03 08	UT, Salt Lake City
White ....Ellen	Nichols ....William	1854 03 19	ENG, Durham
White ....Isabelle	Squire..................William		
White ....Isabelle E.	Jardine ....James	1840 07 17	Scotland
White ....Mary Ann	Holmes................John	1829 06 22	ENG
White ....Mary Elizabeth	Hudson................William	1839	ENG, Derbyshire
White ....Mary Elizabeth	Musser ....Amos Milton	1864 10 01	UT, Salt Lake City
White ....Minerva	Snow...................Erastus	1844 04 02	IL, Nauvoo
White ....Ortentia	Leonard...............Truman		
White ....Sarah Ann	Olpin...................Henry	1835 10 25	ENG, Coaley
White ....Sarah Elizabeth	Burningham.........Thomas	1826 05 29	ENG, Surrey
White ....Susanna E.	Dunn ....Joseph Moroni	1866 12 27	UT, Tooele
Whitehead ....Julia Ellen	James ....William Francis	1877 08 09	UT, Ogden
Whitehead ....Mary	Chadwick ....Joseph	1832 11 19	ENG, Lancashire
Whitehead ....Rose Hannah	Pears...................John Burton	1822 01 30	ENG
Whitesides ......Mary Ann	Hunter ....Edward	1843 11 05	IL, Nauvoo
Whiting ....Eliza Avery	Deuel..................William H.	1837 01 01	NY, Freedom
Whiting ....Helen Amelia	Buchanan............Archibald W. O.	1855 08 22	
Whitlock..........Mary Jane	....	1853 02 01	
Whitlock..........Sally Rae	Oviatt...................Henry Herman	1853 02 01	UT, Spring City
Whitlock..........Sally Rae	Rogers ....Mark	1849 01 11	
Whitney ....Sarah Ann	Kimball ....Heber Chase	1846 01 12	IL, Nauvoo
Whitney ....Sarah Ann	Smith...................Joseph Jr.	1842 07 27	IL, Nauvoo
Whittaker ....Alice	Grimshaw............John	1836 01 01	ENG, Lancashire
Whittaker ....Elizabeth	Cain....................Joseph	1847 02 01	ENG
Whittaker ....Elizabeth	Richards..............Samuel W.	1859 01 27	UT, Salt Lake City
Whittaker ....Mary	Thornton..............Amos Griswold		
Whittle ....Emeline	Harris ....William	1861 08 20	UT, Richmond
Whittle ....Olive Amelia	Hale....................Aroet	1849 09 05	UT, Salt Lake City
Whork............Elizabeth	Reid....................George	1817 05 14	

Female	Male	Date	Place
Whytock..........Eliza	Wood................William	1888 09 26	UT, Logan
Whytock..........Helen	McKell ....Robert	1846 01 26	Scotland
Whytock..........Helen	Moncur...............Robert	1838 08 14	Scotland
Wiard ....Hannah	Case..................James	1815 12 12	OH, Austinburg
Wickersham.....Mary	Woolley ....Edwin D.	1831 03 24	OH
Wickes............Ann	Taylor................George E. G.	1830 02	ENG
Wicklund.........Christina	Sorensen............Morton	1862 07 19	UT, Salt Lake City
Wickoff............Elizabeth H.	Shreve..............Edwin A.	1844 05 09	
Widdison.........Agnes	Livingston...........James Campbell	1854 06 07	
Widdison.........Hannah	Livingston...........James Campbell	1862 02 15	UT, Salt Lake City
Wiggins...........Catherine	Wilson ....Lewis D. Jr.	1862 12 31	
Wight ....Sarah (Sally)	Cutler ....Sheldon Bela	1850 02 09	IA, Kanesville
Wight ....Sarah (Sally)	Wight................Ephraim		
Wightman ....Jane Elizabeth	Dixon................Christopher F.	1844 09 01	Canada
Wightman ....Mary Elizabeth	Daley................Matthew H.	1863 03 01	UT, Payson
Wilbur ....Phebe Eunice	Walker..............Rufus	1856 01 27	UT, Salt Lake City
Wilcock ....Esther	Lythgoe ....Thomas	1825 04 04	ENG, Lancashire
Wilcox.............Clarissa Jane	Seeley ....Justus W.	1842 03 10	IA, Nashville
Wilcox.............Elizabeth	Mead.................Ezra	1811	
Wilcox.............Elizabeth	Noakes..............Thomas	1852 03 18	UT, Salt Lake City
Wilcox.............Mary	Lowry................John	1824 02 01	MO, Madison Co.
Wild ....Dianna	Waller................Samuel	1819	ENG
Wilde ....Emma	Carruth..............William	1870 05 09	
Wilde ....Martha	Nield.................Luke	1817 06 30	ENG, Prestwich
Wilde ....Mary Ann	Slater................Albert G.	1865 01 01	
Wilde ....Sarah	Lewis................John Moss		
Wilde ....Sarah	Nield.................Luke		
Wilde ....Sarah Jane	Burnett ....David R.		UT, Tooele
Wilder ....Hannah Austin	Child.................Warren Gould	1853 01 06	UT, Ogden
Wilding...........Elizabeth Ann	Hamer...............John	1850 09 24	IA, Ferryville
Wilding...........Ellen	Woolley ....Edwin D.	1843 12 28	IL, Nauvoo
Wildman ....Susan	Mouritsen ....Mourits	1885 10 22	UT, Logan
Wilds...............Ann	Clements............James		
Wilds...............Ann	Clemons............William	1840	ENG
Wilds...............Ann	Conklin ....Clarence	1851	UT
Wilds...............Ann	Neibaur ....Alexander	1852 11 02	
Wilds...............Ann	Thorpe...............Alvin	1855	UT
Wilgus.............Mary Jane	Gibbs.................William	1870	
Wilhelmsen......Maren	Hansen...............Rasmus	1832 10 09	Denmark
Wilhelmsen......Maren	Hemrot		
Wilhelmsen......Maren	Pederson............Anders		Denmark
Wilkerson........Lucretia Ann	Wimmer..............Robert	1831 03 15	IN, Warren Co.
Wilkerson........Margery	Stewart...............Levi	1852 12 31	UT, Salt Lake City
Wilkes.............Mary	Gibbons..............William B.	1852 02 16	UT, Salt Lake City
Wilkes.............Sarah Ann	Allred.................William Lansing	1867 01 25	UT, Salt Lake City
Wilkie..............Ann	Galbraith ....George	1832 07 13	Scotland
Wilkie..............Ann	Hooper ....John	1844 07	
Wilkin.............Elizabeth	Thompson...........Robert	1833 02 24	Scotland
Wilkins ....Ann Priscilla	Garrett...............William A.	1860 04 23	Ocean
Wilkins ....Jane	Brown................John	1851 03 15	ENG
Wilkinson........Elizabeth	Austin................John		
Wilkinson........Elizabeth	Pead.................James	1845	
Wilkinson.........Harriet	Bloomfield ....John	1857 11 11	NJ, Chancerville
Wilkinson.........Lucy	Norton ....Allen	1809 12 31	NY, Granville

Female	Male	Date	Place
Wilkinson ....Lydia	Reeder ....Robert	1861 04 15	UT, Hyde Park
Wilkinson ....Maria	Hortin ....John	1864 12 03	UT, Salt Lake City
Wilkinson ....Sarah	Buchanan............John	1866 04 28	UT, Salt Lake City
Wilkinson ....Susannah	Barton ....John	1835 12 29	PA, Shamokin
Williams ....Amanda	Clark...................Riley Garner	1850 03 20	
Williams ....Amelia Ann	Singleton ....Francis	1840 02	ENG
Williams ....Ann	Aldredge............Joseph		
Williams ....Ann	Harris ....Thomas	1844 03 01	ENG
Williams ....Ann	Owens................William John	1868 02 29	UT, Salt Lake City
Williams ....Ann	Williams..............William		
Williams ....Anne	Rogers ....John	1838 12 13	Wales
Williams ....Anne	Terry...................Parshall	1857 09 13	UT, Salt Lake City
Williams ....Anne	Thomas ....Daniel Stillwell	1853 04 03	UT, Salt Lake City
Williams ....Caroline Marion	Kimball ....David Patten	1857 04 13	UT, Salt Lake City
Williams ....Diana Mary	Ross....................Alexander		
Williams ....Diana Mary	White...................Barnard	1869 03 07	UT, Salt Lake City
Williams ....Eleanor	James ....Thomas	1821 06 06	ENG, Lugwardine
Williams ....Elizabeth	Morris..................Isaac Conway	1852 10 16	Wales
Williams ....Elizabeth Henry	James ....John Sanders	1866 10 06	Wales
Williams ....Emily Electa	Stevenson ....Edward	1857	
Williams ....Grace Ann	Perry ....John	1822 11 14	ENG
Williams ....Hannah	Hibbard ....George	1855	
Williams ....Hannah	Hopkin................Morgan	1841 04 25	Wales
Williams ....Hannah	Jones ....Elias	1856 01 02	
Williams ....Hannah	White...................Thomas Jones	1847 06 20	ENG
Williams ....Harriet Cordelia	Adair...................Wesley	1849 02 08	
Williams ....Harriet Cordelia	Beach..................Rufus	1846	IA, Council Bluffs
Williams ....Harriet Cordelia	Brooks.................Francis William	1851	IL, Warren
Williams ....Harriet Cordelia	Lasell..................James	1873 06 04	
Williams ....Jane	Backhouse ....James	1847	ENG
Williams ....Louisa	Davis...................Joseph C.		
Williams ....Maria	Davis...................Joseph C.	1859 04 01	Wales
Williams ....Martha	Howell ....William	1829 09 26	Wales
Williams ....Martha	Morgan................William	1855 11 13	UT, Willard
Williams ....Mary	Crisman...............Peter	1824 05 21	KY, Hopkinville
Williams ....Mary	Davis...................David Thomas	1860 11 28	UT, Spanish Fork
Williams ....Mary	Elmer...................Elijah	1840 04 29	
Williams ....Mary	Howell ....Louis W.	1878 06 27	UT, Salt Lake City
Williams ....Mary	Parry ....John	1808	Wales
Williams ....Mary Ann	Lee.....................John Alma	1859 01 18	UT
Williams ....Mary Ann	Lee.....................John Doyle	1858	
Williams ....Mary Ann	Moyle ....John Rowe	1868 10 03	UT, Salt Lake City
Williams ....Mary Ann	West...................Jesse	1867 08 31	UT, Salt Lake City
Williams ....Mary Jane	Ball ....James Henry	1876 10 21	UT, Salt Lake City
Williams ....Myra	Clark...................David	1849 11 26	MO, St. Louis
Williams ....Polly	Davies.................James G.	1856	UT, Ft. Harmony
Williams ....Priscilla Jane	Parkinson ....Timothy H.	1881 03 03	
Williams ....Ruth	Price...................John Evan	1841 05	
Williams ....Sarah	Bennion..............Samuel	1853 02 13	UT, Salt Lake City
Williams ....Sarah Ann	Fitzgerald ....John	1858 02 17	UT, Salt Lake City
Williamson ....Eliza	Homer.................Russell King	1836 12 20	NY
Williamson ....Elizabeth	Carlile.................John	1844	ENG
Williamson ....Ellen	Watts..................Benjamin	1857 01 01	UT, Paragonah
Williamson ....Ellen (Eleanor)	Miller ....Daniel Arthur	1857 03 27	UT, Salt Lake City

Female	Male	Date	Place
Williamson ....Ellen (Eleanor)	Wandless ....Thomas	1847 03 28	ENG, Durham
Williamson ......Janetta	Izatt ....Alexander S.	1864 02 27	UT, Salt Lake City
Williamson ....Margaret Rae	Hall.....................Samuel Parley	1864 02 02	UT, Wellsville
Williamson ......Mary Ann	Coons.................Libbeus T.	1831	NY
Williamson ......Pauline Mary	Clinger.................James Henry	1868 02 09	UT, Provo
Willis ....Jemima	Smith..................Paul	1854	Ocean
Willis ....Margaret Jane	Willis...................William W.	1833 03 03	MO, Hamilton Co.
Willis ....Mary Lucretia	Brown.................Thomas D.	1855 10 19	UT, Cedar City
Willis ....Mary Lucretia	Groves ....Elisha Samuel	1863 10 10	
Willis ....Matilda Delila	Thompson ....James L.	1837 10 05	IL, Nauvoo
Willis ....Sarah Ann	Scott...................John	1848 03 24	IL, Nauvoo
Wilson..............Agnes	Nish....................Robert	1855 01 16	ENG, Liverpool
Wilson..............Almira	Hubbard ....Elisha F.	1885 04 02	
Wilson..............Ann	Memmott............William	1835 11 30	ENG, Yorkshire
Wilson..............Ann	Stokes ....Robert W.	1858 05 09	MA, Boston
Wilson..............Annie Mariah	Fenton ....Thomas	1866 05 12	
Wilson..............Caroline R.	Wakefield ....John	1856 07 27	ENG
Wilson..............Eleanor	Barnes................John M.	1852	
Wilson..............Elizabeth P.	Willis...................William T.	1840	
Wilson..............Jane	Stanger ....Thomas	1853 07 09	ENG
Wilson..............Jean	Nibley ....James	1836 04 17	Scotland
Wilson..............Julia	Memmott.............John	1846 03 16	ENG, Yorkshire
Wilson..............Margaret L.	Bennett...............Thomas M.	1837 11 09	IL
Wilson..............Mary	Montgomery ....Robert	1830 09 06	Scotland
Wilson..............Nancy Jane	Hunt ....Andrew Jackson	1864 12 11	
Wilson..............Rachel	Lloyd ....William John	1888 09 02	
Wilson..............Rachel	Pollard................Herbert Jonathan		
Wilson..............Sarah	Paul....................James Patten	1861	
Wimmer ....Eliza Jane	Dimick ....Albert Stanley	1861 11 09	
Wimmer ....Eliza Jane	Hill......................Alexander B.	1857 03 23	
Wimmer ....Eliza Jane	Loveless..............Hyrum Smith	1870 04 27	
Wimmer ....Jemima	Powell ....James	1833 10 06	IN, Henry Co.
Winberg ....Johanna C.	Mansfield............Matthew	1856 06 17	UT, Mill Creek
Winberg ....Johanna C.	Peterson.............Peter	1842 11 18	Sweden
Winchell...........Ada	Clements.............Albert	1821 01 28	NY, Washington
Winegar ....Almira	Stoker.................William	1838 08 20	MO, Far West
Wing ....Deborah	Gifford ....Levi	1816	
Wing ....Eunice	Perry ....Gustavus A.	1816	
Winget ....Melvina	Demill.................Elias	1863 06 12	
Wingrove ....Mary Ann	Price...................John Isaac	1852	NY, New York City
Winn ....Adelia Ann S.	Pine....................Joseph	1814 09 27	NY
Winner ....Leoni Leoti	Wilding ....George	1875	
Winsbrough .....Ann	Western..............Samuel R. R.	1836 03 09	ENG
Winsor ....Elizabeth	Smart ....Hezekiah B.	1860 06 19	ENG
Wintch ....Anna Caroline	Muhlestein..........Nicholas	1868 04 13	
Winter..............Ann	Miller..................William	1854 12 25	ENG
Winter..............Ann	Tremayne ....William Henry	1870 05 30	
Winters ....Helen Melissa	Hickerson............James M. F.	1867 09	
Winters ....Rosannah E.	Loveland ....Chester	1846 01 15	IL, Nauvoo
Wintle ....Elizabeth	Sessions ....Carlos Lyon	1864 04 02	UT, Salt Lake City
Wintle ....Sarah S.	Bitton ....John Evington	1856 05 13	ENG, Norfolk
Wintsch............Anna M.	Reber ....Samuel	1863	UT, Payson
Wintsch............Verena	Bryner ....Hans Ulrich	1826 03 29	Switzerland
Wiscombe........Laura	Sainsbury ....John Henry	1871	

Female	Male	Date	Place
Wiscombe........Martha Ann	Sainsbury ....John Henry	1865 12 08	ENG, Portsmouth
Wise ....Eleanor	Tippets ....John Harvey	1863 12 26	UT, Salt Lake City
Witner ....Christine Diana	Lytle ....John	1827 02 22	
Wolfe ....Catherine	Isom ....William	1861 03 24	ENG, Birmingham
Wood ....Charlotte	Greenwood ....William Houghton	1870 10 31	UT, Salt Lake City
Wood ....Electa	Bullock ....Isaac	1856 12 14	UT, Salt Lake City
Wood ....Elizabeth	Moyle ....James	1856 07 22	UT, Salt Lake City
Wood ....Elizabeth Agnes	Smith..................Benjamin M.	1855 02 28	UT, American Fork
Wood ....Elizabeth Jane	Bennett...............Edward	1877 03 02	UT, St. George
Wood ....Harriet	Woolf.................Absolom	1857 04 19	UT, Salt Lake City
Wood ....Margaret S.	Coffman ....William M.	1854 05 11	MO, Putnam Co.
Wood ....Maria	Robinson............Joseph Lee	1832 07 23	NY, Booneville
Wood ....Mary	Bagley ....Daniel	1849 05 10	IA, Appanoose
Wood ....Mary	Wilson ....Sylvester	1861 05 26	UT
Wood ....Mary Ellen	Allsop ....John	1854 09 12	
Wood ....Nancy Ann	Clark...................Hiram William	1843	
Wood ....Sarah Ann	Oaks...................Hyrum	1846 12 06	IA, Council Bluffs
Wood ....Sarah Ann	Western...............Samuel W.	1866 01 29	UT, Berryville
Woodall ....Caroline	Howard...............Joseph		
Woodard..........Emily Jane	Corbett ....John W.	1863 10 31	UT, Salt Lake City
Woodbury ....Hannah Marie	Haskell ....Thales	1855 10 04	
Woodcock........Encora	Batty...................George Jr.	1844	ENG, Pilley
Woodcock........Mary	Graham ....Richard	1841 03 08	
Woodcock........Mary	Nebeker ....John	1854 09 10	UT, Salt Lake City
Woodfield ....Mary	Hunt ....John Jackson	1854 07 26	MO, Lawrence
Woodfield ....Mary	Jinks...................John Jr.	1823 05 12	ENG, Stone
Woodhams ......Mary Ann	Gingell................William	1840 11 01	ENG
Woodhead ....Alice	Barker ....Josiah	1853 10	
Woodhead ....Charlotte E.	Lofthouse ....James	1856 02 19	UT, Ogden
Woodhead ....Sarah Ann	Berrett ....Robert Griffin	1855 03 04	
Woodhouse .....Annie	Candland.............David	1855 11 05	UT, Salt Lake City
Woodhouse .....Mary Ellen	White..................Samuel O.	1867 10 05	UT, Salt Lake City
Wooding ....Sarah	Smith..................Daniel W.	1815 07 10	ENG, Emberton
Wooding ....Sarah	Turpin.................Jesse	1850 01 08	UT, Salt Lake City
Woodland ....Nancy	Whitaker..............James	1838 01 16	
Woodruff..........Phebe Amelia	Snow ....Lorenzo	1859 04 04	UT, Salt Lake City
Woods ....Charlotte	Carter.................Gideon H.	1833 12 31	
Woods ....Charlotte	Higbee.................Isaac	1841 04 30	
Woods ....Elizabeth	Lewis..................John Moss		
Woodward ....Betsy Barnes	Parkinson ....Henry F.	1860 01 02	UT, Wellsville
Woodward ....Ellen Celeste	Fuller..................Elijah K.	1851 03 11	
Woodward ....Emmeline B. B.	Harris ....James Harvey	1843 07 29	
Woodward ....Emmeline B. B.	Wells ....Daniel H.	1852 10 18	
Woodward ....Emmeline B. B.	Whitney ....Newel Kimball	1845 01 07	IL, Nauvoo
Wool ....Elizabeth	Dinwoodey ....James	1821	ENG, Liverpool
Wool ....Elizabeth	Evans ....John	1839	
Wool ....Elizabeth	Hillyard ....Thomas	1830	ENG, Doddington
Wool ....Elizabeth	Meeks ....Murfitt	1853	ENG
Wooldridge ......Permelia Emily	Hundley...............Jordan Y.	1817 10 27	AL, Madison
Wooldridge ......Permelia Emily	Rooker ....Samuel McRae	1835 07 27	
Woolerton ....Eliza	Dilworth..............Caleb	1812	
Wooley ....Ann Esther	Jackson...............William	1853 03	Ocean
Woolfenden .....Margaret	Goddard ....Robert	1843	ENG
Woolley...........Henrietta	Simmons ....Joseph M.	1858 07	UT, Salt Lake City

Female	Male	Date	Place
Woolley............Mary Edna	Evans.................John Robert	1830 08 24	ENG, Louth
Woolley............Mary Louisa	Clark....................Joshua R.	1870 07 11	UT, Salt Lake City
Woolley............Rachel Emma	Simmons.............Joseph M.	1851 12 18	
Woolley............Sarah	Davis...................Nathan	1836 03 31	OH, Columbus
Woolley............Sarah	Sutton.................John A.	1887 07 24	UT, Logan
Woolsey...........Agatha Ann	Lee......................John Doyle	1833 07 24	IL, Vandelia
Woolsey...........Mary Elizabeth	Lee......................Joseph Hyrum	1863 01 02	
Wooten............Catherine	Smith..................George W.	1845 12 21	ENG, Eaton Bray
Wootton...........Elizabeth	Robinson.............Richard S.	1853	UT, American Fork
Worden............Johanna Case	Keyes.................Elisha B.	1838 03 26	OH, Grafton
Worden............Johanna Case	Teeples..............George Bently	1856 02 20	
Workman.........Caroline	Hess...................John W.	1861 04 12	
Worley.............Catherine	Cowley...............Joseph Enos	1875 07 05	UT, Salt Lake City
Wride..............Ann Davis	Stubbs................Peter	1862 10 10	UT, Salt Lake City
Wride..............Jane	Todd...................George	1869 10 18	UT, Salt Lake City
Wride..............Mary	John...................David	1860 02 08	
Wright.............Alice	Seaman..............John W.	1870 07 18	UT, Salt Lake City
Wright.............Charlotte	Walker................Walter P.	1864 12 17	UT, Salt Lake City
Wright.............Elizabeth	Andrews.............John	1857	
Wright.............Elizabeth E.	Farmer...............Edward John	1858 09 26	PA, Philadelphia
Wright.............Ellen	Jackson..............William W.	1854 07 08	UT, Salt Lake City
Wright.............Elmira	Corbett...............Daniel D.	1834	
Wright.............Emma	Dalley.................James	1850 08 15	IA, Keg Creek
Wright.............Esther B.	Barney................Royal	1857 07 18	UT, Salt Lake City
Wright.............Esther B.	Fletcher..............Francis	1839 07 03	MA, Middlesex
Wright.............Harriet	Folland................Henry	1849 05 05	ENG, Upton Pyne
Wright.............Harriet	Shipley...............Robert	1848 12 03	ENG, Hull
Wright.............Jane	Earl....................Jonathan	1847 03 22	ENG
Wright.............Julia Ann	Petty...................Robert Thomas	1864 01 22	UT, Salt Lake City
Wright.............Lucy	Tristram..............George D.	1841 07 18	ENG
Wright.............Lucy Ann	Rigby..................John	1867 11 08	UT, Salt Lake City
Wright.............Margaret	Dunkley..............Joseph	1868 11 14	UT, Salt Lake City
Wright.............Mary Ann	Webster..............John	1858 07 15	WI
Wright.............Rosetta	Benbow..............John	1851 09 03	
Wright.............Rosetta	King...................Thaddeus	1838 01	
Wright.............Rosetta	Peacock.............William	1847	
Wright.............Sarah	Shupe.................Peter	1814 12 22	
Wright.............Sarah Ann	Jones.................William Roberts	1853 10 12	UT, Salt Lake City
Wrigley............Catherine	Knighton.............George	1824 08 23	ENG, Eastwood
Wrigley............Catherine	Shaw..................Edward Stubbs		
Wycoff............Eliza Ann	Barnard..............John Porter	1826 08 31	NY, Tomkins
Wylie...............Elizabeth	Steele.................James	1851 08 24	ENG
Wylie...............Elizabeth	Wood..................David	1857 07 07	UT, Salt Lake City

X

Xavier.............Elizabeth	Tait.....................William	1850 01 21	India, Bombay

Y

Yager..............Hetty Elizabeth	Benson...............Alford B.	1841 06 17	IL, Nauvoo
Yallop.............Ellen Maria	Ricks..................Thomas Edwin	1866 11 29	UT, Salt Lake City

Female	Male	Date	Place
Yarbrough........Elizabeth	Coon ....Abraham	1829	IL, St. Claire Co.
Yardley ....Esther	Milner ....John Brewitt	1854 03	UT, Salt Lake City
Yardley ....Esther	Thurman.............Thomas Edward	1848 11 06	ENG, Dudley
Yarnell ....Sarah	Evans ....Richard	1844 09 23	ENG
Yarnell ....Sarah	Fenn...................William	1859	UT, Provo
Yarnell ....Sarah	Stradling.............William		
Yarwood ....Mary	Hill ....James	1836 04 05	ENG
Yarwood ....Mary	Roylance ....William J.	1842	IA, Montrose
Yates ....Annie Hannah	Barlow ....Israel Jr.	1863 04 26	UT, Bountiful
Yates ....Harriet	Quigley................Andrew	1856	
Yates ....Margaret	Farnsworth ....Philo T.	1848 10 29	UT, Salt Lake City
Yates ....Mary Ann	Partridge ....Jonathan W.	1857 01 05	UT, Salt Lake City
Yeager............Harriet	Whipple ....Edson	1850 11 04	UT, Salt Lake City
Yeager............Martha Eleanor	Vance................Isaac Y.	1840 11 23	
Yeager............Mary Ann	Whipple ....Edson	1850 11 04	UT, Salt Lake City
Yearsley ....Emma Smith	Wright................William B.	1860 03 15	UT, Ogden
Yearsley ....Mary Jane	Cummings...........Benjamin F.	1856 05 27	UT, Salt Lake City
Yeates ....Elizabeth L.	Franganillo ....A. E.		
Yeates ....Elizabeth L.	Thurgood............William	1863 09 15	UT, Bountiful
Yeates ....Esther	Scott..................John	1860 02 13	UT, Salt Lake City
Yelton ....Mary Margaret	Cherry ....Aaron B.	1829 05 21	KY, Pendleton
York ....Julia Ann K.	Perrish................George W.	1850	
York ....Julia Ann K.	Reidhead............John	1863 10 24	
York ....Mary Tabitha	Coon ....John	1854 03 12	UT, Salt Lake City
York ....Sarah	Carter................William F.	1831	
Yorston ....Cecelia	Johnston ....Hugh	1826 12 12	
Yorston ....Cecelia	Knowlton ....Sidney A.	1855 03 25	
Yost ....Ann	Mayer.................George	1828 03 04	PA
Young ....Alice	Moore.................James	1838	ENG
Young ....Ann	Tingey ....Henry	1839 05 12	ENG
Young ....Christina	Higginson ....William T.	1863 09 27	
Young ....Eathalinda M.	Young.................John W.	1850	UT, Salt Lake City
Young ....Elizabeth	Bailey ....George Brown	1853 02 10	ENG, Gloucester.
Young ....Elizabeth	Ellsworth ....Edmund L.	1842 07 10	
Young ....Elizabeth	Staker.................Alma	1856 02 07	UT
Young ....Eunice Clark	Angell ....Solomon	1828 04 13	RI, North Prov.
Young ....Harriet Maria	Brown.................Joseph G.	1851 12 31	UT, Salt Lake City
Young ....Jane Adeline	Robbins ....Charles B.	1855 11 22	UT, Salt Lake City
Young ....Lavina	Lee ....John Doyle	1847 02 27	NE
Young ....Lydia	Crockett..............David	1830 12 20	ME, Knox Co.
Young ....Margaret	Taylor ....John	1856 09 27	CT, Westport
Young ....Martha Ann	Sweat ....John Henry	1888 09 14	UT, Wallsburg
Young ....Mary	Brown.................John	1836 12 17	
Young ....Mary	Wilcox ....John H. O.	1848 03 14	UT, Salt Lake City
Young ....Mary Vance	Lee ....John Doyle	1847 02 27	NE
Young ....Mercy	Baker..................Simon	1829 12 31	NY, Herker
Young ....Nancy	Kent....................Daniel	1803 01 03	
Young ....Persis Louisa	Richards.............Levi Willard	1884	
Young ....Rebecca	Young.................John	1859 01 12	ENG, Liverpool
Young ....Susannah	Little ....James	1815	NY, Aurelius
Young ....Susannah	Oliphant..............Richard	1825 02	
Young ....Susannah	Pettingill ....Alonzo	1845	MO, St. Louis
Young ....Susannah	Stilson ....William B.	1829	NY, Monroe Co.
Young ....Vilate	Decker................Charles F.	1847 02 04	IA

Z

Female	Male	Date	Place
Zabriskie..........Elizabeth	Perry ....Henry Elisha	1848	
Zerfass ....Susannah	Fullmer................Peter	1802	PA, Schuykill Co.
Zimmerman .....Christina	Hopkins ....Ezekiel	1854 08 06	UT, Salt Lake City
Zimmerman .....Christina	Stevens ....Abraham	1843 01 19	IL, Nauvoo
Zimmerman .....Margaret	Brown..................John		
Zufelt ....Louisa	Bennett...............Eli	1851 03 28	IA, Harris Grove

www.ingramcontent.com/pod-product-compliance
Lightning Source LLC
Chambersburg PA
CBHW080016280326
41934CB00015B/3366